COMPLETE BOOK OF LAW SCHOOLS

COMPLETE BOOK OF LAW SCHOOLS

2004 EDITION

ERIC OWENS

Random House, Inc.
New York
www.PrincetonReview.com

Princeton Review Publishing, L.L.C.
2315 Broadway
New York, NY 10024
E-mail: bookeditor@review.com

© 2003 by Princeton Review Publishing, L.L.C.

All rights reserved under International and Pan-American Copyright Conventions. Published in the United States by Random House, Inc., New York, and simultaneously in Canada by Random House of Canada Limited, Toronto.

ISBN: 0-375-76347-3

Editorial Director: Robert Franek
Production Editor: Julieanna Lambert
Production Coordinator: Scott Harris
Account Manager: Kevin McDonough
Editor: Erica Magrey

Manufactured in the United States of America on partially recycled paper.

9 8 7 6 5 4 3 2 1

2004 Edition

ACKNOWLEDGMENTS

Eric Owens would like to say, "Thank you, John Katzman, for pretty much everything."

Thanks also to Erik Olson for support and guidance on this book and many others and to Bob Spruill for his LSAT expertise.

In addition, much thanks should go to David Soto and Ben Zelevsky for spearheading the law school data collection efforts. Their survey, along with the support and assistance of Yojaira Cordero, Miguel Lopez, Tiffany Titus, and Nathan Firer, allowed for the completion of a totally cohesive stat-packed guide.

Thanks also to our tireless sales team: Matt Doherty, Richard Strattner, Josh Escott, Tore Erickson, Eric Anderson, Nate Anderson, Ronan Campbell, and Thomas Macleod.

As usual, to Chris Wujciak, what would we do without you? Thanks to Chris for his ever-present guidance and patience throughout the book pouring process.

A special thanks must go to our production team: Scott Harris and Julieanna Lambert. Your commitment, flexibility, and attention to detail are always appreciated in both perfect and crunch times.

CONTENTS

Preface	ix
All About Law School	1
Chapter 1 So You Want to Go to Law School . . .	3
Chapter 2 Applying to Law School	13
Chapter 3 The LSAT	21
Chapter 4 Writing a Great Personal Statement	33
Chapter 5 Recommendations	41
Chapter 6 Real Life Work Experience and Community Service	47
Chapter 7 Interviews	51
Chapter 8 Choosing a Law School	53
Chapter 9 Money Matters	59
Chapter 10 Career Matters	67
Chapter 11 Law School 101	71
Chapter 12 How to Excel at Any Law School	79
Chapter 13 How to Use This Book	87
Law School Profiles	97
Indexes	307
Alphabetical List of Schools	309
Law Program Name	311
Location	313
Cost	317
Enrollment of Law School	319
Average LSAT	321
Average Undergrad GPA	323
Average Starting Salary	325
Pass Rate for First-Time Bar	327
About the Author	329

PREFACE

Welcome to the *Complete Book of Law Schools*, The Princeton Review's truly indispensable guide for anyone thinking about entering the law school fray. This is not simply a reprint of the garden-variety fluff from each law school's admissions booklet. What we have attempted to do is provide a significant amount of essential information from a vast array of sources to give you a complete, accurate, and easily digestible snapshot of each and every law school in the country. Here you'll find a wealth of practical advice on admissions, taking and acing the Law School Admissions Test (LSAT), choosing the right school, and doing well once you're there. You'll also find all the information you need on schools' bar exam pass rates, ethnic and gender percentages, tuition, average starting salaries of graduates, and much more. Indeed, with this handy reference, you should be able to narrow your choices from the few hundred law schools in North America to a handful in no time at all.

Never trust any single source too much, though—not even us. Take advantage of all the resources available to you, including friends, family members, the Internet, and your local library. Obviously, the more you explore all the options available to you, the better decision you'll make. We hope you are happy wherever you end up and that we were helpful in your search for the best law school for you.

Best of luck!

ALL ABOUT LAW SCHOOL

CHAPTER 1
So You Want to Go to Law School . . .

Congrats! Law school is a tremendous intellectual challenge and an amazing experience. It can be confusing and occasionally traumatic—especially during the crucial first year—but the cryptic ritual of legal education will make you a significantly better thinker, a consummate reader, and a far more mature person over the course of three years.

The application process is rigorous, but it's not brutal. Here's our advice.

Fascinating Acronyms
LSAC: *Law School Admission Council, headquartered in beautiful Newtown, Pennsylvania*
LSAT: *Law School Admissions Test*
LSDAS: *Law School Data Assembly Service*
ABA: *American Bar Association*

WHAT MAKES A COMPETITIVE APPLICANT?

It depends. One of the great things about law schools in the United States is that there are a lot of them and standards for admission run the gamut from appallingly difficult to not very hard at all.

Let's just say, for example, you have your heart set on Yale Law School, arguably the finest law school in all the land. Let's also say you have stellar academic credentials: a 3.45 GPA and an LSAT score in the 99th percentile of everyone who takes it. With these heady numbers, you've got a whopping 2 percent chance of getting into Yale, at best. On the other hand, with this same 3.45 GPA and LSAT score in the 99th percentile, you are pretty much a lock at legal powerhouses like Duke University School of Law and Boston College Law School. With significantly lower numbers—say, a 3.02 GPA and an LSAT score in the 81st percentile—you stand a mediocre chance of getting into top-flight law schools like Case Western or Indiana. But with a little bit of luck, these numbers might land you at George Washington or UCLA.

This is good news. The even better news is that there are several totally respectable law schools out there that will let you in with a 2.5 GPA and an LSAT of 148 (which is about the 36th percentile). If you end up in the top 10 percent of your class at one of these schools and have even a shred of interviewing skills, you'll get a job that is just as prestigious and pays just as much money as the jobs garnered by Yale grads. Honest to Christmas. Notice the important catch here, though: You *must* graduate in the top 10 percent of your class at so-called "lesser" schools. Almost every Yale Law grad who wants a high-paying job can land one.

Ultimately, there's a law school out there, somewhere, for you. If you want to get into a "top-flight" or "pretty good" school, though, you're in for some pretty stiff competition. Unfortunately, it doesn't help that the law school admissions process is somewhat formulaic; your LSAT score and your GPA are vastly more important to the process than anything else about you. But if your application ends up in the "maybe" pile, your recommendations, your major, the reputation of your college alma mater, a well-written and nongeneric essay, and various other factors will play a larger role in determining your fate.

THE ADMISSIONS INDEX
The first thing most law schools will look at when evaluating your application is your "index." It's a number (which varies from school to school) that is made up of a weighted combination of your undergraduate GPA and LSAT score. In virtually every case, the LSAT is weighted more heavily than the GPA.

While the process differs from school to school, it is generally the case that your index will put you into one of three piles:

(Probably) Accepted. A select few applicants with high LSAT scores and stellar GPAs are admitted pretty much automatically. If your index is very, very strong compared to the school's median or target number, you're as good as in, unless you are a convicted felon or you wrote your personal statement in crayon.

(Probably) Rejected. If your index is very weak compared to the school's median or target number, you are probably going to be rejected without much ado. When admissions officers read weaker applications (yes, at almost every school every application is read) they will be looking for something so outstanding or unique that it makes them willing to take a chance. Factors that can help here include ethnic background, where you are from, or very impressive work or life experience. That said, don't hold your breath, because not many people in this category are going to make the cut.

Admission Decision Criteria
According to the Law School Admission Council (LSAC), there are no less than 20 factors that law schools might consider in deciding to admit or reject applicants. They are:
- LSAT score
- Undergraduate grade point average (UGPA)
- Undergraduate course of study
- College attended
- Graduate work
- Improvement in grades and grade distribution
- Extracurricular activities in college
- Ethnic background
- Character and personality
- Letters of recommendation
- Writing skills
- Personal statement/essay
- Work experience and other relevant experience
- Community activities
- Motivation and reasons for studying law
- State of residency
- Difficulties overcome
- Pre-college preparation
- Past accomplishments and leadership
- That old catchall: anything else about you

Well . . . Maybe. The majority of applicants fall in the middle; their index number is right around the median or target index number. Folks in this category have decent enough LSAT scores and GPAs for the school, just not high enough for automatic admission. Why do most people fall into this category? Because for the most part, people apply to schools they think they have at least a shot of getting into based on their grades and LSAT scores; Yale doesn't see very many applicants who got a 140 on the LSAT. What will determine the fate of those whose applications hang in the balance? One thing law schools often look at is the competitiveness of your undergraduate program. Someone with a 3.3 GPA in an easy major from a school where everybody graduates with a 3.3 or higher will face an uphill battle. On the other hand, someone with the same GPA in a difficult major from a school that has a reputation for being stingy with A's is in better shape. Admissions officers will also pore over the rest of your application—personal statement, letters of recommendation, resume, etc.—for reasons to admit you, reject you, or put you on their waiting list.

ARE YOU MORE THAN YOUR LSAT SCORE?

Aside from LSAT scores and GPAs, what do law schools consider when deciding who's in and who's out? It's the eternal question. On the one hand, we should disabuse you hidebound cynics of the notion that they care about nothing else. On the other hand, if you harbor fantasies that a stunning application can overcome truly substandard scores and grades, you should realize that such hopes are unrealistic.

Nonquantitative factors are particularly important at law schools that receive applications from thousands of numerically qualified applicants. A "Top Ten" law school that receives ten or fifteen applications for every spot in its first-year class has no choice but to "look beyond the numbers," as admissions folks are fond of saying. Such a school will almost surely have to turn away hundreds of applicants with near-perfect LSAT scores and college grades, and those applicants who get past the initial cut will be subjected to real scrutiny.

Waiting Lists

If a law school puts you on its waiting list, it means you may be admitted depending on how many of the applicants they've already admitted decide to go to another school. Most schools rank students on their waiting list; they'll probably tell you where you stand if you give them a call. Also, note that schools routinely admit students from their waiting lists in late August. If you are on a school's waiting list and you really, really want to go there, keep your options at least partially open. You just might be admitted in the middle of first-year orientation.

Less competitive schools are just as concerned, in their own way, with "human criteria" as are the Harvards and Stanfords of the world. They are on the lookout for capable people who have relatively unimpressive GPAs and LSAT scores. The importance of the application is greatly magnified for these students, who must demonstrate their probable success in law school in other ways.

CAN PHYSICS MAJORS GO TO LAW SCHOOL?

"What about my major?" is one of the more popular questions we hear when it comes to law school admissions. The conventional answer to this question goes something like "There is no prescribed, pre-law curriculum, but you should seek a broad and challenging liberal arts education, and yadda, yadda, yadda."

Here's the truth: It really doesn't matter what you major in. Obviously, a major in aviation or hotel and restaurant management is not exactly ideal, but please—we beg you!—don't feel restricted to a few majors simply because you want to attend law school. This is especially true if those particular majors do not interest you. Comparative literature? Fine. American studies? Go to town. Physics? No problem whatsoever. You get the idea.

Think about it. Because most would-be law students end up majoring in the *same* few fields (e.g., political science and philosophy), their applications all look the *same* to the folks in law school admissions offices. You want to stand out, which is why it is a good idea to major in something *different*. Ultimately, you should major in whatever appeals to you. By the way, of course, if you want to major in political science or philosophy (or you already have), well, that's fine too.

DOES GRAD SCHOOL COUNT?

Your grades in graduate school will not be included in the calculation of your GPA (only the UGPA, the undergraduate grade point average, is reported to the schools) but will be taken into account separately by an admissions committee if you make them available. Reporting grad school grades would be to your advantage, particularly if they are better than your college grades. Admissions committees are likely to take this as a sign of improvement with maturation.

Engineering and Math Majors Make Great Law Students
A disproportionate number of law students with backgrounds in the so-called "hard sciences" (math, physics, engineering, etc.) make very high grades in law school, probably because they are trained to think methodically and efficiently about isolated problems (which is what law students are supposed to do on exams).

ADVICE FOR THE "NONTRADITIONAL" APPLICANT

The term "nontraditional" is, of course, used to describe applicants who are a few years or many years older than run-of-the-mill law school applicants.

In a nutshell, there's no time like the present to start law school. It's true that most law students are in their early to mid-twenties, but if you aren't, don't think for a minute that your age will keep you from getting in and having a great experience. It won't. Applicants for full-time and part-time slots at all manner of law schools all over the fruited plain range in age from twenty-one to seventy-one and include every age in between. Some of these older applicants always intended to go to law school and simply postponed it to work, travel, or start a family. Other older applicants never seriously considered law school until after they were immersed in another occupation.

Part-time attendance is especially worth checking into if you've been out of college for a few years. Also, dozens of law schools offer evening programs—particularly in urban centers.

MINORITY LAW SCHOOL APPLICANTS

Things are definitely looking up. Back in 1978, according to figures published by the American Bar Association's Committee on Legal Education, over 90 percent of the law students in the ABA's 167 schools were white. In recent years, though, the number of nonwhites enrolled in law school has nearly doubled, from about 10 percent to approximately 19 percent. Taking an even longer view, figures have tripled since 1972, when minority enrollment was only 6.6 percent. These days, the American Bar Association and the legal profession in general seem pretty committed to seeking and admitting applicants who are members of historically under-represented minority groups.

Pre-Law Advisors Are Your Pals
It really pays to cozy up to them. Love them. Shower them with gifts. They are an invaluable source of insight and information before, during, and even after the law school admission process. If you are thinking about law school, do yourself a favor and introduce yourself to a pre-law advisor at your undergraduate institution just as soon as possible.

Already graduated? Don't be bashful about calling a pre-law advisor at the old alma mater. The odds are, they'll still be more than happy to help you out.

MINORITY REPRESENTATION

Here is a sampling of law schools around the United States that boast notably high minority representation among students.

School Name	% Minority
Arizona State University	29
City University of New York	45
Columbia University	32
George Washington University	31
Loyola Marymount University	39
New College of California	43
North Carolina Central University	63
Northwestern University	30
Santa Clara University	37
Southwestern University	34
St. Mary's University	46
St. Thomas University	47
Stanford University	32
Texas Southern University	77
University of California, Davis	33
University of California, Hastings	33
University of California, Los Angeles	28
University of Florida	28
University of Miami	26
University of New Mexico	35
University of Pennsylvania	28
University of San Francisco	31
University of Southern California	43
University of the District of Columbia	74
University of West Los Angeles	32
Western State University	45
Yale University	32

Making Law Review

Every law school has something called a law review, which is an academic periodical produced and edited by law students. It contains articles about various aspects of law—mostly written by professors. While some schools sponsor more than one law review, there is generally one that is more prestigious than all the others. In order to "make" law review, you will have to finish the all-important first year at (or very, very near) the top of your class or write an article that will be judged by the existing members of the law review. You might have to do both. Making law review is probably the easiest way to guarantee yourself a job at a blue-chip firm, working for a judge, or in academia. In all honesty, it is a credential you will proudly carry for the rest of your life.

WOMEN IN LAW SCHOOL

During the past decade, the number of women lawyers has escalated rapidly, and women undeniably have become more visible in the uppermost echelons of the field. Two women sit on the United States Supreme Court, for instance. Also, according to statistics compiled by the American Bar Association (ABA), more than 15 percent of all law firm partners are women and women comprise 28 percent of the federal judicial department.

More and more women are going to law school as well. At a solid majority of the ABA-approved law schools in the United States, the percentage of women in the student population is 45 percent or higher, and women make up well over half of the students at a handful of schools.

Gender discrimination certainly lingers here and there, though. You might want to check certain statistics on the law schools you are interested in, such as the percentage of women on law review and the percentage of female professors who are tenured or on track to be tenured. (Nationally, nearly 22 percent of all full law school professors are women, but under 6 percent of tenured faculty are women.) Also, go to each law school and talk with female students and female professors about how women are treated at that particular school. Finally, see if the school has published any gender studies about itself. If it has, you obviously ought to check them out, too.

PROPORTION OF FEMALE STUDENTS
Here is a sampling of law schools around the United States and Canada that boast notably high percentages of female students.

School Name	% Female
Boston University	53
California Western	55
City University of New York	60
Emory University	53
Golden Gate University	60
Hamline University	59
Loyola University New Orleans	57
New College of California	55
North Carolina Central University	61
Northeastern University	60
Pace University	60
Seattle University	55
Southwestern University	51
Stetson University	55
Suffolk University	54
University of British Columbia	58
University of California, Davis	56
University of California, Hastings	53
University of Colorado	54
University of Maryland	57
University of New Mexico	60
University of San Francisco	56
University of the District of Columbia	64
University of Victoria	56
University of Windsor	58

Required Reading
These two law review articles plus one study discuss the difficulties women face in law school and the legal profession. Check them out.

Lani Guinier, "Becoming Gentlemen: Women's Experiences at One Ivy League Law School," University of Pennsylvania Law Review, November 1994.

Catherine Weiss and Louise Melling, "The Legal Education of Twenty Women," Stanford Law Review, May 1988.

Deborah L. Rhode, "The Unfinished Agenda: Women and the Legal Profession," ABA Commission on Women in the Profession, 2001.

CHAPTER 2
APPLYING TO LAW SCHOOL

Our advice: Start early. The LSAT alone can easily consume 80 or more hours of prep time, and a single application form might take as much as 30 hours if you take great care with the essay questions. Don't sabotage your efforts through last-minute sloppiness or let this already-annoying process become a gigantic burden.

WHEN TO APPLY

Yale Law School's absolute final due date is February 15, but Loyola University Chicago's School of Law will receive your application up to April 1. There is no pattern. However, the longer you wait to apply to a school, regardless of its deadline, the worse your chances of getting into that school may be. No efficient admissions staff is going to wait for all the applications before starting to make their selections.

If you're reading this in December and hope to get into a law school for the fall but haven't done anything about it, you're in big trouble. If you've got an LSAT score you are happy with, you're in less trouble. However, your applications will get to the law schools after the optimum time and, let's face it, they may appear a bit rushed. The best way to think about applying is to start early in the year, methodically take care of one thing at a time, and *finish by December*.

Early Admissions Options. A few schools have "early admissions" options, so you may know by December if you've been accepted (for instance, New York University's early admission deadline is on or about October 15). Early admission is a good idea for a few reasons. It can give you an indication of what your chances are at other schools. It can relieve the stress of waiting until April to see where you'll be spending the next three years of your life. Also, it's better to get waitlisted in December than April (or whenever you would be notified for regular admission); if there is a "tie" among applicants on the waiting list, they'll probably admit whoever applied first. Of course, not every school's early admission option is the same (and many schools don't even have one).

Rolling Admissions. Many law schools evaluate applications and notify applicants of admission decisions continuously over the course of several months (ordinarily from late fall to midsummer). Obviously, if you apply to one of these schools, it is vital that you apply as early as possible because there will be more places available at the beginning of the process.

Applying on Computer. More and more law schools are allowing applicants to submit applications online, though you will still find some that want their applications typed. While typing is not exactly rocket science, it is a pain in the neck. A few services can make the process easier. The Princeton Review's very own PrincetonReview.com will allow you to fill out law school applications electronically for free on its site. The LSACD, a CD-ROM/online service (215-968-1001 or www.lsac.org; $59/$54 respectively), has a searchable database and applications to ABA-approved schools.

Looking for a Typewriter?
Most libraries will have one you can use for free. Almost all law libraries have typewriters available if you ask nicely.

LAW SCHOOL ADMISSIONS COUNCIL: THE LAW SCHOOL APPLICATION MAFIA

In addition to single-handedly creating and administering the LSAT, an organization called the Law School Admissions Council (LSAC) maintains a stranglehold on communication between you and virtually every law school in the United States. It runs the Law School Data Assembly Service (LSDAS), which provides information (in a standard format) on applicants to the law schools. They—not you—send your grades, your LSAT score, and plenty of other information about you to the schools. You'll send only your actual applications directly to the law schools themselves. Oh, by the way, the fee for this service is almost $100 of your hard-earned money plus $10 (or more) every time you want LSDAS to send a report about you to an additional law school.

THE BIG HURDLES IN THE APPLICATION PROCESS: A BRIEF OVERVIEW

Take the LSAT. The Law School Admission Test is a roughly three-and-a-half-hour multiple-choice test used by law schools to help them select candidates. The LSAT is given in February, June, October (or, occasionally, late

September), and December of each year. It's divided into five multiple-choice sections and one (completely useless) writing sample. All ABA-approved and most non-ABA-approved law schools in the United States and Canada require an LSAT score from each and every applicant.

Register for LSDAS. You can register for the Law School Data Assembly Service at the same time you register to take the LSAT; all necessary forms are contained in the *LSAT and LSDAS Registration Information Book* (hence the name).

Get applications from six or seven schools. Why so many? Better safe than sorry. Fairly early—like in July—select a couple "reach" schools, a couple schools to which you've got a good shot at being accepted, and a couple "safety" schools where you are virtually assured of acceptance. Your safety school—if you were being realistic—will probably accept you pretty quickly. It may take a while to get a final decision from the other schools, but you won't be totally panicked because you'll know your safety school is there for you. If, for whatever reason, your grades or LSAT score are extremely low, you should apply to several safety schools.

Write your personal statement. With any luck, you'll only have to write one personal statement. Many, many schools will simply ask you the same question: basically, "Why do you want to obtain a law degree?" However, you may need to write several personal statements and essays—which is one more reason you need to select your schools fairly early.

Obtain two or three recommendations. Some schools will ask for two recommendations, both of which must be academic. Others want more than two recommendations and want at least one to be from someone who knows you outside traditional academic circles. As part of your LSDAS file, the LSAC will accept up to three letters of recommendation on your behalf, and they will send them to all the schools to which you apply. This is one of the few redeeming qualities of the LSAC. The last thing the writers of your recommendations are going to want to do is sign, package, and send copies of their letters all over the continent.

LSDAS Fees

LSDAS Subscription Fee: $99 (This buys you an LSDAS "subscription" for 12 months and a single, solitary report to one law school.)

LSDAS Law School Reports: $10 (when you initially subscribe)

Additional LSDAS Law School Reports: $12 (after you subscribe)

A Legal Education: Priceless

Update/create your resume. Most law school applicants ask that you submit a resume. Make sure yours is up-to-date and suitable for submission to an academic institution. Put your academic credentials and experience first—no matter what they are. This is just a supplement to the rest of the material; it's probably the simplest part of the application process.

Get your academic transcripts sent to LSDAS. When you subscribe to LSDAS, you must request that the registrar at every undergraduate, graduate, and professional school you ever attended send an official transcript to Law Services. Don't even think about sending your own transcripts anywhere; these people don't trust you any farther than they can throw you. *Make these requests in August.* If you're applying for early decision, start sending for transcripts as early as May. Law schools require complete files before making their decisions, and LSDAS won't send your information to the law schools without your transcripts. Undergraduate institutions can and will screw up and delay the transcript process—even when you go there personally and pay them to provide your records. Give yourself some time to fix problems should they arise.

Write any necessary addenda. An addendum is a brief explanatory letter written to explain or support a "deficient" portion of your application. If your personal and academic life has been fairly smooth, you won't need to include any addenda with your application. If, however, you were ever on academic probation, arrested, or if you have a low GPA, you may need to write one. Other legitimate addenda topics are a low/discrepant LSAT score, DUI/DWI suspensions, or any "time gap" in your academic or professional career.

An addendum is absolutely not the place to go off on polemics about the fundamental unfairness of the LSAT or how that evil campus security officer was only out to get you when you got arrested. If, for example, you have taken the LSAT two or three times and simply did not do very well, even after spending time and money preparing with a test prep company or a private tutor, merely tell the admissions committee that you worked diligently to achieve

---

Fee Waivers

Taking the LSAT, subscribing to LSDAS, and applying to law schools at $50 a pop will cost you an arm and a leg (though these costs are but a drop in the bucket compared to the amount of money you are about to spend on your law school education). The LSAC and most law schools offer fee waiver programs. If you are financially strapped and are accepted into the LSAC program, you get to take the LSAT and subscribe to LSDAS for free. You also get three LSDAS law school reports and a complimentary book of three previously administered LSATs.

You can request a fee waiver packet from Law Services at 215-968-1001, or write to them at:
Law Services
Attn: Fee Waiver Packet
Box 2000
661 Penn Street
Newtown, PA 18940-0998

a high score. Say you explored all possibilities to help you achieve that goal. Whatever the case, lay out the facts, but let them draw their own conclusions. Be brief and balanced. Be fair. Do not go into detailed descriptions of things. Explain the problem and state what you did about it. This is no time to whine.

Send in your seat deposit. Once you are accepted at a particular school, that school will ask you to put at least some of your money where your mouth is. A typical fee runs $200 or more. This amount will be credited to your first-term tuition once you actually register for classes.

Do any other stuff. You may find that there are other steps you must take during the law school application process. You may request a fee waiver, for example. Make extra-special sure to get a copy of the LSAC's *LSAT/LSDAS Registration and Information Book*, which is unquestionably the most useful tool in applying to law school. It has the forms you'll need, a sample LSAT, admissions information, the current Law Forum schedule, and sample application schedules.

The Princeton Review — LAW SCHOOL APPLICATION CHECKLIST
(suitable for framing)

January	• **Take a practice LSAT.** Do it at a library or some place where you won't be interrupted. Also, take it all at once.
February	• **Investigate LSAT prep courses.** If you don't take one with The Princeton Review, do *something*. Just as with any test, you'll get a higher score on this one if you prepare for it first.
March	• **Obtain an *LSAT/LSDAS Registration and Information Book.*** The books are generally published in March of each year. You can get one at any law school, by calling the LSAC at 215-968-1001, or by stopping by The Princeton Review office nearest you.
April	• **Register for the June LSAT.** • **Begin an LSAT prep course.** At the very, very least, use some books or software.
May	• **Continue your LSAT prep.**
June	• **Take the LSAT.** If you take the test twice, most law schools will consider just your highest LSAT score. Some, however, will average them. Your best bet is to take it once, do exceedingly well, and get it out of your hair forever.
July	• **Register for LSDAS.** • **Research law schools.**
August	• **Obtain law school applications.** You can call or write, but the easiest and cheapest way to get applications sent to you is via the Internet. • **Get your undergraduate transcripts sent to LSDAS.** Make sure to contact the registrar at each undergraduate institution you attended.
September	• **Write your personal statements.** Proofread them. Edit them. Edit them again. Have someone else look them over for all the mistakes you missed. • **Update your resume.** Or create a resume if you don't have one. • **Get your recommendations in order.** You want your recommenders to submit recommendations exactly when you send your applications (in October and November).
October	• **Complete and send early decision applications.**
November	• **Complete and send all regular applications.**
December	• **Chill.** • **Buy holiday gifts.** • **Make plans for New Year's.**

CHAPTER 3
The LSAT

Celebrity Lawyers
John Grisham, writer
Geraldo Rivera, talk-show host
Paul Tagliabue, NFL commissioner
Richard Nixon, U.S. president
Cole Porter, musician

As you may know, we at The Princeton Review are pretty much disgusted with most of the standardized tests out there. They make us a lot of money, of course, and we like that, but they are hideously poor indicators of anything besides how well you do on that particular standardized test. They are certainly not intelligence tests. The LSAT is no exception. It is designed to keep you out of law school, not facilitate your entrance into it. For no good reason we can think of, this 101-question test is *the single most important factor in all of law school admissions*, and, at least for the foreseeable future, we're all stuck with it.

Unfortunately, with the possible exception of the MCAT (for medical school), the LSAT is the toughest of all the standardized tests. Only 23–24 of the 101 questions have a "correct" answer (Logic Games), as opposed to Arguments and Reading Comprehension, where you must choose the elusive "best" answer. As ridiculous as they are, the GMAT, GRE, SAT, MCAT, and ACT at least have large chunks of math or science on them. There are verifiably correct answers on these tests, and occasionally you even have to know something to get to them. *Only the LSAT requires almost no specific knowledge of anything whatsoever, which is precisely what makes it so difficult*. The only infallible way to study for the LSAT is to study the LSAT itself. The good news is that *anybody* can get significantly better at the LSAT by working diligently at it. In fact, your score will increase exponentially in relation to the amount of time and work you put into preparing for it.

HOW IMPORTANT IS THE LSAT?
The LSAT figures very prominently in your law school application, especially if you've been out of school for a few years. Some law schools won't even look at your application unless you achieve a certain score on your LSAT. By the way, each score you receive is valid for five years after you take the test.

LSAT STRUCTURE

Section Type	Sections	Questions Per Section	Time
Logical Reasoning (Arguments)	2	24-26	35 minutes
Analytical Reasoning (Games)	1	23-24	35 minutes
Reading Comprehension	1	26-28	35 minutes
Experimental	1	????	35 minutes
Writing Sample	1	1	30 minutes

Each test has 101 questions. Neither the experimental section nor the writing sample counts toward your score. The multiple-choice sections may be given in any order, but the writing sample is always administered last. The experimental section can be any of the three types of multiple-choice sections and is used by the test writers to test out new questions on your time and at your expense.

Not only is the writing sample not scored, but it is also unlikely that anyone other than you will ever read it. However, the law schools to which you apply will receive a copy of your writing sample, so you should definitely do it. A blank page would stand out like a sore thumb, and you wouldn't want the folks in the admissions office to think you were some kind of revolutionary.

WHAT'S ON THE LSAT, EXACTLY?

We asked the experts in the LSAT Course Division of The Princeton Review for the lowdown on the various sections of the LSAT. Here's what they had to say:

Analytical Reasoning: If you've ever worked logic problems in puzzle books, then you're already somewhat familiar with the Analytical Reasoning section of the LSAT. The situations behind these problems—often called "games" or "logic games"—are common ones: deciding in what order to interview candidates, or assigning employees to teams, or arranging dinner guests around a table. The arrangement of "players" in these games is governed by a set of rules you must follow in answering the questions. Each Analytical Reasoning section is made up of four games, with five to seven questions each. Questions may ask you to find out what must be true under the rules or what could be true under the rules, they may add a new condition that applies to just that question, they may ask you to count the number of possible arrangements under the stated conditions. These questions are difficult mostly because of the time constraints under which they must be worked; very few test-takers find themselves able to complete the twenty-three or twenty-four questions on this section in the time allotted.

Logical Reasoning: Because there are two scored sections of them, Logical Reasoning questions on the LSAT are the most important to your score. Each Logical Reasoning— sometimes called "arguments"—question is made up of a short paragraph, often written to make a persuasive point. These small arguments are usually written to contain a flaw—some error of reasoning or unwarranted assumption that you must identify in order to answer the question successfully. Questions may ask you to draw conclusions from the stated information, to weaken or strengthen the argument, to identify its underlying assumptions, or to identify its logical structure or method. There are most often a total of fifty or fifty-one argument questions between the two sections—roughly half of the scored questions on the LSAT.

Registering for the LSAT
You can register for the LSAT by mail, over the phone, or on the Internet. To register by mail, you will need a copy of the Registration and Information Bulletin, which you may either request from Law Services or pick up from your pre-law advisor. You may also register for the LSAT online at www.lsac.org. The LSAT fee is currently a whopping $103; if you're late, it's an extra $54. To avoid late fees, mail your registration form at least six weeks—six weeks—before the test. Also, by registering early, you are more likely to be assigned your first choice of test center.
You can reach the Law School Admissions Council at:
  Phone: 215-968-1001
  www.lsac.org
  lsacinfo@lsac.org

Reading Comprehension: Reading Comprehension is familiar to anyone who's taken the SAT or virtually any other standardized test. The Reading Comprehension section is made up of four passages, each roughly 500 words in length, with six to eight associated questions. The material of these reading passages is often obscure or esoteric, but answering the questions correctly doesn't depend on any specialized knowledge. Questions may ask you to identify the passage's main idea, to identify descriptions of its structure or purpose, to evaluate the purpose of specific examples or contentions, or to understand its argumentation. Although the form of this section is familiar, the language and length of passages, questions, and answer choices make it challenging; like the Analytical Reasoning section, the Reading Comprehension section is for many test-takers simply too long to finish in the time allotted.

You really ought to prep for this test. You certainly don't have to take The Princeton Review's course (or buy our book, *Cracking the LSAT*, or sign up for our awesome distance learning course), as much as we'd obviously like it. There are plenty of books, software products, courses, and tutors out there. The evil minions who make the LSAT will gleefully sell you plenty of practice tests as well. The key is to find the best program for you. Whatever your course of action, though, make sure you remain committed to it so you can be as prepared as possible when you take the actual test.

WHEN SHOULD YOU TAKE THE LSAT?
Here is a quick summary of test dates along with some factors to consider for each.

JUNE
The June administration is the only time the test is given on a Monday afternoon. If you have trouble functioning at the ordinary 8 A.M. start-time, June may be a good option. Furthermore, taking the LSAT in June frees up your summer and fall to research schools and complete applications. On the other hand, if you are still in college, you'll have to balance LSAT preparation with academic course work and, in some cases, final exams. Check your exam schedules before deciding on a June LSAT test date.

OCTOBER/SEPTEMBER

The October test date (which is sometimes in late September) will allow you to prepare for the LSAT during the summer. This is an attractive option if you are a college student with some free time on your hands. Once you've taken the LSAT, you can spend the remainder of your fall completing applications.

DECEMBER

December is the last LSAT administration that most competitive law schools will accept. If disaster strikes and you get a flat tire on test day, you may end up waiting another year to begin law school. December testers also must balance their time between preparing for the LSAT and completing law school applications. Doing so can make for a hectic fall, especially if you're still in college. You should also remember that, while a law school may accept December LSAT scores, taking the test in December could affect your chances of admission. Many law schools use a rolling admissions system, which means that they begin making admissions decisions as early as mid-October and continue to do so until the application deadline. Applying late in this cycle could mean that fewer spots are available. Check with your potential law schools to find out their specific policies.

FEBRUARY

If you want to begin law school in the following fall, the February LSAT will be too late for most law schools. However, if you don't plan to begin law school until the *next* academic year, you can give yourself a head start on the entire admissions process by taking the LSAT in February, then spending your summer researching schools and your fall completing applications.

| UPCOMING LSAT TEST DATES ||||
TEST DATE	Registration Deadline	Late Registration Periods by Mail	Late Registration by Phone/Online
October 4, 2003	September 3	September 4–10	September 4–15
December 6, 2003	November 5	November 6–12	November 6–17
February 7, 2004	January 7	January 8–14	January 8–20

HOW IS THE LSAT SCORED?

LSAT scores currently range from 120 to 180. Why that range? We have no idea. The following table indicates the percentile rating of the corresponding LSAT scores between 141 and 180. This varies slightly from test to test.

This is the case because your raw score (the number of questions you answer correctly) doesn't always produce the same scaled score as previous LSATs. What actually happens is that your raw score is compared to that of everyone else who took the test on the same date you did. The LSAC looks at the scales from every other LSAT given in the past three years and "normalizes" the current scale so that it doesn't deviate widely from those scaled scores in the past.

LSAT Score	Percent Below	LSAT Score	Percent Below
180	99.9	160	83.1
179	99.9	159	80.6
178	99.9	158	77.4
177	99.9	157	74.2
176	99.8	156	70.7
175	99.7	155	67.1
174	99.5	154	63.3
173	99.3	153	59.3
172	99.1	152	55.2
171	98.7	151	51.5
170	98.2	150	47.3
169	97.5	149	43.2
168	97.0	148	39.3
167	95.9	147	35.6
166	94.8	146	32.2
165	93.5	145	28.4
164	91.9	144	25.5
163	90.0	143	22.2
162	88.2	142	19.6
161	85.7	141	16.9

Most law schools will consider just your highest LSAT score, rather than average them, which is what they used to do.

A GOOD LSAT SCORE
A good score on the LSAT is the score that gets you into the law school you want to attend. Remember that a large part of the admissions game is the formula of your UGPA (undergraduate grade point average) multiplied by your LSAT score. Chances are, you are at a point in life where your UGPA is pretty much fixed (if you're reading this early in your college career, start getting very good grades pronto), so the only piece of the formula you can have an impact on is your LSAT score.

A LITTLE IMPROVEMENT GOES A LONG WAY
A student who scores a 154 is in the 63rd percentile of all LSAT-takers. If that student's score were 161, however, that same student would jump to the 86th percentile. Depending upon your score, a 7-point improvement can increase your ranking by over 30 percentile points.

COMPETITIVE LSAT SCORES AROUND THE UNITED STATES
The range of LSAT scores from the 25th to 75th percentile of incoming full-time students at U.S. law schools is pretty broad. Here is a sampling.

Law School	Score
Widener University, School of Law, Harrisburg	146–151
The John Marshall Law School	145–152
Gonzaga University, School of Law	149–155
University of North Dakota, School of Law	148–155
University of Pittsburgh, School of Law	154–161
Temple University, James E. Beasley School of Law	154–160
Northeastern University, School of Law	152–160
Rutgers University—Newark, Rutgers School of Law at Newark	154–160
University of Florida, Levin College of Law	154–162
University of Missouri–Columbia, School of Law	154–160
University of Tennessee, College of Law	155–160
Case Western Reserve University, School of Law	155–160
University of Alabama, School of Law	157–162
Southern Methodist University, School of Law	156–161
Loyola University Chicago, School of Law	157–161
Brigham Young University, J. Reuben Clark Law School	158–164
Boston University, School of Law	163–166
Emory University, School of Law	160–165
University of Southern California Law School	163–166
George Washington University, Law School	160–164
Duke University, School of Law	164–169
University of Michigan, Law School	163–168
Stanford University, School of Law	165–170
New York University, School of Law	167–171
University of Chicago, Law School	165–172
Yale University, Yale Law School	168–174

PREPARING FOR THE LSAT

No matter who you are—whether you graduated *magna cum laude* from Cornell University or you're on academic probation at Cornell College—the first thing you need to do is order a recent LSAT. One comes free with every *Official LSAT Registration Booklet*. Once you get the test, take it, but not casually over the course of two weeks. Bribe someone to be your proctor. Have them administer the test to you under strict time conditions. Follow the test booklet instructions exactly and do it right. Your goal is to simulate an actual testing experience as much as possible. When you finish, score the test honestly. Don't give yourself a few extra points because "you'll do better on test day." The score on this practice test will provide a baseline for mapping your test preparation strategy.

If your practice LSAT score is already at a point where you've got a very high-percentage shot of getting accepted to the law school of your choice, chances are you don't need much preparation. Order a half dozen or so of the most recent LSATs from LSAC and work through them over the course of a few months, making sure you understand why you are making specific mistakes. If your college or university offers a free or very cheap prep course, consider taking it to get more tips on the test. Many of these courses are taught by pre-law advisors who will speak very intelligently about the test and are committed to helping you get the best score you can.

If, after you take a practice LSAT, your score is not what you want or need it to be, you are definitely not alone. Many academically strong candidates go into the LSAT cold because they assume that the LSAT is no more difficult than or about the same as their college courses. Frankly, many students are surprised at how poorly they do the first time they take a dry run. Think about it this way: It's better to be surprised sitting at home with a practice test than while taking the test for real.

If you've taken a practice LSAT under exam conditions and it's, say, 10 or 15 points below where you want it to be, you should probably consult an expert. Test preparation companies spend quite a lot of money and time poring over the tests and measuring the improvements of their students. We sure do. Ask around. Assess your financial situation.

Talk to other people who have improved their LSAT scores and duplicate their strategies.

Whatever you decide to do, make sure you are practicing on real LSAT questions—again and again and again.

SOME ESSENTIAL, DOWN-AND-DIRTY LSAT TIPS

Slow down. Way down. The slower you go, the better you'll do. It's that simple. Any function you perform, from basic motor skills to complex intellectual problems, will be affected by the rate at which you perform that function. This goes for everything from cleaning fish to taking the LSAT. You can get twenty-five questions wrong and still get a scaled score of 160, which is a very good score (it's in the 84th percentile). You can get at least six questions wrong per section or, even better, you can ignore the two or three most convoluted questions per section, *still* get a few *more* questions wrong, and you'll get an excellent overall score. Your best strategy is to find the particular working speed at which you will get the most questions correct.

There is no guessing penalty. If you don't have time to finish the exam, it's imperative that you leave yourself at least 30 seconds at the end of each section in which to grab free points by bubbling in some answer to every question before time is called. Pick a letter of the day—like B—don't bubble in randomly. If you guess totally randomly, you might get every single guess right. Of course, you may also get struck by lightning in the middle of the test. The odds are about the same. *You are far more likely to miss every question if you guess without a plan.* On the other hand, if you stick with the same letter each time you guess, you will definitely be right once in a while. It's a conservative approach, but it is also your best bet for guaranteed points, which is what you want. By guessing the same letter pretty much every time as time runs out, you can pick up anywhere from two to four raw points per section. Be careful about waiting until the very last second to start filling in randomly, though, because proctors occasionally cheat students out of the last few seconds of a section.

Use process of elimination all the time. This is absolutely huge. On 75 percent of the LSAT (all the Logical Reasoning and the Reading Comprehension questions), you are *not*

The Princeton Review's Online LSAT Resources
The Princeton Review combines cutting-edge technology with its standardized-testing expertise to accommodate the needs of LSAT-takers everywhere.

Visit www.PrincetonReview.com for fantastic resources, free practice material, and information on The Princeton Review's classroom and online courses.

> **Law School Trivia**
> The last president to argue a case before the United States Supreme Court was Richard Nixon (a Duke alumnus). He argued the case between his tenure as vice president and his presidency. The case was Time, Inc. v. Hill (1967), a rather complicated First Amendment case.

looking for the *right* answer, only the *best* answer. It says so right there in the instructions. Eliminating even one answer choice increases your chances of getting the question right by 20 to 25 percent. If you can cross off two or three answer choices, you are really in business. Also, very rarely will you find an answer choice that is flawless on the LSAT. Instead, you'll find four answer choices that are definitely wrong and one that is the least of five evils. You should constantly look for reasons to get rid of answer choices so you can eliminate them. This strategy will increase your odds of getting the question right, and you'll be a happier and more successful standardized test-taker. We swear.

Attack! Attack! Attack! Read the test with an antagonistic, critical eye. Read it like it's a contract you are about to sign with the devil; look for holes and gaps in the reasoning of arguments and in the answer choices. Many LSAT questions revolve around what is wrong with a particular line of reasoning. The more you can identify what is wrong with a problem before going to the answer choices, the more successful you'll be.

Write all over your test booklet. Actively engage the exam and put your thoughts on paper. Circle words. *Physically cross out wrong answer choices you have eliminated.* Draw complete and exact diagrams for the logic games. Use the diagrams you draw.

Do the questions in whatever order you wish. Just because a logic game question is first doesn't mean you should do it first. There is *no order of difficulty* on the LSAT—unlike some other standardized tests—so you should hunt down and destroy those questions at which you are personally best. If you are doing a Reading Comprehension question, for example, or tackling an argument, and you don't know what the hell is going on, then cross off whatever you can, guess, and move on. If you have no idea what is going on in a particular logic game, don't focus your energy there. Find a game you can do and milk it for points. Your mission is to gain points wherever you can. By the way, if a particular section is really throwing you, it's probably because it is the dastardly experimental section (which is often kind of sloppy and, thankfully, does not count toward your score).

CHAPTER 4
WRITING A GREAT PERSONAL STATEMENT

There is no way to avoid writing the dreaded personal statement. You'll probably need to write only one personal statement, and it will probably address the most commonly asked question: "Why do you want to obtain a law degree?" This question, in one form or another, appears on virtually every law school application and often represents your only opportunity to string more than two sentences together. Besides your grades and your LSAT score, it is the most important part of your law school application. Your answer should be about two pages long, and it should amount to something significantly more profound than "A six-figure salary really appeals to me," or "Because I watch *Law & Order* every night."

Unlike your application to undergraduate programs, the personal statement on a law school application is not the time to discuss what your trip to Europe meant to you, describe your wacky chemistry teacher, or try your hand at verse. It's a fine line. While you want to stand out, you definitely don't want to be *overly* creative here. You want to be unique, but you don't want to come across as a weirdo or a loose cannon. You want to present yourself as intelligent, professional, mature, persuasive, and concise because these are the qualities law schools seek in applicants.

THE BASICS

Here are the essentials of writing essays and personal statements.

Find your own unique angle. The admissions people read tons of really boring essays about "how great I am" and how "I think there should be justice for everyone." If you must explain why you want to obtain a law degree, strive to find an angle that is interesting and unique to you. If what you write *isn't* interesting to you, we promise that it won't be remotely interesting to an admissions officer. Also, in addition to being more effective, a unique and interesting essay will be far more enjoyable to write.

In general, avoid generalities. Again, admissions officers have to read an unbelievable number of boring essays. You will find it harder to be boring if you write about particulars. It's the details that stick in a reader's mind.

Good writing is writing that is easily understood. You want to get your point across, not bury it in words. Don't talk in circles. Your prose should be clear and direct. If an admissions officer has to struggle to figure out what you are trying to say, you'll be in trouble. Also, legal writing courses make up a significant part of most law school curriculums; if you can show that you have good writing skills, you have a serious edge.

Buy and read *The Elements of Style*, **by William Strunk, Jr. and E. B. White.** We can't recommend it highly enough. In fact, we're surprised you don't have it already. This little book is a required investment for any writer (and, believe us, you'll be doing plenty of writing as a law student and a practicing attorney). You will refer to it forever, and if you do what it says, your writing will definitely improve.

Have three or four people read your personal statement and critique it. If your personal statement contains misspellings and grammatical errors, admissions officers will conclude not only that you don't know how to write but also that you aren't shrewd enough to get help. What's worse, the more time you spend with a piece of your own writing, the less likely you are to spot any errors. You get tunnel vision. Ask friends, boyfriends, girlfriends, professors, brothers, sisters—somebody—to read your essay and comment on it. Use a computer with a spellchecker. *Be especially careful about punctuation!* Another tip: Read your personal statement aloud to yourself or someone else. You will catch mistakes and awkward phrases that would have gotten past you otherwise because it sounded fine in your head.

Don't repeat information from other parts of your application. It's a waste of time and space.

Stick to the length that is requested. It's only common courtesy.

Maintain the proper tone. Your essay should be memorable without being outrageous and easy to read without being too formal or sloppy. When in doubt, err on the formal side.

Being funny is a lot harder than you think. An applicant who can make an admissions officer laugh never gets lost

---

Law School Trivia
Four law schools that can claim both a United States president and a United States supreme court justice as either alumni or one-time students:
Harvard University: Rutherford B. Hayes and Harry Blackmun (among many, many others)
Yale University: William Jefferson Clinton and Clarence Thomas (also among many, many others)
University of Missouri—Kansas City: Harry S Truman (took night classes but did not graduate) and Charles Evans Whittaker
University of Cincinnati: William Howard Taft (who served both as president and as a member of the Supreme Court)

Websites about Getting into Law School

www.PrincetonReview.com
You can access tons of information about law school and the LSAT at our site.

www.lsac.org
This site is home to the people who bring you the LSAT and the LSDAS application processing service.

www.pre-law.com
This is a confidential service designed to answer your questions about how best to prepare for and successfully apply to law school. Once registered, you become eligible for up to a full year of unlimited, personalized, high-quality, pre-law advising for one flat fee.

---

in the shuffle. The clever part of the personal statement is passed around and read aloud. Everyone smiles and the admissions staff can't bear to toss your app into the "reject" pile. But beware! Most people think they're funny, but only a few are able to pull it off in this context. Obviously, stay away from one liners, limericks, and anything remotely off-color.

WHY DO YOU WANT TO GO TO LAW SCHOOL?
Writing about yourself often proves to be surprisingly difficult. It's certainly no cakewalk explaining who you are and why you want to go to law school, and presenting your lifetime of experiences in a mere two pages is nearly impossible. On the bright side, though, the personal statement is the only element of your application over which you have total control. It's a tremendous opportunity to introduce yourself, if you avoid the urge to communicate your entire genetic blueprint. Your goal should be much more modest.

DON'T GET CARRIED AWAY
Although some law schools set no limit on the length of the personal statement, you shouldn't take their bait. You can be certain that your statement will be at least glanced at in its entirety, but admissions officers are human, and their massive workload at admissions time has an understandable impact on their attention spans. You should limit yourself to two or three typed, double-spaced pages. Does this make your job any easier? Not at all. In fact, practical constraints on the length of your essay demand a higher degree of efficiency and precision. Your essay needs to convey what kind of thinking, feeling human being you are, and a two-page limit allows for absolutely no fat.

MAKE YOURSELF STAND OUT
We know you know this, but you will be competing against thousands of well-qualified applicants for admission to just about any law school. Consequently, your primary task in writing your application is to separate yourself from the crowd. Particularly if you are applying directly from college or if you have been out of school for a very

short time, you must do your best to see that the admissions committee cannot categorize you too broadly. Admissions committees will see innumerable applications from bright twenty-two-year-olds with good grades. Your essay presents an opportunity to put those grades in context, to define and differentiate yourself.

WHAT MAKES A GOOD PERSONAL STATEMENT?

Like any good writing, your law school application should tend towards clarity, conciseness, and candor. The first two of these qualities, clarity and conciseness, are usually the products of a lot of reading, rereading, and rewriting. Without question, repeated critical revision by yourself and others is the surest way to trim and tune your prose. The third quality, candor, is the product of proper motivation. Honesty cannot be superimposed after the fact; your writing must be candid from the outset.

In writing your personal statement for law school applications, pay particularly close attention to the way it is structured and the fundamental message it communicates. Admissions committees will read your essay two ways: as a product of your handiwork and as a product of your mind. Don't underestimate the importance of either perspective. A well-crafted essay will impress any admissions officer, but if it does not illuminate, you will not be remembered. You will not stand out. This is bad. Conversely, a thoughtful essay that offers true insight will stand out unmistakably, but if it is not readable, it will not receive serious consideration.

WHAT, PARTICULARLY, TO WRITE ABOUT

Given the most popular topic—"Why do you want to obtain a law degree?"—this one is pretty obvious. If you are having serious writer's block, try to express in a compelling manner some moment in your life, some experience you've had, or some intellectual slant of personal interest that is directing you to law school.

THINGS TO AVOID IN YOUR PERSONAL STATEMENT

"MY LSAT SCORE ISN'T GREAT, BUT I'M JUST NOT A GOOD TEST TAKER."

If you have a low LSAT score, avoid directly discussing it in your personal statement like the plague. Law school is a test-rich environment. In fact, grades in most law-school courses are determined by a single exam at the semester's end, and as a law student, you'll spend your Novembers and Aprils in a study carrel, completely removed from society. Saying that you are not good at tests will do little to convince an admissions committee that you've got the ability to succeed in law school once accepted.

Consider also that a low LSAT score speaks for itself—all too eloquently. It doesn't need you to speak for it, too. The LSAT may be a flawed test but don't go arguing the merits of the test to admissions officers because ordinarily it is the primary factor they use to make admissions decisions. We feel for you, but you'd be barking up the wrong tree here. The attitude of most law school admissions departments is that while the LSAT may be imperfect, it is equally imperfect for all applicants. Apart from extraordinary claims of serious illness on test day, few explanations for poor performance on the LSAT will mean much to the people who read your application.

About the only situation in which a discussion of your LSAT score is necessary is if you have two (or more) LSAT scores and one is significantly better than another. If you did much better in your second sitting than in your first, or vice versa, a brief explanation couldn't hurt. However, your explanation may mean little to the committee, which may have its own hard-and-fast rules for interpreting multiple LSAT scores. Even in this scenario, however, you should avoid bringing up the LSAT in the personal statement. *Save it for an addendum.*

The obvious and preferable alternative to an explicit discussion of a weak LSAT score would be to focus on what you *are* good at. If you really are bad at standardized tests, you must be better at something else, or you wouldn't have gotten as far as you have. If you think you are a marvelous researcher, say so. If you are a wonderful writer, show it.

Let your essay implicitly draw attention away from your weak points by focusing on your strengths. There is no way to convince an admissions committee that they should overlook your LSAT score. You may, however, present compelling reasons for them to look beyond it.

"MY COLLEGE GRADES WEREN'T THAT HIGH, BUT..."
This issue is a bit more complicated than the low LSAT score. Law school admissions committees will be more willing to listen to your interpretation of your college performance, but only within limits. Keep in mind that law schools require official transcripts for a reason. Members of the admissions committee will be aware of your academic credentials before ever getting to your essay. Just like with low LSAT scores, your safest course of action is to *save low grades for an addendum*.

Make no mistake: if your grades are unimpressive, you should offer the admissions committee something else by which to judge your abilities. Again, the best argument for looking past your college grades is evidence of achievement in another area, whether in your LSAT score, your extracurricular activities, your economic hardship as an undergraduate, or your career accomplishments.

"I'VE ALWAYS WANTED TO BE A LAWYER."
Sure you have. Many applicants seem to feel the need to point out that they really, really want to become attorneys. You will do yourself a great service by avoiding such throwaway lines. They'll do nothing for your essay but water it down. Do not convince yourself in a moment of desperation that claiming to have known that the law was your calling since age six (when—let's be honest—you really wanted to be a firefighter) will somehow move your application to the top of the pile. The admissions committee is not interested in how much you want to practice law. They want to know *why*.

"I WANT TO BECOME A LAWYER TO FIGHT INJUSTICE."
No matter how deeply you feel about battling social inequity, between us, writing it down makes you sound like a superhero on a soapbox. Moreover, though some people really do want to fight injustice, way down in the cockles

Law School Trivia
Supreme Court justices William Rehnquist and Sandra O'Connor were classmates at Stanford Law School.

More Celebrity Lawyers
Tony La Russa, manager of the St. Louis
  Cardinals and Oakland A's
Larry Rosenfeld and Rick Flax, founders of
  California Pizza Kitchen
Paul Cézanne, artist
Honoré de Balzac, writer
Igor Stravinsky, musician

of their hearts, most applicants are motivated to attend law school by less altruistic desires. Among the nearly one million practicing lawyers in the United States, there are relatively few who actually earn a living defending the indigent or protecting civil rights. Tremendously dedicated attorneys who work for peanuts and take charity cases are few and far between. We're not saying you don't want to be one of them; we're merely saying that folks in law school admissions won't *believe* you want to be one of them. They'll take your professed altruistic ambitions (and those of the hundreds of other personal statements identical to yours) with a chunk of salt.

If you can in good conscience say that you are committed to a career in the public interest, show the committee something tangible on your application and in your essay that will allow them to see your statements as more than mere assertions. However, if you cannot show that you are already a veteran in the Good Fight, don't claim to be. Law school admissions committees certainly do not regard the legal profession as a Saints vs. Sinners proposition, and neither should you. Do not be afraid of appearing morally moderate. If the truth is that you want the guarantee of the relatively good jobs a law degree practically ensures, be forthright. Nothing is as impressive to the reader of a personal statement as the ring of truth. And what's wrong with a good job, anyhow?

CHAPTER 5
Recommendations

The law schools to which you apply will require two or three letters of recommendation in support of your application. Some schools will allow you to submit as many letters as you like. Others make it clear that any more than the minimum number of letters of recommendation is unwelcome. If you've ever applied to a private school (or perhaps a small public school) then you know the drill.

Unlike the evaluation forms for some colleges and graduate programs, however, law school recommendation forms tend toward absolute minimalism. All but a few recommendation forms for law school applications ask a single, open-ended question. It usually goes something like, "What information about this applicant is relevant that is not to be found in other sources?" The generic quality of the forms from various law schools may be both a blessing and a curse. On the one hand, it makes it possible for those writing your recommendations to write a single letter that will suffice for all the applications you submit. This convenience will make everybody a lot happier. On the other hand, if a free-form recommendation is to make a positive impression on an admissions committee, it must convey real knowledge about you.

WHOM TO ASK

Your letters of recommendation should come from people who know you well enough to offer a truly informed assessment of your abilities. Think carefully before choosing whom to ask to do this favor for you, but, as a general rule, pick respectable people you've known for a long time. The better the writers of your recommendations know you and understand the broader experience that has brought you to your decision to attend law school, the more likely they will be able to write a letter that is specific enough to do you some good. You also want people who can and are willing to contribute to an integrated, cohesive application.

The application materials from most law schools suggest that your letters should come, whenever possible, from people in an academic setting. Some schools want at least two recommendations, both of which must be academic. Others explicitly request that the letters come from someone who has known you in a professional setting, especially if you've been out of school for a while.

HELP YOUR RECOMMENDATION WRITERS HELP YOU

Here, in essence, is the simple secret to great recommendations: Make sure the writers of your recommendations know you, your academic and professional goals, and the overall message you are trying to convey in your application. The best recommendations will fit neatly with the picture you present of yourself in your own essay, even when they make no specific reference to the issues your essay addresses. An effective law school application will present to the admissions committee a cohesive picture, not a pastiche. A great way to point your recommendation writers in the right direction and maximize their ability to contribute to your overall cause is to provide them with copies of your personal statement. Don't be bashful about amiably communicating a few "talking points" that don't appear in your personal statement, as well.

ACADEMIC REFERENCES

Most applicants will (and should) seek recommendations from current or former professors. The academic environment in law school is extremely rigorous. Admissions committees will be looking for assurance that you will be able not just to survive, but to excel. A strong recommendation from a college professor is a valuable corroboration of your ability to succeed in law school.

You want nothing less than stellar academic recommendations. While a perfunctory, lukewarm recommendation is unlikely to damage your overall application, it will obviously do nothing to bolster it. Your best bet is to choose at least one professor from your major field. An enthusiastic endorsement from such a professor will be taken as a sign that you are an excellent student. Second—and we hope that this goes without saying—you should choose professors who do not immediately associate your name with the letter C.

Specifics are of particular interest to admissions officers when they evaluate your recommendations. If a professor can make *specific* reference to a particular project you completed, or at least make substantive reference to your work in a particular course, the recommendation will be strengthened considerably. Make it your responsibility to

---

Helpful Websites
www.findlaw.com
Findlaw has the mother lode of free information about law, law schools, and legal careers.
www.ilrg.com
Mother lode honorable mention.
www.hg.org/students.html
Another honorable mention.
www.canadalawschools.org
Pretty much everything you ever wanted to know about Canadian law schools, eh.
www.jurist.law.pitt.edu
The University of Pittsburgh School of Law's splendid "Legal Education Network" offers a wealth of useful information.

enable your professors to provide specifics. Drop hints, or just lay it out for them. You might, for example, make available a paper you wrote for them of which you are particularly proud. Or you might just chat with the professor for a while to jog those dormant memories. You might feel uncomfortable tooting your own horn, but it's for the best. Unless your professors are well enough acquainted with you to be able to offer a very personal assessment of your potential, they will greatly appreciate a tangible reminder of your abilities on which to base their recommendation.

ESCAPING THE WOODWORK
If you managed to get through college without any professors noticing you, it's not the end of the world. Professors are quite talented at writing recommendations for students they barely know. Most consider it part of their job. Even seemingly unapproachable academic titans will usually be happy to dash off a quick letter for a mere student. However, these same obliging professors are masters of a sort of opaque prose style that screams to an admissions officer, "I really have no idea what to say about this kid who is, in fact, a near-total stranger to me!" Although an admissions committee will not dismiss out of hand such a recommendation, it's really not going to help you much.

REELING IN THE YEARS
Obviously, the longer it has been since you graduated, the tougher it is to obtain academic recommendations. However, if you've held on to your old papers, you may still be able to rekindle an old professor's memory of your genius by sending a decent paper or two along with your request for a recommendation (and, of course, a copy of your personal statement). You want to provide specifics any way you can.

NONACADEMIC REFERENCES
Getting the mayor, a senator, or the CEO of your company to write a recommendation helps only if you have a personal and professional connection with that person. Remember, you want the writers of your recommendations to provide specifics about your actual accomplishments. If

---

Even More Celebrity Lawyers
Henry James, writer
Howard Cosell, sportscaster
David Stern, NBA commissioner
Abraham Lincoln, U.S. president
Tim and Nina Zagat, the people who bring you Zagat's restaurant and hotel guides

you're having trouble finding academic recommendations, choose people from your workplace, from the community, or from any other area of your life that is important to you. If at all possible, talk to your boss or a supervisor from a previous job who knows you well (and, of course, likes you).

SEND A THANK-YOU NOTE

Always a good idea. It should be short and handwritten. Use a blue pen so the recipient knows for sure that your note is no cheap copy. As with any good thank-you note (and any good recommendation), mention a specific. (Send a thank-you note if you have an interview at a law school, too.)

CHAPTER 6
REAL LIFE WORK EXPERIENCE AND COMMUNITY SERVICE

WORK EXPERIENCE IN COLLEGE

Most law school applications will ask you to list any part-time jobs you held while you were in college and how many hours per week you worked. If you had to (or chose to) work your way through your undergraduate years, this should come as good news. A great number of law schools make it clear that they take your work commitments as a college student into consideration when evaluating your undergraduate GPA.

WORK EXPERIENCE IN REAL LIFE

All law school applications will ask you about your work experience beyond college. They will give you three or four lines on which to list such experience. Some schools will invite you to submit a resume. If you have a very good one, you should really milk this opportunity for all it's worth. Even if you don't have a marvelous resume, these few lines on the application and your resume are the only opportunities you'll have to discuss your post-college experience meaningfully—unless you choose to discuss professional experience in your personal statement as well.

The kind of job you've had is not as important as you might think. What interests the admissions committee is what you've made of that job and what it's made of you. Whatever your job was or is, you want to offer credible evidence of your competence. For example, mention in your personal statement your job advancement or any increase in your responsibility. Most importantly, though, remember your overriding goal of cohesive presentation: you want to show off your professional experience within the context of your decision to attend law school. This does not mean that you need to offer a geometric proof of how your experience in the workplace has led you inexorably to a career in the law. You need only explain truthfully how this experience influenced you and how it fits nicely into your thinking about law school.

Would You Believe? . . . Still More Celebrity Lawyers
Steve Young, retired NFL quarterback
Wallace Stevens, poet
Otto Preminger, filmmaker
Mahatma Ghandi, Indian political leader
Franz Kafka, writer

COMMUNITY SERVICE

An overwhelming majority of law schools single out community involvement as one of several influential factors in their admissions decisions. Law schools would like to admit applicants who show a long-standing commitment to something other than their own advancement.

It is certainly understandable that law schools would wish to determine the level of such commitment before admitting an applicant, particularly since so few law students go on to practice public interest law. Be forewarned, however, that nothing—*nothing*—is so obviously bogus as an insincere statement of a commitment to public interest issues. It just reeks. Admissions committees are well aware that very few people take the time out of their lives to become involved significantly in their communities. If you aren't one of them, trying to fake it can only hurt you.

CHAPTER 7
Interviews

Law School Trivia
You probably know about John Marshall, Thurgood Marshall, Oliver Wendell Holmes, and other significant Supreme Court justices, but we bet you can't name the justice appointed by Grover Cleveland whom one newspaper described as "the most obscure man ever appointed Chief Justice."

If you said Melvin Fuller, you really should get out more.

The odds are very good that you won't ever encounter an interview in the law school admissions process. Admissions staffs just aren't very keen on them. They do happen occasionally, though, and if you are faced with one, here are a few tips.

Be prepared. Interviews do make impressions. Some students are admitted simply because they had great interviews; less often, students are rejected because they bombed. Being prepared is the smartest thing you can do.

Don't ask questions that are answered in the brochures you got in the mail. This means you have to read those brochures. At breakfast before the interview is an ideal time.

If there is a popular conception of the school (e.g., Harvard is overly competitive), don't ask about it. Your interviewer will have been through the same song and dance too many times. You don't want to seem off the wall by asking bizarre questions; but even more, you don't want to sound exactly like every other boring applicant before you.

Look good, feel good. Wear nice clothes. If you aren't sure what to wear, *ask the admissions staff*. Say these words: "What should I wear?" Get a respectable haircut. Don't chew gum. Clean your fingernails. Brush your teeth. Wash behind your ears. You can go back to being a slob just as soon as they let you in.

Don't worry about time. Students sometimes are told that the sign of a good interview is that it lasts longer than the time allowed for it. Forget about this. Don't worry if your interview lasts exactly as long as the secretary said it would. And don't try to stretch out the end of your interview by suddenly becoming long-winded or asking a lot of questions you don't care about.

CHAPTER 8
Choosing a Law School

Attend a Law School Forum
These "college fairs" for law schools from all around the United States are held between July and November at different sites around the country. Law School Forums are a terrific way to get a broad overview of the whole field of schools; more than 150 programs send admissions officers to these forums, affording you a chance to gather information from representatives of almost every law school in the country—all in one place. Contact the LSAC or visit their website for more information.

There are some key things you should consider before randomly selecting schools from around the country or just submitting your application to somebody else's list of the Top 10 law schools.

GEOGRAPHY

It's a big deal. If you were born and raised in the state of New Mexico, care deeply about the "Land of Enchantment," wish to practice law there, and want to be the governor someday, then your best bet is to go to the University of New Mexico. A school's reputation is usually greater on its home turf than anywhere else (except for some of the larger-than-life schools, like Harvard and Yale). Also, most law schools tend to teach law that is specific to the states in which they are located. Knowledge of the eccentricities of state law will help you immensely three years down the road when it comes time to pass the bar exam. Even further, the career services office at your school will be strongly connected to the local legal industry. And, as a purely practical matter, it will be much easier to find a job and get to interviews in Boston, for example, if you live there. Still another reason to consider geography is the simple fact that you'll put down professional and social roots and get to know a lot of really great people throughout your law school career. Leaving them won't be any fun. Finally, starting with geographic limitations is the easiest way to dramatically reduce your number of potential schools.

SPECIALIZATION

Word has it that specialization is the trend of the future. General practitioners in law are becoming less common, so it makes sense to let future lawyers begin to specialize in school. At certain schools, you may receive your JD with an official emphasis in, say, taxation. Specialization is a particularly big deal at smaller or newer schools whose graduates cannot simply get by on their school's established reputation of excellence. Just between us, though, it's kind of hard to specialize in anything in most law schools because every graduate has to take this huge exam—the bar—that tests about a dozen topics. Most of your course selections will (and should) be geared toward passing the bar, which leaves precious few hours for specialization.

You'll almost certainly specialize, but it's not something to worry about until you actually look for a job. All of that said, if you already know what kind of law you want to specialize in, you're in good shape. Many schools offer certain specialties because of their location. If you are very interested in environmental law, you'd be better off going to Vermont Law School or Lewis and Clark's Northwestern School of Law than to Brooklyn Law School. Similarly, if you want to work with children as an attorney, check out Loyola University Chicago's Child Law Center. So look at what you want to do in addition to where you want to do it.

JOINT DEGREE PROGRAMS
In addition to offering specialized areas of study, many law schools have instituted formal dual-degree programs. These schools, nearly all of which are directly affiliated with a parent institution, offer students the opportunity to pursue a JD while also working toward some other degree. Although the JD/MBA combination is the most popular joint degree sought, many universities offer a JD program combined with degrees in everything from public policy to public administration to social work. Amidst a perpetually competitive legal market, dual degrees may make some students more marketable for certain positions come job time. However, don't sign up for a dual-degree program on a whim—they require a serious amount of work and often, a serious amount of tuition. (See page 95 for a list of joint degree programs available at some of the schools in this book.)

YOUR CHANCE OF ACCEPTANCE
Who knows how law schools end up with their reputations, but everything else being equal, you really do want to go a to a well-respected school. It will enhance your employment opportunities tremendously. Remember, whoever you are and whatever your background, your best bet is to select a couple "reach" schools, a couple schools at which you've got a good shot at being accepted, and a couple "safety" schools where you are virtually assured of acceptance. Remember also that being realistic about your chances will save you from unnecessary emotional letdowns. Getting in mostly boils down to numbers. Look at the acceptance rates and the average LSATs and GPAs of incoming classes at various schools to assess how you stack up.

Dean's List
According to a letter signed by just about every dean of every ABA-approved law school in the country, here are the factors you should consider when choosing a law school:
- *Breadth and support of alumni network*
- *Breadth of curriculum*
- *Clinical programs*
- *Collaborative research opportunities with faculty*
- *Commitment to innovative technology*
- *Cost*
- *Externship options*
- *Faculty accessibility*
- *Intensity of writing instruction*
- *Interdisciplinary programs*
- *International programming*
- *Law library strengths and services*
- *Loan repayment assistance for low-income lawyers*
- *Location*
- *Part-time enrollment options*
- *Public interest programs*
- *Quality of teaching*
- *Racial and gender diversity within the faculty and student body*
- *Religious affiliation*
- *Size of first-year classes*
- *Skills instruction*
- *Specialized areas of faculty expertise*

The Dreaded Bar Exam
Once you graduate, most states require you to take a bar exam before you can practice law. Some state bar exams are really, really hard. New York and California are examples. If you don't want to take a bar exam, consider a law school in beautiful Wisconsin. Anyone who graduates from a state-certified Wisconsin law school does not need to take the state bar exam to practice law in the Badger State, as long as they are approved by the Board of Bar Examiners.

PERSONAL APPEAL
A student at a prominent law school in the Pacific Northwest once described his law school to us as "a combination wood-grain bomb shelter and Ewok village." Another student at a northeastern law school told us her law school was fine except for its "ski-slope classrooms" and "East German Functionalist" architecture. While the curricula at various law schools are pretty much the same, the weather, the surrounding neighborhoods, the nightlife, and the character of the student populations are startlingly different. An important part of any graduate program is enjoying those moments in life when you're not studying. If you aren't comfortable in the environment you choose, it's likely to be reflected in the quality of work you do and your attitude. Before you make a $10,000 to $80,000 investment in any law school, you really ought to check it out in person. While you are there, talk to students and faculty. Walk around. Kick the tires. *Then* make a decision.

EMPLOYMENT PROSPECTS
Where do alumni work? How much money do they make? What percentage of graduates is employed within six months of graduation? How many major law firms interview on campus? These are massively important questions, and you owe it to yourself to look into the answers before choosing a school.

YOUR VALUES
It is important that you define honestly the criteria for judging law schools. What do you want out of a law school? Clout? A high salary? A hopping social life? To live in a certain city? To avoid being in debt up to your eyeballs? A noncompetitive atmosphere? Think about it.

MAKE A LIST
Using these criteria (and others you find relevant), develop a list of prospective schools. Ideally, you'll find this book useful in creating the list. Assign a level to each new school you add (something like "reach," "good shot," and "safety").

At your "reach" schools, the average LSAT scores and GPAs of incoming students should be higher than yours are. These are law schools that will probably not accept you based on your numbers alone. In order to get in, you'll need to wow them with everything else (personal statement, stellar recommendations, work experience, etc.).

Your "good shot" schools should be the schools you like that accept students with about the same LSAT scores and GPA as yours. Combined with a strong and *cohesive* application, you've got a decent shot at getting into these schools.

At your "safety" schools, the average LSAT scores and GPAs of their current students should be below yours. These schools should accept you pretty painlessly if there are no major blemishes on your application (e.g., a serious run-in with the law) and you don't just phone in the application. They hate that.

Did You Know?
According to the people who make the LSAT, the average applicant applies to between 4 and 5 law schools.

CHAPTER 9
MONEY MATTERS

Law school is a cash cow for colleges and universities everywhere and, especially at a private school, you are going to be gouged for a pretty obscene wad of cash over the next three years. Take New York University School of Law, where tuition is just over $30,000. If you are planning to eat, live somewhere, buy books, and (maybe) maintain health insurance, you are looking at about $47,000 per year. Multiply that by three years of law school. You should get $141,000. Now faint. Correct for inflation (NYU certainly will), add things like computers and other miscellany, and you can easily spend $150,000 to earn a degree. Assume that you have to borrow every penny of that $150,000. Multiply it by 8 percent over 10 years (a common assumption of law school applicants is that they will be able to pay all their debt back in 10 years or less). Your monthly payments will be around $1,825.

Tuition at ABA-accredited schools has increased 127 percent in the last decade or so. Over the past 20 years the increase has been a whopping 570 percent.

On the bright side, while law school is certainly an expensive proposition, the financial rewards of practicing can be immensely lucrative. You won't be forced into bankruptcy if you finance it properly. There are tried-and-true ways to reduce your initial costs, finance the costs on the horizon, and manage the debt you'll leave school with—all without ever asking "Have you been in a serious accident recently?" in a television commercial.

LAW SCHOOL ON THE CHEAP

Private schools aren't the only law schools and you don't have to come out of law school saddled with tens of thousands of dollars of debt. Many state schools have reputations that equal or surpass some of the top privates. It might be worth your while to spend a year establishing residency in a state with one or more good public law schools. Here's an idea: Pack up your belongings and move to a cool place like Minneapolis or Seattle or Berkeley or Austin or Boulder. Spend a year living there. Wait tables, hang out, listen to music, walk the earth, write the Great American Novel, and *then* study law.

COMPARISON SHOPPING

Here are the full-time tuition costs at law schools around the country. They are randomly paired schools in the same region (one public and one private) and are provided to help you get a feel of what law school costs are going to run you. Those schools that have the same tuition in both columns are private law schools.

Law School	In State	Out of State
Florida State University, College of Law	$4,868	$14,173
University of Miami, School of Law	$26,070	$26,070
Indiana University-Bloomington, School of Law	$10,380	$22,627
Notre Dame Law School	$26,110	$26,110
University of Tennessee, College of Law	$6,576	$18,382
Vanderbilt University, Law School	$28,350	$28,350
University of Iowa, College of Law	$10,000	$23,758
Drake University, Law School	$19,450	$19,450
Louisiana State University, Law Center	$6,711	$12,552
Tulane University, School of Law	$26,100	$26,100
University of California, Hastings College of Law	$10,175	$20,182
Golden Gate University, School of Law	$24,476	$24,476
University of Texas, School of Law	$8,520	$16,680
Baylor University, School of Law	$14,719	$14,719
University of Illinois, College of Law	$11,310	$24,398
Northwestern University, School of Law	$32,008	$32,008
University of Pittsburgh, School of Law	$15,936	$24,038
University of Pennsylvania, Law School	$29,310	$29,310
University of Oregon, School of Law	$11,500	$15,600
Lewis and Clark College, Northwestern School of Law	$23,196	$23,196

The Skinny on Loan Repayment Assistance Programs
For a comprehensive listing of assistance programs and for other loan-forgiveness information, call Equal Justice Works at 202-466-3686, or look them up on the Web at www.napil.org.

LOAN REPAYMENT ASSISTANCE PROGRAMS

If you are burdened with loans, we've got more bad news. The National Association of Law Placement (NALP) shows that while salaries for law school graduates who land jobs at the big, glamorous firms have skyrocketed in the past few years, salaries of $35,000–$40,000 are just as common as salaries of $70,000–$130,000 for the general run of law school grads. There are, however, a growing number of law schools and other sources willing to pay your loans for you (it's called loan forgiveness—as if you've sinned by taking out loans) in return for your commitment to employment in public interest law.

While doing a tour of duty in public service law will put off dreams of working in a big firm or becoming the next Johnnie Cochran, the benefits of these programs are undeniable. Here's how just about all of them work. You commit to working for a qualified public service or public interest job. As long as your gross income does not exceed the prevailing public service salary, the programs will pay off a good percentage of your debt. Eligible loans are typically any educational debt financed through your law school, which really excludes only loan sharks and credit-card debts.

MAXIMIZE YOUR AID

A simple but oft-forgotten piece of wisdom: if you don't ask, you usually don't get. Be firm when trying to get merit money from your school. Some schools have reserves of cash that go unused. Try simply asking for more financial aid. The better your grades, of course, the more likely they are to crack open their safe of financial goodies for you. Unfortunately, grants aren't as prevalent for law students as for undergrads. Scholarships are not nearly as widely available, either. To get a general idea of availability of aid at a law school, contact the financial aid office.

PARENTAL CONTRIBUTION?!

If you are operating under the assumption that, as a taxpaying grownup who has been out of school for a number of years, you will be recognized as the self-supporting adult you are, well, you could be in for a surprise. Veterans of financial aid battles will not be surprised to hear that even law school financial aid offices have a difficult time recognizing when apron strings have legitimately been cut. Schools may try to take into account your parents' income in determining your eligibility for financial aid, regardless of your age or tax status. Policies vary widely. Be sure to ask the schools you are considering exactly what their policy is regarding financial independence for the purposes of financial aid.

BORROWING MONEY

It's an amusingly simple process and several companies are in the business of lending large chunks of cash specifically to law students. Your law school financial aid office can tell you how to reach them. You should explore more than one option and shop around for the lowest fees and rates.

WHO'S ELIGIBLE?

Anyone with reasonably good credit, regardless of financial need, can borrow enough money to finance law school. If you have financial need, you will probably be eligible for some types of financial aid if you meet the following basic qualifications:

- You are a United States citizen or a permanent U.S. resident.

- You are registered for Selective Service if you are a male, or you have the documentation to prove that you are exempt.

- You are not in default on student loans already.

- You don't have a horrendous credit history.

- You haven't been busted for certain drug-related crimes, including possession.

WHAT TYPES OF LOANS ARE AVAILABLE?

There are four basic types of loans: federal, state, private, and institutional.

Federal

The federal government funds federal loan programs. Federal loans, particularly the Stafford Loan, are usually the "first resort" for borrowers. Most federal loans are need-based, but some higher-interest loans are available regardless of financial circumstances.

Let the Law School Pick Up the Tab for Phone Calls Whenever Possible
A lot of schools have free telephone numbers that they don't like to publish in books like this one. If the number we have listed for a particular law school is not an 800-number, it doesn't necessarily mean that you have to pay every time you call the school. Check out the school's Internet site, or ask for the 800-number when you call the first time.

TABLE OF LOANS

NAME OF LOAN	SOURCE	ELIGIBILITY	MAXIMUM ALLOCATION
Subsidized Federal Stafford Student Loan (SSL, formerly GSL)	Federal, administered by participating lender	Demonstrated financial need; selective service registration; not in default on any previous student loan	$8,500/year with maximum aggregate of $65,500; aggregate includes undergraduate subsidized loans made under the same program
Unsubsidized Stafford Student Loan	Federal, administered by participating lender	Not need-based; selective service registration; not in default on any previous student loan.	$18,500/year with maximum aggregate of $138,500; aggregate includes undergraduate loans made under the same program and undergraduate and graduate loans made under the Unsubsidized and Subsidized Stafford Student Loan program
Perkins Loan (formerly NDSL)	Federal, administered by school	Demonstrated financial need; selective service registration; not in default on student loans.	$6,000/year with maximum aggregate of $40,000; aggregate includes undergraduate Perkins loans
Law Access Loan (LAL)	Access Group	Not need-based	$120,000 for most schools (up to amount certified by your school)

Private

Private loans are funded by banks, foundations, corporations, and other associations. A number of private loans are targeted to aid particular segments of the population. You may have to do some investigating to identify private loans for which you might qualify. Like always, contact your law school's financial aid office to learn more.

Institutional

The amount of loan money available and the method by which it is disbursed vary greatly from one school to another. Private schools, especially those that are older and more established, tend to have larger endowments and can offer more assistance. To find out about the resources available at a particular school, refer to its catalogue or contact—you guessed it—the financial aid office.

TABLE OF LOANS

REPAYMENT AND DEFERRAL OPTIONS	INTEREST RATE	PROS	CONS
10 years to repay; begin repayment 6 months after graduation; forbearance possible.	Variable, doesn't exceed 8.25%	Most common law school loan; interest is subsidized by the feds during school; once you get a loan, any subsequent loans are made at the same rate	None
10 years to repay; principal is deferred while in school, but interest accrues immediately; begin repayment six months after graduation; forbearance possible	Variable, doesn't exceed 8.25%	Not need based; same interest rates as Federal Stafford; once you get a loan, any subsequent loans are made at the same rate	Interest accrues immediately and is capitalized if deferred.
10 years to repay; begin repayment 9 months after graduation	Fixed, 5%	Low interest rate	Low maximum allocation; primarily restricted to first- and second-year students
20 years to repay; principal repayment begins nine months after graduation.	Varies quarterly; 3-month LIBOR (London Interbank Offered Rate) Rate plus 2.7% or 3.9% determined by your credit history	High maximum allocation, not need based	Importance of credit rating in determining interest rate (for those with a poor credit history)

CHAPTER 10
CAREER MATTERS

A Few Good Books
If you are thinking about law school, here are a few books you might find interesting:

The Princeton Review's Law School Essays That Made a Difference
Check out 34 successful essays written for an assortment of selective schools.

Jeff Deaver, The Complete Law School Companion: How to Excel at America's Most Demanding Post-Graduate Curriculum
This straightforward law school survival guide has much to commend it.

Paul M. Lisnek, Law School Companion: The Ultimate Guide to Excelling in Law School and Launching Your Career
We'd be remiss if we did not recommend our own modest contribution to the pile of books about succeeding in law school. It's worth a look, in our humble opinion.

Okay, it's a long time away, but you really ought to be thinking about your professional career beyond law school from Day One, especially if your goal is to practice with a major law firm. What stands between you and a job as an "associate," the entry-level position at one of these firms, is a three-stage evaluation: first, a review of your resume, including your grades and work experience; second, an on-campus interview; and last, one or more "call-back" interviews at the firm's offices. It's a fairly intimidating ordeal, but there are a few ways to reduce the anxiety and enhance your chances of landing a great job.

YOUR RESUME
The first thing recruiters tend to notice after your name is the name of the law school you attend. Tacky, but true. Perhaps the greatest misconception among law students, however, is that hiring decisions turn largely upon your school's prestige. All those rankings perpetuate this myth. To be sure, there are a handful of schools with reputations above all others, and students who excel at these schools are in great demand. But you are equally well, if not better, situated applying from the top of your class at a strong, less prestigious law school class than from the bottom half of a "Top 10" law school class.

FIRST-YEAR GRADES ARE THE WHOLE ENCHILADA
Fair or not, the first year of law school will unduly influence your legal future. It's vital that you hit the ground running because law school grades are *the* critical factor in recruitment. An even harsher reality is that *first-year grades are by far the most critical in the hiring process.* Decisions about who gets which fat summer jobs are generally handed down before students take a single second-year exam. Consequently, you're left with exactly no time to adjust to law-school life and little chance to improve your transcript if you don't come out on top as a first-year student.

WORK EXPERIENCE

If you're applying to law school right out of college, chances are your most significant work experience has been a summer job. Recruiters don't expect you to have spent these months writing Supreme Court decisions. They are generally satisfied if you have shown evidence that you worked diligently and seriously at each opportunity. Students who took a year or more off after college obviously have more opportunities to impress, but also more of a burden to demonstrate diligence and seriousness.

Work experience in the legal industry—clerkships and paralegal jobs, just for instance—can be excellent sources of professional development. They are fairly common positions among job applicants, though, so don't feel you have to pursue one of these routes just to show your commitment to the law. You'll make a better impression, really, by working in an industry in which you'd like to specialize (e.g., a prospective securities lawyer summering with an investment bank).

THE INTERVIEWS

There are as many "right approaches" to an interview as there are interviewers. That observation provides little comfort, of course, especially if you're counting on a good interview to make up for whatever deficiencies there are on your resume. Think about the purpose of the initial 30-minute interview you are likely to have: it provides a rough sketch not only of your future office personality but also your demeanor under stress. The characteristics you demonstrate and the *impression* you give are more important than anything you say. Composure, confidence, maturity, articulation, an ability to develop rapport—these are characteristics recruiters are looking for. Give them what they want.

CHAPTER 11
LAW SCHOOL 101

> **An Old Law School Adage**
> First year they scare you to death.
> Second year they work you to death.
> Third year they bore you to death.

IS IT REALLY THAT BAD?

The first semester of law school has the well-deserved reputation of being among the greatest challenges to the intellect and stamina that you'll ever face. It is tons and tons of work and, in many ways, it's an exercise in intellectual survival. Just as the gung-ho army recruit must survive boot camp, so too must the bright-eyed law student endure the homogenizing effects of that first year.

Though complex and difficult, the subject matter in first-year law-school courses is probably no more inherently difficult than what is taught in other graduate or professional schools. The particular, private terror that is shared by roughly 40,000 1Ls every year stems more from law school's peculiar *style*. The method of instruction here unapologetically punishes students who would prefer to learn passively.

THE FIRST-YEAR CURRICULUM

The first-year curriculum in the law school you attend will almost certainly be composed of a combination of the following courses:

TORTS

The word comes from the Middle French for "injury." The Latin root of the word means "twisted." Torts are wrongful acts, excluding breaches of contract, over which you can sue people. They include battery, assault, false imprisonment, and intentional infliction of emotional distress. Torts can range from the predictable to the bizarre, from "Dog Bites Man" to "Man Bites Dog" and everything in between. The study of torts mostly involves reading cases in order to discern the legal rationale behind decisions pertaining to the extent of, and limits on, the civil liability of one party for harm done to another.

CONTRACTS

They may seem fairly self-explanatory but contractual relationships are varied and complicated, as two semesters of contracts will teach you. Again, through the study of past court cases, you will follow the largely unwritten law governing the system of conditions and obligations a contract represents, as well as the legal remedies available when contracts are breached.

CIVIL PROCEDURE

Civil procedure is the study of how you get things done in civil (as opposed to criminal) court. "Civ Pro" is the study of the often dizzyingly complex rules that govern not only who can sue whom, but also how, when, and where they can do it. This is not merely a study of legal protocol, for issues of process have a significant indirect effect on the substance of the law. Rules of civil procedure govern the conduct of both the courtroom trial and the steps that might precede it: obtaining information (discovery), making your case (pleading), pretrial motions, etc.

PROPERTY

You may never own a piece of land, but your life will inevitably and constantly be affected by property laws. Anyone interested in achieving an understanding of broader policy issues will appreciate the significance of this material. Many property courses will emphasize the transfer of property and, to varying degrees, economic analysis of property law.

CRIMINAL LAW

Even if you become a criminal prosecutor or defender, you will probably never run into most of the crimes you will be exposed to in this course. Can someone who shoots the dead body of a person he believes to be alive be charged with attempted murder? What if they were both on drugs or had really rough childhoods? Also, you'll love the convoluted exam questions, in which someone will invariably go on a nutty crime spree.

CONSTITUTIONAL LAW

"Con Law" is the closest thing to a normal class you will take in your first year. It emphasizes issues of government structure (e.g., federal power versus state power) and individual rights (e.g., personal liberties, freedom of expression, property protection). You'll spend a great deal of time studying the limits on the lawmaking power of Congress as well.

Good Law School Joke
In contracts class, the professor asked a student, "If you were to give someone an orange, how would you go about it?"
The student replied, "Here's an orange."
The professor was outraged. "No! No!" she exclaimed. "Think like a lawyer!"
The student then replied, "Okay. I'd say, 'I hereby give and convey to you all and singular, my estate and interests, rights, claim, title, and claim of and in, said orange, together with all its rind, juices, pulp, and seeds, and all rights and advantages contained therein, with full power to bite, cut, freeze, and otherwise eat, or give, bequeath, or devise with and without aforementioned rind, juices, pulp, and seeds. Anything herein before or hereinafter or in any deed, or deeds, instruments of whatever nature or kind whatsoever to the contrary in anywise notwithstanding . . .'"

Tips for Classroom Success

Be alert. Review material immediately before class so that it is fresh in your memory. Then review your notes from class later the same day and the week's worth of notes at the end of each week.

Remember that there are few correct answers. The goal of a law school class is generally to analyze, understand, and attempt to resolve issues or problems.

Learn to state and explain legal rules and principles with accuracy.

You don't want to focus on minutiae from cases or class discussions; always be trying to figure out what the law is.

Accept the ambiguity in legal analysis and class discussion; classes are intended to be thought-provoking, perplexing, and difficult.

No one class session will make or break you. Keep in mind how each class fits within the course overall.

Don't write down what other students say. Write down the law. Concentrate your notes on the professor's hypotheticals and emphasis in class.

A simple but effective way of keeping yourself in touch with where the class is at any given time is to review the table of contents in the casebook.

If you don't use a laptop, don't sit next to someone who does. The constant tapping on the keys will drive you crazy, and you may get a sense that they are writing down more than you (which is probably not true).

If you attend class, you don't need to tape record it. There are better uses of your time than to spend hours listening to the comments of students who were just as confused as you were when you first dealt with the material in class.

LEGAL METHODS

One of the few 20th-century improvements on the traditional first-year curriculum that has taken hold nearly everywhere, this course travels under various aliases, such as Legal Research and Writing, or Elements of the Law. In recent years, increased recognition of the importance of legal writing skills has led over half of the U.S. law schools to require or offer a writing course after the first year. This class will be your smallest, and possibly your only, refuge from the Socratic Method. Methods courses are often taught by junior faculty and attorneys in need of extra cash, and are designed to help you acquire fundamental skills in legal research, analysis, and writing. The Methods course may be the least frightening you face, but it can easily consume an enormous amount of time. This is a common lament, particularly at schools where very few credits are awarded for it.

In addition to these course requirements, many law schools require 1Ls to participate in a moot-court exercise. As part of this exercise, students—sometimes working in pairs or even small groups—must prepare briefs and oral arguments for a mock trial (usually appellate). This requirement is often tied in with the methods course so that those briefs and oral arguments will be well researched—and graded.

THE CASE METHOD

In the majority of your law school courses, and probably in all of your first-year courses, your only texts will be things called casebooks. The case method eschews explanation and encourages exploration. In a course that relies entirely on the casebook, you will never come across a printed list of "laws." Instead, you will learn that in many areas of law there is no such thing as a static set of rules, but only a constantly evolving system of principles. You are expected to understand the principles of law—in all of its layers and ambiguity—through a critical examination of a series of cases that were decided according to such principles. You will often feel utterly lost, groping for answers to unarticulated questions. This is not merely normal; it is intended.

In practical terms, the case method works like this: For every class meeting, you will be assigned a number of cases to read from your casebook, which is a collection of (extremely edited) written judicial decisions in actual court cases. The names won't even have been changed to protect the innocent. The cases are the written judicial opinions rendered in court cases that were decided at the appeals or Supreme Court level. (Written opinions are not generally rendered in lower courts.)

Your casebook will contain no instructions and little to no explanation. Your assignments simply will be to read the cases and be in a position to answer questions based on them. There will be no written homework assignments, just cases, cases, and more cases.

You will write, for your own benefit, summaries—or briefs—of these cases. Briefs are your attempts to summarize the issues and laws around which a particular case revolves *By briefing, you figure out what the law is*. The idea is that, over the course of a semester, you will try to integrate the content of your case briefs and your notes from in-class lectures, discussions, or dialogues into some kind of cohesive whole.

THE SOCRATIC METHOD

As unfamiliar as the case method will be to most 1Ls, the real source of anxiety is the way the professor presents it. Socratic instruction entails directed questioning and limited lecturing. Generally, the Socratic professor invites a student to attempt a cogent summary of a case assigned for that day's class. Hopefully, it won't be you (but someday it will be). Regardless of the accuracy and thoroughness of your initial response, the professor then grills you on details overlooked or issues unresolved. Then, the professor will change the facts of the actual case at hand into a hypothetical case that may or may not have demanded a different decision by the court.

The overall goal of the Socratic Method is to forcibly improve your critical reasoning skills. If you are reasonably well prepared, thinking about all these questions will force you beyond the immediately apparent issues in a given case to consider its broader implications. The dia-

> **Watch The Paper Chase. Twice.**
> This movie is the only one ever produced about law school that comes close to depicting the real thing. Watch it before you go to orientation. Watch it again on Thanksgiving break and laugh when you can identify your classmates.

logue between the effective Socratic instructor and the victim-of-the-moment will also force nonparticipating students to question their underlying assumptions of the case under discussion.

WHAT IS CLINICAL LEGAL EDUCATION?

The latest so-called innovation in legal education is ironic in that it's a return to the old emphasis on practical experience. Hands-on training in the practical skills of lawyering now travels under the name "Clinical Legal Education."

HOW IT WORKS

Generally, a clinical course focuses on developing practical lawyering skills. "Clinic" means exactly what you would expect: a working law office where second- and third-year law students counsel clients and serve human beings. (A very limited number of law schools allow first-year students to participate in legal clinics.)

In states that grant upper-level law students a limited right to represent clients in court, students in a law school's clinic might actually follow cases through to their resolution. Some schools have a single on-site clinic that operates something like a general law practice, dealing with cases ranging from petty crime to landlord-tenant disputes. At schools that have dedicated the most resources to their clinical programs, numerous specialized clinics deal with narrowly defined areas of law, such as employment discrimination. The opportunities to participate in such live-action programs, however, are limited.

OTHER OPTIONS

Clinical legal education is a lot more expensive than traditional instruction, which means that few law schools can accommodate more than a small percentage of their students in clinical programs. If that's the case, check out external clinical placements and simulated clinical courses. In a clinical externship, you might work with a real firm or public agency several hours a week and meet with a faculty advisor only occasionally. Though students who participate in these programs are unpaid, they will ordinarily receive academic credit. Also, placements are chosen quite carefully to ensure that you don't become a gopher.

There are also simulated clinical courses. In one of these, you'll perform all of the duties that a student in a live-action clinic would, but your clients are imaginary.

CHAPTER 12
HOW TO EXCEL AT ANY LAW SCHOOL

Contact Law Preview
Law Preview
69 South Moger Avenue, Suite 206
Mount Kisco, NY 10549
Phone: 888-PREP-YOU
E-mail: admin@lawpreview.com
Website: www.lawpreview.com

Preparation for law school is something you should take very seriously. Law school will be one of the most interesting and rewarding experiences of your life, but it's also an important and costly investment. Your academic performance in law school will influence your career for years to come. Consider the following facts when thinking about how important it is to prepare for law school:

- The average full-time law student spends more than $125,000 to attend law school.

- The average law student graduates with over $80,000 of debt.

- The median income for law school graduates is only about $55,000.

As you can see, most law students cannot afford to be mediocre. Money isn't everything, but when you're strapped with close to six figures of debt, money concerns will weigh heavily on your career choices. Even if money is not a concern for you, your academic performance in law school will profoundly affect your employment options after graduation and, ultimately, your legal career. Consider these additional facts:

- Students who excel in law school may have opportunities to earn up to $160,000 right out of law school.

- Only law students who excel academically have opportunities to obtain prestigious judicial clerkships, teaching positions, and distinguished government jobs.

As you can see, law students who achieve academic success enjoy better career options and have a greater ability to escape the crushing debt of law school. The point here is obvious: Your chances of achieving your goals—no matter what you want to do with your career—are far better if you succeed academically.

Now comes the hard part: How do you achieve academic success? You are going to get plenty of advice about how to excel in law school—much of it unsolicited. You certainly don't need any from us. We strongly advise, however, that you pay extra-special attention to what Don Macaulay, the president of Law Preview, has to say about surviving, and thriving, as a law student. Macaulay, like all the founders of Law Preview, graduated at the top of his law school class and worked at a top law firm before he began developing and administering Law Preview's law school prep course in 1998.

While there are many resources that claim to provide a recipe for success in law school, Law Preview is the best of the lot. They have retained some of the most talented legal scholars in the country to lecture during their week-long sessions, and they deliver what they promise—a methodology for attacking and conquering the law school experience.

We asked Macaulay a few questions we thought prospective law students might like to know the answers to:

Q: **It is often said that the "first year" of law school is the most important year. Is this true and, if so, why?**

A: It is true. Academic success during the first year of law school can advance a successful legal career unlike success in any other year, because many of the top legal employers start recruiting so early that your first-year grades are all they will see. Most prestigious law firms hire their permanent attorneys from among the ranks of the firm's "summer associates"—usually second-year law students who work for the firm during the summer between the second and third years of law school. Summer associates are generally hired during the fall semester of the second year, a time when only the first year grades are available. A student who does well during the first year, lands a desirable summer associate position, and then impresses her employer, is well on her way to a secure legal job regardless of her academic performance after the first year.

In addition, first-year grades often bear heavily upon a student's eligibility for law review and other prestigious scholastic activities, including other law journals and moot court. These credentials are considered the most significant signs of law school achievement, often even more than a high grade point average. Many of the top legal employers in the private and the public sectors seek out young lawyers with these credentials, and some employers will not even interview candidates who lack these honors, even after a few years of experience. As a result, a solid performance during the first year of law school can have a serious impact upon your professional opportunities available after graduation.

All B+s put you in the top quarter at most schools, in the top fifth at many.

Websites About Doing Well in Law School

www.lawpreview.com
Law Preview is an intensive week-long seminar designed to help you conquer law school. Learn why hundreds of students have made Law Preview their first step to law review. The site also offers free features such as law school news and a daily advice column written by Atticus Falcon, author of Planet Law School.

www.barristerbooks.com
BarristerBooks.com is the best place to purchase legal study aids, cheap!

Q: How does law school differ from what students experienced as undergraduates?

A: Many students, especially those who enjoyed academic success in college, presume that law school will be a mere continuation of their undergraduate experience, and that, by implementing those skills that brought them success in college, they will enjoy similar success in law school. This couldn't be farther from the truth. Once law school begins, students often find themselves thrown into deep water. They are handed an anchor in the form of a casebook (and they are told it's a life preserver), and they are expected to sink or swim. While almost nobody sinks in law school anymore, most spend all of first year just trying to keep their heads above water. In reality, virtually every student who is admitted into law school possesses the intelligence and work ethic needed to graduate. But in spite of having the tools needed to survive the experience, very few possess the know-how to truly excel and make law review at their schools.

What makes the law school experience unique is its method of instruction and its system of grading. Most professors rely on the case method as a means for illustrating legal rules and doctrines encountered in a particular area of the law. With the case method, students are asked to read a particular case or, in some instances, several cases, that the professor will use to lead a classroom discussion illustrating a particular rule of law. The assigned readings come from casebooks, which are compilations of cases for each area of law. The cases are usually edited to illustrate distinct legal rules, often with very little commentary or enlightenment by the casebook editor. The casebooks often lack anything more than a general structure, and law professors often contribute little to the limited structure. Students are asked to read and analyze hundreds of cases in a vacuum. Since each assigned case typically builds upon a legal rule illustrated in a previous case, it isn't until the end of the semester or, for some classes, the end of the year, that students begin to form an understanding of how these rules interrelate.

One of the objectives of Law Preview's law school prep course is to help students to understand the "big picture" before they begin their classes. We hire some of the most talented law professors from around the country to provide "previews" of the core first-year law school courses:

Civil Procedure, Constitutional Law, Contracts, Criminal Law, Property, and Torts. During their lectures, our professors provide students with a roadmap for each subject by discussing the law's development, legal doctrines, and recurring themes and policies that students will encounter throughout the course. By providing entering law students with a conceptual framework for the material they will study, Law Preview eliminates the frustration that most of them will encounter when reading and analyzing case law in a vacuum.

Q: What is the best way to prepare for law school, and when should you start?

A: When preparing for law school, students should focus on two interrelated tasks: 1) developing a strategy for academic success, and 2) getting mentally prepared for the awesome task ahead. The primary objective for most law students is to achieve the highest grades possible, and a well-defined strategy for success will help you direct your efforts most efficiently and effectively toward that goal. You must not begin law school equipped solely with some vague notion of hard work. Success requires a concrete plan that includes developing a reliable routine for classroom preparation, a proficient method of outlining, and a calculated strategy for exam-taking. The further you progress in law school without such a plan, the more time and energy you will waste struggling through your immense work load without moving discernibly closer toward achieving academic success.

You must also become mentally prepared to handle the rigors of law school. Law school can be extremely discouraging because students receive very little feedback during the school year. Classes are usually graded solely based on final exam scores. Mid-term exams and graded papers are uncommon, and classroom participation is often the only way for students to ascertain if they understand the material and are employing effective study methods. As a result, a winning attitude is critical to success in law school. Faith in yourself will help you continue to make the personal sacrifices during the first year that you need to make to succeed in law school, even when the rewards are not immediately apparent.

Books About Doing Well in Law School

Professors Jeremy Paul and Michael Fischl, Getting To Maybe: How To Excel on Law School Exams
This book is excellent! While many books and professors may preach "IRAC" as a way of structuring exam answers, Getting to Maybe *correctly points out that such advice does not help students first correctly identify legal issues and, more importantly, master the intricacies of legal analysis.*

Atticus Falcon, Planet Law School: What You Need to Know (Before You Go) . . . But Didn't Know to Ask
This is what everyone is reading before going to law school. Pseudonymned author Atticus Falcon gives a critical appraisal of the state of law school education. The author's assessments are usually directed and well-reasoned. This book tells you what the real "rules of the game" are, so you'll know exactly what you are facing. It's also the only book that gives you detailed information — including recommendations of "primers" and other aids — that you can you use to get a head start before you go to law school.

Incoming law students should begin preparing for law school during the summertime prior to first year, and preparation exercises should be aimed at gaining a general understanding of what law school is all about. A solid understanding of what you are expected to learn during the first year will give you the information you need to develop both your strategy for success and the confidence you need to succeed. There are several books on the market that can help in this regard, but those students who are best prepared often attend Law Preview's one-week intensive preparatory course specifically designed to teach beginning law students the strategies for academic success.

Q: What factors contribute to academic success in law school?

A: Academic success means one thing in law school—exam success. The grades that you receive, particularly during the first year, will be determined almost exclusively by the scores you receive on your final exams. Occasionally, a professor may add a few points for class participation, but that is rare. In most classes, your final exam will consist of a three- or four-hour written examination at the end of the semester or—if the course is two semesters long—at the end of the year. The amount of material you must master for each final exam will simply dwarf that of any undergraduate exam you have ever taken. The hope that you can "cram" a semester's worth of information into a one-week reading period is pure fantasy and one that will surely lead to disappointing grades. The focus of your efforts from day one should be success on your final exams. Don't get bogged down in class preparation or in perfecting a course outline if it will not result in some discernible improvement in your exam performance. All of your efforts should be directed at improving your exam performance in some way. It's as simple as that.

Q: What skills are typically tested on law school exams?

A: Law school exams usually test three different skills: 1) the ability to accurately identify legal issues, 2) the ability to recall the relevant law with speed, and 3) the ability to apply the law to the facts efficiently and skillfully. The proper approach for developing these skills differs, depending on the substantive area of law in question and whether your exam is open-book or closed-book.

Identifying legal issues is commonly known as issue-spotting. On most of your exams, you will be given complex, hypothetical fact patterns. From the facts you are given, you must identify the particular legal issues that need to be addressed. This is a difficult skill to perfect and can only be developed through practice. The best way to develop issue-spotting skills is by taking practice exams. For each of your classes, during the first half of the semester you should collect all of the available exams that were given by your professor in the past. Take all of these exams under simulated exam conditions—find an open classroom, get some blue books, time yourself, and take the exams with friends so that you can review them afterwards. It is also helpful for you to practice any legal problems you were given during the semester. Issue-spotting is an important skill for all lawyers to develop. Lawyers utilize this skill on a daily basis when they listen to their clients' stories and are asked to point out places where legal issues might arise.

The ability to recall the law with speed is also very important and frequently tested. On all of your exams, you will be given a series of legal problems, and for each problem you will usually be required to provide the relevant substantive law and apply it to the facts of the problem. Your ability to recall the law with speed is critical, because in most classes, you will be under time constraints to answer all of the problems. The faster you recall the law, the more problems you will complete and the more time you will have to spend on demonstrating your analytical skills. For courses with closed-book exams, this means straight memorization or the use of memory recall devices, such as mnemonics. Do not be passive about learning the law—repeatedly reviewing your outline is not enough. You must actively learn the law by studying definitions and using memory-assistance devices like flash cards. When you have become exceedingly familiar with your flash cards, rewrite them so as to test your memory in different words. This is particularly critical for courses such as Torts and Criminal Law where you must learn a series of definitions with multiple elements. For courses with open-book exams, this means developing an index for your outline that will enable you to locate the relevant law quickly. Create a cover page for your outline that lists the page number for each substantive sub-topic. This will help you get there without any undue delay.

More Books About Doing Well in Law School

Professor Jay Feinman, Law 101: Everything You Need to Know About the American Justice System
This is another excellent book! Professor Feinman has provided an easy-to-understand introduction to the American legal system using simple language and intriguing cases.

Robert H. Miller, Esq, Law School Confidential: A Complete Guide to the Law School Experience
The author—a graduate of Penn Law, member of the law review, and former federal judicial clerk—and his team of "mentors" from law schools across the country pull no punches in providing revealing and honest chronological advice for all three years of the law school experience, from picking the law school that's right for you and funding your legal education, to how to study efficiently and how to make the law review, get judicial clerkships, and properly assess job opportunities. This critically acclaimed book also features the much-discussed interview with Penn Law's dean of admissions, which provides a shockingly candid look into the admissions process at one of the nation's finest law schools.

The final skill you need to develop is the ability to apply the law to the facts efficiently and skillfully. On your exams, once you have correctly identified the relevant issue and stated the relevant law, you must engage in a discussion of how the law applies to the facts that have been given. The ability to engage in such a discussion is best developed by taking practice exams. When you are practicing this skill, you should focus on efficiency. Try to focus on the essential facts, and do not to engage in irrelevant discussions that will waste your energy and your professor's time.

Q: Any final comments for our audience of aspiring law students?

A: The study of law is a wonderful and noble pursuit, one that I thoroughly enjoyed. Law school is not easy, however, and proper preparation can give you a firm foundation for success. I invite you to visit our website (www.lawpreview.com) and contact us with any questions (888-PREP-YOU).

CHAPTER 13
How to Use This Book

It's pretty simple.

The first part of this book provides a wealth of indispensable information covering everything you need to know about selecting and getting into the law school of your choice. There is also a great deal here about what to expect from law school and how to do well. You name it—taking the LSAT, choosing the best school for you, writing a great personal statement, interviewing, paying for it—it's all here.

The second part is the real meat and potatoes of the *Complete Book of Law Schools*. It comprises portraits of more than 200 schools across the United States and Canada. Each school has a directory entry that contains the same basic information and follows the same basic format. Unless noted in the descriptions below, The Princeton Review collected all of the data presented in these directory entries. As is customary with college guides, all data reflects the figures for the academic year prior to publication, unless otherwise indicated. Since law school offerings and demographics vary significantly from one institution to another and some schools report data more thoroughly than others, some entries will not include all the individual data described below.

Some schools have also opted to include a "School Says..." profile, giving extended descriptions of their admissions process, curriculum, internship opportunities, and much more. This is your chance to get in-depth information on programs that interest you. These schools have paid us a small fee for the chance to tell you more about themselves, and the editorial responsibility is solely that of the law school. We think you'll find these profiles add lots to your picture of a school.

WHAT'S IN THE PROFILES

The Heading: The first thing you will see for each profile is (obviously) the school's name. Just below the name, you'll find the school's snail mail address, telephone number, fax number, e-mail address, and Internet site. You can find the name of the admissions office contact person in the heading, too.

INSTITUTIONAL INFORMATION

Public/Private: Indicates whether a school is state-supported or funded by private means.

Affiliation: If the school is affiliated with a particular religion, you'll find that information here.

Environment: Urban, suburban, or rural. Pretty self-explanatory.

Academic Calendar: The schedule of academic terms. Semester—two long terms. Trimester—three terms. Quarter—three terms plus an optional summer term.

Schedule: Whether only full-time or both full- and part-time programs are available.

Student/Faculty Ratio: The ratio of law students to full-time faculty.

Total Faculty: The number of faculty members at the law school.

% Part Time: The percentage of faculty who are part time.

% Female: The percentage of faculty who are women.

% Minority: You guessed it! The percentage of people who teach at the law school who are also members of minority groups.

PROGRAMS

Academic Specialties: Different areas of law and academic programs in which the school prides itself.

Advanced Degrees Offered: Degrees available through the law school, and the length of the program.

Combined Degrees Offered: Programs at this school involving the law school and some other college or degree program within the larger university, and how long it will take you to complete the joint program.

Grading System: Scoring system used by the law school.

Clinical Program Required? Indicates whether clinical programs are required to complete the core curriculum.

Clinical Program Description: Programs designed to give students hands-on training and experience in the practice of some area of law.

Even More Good Books
Law Services, Thinking About Law School: A Minority Guide
This free publication, which offers pointers on finding and getting into the right school for minority applicants, is worth checking out.

Scott Turow, One L: The Turbulent True Story of a First Year at Harvard Law School
This law school primer is equal parts illuminating and harrowing.

HOW TO USE THIS BOOK • 89

Law School Trivia
The least litigated amendment in the Bill of Rights is the Third Amendment, which prohibits the quartering of soldiers in private homes without consent of the owner.

Legal Writing/Methods Course Requirements: The components of the curriculum included to develop the research, analysis, and writing skills vital to the practice of law.

Legal Writing Course Requirement? Tells you whether there is a required course in legal writing.

Legal Writing Description: A description of any course work, required or optional, designed specifically to develop legal writing skills vital to the practice of law.

Legal Method Course Requirements? Indicates whether there is a mandatory curriculum component to cover legal methods.

Legal Methods Description: A description of any course work, required or optional, designed specifically to develop the skills vital to legal analysis.

Legal Research Course Requirements? If a school requires course work specifically to develop legal research skills, this field will tell you.

Legal Research Description: A description of any course work, required or optional, designed specifically to develop legal research skills vital to the practice of law.

Moot Court Requirement? Indicates whether participation in a moot court program is mandatory.

Moot Court Description: Surprise! This will describe any moot court program, mandatory or optional, designed to develop skills in legal research, writing, and oral argument.

Public Interest Law Requirement? If a school requires participation on a public interest law project, we'll let you know here.

Public Interest Law Description: Programs designed to expose students to the public interest law field through clinical work, volunteer opportunities, or specialized course work.

Academic Journals: This field will list any academic journals offered at the school.

STUDENT INFORMATION
Enrollment of Law School: The total number of students enrolled in the law school.

% Out of State: The percentage of full-time students who are from out of state. This field only applies to state schools.

% Male/Female: The percentage of students with an X and a Y chromosome and the percentage of students with two X chromosomes, respectively.

% Full Time: The percentage of students who attend the school on a full-time basis.

% Full Time That Are International: The percentage of students that hails from foreign soil.

% Minority: The percentage of students who represent minority groups.

Average Age of Entering Class: On the whole, how old the 1Ls are.

RESEARCH FACILITIES
Research Resources Available: Online retrieval resources, subscription services, libraries, databases, etc. available for legal research.

% of JD Classrooms Wired: You got it—the percentage of dedicated law school classrooms wired for laptops and Internet access.

Computers/Workstations Available: The number of computers on campus.

Computer Labs: The number of rooms full of computers that you can use for free.

Campuswide Network? Indicates whether the campus is wired.

School-Supported Research Centers: Indicates whether the school has on-campus, internally supported research centers.

EXPENSES/FINANCIAL AID

Annual Tuition (Residents/Nonresidents): What it costs to go to school there for an academic year. For state schools, both in-state and out-of-state tuition is listed.

Room and Board (On/Off campus): This is the school's estimate of what it costs to buy meals and to pay for decent living quarters for the academic year. Where available, on- and off-campus rates are listed.

Books and Supplies: Indicates how much students can expect to shell out for textbooks and other assorted supplies during the academic year.

Financial Aid Application Deadline: The last day on which students can turn in their applications for monetary assistance.

Average Grant: Average amount awarded to students that does not have to be paid back. This figure can include scholarships as well.

Average Loan: Average amount of loan dollars accrued by students for the year.

% of Aid That Is Merit-Based: The percentage of aid not based on financial need

% Receiving Some Sort of Aid: The percentage of the students here presently accumulating a staggering debt.

Average Total Aid Package: How much aid each student here receives on average for the year.

Average Debt: The amount of debt—or, in legal lingo, arrears—you'll likely be saddled with by the time you graduate.

Tuition Per Credit (Residents/Nonresidents): Dollar amount charged per credit hour. For state schools, both in-state and out-of-state amounts are listed when they differ.

Fees Per Credit (Residents/Nonresidents): That mysterious extra money you are required to pay the law school in addition to tuition and everything else, on a per-credit basis. If in-state and out-of-state students are charged differently, both amounts are listed.

ADMISSIONS INFORMATION

Application Fee: The fee is how much it costs to apply to the school.

Regular Application Deadline and "Rolling" Decision: Many law schools evaluate applications and notify applicants of admission decisions on a continuous, "rolling" basis over the course of several months (ordinarily from late fall to midsummer). Obviously, if you apply to one of these schools, you want to apply early because there will be more places available at the beginning of the process.

Regular Notification: The official date on which a law school will release a decision for an applicant who applied using the "regular admission" route.

LSDAS Accepted? A "Yes" here indicates that the school utilizes the Law School Data Assembly Service.

Average GPA/Range of GPA: It's usually on a 4.0 scale.

Average LSAT/Range of LSAT: Indicates the average LSAT score of incoming 1Ls, as reported by the school.

Transfer Students Accepted? Whether transfer students from other schools are considered for admission.

Other Schools to Which Students Applied: The law schools to which applicants to this school also apply. It's important. It's a reliable indicator of the overall academic quality of the applicant pool.

Other Admissions Factors Considered: Additional criteria the law schools considers when admitting applicants.

Number of Applications Received: The number of people who applied to the law school.

Number of Applicants Accepted: The number of people who were admitted to the school's class.

Number of Applicants Enrolled: The number of those admitted who chose to attend that particular institution.

INTERNATIONAL STUDENTS

TOEFL Required/Recommended of International Students? Indicates whether or not international students must take the TOEFL, or Test of English as a Foreign Language, in order to be admitted to the school.

Minimum TOEFL: Minimum score an international student must earn on the TOEFL in order to be admitted.

Law School Trivia
The guarantee that each state must have an equal number of votes in the United States Senate is the only provision in the Constitution of 1787 that cannot be amended.

EMPLOYMENT INFORMATION

The **bar graph** will let you know in which fields a law school's grads are working. The fields are as follows:

Public Interest: The percentage of (mostly) altruistic graduates who got jobs providing legal assistance to folks who couldn't afford it otherwise and fighting the power in general.

Private Practice: The percentage of graduates who got jobs in traditional law firms of various sizes, or "put out a shingle" for themselves as sole practitioners.

Military: The percentage of lawyers who work to represent the Armed Forces in all kinds of legal matters. Like Tom Cruise in *A Few Good Men*. We knew you could handle the truth.

Judicial Clerkships: The number of graduates who got jobs doing research for judges.

Government: Uncle Sam needs lawyers like you wouldn't even believe.

Business/Industry: The number of graduates who got jobs working in business, in corporations, in consulting, etc. These jobs are sometimes law-related and sometimes not.

Academic: The number of graduates who got jobs at law schools, universities, and think tanks.

Rate of Placement: Placement rate into the job market upon completion of the Juris Doctor.

Average Starting Salary: The amount of money the average graduate of this law school makes the first year out of school.

Employers Who Frequently Hire Grads: Firms where past grads have had success finding jobs.

Prominent Alumni: Those who made it.

State for Bar Exam: The state for which most students from the school will take the bar exam.

Number Taking Bar Exam: Number of students taking the bar.

Pass Rate for First-Time Bar: After three years, the percentage of students who passed the bar exam the first time they took it. It's a crucial statistic. You *don't* want to fail your state's bar.

DECODING DEGREES

Many law schools offer joint or combined degree programs with other departments (or sometimes even with other schools) that you can earn along with your Juris Doctor. You'll find the abbreviations for these degrees in the individual school profiles, but we thought we'd give you a little help in figuring out exactly what they are.

AMBA	Accounting Master of Business
BCL	Bachelor of Civil Law
DJUR	Doctor of Jurisprudence
DL	Doctor of Law
DLaw	Doctor of Law
EdD	Doctor of Education
HRIR	Human Resources and Industrial Relations
IMBA	International Master of Business Administration
JD	Juris Doctor
JSD	Doctor of Juridical Science
JSM	Master of the Science of Law
LLB	Bachelor of Law
LLCM	Master of Comparative Law (for international students)
LLM	Master of Law
MA	Master of Arts
MAcc	Master of Accounting
MALD	Masters of Arts in Law and Diplomacy
MAM	Master of Arts Management
MM	Master of Management
MANM	Master of Nonprofit Management
MAPA	Master of Public Administration
MAUA	Masters of Arts in Urban Affairs
MBA	Master of Business Administration
MCJ	Master of Criminal Justice
MCL	Master of Comparative Law
MCP	Master of Community Planning
MCRP	Master of City and Regional Planning

MDiv	Master of Divinity	MSI	Master of Science in Information
ME	Master of Engineering OR Master of Education	MSIA	Master of Industrial Administration
MEd	Master of Education	MSIE	Master of Science in International Economics
MED	Master of Environmental Design	MSJ	Master of Science in Journalism
MEM	Master of Environmental Management	MSPH	Master of Science in Public Health
MFA	Master of Fine Arts	MSW	Master of Social Welfare OR Master of Social Work
MHA	Master of Health Administration	MT	Master of Taxation
MHSA	Master of Health Services Administration	MTS	Master of Theological Studies
MIA	Master of International Affairs	MUP	Master of Urban Planning
MIB	Master of International Business	MUPD	Master of Urban Planning and Development
MIP	Master of Intellectual Property	MURP	Master of Urban and Regional Planning
MIR	Masters in Industrial Relations	PharmD	Doctor of Pharmacy
MIRL	Masters Industrial and Labor Relations	PhD	Doctor of Philosophy
MJ	Master of Jurisprudence	REES	Russian and Eastern European Studies Certificate
MJS	Master of Juridical Study (not a JD)	SJD	Doctor of Juridcial Science
MLIR	Master of Labor and Industrial Relations	DVM	Doctor of Veterinary Medicine
MLIS	Master of Library and Information Sciences	MALIR	Master of Arts in Labor and Industrial Relations
MLS	Master of Library Science		
MMA	Masters Marine Affairs		
MOB	Master of Organizational Behavior		
MPA	Master of Public Administration		
MPAFF	Master of Public Affairs		
MPH	Master of Public Health		
MPP	Master of Public Planning OR Master of Public Policy		
MPPA	Master of Public Policy		
MPPS	Master of Public Policy Sciences		
MPS	Master of Professional Studies in Law		
MRP	Master of Regional Planning		
MS	Master of Science		
MSEL	Master of Studies in Environmental Law		
MSES	Master of Science in Environmental Science		
MSF	Master of Science in Finance		
MSFS	Master of Science in Foreign Service		

LAW SCHOOL PROFILES

ALBANY LAW SCHOOL

Admissions Contact: Assistant Dean of Admissions and Financial Aid, Dawn Chamberlaine
80 New Scotland Avenue, Albany, NY 12208
Admissions Phone: 518-445-2326 • Admissions Fax: 518-445-2369
Admissions E-mail: admissions@mail.als.edu • Web Address: www.als.edu

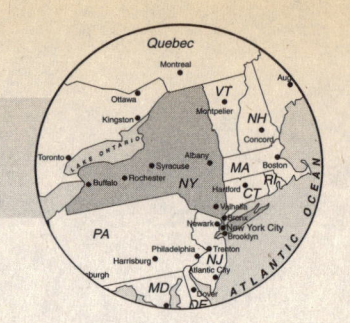

INSTITUTIONAL INFORMATION
Public/Private: Private
Student/Faculty Ratio: 20:1
Total Faculty: 68
% Part Time: 28
% Female: 44
% Minority: 13

PROGRAMS
Academic Specialties: Health Law, Intellectual Property Law, Criminal Law, International Law, Government Administration and Regulation, Environmental Law, Civil Procedure, Constitutional Law, Government Services, Intellectual Property Law, Labor Law, Taxation
Advanced Degrees Offered: JD (3 years), LLM (1 to 3 years), LLM for Foreign Law Graduates (1 year)
Combined Degrees Offered: JD/MBA, JD/MPA, JD/MSW, JD/MRP (all 3.5 to 4 years)
Grading System: A+ (4.3), A (4.0), A– (3.7), B+ (3.3), B (3.0), B– (2.7), C+ (2.3), C (2.0), C– (1.7), D+ (1.3), D (1), D– (0.7), F (0.0)
Clinical Program Required? No
Clinical Program Description: AIDS Law Project, Disabilities Law Project, Domestic Violence Law Project, Low-Income Taxpayer Clinic, Litigation Project, various placement and externships, semester in government programs
Legal Writing Course Requirements? Yes
Legal Writing Description: Introduction to Lawyering gives students an opportunity to begin developing their professional skills in a year-long case simulation that combines legal writing and clinical methodology.
Legal Methods Course Requirements? Yes
Legal Methods Description: 1 week prior to start of classes
Legal Research Course Requirements? Yes
Legal Research Description: See Legal Writing.
Moot Court Requirement? No
Public Interest Law Requirement? No
Academic Journals: *Law Review, Journal of Science and Technology, Environmental Outlook, Literary Review*

STUDENT INFORMATION
Enrollment of Law School: 811
% Out of State: 20
% Male/Female: 48/52
% Full Time: 93
% Full Time That Are International: 3
% Minority: 18
Average Age of Entering Class: 26

RESEARCH FACILITIES
Research Resources Available: Albany Law School is located in the capital of New York State, so students have access to the agencies of state government, the legislature, executive offices, and the state's highest court, the court of appeals.
School-Supported Research Centers: Government Law Center, Schaffer Law Library, Science and Technology Law Center

EXPENSES/FINANCIAL AID
Annual Tuition: $24,125
Room and Board (Off Campus): $6,100
Books and Supplies: $700
Average Grant: $7,400
Average Loan: $24,630
% of Aid That Is Merit-Based: 29
% Receiving Some Sort of Aid: 91
Average Total Aid Package: $28,300
Average Debt: $56,500
Tuition Per Credit: $830

ADMISSIONS INFORMATION
Application Fee: $50
Regular Application Deadline: 3/15
Regular Notification: Rolling
LSDAS Accepted? Yes
Average GPA: 3.2
Range of GPA: 2.9–3.5
Average LSAT: 151
Range of LSAT: 148–154
Transfer Students Accepted? Yes
Other Schools to Which Students Applied: New England School of Law; New York Law School; Pace University; Syracuse University; University at Buffalo, State University of NY
Other Admissions Factors Considered: Strength of academic institution, rigor of undergraduate program, uniqueness of life experience and background, employment experience
Number of Applications Received: 1,663
Number of Applicants Accepted: 856
Number of Applicants Enrolled: 294

INTERNATIONAL STUDENTS
TOEFL Recommended for International Students? Yes

EMPLOYMENT INFORMATION

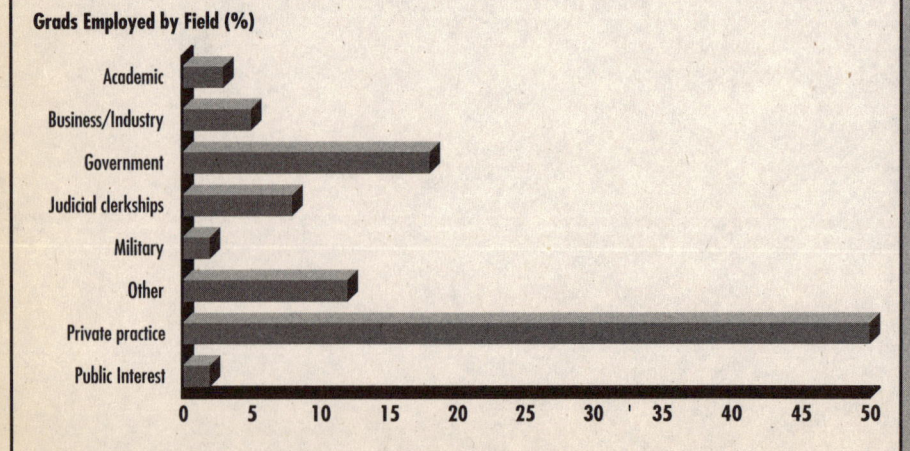

Grads Employed by Field (%)

Field	%
Academic	~2
Business/Industry	~5
Government	~18
Judicial clerkships	~7
Military	~1
Other	~13
Private practice	~50
Public Interest	~3

Rate of Placement: 93%
Average Starting Salary: $53,553
Employers Who Frequently Hire Grads: Private law firms, government agencies, business and industry
Prominent Alumni: Thomas Vilsack, Governor of Iowa; Richard D. Parsons, Chief Executive Officer, AOL–Time Warner; Mary Donohue, Lieutenant Governor, New York State; Andrew Cuomo, former Secretary of U.S. Department of Housing and Urban Development; Victoria Graffeo, Associate Justice, New York State Court of Appeals
State for Bar Exam: NY
Pass Rate for First-Time Bar: 77%

AMERICAN UNIVERSITY
Washington College of Law

Admissions Contact: Director of Admissions, Sandra Oakman
4801 Massachusetts Avenue, NW, Washington, DC 20016
Admissions Phone: 202-274-4101 • Admissions Fax: 202-274-4107
Admissions E-mail: wcladmit@wcl.american.edu • Web Address: www.wcl.american.edu

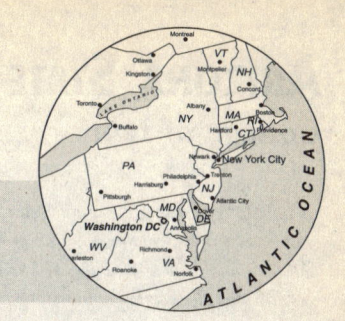

INSTITUTIONAL INFORMATION
Public/Private: Private
Student/Faculty Ratio: 19:1
Total Faculty: 203
% Part Time: 69
% Female: 37
% Minority: 18

PROGRAMS
Academic Specialties: International Law (Human Rights, International Business, International Organizations, Gender), Clinical Education, Externships, Simulation Courses, Experiential Learning, Law and Government, Legal Theory (especially History, Law and Economics, Jurisprudence), Law and Business, Commercial Law, Corporation Securities Law, Environmental Law, Government Services, Intellectual Property Law
Advanced Degrees Offered: LLM International Legal Studies (12 to 18 months), LLM Law and Government (12 months), SJD
Combined Degrees Offered: JD/MBA, JD/MA International Affairs, JD/MS Justice (all 3.5 to 4 years)
Grading System: A, A–, B+, B, B–, C+, C, D, F; no mandatory curve
Clinical Program Required? No
Clinical Program Description: Criminal Justice, DC Law Students in Court (civil litigation—landlord/tenant and small claims), Civil Practice, Domestic Violence, International Human Rights, Tax, Women and the Law, Community and Economic Development, Intellectual Property
Legal Writing Course Requirements? No
Legal Methods Course Requirements? Yes
Legal Methods Description: Small sections; 1-year program on legal research, writing, and rhetoric
Legal Research Course Requirements? Yes
Legal Research Description: Students must complete a 30-page research paper in connection with a seminar, independent study, or law review/journal write-on competition.
Moot Court Requirement? No
Moot Court Description: Students participate in a first-year intraschool moot court competition, an upper-level intraschool competition, and numerous interschool competitions. Our students compete in such international competitions as the Jessup, Rene Cassin (French), and Inter-American (Spanish and English) Moot Courts.
Public Interest Law Requirement? No
Academic Journals: *Administrative Law Review*; *American University International Law Review*; *American University Journal of Gender, Social Policy, and the Law*; *American University Law Review*

STUDENT INFORMATION
Enrollment of Law School: 1,279
% Male/Female: 37/63
% Full Time: 77
% Full Time That Are International: 2
% Minority: 24
Average Age of Entering Class: 23

RESEARCH FACILITIES
Research Resources Available: Research workstations in the library; laptop configuration for access to the network; high-capacity printer access; network and Internet in every classroom; computer lab with 60 Pentium and 8 PowerMac computers; Lexis/Nexis; Amicus case management software; Novell file server

EXPENSES/FINANCIAL AID
Annual Tuition: $27,170
Room and Board: $14,639
Books and Supplies: $865
Financial Aid Application Deadline: 3/1
Average Grant: $9,200
Average Loan: $26,304
% of Aid That Is Merit-Based: 34
% Receiving Some Sort of Aid: 80
Average Total Aid Package: $26,235
Average Debt: $57,402
Tuition Per Credit: $1,007

ADMISSIONS INFORMATION
Application Fee: $65
Regular Application Deadline: 3/1
Regular Notification: Rolling
LSDAS Accepted? Yes
Average GPA: 3.4
Range of GPA: 3.2–3.6
Average LSAT: 158
Range of LSAT: 156–160
Transfer Students Accepted? Yes
Other Schools to Which Students Applied: Boston College, Boston University, Fordham, George Mason, George Washington, Georgetown, Catholic University
Number of Applications Received: 6,808
Number of Applicants Accepted: 2,006
Number of Applicants Enrolled: 518

INTERNATIONAL STUDENTS
TOEFL Required of International Students? Yes
Minimum TOEFL: 600

EMPLOYMENT INFORMATION

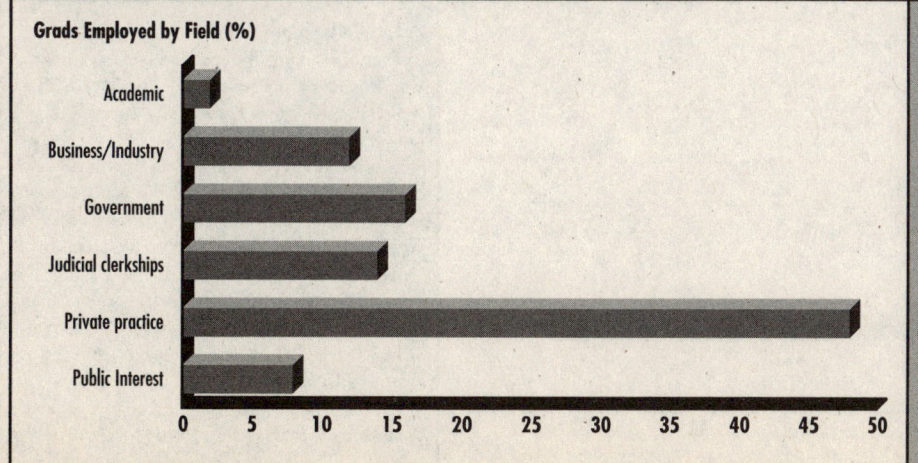

Grads Employed by Field (%)

Field	%
Academic	~2
Business/Industry	~12
Government	~17
Judicial clerkships	~15
Private practice	~48
Public Interest	~6

Rate of Placement: 95%
Average Starting Salary: $69,500
Employers Who Frequently Hire Grads: Akin, Gump, Strauss, Haver, & Feld, LLP; Jones Day Reavis & Pogue; Manhattan District Attorney; U.S. Department of Justice; Sonnenschein, Nath & Rosenthal; Dickstein, Shapiro & Morin, LLP; Latham & Watkins; Womble, Carlyle, Sandridge & Rice; Finnegan, Henderson
Prominent Alumni: Robert Byrd, U.S. Senator (D-W.VA.); Rick Lazio, former Congressman (R-NY); Carol Crawford, former Commissioner, International Trade Commission; Gerald Lee, Judge, U.S. District Court; Sarah Evans Barker, Judge, U.S. District Court
State for Bar Exam: MD
Pass Rate for First-Time Bar: 73%

ARIZONA STATE UNIVERSITY
College of Law

Admissions Contact: Assistant Dean for Admissions, Brenda Brock
PO Box 877906, Tempe, AZ 85287-7906
Admissions Phone: 480-965-1474 • Admissions Fax: 480-727-7930
Admissions E-mail: law.admissions@asu.edu • Web Address: www.law.asu.edu

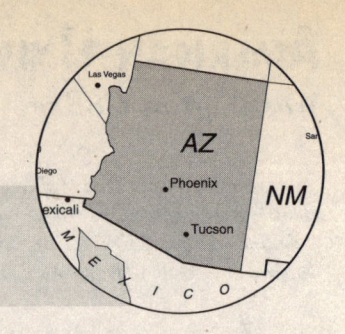

INSTITUTIONAL INFORMATION
Public/Private: Public
Student/Faculty Ratio: 13:1
Total Faculty: 51
% Female: 22
% Minority: 6

PROGRAMS
Academic Specialties: Clinical Program, Indian Legal Program, Constitutional Law, Environmental Law, Intellectual Property Law, Legal Philosophy; Center for the Study of Law, Science and Technology
Advanced Degrees Offered: JD (3 years)
Combined Degrees Offered: JD/MBA (4 years), JD/PhD Justice Studies
Grading System: Distinguished (90–99), Excellent (85–89), Very Good (80–84), Good (75–79), Satisfactory (70–74), Deficient (65–69), Failing (64). A grade of 65 or above is required to receive credit. Some Pass/Fail courses are offered.
Clinical Program Required? No
Clinical Program Description: Criminal Practice Clinic, Public Defender Clinic, Civil Practice Clinic, Mediation Clinic
Legal Writing Course Requirements? Yes
Legal Writing Description: Required as part of the first-year Legal Method and Writing program; 2-semester course includes writing legal memoranda, motions, letters, and other assignments
Legal Methods Course Requirements? Yes
Legal Methods Description: Required as part of the first-year Legal Method and Writing program; 2-semester course covers legal analysis (including case analysis, statutory analysis, synthesis)
Legal Research Course Requirements? Yes
Legal Research Description: Required as part of the first-year Legal Method and Writing program; 2-semester course covers manual legal research (fall) and electronic legal research (spring)
Moot Court Requirement? Yes
Moot Court Description: First-year students are required to participate in Moot Court programs. We offer numerous moot court competitions, including Client Counseling, Jenckes Cup on closing arguments, Oplinger Closing Argument, Michael A. Berch Appellate Argument, Canby Appellate Brief, Donald Froeb Trial Advocacy, First Amendment, National, and Environmental.
Public Interest Law Requirement? No
Academic Journals: Arizona State Law Journal; Jurimetrics Journal of Law, Science and Technology

STUDENT INFORMATION
Enrollment of Law School: 550
% Out of State: 18
% Male/Female: 47/53
% Full Time: 100
% Full Time That Are International: 3
% Minority: 29
Average Age of Entering Class: 28

RESEARCH FACILITIES
Research Resources Available: Student membership in Arizona State Bar Young Lawyers, Lexis, Westlaw
School-Supported Research Centers: Center for the Study of Law, Science and Technology; Indian Legal Program; Law Review; Jurimetrics Journal

EXPENSES/FINANCIAL AID
Annual Tuition (Residents/Nonresidents): $5,758/$14,278
Room and Board (Off Campus): $7,236
Books and Supplies: $748
Financial Aid Application Deadline: 3/3
Average Grant: $4,223
Average Loan: $16,120
% Receiving Some Sort of Aid: 81
Average Total Aid Package: $16,965
Average Debt: $46,888

ADMISSIONS INFORMATION
Application Fee: $45
Regular Application Deadline: 2/15
Regular Notification: Rolling
LSDAS Accepted? Yes
Average GPA: 3.4
Range of GPA: 3.2–3.7
Average LSAT: 160
Range of LSAT: 154–163
Transfer Students Accepted? Yes
Other Schools to Which Students Applied: University of Arizona
Number of Applications Received: 2,767
Number of Applicants Accepted: 481
Number of Applicants Enrolled: 173

INTERNATIONAL STUDENTS
TOEFL Required of International Students? Yes

EMPLOYMENT INFORMATION

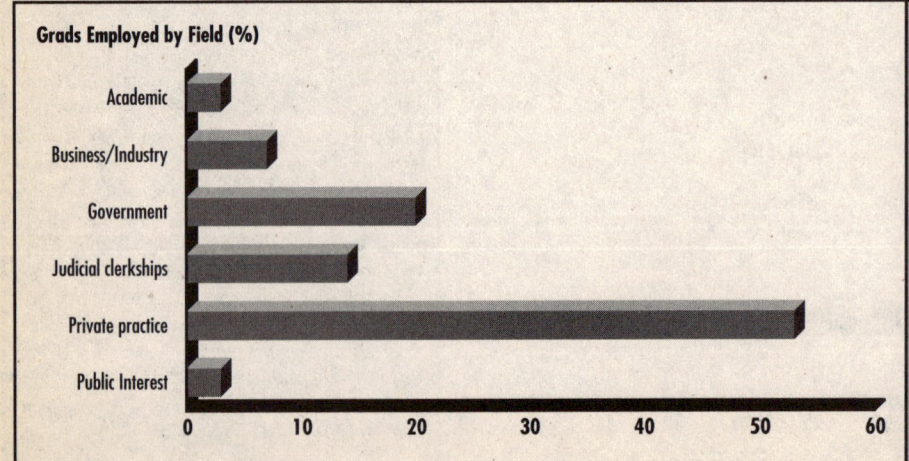

Grads Employed by Field (%)
- Academic
- Business/Industry
- Government
- Judicial clerkships
- Private practice
- Public Interest

Rate of Placement: 93%
Average Starting Salary: $62,903
Employers Who Frequently Hire Grads: Snell & Wilmer; Brown & Bain; Gammage & Birnham; Lewis and Roca; Fennemore Craig; Jennings, Strouss & Salmon; Gallagher & Kennedy; Quarles & Brady Streich Lang; Ryley Carlock & Applewhite; Steptoe Johnson; Morrison Hecker; Mariscal Weeks; Meyer Hendricks; Osborn Maledon; Bryan Cave; Squires, Sanders & Dempsey
Prominent Alumni: Ruth McGregor, Vice Chief Justice, Arizona State Supreme Court; Barry Silverman, U.S. 9th Circuit Court of Appeals; Ed Pastor, U.S. House of Representatives
State for Bar Exam: AZ
Pass Rate for First-Time Bar: 81%

Ave Maria College
School of Law

Admissions Contact: Dean of Admissions, Michael Kenney
3475 Plymouth Road, Ann Arbor, MI 48105
Admissions Phone: 734-827-8063 • Admissions Fax: 734-622-0123
Admissions E-mail: info@avemarialaw.edu • Web Address: www.avemarialaw.edu

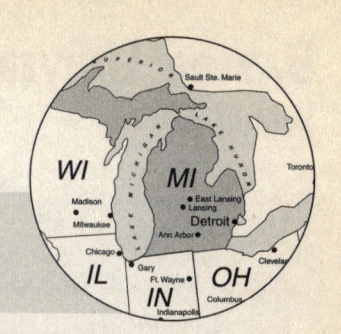

INSTITUTIONAL INFORMATION
Public/Private: Private
Affiliation: Roman Catholic
Student/Faculty Ratio: 12:1
Total Faculty: 29
% Part Time: 20
% Female: 27
% Minority: 3

PROGRAMS
Academic Specialties: Jurisprudence, Commercial Law, Criminal Law, International Law, Trial Advocacy, Constitutional Law, Labor and Employment Law, Torts Law, Canon Law, Contracts, Bioethics, State and Local Government, Civil Procedure, Complex Litigation, Property, Professional Responsibility
Advanced Degrees Offered: JD (3 years)
Grading System: 4.0 scale
Clinical Program Required? No
Legal Writing Course Requirements? Yes
Legal Writing Description: First year, 2 semesters; second year, 1 semester
Legal Methods Course Requirements? No
Legal Research Course Requirements? Yes
Legal Research Description: First year, 2 semesters; second year, 1 semester
Moot Court Requirement? No
Public Interest Law Requirement? No
Academic Journals: *Ave Maria Law Review*

STUDENT INFORMATION
Enrollment of Law School: 74
% Out of State: 70
% Male/Female: 77/23
% Full Time: 100
% Full Time That Are International: 5
% Minority: 16
Average Age of Entering Class: 27

RESEARCH FACILITIES
Research Resources Available: Westlaw, Lexis

EXPENSES/FINANCIAL AID
Annual Tuition: $21,900
Room and Board (Off Campus): $9,738
Books and Supplies: $850
Financial Aid Application Deadline: 6/1
Average Grant: $17,554
Average Loan: $20,100
% Receiving Some Sort of Aid: 97
Average Total Aid Package: $18,709

ADMISSIONS INFORMATION
Application Fee: $0
Regular Application Deadline: 5/1
Regular Notification: Rolling
LSDAS Accepted? Yes
Average GPA: 3.3
Range of GPA: 2.8–3.5
Average LSAT: 160
Range of LSAT: 155–163
Transfer Students Accepted? Yes
Number of Applications Received: 326
Number of Applicants Accepted: 181
Number of Applicants Enrolled: 74

INTERNATIONAL STUDENTS
TOEFL Recommended for International Students? Yes

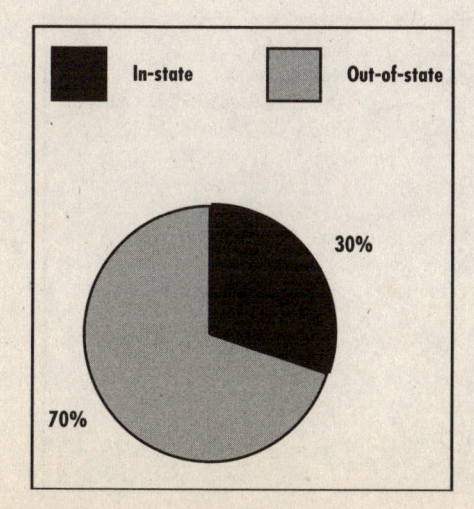

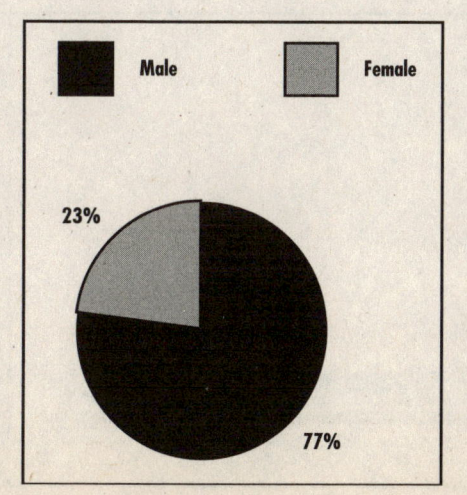

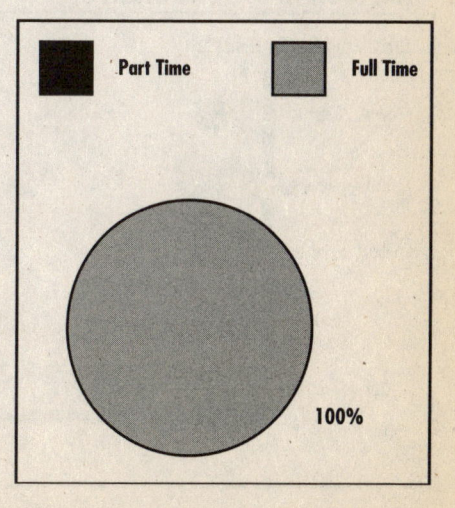

BAYLOR UNIVERSITY
School of Law

Admissions Contact: Admission Director, Becky Beck
PO Box 97288, Waco, TX 76798
Admissions Phone: 254-710-1911 • Admissions Fax: 254-710-2316
Admissions E-mail: becky_becky@baylor.edu • Web Address: law.baylor.edu

INSTITUTIONAL INFORMATION
Public/Private: Private
Affiliation: Southern Baptist
Student/Faculty Ratio: 20:1
Total Faculty: 56
% Part Time: 61
% Female: 20
% Minority: 4

PROGRAMS
Academic Specialties: General Civil Litigation, Business Litigation, Estate Planning, Criminal Practice, Business Transaction, Administrative Practice, Civil Procedure, Criminal Law
Combined Degrees Offered: JD/MBA, JD/M Taxation, JD/MPPA (all 3.5 to 4 years)
Grading System: Letter and numerical system, 4.0 scale: A (4.0), A– (3.5), B (3.0), B– (2.5), C (2.0), D (1.0), F (0.0)
Clinical Program Required? Yes
Clinical Program Description: All students are required to participate in our 2-quarter, 12-credit-hour Practice Court Program with a minimum of 4 trials plus other advocacy training exercises.
Legal Writing Course Requirements? Yes
Legal Writing Description: In the students' third quarter, they take a required 2-credit-hour Legal Analysis, Research and Communications III course. The students are required to write and rewrite an appellate brief.
Legal Methods Course Requirements? Yes
Legal Methods Description: Legal Analysis, Research and Communications. 3-part course for 4 quarter hours taught over 3 quarters. LARC I focuses on legal analysis and memo writing. LARC II concentrates on research skills. For LARC III, students continue with writing exercises and write and argue an appellate brief.
Legal Research Course Requirements? Yes
Legal Research Description: Our 1-credit-hour LARC II course is taken in the students' second quarter of law school. The course concentrates on research skills, both using technology and without the assistance of technology.
Moot Court Requirement? Yes
Moot Court Description: As part of our third-quarter required LARC III course, students are required to write a competition brief and participate in a class moot court round. Students then complete a minimum of 3 rounds as part of the fall or spring intraschool moot court competitions.
Public Interest Law Requirement? No
Academic Journals: *Baylor Law Review*

STUDENT INFORMATION
Enrollment of Law School: 389
% Out of State: 21
% Male/Female: 61/39
% Full Time: 100
% Full Time That Are International: 1
% Minority: 11
Average Age of Entering Class: 27

EXPENSES/FINANCIAL AID
Annual Tuition: $14,719
Room and Board (On/Off Campus): $9,051/$13,194
Books and Supplies: $600
Financial Aid Application Deadline: 5/1
Average Grant: $4,860
Average Loan: $21,170
% of Aid That Is Merit-Based: 32
% Receiving Some Sort of Aid: 98
Average Total Aid Package: $19,512
Average Debt: $46,457
Tuition Per Credit: $359
Fees Per Credit: $20

ADMISSIONS INFORMATION
Application Fee: $40
Regular Application Deadline: 3/1
Regular Notification: Rolling
LSDAS Accepted? Yes
Average GPA: 3.6
Range of GPA: 3.3–3.8
Average LSAT: 161
Range of LSAT: 159–163
Transfer Students Accepted? Yes
Other Schools to Which Students Applied: University of Texas at Austin, University of Houston, Texas Tech University, Southern Methodist University
Other Admissions Factors Considered: Achievements, work and life experiences, evidence of maturity, strong work ethic
Number of Applications Received: 1,259
Number of Applicants Accepted: 461
Number of Applicants Enrolled: 63

EMPLOYMENT INFORMATION

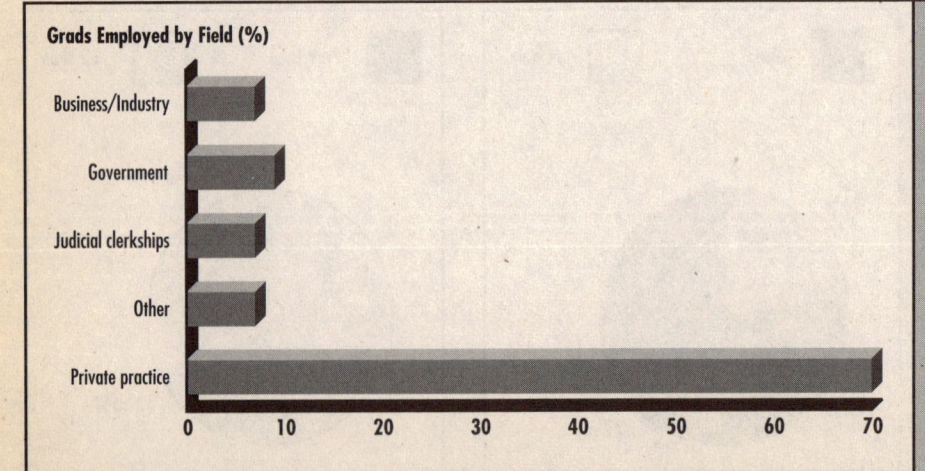

Grads Employed by Field (%)

Field	%
Business/Industry	~7
Government	~10
Judicial clerkships	~8
Other	~5
Private practice	~70

Rate of Placement: 96%
Average Starting Salary: $57,000
Employers Who Frequently Hire Grads: Akin Gump, Jenkins & Gilcrest, Thompson & Knight, Strasburger & Price, Baker & Botts, Haynes & Boone, Bracewell & Patterson, Jackson Walker, Fulbright & Jaworski, Andrews & Kurth, Winstead Sechrest, Liddell Sapp
State for Bar Exam: TX
Pass Rate for First-Time Bar: 89%

BOSTON COLLEGE
Law School

Admissions Contact: Director of Admissions
885 Centre Street, Newton, MA 02459
Admissions Phone: 617-552-4351 • Admissions Fax: 617-552-2917
Admissions E-mail: bclawadmis@bc.edu • Web Address: www.bc.edu/lawschool

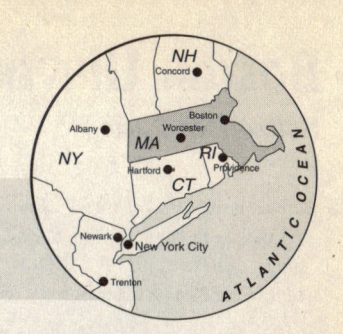

INSTITUTIONAL INFORMATION
Public/Private: Private
Affiliation: Roman Catholic
Student/Faculty Ratio: 13:1
Total Faculty: 78
% Part Time: 35
% Female: 27
% Minority: 11

PROGRAMS
Academic Specialties: Civil Procedure, Commercial Law, Constitutional Law, Corporation Securities Law, Criminal Law, Environmental Law, Human Rights Law, International Law, Labor Law, Legal History, Legal Philosophy, Property, Taxation
Advanced Degrees Offered: JD (3 years)
Combined Degrees Offered: JD/MBA (4 years), JD/MSW (4 years), JD/MEd (3 years)
Grading System: Standard letter system on a 4.0 scale
Clinical Program Required? No
Clinical Program Description: Legal Assistance Bureau, Criminal Process, Attorney General Clinical Program, Judicial Process, Urban Legal Laboratory, Juvenile Rights and Advocacy, Immigration Law Clinic
Legal Writing Course Requirements? Yes
Legal Writing Description: First year, 2 semesters, 5 credits
Legal Methods Course Requirements? Yes
Legal Methods Description: See Legal Writing.
Legal Research Course Requirements? Yes
Legal Research Description: See Legal Writing.
Moot Court Requirement? No
Public Interest Law Requirement? No
Academic Journals: Boston College Law Review, International and Comparative Law Journal, Environmental Law Journal, Third World Law Journal, Uniform Commercial Code Digest

STUDENT INFORMATION
Enrollment of Law School: 805
% Out of State: 63
% Male/Female: 49/51
% Full Time: 100
% Full Time That Are International: 2
% Minority: 19
Average Age of Entering Class: 25

RESEARCH FACILITIES
School-Supported Research Centers: New $16 million library

EXPENSES/FINANCIAL AID
Annual Tuition: $27,080
Room and Board (Off Campus): $12,985
Books and Supplies: $840
Financial Aid Application Deadline: 3/15
Average Grant: $10,063
Average Loan: $26,017
% Receiving Some Sort of Aid: 85
Average Debt: $63,500

ADMISSIONS INFORMATION
Application Fee: $65
Regular Application Deadline: 3/1
Regular Notification: Rolling
LSDAS Accepted? Yes
Average GPA: 3.5
Range of GPA: 3.3–3.7
Average LSAT: 162
Range of LSAT: 159–164
Transfer Students Accepted? Yes
Other Schools to Which Students Applied: Boston University, Fordham University, George Washington University, Georgetown University
Number of Applications Received: 5,363
Number of Applicants Accepted: 1,263
Number of Applicants Enrolled: 276

INTERNATIONAL STUDENTS
TOEFL Required of International Students? Yes

EMPLOYMENT INFORMATION

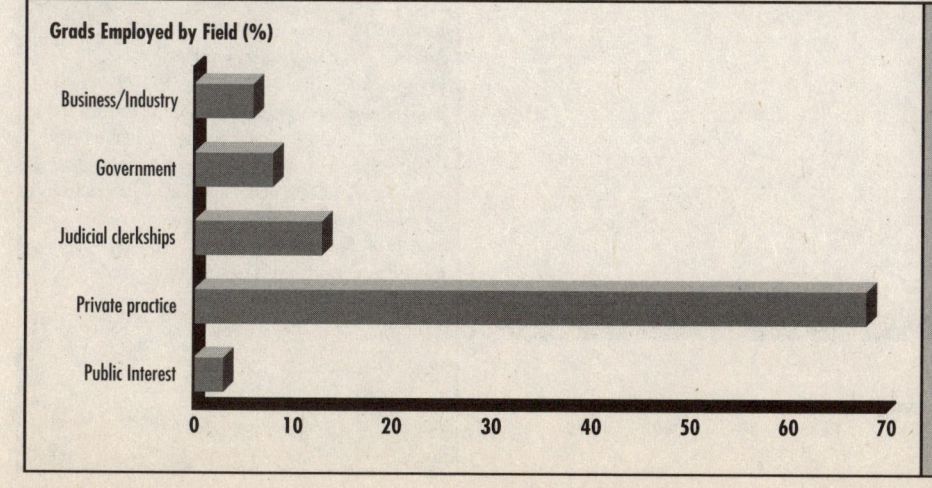

Grads Employed by Field (%)
- Business/Industry
- Government
- Judicial clerkships
- Private practice
- Public Interest

Rate of Placement: 98%
State for Bar Exam: MA
Pass Rate for First-Time Bar: 92%

BOSTON UNIVERSITY
School of Law

Admissions Contact: Director of Admissions and Financial Aid, Joan Horgan
765 Commonwealth Avenue, Boston, MA 02215
Admissions Phone: 617-353-3100 • Admissions Fax: 617-353-0578
Admissions E-mail: bulawadm@bu.edu • Web Address: www.bu.edu/law

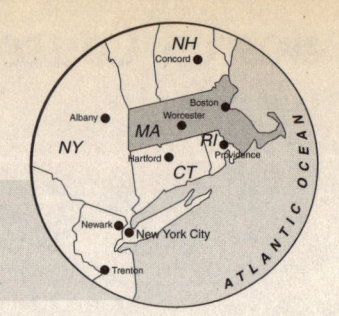

INSTITUTIONAL INFORMATION
Public/Private: Private
Student/Faculty Ratio: 11:1
Total Faculty: 141
% Part Time: 51
% Female: 29
% Minority: 9

PROGRAMS
Academic Specialties: Antitrust, Law and Economics, Constitutional Law, Administrative Law, Health Law, Labor Law, Intellectual Property Law, International Law, Civil Procedure, Legal Philosophy, Litigation and Dispute Resolution, Civil and Criminal Clinical Programs, Corporation Securities Law, Taxation
Advanced Degrees Offered: LLM Taxation (1 year full time, up to 4 years part time), LLM Banking and Financial Law (1 year full time, up to 3 years part time), LLM American Law (1 year full time), LLM Intellectual Property Law (1 year full time)
Combined Degrees Offered: JD/MBA, JD/MBA Health Care Management, JD/MA International Relations, JD/MS Mass Communication, JD/MA Preservation Studies, JD/MPH, JD/MSW, JD/MA Philosophy, JD/LLM Taxation, JD/LLM Banking (all 3.5 to 4 years)
Grading System: Letter and numerical system on a 4.3 scale
Clinical Program Required? No
Clinical Program Description: Legislation Clinics, Legislative Internship Program, Criminal Trial Advocacy (Prosecution and Criminal Defense), Judicial Internship, Legal Externship, Civil Litigation Program (includes Disability Law, Employment Law, Housing Law, Family Law, Immigration/Human Rights Law)
Legal Writing Course Requirements? Yes
Legal Writing Description: Full-year, small-group program for first-years
Legal Methods Course Requirements? No
Legal Research Course Requirements? Yes
Legal Research Description: Full-year, small-group program for first-years
Moot Court Requirement? Yes
Moot Court Description: All first-year students participate in the Esdaile Moot Court Program, in which students prepare a written appellate brief and do an oral argument as part of the first-year Legal Research and Writing Seminar. There are a number of moot court competitions available for upper-class students who wish to participate.
Public Interest Law Requirement? No
Academic Journals: American Journal of Law and Medicine, Annual Review of Banking Law, Boston University Law Review, International Law Journal, Public Interest Law Journal, Journal of Science and Technology Law

STUDENT INFORMATION
Enrollment of Law School: 823
% Out of State: 84
% Male/Female: 47/53
% Full Time: 100
% Full Time That Are International: 3
% Minority: 23
Average Age of Entering Class: 23

EXPENSES/FINANCIAL AID
Annual Tuition: $27,222
Room and Board: $10,030
Books and Supplies: $1,081
Financial Aid Application Deadline: 3/1
Average Grant: $15,000
Average Loan: $27,029
% of Aid That Is Merit-Based: 4
% Receiving Some Sort of Aid: 82
Average Total Aid Package: $26,213
Average Debt: $74,925

ADMISSIONS INFORMATION
Application Fee: $60
Regular Application Deadline: 3/1
Regular Notification: Rolling
LSDAS Accepted? Yes
Average GPA: 3.4
Range of GPA: 3.1–3.6
Average LSAT: 164
Range of LSAT: 163–166
Transfer Students Accepted? Yes
Other Schools to Which Students Applied: American University, Boston College, Fordham University, George Washington University, Georgetown University, New York University
Other Admissions Factors Considered: Grade trends, quality and difficulty of courses taken, leadership ability, motivation for study of law, economic or social obstacles overcome, outstanding nonacademic achievements
Number of Applications Received: 7,265
Number of Applicants Accepted: 1,351
Number of Applicants Enrolled: 286

INTERNATIONAL STUDENTS
TOEFL Required of International Students? Yes
Minimum TOEFL: 600 (250 computer)

EMPLOYMENT INFORMATION

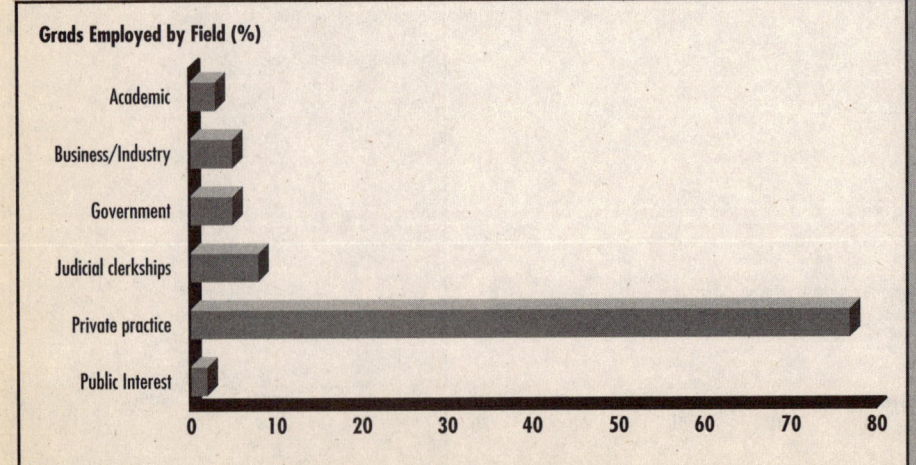

Grads Employed by Field (%)
- Academic
- Business/Industry
- Government
- Judicial clerkships
- Private practice
- Public Interest

Rate of Placement: 100%
Average Starting Salary: $125,000
Prominent Alumni: Judd Gregg, U.S. Senator, New Hampshire; William S. Cohen, former Secretary of Defense; David Kelley, Executive Producer; Gary F. Locke, Governor of Washington; Hon. Sandra L. Lynch, Judge, U.S. 1st Circuit Court of Appeals
State for Bar Exam: MA, NY, CA, IL, NJ
Pass Rate for First-Time Bar: 90%

BRIGHAM YOUNG UNIVERSITY
J. Reuben Clark Law School

Admissions Contact: Director of Admissions, Lola Wilcock
340 JRCB, Brigham Young University Law School, Provo, UT 84602
Admissions Phone: 801-378-4277 • *Admissions Fax:* 801-378-5897
Admissions E-mail: wilcockl@lawgate.byu.edu • *Web Address:* www.law2.byu.edu

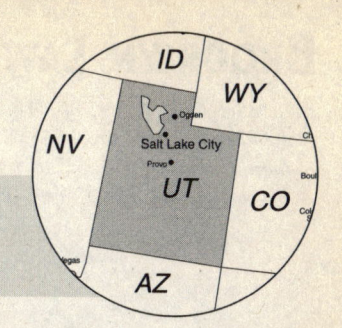

INSTITUTIONAL INFORMATION
Public/Private: Private
Affiliation: Church of Jesus Christ of Latter-day Saints
Student/Faculty Ratio: 17:1
Total Faculty: 70
% Part Time: 46
% Female: 26
% Minority: 7

PROGRAMS
Academic Specialties: The faculty and curriculum are strong across the board, but have particular curricular strengths in Intellectual Property, International and Comparative Law, Federal Taxation, Commercial Law, Constitutional Law, and Skills Training.
Advanced Degrees Offered: Comparative Law (1 year)
Combined Degrees Offered: JD/MBA, JD/MPA, JD/Macc, JD/MOB, JD/MEd (all 4 years); JD/EdD (5 years)
Grading System: 4.0 scale; a set median of 3.2; no credit for grades below 2.2
Clinical Program Required? No
Legal Writing Course Requirements? Yes
Legal Writing Description: Advocacy I and II are required first-year courses focusing on legal writing, research, analysis, and appellate oral advocacy. Students prepare 3 predictive memoranda in the fall semester and prepare an appellate brief and orally argue a case during the winter semester.
Legal Methods Course Requirements? No
Legal Research Course Requirements? Yes
Legal Research Description: As part of first-year Advocacy, students develop skills using both manual and electronic legal research sources. They also acquire and exercise research strategy skills as they work with fact situations and prepare memoranda and briefs. An Advanced Legal Research course is required during the second or third year.
Moot Court Requirement? Yes
Moot Court Description: All first-year students participate in a moot court competition as part of their Advocacy course.
Public Interest Law Requirement? No
Academic Journals: Law Review, Journal of Public Law, Education and Law Journal

STUDENT INFORMATION
Enrollment of Law School: 480
% Out of State: 57
% Male/Female: 69/31
% Full Time: 100
% Full Time That Are International: 2
% Minority: 18
Average Age of Entering Class: 26

RESEARCH FACILITIES
Research Resources Available: Central European University (Budapest, Hungary); T.C. Beirne School of Law at the University of Queensland (Brisbane, Australia)
School-Supported Research Centers: World Family Policy Center, Center for Law and Religion Studies, Rex E. Lee Advocacy Program

EXPENSES/FINANCIAL AID
Annual Tuition: $6,140
Room and Board (On/Off Campus): $6,100/$7,375
Books and Supplies: $1,230
Financial Aid Application Deadline: 6/1
Average Grant: $2,500
Average Loan: $12,000
% of Aid That Is Merit-Based: 33
% Receiving Some Sort of Aid: 89
Average Total Aid Package: $10,000
Average Debt: $24,000
Tuition Per Credit: $342

ADMISSIONS INFORMATION
Application Fee: $50
Regular Application Deadline: 2/1
Regular Notification: Rolling
LSDAS Accepted? Yes
Average GPA: 3.7
Range of GPA: 3.4–3.8
Average LSAT: 161
Range of LSAT: 158–164
Transfer Students Accepted? Yes
Other Schools to Which Students Applied: Georgetown University; Loyola Marymount University; University of Texas at Austin; University of Nevada, Las Vegas; University of Southern California; University of Utah
Number of Applications Received: 677
Number of Applicants Accepted: 240
Number of Applicants Enrolled: 153

INTERNATIONAL STUDENTS
TOEFL Required of International Students? Yes
Minimum TOEFL: 590 (242 computer)

EMPLOYMENT INFORMATION

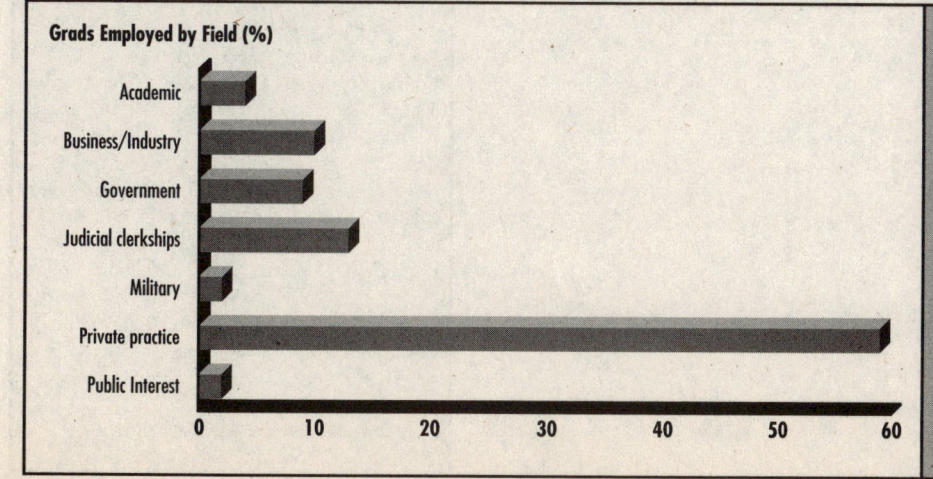

Grads Employed by Field (%): Academic, Business/Industry, Government, Judicial clerkships, Military, Private practice, Public Interest

Rate of Placement: 100%
Average Starting Salary: $76,453
Employers Who Frequently Hire Grads: Alston & Bird; Alverson Taylor; Baker & McKenzie; Ballard Spahr; Best Best & Krieger; Blackwell Sanders Peper Martin; Blakely Sokoloff Taylor & Zafman; Covington & Burling; Dechert; Deloitte & Touche; Dorsey & Whitney; Ernst & Young; Federal and State Courts; Fennemore Craig; Foley & Lardner; Hale Lane Peek Dennison Howard & Anderson; Gallagher & Kennedy; Gibson Dunn & Crutcher; Gray Cary Ware & Freidenrich; Hughes & Luce; JAGs; Jones Day Reavis & Pogue; Kirkland & Ellis
State for Bar Exam: UT, CA, NV, AZ, TX
Pass Rate for First-Time Bar: 92%

BROOKLYN LAW SCHOOL

Admissions Contact: Dean of Admissions and Financial Aid, Henry W. Haverstick III
250 Joralemon Street, Brooklyn, NY 11201
Admissions Phone: 718-780-7906 • Admissions Fax: 718-780-0395
Admissions E-mail: admitq@brooklaw.edu • Web Address: www.brooklaw.edu

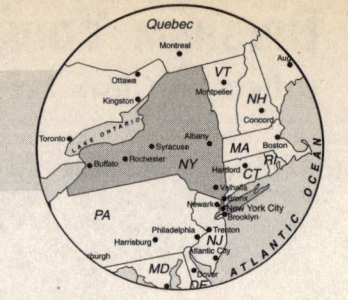

INSTITUTIONAL INFORMATION
Public/Private: Private
Student/Faculty Ratio: 18:1
Total Faculty: 130
% Part Time: 52
% Female: 39
% Minority: 6

PROGRAMS
Academic Specialties: Advocacy, International Business Law, International Human Rights, Liability, Public Interest, Litigation, Health Law, Civil Procedure, Commercial Law, Constitutional Law, Corporation Securities Law, Criminal Law, Government Services, Intellectual Property Law, Legal History, Legal Philosophy, Property, Taxation
Combined Degrees Offered: JD/MA Political Science, JD/MS Planning, JD/MBA, JD/MS Library/Information Science, JD/MUP, JD/MPA
Grading System: Letter system
Clinical Program Required? No
Clinical Program Description: Capital Defender Clinic, Consumer Counseling and Bankruptcy Clinic, Corporate and Real Estate Clinic, Elder Law Clinic, Federal Litigation Clinic, Safe Harbor Project (Immigration), Second Look Program, Securities Arbitration Clinic, Children's Law Center, Civil Practice Internship, Criminal Appeals—Manhattan DA Clinic, Criminal Appeals—Legal Aid Society, Criminal Practice Internship, Judicial Clerkship Internship, Mediation Clinic, Prosecutors Clinic—U.S. Attorney, EDNY
Legal Writing Course Requirements? Yes
Legal Writing Description: Legal Writing—1 year plus 1 upper-division writing elective; Legal Process—1 semester in first year
Legal Methods Course Requirements? Yes
Legal Methods Description: See Legal Writing.
Legal Research Course Requirements? Yes
Legal Research Description: Part of Legal Writing course
Moot Court Requirement? Yes
Moot Court Description: First-year Moot Court Competition as part of Legal Writing course
Public Interest Law Requirement? No
Academic Journals: *Brooklyn Law Review*, *Brooklyn Journal of International Law*, *Journal of Law and Policy*

STUDENT INFORMATION
Enrollment of Law School: 1,530
% Out of State: 34
% Male/Female: 48/52
% Full Time: 77
% Full Time That Are International: 2
% Minority: 18
Average Age of Entering Class: 25

RESEARCH FACILITIES
School-Supported Research Centers: Center for the Study of International Business Law; Edward Sparer Public Interest Law Fellowship Program; Center for Law, Language and Cognition; Center for Health Law and Policy

EXPENSES/FINANCIAL AID
Annual Tuition: $28,900
Room and Board (Off Campus): $13,907
Books and Supplies: $1,200
Financial Aid Application Deadline: 3/15
Average Grant: $6,459
Average Loan: $26,070
% of Aid That Is Merit-Based: 73
% Receiving Some Sort of Aid: 44
Average Total Aid Package: $28,058
Average Debt: $78,486
Tuition Per Credit: $21,675
Fees Per Credit: $130

ADMISSIONS INFORMATION
Application Fee: $65
Regular Application Deadline: Rolling
Regular Notification: Rolling
LSDAS Accepted? Yes
Average GPA: 3.4
Range of GPA: 3.1–3.6
Average LSAT: 160
Range of LSAT: 158–162
Transfer Students Accepted? Yes
Other Schools to Which Students Applied: Fordham University, University of Miami, Yeshiva University
Other Admissions Factors Considered: Quality of undergraduate institution; major; grade trends; grade inflation; advanced degree; maturity; moral character; geographic diversity; economic, racial/ethnic, and cultural background; alumni relationship; honors
Number of Applications Received: 3,961
Number of Applicants Accepted: 1,160
Number of Applicants Enrolled: 407

INTERNATIONAL STUDENTS
TOEFL Recommended for International Students? Yes

EMPLOYMENT INFORMATION

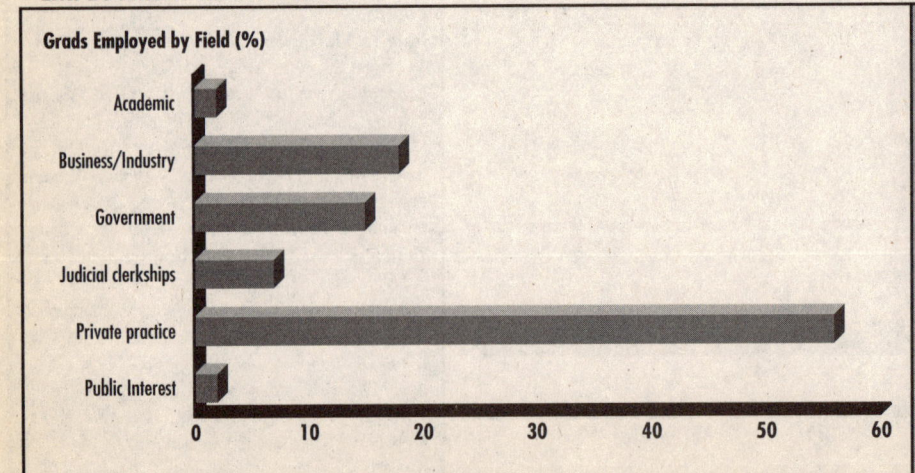

Grads Employed by Field (%)
- Academic
- Business/Industry
- Government
- Judicial clerkships
- Private practice
- Public Interest

Rate of Placement: 98%
Average Starting Salary: $94,174
Employers Who Frequently Hire Grads: Fried, Frank, Harris, Shriver & Jacobson; Pillsbury, Winthrop; Proskauer Rose; Kings County District Attorney's Office; New York City Law Department; Skadden, Arps, Slate, Meagher & Flom; Stroock & Stroock & Lavan; Administration for Children's Services
Prominent Alumni: David Dinkins, former Mayor, City of New York; Hon. Edward R. Korman, Chief Judge, U.S. District, EDNY; Russell Lewis, President and CEO, New York Times Company; Carlos Ortiz, General Counsel, Goya Foods
State for Bar Exam: NY, NJ
Pass Rate for First-Time Bar: 82%

CAL NORTHERN SCHOOL OF LAW

Admissions Contact: Dean, Sandra L. Brooks
1395 Ridgewood Drive, Chico, CA 95973
Admissions Phone: 530-891-6900 • Admissions Fax: 530-891-3429
Admissions E-mail: info@calnorthern.edu • Web Address: www.calnorthern.edu

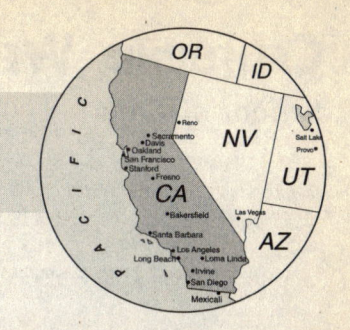

INSTITUTIONAL INFORMATION
Public/Private: Private
Student/Faculty Ratio: 4:1
Total Faculty: 18
% Part Time: 100
% Female: 28

PROGRAMS
Academic Specialties: All faculty are practicing attorneys or sitting judges.
Advanced Degrees Offered: JD (4 years)
Clinical Program Required? No
Legal Writing Course Requirements? Yes
Legal Writing Description: Legal Writing is required in the first year, Advanced Legal Writing required in the fourth year
Legal Methods Course Requirements? Yes
Legal Methods Description: See Legal Writing.
Legal Research Course Requirements? Yes
Legal Research Description: Legal Research required in the first year
Moot Court Requirement? Yes
Moot Court Description: Fourth-year Trial Advocacy, 15 weeks
Public Interest Law Requirement? No

STUDENT INFORMATION
Enrollment of Law School: 75
% Male/Female: 100/0
Average Age of Entering Class: 35

RESEARCH FACILITIES
Research Resources Available: California State University, Chico and Butte County Law Library

EXPENSES/FINANCIAL AID
Annual Tuition: $7,590
Books and Supplies: $400
Average Grant: $250
Average Loan: $7,600
% Receiving Some Sort of Aid: 5
Tuition Per Credit: $330

ADMISSIONS INFORMATION
Application Fee: $50
Regular Application Deadline: 6/3
Regular Notification: 7/3
LSDAS Accepted? No
Average GPA: 3.1
Average LSAT: 145
Transfer Students Accepted? Yes
Number of Applications Received: 43
Number of Applicants Accepted: 41
Number of Applicants Enrolled: 32

INTERNATIONAL STUDENTS
TOEFL Recommended for International Students? Yes

EMPLOYMENT INFORMATION
Prominent Alumni: Rick Keene, California Assemblyman
State for Bar Exam: CA
Pass Rate for First-Time Bar: 54%

CALIFORNIA WESTERN
School of Law

Admissions Contact: Director of Admissions, Traci Howard
225 Cedar Street, San Diego, CA 92101
Admissions Phone: 619-525-1401 • Admissions Fax: 619-615-1401
Admissions E-mail: admissions@cwsl.edu • Web Address: www.californiawestern.edu

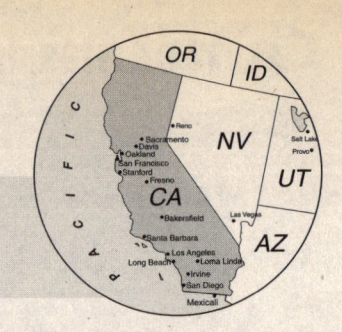

INSTITUTIONAL INFORMATION
Public/Private: Private
Student/Faculty Ratio: 29:1
Total Faculty: 37
% Part Time: 20
% Female: 41
% Minority: 11

PROGRAMS
Academic Specialties: Constitutional Law, Criminal Law, Environmental Law, Intellectual Property Law, International Law, Labor Law, Taxation
Advanced Degrees Offered: JD (2 to 3 years), MCL/LLM (9 months), LLM Trial Advocacy (1 year)
Combined Degrees Offered: JD/MSW (4 years), JD/MBA (4 years), JD/PhD Political Science or History (5 years)
Grading System: 50–95 scale with mandatory curve
Clinical Program Required? No
Legal Writing Course Requirements? Yes
Legal Writing Description: 3-course series required in first, second, third, or fourth trimester
Legal Methods Course Requirements? Yes
Legal Methods Description: See Legal Writing.
Legal Research Course Requirements? Yes
Legal Research Description: See Legal Writing.
Moot Court Requirement? No
Public Interest Law Requirement? No
Academic Journals: *California Western Law Review, California Western International Law Journal*

STUDENT INFORMATION
Enrollment of Law School: 1,000
% Out of State: 37
% Male/Female: 45/55
% Full Time: 86
% Full Time That Are International: 3
% Minority: 25
Average Age of Entering Class: 26

EXPENSES/FINANCIAL AID
Annual Tuition: $26,200
Room and Board (Off Campus): $15,816
Books and Supplies: $1,088
Financial Aid Application Deadline: 3/14
Average Grant: $10,000
Average Loan: $38,000
% of Aid That Is Merit-Based: 10
% Receiving Some Sort of Aid: 87
Average Total Aid Package: $35,000
Average Debt: $87,639
Tuition Per Credit: $920
Fees Per Credit: $10

ADMISSIONS INFORMATION
Application Fee: $45
Regular Application Deadline: 4/2
Regular Notification: Rolling
LSDAS Accepted? Yes
Average GPA: 3.2
Range of GPA: 2.9–3.5
Average LSAT: 151
Range of LSAT: 147–154
Transfer Students Accepted? Yes
Other Schools to Which Students Applied: University of San Diego
Other Admissions Factors Considered: Work experience, volunteer and extracurricular activities, diversity (ethnicity, culture, age)
Number of Applications Received: 2,088
Number of Applicants Accepted: 1,383
Number of Applicants Enrolled: 453

INTERNATIONAL STUDENTS
TOEFL Required of International Students? Yes
Minimum TOEFL: 600

EMPLOYMENT INFORMATION

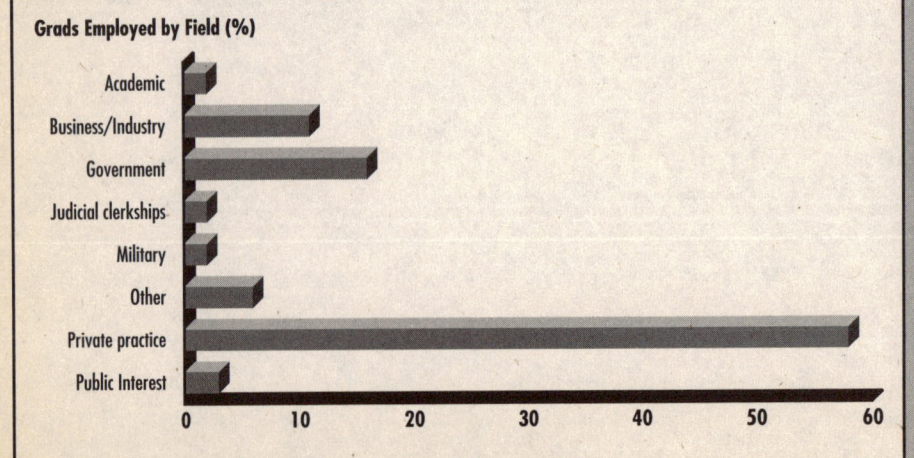

Grads Employed by Field (%)

Field	%
Academic	~0
Business/Industry	~11
Government	~17
Judicial clerkships	~3
Military	~1
Other	~6
Private practice	~58
Public Interest	~3

Rate of Placement: 85%
Average Starting Salary: $55,232
Employers Who Frequently Hire Grads: Multiple private, public, and nonprofit employers of all sizes from many regions nationally
Prominent Alumni: Lisa Haile, Partner, Gray, Cary, Ware, and Freidenrich; Garland Burrell, Judge, U.S. District Court; Roy Bell, Partner, Ross, Dixon, and Bell; David Roger, D.A., Clark County, Nevada; James Herman, President, State Bar of California
State for Bar Exam: CA, NV, AZ, NY, HI
Pass Rate for First-Time Bar: 82%

CAMPBELL UNIVERSITY
Norman Adrian Wiggins School of Law

Admissions Contact: Associate Dean for Admissions, Alan D. Woodlief, Jr.
Box 158, Buies Creek, NC 27506
Admissions Phone: 910-893-1754 • Admissions Fax: 910-893-1780
Admissions E-mail: culaw@webster.campbell.edu • Web Address: www.law.campbell.edu

INSTITUTIONAL INFORMATION
Public/Private: Private
Affiliation: Baptist
Student/Faculty Ratio: 17:1
Total Faculty: 41
% Part Time: 51
% Female: 17
% Minority: 2

PROGRAMS
Academic Specialties: Our trial and appellate advocacy program is a special strength of our curriculum. A business/transactions concentration or track is also offered.
Advanced Degrees Offered: JD (3 years, 90 semester hours)
Combined Degrees Offered: JD/MBA
Grading System: Superior (93–99), Above Average (84–92), Satisfactory (75–83), Unsatisfactory But Passing (68–74), Failing (60–67). Certain elective courses: Honors, Satisfactory, Unsatisfactory Pass, Unsatisfactory Fail.
Clinical Program Required? No
Legal Writing Course Requirements? Yes
Legal Writing Description: Part of the Legal Methods course
Legal Methods Course Requirements? Yes
Legal Methods Description: 3-semester course. The first fall semester focuses on legal research. The spring semester focuses on an introduction to legal writing, with students preparing various legal documents including complaints, motions, and legal memoranda. The second fall semester focuses on appellate advocacy, with students preparing an appellate brief and presenting an oral argument before a panel of alumni and judges.
Legal Research Course Requirements? Yes
Legal Research Description: Part of the Legal Methods course
Moot Court Requirement? Yes
Moot Court Description: Students prepare an appellate brief and present an oral argument during the fall semester of their second year as part of the Legal Methods course.
Public Interest Law Requirement? No
Academic Journals: *Campbell Law Review*, *Campbell Law Observer*

STUDENT INFORMATION
Enrollment of Law School: 336
% Male/Female: 54/46
% Full Time: 100
% Minority: 7
Average Age of Entering Class: 26

EXPENSES/FINANCIAL AID
Annual Tuition: $19,950
Room and Board (On/Off Campus): $9,075/$11,595
Books and Supplies: $1,050
Financial Aid Application Deadline: 4/15
Average Grant: $3,250
Average Loan: $19,854
% Receiving Some Sort of Aid: 77
Average Debt: $59,563

ADMISSIONS INFORMATION
Application Fee: $50
Regular Application Deadline: Rolling
Regular Notification: Rolling
LSDAS Accepted? Yes
Average GPA: 3.3
Range of GPA: 3.0–3.5
Average LSAT: 154
Range of LSAT: 151–156
Transfer Students Accepted? Yes
Other Schools to Which Students Applied: Mercer University, North Carolina Central University, University of North Carolina at Chapel Hill, University of Richmond, University of South Carolina, Wake Forest University
Number of Applications Received: 870
Number of Applicants Accepted: 237
Number of Applicants Enrolled: 136

INTERNATIONAL STUDENTS
TOEFL Recommended for International Students? Yes

EMPLOYMENT INFORMATION

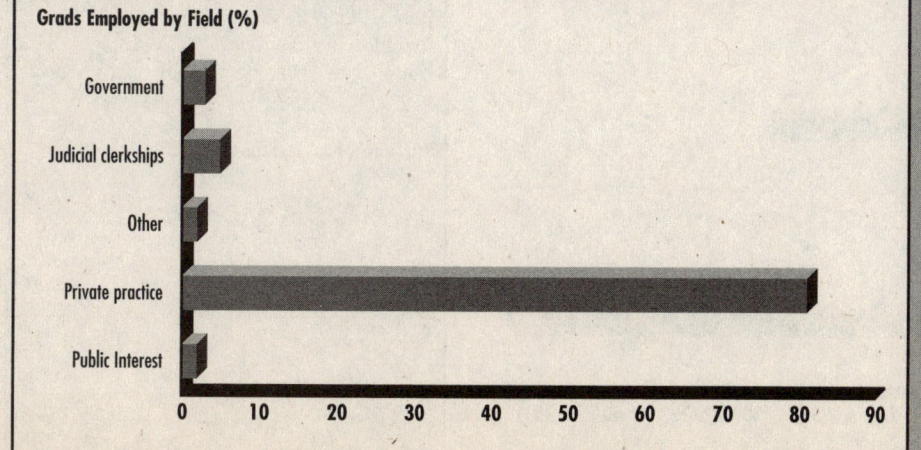

Grads Employed by Field (%)
- Government
- Judicial clerkships
- Other
- Private practice
- Public Interest

Rate of Placement: 94%
Average Starting Salary: $43,300
Employers Who Frequently Hire Grads: Small to medium-size private firms
Prominent Alumni: Elaine Marshall, Secretary of State, North Carolina; John Tyson, Judge, North Carolina Court of Appeals; Meg Scott Phipps, Secretary of Agriculture, North Carolina; Ann Marie Calabria, Judge, North Carolina Court of Appeals; Laura Bridges, Judge, North Carolina District Court
State for Bar Exam: NC
Pass Rate for First-Time Bar: 90%

CAPITAL UNIVERSITY
Law School

Admissions Contact: Assistant Dean of Admissions and Financial Aid, Linda J. Mihely
303 East Broad Street, Columbus, OH 43215-3200
Admissions Phone: 614-236-6310 • Admissions Fax: 614-236-6972
Admissions E-mail: admissions@law.capital.edu • Web Address: www.law.capital.edu

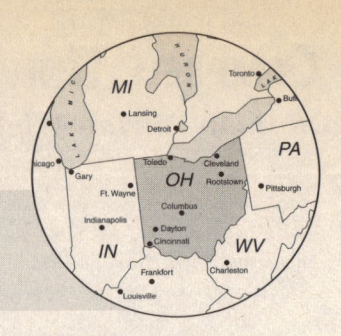

INSTITUTIONAL INFORMATION
Public/Private: Private
Affiliation: Lutheran
Student/Faculty Ratio: 23:1
Total Faculty: 29
% Part Time: 36
% Female: 21
% Minority: 14

PROGRAMS
Academic Specialties: Corporation Securities Law, International Law, Labor Law, Dispute Resolution, Business Law, Environmental Law, Family Law, Taxation, and Government Law are among the faculty's specialties. Strengths include commitment to teaching, innovative centers and institutes, positive relationships with students, and open access to students.
Advanced Degrees Offered: LLM Taxation, LLM Business, LLM Business and Taxation, MT (all 1 to 6 years)
Combined Degrees Offered: JD/MBA (3.5 to 6 years), JD/MSN (3.5 to 6 years), JD/MSA (3.5 to 4 years), JD/MTS (4 to 6 years)
Grading System: 4.0 scale
Clinical Program Required? No
Clinical Program Description: General Civil Litigation Clinic, Mediation Clinic, General Criminal Litigation Clinic, Domestic Violence Clinic, Externships
Legal Writing Course Requirements? Yes
Legal Writing Description: Year-long course covering research, writing, and methods
Legal Methods Course Requirements? Yes
Legal Methods Description: See Legal Writing.
Legal Research Course Requirements? Yes
Legal Research Description: See Legal Writing.
Moot Court Requirement? No
Moot Court Description: Active intercollegiate moot court program as well as a first-year student moot court competition
Public Interest Law Requirement? No
Public Interest Law Description: Although not required, students may receive a certificate for participation in the Pro Bono Program.
Academic Journals: *Capital University Law Review*

STUDENT INFORMATION
Enrollment of Law School: 726
% Out of State: 27
% Male/Female: 50/50
% Full Time: 56
% Minority: 13
Average Age of Entering Class: 25

RESEARCH FACILITIES
Research Resources Available: Supreme Court Law Library, Columbus Law Library Association, University Computer Lab, University Clinic and Recreation Center
School-Supported Research Centers: Center for Dispute Resolution, Institute for International Legal Education, Institute for Citizen Education, Institute for Adoption Law

EXPENSES/FINANCIAL AID
Annual Tuition: $18,009
Room and Board (Off Campus): $9,471
Books and Supplies: $887
Financial Aid Application Deadline: 4/1
Average Grant: $6,000
Average Loan: $20,400
% of Aid That Is Merit-Based: 40
% Receiving Some Sort of Aid: 93
Average Total Aid Package: $28,737
Average Debt: $53,485
Tuition Per Credit: $621
Fees Per Credit: $621

ADMISSIONS INFORMATION
Application Fee: $35
Regular Application Deadline: Rolling
Regular Notification: Rolling
LSDAS Accepted? Yes
Average GPA: 3.1
Range of GPA: 3.0–3.4
Average LSAT: 150
Range of LSAT: 147–154
Transfer Students Accepted? Yes
Other Schools to Which Students Applied: Ohio State, University of Dayton, University of Akron, University of Toledo, Cleveland State, Ohio Northern, University of Cincinnati
Other Admissions Factors Considered: Writing skills, employment history, graduate course work, socioeconomic status, demonstrated ability to overcome hardship, diversity, leadership ability, commitment to justice
Number of Applications Received: 1,034
Number of Applicants Accepted: 599
Number of Applicants Enrolled: 276

INTERNATIONAL STUDENTS
TOEFL Recommended for International Students? Yes

EMPLOYMENT INFORMATION

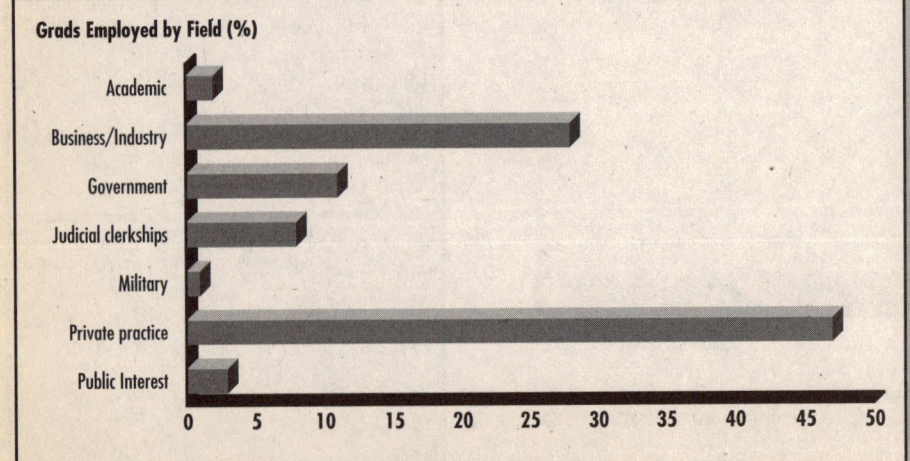

Grads Employed by Field (%)
- Academic: ~1
- Business/Industry: ~28
- Government: ~12
- Judicial clerkships: ~5
- Military: ~1
- Private practice: ~47
- Public Interest: ~3

Rate of Placement: 95%
Average Starting Salary: $55,069
Employers Who Frequently Hire Grads: Law firms, government agencies, business and corporate employers
State for Bar Exam: OH
Pass Rate for First-Time Bar: 62%

CARDOZO SCHOOL OF LAW
Yeshiva University

Admissions Contact: Associate Dean for Admissions, Robert L. Schwartz
55 Fifth Avenue, New York, NY 10003
Admissions Phone: 212-790-0274 • Admissions Fax: 212-790-0482
Admissions E-mail: lawinfo@ymail.yu.edu • Web Address: www.cardozo.yu.edu

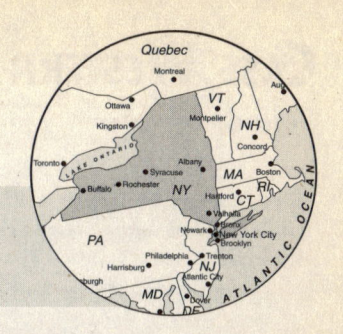

INSTITUTIONAL INFORMATION
Public/Private: Private
Affiliation: Jewish
Student/Faculty Ratio: 19:1
Total Faculty: 105
% Part Time: 54
% Female: 23
% Minority: 4

PROGRAMS
Academic Specialties: Commercial Law, Litigation, Constitutional Law and Theory, Civil Procedure, Corporation Securities Law, Criminal Law, Intellectual Property Law, International Law, Labor Law, Legal History, Legal Philosophy, Property, Taxation
Advanced Degrees Offered: JD (2 to 3 years), LLM (1 to 3 years)
Combined Degrees Offered: JD/LLM Intellectual Property Law (7 semesters); JD/MSW (4 years); JD/MA Economics, Philosophy, Political Science, or Sociology (4 years)
Grading System: A+ to D, F; curve for all first-year and large upper-level courses
Clinical Program Required? No
Clinical Program Description: Bet Tzedek Legal Services Clinic, Corporate Counsel's Appellate Internship, Criminal Appeals Clinic, Criminal Law Clinic, Family Court Clinic, Heyman/ACCA In-House Counsel Internship, Holocaust Claims Restitution Clinic, Immigration Law Clinic, Innocence Project, Intellectual Property Externship, International Law Practicum, Judicial Internship, Labor and Employment Law Externship, Mediation Clinic, Prosecutor Practicum, Tax Clinic, Telecommunications Workshop, U.S. Attorney's Office Externship, United Nations Commission on Civil and Political Rights Internship
Legal Writing Course Requirements? Yes
Legal Writing Description: Lawyering skills, legal writing, and research in the first semester; litigation and appellate oral and written advocacy in the second semester
Legal Methods Course Requirements? Yes
Legal Methods Description: 2 credits, taught during the first half of the first semester
Legal Research Course Requirements? Yes
Legal Research Description: Advanced Legal Research, second or third year
Moot Court Requirement? No
Public Interest Law Requirement? No
Academic Journals: Cardozo Law Review, Cardozo Arts and Entertainment Law Journal, Cardozo Women's Law Journal, Cardozo Journal of International and Comparative Law, Cardozo Online Journal of Conflict Resolution, Cardozo Public Law, Policy and Ethics Journal

STUDENT INFORMATION
Enrollment of Law School: 987
% Out of State: 45
% Male/Female: 49/51
% Full Time: 93
% Full Time That Are International: 2
% Minority: 19
Average Age of Entering Class: 25

RESEARCH FACILITIES
Research Resources Available: Courses and facilities at other divisions of Yeshiva and at New School University. Library on site access arrangements with area academic libraries.

School-Supported Research Centers: Jacob Burns Institute for Advanced Legal Studies; Heyman Center on Corporate Governance; Diener Institute of Jewish Law; Squadron Program in Law, Media and Society; Jacob Burns Ethics Center; Floersheimer Center for Constitutional Democracy; Kukin Program for Conflict Resolution; Center for Public Service Law; Siegel Progam in Real Estate Law

EXPENSES/FINANCIAL AID
Annual Tuition: $28,900
Room and Board (Off Campus): $20,727
Books and Supplies: $989
Financial Aid Application Deadline: 4/15
Average Grant: $8,000
Average Loan: $15,500
% of Aid That Is Merit-Based: 62
% Receiving Some Sort of Aid: 91
Average Total Aid Package: $30,000
Average Debt: $82,000
Tuition Per Credit: $1,300

ADMISSIONS INFORMATION
Application Fee: $60
Regular Application Deadline: 4/1
Regular Notification: Rolling
LSDAS Accepted? Yes
Average GPA: 3.5
Average LSAT: 160
Transfer Students Accepted? Yes
Other Schools to Which Students Applied: Boston University, Brooklyn Law, Columbia, Fordham, George Washington, New York Law, NYU
Number of Applications Received: 3,978
Number of Applicants Accepted: 1,074
Number of Applicants Enrolled: 312

EMPLOYMENT INFORMATION

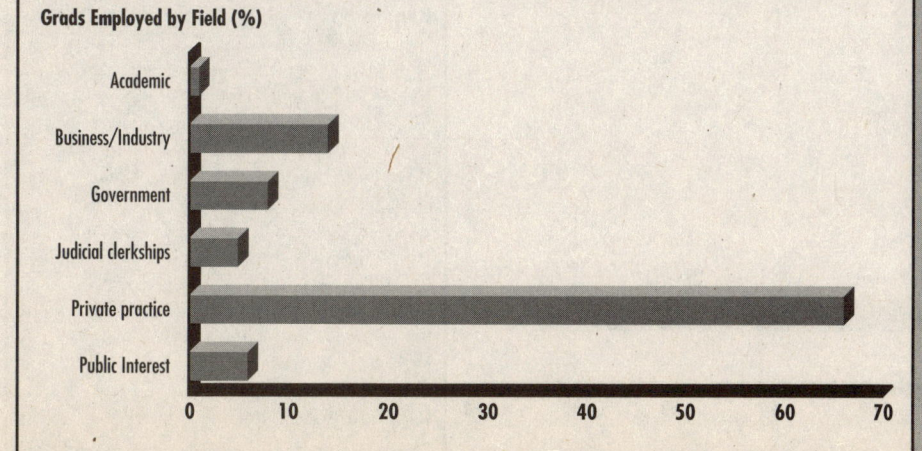

Grads Employed by Field (%)
- Academic: ~1
- Business/Industry: ~15
- Government: ~10
- Judicial clerkships: ~8
- Private practice: ~67
- Public Interest: ~5

Rate of Placement: 98%
Average Starting Salary: $89,670
Employers Who Frequently Hire Grads: International and national law firms of all sizes; federal and state judges nationwide; district attorney's offices and other state and federal government entities; public interest organizations
State for Bar Exam: NY
Pass Rate for First-Time Bar: 83%

CASE WESTERN RESERVE UNIVERSITY
School of Law

Admissions Contact: Director of Admissions, Christopher Lucak
11075 East Boulevard, Cleveland, OH 44106
Admissions Phone: 800-756-0036 • Admissions Fax: 216-368-1042
Admissions E-mail: lawadmissions@cwru.edu • Web Address: www.law.cwru.edu

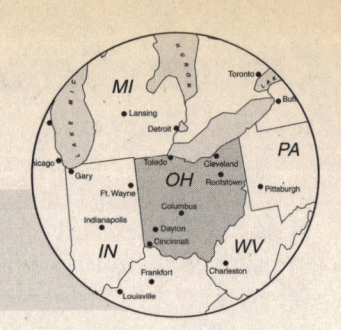

INSTITUTIONAL INFORMATION
Public/Private: Private
Student/Faculty Ratio: 15:1
Total Faculty: 51
% Female: 31
% Minority: 4

PROGRAMS
Academic Specialties: Our curriculum is distinguished for both its breadth and depth. Students will find a wide offering of courses in virtually every area of the law. More than 75 new courses and seven new concentrations (Law, Technology, and the Arts; Health Law; International Law; Criminal Law; Business Organizations; Public Law; and Litigation) have been added since 1999. Also available are Commercial Law, Constitutional Law, Corporation Securities Law, Government Services, Human Rights Law, Intellectual Property Law, and Taxation.
Advanced Degrees Offered: LLM U.S. Legal Studies (1 year for international lawyers)
Combined Degrees Offered: JD/MBA, JD/MNO Nonprofit Management, JD/MSSA Social Work, JD/MA Legal History, JD/MA Bioethics, JD/MPH (all 4 years); JD/Certificate in Nonprofit Management (3 years); JD/MD (7 years)
Grading System: A, A–, B+, B, B–, C+, C, C–, D+, D, D–, P, F, WF, W, N
Clinical Program Required? No
Clinical Program Description: Third-year students may take a clinics as an elective. Each offers first-chair experience: Civil Law, Criminal Law, Immigration Law, Community Development Law, and Health Law.
Legal Writing Course Requirements? Yes
Legal Writing Description: Our first-year writing program, known as RAW (Research, Analysis, and Writing), is a 2-semester course. Each RAW section meets in a small group of 20–25 students. Students undertake a rigorous program of research and legal writing, from legal memoranda and contracts to trial briefs and appellate briefs.
Legal Methods Course Requirements? No
Legal Research Course Requirements? No
Moot Court Requirement? No
Moot Court Description: Our Moot Court Board sponsors both intramural and interschool competitions. Students refine their brief writing and oral advocacy skills through second-year competition; the most outstanding candidates represent the school in national competition during their third year.
Public Interest Law Requirement? No
Academic Journals: *Law Review, Health Matrix: The Journal of Law and Medicine, The Journal of International Law*

STUDENT INFORMATION
Enrollment of Law School: 664
% Out of State: 60
% Male/Female: 55/45
% Full Time: 100
% Minority: 16
Average Age of Entering Class: 24

RESEARCH FACILITIES
School-Supported Research Centers: Law-Medicine Center; International Law Center; Center for Law, Technology, and the Arts; Milton A. Kramer Law Clinic Center; Center for Professional Ethics

EXPENSES/FINANCIAL AID
Annual Tuition: $25,900
Room and Board: $12,370
Books and Supplies: $980
Financial Aid Application Deadline: 5/1
Average Grant: $13,750
Average Loan: $24,200
% of Aid That Is Merit-Based: 100
% Receiving Some Sort of Aid: 82
Average Total Aid Package: $31,700
Average Debt: $58,700
Tuition Per Credit: $1,079

ADMISSIONS INFORMATION
Application Fee: $40
Regular Application Deadline: 4/1
Regular Notification: Rolling
LSDAS Accepted? Yes
Average GPA: 3.2
Range of GPA: 3.0–3.5
Average LSAT: 157
Range of LSAT: 155–160
Transfer Students Accepted? Yes
Number of Applications Received: 2,434
Number of Applicants Accepted: 774
Number of Applicants Enrolled: 244

EMPLOYMENT INFORMATION

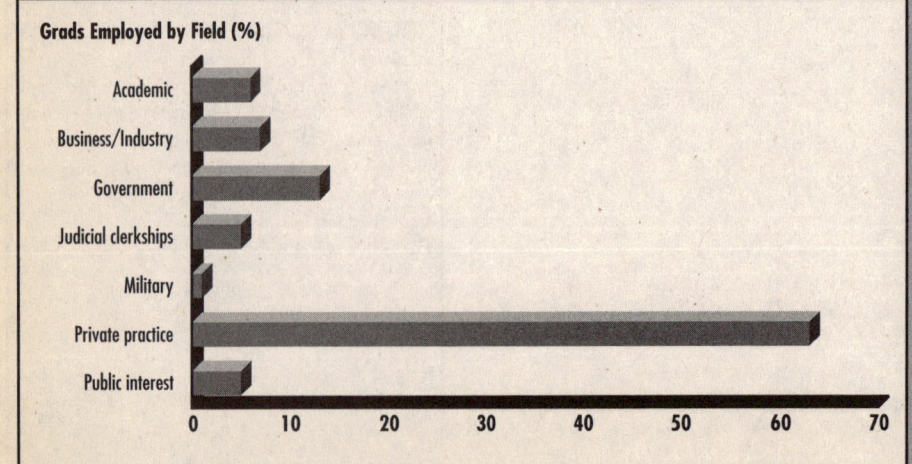

Grads Employed by Field (%)
- Academic
- Business/Industry
- Government
- Judicial clerkships
- Military
- Private practice
- Public interest

Employers Who Frequently Hire Grads: Jones Day Reavis & Pogue; Squire, Sanders and Dempsey; Baker & Hostetler; Jenner & Block; Ernst & Young; PriceWaterhouse Coopers; Altheimer & Gray; federal government; Department of Justice; state and federal judiciaries
Prominent Alumni: Fred Gray, Senior Partner and Civil Rights Attorney who represented Rosa Parks; Lincoln R. Diaz-Balart, Congressman, U.S. House of Representatives; James L. Bildner, Chairman and CEO, Tier Technologies, Inc.; Jane Kober, Senior VP, General Counsel, and Secretary, Biopure Corp.; Nicholas E. Calio, Assistant to the President of the United States
State for Bar Exam: OH, NY, CA, DC, PA
Pass Rate for First-Time Bar: 81%

CATHOLIC UNIVERSITY OF AMERICA
Columbus School of Law

Admissions Contact: Director of Admissions, Eric Eden
Cardinal Station, Washington, DC 20064
Admissions Phone: 202-319-5151 • Admissions Fax: 202-319-6285
Admissions E-mail: admissions@law.edu • Web Address: www.law.cua.edu

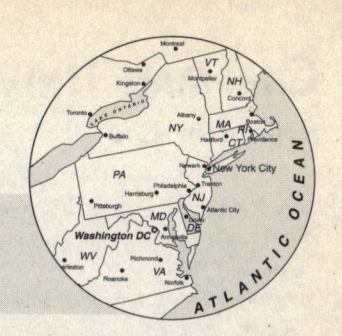

INSTITUTIONAL INFORMATION
Public/Private: Private
Affiliation: Roman Catholic
Student/Faculty Ratio: 21:1
Total Faculty: 93
% Part Time: 53
% Female: 34
% Minority: 13

PROGRAMS
Academic Specialties: Four Institutes/Certificate Programs, Institute for Communications Law Studies, Comparative and International Law Institute, Law and Public Policy, Health Law Corporation, Securities Law, Labor Law
Advanced Degrees Offered: JD (3 years full time, 4 years part time)
Combined Degrees Offered: JD/MA in Accounting, Canon Law, History, Philosophy, Psychology, Politics, Library Science, Economics, or Social Work (3 to 4 years)
Grading System: Letter system
Clinical Program Required? No
Clinical Program Description: General Practice Clinic, Families and the Law Clinic, Advocacy for the Elderly, Criminal Prosecution Clinic, DC Law Students in Court, Legal Externships; SEC Training Program
Legal Writing Course Requirements? No
Legal Methods Course Requirements? Yes
Legal Methods Description: 2 semesters in first year focusing on legal research, writing, and advocacy
Legal Research Course Requirements? No
Moot Court Requirement? No
Public Interest Law Requirement? No
Academic Journals: *Catholic University Law Review, Journal of Communications Law and Policy, Journal of Contemporary Health Law and Policy*

STUDENT INFORMATION
Enrollment of Law School: 955
% Out of State: 99
% Male/Female: 47/53
% Full Time: 70
% Full Time That Are International: 1
% Minority: 19
Average Age of Entering Class: 25

RESEARCH FACILITIES
Research Resources Available: Lexis/Nexis, Westlaw

EXPENSES/FINANCIAL AID
Annual Tuition: $26,140
Room and Board (On/Off Campus): $6,772/$7,080
Books and Supplies: $824
Financial Aid Application Deadline: 3/15
Average Grant: $6,600
Average Loan: $27,000
% of Aid That Is Merit-Based: 5
% Receiving Some Sort of Aid: 93
Average Total Aid Package: $35,250
Average Debt: $79,000
Tuition Per Credit: $955

ADMISSIONS INFORMATION
Application Fee: $55
Regular Application Deadline: 3/1
Regular Notification: Rolling
LSDAS Accepted? Yes
Average GPA: 3.3
Range of GPA: 3.0–3.5
Average LSAT: 157
Range of LSAT: 154–158
Transfer Students Accepted? Yes
Number of Applications Received: 2,194
Number of Applicants Accepted: 761
Number of Applicants Enrolled: 203

INTERNATIONAL STUDENTS
TOEFL Required of International Students? Yes

EMPLOYMENT INFORMATION

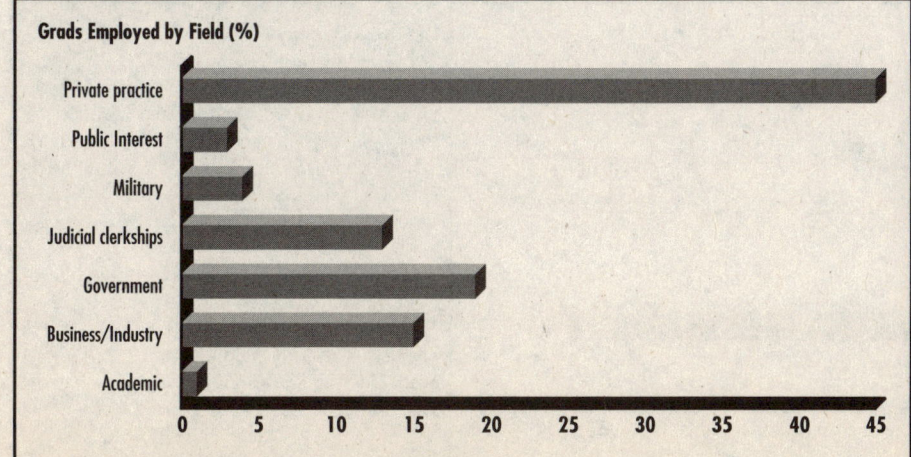

Grads Employed by Field (%)
- Private practice: ~45
- Public Interest: ~3
- Military: ~3
- Judicial clerkships: ~13
- Government: ~19
- Business/Industry: ~15
- Academic: ~1

Rate of Placement: 98%
Average Starting Salary: $63,014
Employers Who Frequently Hire Grads: Akin, Gump, Strauss, Hauer and Feld, LLP; Clifford, Chance, Rogers and Wells; Couder and Brothers
State for Bar Exam: MD, VA, PA, NY, NJ

CHAPMAN UNIVERSITY
School of Law

Admissions Contact: Director of Admissions, Demetrius Greer
One University Drive, Orange, CA 92866
Admissions Phone: 714-628-2500 • Admissions Fax: 714-628-2501
Admissions E-mail: lawadm@chapman.edu • Web Address: www.chapman.edu/law

INSTITUTIONAL INFORMATION
Public/Private: Private
Affiliation: Disciples of Christ
Student/Faculty Ratio: 15:1
Total Faculty: 22
% Female: 36
% Minority: 14

PROGRAMS
Academic Specialties: Land Use/Environment/Property, Elder Law, Business/Commercial Law, Constitutional Law, Criminal Law, Taxation
Advanced Degrees Offered: JD (3 years full time, 4 years part time)
Combined Degrees Offered: JD/MBA (4 years full time)
Grading System: 4.0 scale using plus and minus grades; 2.0 required for good academic standing and graduation
Clinical Program Required? No
Clinical Program Description: Live client clinics in taxation, bankruptcy, and elder law; numerous simulation courses in advocacy, dispute resolution, and trial practice
Legal Writing Course Requirements? Yes
Legal Writing Description: First year, 2 semesters, 5 credits, plus a paper of publishable quality in the second or third year
Legal Methods Course Requirements? Yes
Legal Methods Description: Part of the Legal Writing course
Legal Research Course Requirements? Yes
Legal Research Description: Part of the Legal Writing course

Moot Court Requirement? No
Public Interest Law Requirement? No
Academic Journals: *Chapman Law Review*; *Nexus, A Journal of Opinion*

STUDENT INFORMATION
Enrollment of Law School: 372
% Out of State: 16
% Male/Female: 52/48
% Full Time: 71
% Full Time That Are International: 2
% Minority: 25
Average Age of Entering Class: 25

RESEARCH FACILITIES
School-Supported Research Centers: Because our building is new, it is state-of-the-art, with computerized classrooms, labs, and the newest technology in courtrooms.

EXPENSES/FINANCIAL AID
Annual Tuition: $24,250
Room and Board (On/Off Campus): $10,017/$10,535
Books and Supplies: $1,000
Financial Aid Application Deadline: 3/2
Average Grant: $13,039
Average Loan: $21,345
% of Aid That Is Merit-Based: 45
% Receiving Some Sort of Aid: 85
Average Total Aid Package: $26,692
Average Debt: $58,530
Tuition Per Credit: $760

ADMISSIONS INFORMATION
Application Fee: $50
Regular Application Deadline: Rolling
Regular Notification: Rolling
LSDAS Accepted? Yes
Average GPA: 3.2
Range of GPA: 2.9–3.4
Average LSAT: 154
Range of LSAT: 151–157
Transfer Students Accepted? Yes
Other Schools to Which Students Applied: California Western, Loyola Marymount University, Pepperdine University, Southwestern University School of Law, University of San Diego, University of Southern California, Whittier College
Other Admissions Factors Considered: Writing ability, community service
Number of Applications Received: 1,151
Number of Applicants Accepted: 417
Number of Applicants Enrolled: 152

INTERNATIONAL STUDENTS
TOEFL Required of International Students? Yes
Minimum TOEFL: 600 (250 computer)

EMPLOYMENT INFORMATION

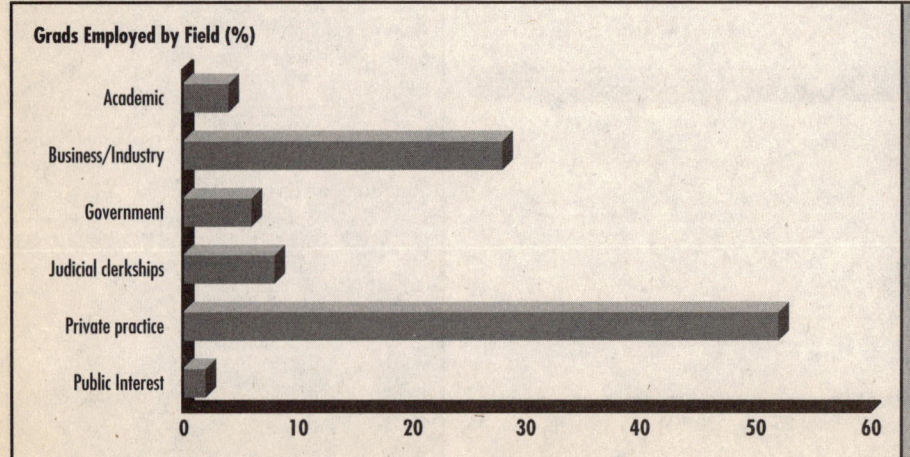

Grads Employed by Field (%)

Field	%
Academic	~0
Business/Industry	~28
Government	~5
Judicial clerkships	~8
Private practice	~53
Public Interest	~1

Rate of Placement: 89%
Average Starting Salary: $55,374
Employers Who Frequently Hire Grads: O'Melveny & Myers, Orange County District Attorney, Orange County Public Defender, United States District Courts, Los Angeles District Attorney, Knobbe Martens, Berger Khan, Riverside District Attorney, Bonne Bridges Mueller O'Keefe and Nichols
Prominent Alumni: Allison LeMoine-Bui, Associate, Rutan & Tucker; Bryan Godol, Associate, Morrison, Foerester; Melanie Triebel, Clerk, U.S. District Court for Central California
State for Bar Exam: CA, AZ
Pass Rate for First-Time Bar: 74%

CITY UNIVERSITY OF NEW YORK
CUNY School of Law at Queens College

Admissions Contact: Assistant Dean for Enrollment Management and Director of Admissions, Yvonne Cherena Pacheco
65-21 Main Street, Flushing, NY 11367-1358
Admissions Phone: 718-340-4210 • Admissions Fax: 718-340-4435
Admissions E-mail: admissions@mail.law.cuny.edu • Web Address: www.law.cuny.edu

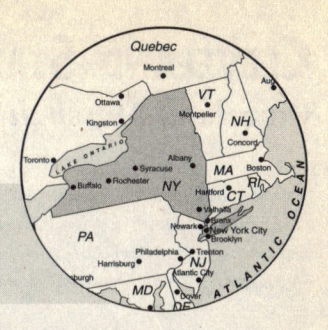

INSTITUTIONAL INFORMATION
Public/Private: Public
Student/Faculty Ratio: 14:1
Total Faculty: 50
% Part Time: 30
% Female: 62
% Minority: 36

PROGRAMS
Academic Specialties: We are a public interest/public service law school. Our curriculum is designed to build on the traditional doctrinal core to include policy and lawyering perspectives most relevant to public interest/public service lawyers. All students are required to enroll in a 12- to 16-credit concentration (externship) or clinical program in their third year, which builds on a foundation of 12 credits of lawyering seminars spread over the first 2 years. The academic specialties of our faculty include International Human Rights, Civil Rights, Women's Rights, Health Law, Labor and Workers Law, Environmental Law, Community Lawyering, Criminal Law, and International Law.
Advanced Degrees Offered: JD (3 years full time)
Grading System: A, A–, B+, B, B–, C+, C, C–, D, F, Credit/No Credit
Clinical Program Required? Yes
Clinical Program Description: Clinics in Battered Women's Rights, Defender, Elder Law, Immigrant and Refugee Rights, International Women's Human Rights, Mediation, Equality Concentration, Health Law Concentration
Legal Writing Course Requirements? Yes
Legal Writing Description: Students spend 4 hours each week of first year in Lawyering Seminar.
Legal Methods Course Requirements? Yes
Legal Methods Description: Another primary component of Lawyering Seminar is the teaching and learning of lawyering skills (including interviewing, negotiation, and oral advocacy).
Legal Research Course Requirements? Yes
Legal Research Description: The third core component of Lawyering Seminar is Legal Research, taught by the library faculty.
Moot Court Requirement? No
Moot Court Description: Any student may participate in the competitive selection process for Moot Court, a student-run organization, or a 2-credit Moot Court course.
Public Interest Law Requirement? Yes
Public Interest Law Description: Minimum of 12 credits of live-client clinical experience required. The 6 in-house clinics and 2 concentrations available to satisfy this requirement are all directly related to the school's mission to prepare each student for "Law in the Service of Human Needs" careers in public interest law.
Academic Journals: *NY City Law Review* (not an official publication of the law school).

STUDENT INFORMATION
Enrollment of Law School: 442
% Out of State: 31
% Male/Female: 40/60
% Full Time: 100
% Full Time That Are International: 3
% Minority: 45
Average Age of Entering Class: 29

RESEARCH FACILITIES
Research Resources Available: New York Joint International Program, Immigrants' Initiatives

EXPENSES/FINANCIAL AID
Annual Tuition (Residents/Nonresidents): $5,700/$8,930
Books and Supplies: $500
Financial Aid Application Deadline: 5/1
Average Grant: $3,000
Average Loan: $9,250
% Receiving Some Sort of Aid: 84
Average Total Aid Package: $18,416
Average Debt: $39,067

ADMISSIONS INFORMATION
Application Fee: $40
Regular Application Deadline: 3/15
Regular Notification: 5/31
LSDAS Accepted? Yes
Average GPA: 3.1
Range of GPA: 2.8–3.3
Average LSAT: 149
Range of LSAT: 145–153
Transfer Students Accepted? Yes
Other Schools to Which Students Applied: Fordham University, New York Law School, Rutgers University—Camden, St. John's University
Other Admissions Factors Considered: Experience in public interest or public service
Number of Applications Received: 1,842
Number of Applicants Accepted: 479
Number of Applicants Enrolled: 170

INTERNATIONAL STUDENTS
TOEFL Recommended for International Students? Yes

EMPLOYMENT INFORMATION

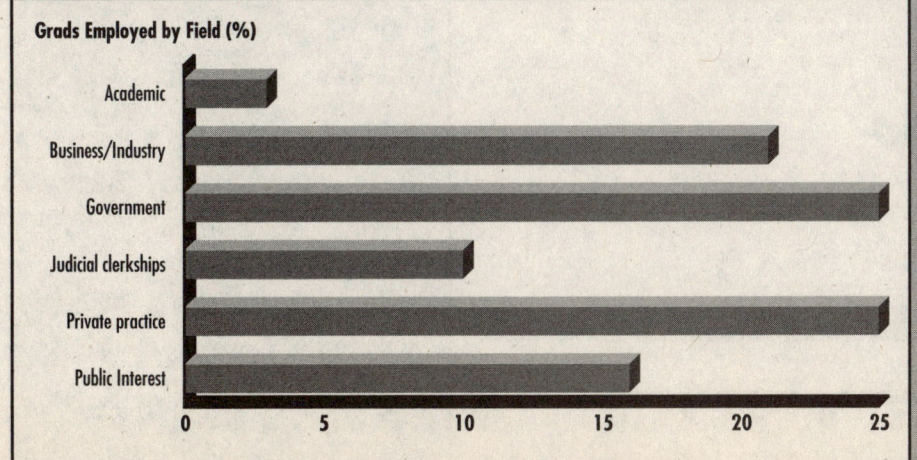

Grads Employed by Field (%)

Field	%
Academic	~3
Business/Industry	~21
Government	~25
Judicial clerkships	~10
Private practice	~21
Public Interest	~16

Rate of Placement: 77%
Average Starting Salary: $45,000
Employers Who Frequently Hire Grads: Legal Aid Society; NY City Law Department; Legal Services; District Attorney's Offices; U.S. Court of Appeals; NY State Court of Appeals; U.S. magistrate judges; U.S. Department of Justice Honors Program
Prominent Alumni: Hon. Diccia Pineda-Kirwan, Judge, Queens County Civil Court; Carmen Rita Torrent, Executive Director, Mayor's Commission on Women; Daniel O'Donnell, New York State Assemblyman; Kari Moss, Executive Director, ACLU; James Lawrence, Police Commissioner, Nassau County
State for Bar Exam: NY
Pass Rate for First Time Bar: 76%

CLEVELAND STATE UNIVERSITY
Cleveland-Marshall College of Law

Admissions Contact: Assistant Dean for Admissions, Melody Stewart
2121 Euclid Avenue, LB 138, Cleveland, OH 44115-2214
Admissions Phone: 216-687-2304 • Admissions Fax: 216-687-6881
Admissions E-mail: admissions@law.csuohio.edu • Web Address: www.law.csuohio.edu

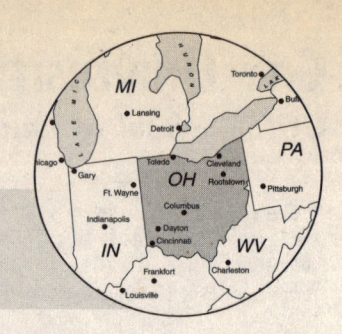

INSTITUTIONAL INFORMATION
Public/Private: Public
Student/Faculty Ratio: 20:1
Total Faculty: 78
% Part Time: 35
% Female: 28
% Minority: 8

PROGRAMS
Academic Specialties: Public Interest/Public Service/Governmental Placements, Business and Tax course offerings. Concentrations are offered in Business Law, Civil Litigation and Dispute Resolution, Criminal Law, Employment and Labor Law, Advocacy, Health Law, Commercial Law, Corporation Securities Law, Environmental Law, International Law, and Taxation.
Advanced Degrees Offered: LLM (1 to 4 years, 20 to 24 credits)
Combined Degrees Offered: JD/MPA, JD/MUPDD, JD/MAES, JD/MBA (all 4 years full time)
Grading System: 4.0 scale; A, B+, B, C+, C, D+, D, F. Limited Pass/D+/D/F option
Clinical Program Required? No
Clinical Program Description: Community Advocacy Clinic, Employment Law Clinic, Environmental Law Clinic, Fair Housing Law Clinic, Non-Profit Corporation Clinic, Judicial Externship, U.S. Attorney Externship, Public Service Externship, Independent Externship
Legal Writing Course Requirements? Yes
Legal Writing Description: First-year Legal Writing is a 5-credit course that introduces legal research, legal method, case briefing, and legal writing including memoranda and briefs on motions. Students must elect a course providing a third semester of legal writing. Students must also complete an upper-level writing project, which requires a substantial research paper.
Legal Methods Course Requirements? Yes
Legal Methods Description: See Legal Writing.
Legal Research Course Requirements? Yes
Legal Research Description: See Legal Writing. An upper-level elective in Advanced Legal Research is sometimes offered.
Moot Court Requirement? No
Moot Court Description: Second-year students who have taken an elective course called Advanced Brief Writing may participate in Spring Moot Court competition; up to 18 students are selected for interscholastic competition the following year. Up to 6 first-year students are selected for interscholastic competition in their second year.
Public Interest Law Requirement? No
Public Interest Law Description: While we do not require public service, we do recognize students who serve 50 hours or more in a variety of pro bono and community service projects. We also have a number of awards and scholarships for students who distinguish themselves in public service activities.
Academic Journals: *Cleveland State Law Review*, *Journal of Law and Health*

STUDENT INFORMATION
Enrollment of Law School: 828
% Male/Female: 59/41
% Full Time: 65
% Full Time That Are International: 1
% Minority: 10
Average Age of Entering Class: 27

EXPENSES/FINANCIAL AID
Annual Tuition (Residents/Nonresidents): $9,964/$19,928
Room and Board: $10,350
Books and Supplies: $700
Financial Aid Application Deadline: 4/1
Average Grant: $4,848
Average Loan: $16,593
% of Aid That Is Merit-Based: 90
% Receiving Some Sort of Aid: 89
Average Total Aid Package: $22,025
Average Debt: $41,872
Tuition Per Credit (Residents/Nonresidents): $383/$766
Fees Per Credit (Res./Nonres.): $22/$38

ADMISSIONS INFORMATION
Application Fee: $35
Regular Application Deadline: 4/1
Regular Notification: 5/1
LSDAS Accepted? Yes
Average GPA: 3.1
Range of GPA: 2.8–3.4
Average LSAT: 152
Range of LSAT: 149–154
Transfer Students Accepted? Yes
Other Schools to Which Students Applied: Case Western Reserve University, University of Akron
Other Admissions Factors Considered: Work and life experiences, graduate degree, recommendation, résumé, personal statement
Number of Applications Received: 1,410
Number of Applicants Accepted: 592
Number of Applicants Enrolled: 264

EMPLOYMENT INFORMATION

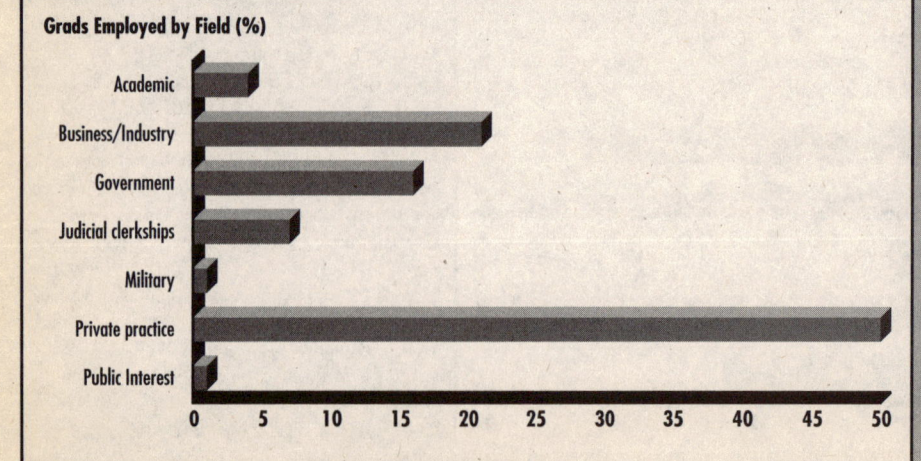

Grads Employed by Field (%)
- Academic
- Business/Industry
- Government
- Judicial clerkships
- Military
- Private practice
- Public Interest

Rate of Placement: 95%
Average Starting Salary: $59,500
Employers Who Frequently Hire Grads: Jones Day; Thompson, Hine; Squire, Sanders & Dempsey; Calfee, Halter & Griswold; Arter & Hadden; Ernst & Young; Benesch, Friedlander, Coplan & Arnold; Hahn, Loeser & Parks, LLP; Fay, Sharpe, Fagan, Minnich & McKee LLP; Porter, Wright, Morris & Arthur; Duvin, Cahn & Hutton; Gallagher, Sharpe, Fulton & Norman; Janik & Dorman
Prominent Alumni: Tim Russert Sr., VP, NBC News; Hon. Louis Stokes, U.S. House of Representatives (retired); Maureen O'Connor, Justice, Ohio Supreme Court
State for Bar Exam: OH, NY, CA, FL, IL
Pass Rate for First-Time Bar: 73%

COLLEGE OF WILLIAM AND MARY
Law School

Admissions Contact: Associate Dean, Faye Shealy
Office of Admission, PO Box 8795, Williamsburg, VA 23187-8795
Admissions Phone: 757-221-3785 • Admissions Fax: 757-221-3261
Admissions E-mail: lawadm@wm.edu • Web Address: www.wm.edu/law

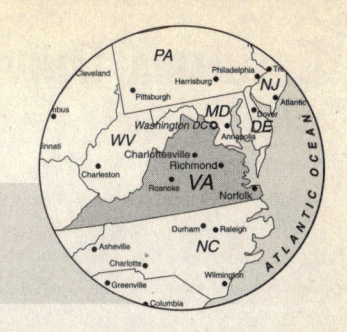

INSTITUTIONAL INFORMATION
Public/Private: Public
Student/Faculty Ratio: 17:1
Total Faculty: 86
% Part Time: 64
% Female: 26
% Minority: 8

PROGRAMS
Academic Specialties: Constitutional Law, especially Bill of Rights study and public programs; Environmental Science and Policy; Courtroom Technology, Research, and Application. Also offered are Civil Procedure, Commercial Law, Corporation Securities Law, Criminal Law, Government Services, Human Rights Law, Intellectual Property Law, International Law, Labor Law, Legal History, Legal Philosophy, Property, Taxation
Advanced Degrees Offered: LLM American Legal System (1 year)
Combined Degrees Offered: JD/MPP, JD/MBA, JD/MA American Studies (all 4 years)
Grading System: 4.0 scale; A, B+, B, B–, C+, C, C–, D, F
Clinical Program Required? No
Clinical Program Description: Federal Tax Practice Clinic, Domestic Violence and Legal Aid Clinic; externships: General Practice, Non-Profit Organizations, Department of Employment Dispute Resolution, Virginia Court of Appeals, Attorney General, Supreme Court of Virginia, Judicial Clerk
Legal Writing Course Requirements? Yes
Legal Writing Description: The teaching of Legal Writing or Legal Methods is incorporated within our mandatory Legal Skills Program.
Legal Methods Course Requirements? Yes
Legal Methods Description: See Legal Writing.
Legal Research Course Requirements? No
Moot Court Requirement? No
Moot Court Description: Intraschool competition in the fall of the second year; winners are placed in interschool teams in their third year.
Public Interest Law Requirement? No
Academic Journals: W&M Bill of Rights Journal, W&M Environmental Law and Policy Review, W&M Journal of Women and the Law, W&M Law Review

STUDENT INFORMATION
Enrollment of Law School: 557
% Out of State: 46
% Male/Female: 58/42
% Full Time: 100
% Full Time That Are International: 1
% Minority: 16
Average Age of Entering Class: 24

RESEARCH FACILITIES
Research Resources Available: National Center for State Courts, William and Mary Environmental Science and Policy Cluster, Virginia Institute for Marine Science
School-Supported Research Centers: Courtroom 21 Project; Institute of Bill of Rights Law

EXPENSES/FINANCIAL AID
Annual Tuition (Residents/Nonresidents): $11,500/$21,690
Room and Board: $6,300
Books and Supplies: $1,000
Financial Aid Application Deadline: 2/15
Average Grant: $4,181
Average Loan: $20,145
% of Aid That Is Merit-Based: 75
% Receiving Some Sort of Aid: 85
Average Total Aid Package: $22,903
Average Debt: $59,700
Tuition Per Credit (Residents/Nonresidents): $374/$687

ADMISSIONS INFORMATION
Application Fee: $40
Regular Application Deadline: 3/1
Regular Notification: 4/1
LSDAS Accepted? Yes
Average GPA: 3.6
Range of GPA: 3.3–3.8
Average LSAT: 163
Range of LSAT: 160–165
Transfer Students Accepted? Yes
Other Schools to Which Students Applied: Boston College, Boston U., George Mason, George Washington, Georgetown, U. of Virginia, Washington and Lee
Other Admissions Factors Considered: Quality of school(s) attended, difficulty of major, outside employment or extracurricular activities
Number of Applications Received: 3,384
Number of Applicants Accepted: 686
Number of Applicants Enrolled: 189

INTERNATIONAL STUDENTS
TOEFL Required of International Students? Yes
Minimum TOEFL: 600 (250 computer)

EMPLOYMENT INFORMATION

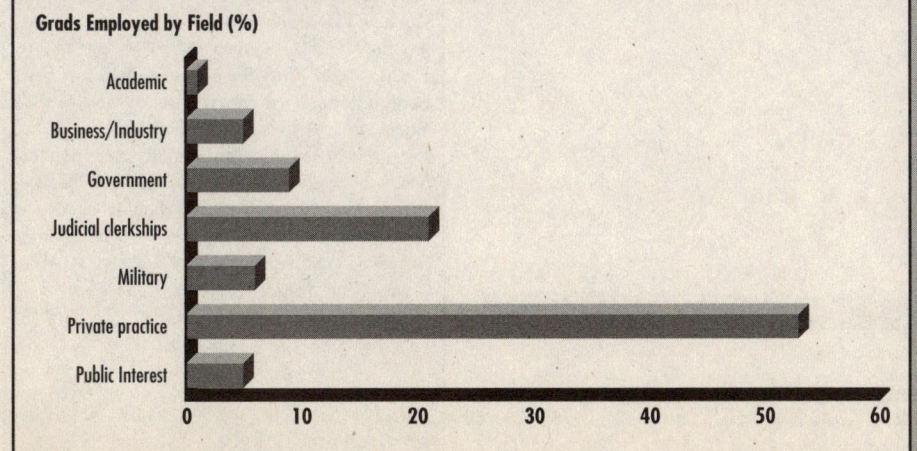

Grads Employed by Field (%)

Field	%
Academic	~1
Business/Industry	~5
Government	~10
Judicial clerkships	~21
Military	~2
Private practice	~53
Public Interest	~3

Rate of Placement: 99%
Average Starting Salary: $85,000
State for Bar Exam: VA, NY, MD, PA
Pass Rate for First-Time Bar: 88%

COLUMBIA UNIVERSITY
School of Law

Admissions Contact: Dean of Admissions, James Milligan
435 West 116th Street, Box A–3, New York, NY 10027
Admissions Phone: 212-854-2670 • Admissions Fax: 212-854-1109
Admissions E-mail: admissions@law.columbia.edu • Web Address: www.law.columbia.edu

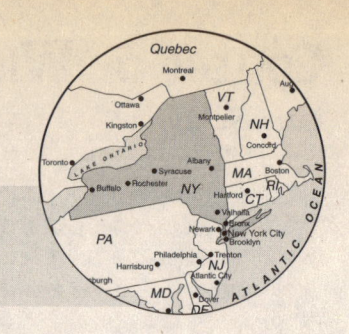

INSTITUTIONAL INFORMATION
Public/Private: Private
Student/Faculty Ratio: 13:1
Total Faculty: 167
% Part Time: 30
% Female: 25
% Minority: 19

PROGRAMS
Academic Specialties: Clinical Education, Comparative Law, Profession of Law (Professional Responsibility), Critical Race Theory, Feminist Jurisprudence, Civil Procedure, Commercial Law, Constitutional Law, Corporation Securities Law, Criminal Law, Environmental Law, Government Services, Human Rights Law, Intellectual Property Law, International Law, Labor Law, Legal History, Legal Philosophy, Property, Taxation
Advanced Degrees Offered: LLM (1 year), JSD (2 semesters in residence plus dissertation)
Combined Degrees Offered: JD/PhD History, Philosophy, Anthropology, Economics, Political Science, Psychology, or Sociology (7 years); JD/MBA (3 to 4 years); JD/MS Journalism (3.5 years); JD/MFA Arts Administration, JD/MSW, JD/MUP, JD/MIA, JD/MPA with Columbia or Princeton (all 4 years)
Grading System: A+, A, A–, B+, B, B–, C, F, CR
Clinical Program Required? No
Clinical Program Description: Child Advocacy, Human Rights, Mediation, Non-Profit Organizations/Small Business, Prisoners and Families, Law and the Arts, Environmental Law, Lawyering in the Digital Age
Legal Writing Course Requirements? Yes
Legal Writing Description: First-year, fall semester; students create, revise, and hone a series of legal documents

Legal Methods Course Requirements? Yes
Legal Methods Description: An introduction to legal institutions, processes, and skills.
Legal Research Course Requirements? Yes
Legal Research Description: Students must write two research papers.
Moot Court Requirement? Yes
Moot Court Description: Done over the course of the spring semester of the first year. There are specialized moot court opportunities for upper-class students.
Public Interest Law Requirement? Yes
Public Interest Law Description: Must devote 40 hours of uncompensated time to field work.
Academic Journals: *American Journal of International Arbitration, Columbia Business Law Review, Columbia Human Rights Law Review, Columbia Journal of European Law, Columbia Journal of Asian Law,* and many others

STUDENT INFORMATION
Enrollment of Law School: 1,176
% Out of State: 78
% Male/Female: 51/49
% Full Time: 100
% Full Time That Are International: 7
% Minority: 32
Average Age of Entering Class: 24

RESEARCH FACILITIES
Research Resources Available: Computer resources, specialized technology teaching and learning consultation by the Center for New Media
School-Supported Research Centers: Center for Law and the Arts; Julius Silver Program in Law, Science and Technology; Center for Japanese Legal Studies; Center for Chinese Legal Studies; Center for Law and Economics; Legislative Drafting Research Fund; Center for Public Interest Law; Parker School of Foreign and Comparative Law; Human Rights Institute; European Legal Studies Center; Center for Law and Philosophy

EXPENSES/FINANCIAL AID
Annual Tuition: $32,700
Room and Board (On/Off Campus): $16,130/$15,200
Books and Supplies: $930
Financial Aid Application Deadline: 3/1
Average Grant: $14,653
Average Loan: $32,600
% of Aid That Is Merit-Based: 38
% Receiving Some Sort of Aid: 83
Average Total Aid Package: $35,650
Average Debt: $87,000
Fees Per Credit: $1,636

ADMISSIONS INFORMATION
Application Fee: $70
Regular Application Deadline: 2/15
Regular Notification: Rolling
LSDAS Accepted? Yes
Range of GPA: 3.5–3.9
Range of LSAT: 166–173
Transfer Students Accepted? Yes
Other Schools to Which Students Applied: Harvard, NYU, Stanford, Yale
Other Admissions Factors Considered: Personal statement, letters of recommendation, course selection, extracurricular involvment, community service
Number of Applications Received: 8,072
Number of Applicants Accepted: 1,172
Number of Applicants Enrolled: 377

EMPLOYMENT INFORMATION

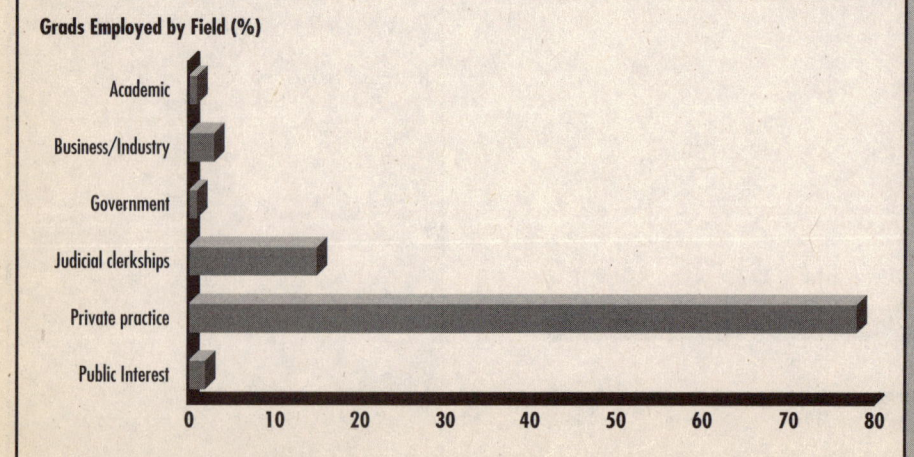

Grads Employed by Field (%)

Field	%
Academic	~1
Business/Industry	~2
Government	~1
Judicial clerkships	~15
Private practice	~78
Public Interest	~2

Rate of Placement: 99%
Average Starting Salary: $125,000
Employers Who Frequently Hire Grads: Large international corporate law firms, federal judges, federal government agencies
Prominent Alumni: Ruth Bader Ginsburg, Justice, U.S. Supreme Court; George Pataki, Governor of New York; Franklin D. Roosevelt, former President of U.S.; Paul Robeson, performing artist and civil rights activist; Charles Evans Hughes, former Chief Justice, U.S. Supreme Court
State for Bar Exam: NY, NJ, CA, FL, TX
Pass Rate for First-Time Bar: 94%

CORNELL UNIVERSITY
Law School

Admissions Contact: Dean of Admissions, Richard Geiger
Myron Taylor Hall, Ithaca, NY 14853-4901
Admissions Phone: 607-255-5141 • Admissions Fax: 607-255-7193
Admissions E-mail: lawadmit@postoffice.law.cornell.edu • Web Address: www.lawschool.cornell.edu

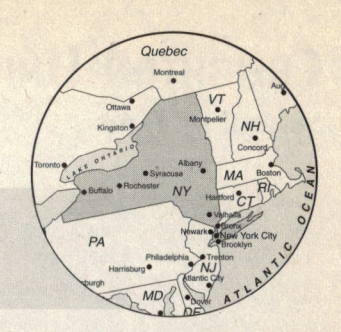

INSTITUTIONAL INFORMATION
Public/Private: Private
Student/Faculty Ratio: 13:1
Total Faculty: 45
% Female: 42
% Minority: 16

PROGRAMS
Academic Specialties: International Law
Advanced Degrees Offered: JD (3 years) LLM (1 year), JSD (2 years)
Combined Degrees Offered: JD/MBA; JD/MPA; JD/MA; JD/PhD; JD/MRP; JD/MILR; JD/LLM International and Comparative Law (3 years); JD/Maitrise en Droit (4 years); JD/MLLP German and European (4 years)
Grading System: Letter system
Clinical Program Required? No
Clinical Program Description: Legal Aid, Capital Punishment, Appellate Advocacy, Civil Liberties, Government Benefits, Women and the Law, Judicial Externship, Legislative Externship, Neighborhood Legal Services Externship, Public International Law Clinic, Law Guardian Externship, Religious Liberty Clinic
Legal Writing Course Requirements? No
Legal Methods Course Requirements? Yes
Legal Methods Description: Legal Methods is a full-year skills course designed to introduce first-year students to the techniques of research, analysis, and writing that are necessary in legal practice. Instruction in the fall semester focuses on legal research and the written communication of objective legal analysis. Students complete a series of research and writing assignments that develop and test their skills in these areas. Instruction in the spring semester focuses on written and oral advocacy. In the context of a simulated civil or criminal trial, students complete the necessary research and then draft and rewrite a trial or appellate brief advocating their client's position on one or more legal issues. The spring semester culminates with a moot court exercise designed to introduce the students to the techniques and logistics of oral advocacy in a courtroom setting. Instruction occurs in small sections of approximately 30 students and in individual conferences. Each student receives extensive editorial and evaluative feedback on each written assignment.
Legal Research Course Requirements? No
Moot Court Requirement? No
Public Interest Law Requirement? No
Academic Journals: Law Review, International Law Journal, Journal of Law and Public Policy, LII Bulletin

STUDENT INFORMATION
Enrollment of Law School: 570
% Out of State: 75
% Male/Female: 51/49
% Full Time: 100
% Full Time That Are International: 2
% Minority: 26
Average Age of Entering Class: 25

RESEARCH FACILITIES
Research Resources Available: Vast resources of Cornell University; students can take 12 credits in another graduate program at Cornell for law school credit.

School-Supported Research Centers: Legal Information Institute (school's legal research website); James R. Withrow Jr. Program on Legal Ethics; Empirical Studies on Federal and State Court Cases; Olin Program in Law and Economics; Death Penalty Project; Religious Liberty Institute; Feminism Legal Theory Project; Gender, Sexuality, and Family Project

EXPENSES/FINANCIAL AID
Annual Tuition: $31,250
Room and Board: $7,870
Books and Supplies: $760
Financial Aid Application Deadline: 3/15
Average Grant: $9,000
% Receiving Some Sort of Aid: 75

ADMISSIONS INFORMATION
Application Fee: $65
Regular Application Deadline: 2/1
Regular Notification: Rolling
LSDAS Accepted? Yes
Average GPA: 3.6
Range of GPA: 3.5–3.7
Average LSAT: 165
Range of LSAT: 164–166
Transfer Students Accepted? Yes
Other Admissions Factors Considered: Undergraduate and graduate course work, work experience, extracurricular activities, community involvement, leadership
Number of Applications Received: 4,102
Number of Applicants Accepted: 789
Number of Applicants Enrolled: 212

EMPLOYMENT INFORMATION

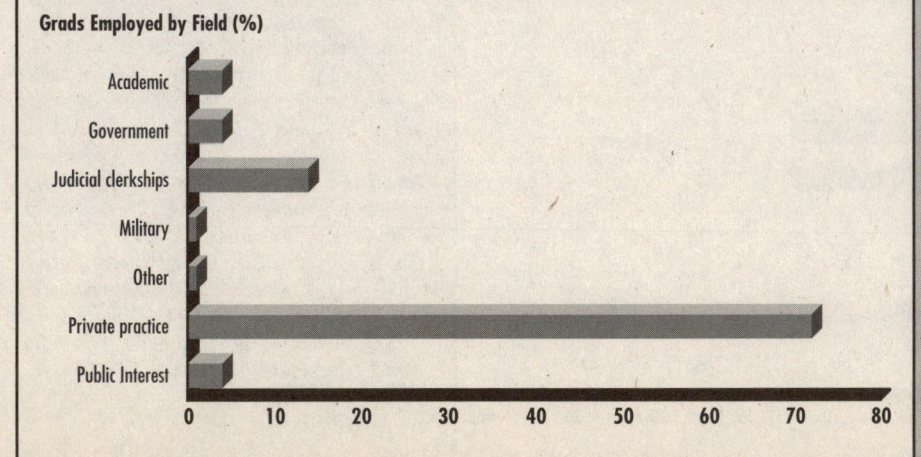

Grads Employed by Field (%)

Field	%
Academic	~2
Government	~3
Judicial clerkships	~15
Military	0
Other	~1
Private practice	~72
Public Interest	~3

Rate of Placement: 100%
Average Starting Salary: $103,247
State for Bar Exam: NY
Pass Rate for First-Time Bar: 97%

CREIGHTON UNIVERSITY
School of Law

Admissions Contact: Assistant Dean, Andrea D. Bashara
2500 California Plaza, Omaha, NE 68178
Admissions Phone: 402-280-2872 • Admissions Fax: 402-280-3161
Admissions E-mail: lawadmit@creighton.edu • Web Address: culaw.creighton.edu

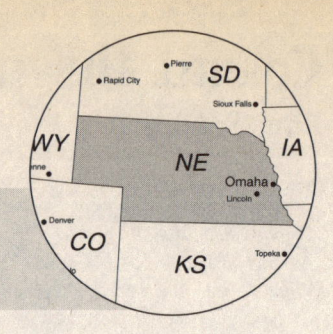

INSTITUTIONAL INFORMATION
Public/Private: Private
Affiliation: Roman Catholic
Student/Faculty Ratio: 17:1
Total Faculty: 69
% Part Time: 59
% Female: 33
% Minority: 6

PROGRAMS
Academic Specialties: Small classes in the first year; strong skills programs in trial practice, negotiations, and client counseling; Constitutional Law; Evidence/Litigation and Alternate Dispute Resolution; Civil Procedure/Federal Courts/Conflict of Laws; International Law; Commercial Law; Corporation Securities Law; Criminal Law; Taxation
Combined Degrees Offered: JD/MBA (3 years), JD/MS Electronic Commerce (3 years)
Grading System: 50–100 scale
86-100 = A
75-85 = B
65-74 = C
57-64 = D
50-56 = F
Clinical Program Required? No
Clinical Program Description: Milton R. Abrahams Legal Clinic; clinical and judicial internships with government and legal aid offices
Legal Writing Course Requirements? Yes
Legal Writing Description: 2 semesters
Legal Methods Course Requirements? No
Legal Research Course Requirements? Yes
Legal Research Description: 1 semester
Moot Court Requirement? Yes
Moot Court Description: Brief writing and oral argument, elimination rounds, part of Legal Writing II
Public Interest Law Requirement? No
Academic Journals: *Creighton Law Review*

STUDENT INFORMATION
Enrollment of Law School: 163
% Out of State: 60
% Male/Female: 59/41
% Full Time: 94
% Full Time That Are International: 1
% Minority: 7
Average Age of Entering Class: 25

RESEARCH FACILITIES
School-Supported Research Centers: The Klutznick Law Library is maintained to support the curriculum of the law school and faculty and student research. The library contains more than 275,000 volumes and access to a wide range of online research products.

EXPENSES/FINANCIAL AID
Annual Tuition: $19,432
Room and Board: $10,350
Books and Supplies: $1,250
Financial Aid Application Deadline: 3/1
Average Grant: $7,117
Average Loan: $20,500
% of Aid That Is Merit-Based: 33
% Receiving Some Sort of Aid: 92
Average Total Aid Package: $23,000
Average Debt: $63,388
Tuition Per Credit: $650
Fees Per Credit: $114

ADMISSIONS INFORMATION
Application Fee: $45
Regular Application Deadline: 5/1
Regular Notification: Rolling
LSDAS Accepted? Yes
Average GPA: 3.3
Range of GPA: 3.0–3.5
Average LSAT: 153
Range of LSAT: 149–157
Transfer Students Accepted? Yes
Other Schools to Which Students Applied: Drake University, Gonzaga University, University of Nebraska—Lincoln
Other Admissions Factors Considered: Type of courses completed, grade trends, military achievements, graduate studies, adjustment to individual hardship
Number of Applications Received: 821
Number of Applicants Accepted: 426
Number of Applicants Enrolled: 153

INTERNATIONAL STUDENTS
TOEFL Recommended for International Students? Yes

EMPLOYMENT INFORMATION

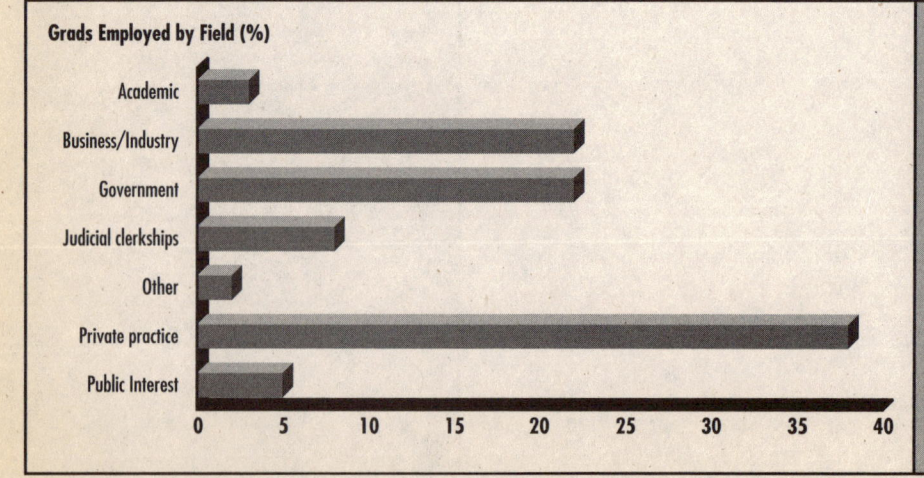

Grads Employed by Field (%)
- Academic: ~2
- Business/Industry: ~22
- Government: ~22
- Judicial clerkships: ~8
- Other: ~3
- Private practice: ~38
- Public Interest: ~5

Rate of Placement: 93%
Average Starting Salary: $45,986
Employers Who Frequently Hire Grads: McGrath North, Kutak Rock, Fraser Stryker, Baird Holm, Koley Jessen, Blackwell Sanders, Stinson Morrison, Erickson Sederstrom, Fitzgerald Schorr
Prominent Alumni: Michael O. Johanns, Governor of Nebraska; Bruce C. Rohde, President, CEO, and Chairman, ConAgra Inc.; Hon. Michael J. McCormack, Justice, Nebraska Supreme Court; Hon. William M. Connolly, Justice, Nebraska Supreme Court; Hon. Robert W. Pratt, United States District Court, District of Iowa
State for Bar Exam: NE
Pass Rate for First-Time Bar: 77%

DALHOUSIE UNIVERSITY
Law School

Admissions Contact: Director of Admissions and Placement, Rose Godfrey
Dalhousie Law School, Halifax, NS B3P 1P8 Canada
Admissions Phone: 902-494-1018 • Admissions Fax: 902-494-1316
Admissions E-mail: rose.godfrey@dal.ca • Web Address: www.dal.ca/law/admission.html

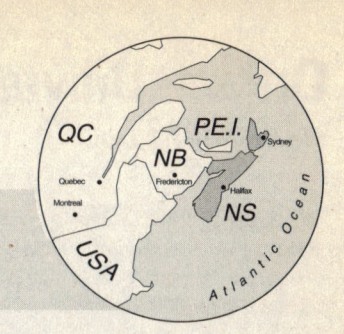

INSTITUTIONAL INFORMATION
Public/Private: Public
Student/Faculty Ratio: 13:1
Total Faculty: 35
% Female: 45
% Minority: 6

PROGRAMS
Academic Specialties: Environmental Law, International Law, Marine Law, Maritime Law
Advanced Degrees Offered: LLM, JSD
Combined Degrees Offered: LLB/MBA, LLB/MLIS, LLB/MPA, LLB/MHSA (4 years)
Grading System: Pass/Fail
Clinical Program Required? No
Clinical Program Description: Legal Aid Clinic, Criminal Clinic
Legal Writing/Methods Course Requirements: Full year

STUDENT INFORMATION
Enrollment of Law School: 458
% Male/Female: 50/50
% Part Time: 4
% Full Time: 96
% Minority: 12
Average Age of Entering Class: 25

RESEARCH FACILITIES
Computers/Workstations Available: 60

EXPENSES/FINANCIAL AID
Annual Tuition: $5,900
Room and Board (On Campus): $3,500
Books and Supplies: $1,200
Average Grant: $4,212
% of Aid That Is Merit-Based: 43
% Receiving Some Sort of Aid: 57%
Average Total Aid Package: $1,257

ADMISSIONS INFORMATION
Application Fee: $65
Regular Application Deadline: 2/8
Regular Notification: 4/1
Average GPA: 3.7
Average LSAT: 158
Transfer Students Accepted? Yes
Other Schools to Which Students Applied: University of British Columbia, University of New Brunswick, Western University, McGill University, University of Toronto, Queens University, Winsor University, Osgoode University
Number of Applications Received: 1,077
Number of Applicants Accepted: 317
Number of Applicants Enrolled: 161

INTERNATIONAL STUDENTS
TOEFL Required of International Students? Yes
Minimum TOEFL: 600

EMPLOYMENT INFORMATION

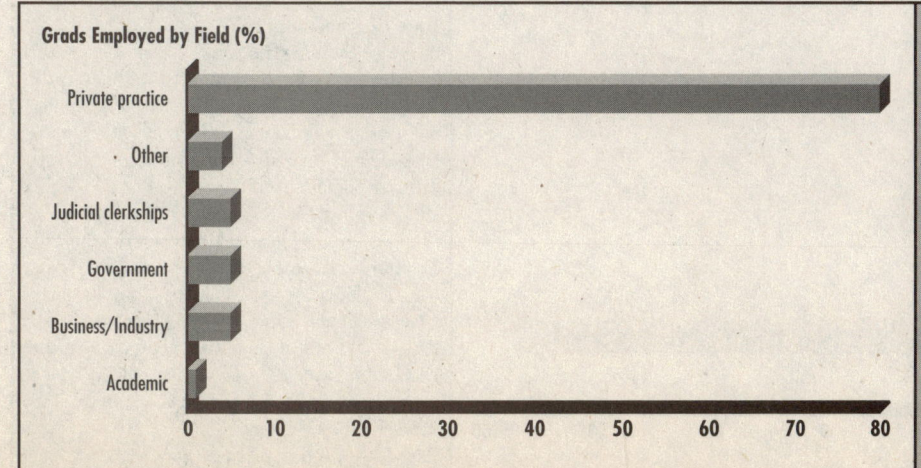

Grads Employed by Field (%)
- Private practice: ~80
- Other: ~3
- Judicial clerkships: ~5
- Government: ~5
- Business/Industry: ~5
- Academic: ~1

Rate of Placement: 90%
Employers Who Frequently Hire Grads: Law firms, government, courts
Prominent Alumni: Sir Graham Day, chancellor, Dalhousie University; Purdy A. Crawford, chairman, Imasco Limited; The Honourable Anne MacLellan, justice minister, Canada

DePaul University
College of Law

Admissions Contact: Director of Admission, Dennis Shea
25 East Jackson Boulevard, Chicago, IL 60604
Admissions Phone: 312-362-6831 • Admissions Fax: 312-362-5280
Admissions E-mail: lawinfo@depaul.edu • Web Address: www.law.depaul.edu

INSTITUTIONAL INFORMATION
Public/Private: Private
Affiliation: Roman Catholic
Student/Faculty Ratio: 22:1

PROGRAMS
Academic Specialties: Health Law, International Human Rights Law, Commercial Law, Criminal Law, Intellectual Property Law, International Law, Taxation
Advanced Degrees Offered: LLM Health Law (2 to 3 years), LLM Taxation (2 to 4 years)
Combined Degrees Offered: JD/MBA (3 to 4 years), JD/MS Public Service Management (4 years), JD/MA International Studies (4 years)
Grading System: A, B+, B, C+, C, D, F; curve in all years
Clinical Program Required? No
Clinical Program Description: Asylum/Immigration, Criminal Appeals, Community Development, Death Penalty, Disability Rights, Technology/Intellectual Property
Legal Writing Course Requirements? Yes
Legal Writing Description: 1 year required (2 courses); multiple electives in upper years
Legal Methods Course Requirements? No
Legal Research Course Requirements? No
Moot Court Requirement? No
Public Interest Law Requirement? No
Academic Journals: DePaul Law Review, DePaul Business and Commercial Law Journal, DePaul Journal of Health Law, DePaul-LCA Journal of Art and Entertainment Law, DePaul Online Journal of Sports Law and Contemporary Problems

STUDENT INFORMATION
Enrollment of Law School: 1,000
% Out of State: 45
% Male/Female: 45/55
% Full Time: 73
% Full Time That Are International: 1
% Minority: 20
Average Age of Entering Class: 25

RESEARCH FACILITIES
Research Resources Available: Numerous state, local, and federal libraries as well as Chicago and Illinois bar associations and libraries
School-Supported Research Centers: Health Law Institute, International Human Rights Law Institute, Center for Church/State Studies, Center for Family Law, Center for Intellectual Property Law and Information Technology, Center for Justice in Capital Cases, Center for Law and Science

EXPENSES/FINANCIAL AID
Annual Tuition: $25,000
Room and Board (Off Campus): $13,182
Books and Supplies: $900
Financial Aid Application Deadline: 3/1
Average Grant: $6,223
Average Loan: $29,146
% of Aid That Is Merit-Based: 12
% Receiving Some Sort of Aid: 87
Average Total Aid Package: $34,096
Average Debt: $76,500
Tuition Per Credit: $825
Fees Per Credit: $140

ADMISSIONS INFORMATION
Application Fee: $60
Regular Application Deadline: 4/1
Regular Notification: 2/1
LSDAS Accepted? Yes
Average GPA: 3.4
Range of GPA: 3.2–3.4
Average LSAT: 156
Range of LSAT: 153–158
Transfer Students Accepted? Yes
Number of Applications Received: 3,197
Number of Applicants Accepted: 1,014
Number of Applicants Enrolled: 361

INTERNATIONAL STUDENTS
TOEFL Required of International Students? Yes
Minimum TOEFL: 550

EMPLOYMENT INFORMATION

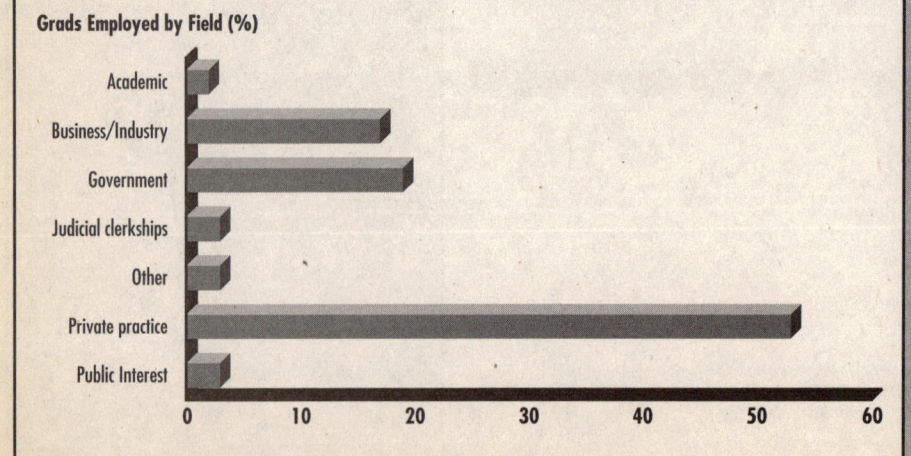

Grads Employed by Field (%)
- Academic: ~1
- Business/Industry: ~18
- Government: ~20
- Judicial clerkships: ~3
- Other: ~3
- Private practice: ~53
- Public Interest: ~3

Rate of Placement: 90%
Average Starting Salary: $63,854
Employers Who Frequently Hire Grads: Andersen LLP; Bell Boyd & Lloyd; Chapman and Cutler; Hinshaw & Culbertson; Kirkland & Ellis; Legal Assistance Foundation of Chicago; Tressler Soderstrom Maloney & Priess; Vedder Price Kaufman & Kammholz; Wildman Harrold Allen & Dixon; Williams Montgomery John Ltd.
Prominent Alumni: Richard M. Daley, Mayor, City of Chicago; Mary Dempsey, Commissioner, Chicago Public Library System; Frank Clark, President, ComEd; Jack Greenberg, Chair and CEO, McDonald's Corporation; William Bauer, Circuit Judge, U.S. 7th Circuit Court of Appeals
State for Bar Exam: IL
Pass Rate for First-Time Bar: 79%

DRAKE UNIVERSITY
Law School

Admissions Contact: Director of Admissions and Financial Aid, Kara Blanchard
2507 University Avenue, Des Moines, IA 50311
Admissions Phone: 515-271-2782 • Admissions Fax: 515-271-1990
Admissions E-mail: lawadmit@drake.edu • Web Address: www.law.drake.edu

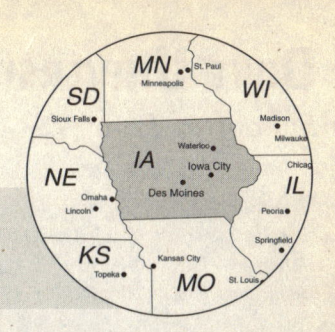

INSTITUTIONAL INFORMATION
Public/Private: Private
Student/Faculty Ratio: 13:1
Total Faculty: 47
% Part Time: 67
% Female: 28
% Minority: 3

PROGRAMS
Academic Specialties: Constitutional Law Resource Center, Agricultural Law Center, Clinics and Internships, Legislative Center, Center for Children's Rights, Constitutional Law, Environmental Law; very strong in Corporate/Commercial and Trial Practice/Litigation
Advanced Degrees Offered: JD (3 years)
Combined Degrees Offered: JD/MBA (6 semesters, 2 summers); JD/MPA (6 semesters, 2 summers); JD/PharmD; JD/MA Mass Communication, JD/MA Political Science, JD/MS Agricultural Economics (all 6 semesters, 1 summer)
Grading System: A (4.0), A– (3.7), B+ (3.3), B (3.0), B– (2.7), C+ (2.3), C (2.0), C– (1.7), D+ (1.3), D (1.0), F (0.0), CR (Credit), I (Incomplete), IP (In Progress)
Clinical Program Required? No
Clinical Program Description: General Civil Practice, Criminal Defense, Advanced Civil Defense—Trial, Advance Civil Defense—Appeals, Elder Law, Administrative Law, Children's Rights
Legal Writing Course Requirements? Yes
Legal Writing Description: First-semester course that must be taken concurrently with Legal Research
Legal Methods Course Requirements? Yes
Legal Methods Description: Legal Research, Writing, and Appellate Practice required in second semester
Legal Research Course Requirements? Yes
Legal Research Description: First-semester course that must be taken concurrently with Legal Writing
Moot Court Requirement? Yes
Moot Court Description: First-year students prepare a brief and participate in at least 2 oral arguments. Many elective Moot Court opportunities are available.
Public Interest Law Requirement? No
Academic Journals: *Drake Law Review, Drake Agricultural Law Review*

STUDENT INFORMATION
Enrollment of Law School: 408
% Out of State: 40
% Male/Female: 49/51
% Full Time: 98
% Full Time That Are International: 1
% Minority: 8
Average Age of Entering Class: 26

RESEARCH FACILITIES
Research Resources Available: Iowa State Law Library
School-Supported Research Centers: Agricultural Law Center, Constitutional Law Center, Legal Clinic, Joan and Lyle Middleton Center for Children's Rights, Center for Legislative Practice

EXPENSES/FINANCIAL AID
Annual Tuition: $19,450
Room and Board: $7,100
Books and Supplies: $1,100
Financial Aid Application Deadline: 3/1
Average Grant: $9,714
Average Loan: $23,450
% of Aid That Is Merit-Based: 71
% Receiving Some Sort of Aid: 93
Average Total Aid Package: $31,500
Average Debt: $60,000
Tuition Per Credit: $660

ADMISSIONS INFORMATION
Application Fee: $40
Regular Application Deadline: Rolling
Regular Notification: Rolling
LSDAS Accepted? Yes
Average GPA: 3.4
Range of GPA: 3.1–3.6
Average LSAT: 153
Range of LSAT: 151–156
Transfer Students Accepted? Yes
Other Schools to Which Students Applied: Creighton University, Hamline University, University of Iowa
Number of Applications Received: 1,055
Number of Applicants Accepted: 490
Number of Applicants Enrolled: 136

INTERNATIONAL STUDENTS
TOEFL Required of International Students? Yes
Minimum TOEFL: 560

EMPLOYMENT INFORMATION

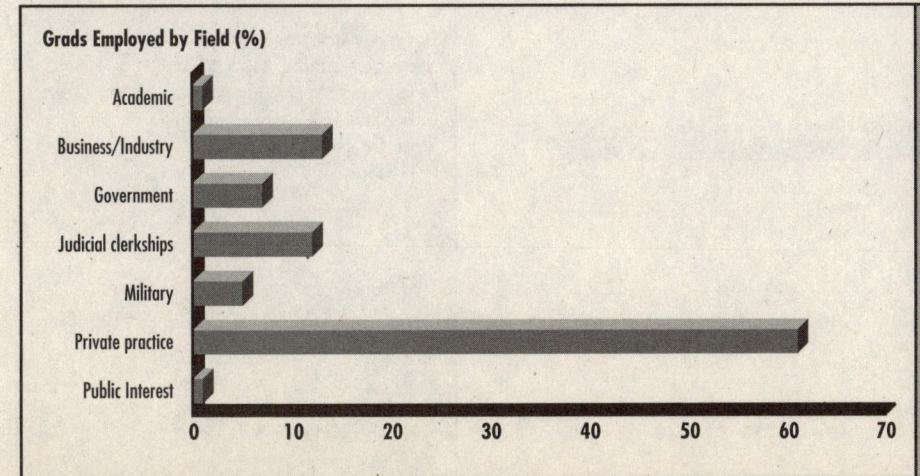

Grads Employed by Field (%)
- Academic
- Business/Industry
- Government
- Judicial clerkships
- Military
- Private practice
- Public Interest

Rate of Placement: 92%
Average Starting Salary: $50,718
Employers Who Frequently Hire Grads: Davis, Brown; Nyemaster, Goode; Department of Justice; JAG Corps; Blackwell Sanders; Shughart Thompson; Bryan Cave
Prominent Alumni: Dwight D. Opperman, CEO, publishing company; Louis Lavarato, Chief Justice, Iowa Supreme Court; Robert Ray, former Governor; Terry Branstad, former Governor; General Russell Davis, Head of U.S. National Guard
State for Bar Exam: IA, MN, MO, IL
Pass Rate for First-Time Bar: 89%

DUKE UNIVERSITY
School of Law

Admissions Contact: Associate Dean for Admissions and Financial Aid, Dennis Shields
PO Box 90393, Durham, NC 27708-0393
Admissions Phone: 919-613-7020 • Admissions Fax: 919-613-7257
Admissions E-mail: admissions@law.duke.edu • Web Address: admissions.law.duke.edu

INSTITUTIONAL INFORMATION
Public/Private: Private
Student/Faculty Ratio: 13:1
Total Faculty: 67
% Part Time: 39
% Female: 33
% Minority: 7

PROGRAMS
Academic Specialties: International and Comparative Law, Intellectual Property Law, Gender Law, Corporate Law, Environmental Law, Constitutional Law and Civil Rights, Alternative Dispute Resolution
Advanced Degrees Offered: JD (3 years), LLM (1 year), SJD (1 year for international students only)
Combined Degrees Offered: JD/MA English, History, Humanities, Philosophy, Romance Studies, Cultural Anthropology, Economics, Political Science, Psychology, Forestry and Environmental Studies, Public Policy Studies, or Religion (3.5 years); JD/MS Mechanical Engineering (3.5 years); JD/MBA, JD/MPP, JD/MEM, JD/MTS (all 4 years); JD/MD (6 years); JD/PhD (7 years); JD/LLM International and Comparative Law (3.5 years)
Grading System: 4.0 scale
Clinical Program Required? No
Clinical Program Description: AIDS Legal Assistance Project, Death Penalty Clinic, Pro Bono Project, Children's Education Law Clinic, Community Economic Development Clinic, International Legal Clinic for Special Court for Sierra Leone
Legal Writing Course Requirements? Yes
Legal Writing Description: Legal Analysis, Research and Writing is a required two-semester course taken in the first year.
Legal Methods Course Requirements? Yes
Legal Methods Description: See Legal Writing.
Legal Research Course Requirements? Yes
Legal Research Description: See Legal Writing.
Moot Court Requirement? Yes
Moot Court Description: All first-year students particpate in moot court competition as part of Legal Analysis, Research and Writing.
Public Interest Law Requirement? No
Academic Journals: *Duke Law Journal, Law and Contemporary Problems, Duke Environmental Law and Policy Forum, Alaska Law Review, Duke Journal of Comparative and International Law, Duke Law and Technology Review, Duke Journal of Gender Law and Policy*

STUDENT INFORMATION
Enrollment of Law School: 651
% Male/Female: 53/47
% Full Time: 100
% Minority: 21

EXPENSES/FINANCIAL AID
Annual Tuition: $29,920
Room and Board (Off Campus): $8,170
Books and Supplies: $1,266
Financial Aid Application Deadline: 3/15
Average Grant: $6,000
Average Loan: $31,519
Average Debt: $77,000

ADMISSIONS INFORMATION
Application Fee: $70
Regular Application Deadline: 1/1
Regular Notification: Rolling
LSDAS Accepted? Yes
Average GPA: 3.6
Range of GPA: 3.3–3.8
Average LSAT: 168
Range of LSAT: 164–169
Transfer Students Accepted? Yes
Other Admissions Factors Considered: Demonstrated leadership, community service, excellence in a field, graduate study in another discipline, work experience, other information indicating academic or professional potential
Number of Applications Received: 4,093
Number of Applicants Accepted: 839
Number of Applicants Enrolled: 201

INTERNATIONAL STUDENTS
TOEFL Required of International Students? Yes
Minimum TOEFL: 600

EMPLOYMENT INFORMATION

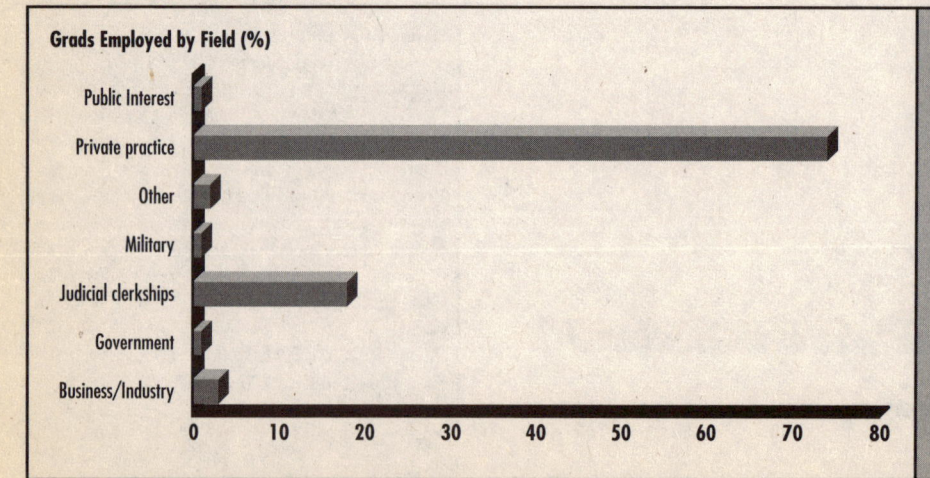

Grads Employed by Field (%)
- Public Interest
- Private practice
- Other
- Military
- Judicial clerkships
- Government
- Business/Industry

Rate of Placement: 100%
Average Starting Salary: $86,000
Employers Who Frequently Hire Grads: More than 400 law firms annually
State for Bar Exam: NY, NC, CA, MD, VA
Pass Rate for First-Time Bar: 92%

DUQUESNE UNIVERSITY
School of Law

Admissions Contact: Director of Admissions, Joseph P. Campion, Jr.
900 Locust Street, Pittsburgh, PA 15282
Admissions Phone: 412-396-6296 • Admissions Fax: 412-396-1073
Admissions E-mail: campion@duq.edu • Web Address: www.law.duq.edu

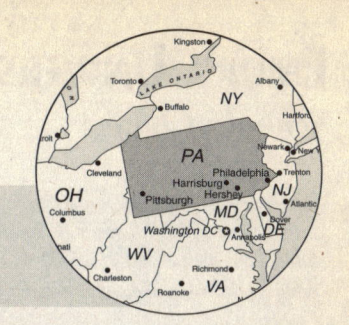

INSTITUTIONAL INFORMATION
Public/Private: Private
Student/Faculty Ratio: 23:1
Total Faculty: 26
% Female: 21
% Minority: 16

PROGRAMS
Academic Specialties: Strong faculty
Combined Degrees Offered: JD/MDiv (5 years); JD/MBA, JD/M Environmental Science and Management, JD/MS Taxation (all 4 years)
Grading System: Numerical system on a 4.0 scale; minimum 3.0 required for graduation
Clinical Program Required? No
Clinical Program Description: Development Law Clinic, Criminal Justice Clinic, Family and Poverty Law Clinic
Legal Writing Course Requirements? Yes
Legal Methods Course Requirements? Yes
Legal Research Course Requirements? Yes
Moot Court Requirement? No
Public Interest Law Requirement? No

STUDENT INFORMATION
Enrollment of Law School: 639
% Out of State: 38
% Male/Female: 50/50
% Full Time: 65
% Minority: 7
Average Age of Entering Class: 23

EXPENSES/FINANCIAL AID
Annual Tuition: $19,394
Room and Board (Off Campus): $8,000
Books and Supplies: $1,000
Average Grant: $4,500
Average Loan: $12,000
% of Aid That Is Merit-Based: 50
% Receiving Some Sort of Aid: 35
Average Total Aid Package: $11,000
Average Debt: $35,000

ADMISSIONS INFORMATION
Application Fee: $50
Regular Application Deadline: 4/1
Regular Notification: Rolling
LSDAS Accepted? Yes
Average GPA: 3.3
Average LSAT: 153
Transfer Students Accepted? Yes

INTERNATIONAL STUDENTS
TOEFL Required of International Students? Yes
Minimum TOEFL: 600

EMPLOYMENT INFORMATION

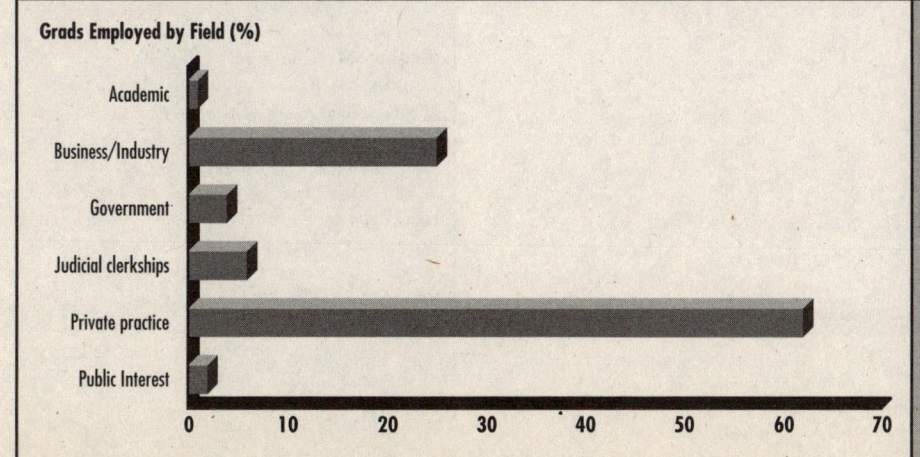

Grads Employed by Field (%):
- Academic: ~1
- Business/Industry: ~25
- Government: ~3
- Judicial clerkships: ~5
- Private practice: ~62
- Public Interest: ~1

Rate of Placement: 97%
Average Starting Salary: $59,693
Employers Who Frequently Hire Grads: Reed Smith, Kirkpatrick & Lockhart, Buchanon Ingersoll, Eckert, Seamans
State for Bar Exam: PA
Pass Rate for First-Time Bar: 78%

EMORY UNIVERSITY
School of Law

Admissions Contact: Assistant Dean for Admission, Lynell A. Cadray
1301 Clifton Road, Atlanta, GA 30322-2770
Admissions Phone: 404-727-6802 • Admissions Fax: 404-727-2477
Admissions E-mail: lawinfo@law.emory.edu • Web Address: www.law.emory.edu

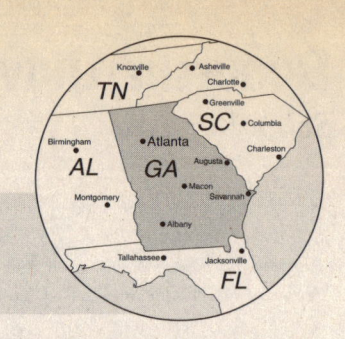

INSTITUTIONAL INFORMATION
Public/Private: Private
Affiliation: Methodist
Student/Faculty Ratio: 19:1
Total Faculty: 56
% Part Time: 7
% Female: 36
% Minority: 7

PROGRAMS
Academic Specialties: Law and Religion, Commercial Law, Corporate Law, Constitutional Law, Criminal Law, Environmental Law, Human Rights Law, International Law, Labor Law, Taxation
Advanced Degrees Offered: LLM (1 year)
Combined Degrees Offered: JD/PhD Religion; JD/REES (3 years); JD/Mdiv (5 years); JD/MPH (3.5 years); JD/LLM, JD/MA Judaic Studies, JD/MBA, JD/MTS (all 4 years)
Grading System: A+ (4.3), A (4.0), A– (3.7), B+ (3.3), B (3.0), B– (2.7), C+ (2.3), C (2.0), C– (1.7), D+ (1.3), D (1.0), D– (0.7), F (0.0); 2.25 required for good standing and graduation
Clinical Program Required? No
Clinical Program Description: Turner Environmental Law Clinic, Barton Child Law and Policy Clinic. More than 27 companies and organizations offer field placement opportunities.
Legal Writing Course Requirements? Yes
Legal Writing Description: Legal Writing, Research, and Appellate Advocacy (LWRAP) is a 2-credit course required in both semesters of the first year that includes an introduction to law and sources of law, legal bibliography, research techniques and strategies, analysis of problems in legal terms, writing of an office memorandum of law and an appellate brief, and the presentation of a case in appellate oral argument.
Legal Methods Course Requirements? Yes
Legal Methods Description: Legal Methods is a 3-credit course taken in the first year that explores the essential sources, institutions, process, and traditions of modern American law. The emphasis is on the role of judges and legislatures in making law. Students will be introduced to the doctrines of precedent and stare decisis, as well as approaches to statutory interpretation. In addition, a variety of perspectives on the jurisprudence of law making will be examined.
Legal Research Course Requirements? Yes
Legal Research Description: Part of the LWRAP course
Moot Court Requirement? No
Public Interest Law Requirement? No
Academic Journals: Emory Law Journal, Emory International Law Review, Emory Bankruptcy Developments Journal

STUDENT INFORMATION
Enrollment of Law School: 702
% Out of State: 85
% Male/Female: 47/53
% Full Time: 100
% Full Time That Are International: 1
% Minority: 19
Average Age of Entering Class: 23

EXPENSES/FINANCIAL AID
Annual Tuition: $27,634
Room and Board: $11,628
Books and Supplies: $1,100
Average Grant: $17,602
Average Loan: $29,379
% of Aid That Is Merit-Based: 1
% Receiving Some Sort of Aid: 86
Average Total Aid Package: $33,776
Average Debt: $74,265
Tuition Per Credit: $1,151

ADMISSIONS INFORMATION
Application Fee: $65
Regular Application Deadline: 3/1
Regular Notification: Rolling
LSDAS Accepted? Yes
Average GPA: 3.5
Range of GPA: 3.4–3.7
Average LSAT: 161
Range of LSAT: 160–165
Transfer Students Accepted? Yes
Other Admissions Factors Considered: Letters of recommendation, significant obstacles overcome, personal essays, community service, leadership ability, quality and difficulty of undergraduate work, work experince
Number of Applications Received: 3,597
Number of Applicants Accepted: 1,033
Number of Applicants Enrolled: 258

INTERNATIONAL STUDENTS
TOEFL Required of International Students? Yes
Minimum TOEFL: 600 (250 computer)

EMPLOYMENT INFORMATION

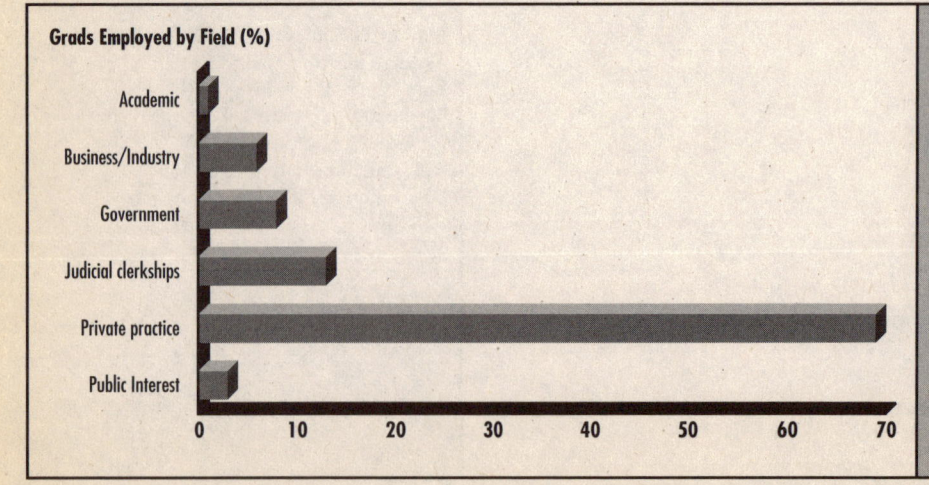

Grads Employed by Field (%):
- Academic: ~2
- Business/Industry: ~5
- Government: ~7
- Judicial clerkships: ~13
- Private practice: ~68
- Public Interest: ~3

Rate of Placement: 95%
Average Starting Salary: $80,546
Employers Who Frequently Hire Grads: Dewey Ballantine; Milbank, Tweed, Hadley & McCloy; Skadden, Arps, Slate, Meagher & Flom; Alston & Bird; King & Spalding; Troutman Sanders; Arnold & Porter; Chadbourne & Parke; Davis Polk & Wardwell; Shearman & Sterling
Prominent Alumni: Hon. Tillie Kidd Fowler, former U.S. Congresswoman; Hon. W. Wyche Fowler, Ambassador to Saudi Arabia; Hon. Sam A. Nunn, former U.S. Senator; Hon. Edward E. Elson, former Ambassador to Denmark; Hon. Stanley F. Birch, Judge, 11th Circuit Court of Appeals
State for Bar Exam: GA, NY
Pass Rate for First-Time Bar: 90%

EMPIRE COLLEGE
School of Law

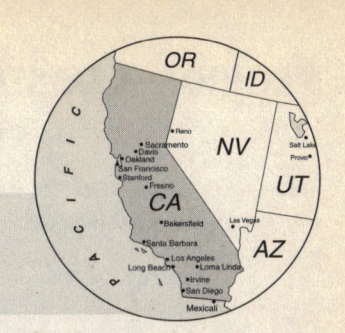

Admissions Contact: Admissions Officer, Aimee M. Lute
3035 Cleveland Avenue, Santa Rosa, CA 95403
Admissions Phone: 707-546-4000 • Admissions Fax: 707-546-4058
Admissions E-mail: alute@empirecollege.com • Web Address: www.empcol.com

INSTITUTIONAL INFORMATION
Public/Private: Private
Student/Faculty Ratio: 40:1
Total Faculty: 45
% Part Time: 100
% Female: 22

PROGRAMS
Academic Specialties: All faculty are practicing attorneys or judges; small class ratio; wide variety of elective courses offered
Grading System: A (100–90), B (89–80), C (79–70), D (69–65), F (below 65)
Clinical Program Required? No
Clinical Programs Description: Students may clerk in law offices, the Public Defender's office, or the District Attorney's office.
Legal Writing Course Requirements? Yes
Legal Writing Description: 1 year
Legal Methods Course Requirements? No
Legal Research Course Requirements? Yes
Legal Research Description: 1 semester
Moot Court Requirement? Yes
Moot Court Description: 1 semester
Public Interest Law Requirement? No

STUDENT INFORMATION
Enrollment of Law School: 142
% Out of State: 0
% Male/Female: 100/0
% Full Time That Are International: 0
% Minority: 2
Average Age of Entering Class: 43

EXPENSES/FINANCIAL AID
Annual Tuition: $5,400
Books and Supplies: $600
Tuition Per Credit: $270
Fees Per Credit: $195

ADMISSIONS INFORMATION
Application Fee: $95
Regular Application Deadline: Rolling
Regular Notification: Rolling
LSDAS Accepted? No
Average GPA: 3.1
Range of GPA: 2.3–3.8
Average LSAT: 147
Transfer Students Accepted? Yes
Number of Applications Received: 56
Number of Applicants Accepted: 52

EMPLOYMENT INFORMATION
Employers Who Frequently Hire Grads: Office of the District Attorney, Public Defender's office
State for Bar Exam: CA
Pass Rate for First-Time Bar: 75%

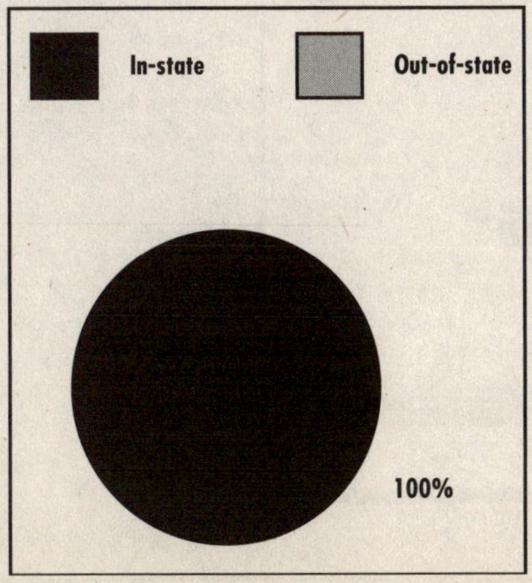

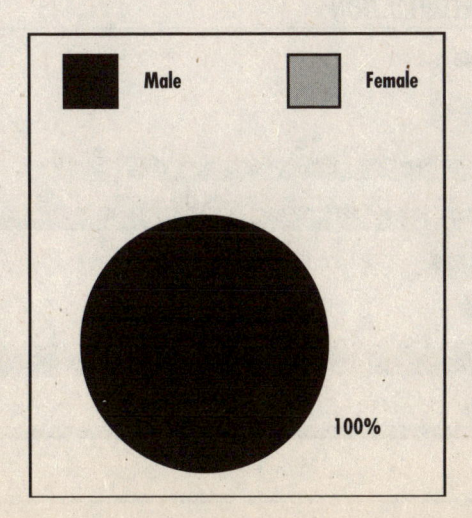

Florida Coastal School of Law

Admissions Contact: Director of Admissions, Steve Jones
7555 Beach Boulevard, Jacksonville, FL 32216
Admissions Phone: 904-680-7710 • Admissions Fax: 904-680-7777
Admissions E-mail: admissions@fcsl.edu • Web Address: www.fcsl.edu

INSTITUTIONAL INFORMATION
Public/Private: Private
Student/Faculty Ratio: 17:1
Total Faculty: 49
% Part Time: 43
% Female: 37
% Minority: 25

PROGRAMS
Academic Specialties: Civil Procedure, Commercial Law, Constitutional Law, Corporation Securities Law, Criminal Law, Environmental Law, Government Services, Human Rights Law, Intellectual Property Law, International Law, Labor Law, Legal History, Legal Philosophy, Property, Taxation
Advanced Degrees Offered: JD (2.5 to 3 years full time, 3.5 to 4 years part time)
Grading System: 4.0 scale
Clinical Program Required? Yes
Clinical Program Description: Criminal Law Clinic, Civil Practice Clinic, Domestic Violence Clinic, Municipal Law Clinic, International Law Clinic
Legal Writing Course Requirements? Yes
Legal Writing Description: All students take Legal Writing in their first year and are required to take an advanced Legal Writing course in the second or third year. Lawyering Process I focuses on basic research and writing and culminates in the submission of an objective memorandum of law. Lawyering Process II focuses on persuasive writing techniques and culminates in submission of an appellate brief. Students also practice basic oral advocacy skills and participate in appellate arguments.
Legal Methods Course Requirements? Yes
Legal Methods Description: First-year students are required to develop legal problem-solving, research, and writing skills and to focus upon development and enhancement of lawyering skills in rule-related and professional-responsibility contexts.
Legal Research Course Requirements? Yes
Legal Research Description: All students take Legal Research in their first year and can elect to take an advanced Legal Research course in their second or third year.
Moot Court Requirement? No
Moot Court Description: The Moot Court Program is voluntary. Students compete in a intramural competition after completion of Lawyering Process II. Students that are selected for Moot Court may receive academic credit and may compete in national competitions.
Public Interest Law Requirement? No
Academic Journals: *Florida Coastal Law Journal*

STUDENT INFORMATION
Enrollment of Law School: 519
% Out of State: 48
% Male/Female: 56/44
% Full Time: 56
% Full Time That Are International: 2
% Minority: 14
Average Age of Entering Class: 26

RESEARCH FACILITIES
Research Resources Available: University of North Florida, Jacksonville University
School-Supported Research Centers: CALI, Lexis, Westlaw, Loislaw, CCH

EXPENSES/FINANCIAL AID
Annual Tuition: $18,420
Room and Board (Off Campus): $12,168
Books and Supplies: $800
Financial Aid Application Deadline: 8/2
Average Grant: $6,200
Average Loan: $18,500
% of Aid That Is Merit-Based: 11
% Receiving Some Sort of Aid: 71
Average Total Aid Package: $18,500
Average Debt: $28,883
Fees Per Credit: $880

ADMISSIONS INFORMATION
Application Fee: $50
Regular Application Deadline: Rolling
Regular Notification: Rolling
LSDAS Accepted? Yes
Average GPA: 3.0
Range of GPA: 2.6–3.3
Average LSAT: 151
Range of LSAT: 149–154
Transfer Students Accepted? Yes
Other Schools to Which Students Applied: Florida State University, Mercer University, Nova Southeastern University, St. Thomas University, Stetson University, University of Florida, University of Miami
Other Admissions Factors Considered: Outstanding academic ability, leadership ability, maturity, organization skills, history of overcoming disadvantage, extraordinary accomplishment, success in a previous career
Number of Applications Received: 2,357
Number of Applicants Accepted: 858
Number of Applicants Enrolled: 190

INTERNATIONAL STUDENTS
TOEFL Required of International Students? Yes

EMPLOYMENT INFORMATION

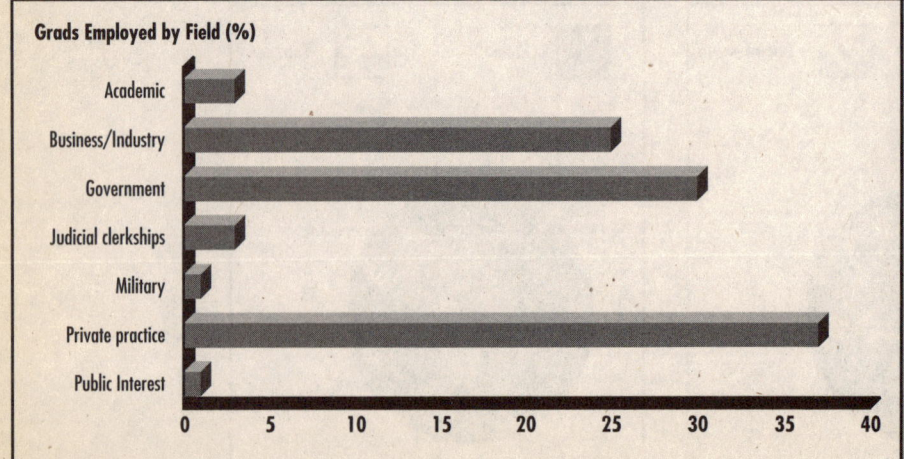

Grads Employed by Field (%)
- Academic
- Business/Industry
- Government
- Judicial clerkships
- Military
- Private practice
- Public Interest

Rate of Placement: 82%
Average Starting Salary: $47,654
State for Bar Exam: FL, GA, TX, TN, SC
Pass Rate for First-Time Bar: 80%

FLORIDA STATE UNIVERSITY
College of Law

Admissions Contact: Director of Admissions and Records, Sharon J. Booker
425 West Jefferson Street, Tallahassee, FL 32306-1601
Admissions Phone: 850-644-3787 • Admissions Fax: 850-644-7284
Admissions E-mail: admissions@law.fsu.edu • Web Address: www.law.fsu.edu

INSTITUTIONAL INFORMATION
Public/Private: Public
Student/Faculty Ratio: 20:1

PROGRAMS
Academic Specialties: Environmental and Land Use Law, Administrative Law, Intellectual Property Law, International Law
Advanced Degrees Offered: JD (minimum 88 credits)
Combined Degrees Offered: JD/MBA, JD/MS URP, JD/MS IA, JD/MS Economics, JD/MPA, JD/MS Social Work, JD/MS LIS (most are 4 years)
Grading System: 100–60 numerical system with corresponding letter grades from A+ to F
Clinical Program Required? No
Clinical Program Description: Students typically earn 6 to 12 credits while learning to assume the role of attorney or judicial clerk in the litigation and adjudication of real cases.
Legal Writing Course Requirements? Yes
Legal Writing Description: In the first year, Legal Writing and Research is required, carrying 2 credits each semester. Students must satisfy an upper-level writing requirement by completing a course, seminar, or Directed Individual Study with a research paper of substantial length which involves responding to at least one critique of a rough draft.
Legal Methods Course Requirements? Yes
Legal Methods Description: See Legal Writing.
Legal Research Course Requirements? Yes
Legal Research Description: See Legal Writing.
Moot Court Requirement? No

Moot Court Description: Composed of 30 members, the team annually attends regional, national, and international competitions. Up to 15 new members are selected each spring from the first-year class for a 2-year membership.
Public Interest Law Requirement? Yes
Public Interest Law Description: Minimum of 20 hours of pro bono legal work during their second or third year.
Academic Journals: Law Review, Journal of Land Use and Environmental Law, Journal of Transnational Law and Policy

STUDENT INFORMATION
Enrollment of Law School: 766
% Male/Female: 55/45
% Full Time: 100
% Minority: 22
Average Age of Entering Class: 25

RESEARCH FACILITIES
Research Resources Available: Access to the main university library and its branches, as well as to all the libraries of the state universities of Florida
School-Supported Research Centers: The law library is open to law students 24 hours a day.

EXPENSES/FINANCIAL AID
Annual Tuition (Residents/Nonresidents): $4,868/$14,173
Room and Board: $14,254
Books and Supplies: $1,800
Financial Aid Application Deadline: 2/15
Average Grant: $1,200
Average Loan: $13,735
% of Aid That Is Merit-Based: 10
Average Debt: $47,201

ADMISSIONS INFORMATION
Application Fee: $20
Regular Application Deadline: 2/15
Regular Notification: Rolling
LSDAS Accepted? Yes
Average GPA: 3.4
Range of GPA: 3.2–3.7
Average LSAT: 155
Range of LSAT: 153–157
Transfer Students Accepted? Yes
Other Schools to Which Students Applied: American, Emory, Stetson, Tulane, U. of Florida, U. of Georgia, U. of Miami
Other Admissions Factors Considered: Personal statement, writing samples, recommendations, strength of undergraduate program, graduate study, significant activities of leadership, unique work or service experience, economic or social hardships, contribution to a diverse academic environment in terms of life experiences
Number of Applications Received: 2,647
Number of Applicants Accepted: 842
Number of Applicants Enrolled: 293

INTERNATIONAL STUDENTS
TOEFL Required of International Students? Yes
Minimum TOEFL: 550

EMPLOYMENT INFORMATION

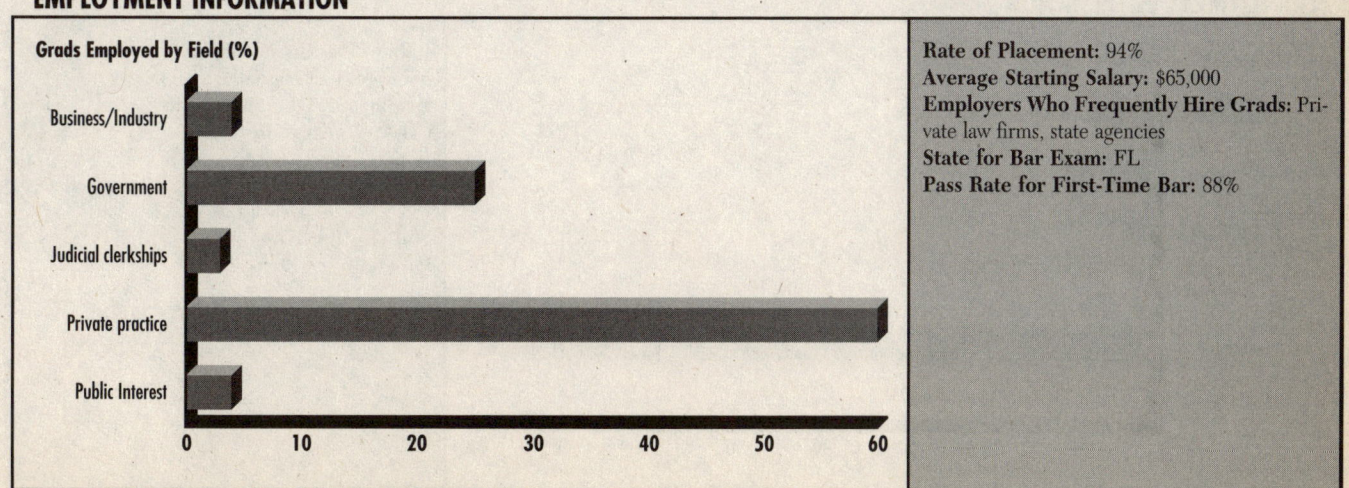

Grads Employed by Field (%):
- Business/Industry: ~3
- Government: ~25
- Judicial clerkships: ~5
- Private practice: ~60
- Public Interest: ~4

Rate of Placement: 94%
Average Starting Salary: $65,000
Employers Who Frequently Hire Grads: Private law firms, state agencies
State for Bar Exam: FL
Pass Rate for First-Time Bar: 88%

Fordham University
School of Law

Admissions Contact: Director of Admissions, John Chalmers
140 West 62nd Street, New York, NY 10023
Admissions Phone: 212-636-6810 • Admissions Fax: 212-636-7984
Admissions E-mail: lawadmissions@law.fordham.edu • Web Address: www.law.fordham.edu

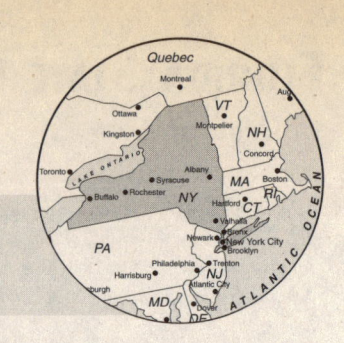

INSTITUTIONAL INFORMATION
Public/Private: Private
Affiliation: Roman Catholic
Student/Faculty Ratio: 17:1
Total Faculty: 214
% Part Time: 71
% Female: 28
% Minority: 8

PROGRAMS
Academic Specialties: Constitutional, Constitutional History, Professional Responsibility and Ethics, Business and Financial, Evidence, Human Rights, Public Interest, Bankruptcy, Church and State Relations, Law and Religion, AIDS and the Law, Employment and Disability Rights, Social Welfare, Employment Discrimination, Arbitration, Collective Bargaining, Feminist and Critical Race Theory, Asian Legal Systems, Freedom of Speech and of the Press, Copyright, Intellectual Property, Feminist Jurisprudence, Legal History, Real Estate, Islamic, Trusts and Estates, Land Use, Negotiation and Alternative Dispute Resolution, Mediation, Antitrust, Domestic Relations, Voting Rights, Entertainment Law, Environmental Law, and many other areas of law
Advanced Degrees Offered: JD (3 years full time, 4 years part time), LLM (1 year full time)
Combined Degrees Offered: JD/MBA with Fordham (4 years full time), JD/MSW with Fordham (4 years full time), JD/MA
Grading System: Letter system; mandatory curve for first year
Clinical Program Required? No

Clinical Program Description: Battered Women's Rights Clinic, Children's Disability and Special Education Clinic, Civil Rights Clinic, Criminal Defense Clinic, Family and Child Protection Clinic, Justice and Welfare Clinic, Mediation Clinic, Securities Arbitration Clinic, Community Economic Development Clinic, Tax Clinic
Legal Writing Course Requirements? Yes
Legal Writing Description: 1 year
Legal Methods Course Requirements? Yes
Legal Methods Description: Writing and Research (first year)
Legal Research Course Requirements? Yes
Legal Research Description: Part of Legal Writing course
Moot Court Requirement? No
Public Interest Law Requirement? No
Academic Journals: Law Review, International Law Journal, Urban Law Journal, Enviromental Law Journal, IP and Entertainment/Media Law Journal, Tax Law Journal

STUDENT INFORMATION
Enrollment of Law School: 1,459
% Out of State: 30
% Male/Female: 51/49
% Full Time: 76
% Full Time That Are International: 2
% Minority: 23
Average Age of Entering Class: 25

RESEARCH FACILITIES
Research Resources Available: Libraries at Fordham, Columbia, NYU, Penn, and Yale.
School-Supported Research Centers: Law students have access to all university libraries.

EXPENSES/FINANCIAL AID
Annual Tuition: $29,976
Room and Board: $19,000
Books and Supplies: $725
Average Grant: $7,200
Average Loan: $6,000
% of Aid That Is Merit-Based: 10
% Receiving Some Sort of Aid: 44
Average Total Aid Package: $7,200
Average Debt: $71,190
Tuition Per Credit: $938

ADMISSIONS INFORMATION
Application Fee: $65
Regular Application Deadline: 3/1
Regular Notification: Rolling
LSDAS Accepted? Yes
Average GPA: 3.6
Average LSAT: 164
Transfer Students Accepted? Yes
Other Schools to Which Students Applied: Boston College, Boston U., Brooklyn Law, Yeshiva, George Washington, Georgetown, Columbia
Other Admissions Factors Considered: Prior employment, student activities, community service, leadership, public service, communication skills, grade trend, course selection, grades in the major, choice of major, undergradate institution
Number of Applications Received: 7,020
Number of Applicants Accepted: 1,466
Number of Applicants Enrolled: 502

INTERNATIONAL STUDENTS
TOEFL Recommended for International Students? Yes
Minimum TOEFL: 600

EMPLOYMENT INFORMATION

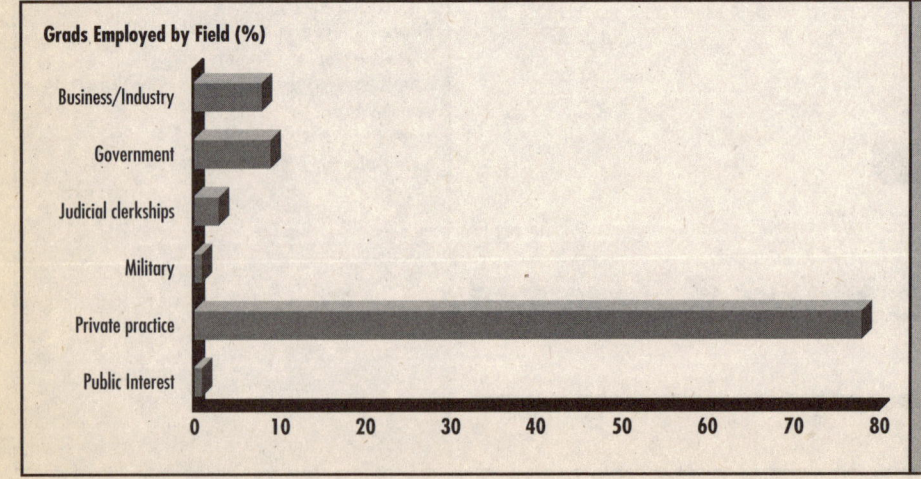

Grads Employed by Field (%)
- Business/Industry
- Government
- Judicial clerkships
- Military
- Private practice
- Public Interest

Rate of Placement: 96%
Average Starting Salary: $102,000
Employers Who Frequently Hire Grads: Cahill Gordon & Reindel; U.S. Department of Justice; Simpson, Thacher & Bartlett; New York Legal Aid; Skadden, Arps, Slate, Meagher & Flom; AT&T; Merrill Lynch; U.S. Courts
State for Bar Exam: NY, DC, FL, CA, MA
Pass Rate for First-Time Bar: 83%

FRANKLIN PIERCE LAW CENTER

Admissions Contact: Assistant Dean for Admissions, Katie McDonald
2 White Street, Concord, NH 03301
Admissions Phone: 603-228-9217 • *Admissions Fax:* 603-224-4661
Admissions E-mail: admissions@piercelaw.edu • *Web Address:* www.piercelaw.edu

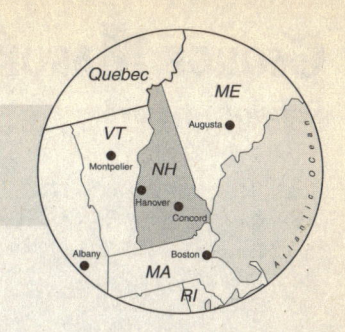

INSTITUTIONAL INFORMATION
Public/Private: Private
Student/Faculty Ratio: 20:1
Total Faculty: 81
% Part Time: 58
% Female: 24
% Minority: 1

PROGRAMS
Academic Specialties: Intellectual Property, Patents, Trademarks, Licensing, Management, Information Law, Entertainment Law, Public Interest and Community Lawyering, Children's Law, Education Law, Health Law, Criminal Law, Non-Profit Organization Law, Civil Procedure, Commercial Law, International Law
Advanced Degrees Offered: LLM (1 year); MIP (1 year); MEL, CAGS in Law (pending ABA acquiescence)
Combined Degrees Offered: JD/MIP (3 years)
Grading System: Anonymous grading using A+ to F. Electives may be Pass/Fail. In classes with more than 15 students, the mean grade will be no higher than B.
Clinical Program Required? No
Clinical Program Description: Children's Advocacy Clinic, Civil Practice Clinic, Administrative Law and Advocacy, Advanced Civil Practice Clinic, Appellate Defender Clinic, Criminal Practice Clinic, Dispute Resolution in Action, Innovation Clinic, Juvenile Corrections, Small Claims Mediation Program, Non-Profit Organizations Clinic

Legal Writing Course Requirements? No
Legal Methods Course Requirements? Yes
Legal Research Course Requirements? No
Moot Court Requirement? No
Public Interest Law Requirement? No

STUDENT INFORMATION
Enrollment of Law School: 370
% Out of State: 73
% Male/Female: 56/44
% Full Time: 100
% Full Time That Are International: 6
% Minority: 14
Average Age of Entering Class: 27

RESEARCH FACILITIES
School-Supported Research Centers: High-tech courtroom

EXPENSES/FINANCIAL AID
Annual Tuition: $19,962
Room and Board (Off Campus): $10,491
Books and Supplies: $600
Average Grant: $2,000
Average Loan: $21,700
% of Aid That Is Merit-Based: 57
% Receiving Some Sort of Aid: 85
Average Total Aid Package: $25,200
Average Debt: $72,100
Tuition Per Credit: $681

ADMISSIONS INFORMATION
Application Fee: $55
Regular Application Deadline: 4/1
Regular Notification: Rolling
LSDAS Accepted? Yes
Average GPA: 3.2
Range of GPA: 2.9–3.4
Average LSAT: 152
Range of LSAT: 148–156
Transfer Students Accepted? Yes
Other Admissions Factors Considered: Personal or academic achievement, professional or life experience, maturity, initiative, public service
Number of Applications Received: 768
Number of Applicants Enrolled: 134

INTERNATIONAL STUDENTS
TOEFL Required of International Students? Yes
Minimum TOEFL: 600 (250 computer)

EMPLOYMENT INFORMATION

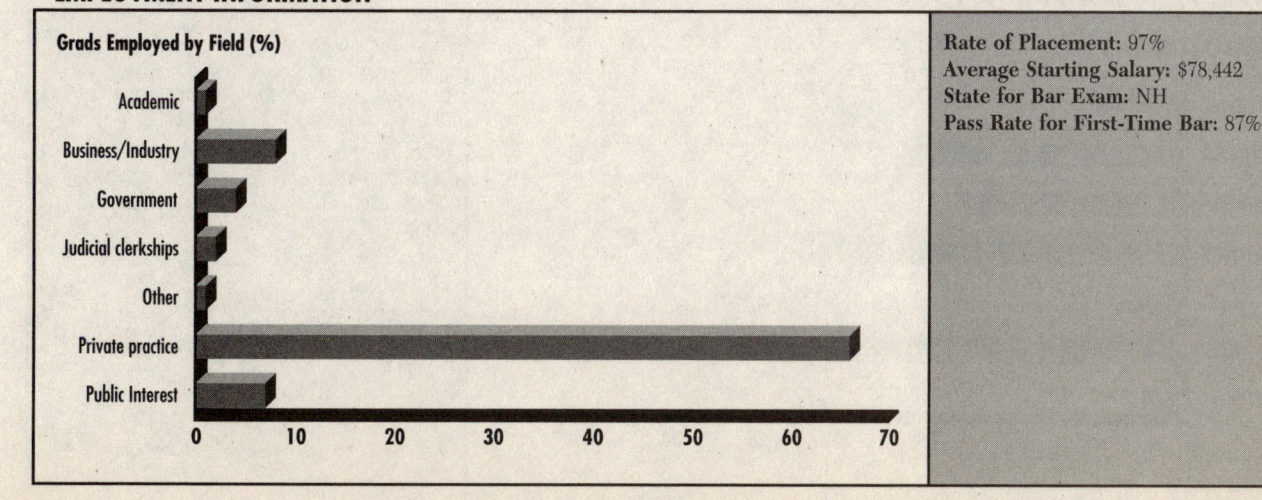

Grads Employed by Field (%):
- Academic
- Business/Industry
- Government
- Judicial clerkships
- Other
- Private practice
- Public Interest

Rate of Placement: 97%
Average Starting Salary: $78,442
State for Bar Exam: NH
Pass Rate for First-Time Bar: 87%

GEORGE MASON UNIVERSITY
School of Law

Admissions Contact: Assistant Dean and Director of Admissions, Anne M. Richard
3301 North Fairfax Drive, Arlington, VA 22201
Admissions Phone: 703-993-8010 • Admissions Fax: 703-993-8088
Admissions E-mail: arichar5@gmu.edu • Web Address: www.law.gmu.edu

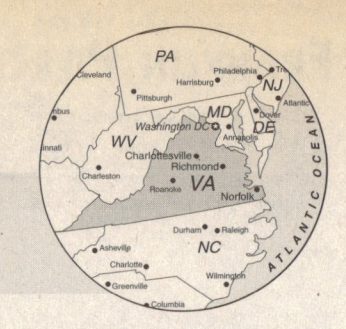

INSTITUTIONAL INFORMATION
Public/Private: Public
Student/Faculty Ratio: 15:1
Total Faculty: 101
% Part Time: 65
% Female: 19
% Minority: 6

PROGRAMS
Academic Specialties: Law and Economics, Intellectual Property Law Program, Technology Law, Civil Procedure, Corporation Securities Law, Criminal Law, Government Services, International Law, Taxation
Advanced Degrees Offered: Juris Master in Policy Analysis (2 years part time, evening)
Combined Degrees Offered: Details of dual-degree programs may be found on our website.
Grading System: 4.33 scale
Clinical Program Required? No
Clinical Program Description: Legal Clinic, Law and Mental Illness Clinic, Public Interest Clinic, Board of Immigration Appeals Clinic, supervised externships
Legal Writing Course Requirements? Yes
Legal Writing Description: 3 years, 4 semesters of Legal Research, Writing, and Analysis, plus at least 2 additional writing courses beyond the first 2 years
Legal Methods Course Requirements? No
Legal Research Course Requirements? Yes
Legal Research Description: See Legal Writing.
Moot Court Requirement? Yes
Moot Court Description: First-year students are required to participate in the first-year moot court competition. After that, students may participate in moot court activities internally or externally as they so desire.
Public Interest Law Requirement? No
Public Interest Law Description: Public Interest Law Clinic and Association for Public Interest Law
Academic Journals: *Civil Rights Law Journal, Federal Circuit Bar Journal, George Mason Law Review*

STUDENT INFORMATION
Enrollment of Law School: 787
% Out of State: 21
% Male/Female: 59/41
% Full Time: 49
% Full Time That Are International: 4
% Minority: 9
Average Age of Entering Class: 27

RESEARCH FACILITIES
Research Resources Available: More than 1 million print volumes; 14 academic labs; print, video, and electronic resources; 4 study rooms; 2 media viewing rooms; focused media and periodicals collection; reference and circulating books; library instruction space; 20 Pentium Processor PCs with access to the library catalog, networked CD-ROMs, and the Internet; 5 reservable labs with 175 Pentium PCs; 1 Mac lab with 20 MacIntosh Power PCs; 84 nonreservable PCs
School-Supported Research Centers: International Commerce and Policy Program

EXPENSES/FINANCIAL AID
Annual Tuition (Residents/Nonresidents): $9,123/$19,232
Room and Board (Off Campus): $15,574
Books and Supplies: $750
Financial Aid Application Deadline: 3/1
Average Grant: $1,567
Average Loan: $16,373
% of Aid That Is Merit-Based: 2
% Receiving Some Sort of Aid: 70
Average Total Aid Package: $16,471
Average Debt: $32,352
Tuition Per Credit (Residents/Nonresidents): $326/$687

ADMISSIONS INFORMATION
Application Fee: $35
Regular Application Deadline: 3/15
Regular Notification: 4/15
LSDAS Accepted? Yes
Average GPA: 3.4
Range of GPA: 3.1–3.7
Average LSAT: 160
Range of LSAT: 156–162
Transfer Students Accepted? Yes
Other Schools to Which Students Applied: American, College of William and Mary, George Washington, Georgetown, U. of Maryland, U. of Richmond, U. of Virginia
Other Admissions Factors Considered: LSAT writing sample and personal statement, difficulty of undergraduate curriculum, undergraduate institution, graduate degrees, public and community service
Number of Applications Received: 4,383
Number of Applicants Accepted: 686
Number of Applicants Enrolled: 260

EMPLOYMENT INFORMATION

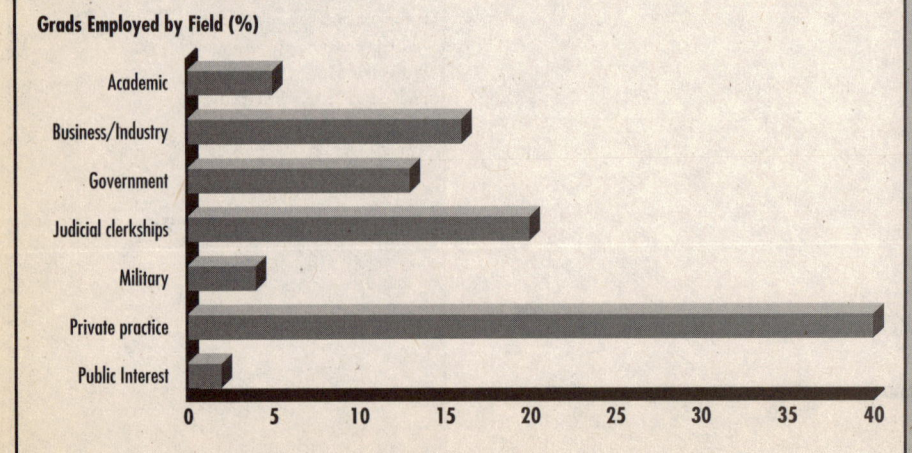

Grads Employed by Field (%)
- Academic: ~1
- Business/Industry: ~15
- Government: ~13
- Judicial clerkships: ~20
- Military: ~3
- Private practice: ~40
- Public Interest: ~2

Rate of Placement: 99%
Average Starting Salary: $72,979
Employers Who Frequently Hire Grads: Hunton & Williams; McGuire Woods LLP; Finnegan, Henderson, Farabow, Garrett & Dunner, LLP; U.S. Government; Shaw Pittman; Wiley, Rein, and Fielding; Sterne, Kessler, Goldstein, and Fox; Sutherland, Asbill, and Brennan; Crowell & Moring; Fried, Frank, Harris, Shriver & Jacobsen; Reed Smith; Morrison & Foerster; Venable
Prominent Alumni: Richard Young, Judge, U.S. District Court; Leslie Alden, Judge, Fairfax County Circuit Court; Paul Misener, VP of Global Policy, Amazon.com; J. Gregory Bedner, President and CEO, Perot Systems Government Services
State for Bar Exam: VA, MD, DC, CA, NY

GEORGE WASHINGTON UNIVERSITY
Law School

Admissions Contact: Associate Dean for Admissions and Financial Aid, Robert V. Stanek
700 20th Street, NW, Washington, DC 20052
Admissions Phone: 202-994-7230 • Admissions Fax: 202-994-3597
Admissions E-mail: jdadmit@law.gwu.edu • Web Address: www.law.gwu.edu

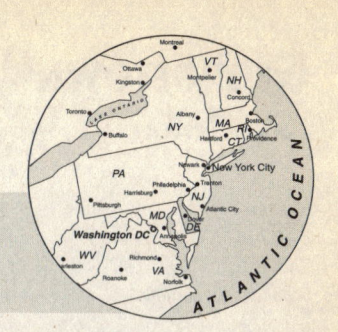

INSTITUTIONAL INFORMATION
Public/Private: Private
Student/Faculty Ratio: 18:1
Total Faculty: 296
% Part Time: 70
% Female: 30
% Minority: 9

PROGRAMS
Academic Specialties: The JD curriculum is very diverse, with more than 200 elective courses. Specialized areas of the curriculum include International and Comparative Law, Government Procurement Law, Civil Procedure, Commercial Law, Constitutional Law, Corporation Securities Law, Criminal Law, Environmental Law, Government Services, Human Rights Law, Intellectual Property Law, Labor Law, Legal History, Legal Philosophy, Property, and Taxation.
Advanced Degrees Offered: JD (3 years full time, 4 years part time), LLM (1 to 2 years) SJD (3 years)
Combined Degrees Offered: JD/MBA; JD/MPA; JD/MA International Affairs, History, or Women's Studies; JD/MPH (all 4 years full time)
Grading System: A+ to F (4.33 to 0.0)
Clinical Program Required? No
Legal Writing Course Requirements? No
Legal Methods Course Requirements? Yes
Legal Methods Description: In the first year, students take Legal Research and Writing in the fall and Introduction to Advocacy in the spring. Both courses are taught in small sections.
Legal Research Course Requirements? No
Moot Court Requirement? No
Public Interest Law Requirement? No
Academic Journals: *The George Washington Law Review, The George Washington International Law Review, The Environmental Lawyer, The American Intellectual Property Law Association Quarterly Journal, The Public Contract Law Journal*

STUDENT INFORMATION
Enrollment of Law School: 1,458
% Out of State: 94
% Male/Female: 52/48
% Full Time: 83
% Full Time That Are International: 5
% Minority: 31
Average Age of Entering Class: 24

RESEARCH FACILITIES
School-Supported Research Centers: Dedicated information portal

EXPENSES/FINANCIAL AID
Annual Tuition: $29,240
Room and Board: $10,300
Books and Supplies: $840
Average Grant: $12,000
Average Loan: $20,500
% of Aid That Is Merit-Based: 20
% Receiving Some Sort of Aid: 82
Average Total Aid Package: $30,500
Average Debt: $78,300
Tuition Per Credit: $1,035

ADMISSIONS INFORMATION
Application Fee: $65
Regular Application Deadline: 3/1
Regular Notification: Rolling
LSDAS Accepted? Yes
Average GPA: 3.5
Range of GPA: 3.3–3.6
Average LSAT: 163
Range of LSAT: 160–164
Transfer Students Accepted? Yes
Other Schools to Which Students Applied: American University, Boston College, Boston University, Columbia University, Fordham University, Georgetown University, North Carolina Central University
Number of Applications Received: 10,774
Number of Applicants Accepted: 2,061
Number of Applicants Enrolled: 462

EMPLOYMENT INFORMATION

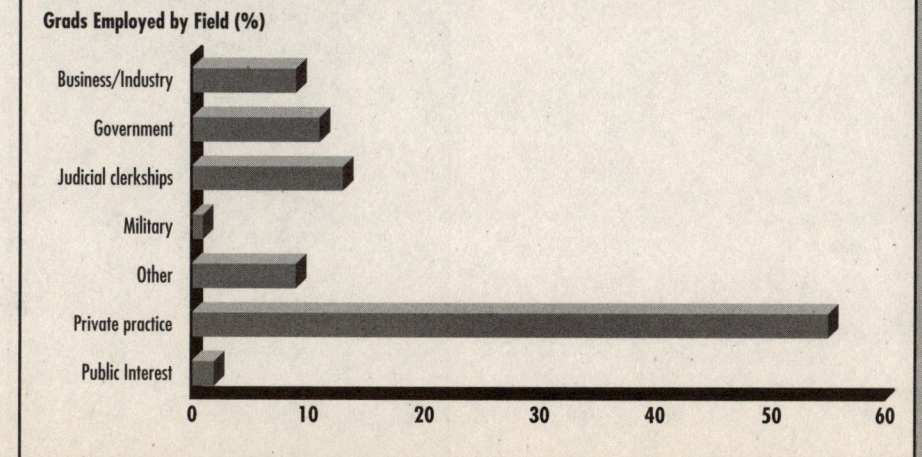

Grads Employed by Field (%)

Field	%
Business/Industry	~8
Government	~12
Judicial clerkships	~14
Military	~2
Other	~8
Private practice	~55
Public Interest	~2

Rate of Placement: 98%
Average Starting Salary: $96,034
Employers Who Frequently Hire Grads: Department of Justice; Howrey & Simon; Finnegan, Henderson et al.; Akin, Gump, et al.; Shearman & Sterling; Arnold & Porter; Wiley, Rein & Fielding; Arent Fox; various government agencies
State for Bar Exam: NY
Pass Rate for First-Time Bar: 90%

GEORGETOWN UNIVERSITY
Law Center

Admissions Contact: Assistant Dean of Admissions, Andrew P. Cornblatt
600 New Jersey Avenue, NW, Room 589, Washington, DC 20001
Admissions Phone: 202-662-9010 • Admissions Fax: 202-662-9439
Admissions E-mail: admis@law.georgetown.edu • Web Address: www.law.georgetown.edu

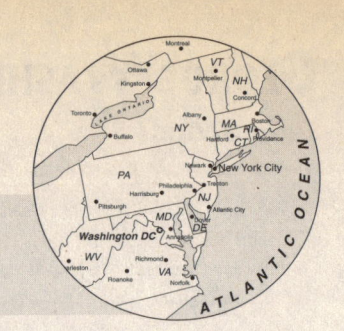

INSTITUTIONAL INFORMATION
Public/Private: Private
Affiliation: Roman Catholic
Student/Faculty Ratio: 15:1
Total Faculty: 189
% Female: 37
% Minority: 11

PROGRAMS
Academic Specialties: Administrative Law, Alternate Dispute Resolution, Communications Law, Constitutional Law, Corporate and Securities Law, Criminal Law, Environmental Law, Health Law and Policy, Immigration and Refugee Law, Intellectual Property Law, International and Comparative Law, International and National Security, Legal Ethics, Legal History, Legal Philosophy, Litigation and Judicial Process, Public Interest Law, Civil Procedure, Commercial Law, Government Services, Human Rights Law, Labor Law, Property, Taxation
Advanced Degrees Offered: JD (3 years full time, 4 years part time); SJD (2 to 5 years); LLM Taxation, Securities and Financial Regulation, International and Comparative Law, or individualized (1 to 3 years); LLM General Studies or International Legal Studies—foreign students only (1 year); Certificate in Employee Benefits (10 credits, 1 to 3 years part time only)
Combined Degrees Offered: JD/MBA (4 years); JD/MPH (4 years), JD/MPP (4 years), JD/MSFS (4 years), JD/PhD Government (4+ years), JD/PhD or MA Philosophy (4+ years)
Grading System: 4.0 scale; A, A–, B+, B, B–, C+, C, C–, D, F
Clinical Program Required? No

EMPLOYMENT INFORMATION

Clinical Program Description: Clinics in Appellate Litigation, Center for Applied Legal Studies, Criminal Justice, DC Law Students in Court, Domestic Violence, Family Advocacy, Federal Legislation, Harrison Institute Housing and Community Development, Harrison Institute Policy, Institute for Public Representation, International Women's Human Rights, Juvenile Justice, Street Law in High Schools, Street Law in the Community
Legal Writing Course Requirements? Yes
Legal Writing Description: A year-long program in the first year introduces students to legal discourse through problem analysis, legal research, writing, oral skills, and legal citation. Law fellows lead weekly workshops that focus on specific tasks of research, analysis, writing, and citation.
Legal Methods Course Requirements? Yes
Legal Methods Description: See Legal Writing.
Legal Research Course Requirements? Yes
Legal Research Description: See Legal Writing.
Moot Court Requirement? No
Moot Court Description: The Moot Court Program competes in national and international competitions.
Public Interest Law Requirement? No
Public Interest Law Description: The voluntary Pro Bono Pledge encourages every student to perform 75 hours of law-related pro bono work prior to graduation.
Academic Journals: *Georgetown Law Journal, American Criminal Law Review, Georgetown Journal on Poverty Law and Policy, The Georgetown Journal of Gender and the Law, Georgetown Immigration Law Journal*, and several others

STUDENT INFORMATION
Enrollment of Law School: 2,020
% Male/Female: 51/49
% Full Time: 80
% Full Time That Are International: 3
% Minority: 23
Average Age of Entering Class: 27

RESEARCH FACILITIES
Research Resources Available: Library of Congress, National Library of Medicine
School-Supported Research Centers: Edward Bennett William Law Library, Joseph Mark Lauinger Library, John Vinton Dahlgren Library

EXPENSES/FINANCIAL AID
Annual Tuition: $29,440
Room and Board: $14,325
Books and Supplies: $2,235
Financial Aid Application Deadline: 3/1
Average Grant: $9,650
Average Loan: $28,700
% Receiving Some Sort of Aid: 87
Average Total Aid Package: $32,100
Average Debt: $86,035
Tuition Per Credit: $1,060

ADMISSIONS INFORMATION
Application Fee: $70
Regular Application Deadline: 2/1
Regular Notification: Rolling
LSDAS Accepted? Yes
Average GPA: 3.6
Range of GPA: 3.5–3.8
Average LSAT: 168
Range of LSAT: 165–169
Transfer Students Accepted? Yes
Number of Applications Received: 11,512
Number of Applicants Accepted: 2,188
Number of Applicants Enrolled: 578

Rate of Placement: 97%
Average Starting Salary: $11,000

Grads Employed by Field (%)

Field	%
Academic	~1
Business/Industry	~4
Government	~5
Judicial clerkships	~9
Military	~1
Other	~3
Private practice	~70
Public Interest	~2

GEORGIA STATE UNIVERSITY
College of Law

Admissions Contact: Director of Admissions, Dr. Cheryl Jester Jeckson
PO Box 4049, Atlanta, GA 30302-4049
Admissions Phone: 404-651-2048 • Admissions Fax: 404-651-1244
Admissions E-mail: admissions@gsulaw.gsu.edu • Web Address: law.gsu.edu

INSTITUTIONAL INFORMATION
Public/Private: Public
Student/Faculty Ratio: 16:1
Total Faculty: 76
% Part Time: 26
% Female: 34
% Minority: 17

PROGRAMS
Academic Specialties: Constitutional Law, Alternative Dispute Resolution, Law and Technology, Civil Procedure, Commercial Law, Corporation Securities Law, Criminal Law, Environmental Law, Human Rights Law, International Law, Taxation; joint degree programs in Law and Business, Law and Policy, Law and Philosophy
Combined Degrees Offered: JD/MBA, JD/MPA, JD/MA Philosophy (all 4 years)
Grading System: A (90–100), B (80–89), C (70–79), D (60–69), F (55–59)
Clinical Program Required? No
Clinical Program Description: Tax Clinic, Externship Program
Legal Writing Course Requirements? Yes
Legal Methods Course Requirements? No
Legal Research Course Requirements? Yes
Moot Court Requirement? No
Public Interest Law Requirement? No
Academic Journals: *Law Review*

STUDENT INFORMATION
Enrollment of Law School: 672
% Out of State: 12
% Male/Female: 47/53
% Full Time: 71
% Full Time That Are International: 3
% Minority: 15
Average Age of Entering Class: 27

RESEARCH FACILITIES
School-Supported Research Centers: Access to the university's computer centers

EXPENSES/FINANCIAL AID
Annual Tuition (Residents/Nonresidents): $3,918/$15,672
Room and Board (On/Off Campus): $4,680/$8,700
Books and Supplies: $690
Financial Aid Application Deadline: 4/1
Average Grant: $3,542
Average Loan: $10,000
% Receiving Some Sort of Aid: 56
Average Total Aid Package: $18,500
Average Debt: $37,811
Tuition Per Credit (Residents/Nonresidents): $164/$653
Fees Per Credit: $398

ADMISSIONS INFORMATION
Application Fee: $30
Regular Application Deadline: 3/15
Regular Notification: Rolling
LSDAS Accepted? Yes
Average GPA: 3.3
Range of GPA: 3.0–3.5
Average LSAT: 157
Range of LSAT: 154–160
Transfer Students Accepted? Yes
Other Schools to Which Students Applied: Emory University, Mercer University, University of Florida, University of Georgia
Other Admissions Factors Considered: Letters of recommendation, personal statement, school and community activities, employment experience, advanced study or degrees
Number of Applications Received: 2,899
Number of Applicants Accepted: 572
Number of Applicants Enrolled: 234

INTERNATIONAL STUDENTS
TOEFL Recommended for International Students? Yes
Minimum TOEFL: 680

EMPLOYMENT INFORMATION

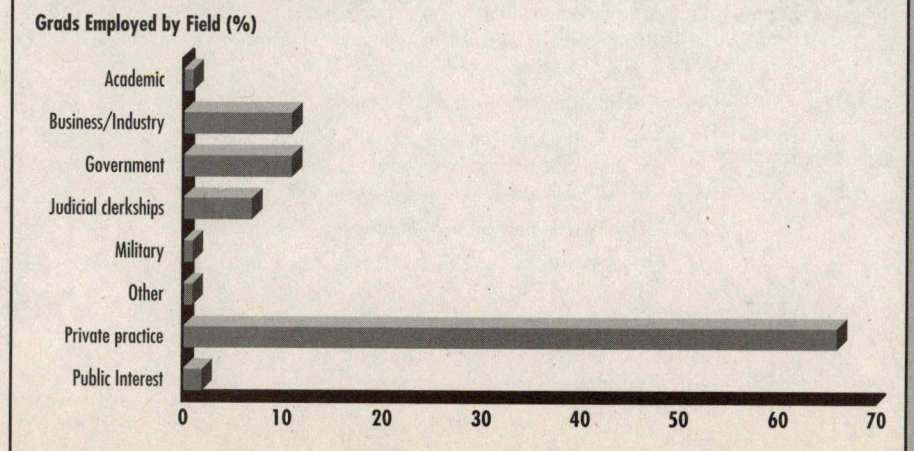

Grads Employed by Field (%)
- Academic
- Business/Industry
- Government
- Judicial clerkships
- Military
- Other
- Private practice
- Public Interest

Rate of Placement: 92%
Average Starting Salary: $72,314
Employers Who Frequently Hire Grads: Alston & Bird; Arnall Golden & Gregory; Drew Eckl; Greenberg Traurig; Kilpatrick & Stockton; Holland & Knight; Hunton and Williams; King & Spalding; Mckennel Long Aldridge; Paul Hastings, Janofosky and Walker; Powell Goldstein Frazer & Murphy; Troutman & Sanders; Fisher & Phillips
Prominent Alumni: Dr. Claudia Adkison, Executive Associate Dean, Emory School of Medicine; Evelyn Ann Ashley, Partner and Founder, Red Hot Law Group of Ashley LLC; Mary M. Brockington, Partner, Holland and Knight
State for Bar Exam: GA
Pass Rate for First-Time Bar: 93%

GOLDEN GATE UNIVERSITY

AT A GLANCE

Founded in 1901, Golden Gate University School of Law is an urban law school that draws on the dynamic environment of the legal/business district of San Francisco. Situated in the middle of the legal and financial districts, the law school is a short walk from law offices, the business center, and courts.

Students can attend a full-time day program or a part-time evening program. Full-time students may begin their studies in August or January. The low student/faculty ratio of 18:1 strengthens the bond of communication between students and teachers. The School of Law's 800 students include working professionals and recent college graduates from more than 100 undergraduate and graduate institutions. They come from across the United States and from a number of other nations, and represent a wide spectrum of ethnic, economic, and cultural backgrounds.

Golden Gate University School of Law is accredited by the American Bar Association (ABA) and the Committee of Bar Examiners of the State of California and is a member of the Association of American Law Schools (AALS). Graduates qualify to take the bar exam in all 50 states and in the District of Columbia.

CAMPUS AND LOCATION

Golden Gate University School of Law is located in the heart of downtown San Francisco, gateway to the Pacific Rim and one of the most beautiful cities in the world. Golden Gate is an urban facility that is centrally located near arts centers, the financial and legal districts, and courts. The School of Law is accessible by all forms of public transportation—local San Francisco bus and streetcar traffic, Bay Area Rapid Transit (BART), and buses that travel to the East Bay and North Bay.

DEGREES OFFERED

Golden Gate University School of Law has developed a reputation for providing a strong balance of theory and practical education. The School of Law has one of the most extensive clinical programs in the country, offering students excellent opportunities to experience hands-on, practical legal training. Students can participate in three on-site clinics: the Women's Employment Rights Clinic, the Environmental Law and Justice Clinic, and the Innocence Project.

Nine field-placement clinics give students experience in a variety of legal areas, including Criminal Law, Family Law, Immigration and Refugee Policy, Landlord-Tenant Issues, Public Interest Law, and Real Estate Law.

The School of Law also has a comprehensive litigation program, with small classes that allow all students full participation in litigation skills training. Courses such as Trial Advocacy, Mock Trial, and Criminal Litigation give students practical, hands-on experience in preparing for all aspects of trials.

Students may earn a combined JD/MBA with Golden Gate University's Ageno School of Business. Students may also earn a combined JD/PhD in Clinical Psychology, earning a JD from Golden Gate University and a PhD from the Pacific Graduate School of Psychology.

After earning their JD, students can attend Golden Gate University School of Law to earn an LLM in one of five programs: Environmental Law, Intellectual Property Law, International Legal Studies, Taxation, or U.S. Legal Studies. The School of Law also offers an SJD in International Legal Studies.

PROGRAMS AND CURRICULUM

Special Honors Program

In addition to the standard JD program, Golden Gate University offers the unique Honors Lawyering Program. This innovative honors program allows students to get the most out of their classroom legal education by combining it with substantive practical experience.

After a first year of foundational courses, Honors students follow a different schedule in their second and third years. During their second and third summers, they study in intensive simulated law firm settings. In the fall semesters of their second and third years, they participate in full-time, semester-long professional apprenticeships in law offices and other legal settings. These apprenticeships link work in the legal community with the theory, skills, and values learned in the classroom.

Certificate and Combined Programs

JD students can earn specialization certificates in Business Law, Criminal Law, Environmental Law, Intellectual Property Law, International Law, Labor and Employment Law, Litigation, Public Interest Law, or Real Estate Law. Students may also earn a combined JD/MBA with a focus in a variety of business areas or a JD/PhD in Clinical Psychology.

Graduate Programs

In recent years, the School of Law has become a center for graduate legal studies, offering five Master of Laws (LLM) degree programs: Environmental Law, Intellectual Property Law, International Legal Studies, Taxation, and United States Legal Studies. In addition, students with an LLM can earn a Doctor of Laws (SJD) in International Legal Studies.

EXPENSES AND FINANCIAL AID

Golden Gate University School of Law has a full range of programs to help students who need financial assistance. The Admissions and Financial Aid Office provides budget and debt management counseling, evaluates students' financial needs, and determines financial aid awards. Tuition for the 2003–2004 year is $877 per unit. For more information on fees and expenses, see our website at www.ggu.edu.

Merit Scholarships

To attract a highly qualified student body, the School of Law awards to entering students a number of full-tuition and partial-tuition scholarships based solely on academic merit. Criteria include past academic achievement and LSAT results. Last year, a significant number of entering students received merit scholarships. There is no formal application for merit scholarships.

Minority Scholarship

The School of Law awards minority scholarships of $5,000 to entering students of all races and ethnicities who have, through past efforts, demonstrated a substantial and meaningful commitment to serve minority communities. This scholarship is awarded for one year only.

Public Interest Scholars Program

Entering students interested in careers in public interest law are considered for the public interest law scholars program. Participants are offered a $5,000 stipend each year as long as they remain in good academic standing.

First-Year Endowed Scholarships

All eligible first-year students are considered for a variety of endowed scholarships.

School of Law

FACULTY

Students at Golden Gate University School of Law are taught by an accomplished, diverse faculty who practiced law before teaching. They are experts in a wide range of legal areas—from litigation to labor law, corporate law to criminal law, property development to public interest, environmental law to entertainment law, international law to intellectual property law—and much more.

The School of Law has 45 full-time faculty members and more than 100 adjunct faculty members.

Our student/teacher ratio is 18:1, and our professors are committed to being accessible to students.

STUDENTS

The approximately 800 students at Golden Gate University School of Law reflect a wide variety of ages, work experience, and cultural, ethnic, and religious backgrounds. Our student population includes students fresh out of undergraduate programs, students with advance degrees, and students returning to school after years in the work force.

More than 20 student organizations address the many interests of our diverse student population.

ADMISSIONS

Admissions Contact: Assistant Dean for Admissions and Financial Aid
Address: 536 Mission Street, San Francisco, CA 94105-2968
Admissions Phone: 415-442-6630 or 800-GGU-4YOU
Admissions Fax: 415-442-6631
Admissions E-mail: lawadmit@ggu.edu
Web Address: www.ggu.edu/law

Application Deadlines:

April 15 for fall full-time day program

June 2 for fall part-time evening program

November 14 for January mid-year admission program

SPECIAL PROGRAMS

Clinical Program

Golden Gate University School of Law has one of the most extensive clinical programs in the country, offering students excellent opportunities to experience hands-on, practical legal training. Students can participate in three on-site clinics: the Women's Employment Rights Clinic, the Environmental Law and Justice Clinic, and the Innocence Project.

Nine field-placement clinics give students experience in a variety of legal areas, including Criminal Law, Family Law, Landlord-Tenant Issues, Public Interest Law, and Real Estate Law.

Flexible Program

Through the mid-year admission program, students can begin law school either in August or in January. Students may also study full time during the day or part time in the evening, making Golden Gate a good law school for working adults.

Special Honors Program

In addition to the standard JD program, Golden Gate University offers the unique Honors Lawyering Program, which allows students to get the most out of their classroom legal education by combining it with substantive practical experience.

After a first year of foundational courses, Honors students follow a different schedule in their second and third years. During their second and third summers, they study in intensive simulated law firm settings. In the fall semesters of their second and third year, they participate in full-time, semester-long professional apprenticeships in law offices and other legal settings. These apprenticeships link work in the legal community with the theory, skills, and values learned in the classroom.

ADDITIONAL INFORMATION

Multiple programs allow students to attend day or evening classes and start law school in January or August:

- Special Honors Lawyering Program, in which students work in two full-time, semester-long apprenticeships
- Extensive clinical program offering students excellent opportunities to receive hands-on, practical legal training
- Specialization certificates available in nine areas
- Comprehensive litigation program with small classes
- Combined degree programs include JD/MBA and JD/PhD in Clinical Psychology
- Graduate programs in Environmental Law, Intellectual Property Law, International Legal Studies, Taxation, and U.S. Legal Studies
- An excellent downtown location in San Francisco near law firms, government agencies, and courts

CAREER SERVICES AND PLACEMENT

The Law Career Services Office (LCS) provides a wide variety of services, resources, and programs to guide students and graduates through the career planning process.

Services for all first-year students include an online job search guide, a one-on-one orientation session, workshops on resumes and cover letters.

Services for all JD and LLM students and graduates include print and online job listings, presentations by graduates on their career experiences, career counseling, job search skills workshops, resume and cover letter review, mock interviews with alumni working in various fields of the legal profession, recruitment programs, specialty area and regional job fairs, and more.

The average starting salary of recent graduates was $59,418, and they were employed as follows: private practice: 52%, business/industry: 22%, government: 12%, judicial clerkships: 2%, public interest: 9%, academic: 2%, and military: 1%.

GOLDEN GATE UNIVERSITY
School of Law

Admissions Contact: Assistant Dean, Tracy Simmons
536 Mission Street, San Francisco, CA 94105
Admissions Phone: 415-442-6630 • Admissions Fax: 415-442-6631
Admissions E-mail: lawadmit@ggu.edu • Web Address: www.ggu.edu/law

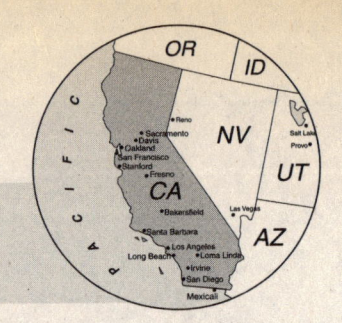

INSTITUTIONAL INFORMATION
Public/Private: Private
Student/Faculty Ratio: 18:1
Total Faculty: 160
% Part Time: 75
% Female: 41
% Minority: 10

PROGRAMS
Academic Specialties: Real Estate Law, Litigation, Immigration Law, Civil Rights Law (includes Affirmative Action, Homeless Rights, Minority, Women, and Gay and Lesbian Issues), Criminal Law, Environmental Law, Intellectual Property Law, International Law, Labor Law, Property
Advanced Degrees Offered: JD (3 years full time, 4 years part time), LLM (1 year)
Combined Degrees Offered: JD/MBA (3 to 4 years), JD/PhD (7 years)
Grading System: Letter and numerical system on a 4.0 scale
Clinical Program Required? No
Clinical Program Description: 2 on-site clinics, 11 field placement clinics
Legal Writing Course Requirements? Yes
Legal Writing Description: 2 semesters of Writing and Research in first year, Appellate Advocacy required in second year
Legal Methods Course Requirements? No
Legal Research Course Requirements? Yes
Legal Research Description: See Legal Writing.
Moot Court Requirement? No
Moot Court Description: Teams attend various national and international contests, including the Jessup Moot Court Competition.
Public Interest Law Requirement? No
Academic Journals: *Golden Gate University Law Review*

STUDENT INFORMATION
Enrollment of Law School: 265
% Out of State: 6
% Male/Female: 40/60
% Full Time: 85
% Full Time That Are International: 2
% Minority: 32
Average Age of Entering Class: 26

RESEARCH FACILITIES
Research Resources Available: CALI, Dialog, Dow Jones, Infotrac, LegalTrac, Lexis/Nexis, Loislaw, Mathew Bender, Westlaw

EXPENSES/FINANCIAL AID
Annual Tuition: $24,476
Room and Board (Off Campus): $12,490
Books and Supplies: $870
Financial Aid Application Deadline: 4/15
Average Grant: $7,693
Average Loan: $35,535
% of Aid That Is Merit-Based: 85
% Receiving Some Sort of Aid: 80
Average Total Aid Package: $38,000
Average Debt: $68,787
Tuition Per Credit: $877
Fees Per Semester: $120

ADMISSIONS INFORMATION
Application Fee: $55
Regular Application Deadline: 4/15
Regular Notification: Rolling
LSDAS Accepted? Yes
Average GPA: 3.1
Range of GPA: 2.6–4.0
Average LSAT: 150
Range of LSAT: 138–165
Transfer Students Accepted? Yes
Other Admissions Factors Considered: Undergraduate program, work experience that engages/develops writing and research skills
Number of Applications Received: 1,974
Number of Applicants Accepted: 1,094
Number of Applicants Enrolled: 227

EMPLOYMENT INFORMATION

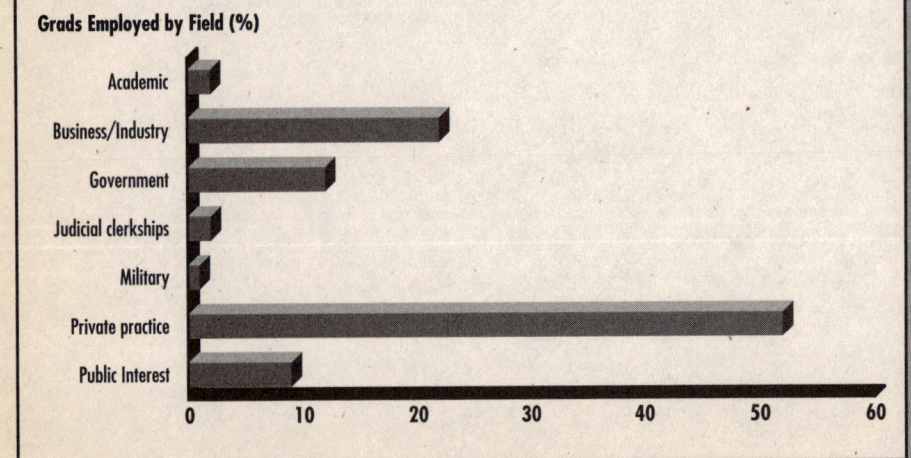

Grads Employed by Field (%)
- Academic
- Business/Industry
- Government
- Judicial clerkships
- Military
- Private practice
- Public Interest

Rate of Placement: 76%
Average Starting Salary: $59,418
Employers Who Frequently Hire Grads: Small, medium, and large firms; government agencies; public interest organizations; businesses and corporations
State for Bar Exam: CA
Pass Rate for First-Time Bar: 53%

GONZAGA UNIVERSITY
School of Law

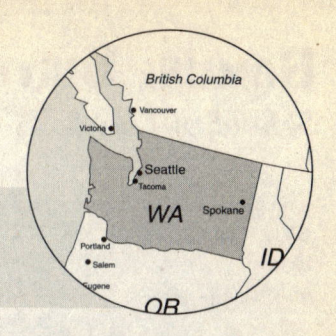

Admissions Contact: Assistant Director of Admissions, Lisa Smythe-Rodino
PO Box 3528, Spokane, WA 99220
Admissions Phone: 800-793-1710 • Admissions Fax: 509-323-3697
Admissions E-mail: admissions@lawschool.gonzaga.edu • Web Address: law.gonzaga.edu

INSTITUTIONAL INFORMATION
Public/Private: Private
Affiliation: Roman Catholic
Student/Faculty Ratio: 24:1
Total Faculty: 78
% Part Time: 57
% Female: 30
% Minority: 6

PROGRAMS
Academic Specialties: Integrated curriculum has skills training and professional ethics and values emphasized throughout; award-winning clinic has three options: university legal assistance (15 credits over two semesters), mini-clinics (3 to 5 credits), and externship placements; Environmental Law; Taxation
Combined Degrees Offered: JD/MBA, JD/Master of Accountancy (3.5 to 4 years)
Grading System: Letter and numerical system on a 4.0 scale; minimum 2.2 required
Clinical Program Required? No
Legal Writing Course Requirements? Yes
Legal Writing Description: 2 credits per semester in first year, 1 credit per semester in second year
Legal Methods Course Requirements? No
Legal Research Course Requirements? Yes
Legal Research Description: 2 credits per semester in first year, 1 credit per semester in second year
Moot Court Requirement? No
Moot Court Description: Intra- and intermural teams

Public Interest Law Requirement? Yes
Public Interest Law Description: 30 hours of public service
Academic Journals: *Gonzaga Law Review, Across Borders International On-Line Journal*

STUDENT INFORMATION
Enrollment of Law School: 575
% Out of State: 52
% Male/Female: 54/46
% Full Time: 95
% Minority: 15
Average Age of Entering Class: 27

RESEARCH FACILITIES
School-Supported Research Centers: Foley Center Library

EXPENSES/FINANCIAL AID
Annual Tuition: $21,600
Room and Board (Off Campus): $7,875
Books and Supplies: $900
Financial Aid Application Deadline: 2/1
Average Grant: $9,000
Average Loan: $30,000
% of Aid That Is Merit-Based: 25
% Receiving Some Sort of Aid: 95
Average Total Aid Package: $35,215
Average Debt: $75,000
Tuition Per Credit: $720
Fees Per Credit: $98

ADMISSIONS INFORMATION
Application Fee: $40
Regular Application Deadline: 7/3
Regular Notification: Rolling
LSDAS Accepted? Yes
Average GPA: 3.2
Range of GPA: 2.9–3.5
Average LSAT: 152
Range of LSAT: 149–155
Transfer Students Accepted? Yes
Other Schools to Which Students Applied: Arizona State University, California Western, Lewis and Clark College, Seattle University, University of Denver, University of Washington, Willamette University
Other Admissions Factors Considered: Personal statement, life and work experience, letters of recommendation, community service
Number of Applications Received: 1,232
Number of Applicants Accepted: 609
Number of Applicants Enrolled: 237

INTERNATIONAL STUDENTS
TOEFL Required of International Students? Yes
Minimum TOEFL: 650

EMPLOYMENT INFORMATION

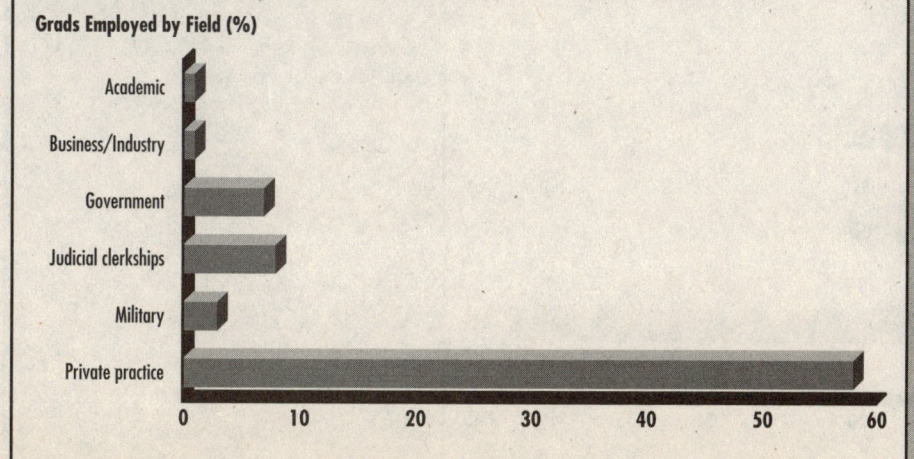

Grads Employed by Field (%)

Field	%
Academic	~1
Business/Industry	~3
Government	~7
Judicial clerkships	~7
Military	~2
Private practice	~58

Rate of Placement: 78%
Average Starting Salary: $44,576
Employers Who Frequently Hire Grads: Various law firms in Spokane and throughout Washington; various local and state government entities
Prominent Alumni: Christine Gregoire, Attorney General, State of Washington; Barbara Madsen, Justice, Washington Supreme Court; George Nethercutt, U.S. House of Representatives; Paul Luvera, lead plaintiff's attorney in tobacco case; Mary Fairhurst, Justice, Washington Supreme Court
State for Bar Exam: WA
Pass Rate for First-Time Bar: 64%

HAMLINE UNIVERSITY
School of Law

Admissions Contact: Director, Michael States
1536 Hewitt Avenue, St. Paul, MN 55104-1284
Admissions Phone: 651-523-2461 • Admissions Fax: 651-523-3064
Admissions E-mail: lawadm@gw.hamline.edu • Web Address: www.hamline.edu/law

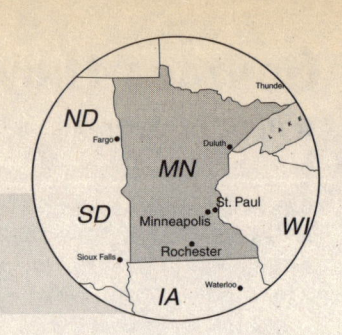

INSTITUTIONAL INFORMATION
Public/Private: Private
Affiliation: Methodist
Student/Faculty Ratio: 20:1
Total Faculty: 36
% Part Time: 8
% Female: 50
% Minority: 8

PROGRAMS
Academic Specialties: Law, Religion, and Ethics; Commercial Law; Children and the Law; Government and Regulatory Affairs; Labor and Employment Law; Criminal Law; Law and Slavery; Alternative Dispute Resolution; Corporation Securities Law; Intellectual Property Law; International Law
Advanced Degrees Offered: JD (3 years), LLM for international lawyers (1 year)
Combined Degrees Offered: JD/MAPA, JD/AMBA, JD/MANM, JD/MAM, JD/MLIS, JD/MAOL (all 4 years)
Grading System: 4.0 scale; A, A–, B+, B, B–, C+, C, C–, D+, D, D–, F, Pass/No Pass
Clinical Program Required? No
Clinical Program Description: Trial Practice Clinic, Mediation, Child Advocacy, Legal Assistance to Minnesota Prisoners (LAMP), Alternative Dispute Resolution Clinic, Education Law Clinic, Small Business/Non-Profit Clinic, Immigration Law Clinic, Innocence Clinic
Legal Writing Course Requirements? Yes
Legal Writing Description: Legal Research and Writing is a full-year course required of all first-year students, taught by full-time instructors in classes of approximately 20 students.
Legal Methods Course Requirements? No
Legal Research Course Requirements? Yes
Legal Research Description: See Legal Writing.
Moot Court Requirement? No
Public Interest Law Requirement? No
Academic Journals: *Hamline Law Review, Hamline Journal of Public Law and Policy, Journal of Law and Religion*

STUDENT INFORMATION
Enrollment of Law School: 583
% Out of State: 38
% Male/Female: 41/59
% Full Time: 81
% Full Time That Are International: 1
% Minority: 11
Average Age of Entering Class: 27

RESEARCH FACILITIES
Research Resources Available: Minnesota Innocence Project, Mediation Center for Dispute Resolution
School-Supported Research Centers: Dispute Resolution Institute

EXPENSES/FINANCIAL AID
Annual Tuition: $20,620
Room and Board (On/Off Campus): $9,210/$12,051
Books and Supplies: $800
Average Grant: $6,435
Average Loan: $23,000
% of Aid That Is Merit-Based: 98
% Receiving Some Sort of Aid: 88
Average Debt: $69,884
Tuition Per Credit: $742
Fees Per Credit: $5

ADMISSIONS INFORMATION
Application Fee: $40
Regular Application Deadline: Rolling
Regular Notification: Rolling
LSDAS Accepted? Yes
Average GPA: 3.3
Range of GPA: 3.0–3.6
Average LSAT: 152
Range of LSAT: 148–156
Transfer Students Accepted? Yes
Other Schools to Which Students Applied: Drake University, Marquette University, University of Minnesota, University of Wisconsin, William Mitchell College of Law
Other Admissions Factors Considered: Motivation, personal experiences, employment history, graduate education, maturity, letters of recommendation, ability to articulate one's interest in and suitability for the study of law
Number of Applications Received: 1,133
Number of Applicants Accepted: 631
Number of Applicants Enrolled: 228

INTERNATIONAL STUDENTS
TOEFL Required of International Students? Yes
Minimum TOEFL: 600 (250 computer)

EMPLOYMENT INFORMATION

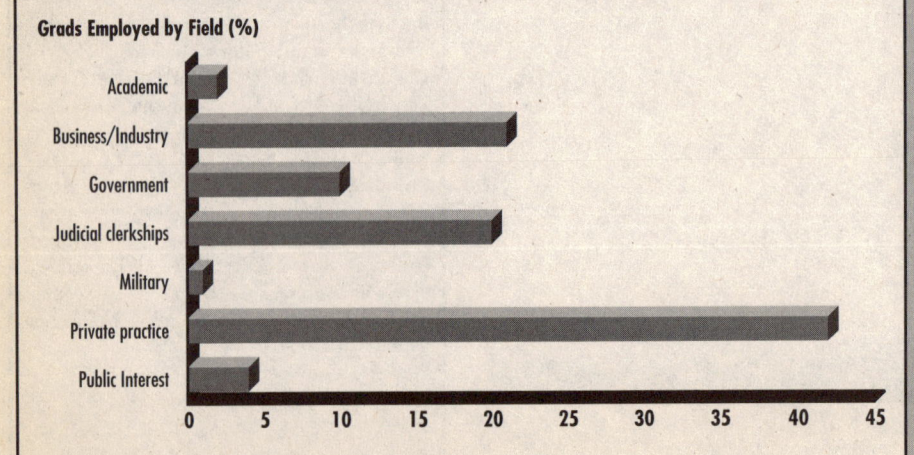

Grads Employed by Field (%)
- Academic: ~1
- Business/Industry: ~21
- Government: ~10
- Judicial clerkships: ~21
- Military: ~0
- Private practice: ~42
- Public Interest: ~3

Rate of Placement: 88%
Average Starting Salary: $44,808
State for Bar Exam: MN, WI
Pass Rate for First-Time Bar: 89%

HARVARD UNIVERSITY
Law School

Admissions Contact: Assistant Dean for Admissions and Financial Aid
1563 Massachusetts Avenue, Cambridge, MA 02138
Admissions Phone: 617-495-3109
Admissions E-mail: jdadmiss@law.harvard.edu • Web Address: www.law.harvard.edu

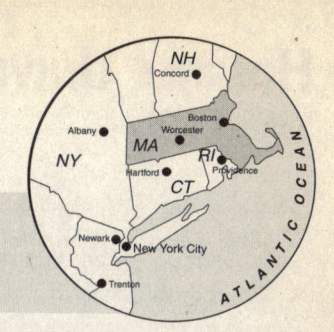

INSTITUTIONAL INFORMATION
Public/Private: Private
Student/Faculty Ratio: 19:1
Total Faculty: 142
% Part Time: 44
% Female: 20
% Minority: 11

PROGRAMS
Academic Specialties: International Law, Taxation, Constitutional Law, Negotiation/ADR, Comparative Law, Family Law, Civil Procedure, Commercial Law, Corporation Securities Law, Criminal Law, Environmental Law, Government Services, Human Rights Law, Labor Law, Legal History, Legal Philosophy, Property; 265 elective courses offered
Advanced Degrees Offered: LLM (18 to 20 credits with optional paper), SJD
Combined Degrees Offered: JD/MBA (4 years), JD/MPP, JD/MALD
Grading System: A+ to F
Clinical Program Required? No
Legal Methods Course Requirements? Yes
Legal Methods Description: Fall semester

STUDENT INFORMATION
Enrollment of Law School: 1,685
% Out of State: 95
% Male/Female: 55/45
% Full Time: 100
% Full Time That Are International: 3
% Minority: 27
Average Age of Entering Class: 24

RESEARCH FACILITIES
Research Resources Available: Harvard University
School-Supported Research Centers: 19 research and special programs

EXPENSES/FINANCIAL AID
Annual Tuition: $29,500
Room and Board: $14,670
Books and Supplies: $972
Average Grant: $13,300
Average Loan: $24,500
% Receiving Some Sort of Aid: 80
Average Total Aid Package: $35,000
Average Debt: $74,000

ADMISSIONS INFORMATION
Application Fee: $75
Regular Application Deadline: 2/1
Regular Notification: Rolling
LSDAS Accepted? Yes
Average GPA: 3.8
Range of GPA: 3.7–3.9
Average LSAT: 170
Range of LSAT: 167–173
Transfer Students Accepted? Yes
Number of Applications Received: 6,924
Number of Applicants Accepted: 872
Number of Applicants Enrolled: 557

EMPLOYMENT INFORMATION

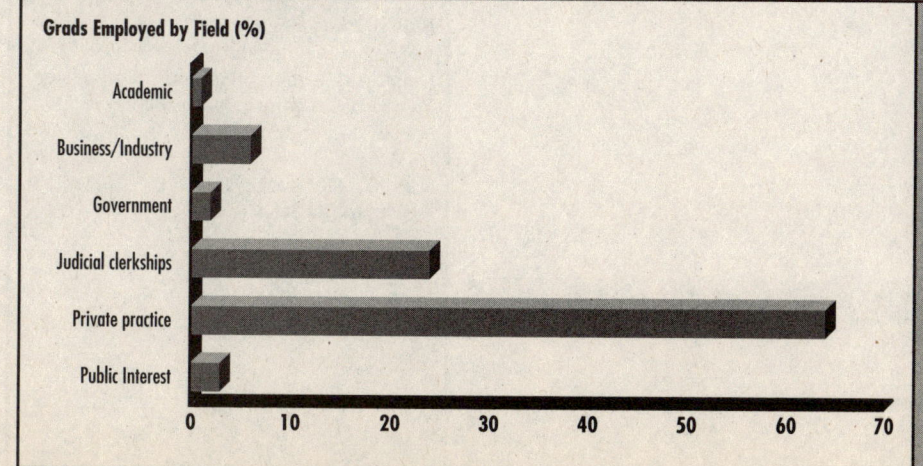

Grads Employed by Field (%)
- Academic
- Business/Industry
- Government
- Judicial clerkships
- Private practice
- Public Interest

Rate of Placement: 98%
Average Starting Salary: $90,000
Employers Who Frequently Hire Grads: Major national law firms, federal and state government, investment banks, consulting firms, law schools
State for Bar Exam: MA
Pass Rate for First-Time Bar: 100%

HOFSTRA UNIVERSITY
School of Law

Admissions Contact: Assistant Dean for Enrollment Management, Tina Sneed
121 Hofstra University, Hempstead, NY 11549
Admissions Phone: 516-463-5916 • Admissions Fax: 516-463-6264
Admissions E-mail: lawadmissions@hofstra.edu • Web Address: www.hofstra.edu/law

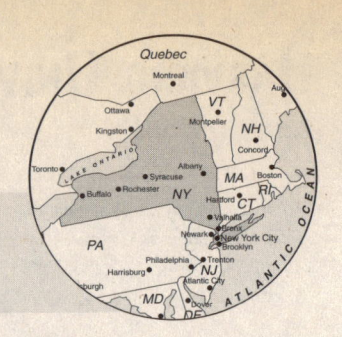

INSTITUTIONAL INFORMATION
Public/Private: Private
Student/Faculty Ratio: 17:1
Total Faculty: 86
% Part Time: 52
% Female: 22
% Minority: 5

PROGRAMS
Academic Specialties: Hofstra has a history of excellence in skills training and trial advocacy, including three clinical programs and an extensive array of simulation-based skills courses, both in Traditional Litigation and Alternative Dispute Resolution. The Center for Children, Families, and the Law offers an innovative interdisciplinary curriculum in Child Advocacy and Family Law. Specialties include Litigation, Civil Procedure, Commercial Law, Constitutional Law, Corporation Securities Law, Criminal Law, Environmental Law, Government Services, Intellectual Property Law, International Law, Labor Law, Property, and Taxation.
Advanced Degrees Offered: JD (3 years full time, 4 years part time), LLM (1 year full time, 2 years part time)
Combined Degrees Offered: JD/MBA (4 years)
Grading System: A to F (4.0–0.0)
Clinical Program Required? No
Clinical Program Description: Child Advocacy Clinic, Criminal Justice Clinic, Housing Rights Clinic
Legal Writing Course Requirements? Yes
Legal Writing Description: Legal Writing is taken in the second semester of the first year for 2 credits.
Legal Methods Course Requirements? Yes
Legal Methods Description: 2-week introduction prior to orientation; variety of sessions during the first semester of the first year
Legal Research Course Requirements? Yes
Legal Research Description: Legal Research, while not a separate course, begins in the first semester of the first year and continues in the Legal Writing course.
Moot Court Requirement? Yes
Moot Court Description: Appellate Advocacy (2 credits) is a required course taken in the first semester; second year includes a required appellate argument.
Public Interest Law Requirement? No
Academic Journals: *Law Review, Labor and Employment Law Journal, Family Courts Review*

STUDENT INFORMATION
Enrollment of Law School: 819
% Out of State: 22
% Male/Female: 53/47
% Full Time: 87
% Minority: 26
Average Age of Entering Class: 26

RESEARCH FACILITIES
Research Resources Available: Discount Internet service accounts with local service providers
School-Supported Research Centers: Wireless Internet and network access inside and outside the building

EXPENSES/FINANCIAL AID
Annual Tuition: $25,752
Room and Board (On/Off Campus): $8,350/$15,600
Books and Supplies: $900
Financial Aid Application Deadline: 6/1
Average Grant: $8,553
Average Loan: $3,161
% of Aid That Is Merit-Based: 66
% Receiving Some Sort of Aid: 96
Average Total Aid Package: $9,352

ADMISSIONS INFORMATION
Application Fee: $60
Regular Application Deadline: Rolling
Regular Notification: Rolling
LSDAS Accepted? Yes
Average GPA: 3.3
Range of GPA: 2.9–3.6
Average LSAT: 156
Range of LSAT: 152–158
Transfer Students Accepted? Yes
Other Schools to Which Students Applied: Brooklyn Law School, Fordham University, New York Law School, New York University, St. John's University, Touro College, Yeshiva University
Other Admissions Factors Considered: LSAT, GPA, undergraduate school curriculum, work experience, extracurricular activities, recommendations
Number of Applications Received: 2,678
Number of Applicants Accepted: 966
Number of Applicants Enrolled: 206

INTERNATIONAL STUDENTS
Minimum TOEFL: 580

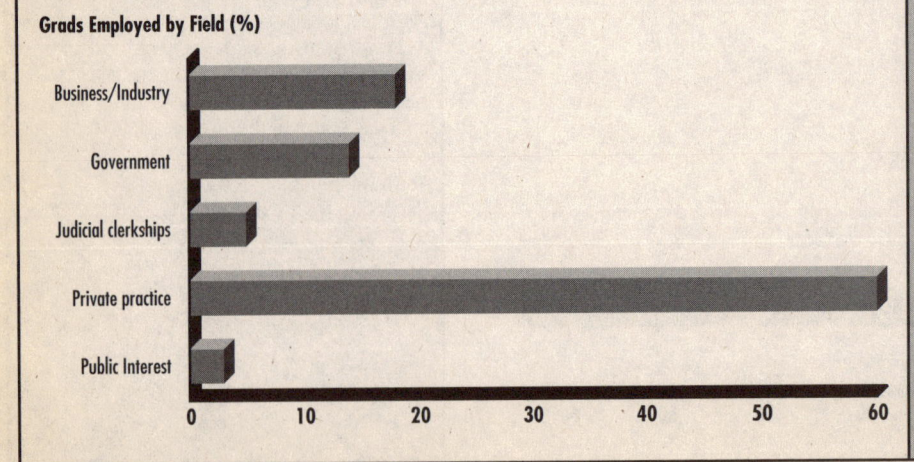

EMPLOYMENT INFORMATION

Grads Employed by Field (%)

Field	%
Business/Industry	~18
Government	~14
Judicial clerkships	~5
Private practice	~60
Public Interest	~2

Rate of Placement: 98%
Average Starting Salary: $68,799
Employers Who Frequently Hire Grads: Prestigious law firms in New York City and Long Island; government agencies, public interest organizations
State for Bar Exam: NY, NJ, CT, FL, CA
Pass Rate for First-Time Bar: 84%

HOWARD UNIVERSITY
School of Law

Admissions Contact: Assistant Dean, Ruby J. Sherrod
2900 Van Ness Street NW, Washington, DC 20008
Admissions Phone: 202-806-8008 • Admissions Fax: 202-806-8162
Admissions E-mail: admissions@law.howard.edu • Web Address: www.law.howard.edu

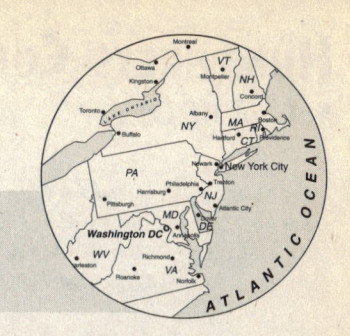

INSTITUTIONAL INFORMATION
Public/Private: Private
Environment: Urban
Academic Calendar: Semester
Schedule: Full time only
Student/Faculty Ratio: 16:1
Total Faculty: 56
% Part Time: 14
% Female: 35
% Minority: 60

PROGRAMS
Academic Specialties: Strong faculty with a wide range of interests including Antitrust Law and Religion, Evidence, Critical Race Scholarship, Feminist Scholarship
Advanced Degrees Offered: LLM (foreign lawyers only) (1–2 years)
Combined Degrees Offered: JD/MBA (4 years)
Grading System: Numerical system; grading is subject to a normalization system
Clinical Program Required? No
Clinical Program Description: Criminal Law, Elder Law, Civil Law, Immigration Law, Small Business Law
Legal Writing/Methods Course Requirements: Integrated program across 3 years

STUDENT INFORMATION
Enrollment of Law School: 415
% Male/Female: 40/60
% Full Time: 100
% Minority: 94
Average Age of Entering Class: 25

RESEARCH FACILITIES
Computers/Workstations Available: 100
School-Supported Research Centers: Law students have access to numerous research libraries in Washington, D.C., and the surrounding area, including the Library of Congress and numerous other public research centers.

EXPENSES/FINANCIAL AID
Annual Tuition: $12,650
Room and Board: $9,051
Books and Supplies: $1,050
Financial Aid Application Deadline: 2/1
Average Grant: $12,000
Average Loan: $15,000
% of Aid That Is Merit-Based: 28
% Receiving Some Sort of Aid: 95
Average Total Aid Package: $23,000
Average Debt: $55,500
Tuition Per Credit: $505
Fees Per Credit: $703

ADMISSIONS INFORMATION
Application Fee: $60
Regular Application Deadline: 3/31
Regular Notification: Rolling
Average GPA: 3.0
Range of GPA: 2.7–3.2
Average LSAT: 152
Range of LSAT: 148–154
Transfer Students Accepted? Yes
Other Schools to Which Students Applied: Georgetown University, University of Maryland, George Washington University, American University, New York University, Temple University, University of Baltimore, Harvard University
Number of Applications Received: 1,225
Number of Applicants Accepted: 372
Number of Applicants Enrolled: 140

INTERNATIONAL STUDENTS
TOEFL Required of International Students? Yes
Minimum TOEFL: 550

EMPLOYMENT INFORMATION

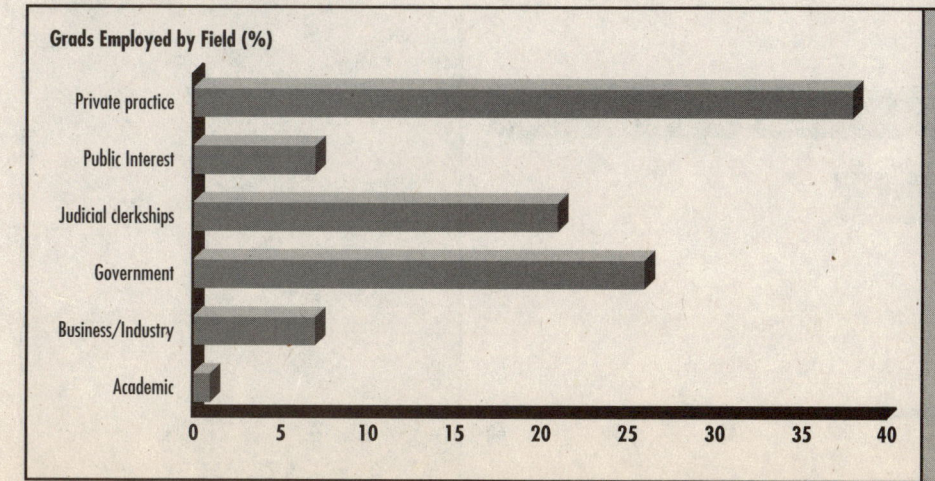

Grads Employed by Field (%)

Field	%
Private practice	~39
Public Interest	~7
Judicial clerkships	~21
Government	~26
Business/Industry	~7
Academic	~1

Average Starting Salary: $85,200
State for Bar Exam: MD/NY
Number Taking Bar Exam: 41/17
Pass Rate for First-Time Bar: 29%/82%

HUMPHREYS COLLEGE
School of Law

Admissions Contact: Admission Officer, Santa Lopez
6650 Inglewood Avenue, Stockton, CA 95207
Admissions Phone: 209-478-0800 • Admissions Fax: 209-478-8721
Admissions E-mail: admissions@humphreys.edu • Web Address: www.humphreys.edu

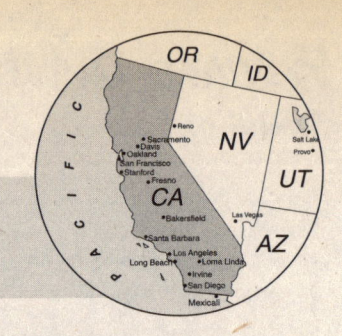

INSTITUTIONAL INFORMATION
Public/Private: Private
Academic Calendar: Quarter
Schedule: Part time only
Student/Faculty Ratio: 6:1
Total Faculty: 12
% Part Time: 83
% Female: 17
% Minority: 0

PROGRAMS
Academic Specialties: All faculty are practicing attorneys, including private practitioners and public defenders. Several judges are on the faculty.
Grading System: 100–90 Excellent, 89–80 Good, 79–70 Satisfactory, 69–55 Unsatisfactory, below 55 Failure
Clinical Program Required? No
Legal Writing/Methods Course Requirements: 1 quarter in first year and in fourth year

STUDENT INFORMATION
Enrollment of Law School: 60
% Male/Female: 100/0
% Full Time: 0
% Full Time That Are International: 0
% Minority: 0
Average Age of Entering Class: 33

EXPENSES/FINANCIAL AID
Annual Tuition: $7,062
Books and Supplies: $650
Average Loan: $14,658
% Receiving Some Sort of Aid: 66
Average Total Aid Package: $14,658
Average Debt: $48,000
Fees Per Credit: $214

ADMISSIONS INFORMATION
Application Fee: $20
Regular Application Deadline: 6/1
Regular Notification: Rolling
LSDAS Accepted? No
Average GPA: 2.8
Average LSAT: 149
Transfer Students Accepted? Yes
Other Schools to Which Students Applied: California State University—Stanislaus, Delta College, California State University—Sacramento
Number of Applications Received: 52
Number of Applicants Accepted: 32
Number of Applicants Enrolled: 19

INTERNATIONAL STUDENTS
TOEFL Required of International Students? Yes
Minimum TOEFL: 450

EMPLOYMENT INFORMATION

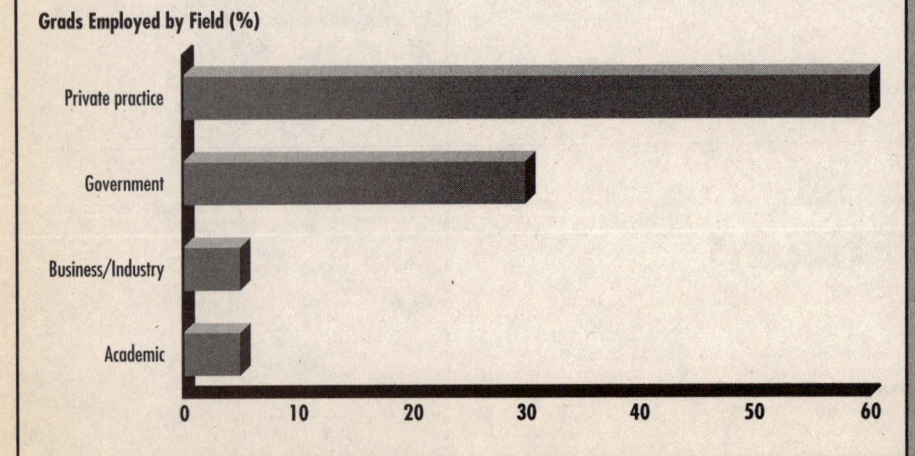

Grads Employed by Field (%)
- Private practice: 60
- Government: 30
- Business/Industry: 5
- Academic: 5

Employers Who Frequently Hire Grads: District Attorney's Offices; police departments
Prominent Alumni: Patti Gharamendi

ILLINOIS INSTITUTE OF TECHNOLOGY
Chicago-Kent College of Law

Admissions Contact: Assistant Dean for Admissions, Michael S. Burns
565 West Adams Street, Chicago, IL 60661
Admissions Phone: 312-906-5020 • Admissions Fax: 312-906-5274
Admissions E-mail: admit@kentlaw.edu • Web Address: www.kentlaw.edu

INSTITUTIONAL INFORMATION
Public/Private: Private
Student/Faculty Ratio: 5:1
Total Faculty: 180
% Part Time: 62
% Female: 26
% Minority: 5

PROGRAMS
Academic Specialties: Biotechnology, Information Technology, Environmental Protection, International Business Transactions, New Paradigms in Products Liability, International Criminal Tribunals, Corporation Securities Law, Criminal Law, Human Rights Law, Intellectual Property Law, International Law, Labor Law, Taxation
Advanced Degrees Offered: JD (3 years full time, 4 years part time), LLM (2 to 8 semesters)
Combined Degrees Offered: JD/MBA, JD/MPA, JD/MS in Environmental Management (all 3.5 to 5 years); JD/LLM (4 to 5 years); JD/MS Financial Markets (4 to 5 years); JD/MPH (3.5 years)
Grading System: Letter and numerical system from A (4.0) to E (0.0); minimum 2.3 required
Clinical Program Required? No
Clinical Program Description: Employment Discrimination/Civil Rights Litigation plus General Practice Program, Criminal Defense Litigation Program, Health Law Litigation Program, Alternative Dispute Resolution (ADR) Program, Tax Litigation Program, Advice Desk Program, Mediation Program, Judicial Externship Program, Advanced Externship Program, Business Entity Formation, Business Entity Transactions

EMPLOYMENT INFORMATION

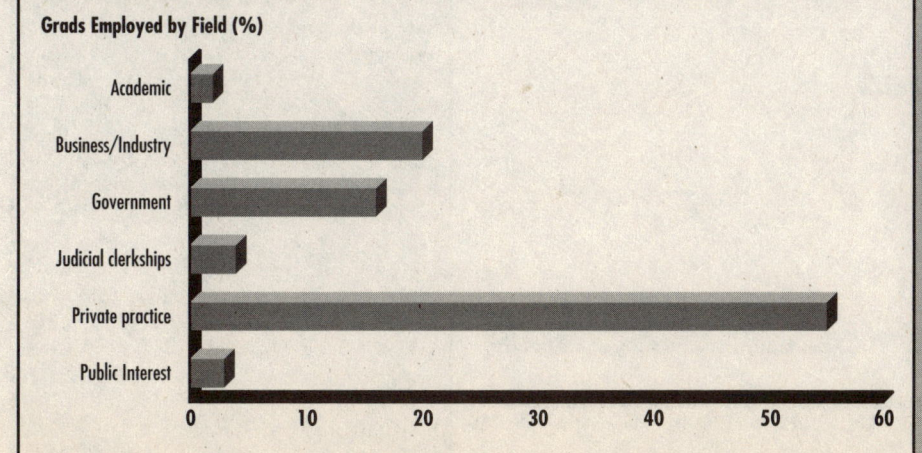

Legal Writing Course Requirements? Yes
Legal Writing Description: The 3-year, 5-course curriculum teaches students to analyze a wide range of legal problems and to write about them persuasively.
Legal Methods Course Requirements? No
Legal Research Course Requirements? Yes
Legal Research Description: First year: basic legal research and writing courses. Second year: two additional courses and advanced training.
Moot Court Requirement? Yes
Moot Court Description: During the second semester of the first year, students participate in competition. Students who distinguish themselves are invited to join the Moot Court Honor Society.
Public Interest Law Requirement? No
Public Interest Law Description: The Public Interest Resource Center
Academic Journals: Chicago-Kent Law Review, Employee Rights and Employment Policy Journal, Illinois Public Employee Relations Report, Chicago-Kent Journal of Intellectual Property, Chicago-Kent Journal of International and Comparative Law

STUDENT INFORMATION
Enrollment of Law School: 970
% Out of State: 37
% Male/Female: 49/51
% Full Time: 73
% Full Time That Are International: 1
% Minority: 13
Average Age of Entering Class: 25

RESEARCH FACILITIES
Research Resources Available: Nearby are the U.S. District Court for the Northern District of Illinois, the U.S. Court of Appeals for the Seventh Circuit, the Illinois state courts, and LaSalle Street, the hub of law practice in Chicago.
School-Supported Research Centers: Global Law and Policy Initiative; Institute for Law and the Humanities; Institute for Law and the Workplace; Institute for Science, Law, and Technology

EXPENSES/FINANCIAL AID
Annual Tuition: $25,200
Room and Board (On/Off Campus): $6,631/$13,860
Books and Supplies: $890
Financial Aid Application Deadline: 4/15
Average Grant: $8,936
Average Loan: $29,164
% of Aid That Is Merit-Based: 17
% Receiving Some Sort of Aid: 91
Average Total Aid Package: $31,917
Average Debt: $78,478
Tuition Per Credit: $890

ADMISSIONS INFORMATION
Application Fee: $50
Regular Application Deadline: 3/1
Regular Notification: Rolling
LSDAS Accepted? Yes
Range of GPA: 3.1–3.5
Range of LSAT: 155–159
Transfer Students Accepted? Yes
Other Schools to Which Students Applied: American, DePaul, Loyola, Northwestern, John Marshall, University of Chicago, University of Illinois
Other Admissions Factors Considered: Academic letters of recommendation, writing sample
Number of Applications Received: 2,463
Number of Applicants Accepted: 920
Number of Applicants Enrolled: 250

Rate of Placement: 95%
Average Starting Salary: $71,396
Employers Who Frequently Hire Grads: Small firms (2–25 attorneys) medium to large firms (26–500+ attorneys); government, public interest, and judicial clerkship positions
Prominent Alumni: Hon. Abraham Lincoln Marovitz, Senior Judge, U.S. District Court, IL; Hon. Ilana Diamond Rovner, U.S. 7th Circuit Court of Appeals; Thomas Demetrio, Partner, Corboy & Demetrio; Robert Hershenhorn, Chairman of the Board, First Bank and Trust Co. of IL
State for Bar Exam: IL
Pass Rate for First-Time Bar: 81%

INDIANA UNIVERSITY — BLOOMINGTON
School of Law

Admissions Contact: Director of Admissions, Patricia S. Clark
211 South Indiana Avenue, Bloomington, IN 47405-1001
Admissions Phone: 812-855-4765 • Admissions Fax: 812-855-0555
Admissions E-mail: lawadmis@indiana.edu • Web Address: www.law.indiana.edu

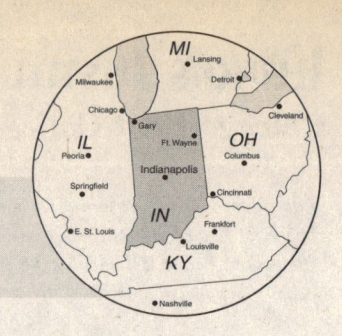

INSTITUTIONAL INFORMATION
Public/Private: Public
Student/Faculty Ratio: 14:1
Total Faculty: 48
% Part Time: 6
% Female: 29
% Minority: 6

PROGRAMS
Academic Specialties: Communications, Interdisciplinary Study (Law and Economics, Law and Psychology, Law and Social Science, etc.), Biotechnology, Civil Procedure, Commercial Law, Constitutional Law, Corporation Securities Law, Criminal Law, Environmental Law, Government Services, Human Rights Law, Intellectual Property Law, International/Global Law, Labor Law, Legal History, Legal Philosophy, Property, Taxation
Advanced Degrees Offered: SJD (1 year in residence plus dissertation), LLM (20 credits plus thesis or 24 credits plus practicum), MCL (21 credits plus practicum)
Combined Degrees Offered: JD/MBA, JD/MPA, JD/MSES, JD/MLIS, JD/MA or MS Telecom, PhD Law and Social Science, JD/MA Journalism (all 4 years)
Grading System: 4.0 scale
Clinical Program Required? No
Clinical Program Description: Community Clinic, Child Advocacy, Protective Order Project, Federal Courts Clinic
Legal Writing Course Requirements? Yes
Legal Writing Description: 3-year initiative created to develop proficiency in legal writing.
Legal Methods Course Requirements? No
Legal Research Course Requirements? Yes
Legal Research Description: See Legal Writing.
Moot Court Requirement? No
Moot Court Description: Sherman Minton Moot Court Competition for second-year students. Nearly half of second-years participate in the competition; a similar competition for third-years is being inaugurated.
Public Interest Law Requirement? No
Public Interest Law Description: About 200 students every year are involved in pro bono services. In addition to IU clinics and the Protective Order Project, students participate in the Environmental Law Research Group, the Inmate Legal Assistance Project, the Outreach for Legal Literacy, and the Public Interest Law Foundation.
Academic Journals: Indiana Law Journal, Federal Communications Law Journal, Indiana Journal of Global Legal Studies

STUDENT INFORMATION
Enrollment of Law School: 656
% Out of State: 46
% Male/Female: 56/44
% Full Time: 99
% Full Time That Are International: 1
% Minority: 16
Average Age of Entering Class: 24

RESEARCH FACILITIES
Research Resources Available: Lexis, Westlaw, expanding national and international networks
School-Supported Research Centers: Online catalog, Web-based and CD-ROM technology, 3-room media center provides the latest in computer equipment

EXPENSES/FINANCIAL AID
Annual Tuition (Residents/Nonresidents): $10,380/$22,627
Room and Board: $6,690
Books and Supplies: $1,064
Financial Aid Application Deadline: 4/1
Average Grant: $5,429
Average Loan: $21,374
% of Aid That Is Merit-Based: 69
% Receiving Some Sort of Aid: 92
Average Total Aid Package: $23,374
Average Debt: $60,250

ADMISSIONS INFORMATION
Application Fee: $35
Regular Application Deadline: Rolling
Regular Notification: Rolling
LSDAS Accepted? Yes
Average GPA: 3.4
Average LSAT: 161
Transfer Students Accepted? Yes
Other Schools to Which Students Applied: George Washington, Ohio State, U. of Illinois, U. of Michigan, Notre Dame, U. of Wisconsin, Washington University
Other Admissions Factors Considered: Faculty evaluations, strong writing and analytic skills, personal statement, activities, major
Number of Applications Received: 2,459
Number of Applicants Accepted: 824
Number of Applicants Enrolled: 233

INTERNATIONAL STUDENTS
TOEFL Required of International Students? Yes
Minimum TOEFL: 600 (250 computer)

EMPLOYMENT INFORMATION

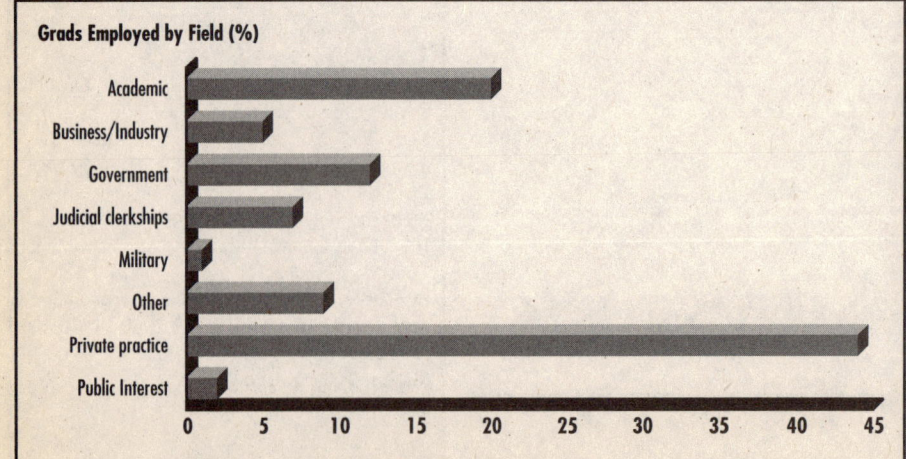

Grads Employed by Field (%)
- Academic: ~20
- Business/Industry: ~5
- Government: ~13
- Judicial clerkships: ~7
- Military: ~1
- Other: ~5
- Private practice: ~45
- Public Interest: ~2

Rate of Placement: 91%
Average Starting Salary: $65,000
Employers Who Frequently Hire Grads: Barnes & Thornburg; U.S. District Courts; Indiana Court of Appeals; Ice Miller Donadio & Ryan; Baker & Daniels; Warner Norcross & Judd; Lord Bissell & Brook; Katten Muckin & Zavis; Kirkland & Ellis; Arnold & Porter
Prominent Alumni: Shirley Abrahamson, Chief Justice, Wisconsin Supreme Court; Frank O'Bannon, Governor of Indiana; Alecia DeCoudreaux, Deputy General Counsel, Eli Lilly; Robert Long, Attorney, Latham & Watkins; Raphael Prevot, Labor Relations Counsel, NFL
State for Bar Exam: IN
Pass Rate for First-Time Bar: 90%

INDIANA UNIVERSITY — INDIANAPOLIS
School of Law

Admissions Contact: Assistant Dean for Admissions, Angela Espada
530 West New York Street, Indianapolis, IN 46202-3225
Admissions Phone: 317-274-2459 • Admissions Fax: 317-278-4780
Admissions E-mail: khmiller@iupui.edu • Web Address: www.indylaw.indiana.edu

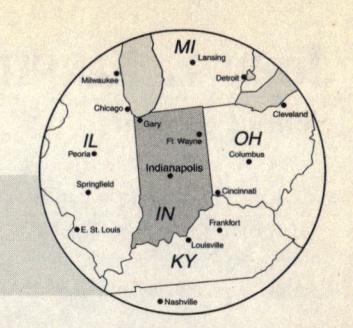

INSTITUTIONAL INFORMATION
Public/Private: Public
Student/Faculty Ratio: 18:1
Total Faculty: 49
% Part Time: 27
% Female: 31
% Minority: 1

PROGRAMS
Academic Specialties: Copyright Law, Health Law, Constitutional Law, Criminal Law, Government Services, Human Rights Law, International Law, Labor Law, Taxation; we have practitioners as well as scholars, and our faculty and curriculum reflect the influence of both.
Combined Degrees Offered: JD/MPA, JD/MBA, JD/MHA, JD/MPH (all 4 years)
Grading System: 4.0 scale with a recommended curve
Clinical Program Required? No
Clinical Program Description: Civil, Disability, Criminal Law
Legal Writing Course Requirements? Yes
Legal Writing Description: 1 year
Legal Methods Course Requirements? Yes
Legal Research Course Requirements? Yes
Legal Research Description: 1 year
Moot Court Requirement? No
Public Interest Law Requirement? No
Academic Journals: Indiana Law Review, Indiana International and Comparative Law Review

STUDENT INFORMATION
Enrollment of Law School: 848
% Out of State: 10
% Male/Female: 69/31
% Full Time: 65
% Full Time That Are International: 2
% Minority: 17
Average Age of Entering Class: 27

RESEARCH FACILITIES
School-Supported Research Centers: Center for Law and Health, Center for State and Local Government

EXPENSES/FINANCIAL AID
Annual Tuition (Residents/Nonresidents): $9,340/$19,696
Room and Board: $13,902
Books and Supplies: $800
Average Grant: $5,300
Average Loan: $12,500
% of Aid That Is Merit-Based: 80
% Receiving Some Sort of Aid: 60
Average Total Aid Package: $4,500
Average Debt: $39,000
Tuition Per Credit (Residents/Nonresidents): $301/$635
Fees Per Credit: $451

ADMISSIONS INFORMATION
Application Fee: $45
Regular Application Deadline: 3/1
Regular Notification: Rolling
LSDAS Accepted? Yes
Average GPA: 3.4
Range of GPA: 3.1–3.6
Average LSAT: 156
Range of LSAT: 154–159
Transfer Students Accepted? Yes
Other Admissions Factors Considered: International students: test of written English, law degree from another institution in the home country
Number of Applications Received: 1,460
Number of Applicants Accepted: 481
Number of Applicants Enrolled: 276

INTERNATIONAL STUDENTS
TOEFL Required of International Students? Yes
Minimum TOEFL: 550 (213 computer)

EMPLOYMENT INFORMATION

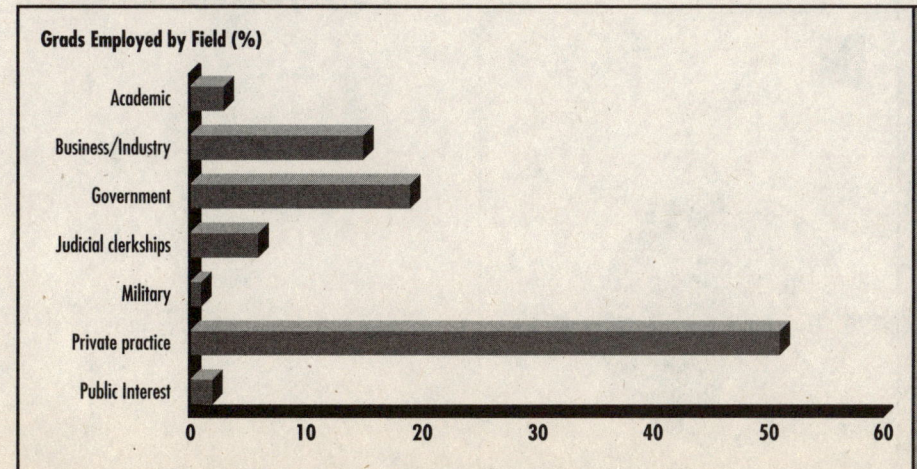

Grads Employed by Field (%):
- Academic: ~2
- Business/Industry: ~15
- Government: ~20
- Judicial clerkships: ~7
- Military: ~1
- Private practice: ~52
- Public Interest: ~2

Rate of Placement: 92%
Average Starting Salary: $57,693
Employers Who Frequently Hire Grads: Private law firms; Baker & Daniels; Barnes & Thornburg; Ice Miller
Prominent Alumni: Dan Coats, former Senator; Edgar Whitcomb, former Governor; Rebecca Kendall, VP and General Counsel, Eli Lilly & Co.; Mark Roesler, President and CEO, CMG Worldwide, Inc.; Alan Cohen, Chairman, President, and CEO, The Finish Line, Inc.
State for Bar Exam: IN
Pass Rate for First-Time Bar: 85%

JOHN F. KENNEDY UNIVERSITY
School of Law

Admissions Contact: Admission Director, Ellena Bloedorn
547 Ygnacio Valley Road, Walnut Creek, CA 94596
Admissions Phone: 925-295-1800 • Admissions Fax: 925-933-0917
Admissions E-mail: law@jfku.edu • Web Address: www.jfku.edu/law

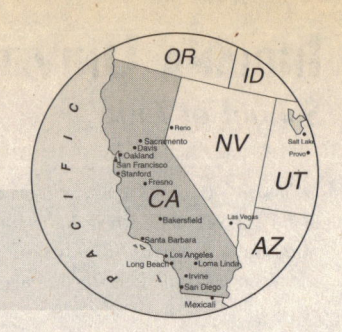

INSTITUTIONAL INFORMATION
Public/Private: Private
Student/Faculty Ratio: 30:1

PROGRAMS
Academic Specialties: Corporation Securities Law
Clinical Program Required? No
Legal Methods Course Requirements? No

STUDENT INFORMATION
Enrollment of Law School: 249
% Male/Female: 50/50
% Minority: 24
Average Age of Entering Class: 36

EXPENSES/FINANCIAL AID
Annual Tuition: $7,823

ADMISSIONS INFORMATION
Regular Application Deadline: 5/30
Regular Notification: Rolling
LSDAS Accepted? No
Transfer Students Accepted? No
Other Schools to Which Students Applied: University of California—Berkeley, Golden Gate University, Syracuse University, University of San Francisco, Stanford University

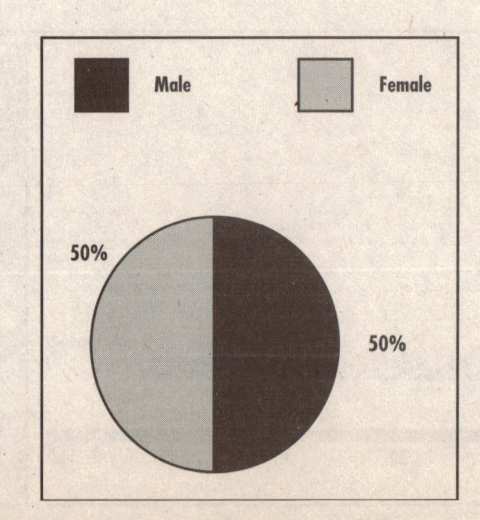

JOHN MARSHALL LAW SCHOOL

Admissions Contact: Associate Dean for Admission and Student Affairs, William B. Powers
315 South Plymouth Court, Chicago, IL 60604
Admissions Phone: 800-537-4280 • Admissions Fax: 312-427-5136
Admissions E-mail: admission@jmls.edu • Web-Address: www.jmls.edu

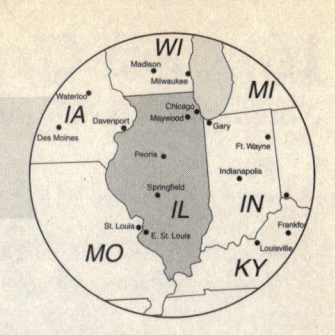

INSTITUTIONAL INFORMATION
Public/Private: Private
Student/Faculty Ratio: 15:1
Total Faculty: 290
% Part Time: 81
% Female: 17
% Minority: 4

PROGRAMS
Academic Specialties: Lawyering Skills, Trial Advocacy, Moot Court, International Law, Property, Taxation
Advanced Degrees Offered: LLM (1 year full time), MS Information Technology
Combined Degrees Offered: JD/MBA, JD/MPA, JD/MA, JD/LLM
Grading System: A+ (4.01), A (4.0), A– (3.5), B (3.0), B– (2.5), C (2.0), C– (1.5), D (1.0), F (0.0)
Clinical Program Required? Yes
Clinical Program Description: Trial Advocacy, Fair Housing Clinic, Extensive Legal Writing Program, numerous externships and simulation courses
Legal Methods Course Requirements? Yes
Legal Methods Description: 4 semesters, 10 semester hours

STUDENT INFORMATION
Enrollment of Law School: 1,152
% Out of State: 35
% Male/Female: 54/46
% Full Time: 62
% Full Time That Are International: 1
% Minority: 19
Average Age of Entering Class: 24

RESEARCH FACILITIES
School-Supported Research Centers: Center for Advocacy and Dispute Resolution, Center for Information and Privacy Law, Center for Intellectual Property Law, Center for International and Comparative Studies, Center for Real Estate Law, Center for Tax Law and Employee Benefits

EXPENSES/FINANCIAL AID
Annual Tuition: $21,000
Room and Board (Off Campus): $13,492
Books and Supplies: $700
Average Grant: $8,400
Average Loan: $9,999
% of Aid That Is Merit-Based: 10
% Receiving Some Sort of Aid: 90
Average Total Aid Package: $18,500
Average Debt: $65,269
Tuition Per Credit: $700

ADMISSIONS INFORMATION
Application Fee: $50
Regular Application Deadline: 3/1
Regular Notification: Rolling
LSDAS Accepted? Yes
Average GPA: 3.0
Range of GPA: 2.7–3.2
Average LSAT: 150
Range of LSAT: 145–152
Transfer Students Accepted? Yes
Other Schools to Which Students Applied: University of Scranton, Illinois Institute of Technology, Stony Brook University
Number of Applications Received: 1,543
Number of Applicants Accepted: 964
Number of Applicants Enrolled: 287

INTERNATIONAL STUDENTS
TOEFL Required of International Students? Yes
Minimum TOEFL: 600

EMPLOYMENT INFORMATION

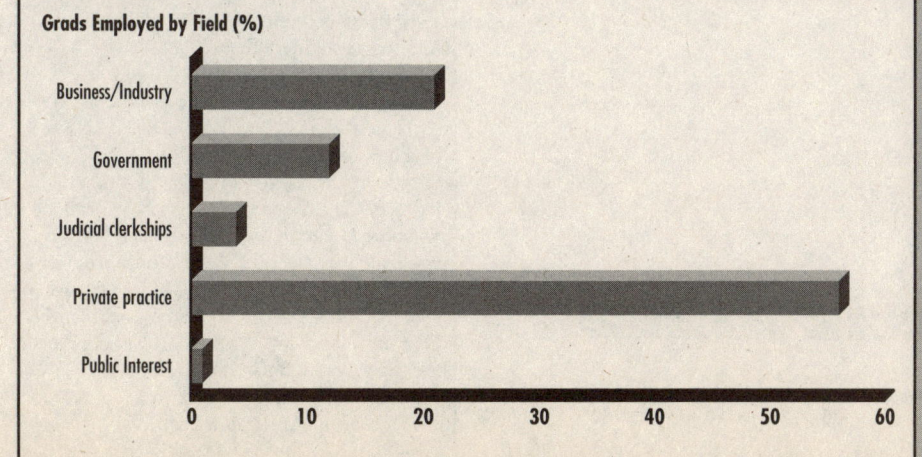

Grads Employed by Field (%)
- Business/Industry: ~22
- Government: ~12
- Judicial clerkships: ~4
- Private practice: ~57
- Public Interest: ~1

Rate of Placement: 89%
Average Starting Salary: $45,076
Employers Who Frequently Hire Grads: Hinshaw & Culbertson, Cook County State's Attorney, Clausen Miller, City of Chicago Law Department
State for Bar Exam: IL
Pass Rate for First-Time Bar: 79%

LEWIS AND CLARK COLLEGE
Northwestern School of Law

Admissions Contact: Associate Director of Admissions, Shannon Burns
10015 SW Terwilliger Boulevard, Portland, OR 97219
Admissions Phone: 503-768-6613 • Admissions Fax: 503-768-6793
Admissions E-mail: lawadmss@lclark.edu • Web Address: law.lclark.edu

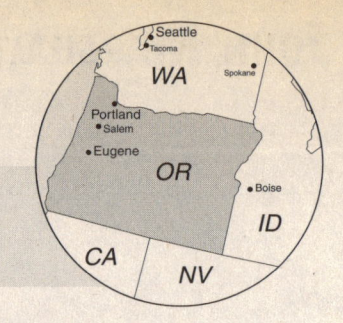

INSTITUTIONAL INFORMATION
Public/Private: Private
Student/Faculty Ratio: 13:1
Total Faculty: 84
% Part Time: 35
% Female: 32
% Minority: 5

PROGRAMS
Academic Specialties: We have a top-ranked Environmental and Natural Resources program, as well as strong programs and certificates in Business Law, Tax Law, and Criminal Law; a respected specialty in Intellectual Property; and a curriculum that supports specialization in several other subject areas, including but not limited to Tort Litigation, Public Interest Law, Family Law, Children's Rights, Real Estate Transactions, Employment Law, Commercial Law, Corporation Securities Law, Government Services, Labor Law, and Property.
Advanced Degrees Offered: LLM Environmental and Natural Resources (12 to 18 months)
Grading System: A+ to F (4.3–0.0)
Clinical Program Required? No
Clinical Program Description: We have a live client clinic in downtown Portland, clinical internship seminars in specific subject areas, summer and full-semester externships, and an environmental practicum. The live clinic offers experience in law, employment, debtor/creditor, small business, tax, landlord/tenant, and domestic violence.
Legal Writing Course Requirements? Yes
Legal Writing Description: Legal Analysis and Writing is required for first-year students. This year-long course includes a number of research and drafting assignments, including an appellate brief and a moot court argument.
Legal Methods Course Requirements? Yes
Legal Methods Description: See Legal Writing.
Legal Research Course Requirements? Yes
Legal Research Description: See Legal Writing.
Moot Court Requirement? No
Public Interest Law Requirement? No
Academic Journals: *Environmental Law Review, The Journal of Small and Emerging Business Law, Animal Law Journal, International Legal Perspectives*

STUDENT INFORMATION
Enrollment of Law School: 711
% Out of State: 65
% Male/Female: 49/51
% Full Time: 72
% Full Time That Are International: 2
% Minority: 17
Average Age of Entering Class: 27

RESEARCH FACILITIES
School-Supported Research Centers: Boley Law Library, U.S. Patent Trademark Depository, Pearl Environmental Law Library, Johnson Public Land Law Collection

EXPENSES/FINANCIAL AID
Annual Tuition: $23,196
Room and Board (Off Campus): $9,000
Books and Supplies: $800
Financial Aid Application Deadline: 3/2
Average Grant: $8,873
Average Loan: $21,104
% of Aid That Is Merit-Based: 18
% Receiving Some Sort of Aid: 90
Average Total Aid Package: $20,632
Average Debt: $66,022

ADMISSIONS INFORMATION
Application Fee: $50
Regular Application Deadline: 3/1
Regular Notification: Rolling
LSDAS Accepted? Yes
Average GPA: 3.4
Range of GPA: 3.2–3.7
Average LSAT: 160
Range of LSAT: 156–163
Transfer Students Accepted? Yes
Other Schools to Which Students Applied: University of Oregon, University of Washington, Willamette University, University of Colorado
Number of Applications Received: 2,268
Number of Applicants Accepted: 830
Number of Applicants Enrolled: 228

INTERNATIONAL STUDENTS
TOEFL Recommended for International Students? Yes
Minimum TOEFL: 600 (250 computer)

EMPLOYMENT INFORMATION

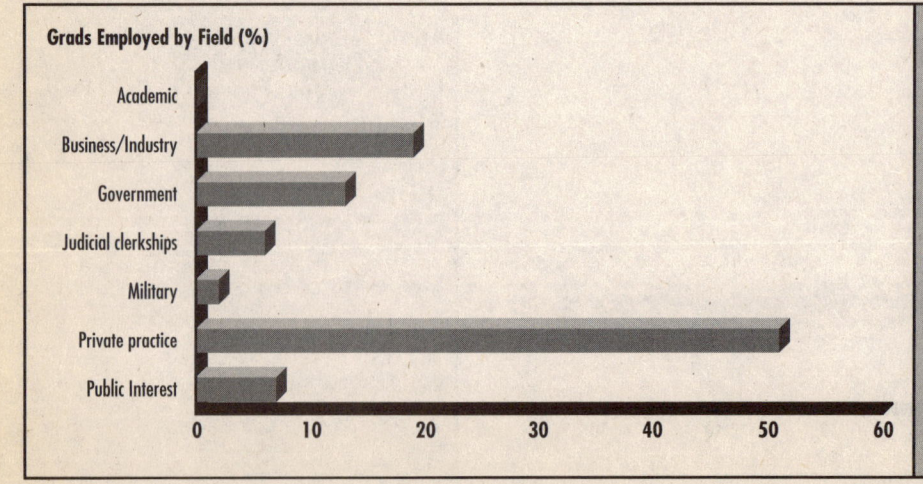

Grads Employed by Field (%)

Field	%
Academic	~0
Business/Industry	~20
Government	~15
Judicial clerkships	~12
Military	~0
Private practice	~52
Public Interest	~7

Rate of Placement: 94%
Average Starting Salary: $58,413
Employers Who Frequently Hire Grads: Numerous small and medium-size firms; State government (Oregon, Washington, Idaho, Alaska); Multnomah, Washington, and Clackamas Counties; United States Government; state and federal judiciary; Stoel Rives LLP; Schwabe Williamson
Prominent Alumni: Earl Blumenauer, U.S. Representative; Heidi Heitkamp, former Attorney General of North Dakota and 2000 Governor nominee; Hon. Robert E. Jones, U.S. District Court for the District of Oregon; Wayne Perry, CEO, Edge Wireless; Isao Tsuruta, Senior VP, AEON (USA), Inc.
State for Bar Exam: OR, CA, WA
Pass Rate for First-Time Bar: 73%

LINCOLN LAW SCHOOL OF SACRAMENTO

Admissions Contact: Registrar, Angelia Harlow
3140 J Street, Sacramento, CA 95816
Admissions Phone: 916-446-1275 • Admissions Fax: 916-446-5641
Admissions E-mail: lincolnlaw@lincolnlaw.edu • Web Address: www.lincolnlaw.edu

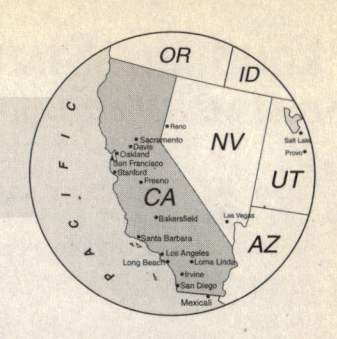

INSTITUTIONAL INFORMATION
Public/Private: Private
Student/Faculty Ratio: 50:1
Total Faculty: 25
% Part Time: 100
% Female: 20
% Minority: 10

PROGRAMS
Academic Specialties: Civil Procedure, Constitutional Law, Corporation Securities Law, Criminal Law, Environmental Law, Government Services, Intellectual Property Law, Labor Law, Legal History, Legal Philosophy, Property, Taxation; all faculty members teach in their field of expertise
Advanced Degrees Offered: JD (4 years)
Grading System: 4.0 scale
Clinical Program Required? No
Legal Writing Course Requirements? Yes
Legal Writing Description: 2 semesters required for first-year students
Legal Methods Course Requirements? Yes
Legal Methods Description: Writing Law School Exams (2 semesters)
Legal Research Course Requirements? Yes
Legal Research Description: 1 semester required for second-year students
Moot Court Requirement? Yes
Moot Court Description: Summer semester required for second-year students
Public Interest Law Requirement? No

STUDENT INFORMATION
Enrollment of Law School: 275
% Male/Female: 100/0
Average Age of Entering Class: 35

RESEARCH FACILITIES
Research Resources Available: Lexis/Nexis

EXPENSES/FINANCIAL AID
Annual Tuition: $6,000
Room and Board (Off Campus): $6,000
Books and Supplies: $500
Financial Aid Application Deadline: 6/1
Average Grant: $500
Average Loan: $10,000
% of Aid That Is Merit-Based: 2
% Receiving Some Sort of Aid: 25
Average Total Aid Package: $5,000
Average Debt: $10,500
Tuition Per Credit: $330
Fees Per Credit: $25

ADMISSIONS INFORMATION
Application Fee: $30
Regular Application Deadline: Rolling
Regular Notification: Rolling
LSDAS Accepted? Yes
Average GPA: 2.8
Range of GPA: 2.1–4.0
Average LSAT: 145
Transfer Students Accepted? Yes
Number of Applications Received: 150
Number of Applicants Accepted: 105
Number of Applicants Enrolled: 95

INTERNATIONAL STUDENTS
TOEFL Recommended for International Students? Yes

EMPLOYMENT INFORMATION

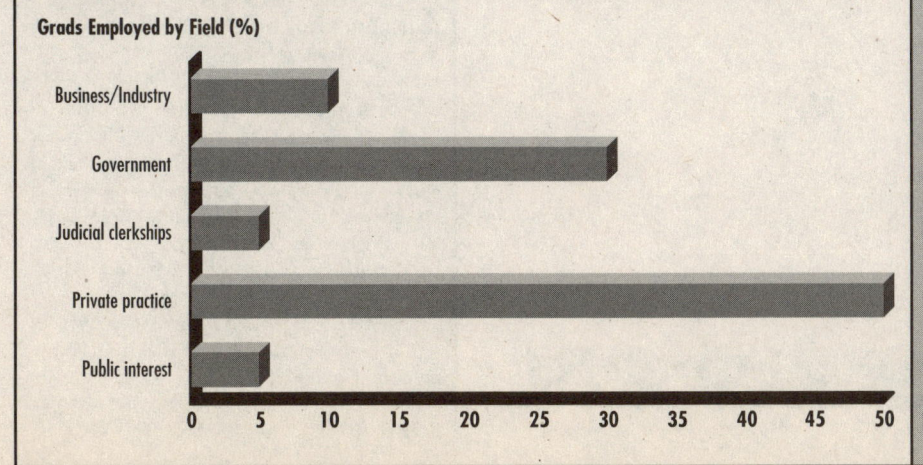

Grads Employed by Field (%)
- Business/Industry: 10
- Government: 30
- Judicial clerkships: 5
- Private practice: 50
- Public interest: 5

Rate of Placement: 80%
Average Starting Salary: $40,000
Employers Who Frequently Hire Grads: District Attorney's Office; Attorney General's Office; Public Defender's Office
Prominent Alumni: Jan Scully, District Attorney, Sacramento County; Brad Fenocchio, District Attorney, Placer County; Robert Holzapfel, District Attorney, Glenn County; Hon. Gerald Bakarich, Judge, Sacramento County Superior Court; Hon. Sue Harlan, Judge, Amador County Superior Court
State for Bar Exam: CA
Pass Rate for First-Time Bar: 60%

SCHOOL PROFILES • 151

LOUISIANA STATE UNIVERSITY
Paul M. Hebert Law Center

Admissions Contact: Director of Admissions/Student Affairs, Michele Forbes
102 Law Center, Baton Rouge, LA 70803
Admissions Phone: 225-578-8646 • Admissions Fax: 225-578-8647
Admissions E-mail: admissions@law.lsu.edu • Web Address: www.law.lsu.edu

INSTITUTIONAL INFORMATION
Public/Private: Public
Student/Faculty Ratio: 20:1
Total Faculty: 60
% Part Time: 47
% Female: 10
% Minority: 5

PROGRAMS
Academic Specialties: The faculty is particularly strong in the areas of Civil Law and International Law. The curriculum is rich in Civil Law offerings.
Advanced Degrees Offered: LLM (1 year), MCL (1 year)
Combined Degrees Offered: JD/MPA (3 years), JD/MBA (4 years)
Grading System: 4.0 scale; A (82–89), A (76–81), B (65–75), C (55–64), D, F
Clinical Program Required? Yes
Clinical Program Description: Trial Advocacy, Appellate Advocacy
Legal Writing Course Requirements? No
Legal Methods Course Requirements? Yes
Legal Methods Description: First year, 2 semesters, 1 hour per week
Legal Research Course Requirements? No
Moot Court Requirement? No
Public Interest Law Requirement? No

STUDENT INFORMATION
Enrollment of Law School: 637
% Out of State: 11
% Male/Female: 54/46
% Full Time: 100
% Full Time That Are International: 1
% Minority: 10

RESEARCH FACILITIES
School-Supported Research Centers: Center of Civil Law Studies

EXPENSES/FINANCIAL AID
Annual Tuition (Residents/Nonresidents): $6,711/$12,552
Room and Board (On/Off Campus): $10,550/$18,950
Books and Supplies: $1,500
Average Grant: $4,729
% of Aid That Is Merit-Based: 22
% Receiving Some Sort of Aid: 24

ADMISSIONS INFORMATION
Application Fee: $25
Regular Application Deadline: 2/2
Regular Notification: 1/2
LSDAS Accepted? Yes
Average GPA: 3.3
Range of GPA: 3.1–3.5
Average LSAT: 153
Range of LSAT: 149–156
Transfer Students Accepted? Yes
Number of Applications Received: 998
Number of Applicants Accepted: 553
Number of Applicants Enrolled: 261

INTERNATIONAL STUDENTS
TOEFL Required of International Students? Yes
Minimum TOEFL: 600 (250 computer)

EMPLOYMENT INFORMATION

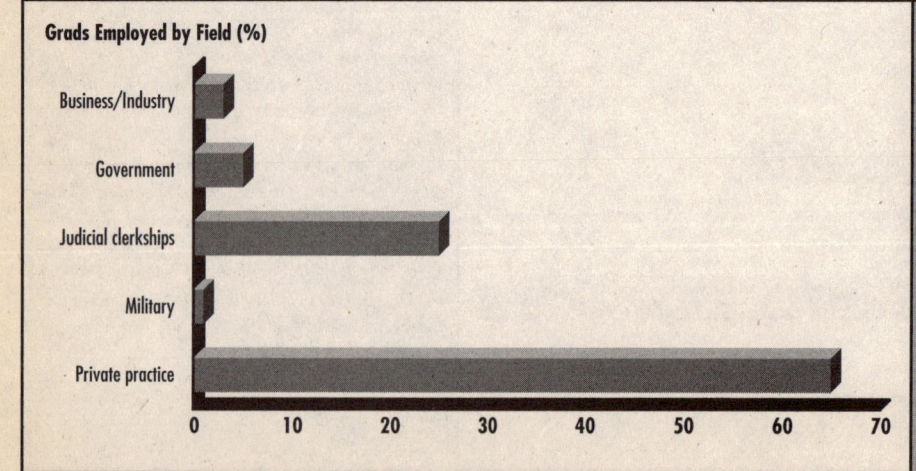

Grads Employed by Field (%)
- Business/Industry
- Government
- Judicial clerkships
- Military
- Private practice

Rate of Placement: 99%
Average Starting Salary: $49,195
Employers Who Frequently Hire Grads: Adams & Reese; Baker & Hostetler; Breazeale Sachse & Wilson; Phelps Dunbar; McGinchey Stafford Lang; Taylor Porter Brooks & Phillips; Stone Pigman; Vinson & Elkins; Chaffe McCall Phillips Toler & Sarpy; Cook Yancey King & Galloway; Correro Fishman Haygood Phelps Weiss; Courtenay Forstall Hunter & Fontana; Cox & Smith; Crawford & Lewis; Deutsch Kerrigan & Stiles; Fisher & Phillips; Jackson & Walker; Jenkins & Gilchrist; Jones Walker Waechter Poitevent Carrerre; Kantrow Spaht Weaver & Blitzer
State for Bar Exam: LA
Pass Rate for First-Time Bar: 89%

LOYOLA MARYMOUNT UNIVERSITY
Loyola Law School

Admissions Contact: *Assistant Director of Admissions, Betty Vu*
919 Albany Street, Los Angeles, CA 90015
Admissions Phone: 213-736-1180 • Admissions Fax: 213-736-6523
Admissions E-mail: admissions@lls.edu • Web Address: www.lls.edu

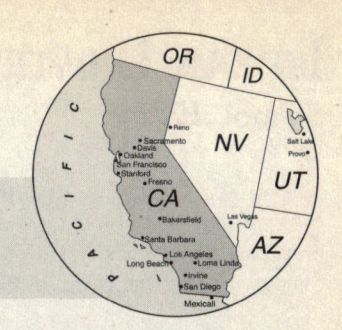

INSTITUTIONAL INFORMATION
Public/Private: Private
Student/Faculty Ratio: 17:1
Total Faculty: 134
% Part Time: 69
% Female: 46
% Minority: 14

PROGRAMS
Academic Specialties: International and Comparative Law, Law and Social Policy, Legal Skills and Litigation, Jurisprudence, Entertainment/Intellectual Property, Civil Procedure, Commercial Law, Constitutional Law, Corporation Securities Law, Criminal Law, Environmental Law, Government Services, Human Rights Law, Labor Law, Legal History, Legal Philosophy, Property, Taxation
Advanced Degrees Offered: LLM Taxation (1 year full time, 3 years part time)
Combined Degrees Offered: JD/MBA (4 years)
Clinical Program Required? No
Clinical Program Description: Business and Commercial, Civil Practice—Public Interest, Trial Advocacy, Judicial Administration, State and Local Government, Mediation, Entertainment Law
Legal Writing Course Requirements? No
Legal Methods Course Requirements? Yes
Legal Methods Description: This course teaches students the basics of legal research and writing. Students are divided into small sections. Research topics covered include ethical obligations to research, court structure, stare decisis, case reporting and precedent, digests, state and federal statutes, administrative law, periodicals, encyclopedias and treatises, citations form, research strategies, and computerized legal research. Students learn the fundamentals of drafting objective and persuasive legal documents. Students will prepare an office memorandum, a brief or memorandum of points and authorities, and other written work.
Legal Research Course Requirements? No
Moot Court Requirement? No
Public Interest Law Requirement? No
Academic Journals: *Loyola of Los Angeles Law Review, Loyola of Los Angeles Entertainment Law Review, Loyola of Los Angeles International Law Review*

STUDENT INFORMATION
Enrollment of Law School: 1,351
% Male/Female: 49/51
% Full Time: 75
% Minority: 39

EXPENSES/FINANCIAL AID
Annual Tuition: $26,546
Room and Board (Off Campus): $9,405
Books and Supplies: $683
Financial Aid Application Deadline: 3/3
Average Grant: $19,000
Average Loan: $26,575
Average Debt: $83,779

ADMISSIONS INFORMATION
Application Fee: $50
Regular Application Deadline: Rolling
Regular Notification: Rolling
LSDAS Accepted? Yes
Average GPA: 3.3
Range of GPA: 3.1–3.6
Average LSAT: 159
Range of LSAT: 157–162
Transfer Students Accepted? Yes
Other Admissions Factors Considered: Undergraduate record, LSAT score, personal statement, letters of reccomendation, community/extracurricular involvement, work experience
Number of Applications Received: 3,379
Number of Applicants Accepted: 1,036
Number of Applicants Enrolled: 350

INTERNATIONAL STUDENTS
TOEFL Required of International Students? Yes
Minimum TOEFL: 600 (250 computer)

EMPLOYMENT INFORMATION

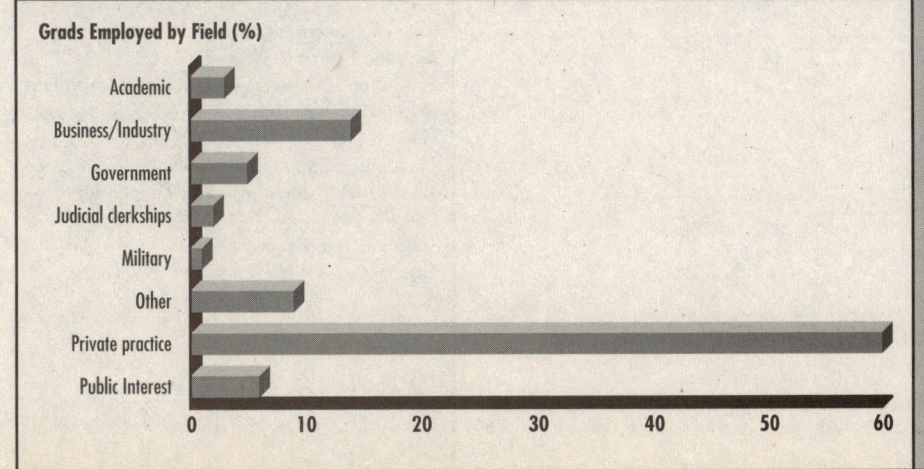

Grads Employed by Field (%)
- Academic
- Business/Industry
- Government
- Judicial clerkships
- Military
- Other
- Private practice
- Public Interest

Rate of Placement: 95%
Average Starting Salary: $80,152
Employers Who Frequently Hire Grads: O'Melveny & Myers; Manatt, Phelps & Phillips; CA Attorney General; Los Angeles District Attorney; Dependency Court Legal Services; Skadden, Arps, Slate, Meagher & Flom; Legal Aid Foundation of L.A.; Paul Hastings; Jones Day Reavis & Pogue; Brobeck, Phleger & Harrison; Shepherd, Mullin, Richter & Hampton; Gibson, Dunn & Crutcher

LOYOLA UNIVERSITY CHICAGO
School of Law

Admissions Contact: Office of Admission and Financial Assistance
1 East Pearson, 4th Floor, Chicago, IL 60611
Admissions Phone: 312-915-7170 • Admissions Fax: 312-915-7906
Admissions E-mail: law-admissions@luc.edu • Web Address: www.luc.edu/schools/law

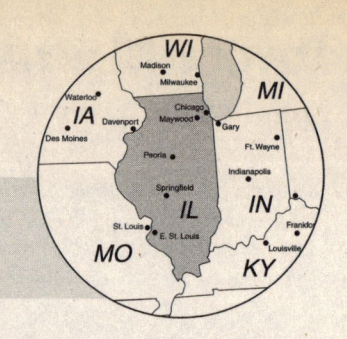

INSTITUTIONAL INFORMATION
Public/Private: Private
Affiliation: Roman Catholic
Student/Faculty Ratio: 15:1
Total Faculty: 121
% Part Time: 76
% Female: 44
% Minority: 7

PROGRAMS
Academic Specialties: Health Law, Child and Family Law, Litigation, Corporation Securities Law, Intellectual Property Law, International Law, Labor Law, Taxation
Advanced Degrees Offered: MJ (22 credits), LLM (24 credits), SJD (2 years full time)
Combined Degrees Offered: JD/MBA, JD/MSW, JD/HRIR, JD/MA Political Science (all 4 years)
Grading System: Letter and numerical system on a 4.0 scale
Clinical Program Required? No
Clinical Program Description: Community Law, Tax Law, Child and Family Law, Business Law, Elder Law
Legal Writing Course Requirements? Yes
Legal Writing Description: 3 semesters (2 semesters in Illinois, third semester Advocacy)
Legal Methods Course Requirements? No
Legal Research Course Requirements? Yes
Legal Research Description: 1 semester
Moot Court Requirement? Yes
Moot Court Description: 1 semester, including intraschool competition

Public Interest Law Requirement? No
Academic Journals: *Law Journal, Consumer Law Review, Annals of Health Law, Public Interest Law Reporter, Child Rights Journal, Forum on International Law*

STUDENT INFORMATION
Enrollment of Law School: 947
% Out of State: 34
% Male/Female: 48/52
% Full Time: 60
% Full Time That Are International: 1
% Minority: 21
Average Age of Entering Class: 26

RESEARCH FACILITIES
Research Resources Available: Free home Internet access via the University. Westlaw and Lexis available for home use for a small fee. All journals and publications have access to dedicated computer resource and high-end printing resources. Freestanding general-access computer stations will attach printers throughout the Law Library. Freestanding general-access kiosk computers throughout the Law School. Free networked laser printing throughout the school and Law Library.
School-Supported Research Centers: Gryphon Project, Child Law Computer Resource Center, Community Law Computer Resource Center, Health Law Institute Computer Resources, Tax Clinic Computer Resource Center, Pro Bono Students America, National Institute of Trail Advocacy

EXPENSES/FINANCIAL AID
Annual Tuition: $25,223
Room and Board (Off Campus): $13,240
Books and Supplies: $900
Financial Aid Application Deadline: 3/1
Average Grant: $6,900
Average Loan: $18,500
% of Aid That Is Merit-Based: 41
% Receiving Some Sort of Aid: 90
Average Total Aid Package: $24,200
Average Debt: $60,000
Tuition Per Credit: $863

ADMISSIONS INFORMATION
Application Fee: $50
Regular Application Deadline: 4/1
Regular Notification: Rolling
LSDAS Accepted? Yes
Average GPA: 3.3
Range of GPA: 3.1–3.5
Average LSAT: 160
Range of LSAT: 157–161
Transfer Students Accepted? Yes
Other Schools to Which Students Applied: American University, DePaul University, Illinois Institute of Technology, Northwestern University, University of Illinois, George Washington University, Boston University
Other Admissions Factors Considered: Work experience, rigor of academic curriculum, ability to overcome hardships or disabilities
Number of Applications Received: 3,235
Number of Applicants Accepted: 791
Number of Applicants Enrolled: 177

INTERNATIONAL STUDENTS
TOEFL Required of International Students? Yes
Minimum TOEFL: 650 (280 computer)

EMPLOYMENT INFORMATION

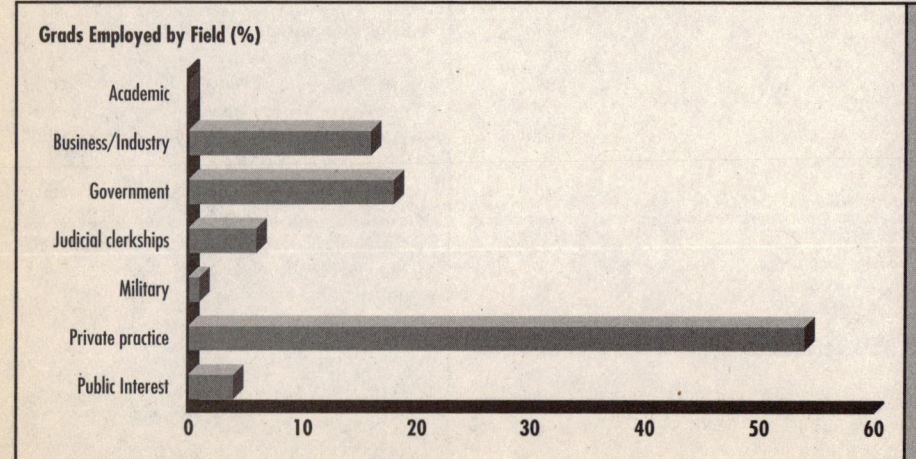

Grads Employed by Field (%)
- Academic
- Business/Industry
- Government
- Judicial clerkships
- Military
- Private practice
- Public Interest

Rate of Placement: 95%
Average Starting Salary: $73,162
Prominent Alumni: Lisa Madigan, Attorney General of Illinois; Henry Hyde, U.S. Senator; Philip Corboy, Attorney; Jeff Jacobs, former President, Harpo Entertainment; Mary Ann McMorrow, Chief Justice, Illinois Supreme Court
State for Bar Exam: IL
Pass Rate for First-Time Bar: 87%

154 • COMPLETE BOOK OF LAW SCHOOLS

LOYOLA UNIVERSITY NEW ORLEANS
School of Law

Admissions Contact: Dean of Admissions, K. Michele Allison-Davis
7214 Saint Charles Avenue, Box 904, New Orleans, LA 70118
Admissions Phone: 504-861-5575 • Admissions Fax: 504-861-5772
Admissions E-mail: ladmit@loyno.edu • Web Address: law.loyno.edu

INSTITUTIONAL INFORMATION
Public/Private: Private
Affiliation: Roman Catholic
Student/Faculty Ratio: 21:1
Total Faculty: 85
% Part Time: 69
% Female: 25
% Minority: 1

PROGRAMS
Academic Specialties: Our faculty members have a variety of specialties, including Civil Law, Tax Law, Reproductive Law Issues, Public Interest Law, Evidence, and International Law.
Combined Degrees Offered: JD/MBA; JD/M Religious Studies, Communications, or Urban and Regional Planning; JD/MPA (all add 1 year to the JD program)
Grading System: A, B+, B, C+, C, D+, D, F
Clinical Program Required? No
Clinical Program Description: Criminal Prosecution and Defense, Immigration, Civil, Juvenile, Domestic, Civil Rights
Legal Writing Course Requirements? Yes
Legal Writing Description: Legal Research and Writing required in the fall semester of the first year for 2 credits.
Legal Methods Course Requirements? Yes
Legal Methods Description: See Legal Writing.
Legal Research Course Requirements? Yes
Legal Research Description: See Legal Writing.
Moot Court Requirement? Yes
Moot Court Description: First year, spring semester, 2 credits. Appellate briefs are submitted and oral arguments presented for grades.
Public Interest Law Requirement? Yes
Public Interest Law Description: Students must take the Law and Poverty course; they may substitute participation in the Pro Bono project, which requires 50 hours of pro bono work, or enrollment in the Street Law course.
Academic Journals: *Loyola Law Review, Journal of Public Interest Law, Maritime Law Journal*

STUDENT INFORMATION
Enrollment of Law School: 854
% Out of State: 33
% Male/Female: 43/57
% Full Time: 73
% Full Time That Are International: 1
% Minority: 20
Average Age of Entering Class: 25

EXPENSES/FINANCIAL AID
Annual Tuition: $22,568
Room and Board (On/Off Campus): $5,000/$8,600
Books and Supplies: $1,000
Average Grant: $8,591
Average Loan: $21,099
% of Aid That Is Merit-Based: 41
Average Debt: $62,863
Tuition Per Credit: $728
Fees Per Credit: $642

ADMISSIONS INFORMATION
Application Fee: $40
Regular Application Deadline: Rolling
Regular Notification: Rolling
LSDAS Accepted? Yes
Average GPA: 3.2
Range of GPA: 2.9–3.4
Average LSAT: 153
Range of LSAT: 150–155
Transfer Students Accepted? Yes
Other Schools to Which Students Applied: American University, Florida State University, Louisiana State University, Tulane University, University of Denver, University of Miami
Other Admissions Factors Considered: Graduate school GPA, date of undergraduate degree, age, undergraduate major, undergraduate institution, diversity, letters of recommendation, work experience, explanation of multiple LSAT scores and below-par GPA
Number of Applications Received: 2,030
Number of Applicants Accepted: 757
Number of Applicants Enrolled: 300

INTERNATIONAL STUDENTS
TOEFL Recommended for International Students? Yes
Minimum TOEFL: 580 (237 computer)

EMPLOYMENT INFORMATION

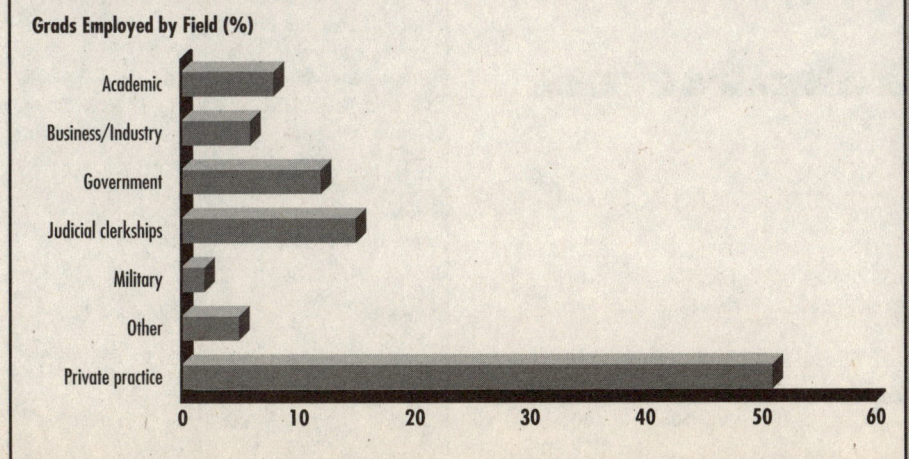

Grads Employed by Field (%)
- Academic: ~3
- Business/Industry: ~7
- Government: ~15
- Judicial clerkships: ~15
- Military: ~1
- Other: ~5
- Private practice: ~52

Rate of Placement: 95%
Employers Who Frequently Hire Grads: Private firms, judiciary, government agencies
Prominent Alumni: Pascal Calogero, Chief Justice, Louisiana Supreme Court; Moon Landrieu, Secretary of HUD and Mayor of New Orleans; Carl Stewart, U.S. 5th Circuit Court of Appeals; Cassandra Chandler, Director of Training, FBI; Paul Pastorek, Chief Counsel, NASA
State for Bar Exam: LA
Pass Rate for First-Time Bar: 65%

MARQUETTE UNIVERSITY
Law School

Admissions Contact: Assistant Dean for Admissions, Edward A. Kawczynski Jr.
1103 West Wisconsin Avenue, Milwaukee, WI 53201
Admissions Phone: 414-288-6767 • Admissions Fax: 414-288-0676
Admissions E-mail: law.admission@marquette.edu • Web Address: www.marquette.edu/law

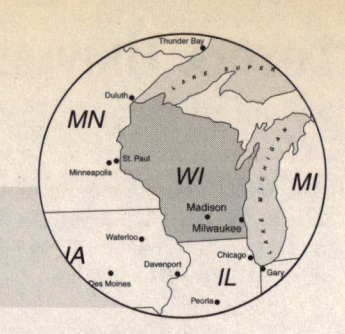

INSTITUTIONAL INFORMATION
Public/Private: Private
Affiliation: Roman Catholic
Student/Faculty Ratio: 15:1
Total Faculty: 35
% Female: 30
% Minority: 3

PROGRAMS
Academic Specialties: Intellectual Property Law, Sports Law, Criminal Law, Civil Litigation, Alternative Dispute Resolution, Civil Procedure, Commercial Law, Constitutional Law, Corporation Securities Law, Environmental Law, Government Services, International Law, Labor Law, Legal History, Property, Taxation
Combined Degrees Offered: JD/MBA, JD/MA Political Science, JD/MA International Relations, JD/MA Bioethics (all 4-year programs)
Grading System: A, B, C, D, F
Clinical Program Required? No
Legal Writing Course Requirements? Yes
Legal Writing Description: Communication skills are emphasized in all core classes. In addition, all students must take specific introductory courses in legal writing, research, and communication.
Legal Methods Course Requirements? Yes
Legal Methods Description: See Legal Writing; students must also take specially designated courses to meet advanced research and advanced oral communication requirements.
Legal Research Course Requirements? Yes
Legal Research Description: Advanced research required
Moot Court Requirement? No
Public Interest Law Requirement? No
Academic Journals: *Marquette Law Review, Intellectual Property Law Review, Sports Law Review, Elder's Advisor*

STUDENT INFORMATION
Enrollment of Law School: 587
% Out of State: 38
% Male/Female: 55/45
% Full Time: 81
% Full Time That Are International: 0
% Minority: 11
Average Age of Entering Class: 25

RESEARCH FACILITIES
Research Resources Available: Westlaw, Lexis/Nexis

EXPENSES/FINANCIAL AID
Annual Tuition: $21,550
Room and Board: $8,290
Books and Supplies: $1,065
Financial Aid Application Deadline: 3/1
Average Grant: $10,000
Average Loan: $30,000
% of Aid That Is Merit-Based: 25
% Receiving Some Sort of Aid: 90
Average Total Aid Package: $21,550
Average Debt: $62,000
Tuition Per Credit: $895

ADMISSIONS INFORMATION
Application Fee: $40
Regular Application Deadline: 4/1
Regular Notification: Rolling
LSDAS Accepted? Yes
Average GPA: 3.3
Range of GPA: 2.9–3.5
Average LSAT: 155
Range of LSAT: 152–157
Transfer Students Accepted? Yes
Other Schools to Which Students Applied: University of Wisconsin—Madison, Loyola University Chicago, DePaul University, Hamline University
Other Admissions Factors Considered: Cultural, educational, and experiential diversity
Number of Applications Received: 984
Number of Applicants Accepted: 490
Number of Applicants Enrolled: 151

INTERNATIONAL STUDENTS
TOEFL Required of International Students? Yes
Minimum TOEFL: 250

EMPLOYMENT INFORMATION

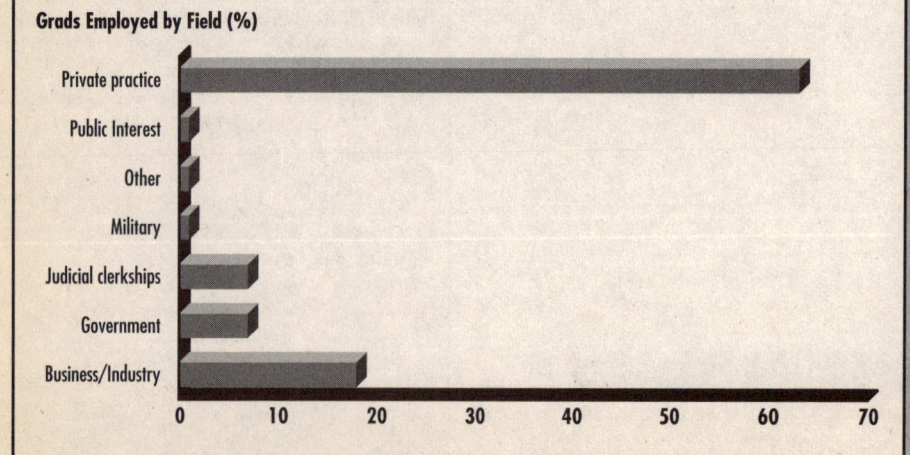

Grads Employed by Field (%)
- Private practice: ~64
- Public Interest: ~2
- Other: ~3
- Military: ~2
- Judicial clerkships: ~5
- Government: ~7
- Business/Industry: ~17

Rate of Placement: 95%
Average Starting Salary: $58,500
Employers Who Frequently Hire Grads: Michael, Best & Friedrich; Quarles & Brady; Godfrey & Kahn; Von Briesen, Purtell & Roport; Foley & Lardner; Davis & Kualthay, SC; Whyte, Hirschboeck, Dudek.
State for Bar Exam: WI
Pass Rate for First-Time Bar: 100%

MERCER UNIVERSITY
Walter F. George School of Law

Admissions Contact: Assistant Dean of Admissions and Financial Aid, Marilyn E. Sutton
1021 Georgia Avenue, Macon, GA 31207
Admissions Phone: 478-301-2605 • Admissions Fax: 478-301-2989
Admissions E-mail: martin_sv@mercer.edu • Web Address: www.law.mercer.edu

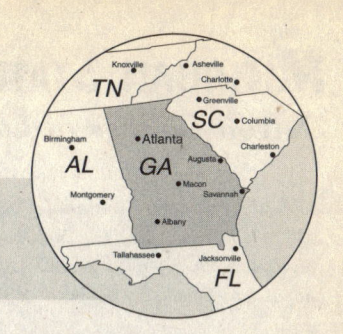

INSTITUTIONAL INFORMATION
Public/Private: Private
Affiliation: Baptist
Student/Faculty Ratio: 16:1
Total Faculty: 52
% Part Time: 37
% Female: 27
% Minority: 10

PROGRAMS
Academic Specialties: Our curriculum is designed to provide an innovative progression toward the practice of law. In 1996, Mercer received the Gambrell Professionalism Award from the ABA because of the depth and excellence of the curriculum and its commitment to professionalism. Specialties include Civil Procedure, Commercial Law, Constitutional Law, Corporation Securities Law, Criminal Law, Environmental Law, Government Services, Intellectual Property Law, International Law, Labor Law, Legal History, Property, and Taxation.
Advanced Degrees Offered: JD (3 years)
Combined Degrees Offered: JD/MBA (4 years)
Grading System: A (90–99), A (82–89), B (76–81), C (70–75), D (65–69)
Clinical Program Required? No
Legal Writing Course Requirements? Yes
Legal Writing Description: 3-year, 4-semester series of writing courses that progress in difficulty and rigor as the student moves toward excellence in writing for legal practice
Legal Methods Course Requirements? Yes
Legal Methods Description: First year, fall semester. Legal Analysis covers formulating a rule of law from one or more legal authorities, placing the rule in a rule structure, analyzing the application of that rule to a set of facts, and organizing a written legal discussion of that analysis.
Legal Research Course Requirements? Yes
Legal Research Description: Introduction to Legal Research is a 1-credit, graded course that meets during the first year. Taught by professional librarians, it covers print and electronic formats used for researching state and federal judicial, administrative, statutory, and secondary sources. Training in legal research continues throughout the Legal Writing program.
Moot Court Requirement? Yes
Moot Court Description: During the fall semester of the second year, all students, as part of our Legal Writing program, draft appellate briefs and present oral arguments.
Public Interest Law Requirement? No
Academic Journals: Mercer Law Review, Journal of Southern Legal History

STUDENT INFORMATION
Enrollment of Law School: 439
% Out of State: 35
% Male/Female: 53/47
% Full Time: 99
% Full Time That Are International: 1
% Minority: 15
Average Age of Entering Class: 23

EXPENSES/FINANCIAL AID
Annual Tuition: $22,313
Room and Board (Off Campus): $12,000
Books and Supplies: $1,000
Financial Aid Application Deadline: 4/1
Average Grant: $16,000
Average Loan: $24,000
% of Aid That Is Merit-Based: 20
% Receiving Some Sort of Aid: 85
Average Total Aid Package: $29,000
Average Debt: $68,969
Tuition Per Credit: $930

ADMISSIONS INFORMATION
Application Fee: $50
Regular Application Deadline: 3/15
Regular Notification: Rolling
LSDAS Accepted? Yes
Average GPA: 3.3
Range of GPA: 2.9–3.5
Average LSAT: 153
Range of LSAT: 151–156
Transfer Students Accepted? Yes
Other Schools to Which Students Applied: Emory, Florida State, Georgia State, Samford, University of Georgia, University of South Carolina, Wake Forest
Other Admissions Factors Considered: Letters of recommendation; personal statement; grade trend; military, work, and community service experience; obstacles overcome; writing proficiency
Number of Applications Received: 1,134
Number of Applicants Accepted: 405
Number of Applicants Enrolled: 158

INTERNATIONAL STUDENTS
TOEFL Recommended for International Students? Yes
Minimum TOEFL: 600

EMPLOYMENT INFORMATION

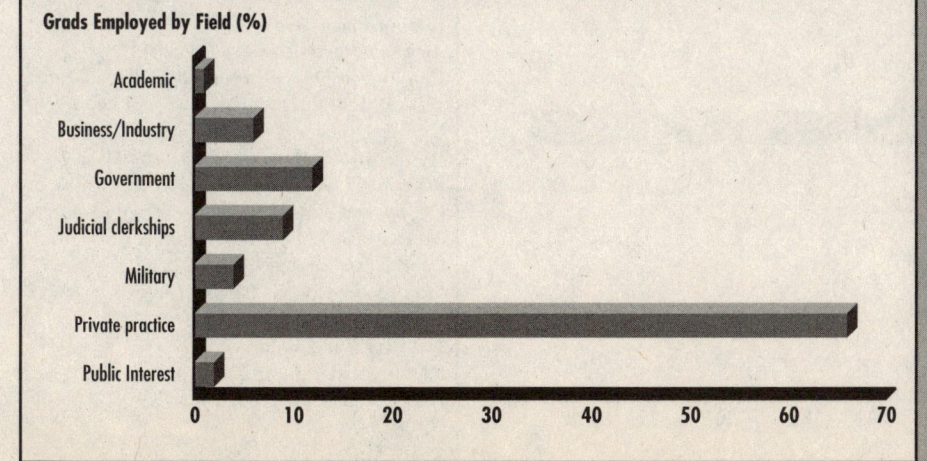

Grads Employed by Field (%)
- Academic
- Business/Industry
- Government
- Judicial clerkships
- Military
- Private practice
- Public Interest

Rate of Placement: 94%
Average Starting Salary: $55,119
Employers Who Frequently Hire Grads: King & Spalding; McKenna, Long, and Aldridge; Moore, Ingram, Johnson & Steele; Martin Snow, LLP; Alston & Bird; James, Bates, Pope, and Spivey
Prominent Alumni: Griffin Bell, former Attorney General; Cathy Cox, Secretary of State, GA; John Oxendine, Insurance Commissioner; Hugh Thompson, Georgia Supreme Court
State for Bar Exam: GA
Pass Rate for First-Time Bar: 84%

MICHIGAN STATE UNIVERSITY
Detroit College of Law

Admissions Contact: Director of Admissions, Andrea Heatley
316 Law Building, East Lansing, MI 48824-1300
Admissions Phone: 517-432-0222 • Admissions Fax: 517-432-0098
Admissions E-mail: law@msu.edu • Web Address: www.dcl.edu

INSTITUTIONAL INFORMATION
Public/Private: Private
Environment: Urban
Schedule: Full time or part time
Student/Faculty Ratio: 23:1
Total Faculty: 30
% Part Time: 40
% Female: 30
% Minority: 2

PROGRAMS
Academic Specialties: 2 concentrations, International Law and Taxation; summer programs in Romania and Ottawa, Canada; joint JD/MBA program
Combined Degrees Offered: JD/MBA (4 years), JD/MPA (4 years), JD/MLIR (4 years), JD/MA (4 years)
Grading System: A (4.0) to F (0)
Clinical Program Required? No
Clinical Program Description: Externships with various courts and government agencies

STUDENT INFORMATION
Enrollment of Law School: 715
% Male/Female: 61/39
% Full Time: 78
% Full Time That Are International: 3
% Minority: 19
Average Age of Entering Class: 28

RESEARCH FACILITIES
Computers/Workstations Available: 70
School-Supported Research Centers: The Michigan State University Library System

EXPENSES/FINANCIAL AID
Annual Tuition: $15,584
Room and Board: $6,364
Books and Supplies: $872
Financial Aid Application Deadline: 6/30
Average Grant: $17,000
Average Loan: $16,925
% of Aid That Is Merit-Based: 7
% Receiving Some Sort of Aid: 80
Average Total Aid Package: $18,300
Average Debt: $59,381
Fees Per Credit: $535

ADMISSIONS INFORMATION
Application Fee: $50
Regular Application Deadline: Rolling
Regular Notification: Rolling
Average GPA: 3.2
Range of GPA: 2.9–3.4
Average LSAT: 152
Range of LSAT: 149–156
Transfer Students Accepted? Yes
Other Schools to Which Students Applied: Wayne State University
Number of Applications Received: 1,055
Number of Applicants Accepted: 701
Number of Applicants Enrolled: 210

INTERNATIONAL STUDENTS
TOEFL Required of International Students? Yes
Minimum TOEFL: 600

EMPLOYMENT INFORMATION

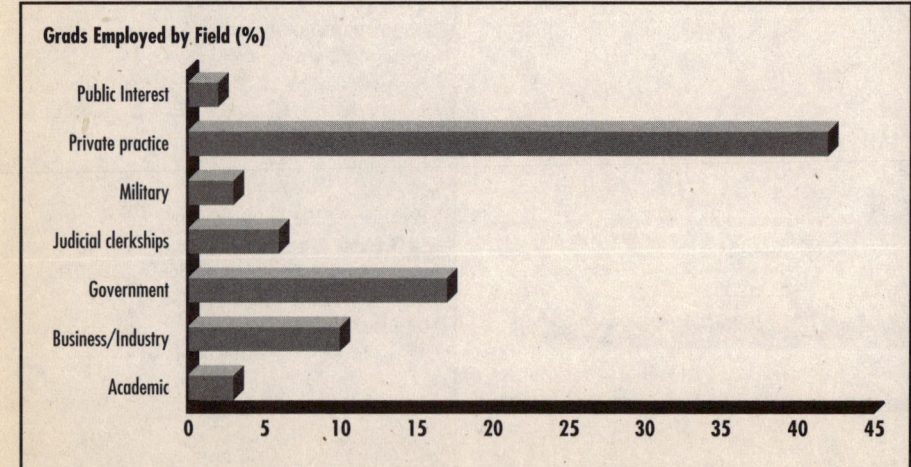

Grads Employed by Field (%)

Field	%
Public Interest	~2
Private practice	~42
Military	~1
Judicial clerkships	~5
Government	~17
Business/Industry	~10
Academic	~3

Rate of Placement: 92%
Average Starting Salary: $43,285
Employers Who Frequently Hire Grads: Clark Hill, PLC; Dykema Gossett, PLLC; Kitch, Drutchas, Wagner and Kenney, PC; Secrest, Wardle, Lynch, Hampton; Truex and Morley
Prominent Alumni: Dennis Archer, mayor of Detroit and former Michigan Supreme Court judge, Hon. Richard Suhrheinrich, judge, U.S. Court of Appeals 6th District Circuit, Michael G. Morris, president and CEO of Consumers Power Company
State for Bar Exam: MI
Number Taking Bar Exam: 194
Pass Rate for First-Time Bar: 76%

Mississippi College
School of Law

Admissions Contact: Director of Admissions, Patricia H. Evans
151 East Griffith Street, Jackson, MS 39201
Admissions Phone: 601-925-7150 • Admissions Fax: 601-925-7185
Admissions E-mail: hweaver@mc.edu • Web Address: www.law.mc.edu

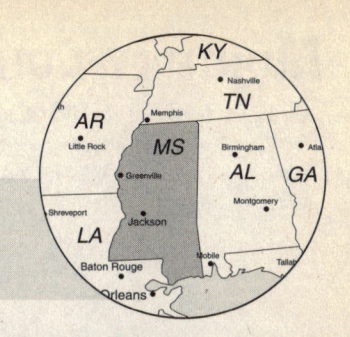

INSTITUTIONAL INFORMATION
Public/Private: Private
Affiliation: Southern Baptist
Student/Faculty Ratio: 18:1
Total Faculty: 36
% Part Time: 17
% Female: 50
% Minority: 7

PROGRAMS
Academic Specialties: The faculty includes nationally recognized experts in Antitrust, Evidence, and Bankruptcy Law. The curriculum emphasizes both substantive law and skills training.
Advanced Degrees Offered: JD (3 years)
Combined Degrees Offered: JD/MBA (4 years)
Grading System: Letter system
Clinical Program Required? No
Legal Writing Course Requirements? No
Legal Methods Course Requirements? Yes
Legal Methods Description: 2 semesters in the first year, upper-level writing requirement
Legal Research Course Requirements? No
Moot Court Requirement? No
Public Interest Law Requirement? No

STUDENT INFORMATION
Enrollment of Law School: 383
% Out of State: 48
% Male/Female: 56/44
% Full Time: 100
% Full Time That Are International: 0
% Minority: 9
Average Age of Entering Class: 26

EXPENSES/FINANCIAL AID
Annual Tuition: $15,600
Room and Board (On/Off Campus): $3,900/$7,400
Books and Supplies: $900
Financial Aid Application Deadline: 5/1
Average Grant: $9,000
Average Loan: $18,500
% of Aid That Is Merit-Based: 25
% Receiving Some Sort of Aid: 93
Average Total Aid Package: $24,000
Average Debt: $55,000
Tuition Per Credit: $499

ADMISSIONS INFORMATION
Application Fee: $40
Regular Application Deadline: Rolling
Regular Notification: Rolling
LSDAS Accepted? Yes
Average GPA: 3.1
Range of GPA: 2.8–3.4
Average LSAT: 149
Range of LSAT: 145–152
Transfer Students Accepted? Yes
Other Admissions Factors Considered: Extracurricular activities, work experience, letters of recommendation
Number of Applications Received: 574
Number of Applicants Accepted: 342
Number of Applicants Enrolled: 143

EMPLOYMENT INFORMATION

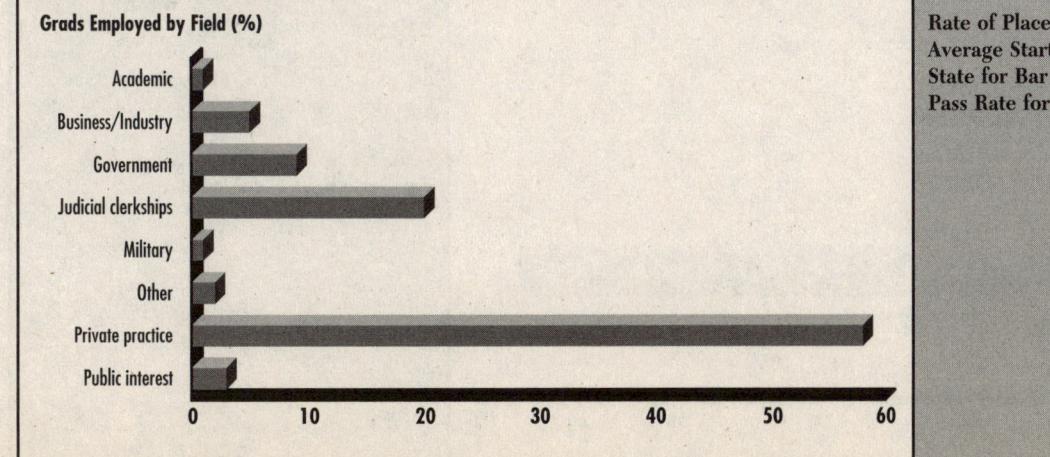

Grads Employed by Field (%)
- Academic: ~1
- Business/Industry: ~5
- Government: ~8
- Judicial clerkships: ~20
- Military: ~2
- Other: ~3
- Private practice: ~58
- Public interest: ~2

Rate of Placement: 92%
Average Starting Salary: $39,171
State for Bar Exam: MS, AL, TN, GA, FL
Pass Rate for First-Time Bar: 85%

MONTEREY COLLEGE OF LAW

Admissions Contact: Director of Admissions and Student Services
404 West Franklin Street, Monterey, CA 93940
Admissions Phone: 831-373-3301 • Admissions Fax: 831-373-0143
Admissions E-mail: wfl@montereylaw.edu • Web Address: www.montereylaw.edu

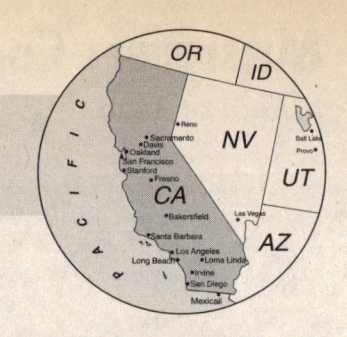

INSTITUTIONAL INFORMATION
Public/Private: Private
Student/Faculty Ratio: 25:1
Total Faculty: 44
% Part Time: 100
% Female: 23
% Minority: 2

PROGRAMS
Academic Specialties: Civil Procedure, Commercial Law, Constitutional Law, Corporation Securities Law, Criminal Law, Environmental Law, Government Services, Human Rights Law, Intellectual Property Law, Property, Taxation; recognizing the special needs of individuals who wish to receive a law degree but cannot attend a full-time program, we provide convenient evening classes taught by practicing attorneys and judges who bring real-world perspective and experiences into the classroom.
Advanced Degrees Offered: JD (4 years evening)
Grading System: Numerical system (0–100)
Clinical Program Required? Yes
Clinical Program Description: Under the supervision of a Clinical Studies professor, students give legal advice to clients in a pro bono legal clinic focusing on small claims issues.
Legal Writing Course Requirements? Yes
Legal Writing Description: 2-semester Legal Writing course in the first year, 2-semester Advanced Legal Writing course in the second year
Legal Methods Course Requirements? Yes
Legal Methods Description: Legal Writing classes are required in the first and second years. In the third and fourth years, they are integrated into the curriculum.
Legal Research Course Requirements? Yes
Legal Research Description: Legal Research is a required course for first-year students. Computer Assisted Legal Research is an elective course available after the student's second year.
Moot Court Requirement? Yes
Moot Court Description: The Heisler Moot Court gives students an opportunity to study and write about constitutional issues. Starting with drafting an appellate brief, the semester culminates in a series of hearings, where local judges hear the students' oral arguments on each side of a current civil liberties issue.
Public Interest Law Requirement? No

STUDENT INFORMATION
Enrollment of Law School: 100
% Male/Female: 100/0
% Minority: 0
Average Age of Entering Class: 37

RESEARCH FACILITIES
Research Resources Available: Monterey Courthouse Law Library, Santa Cruz County Law Library, Salinas Law Library, Watsonville Law Library

EXPENSES/FINANCIAL AID
Average Grant: $750
Average Loan: $5,000
% of Aid That Is Merit-Based: 30
% Receiving Some Sort of Aid: 55
Tuition Per Credit: $400
Fees Per Credit: $70

ADMISSIONS INFORMATION
Application Fee: $75
Regular Application Deadline: 6/2
Regular Notification: 7/31
LSDAS Accepted? No
Average GPA: 3.0
Range of GPA: 2.6–3.5
Average LSAT: 148
Range of LSAT: 140–160
Transfer Students Accepted? Yes
Other Schools to Which Students Applied: Lincoln Law School
Number of Applications Received: 47
Number of Applicants Accepted: 29
Number of Applicants Enrolled: 28

INTERNATIONAL STUDENTS
TOEFL Recommended for International Students? Yes

EMPLOYMENT INFORMATION

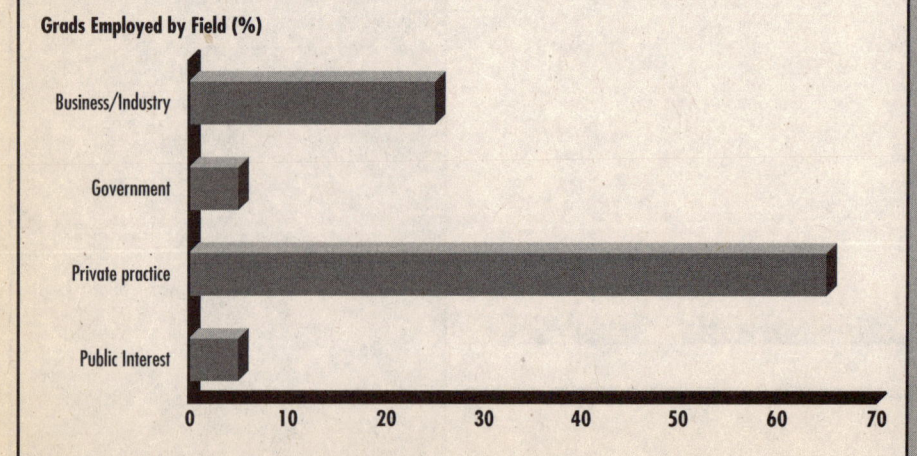

Grads Employed by Field (%)
- Business/Industry: ~25
- Government: ~5
- Private practice: ~65
- Public Interest: ~5

Rate of Placement: 87%
Employers Who Frequently Hire Grads: Governmental offices, public agencies, private law firms, public defender's office, district attorney's office
State for Bar Exam: CA
Pass Rate for First-Time Bar: 54%

NEW COLLEGE OF CALIFORNIA
School of Law

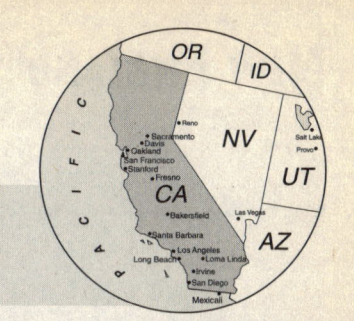

Admissions Contact: Assistant Dean of Admissions, Sabrina Baptiste, JD
50 Fell Street, San Francisco, CA 94102
Admissions Phone: 415-241-1374 • Admissions Fax: 415-241-9525
Admissions E-mail: brina72@aol.com • Web Address: www.newcollege.edu

INSTITUTIONAL INFORMATION
Public/Private: Private
Student/Faculty Ratio: 15:1

PROGRAMS
Academic Specialties: Constitutional Law, Environmental Law, Government Services, Human Rights Law, Labor Law, Property
Grading System: Letter system
Clinical Program Required? No
Legal Writing Course Requirements? Yes
Legal Writing Description: 1 year
Legal Methods Course Requirements? Yes
Legal Methods Description: 1 semester
Legal Research Course Requirements? Yes
Legal Research Description: 1 year
Moot Court Requirement? No
Public Interest Law Requirement? Yes
Public Interest Law Description: 600–800 hours of Public Interest Internship
Academic Journals: *Journal of Public Interest Law*

STUDENT INFORMATION
Enrollment of Law School: 160
% Male/Female: 45/55
% Full Time: 75
% Full Time That Are International: 4
% Minority: 43

EXPENSES/FINANCIAL AID
Annual Tuition: $10,540
Books and Supplies: $400
Average Loan: $18,500

ADMISSIONS INFORMATION
Application Fee: $45
Regular Application Deadline: 5/1
Regular Notification: Rolling
LSDAS Accepted? Yes
Average GPA: 3.0
Range of GPA: 2.0–4.0
Average LSAT: 145
Transfer Students Accepted? Yes
Number of Applications Received: 150
Number of Applicants Accepted: 78
Number of Applicants Enrolled: 58

EMPLOYMENT INFORMATION
State for Bar Exam: CA
Pass Rate for First-Time Bar: 38%

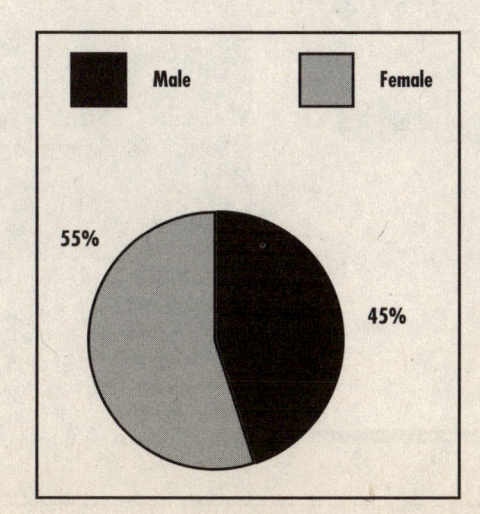

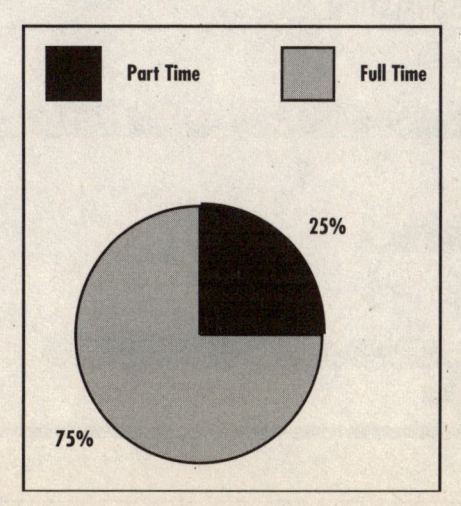

NEW ENGLAND SCHOOL OF LAW

Admissions Contact: Director of Admissions, Pamela Jorgensen
154 Stuart Street, Boston, MA 02116
Admissions Phone: 617-422-7210 • Admissions Fax: 617-422-7200
Admissions E-mail: admit@admin.nesl.edu • Web Address: www.nesl.edu

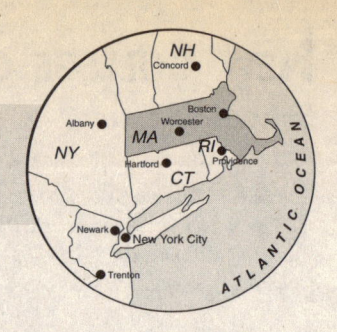

INSTITUTIONAL INFORMATION
Public/Private: Private
Environment: Urban
Academic Calendar: Semester
Schedule: Full time or part time
Student/Faculty Ratio: 20:1
Total Faculty: 93
% Part Time: 60
% Female: 27
% Minority: 8

PROGRAMS
Academic Specialties: International Law, Environmental Law, Business and Tax Law
Grading System: Letter and numerical system on a 4.0 scale
Clinical Program Required? No
Clinical Program Description: The Lawyering Process (Civil Litigation Clinic), The Lawyering Process (Summer Version), The Government Lawyer, Tax Clinic, Administrative Law Clinic, Criminal Procedure II Clinic, Environmental Law Clinic, Family Law Clinic, Health and Hospital Law Clinic
Legal Writing/Methods Course Requirements: There are five major objectives of the Legal Methods program: 1) learning to find and analyze the law and to place the law into a variety of legal formats; 2) learning the legal process from initial client interview through final disposition; 3) learning the relationship between courts and other branches of government; 4) learning how legal doctrines develop and change; and 5) learning to recognize and resolve ethical issues that arise in the practice of law.

STUDENT INFORMATION
Enrollment of Law School: 937
% Male/Female: 48/52
% Full Time: 61
% Full Time That Are International: 1
% Minority: 24
Average Age of Entering Class: 27

RESEARCH FACILITIES
Computers/Workstations Available: 79
School-Supported Research Centers: Memberships: New England Law Library Consortium (NELLCO) provides access to 19 major law libraries in the Northeast. Boston Regional Library System (BRLS) provides research and interlibrary loan service amongst its members—from the largest university library, to mid-size public libraries to small corporate libraries. Bilateral agreements exist between New England and Tufts Health Sciences Library and between New England and Wentworth Institute of Technology Library.

EXPENSES/FINANCIAL AID
Annual Tuition: $15,950
Room and Board (Off Campus): $12,600
Books and Supplies: $850
Financial Aid Application Deadline: 4/15
Average Grant: $5,340
Average Loan: $19,125
% of Aid That Is Merit-Based: 65
% Receiving Some Sort of Aid: 78
Average Total Aid Package: $20,950
Average Debt: $62,870
Tuition Per Credit: $610

ADMISSIONS INFORMATION
Application Fee: $50
Regular Application Deadline: 6/1
Regular Notification: Rolling
LSDAS Accepted? Yes
Range of GPA: 2.7–3.3
Average LSAT: 148
Range of LSAT: 143–153
Transfer Students Accepted? Yes
Other Schools to Which Students Applied: Suffolk University, Boston College, Northeastern University, Boston University, Western New England College, New York Law School, Syracuse University, Quinnipac University School of Law
Number of Applications Received: 2,224
Number of Applicants Accepted: 1,524
Number of Applicants Enrolled: 337

INTERNATIONAL STUDENTS
TOEFL Required of International Students? Yes

EMPLOYMENT INFORMATION

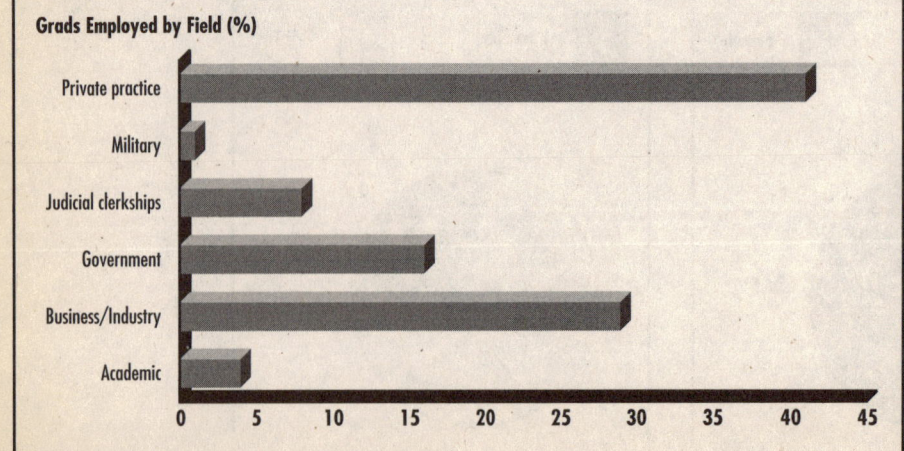

Grads Employed by Field (%)
- Private practice: ~42
- Military: ~1
- Judicial clerkships: ~8
- Government: ~16
- Business/Industry: ~29
- Academic: ~4

Rate of Placement: 89%
Average Starting Salary: $46,287
Employers Who Frequently Hire Grads: A partial list of employers who have hired New England School of Law graduates can be found on our website www.nesl.edu/career/employ.htm
Prominent Alumni: Susan Crawford, judge, U.S. Court of Appeals for the Armed Forces; John Simpson, former director of the Secret Service; Gregory Phillips, presiding justice, Roxbury District Court; Joyce London Alexander, chief U.S. magistrate judge, U.S. District Court for District of Massachusetts; Judge Thomas A. Adams, New York Supreme Court; Joseph Mondello, Republican National Comitteeman for New York

NEW YORK LAW SCHOOL

Admissions Contact: Assistant Dean/Director of Admissions, Thomas Matos
57 Worth Street, New York, NY 10013
Admissions Phone: 212-431-2888 • Admissions Fax: 212-966-1522
Admissions E-mail: admissions@nyls.edu • Web Address: www.nyls.edu

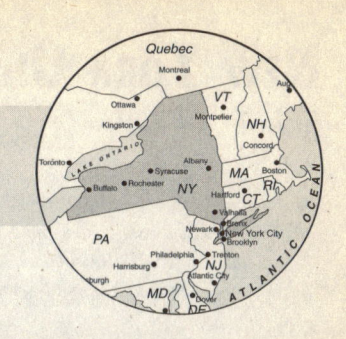

INSTITUTIONAL INFORMATION
Public/Private: Private
Student/Faculty Ratio: 21:1
Total Faculty: 124
% Part Time: 56
% Female: 32
% Minority: 8

PROGRAMS
Academic Specialties: Externships and Judical Internships, Civil and Human Rights Law, Corporations and Business Transactions, Communications and Media Law, New York City Law, Commercial Law, Constitutional Law, Corporation Securities Law, Criminal Law, Government Services, International Law
Advanced Degrees Offered: JD (3 years full time, 4 years part time)
Combined Degrees Offered: JD/MBA with Baruch (4 years full time)
Grading System: A to F; some courses designated Pass/Fail
Clinical Program Required? Yes
Clinical Program Description: Civil and Human Rights Clinic
Legal Methods Course Requirements? Yes

STUDENT INFORMATION
Enrollment of Law School: 1,405
% Male/Female: 52/48
% Full Time: 66
% Full Time That Are International: 1
% Minority: 23
Average Age of Entering Class: 27

RESEARCH FACILITIES
School-Supported Research Centers: Center for International Law, Center for New York City Law, Media and Communications Law Center

EXPENSES/FINANCIAL AID
Annual Tuition: $22,114
Room and Board (Off Campus): $9,945
Books and Supplies: $800
Average Grant: $7,150
Average Loan: $21,000
% Receiving Some Sort of Aid: 84
Average Total Aid Package: $29,000
Average Debt: $49,000

ADMISSIONS INFORMATION
Application Fee: $50
Regular Application Deadline: Rolling
Regular Notification: Rolling
LSDAS Accepted? Yes
Average GPA: 3.1
Range of GPA: 2.9–3.3
Average LSAT: 154
Range of LSAT: 151–156
Transfer Students Accepted? Yes
Other Schools to Which Students Applied: American University, Brooklyn Law School, Fordham University, Hofstra University, Roger Williams University, Seton Hall University, St. John's University
Other Admissions Factors Considered: NES transcript evaluation required of international students
Number of Applications Received: 4,240
Number of Applicants Accepted: 2,035
Number of Applicants Enrolled: 509

INTERNATIONAL STUDENTS
TOEFL Required of International Students? Yes
Minimum TOEFL: 600

EMPLOYMENT INFORMATION

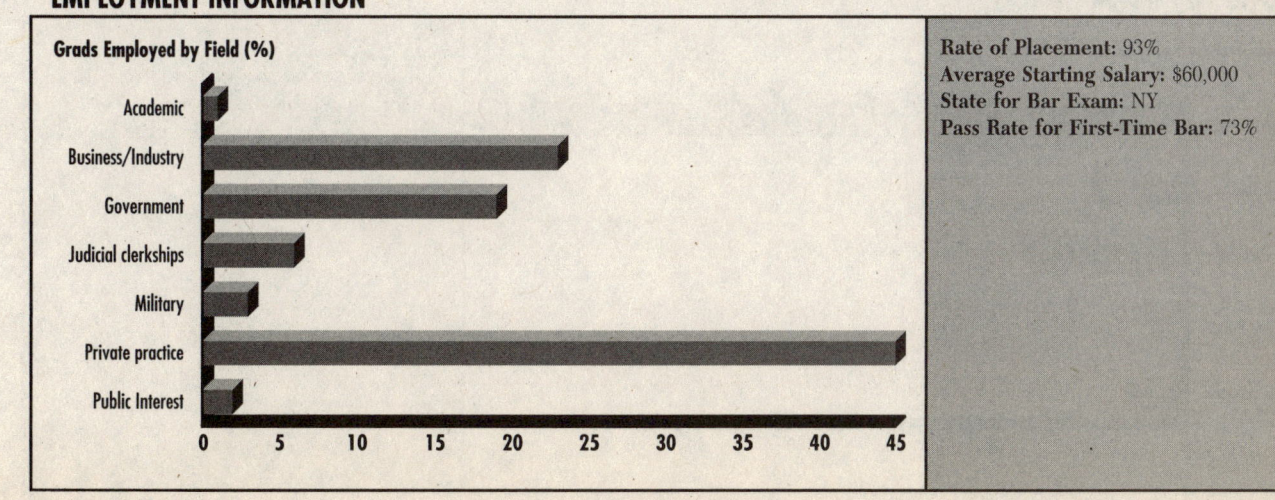

Grads Employed by Field (%)
- Academic: ~1
- Business/Industry: ~23
- Government: ~20
- Judicial clerkships: ~6
- Military: ~3
- Private practice: ~45
- Public Interest: ~3

Rate of Placement: 93%
Average Starting Salary: $60,000
State for Bar Exam: NY
Pass Rate for First-Time Bar: 73%

NEW YORK UNIVERSITY
School of Law

Admissions Contact: Assistant Dean of Admissions
110 West Third Street, New York, NY 10012
Admissions Phone: 212-998-6060 • Admissions Fax: 212-995-4527
Admissions E-mail: law.moreinfo@nyu.edu • Web Address: www.law.nyu.edu

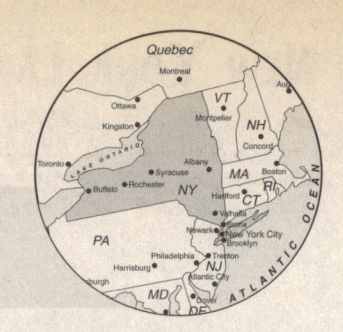

INSTITUTIONAL INFORMATION
Public/Private: Private
Student/Faculty Ratio: 13:1
Total Faculty: 197
% Part Time: 37
% Female: 33
% Minority: 8

PROGRAMS
Academic Specialties: NYU's curriculum is distinguished by its strength in traditional areas of legal study, interdisciplinary study, and clinical education, and has long been committed to educating lawyers who will use their degrees to serve the public. The Root-Tilden-Kern Program and the Public Interest Center sponsor speakers, offer academic and career counseling, and administer summer internship, volunteer, and mentoring programs. Specialties include Commercial Law, Constitutional Law, Corporation Securities Law, Criminal Law, Environmental Law, Human Rights Law, International Law, Labor Law, Legal History, Legal Philosophy, and Taxation.
Advanced Degrees Offered: LLM, JSD
Combined Degrees Offered: JD/LLM, JD/MBA, JD/MPA, JD/MUP, JD/MSW, JD/MA, JD/PhD
Clinical Program Required? No
Clinical Programs Description: 15 different clinics offered

Legal Writing Course Requirements? No
Legal Methods Course Requirements? No
Legal Research Course Requirements? No
Moot Court Requirement? No
Public Interest Law Requirement? No
Academic Journals: Student-edited publications are *New York University Law Review, Annual Survey of American Law, Clinical Law Review, Eastern European Constitutional Review, Environmental Law Review, Journal of International Law and Politics, Journal of Legislation and Public Policy, Review Law and Social Change,* and *Tax Law Review.* The *Commentator* is the law school newspaper.

STUDENT INFORMATION
Enrollment of Law School: 1,368
% Male/Female: 50/50
% Full Time: 100
% Full Time That Are International: 4
% Minority: 25

EXPENSES/FINANCIAL AID
Annual Tuition: $30,024
Room and Board: $19,025
Books and Supplies: $650
Financial Aid Application Deadline: 4/15
Average Grant: $15,000

ADMISSIONS INFORMATION
Application Fee: $65
Regular Application Deadline: 2/1
Regular Notification: 4/15
LSDAS Accepted? Yes
Average GPA: 3.7
Range of GPA: 3.6–3.8
Average LSAT: 169
Range of LSAT: 167–171
Transfer Students Accepted? Yes
Other Admissions Factors Considered: Evidence of significant nonacademic or professional achievement, rigor of thought, maturity, judgement, motivation, leadership, imagination, social commitment
Number of Applications Received: 6,954
Number of Applicants Accepted: 1,547
Number of Applicants Enrolled: 426

EMPLOYMENT INFORMATION

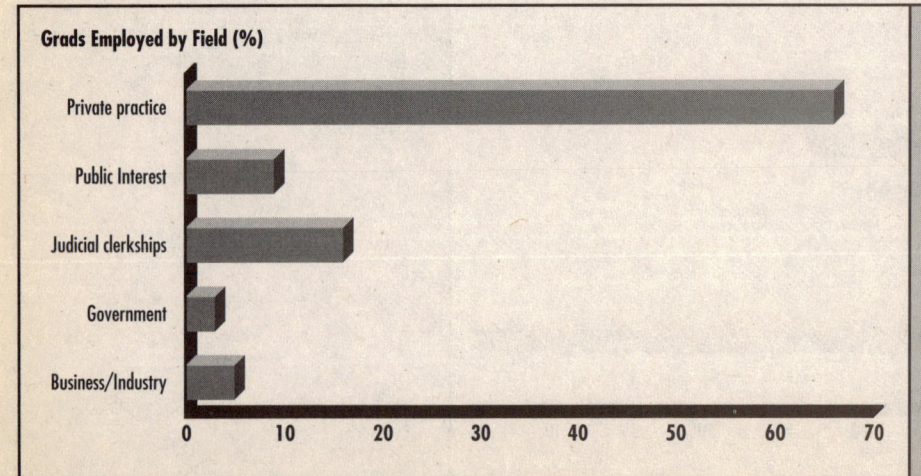

Grads Employed by Field (%)

Field	%
Private practice	~67
Public Interest	~7
Judicial clerkships	~17
Government	~4
Business/Industry	~3

Rate of Placement: 100%
Employers Who Frequently Hire Grads: Private law firms, public interest organizations, government agencies, corporations, public accounting firms
State for Bar Exam: NY
Pass Rate for First-Time Bar: 94%

NORTH CAROLINA CENTRAL UNIVERSITY
School of Law

Admissions Contact: Interim Director of Recruitment/Enrollment Manager, Karen Frasier Alston
1512 South Alston Avenue, Durham, NC 27707
Admissions Phone: 919-530-7173 • Admissions Fax: 919-560-6339
Admissions E-mail: recruiter@wpo.nccu.edu • Web Address: www.nccu.edu/law

INSTITUTIONAL INFORMATION
Public/Private: Public
Student/Faculty Ratio: 17:1

PROGRAMS
Advanced Degrees Offered: JD (3 years day, 4 years evening)
Combined Degrees Offered: JD/MBA (4 years), JD/MLS (4 years)
Grading System: Letter system
Clinical Program Required? No
Clinical Program Description: Civil Litigation Clinic, Criminal Litigation Clinic, Family Law Clinic, Alternative Dispute Resolution Clinic, Pro Bono Legal Clinic, Small Business Clinic, Juvenile Justice Clinic
Legal Writing Course Requirements? Yes
Legal Writing Description: An intensive writing program begins in the first semester and continues through the student's tenure. Required upper-level writing courses require students to engage in complex critical analysis resulting in comprehensive written documents.
Legal Methods Course Requirements? Yes
Legal Methods Description: First-year students must successfully complete Legal Reasoning and Analysis I and II. Legal Reasoning and Analysis I introduces students to the basics of legal reasoning, analysis, and writing, such as preparation of case briefs, issue identification, identification of key facts, analogy, distinction, case synthesis, and statutory construction. The course concludes with a closed-research, objective memorandum of law. Legal Reasoning and Analysis II covers legal research, analysis, writing, and citation form. Students prepare a research outline and an open-research, objective memorandum of law using the same case problem that was introduced in Legal Reasoning and Analysis I.
Legal Research Course Requirements? Yes
Legal Research Description: Legal Bibliography is a required first-year, first-semester course that includes an overview of legal concepts, such as the structure of the court system and how law is made. It identifies and describes the sources of law and their finding tools in print and electronic format. Students are introduced to computer-assisted legal research.
Moot Court Requirement? No
Moot Court Description: Student who excel in Appellate Advocacy I are chosen, through in-house moot court competitions, to participate in various regional and national moot court competitions. Participating students must prepare an appellate brief and present an oral argument in a certified competition in order to obtain Senior Board status and to earn a grade.
Public Interest Law Requirement? No
Academic Journals: Law Journal

STUDENT INFORMATION
Enrollment of Law School: 344
% Out of State: 0
% Male/Female: 39/61
% Full Time: 74
% Full Time That Are International: 0
% Minority: 63

RESEARCH FACILITIES
School-Supported Research Centers: PC environment running Windows 98 and 2000; 2 computer labs for word processing, legal research, Internet access, and e-mail in the Law Library

EXPENSES/FINANCIAL AID
Annual Tuition (Residents/Nonresidents): $2,956/$12,060
Room and Board (On/Off Campus): $6,500/$10,205
Books and Supplies: $1,250
Financial Aid Application Deadline: 4/15
Average Grant: $2,200
Average Loan: $16,500
% of Aid That Is Merit-Based: 65
% Receiving Some Sort of Aid: 97

ADMISSIONS INFORMATION
Application Fee: $40
Regular Application Deadline: 4/15
Regular Notification: 5/31
LSDAS Accepted? Yes
Average GPA: 3.0
Range of GPA: 2.7–3.5
Average LSAT: 149
Range of LSAT: 143–159
Transfer Students Accepted? Yes
Other Admissions Factors Considered: Intellectual ability; academic credentials; diverse talents and personal experiences; economic, societal, or educational obstacles overcome
Number of Applications Received: 996
Number of Applicants Accepted: 256
Number of Applicants Enrolled: 132

INTERNATIONAL STUDENTS
TOEFL Required of International Students? Yes

EMPLOYMENT INFORMATION

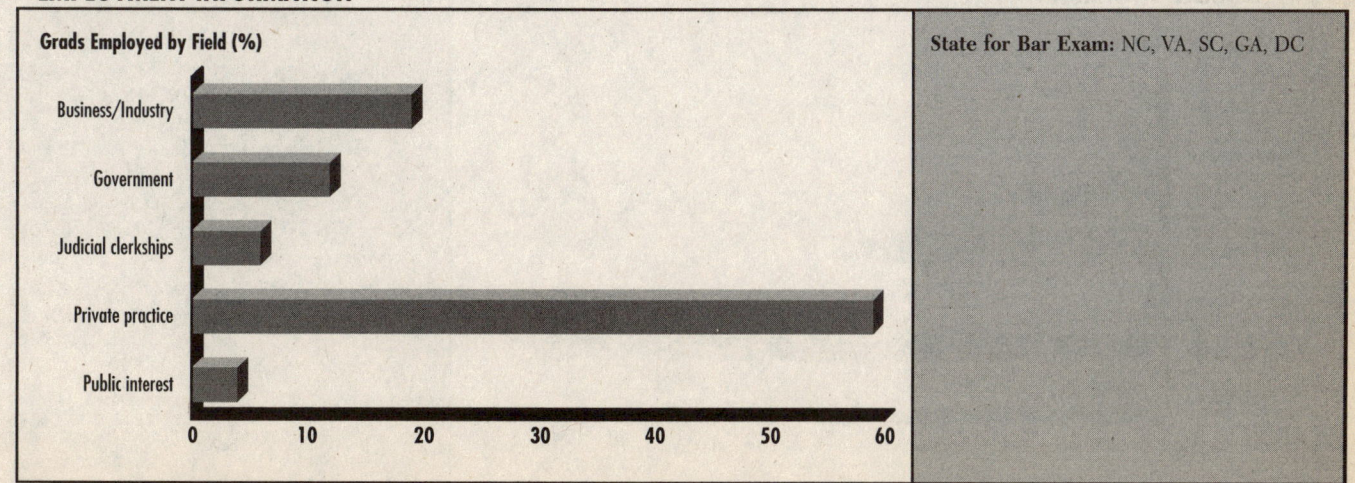

Grads Employed by Field (%)
- Business/Industry: ~20
- Government: ~12
- Judicial clerkships: ~5
- Private practice: ~60
- Public interest: ~3

State for Bar Exam: NC, VA, SC, GA, DC

NORTHEASTERN UNIVERSITY
School of Law

Admissions Contact: Assistant Dean and Director of Admissions, M.J. Knoll
400 Huntington Avenue, Boston, MA 02115
Admissions Phone: 617-373-2395 • Admissions Fax: 617-373-8865
Admissions E-mail: lawadmissions@neu.edu • Web Address: www.slaw.neu.edu

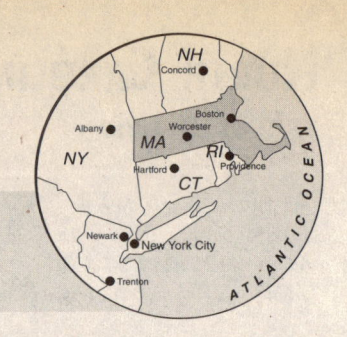

INSTITUTIONAL INFORMATION
Public/Private: Private
Student/Faculty Ratio: 20:1
Total Faculty: 81
% Part Time: 59
% Female: 25
% Minority: 10

PROGRAMS
Academic Specialties: We offer the only Cooperative Legal Education Program in the country, as well as six clinical programs for students interested in hands-on experience during their academic quarters: Ceriorari/Criminal Appeals, Criminal Advocacy, Domestic Violence, Poverty Law and Practice, Prisoners' Rights, and Tobacco Control. The faculty combines energetic and innovative teaching, participation in scholarly debate on pressing contemporary issues of law and social policy, and active involvement in the local, national, and international communities. Specializations include Employment law, Civil Procedure, Commercial Law, Constitutional Law, Corporation Securities Law, Criminal Law, Environmental Law, Human Rights Law, Intellectual Property Law, International Law, Property, and Taxation.
Combined Degrees Offered: JD/MBA (45 months), JD/MBA/Macc (45 months), JD/MPH (42 months)
Grading System: Students receive narrative evaluations in each course in lieu of letter or numerical grades.
Clinical Program Required? No
Clinical Program Description: Certiorari/Criminal Appeals Clinic, Criminal Advocacy Clinic, Domestic Violence Clinic, Poverty Law and Practice Clinic, Prisoners' Rights Clinic, Tobacco Control Clinic
Legal Writing Course Requirements? Yes
Legal Writing Description: Legal Practice is a 6-month, 2-quarter research and writing course required in the first year. Students build legal skills through the simulated-case method.
Legal Methods Course Requirements? Yes
Legal Methods Description: See Legal Writing.
Legal Research Course Requirements? No
Moot Court Requirement? No
Public Interest Law Requirement? Yes
Public Interest Law Description: The requirement can be satisfied by successfully completing a public interest co-op, an approved clinical program, a 30-hour pro bono public interest project, or a special-credit public interest independent study project.

STUDENT INFORMATION
Enrollment of Law School: 590
% Out of State: 66
% Male/Female: 40/60
% Full Time: 100
% Full Time That Are International: 3
% Minority: 27
Average Age of Entering Class: 25

RESEARCH FACILITIES
School-Supported Research Centers: Domestic Violence Institute, Tobacco Products Liability Project, Urban Law and Public Policy Institute, Disability Resource Center

EXPENSES/FINANCIAL AID
Annual Tuition: $26,820
Room and Board (On/Off Campus): $6,500/$12,150
Books and Supplies: $1,200
Financial Aid Application Deadline: 2/15
Average Grant: $8,000
% Receiving Some Sort of Aid: 83
Average Debt: $60,000

ADMISSIONS INFORMATION
Application Fee: $65
Regular Application Deadline: 3/1
Regular Notification: 4/15
LSDAS Accepted? Yes
Average GPA: 3.2
Range of GPA: 3.0–3.5
Average LSAT: 157
Range of LSAT: 152–160
Transfer Students Accepted? Yes
Other Schools to Which Students Applied: American, Boston College, Boston U., Fordham, George Washington, New England School of Law, Suffolk
Other Admissions Factors Considered: Work experience, community service, diversity
Number of Applications Received: 1,980
Number of Applicants Accepted: 793
Number of Applicants Enrolled: 206

INTERNATIONAL STUDENTS
TOEFL Required of International Students? Yes
Minimum TOEFL: 600 (250 computer)

EMPLOYMENT INFORMATION

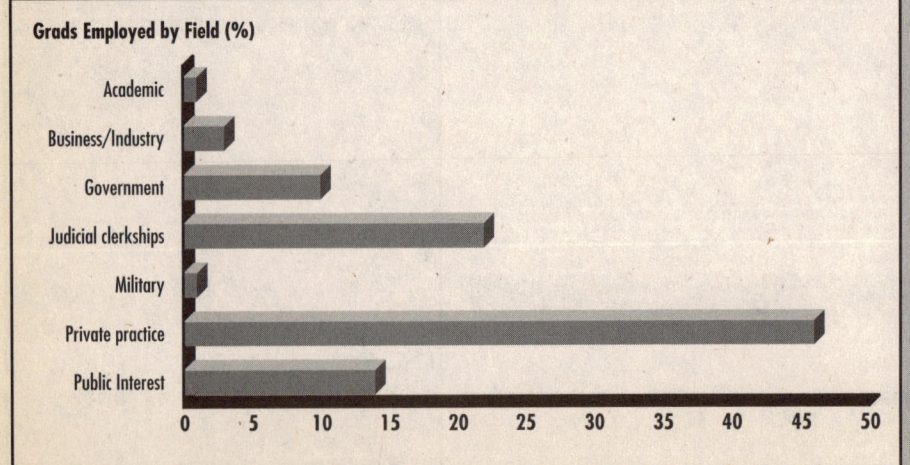

Grads Employed by Field (%)

Field	%
Academic	~1
Business/Industry	~9
Government	~10
Judicial clerkships	~22
Military	~1
Private practice	~46
Public Interest	~14

Rate of Placement: 91%
Average Starting Salary: $65,000
Employers Who Frequently Hire Grads: Mintz, Levin, Cohen, Ferris, Glovsky, & Popeo, P.C.; Testa, Hurwitz & Thibeault, P.C.; Foley, Hoag & Eliot, LLP; Massachusetts Superior Court and Appeals Court; Greater Boston Legal Services; U.S. Department of Justice; Health Law Advocates
State for Bar Exam: MA, NY, CA, FL
Pass Rate for First-Time Bar: 84%

NORTHERN ILLINOIS UNIVERSITY
College of Law

Admissions Contact: Director of Admission and Financial Aid, Judith L. Malen
Swen Parson Hall, Room 276, De Kalb, IL 60115
Admissions Phone: 815-753-8559 • Admissions Fax: 815-753-4501
Admissions E-mail: lawadm@niu.edu • Web Address: www.niu.edu/col

INSTITUTIONAL INFORMATION
Public/Private: Public
Student/Faculty Ratio: 14:1
Total Faculty: 40
% Part Time: 35
% Female: 25
% Minority: 20

PROGRAMS
Academic Specialties: Public Interest, Mediation and Alternative Dispute Resolution, Civil Procedure, Commercial Law, Constitutional Law, Corporation Securities Law, Criminal Law, Environmental Law, Government Services, Human Rights Law, International Law, Labor Law, Property, Taxation
Combined Degrees Offered: JD/MBA, JD/MPA (4 to 5 years)
Grading System: Letter system on a 4.0 scale
Clinical Program Required? Yes
Clinical Program Description: Zeke Giorgi Legal Clinic, Criminal and Civil Externships, Judicial Externship, Appellate Defender Clinic
Legal Writing Course Requirements? Yes
Legal Writing Description: Legal Writing and Advocacy (4 credits) and Basic Legal Research (1 credit) are a 2-part course in the first year.
Legal Methods Course Requirements? Yes
Legal Methods Description: See Legal Writing.
Legal Research Course Requirements? Yes
Legal Research Description: Basic Legal Research (2 credits)

Moot Court Requirement? No
Moot Court Description: Students have the opportunity to participate in the moot court experience during their second year. The Moot Court Society also sends teams nationally and regionally to participation in various competitions.
Public Interest Law Requirement? No
Academic Journals: *Northern Illinois University Law Review*

STUDENT INFORMATION
Enrollment of Law School: 332
% Out of State: 15
% Male/Female: 50/50
% Full Time: 95
% Full Time That Are International: 1
% Minority: 22
Average Age of Entering Class: 27

RESEARCH FACILITIES
Research Resources Available: Westlaw/Dow Jones and Lexis/Nexis through interlibrary loan, access to library resources nationwide and abroad, Internet access, some wireless access

EXPENSES/FINANCIAL AID
Annual Tuition (Residents/Nonresidents): $6,916/$13,833
Room and Board (On/Off Campus): $5,530/$6,430
Books and Supplies: $1,500
Financial Aid Application Deadline: 3/1
Average Grant: $4,735
Average Loan: $15,912
% Receiving Some Sort of Aid: 72
Average Total Aid Package: $18,700
Average Debt: $38,000
Tuition Per Credit (Residents/Nonresidents): $288/$576
Fees Per Credit: $51

ADMISSIONS INFORMATION
Application Fee: $50
Regular Application Deadline: Rolling
Regular Notification: Rolling
LSDAS Accepted? Yes
Average GPA: 3.2
Range of GPA: 2.9–3.5
Average LSAT: 154
Range of LSAT: 151–157
Transfer Students Accepted? Yes
Other Admissions Factors Considered: Leadership qualities, good citizenship, integrity, initiative
Number of Applications Received: 1,116
Number of Applicants Accepted: 367
Number of Applicants Enrolled: 128

INTERNATIONAL STUDENTS
TOEFL Required of International Students? Yes
Minimum TOEFL: 550 (250 computer)

EMPLOYMENT INFORMATION

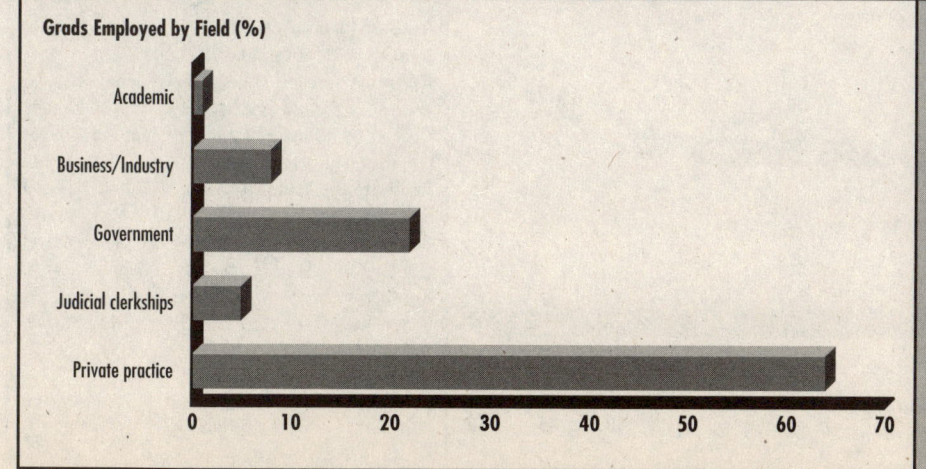

Grads Employed by Field (%)
- Academic
- Business/Industry
- Government
- Judicial clerkships
- Private practice

Rate of Placement: 94%
Employers Who Frequently Hire Grads: State's attorneys, public defenders, Illinois attorney general, private firms
Prominent Alumni: Kathleen Zellner, attorny who won reversals of 7 murder convictions by DNA; Cheryl Niro, one of the top 10 female Illinois lawyers and former President of IBA; Dr. Kenneth Chessick, whose firm specializes in medical negligence litigation; Hon. Patricia Martin-Bishop, Judge, Cook County Circuit Court
State for Bar Exam: IL, WI, IA, TX, AR
Pass Rate for First-Time Bar: 81%

NORTHERN KENTUCKY UNIVERSITY
Salmon P. Chase College of Law

Admissions Contact: Admissions Specialist, Gina Bray
Nunn Hall, Room 541, Highland Heights, KY 41099
Admissions Phone: 859-572-6476 • Admissions Fax: 859-572-6081
Admissions E-mail: brayg@nku.edu • Web Address: www.nku.edu

INSTITUTIONAL INFORMATION
Public/Private: Public
Student/Faculty Ratio: 13:1
Total Faculty: 65
% Part Time: 60
% Female: 34
% Minority: 12

PROGRAMS
Academic Specialties: Every first-year student is placed in a small section of one of his or her classes. Each teacher in a small section uses varied teaching techniques and gives students individualized attention. We also offer the Academic Developement Program to help students learn time management and study techniques. The Academic Learning Center offers a central clearinghouse for academic support and development programs. Specialties include Constitutional Law, Environmental Law, and Labor Law.
Combined Degrees Offered: JD/MBA (3 years full time, 4 years part time)
Grading System: Letter system on a 4.3 scale, Incomplete, Satisfactory, Unsatisfactory, Pass, Credit, No Credit, Withdrew, Audit
Clinical Program Required? No
Clinical Program Description: The Clinical Extern Program includes placement with state and federal judges, prosecutors and public defenders, legal aid programs, and various governmental agencies.
Legal Writing Course Requirements? Yes
Legal Writing Description: Year-long course of skills instruction, exercises in legal research, analysis of common and statutory law, legal writing and reasoning, and written and oral advocacy
Legal Methods Course Requirements? No
Legal Research Course Requirements? Yes
Legal Research Description: See Legal Writing.
Moot Court Requirement? No
Moot Court Description: The Moot Court Program provides opportunities for students to develop various legal skills including research, brief writing, and presentation of oral arguments. The Moot Court Board conducts 2 intramural competitions annually and administers the National Environmental Law Moot Court Competition.
Public Interest Law Requirement? No
Academic Journals: *Northern Kentucky Law Review*

STUDENT INFORMATION
Enrollment of Law School: 473
% Out of State: 31
% Male/Female: 54/46
% Full Time: 55
% Minority: 5
Average Age of Entering Class: 29

EXPENSES/FINANCIAL AID
Annual Tuition (Residents/Nonresidents): $7,824/$17,808
Room and Board: $12,950
Books and Supplies: $750
Financial Aid Application Deadline: 3/1
Average Grant: $7,720
Average Loan: $16,673
% of Aid That Is Merit-Based: 10
% Receiving Some Sort of Aid: 66
Average Total Aid Package: $18,486
Average Debt: $56,856
Tuition Per Credit (Residents/Nonresidents): $326/$742

ADMISSIONS INFORMATION
Application Fee: $30
Regular Application Deadline: 3/1
Regular Notification: Rolling
LSDAS Accepted? Yes
Average GPA: 3.2
Range of GPA: 2.9–3.6
Average LSAT: 151
Range of LSAT: 149–154
Transfer Students Accepted? Yes
Other Schools to Which Students Applied: University of Cincinnati, University of Dayton, University of Kentucky, University of Louisville, Capital University
Other Admissions Factors Considered: Undergraduate institution, undergraduate major, work experience, writing ability
Number of Applications Received: 733
Number of Applicants Accepted: 368
Number of Applicants Enrolled: 202

INTERNATIONAL STUDENTS
TOEFL Required of International Students? Yes

EMPLOYMENT INFORMATION

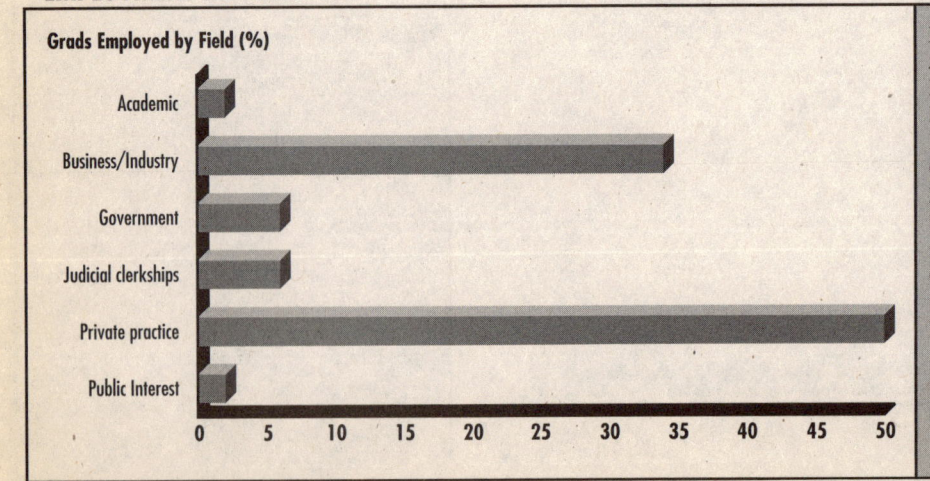

Grads Employed by Field (%)

Field	%
Academic	~2
Business/Industry	~35
Government	~5
Judicial clerkships	~7
Private practice	~50
Public Interest	~2

Rate of Placement: 93%
Average Starting Salary: $52,625
Employers Who Frequently Hire Grads: Procter & Gamble; Taft, Stettinius & Hollister; Lerner, Sampson & Rothfuss; Hamilton County Court of Common Pleas
Prominent Alumni: Steve Chabot, United States Representative for Ohio; Susan Court, General Counsel, Federal Energy Regulations Commission; Hon. Daniel T. Guidugli, Judge, Kentucky Court of Appeals; Hon. Robert P. Ruwe, Judge, U.S. Tax Court; Katie Kratz Stine, Senator, 24th District, Kentucky
State for Bar Exam: KY, OH, IN
Pass Rate for First-Time Bar: 85%

NORTHWESTERN UNIVERSITY
School of Law

Admissions Contact: Associate Dean of Enrollment, Don Rebstock
357 East Chicago Avenue, Chicago, IL 60611
Admissions Phone: 312-503-8465 • Admissions Fax: 312-503-0178
Admissions E-mail: nulawadm@law.northwestern.edu • Web Address: www.law.northwestern.edu

INSTITUTIONAL INFORMATION
Public/Private: Private
Student/Faculty Ratio: 12:1
Total Faculty: 210
% Part Time: 68
% Female: 25
% Minority: 5

PROGRAMS
Academic Specialties: Civil Rights, Constitutional Law, Contracts, Corporate Law, Criminal Law, Dispute Resolution, Employment/Labor Law, Environmental Law, Feminist Legal Theory, Health Law, International Private Law, International Human Rights, Intellectual Property, Jury Selection/Psychology, Law and Economics, Legal History, Public Interest, Torts, Trial Advocacy, Corporation Securities Law, International Law, Taxation
Advanced Degrees Offered: JD (3 years), LLM (1 year), SJD (2 years)
Combined Degrees Offered: JD/MBA (3 years), JD/PhD (6 years), JD/MA (4 years), LLM/Certificate in Management (1 year)
Grading System: Letter system
Clinical Program Required? No
Clinical Program Description: Bluhm Legal Clinic—Children's and Family Justice Center, Center for International Human Rights, Trial Advocacy Program, Center on Wrongful Convictions, Small Business Opportunity Center, various civil clinical opportunities

Legal Writing Course Requirements? Yes
Legal Writing Description: Communication and Legal Reasoning is a 1-year required course for first-year students.
Legal Methods Course Requirements? No
Legal Research Course Requirements? Yes
Legal Research Description: See Legal Writing.
Moot Court Requirement? Yes
Moot Court Description: First year, part of the Communication and Legal Reasoning Program
Public Interest Law Requirement? Yes
Public Interest Law Description: 40 hours of community service
Academic Journals: *Northwestern University Law Review, Journal of Criminal Law and Criminalogy, Journal of International Law and Business, Journal of Intellectual Property and Technology*

STUDENT INFORMATION
Enrollment of Law School: 675
% Out of State: 80
% Male/Female: 50/50
% Full Time: 100
% Full Time That Are International: 2
% Minority: 30
Average Age of Entering Class: 25

EXPENSES/FINANCIAL AID
Annual Tuition: $32,008
Room and Board: $11,790
Books and Supplies: $10,245
Financial Aid Application Deadline: 2/15
Average Grant: $15,000
Average Loan: $25,000
% of Aid That Is Merit-Based: 30
% Receiving Some Sort of Aid: 80
Average Total Aid Package: $40,000
Average Debt: $85,000

ADMISSIONS INFORMATION
Application Fee: $85
Regular Application Deadline: 2/15
Regular Notification: Rolling
LSDAS Accepted? Yes
Average GPA: 3.5
Range of GPA: 3.3–3.7
Average LSAT: 168
Range of LSAT: 165–169
Transfer Students Accepted? Yes
Other Schools to Which Students Applied: Columbia University, Duke University, Georgetown University, New York University, University of Chicago, University of Michigan, University of Pennsylvania
Other Admissions Factors Considered: Interview
Number of Applications Received: 4,436
Number of Applicants Accepted: 771
Number of Applicants Enrolled: 242

EMPLOYMENT INFORMATION

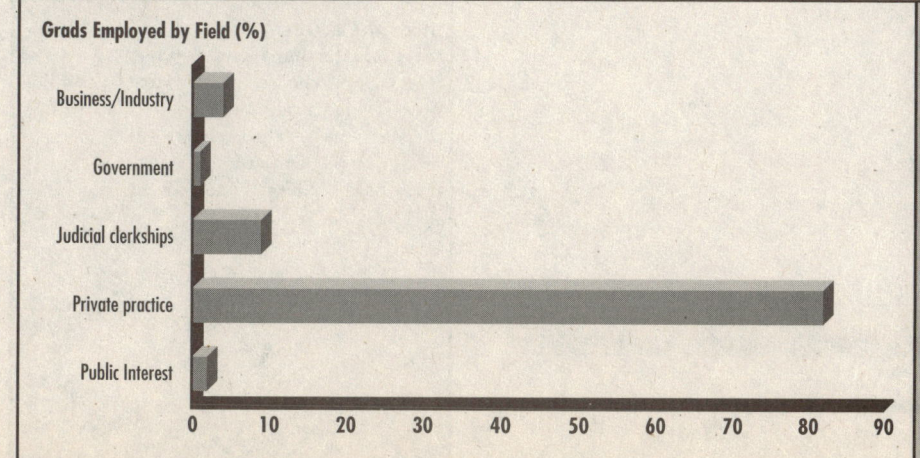

Grads Employed by Field (%)

Field	%
Business/Industry	~3
Government	~5
Judicial clerkships	~10
Private practice	~80
Public Interest	~3

Rate of Placement: 99%
Average Starting Salary: $125,000
Employers Who Frequently Hire Grads: Sidley & Austin; Kirkland & Ellis; Latham & Watkins; Jones Day Reavis & Pogue; Katten, Muchin & Zavis; Morrison & Foerster; Winston & Strawn; Baker & McKenzie; Mayer, Brown & Platt; Schiff, Hardin & Waite **Prominent Alumni:** John Paul Stevens, Justice, Supreme Court; Arthur Goldberg, Justice, Supreme Court; Donald Washburn, Chairman and President, of Northwest Airlines; NIcholas Chabraja, Chairman and CEO, General Dynamics; Kenesaw Landis, first Commissioner of Major League Baseball
State for Bar Exam: IL
Pass Rate for First-Time Bar: 95%

NOVA SOUTHEASTERN UNIVERSITY
Shepard Broad Law Center

Admissions Contact: Director of Admissions, Nancy Kelly Sanguigni
3305 College Avenue, Fort Lauderdale, FL 33314
Admissions Phone: 954-452-6117 • Admissions Fax: 954-262-3844
Admissions E-mail: admission@nsu.law.nova.edu • Web Address: www.nsulaw.nova.edu

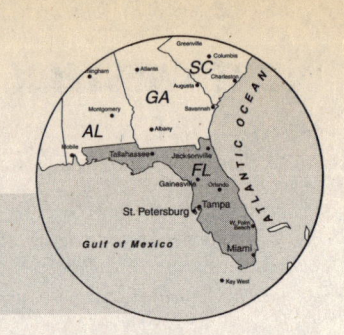

INSTITUTIONAL INFORMATION
Public/Private: Private
Student/Faculty Ratio: 16:1
Total Faculty: 116
% Part Time: 59
% Female: 34
% Minority: 18

PROGRAMS
Academic Specialties: Alternative Dispute Resolution, Business Practice, Children and Families, Criminal Justice, Environmental and Land Use Law, International Practice, Personal Injury, Civil Procedure, Commercial Law, Constitutional Law, Corporation Securities Law, Government Services, Human Rights Law, Intellectual Property Law, Labor Law, Legal History, Property, Taxation
Combined Degrees Offered: JD/MBA; JD/MS Psychology, Dispute Resolution, or Computer; JD/MURP
Grading System: A (4.0), B+ (3.5), B (3.0), C+ (2.5), C (2.0), D+ (1.5), D (1.0), F (0.0)
Clinical Program Required? No
Legal Writing Course Requirements? Yes
Legal Writing Description: Lawyering Skills and Values (LSV) introduces an innovative approach to legal education that integrates legal theory with practice, professionalism, and technology. LSV I and II combine instruction in legal research, writing, and analysis with other lawyering skills such as interviewing, counseling, negotiating, legal drafting, and pre-trial practice.
Legal Methods Course Requirements? No
Legal Research Course Requirements? Yes
Legal Research Description: See Legal Writing.
Moot Court Requirement? Yes
Moot Court Description: Motion practice requirement for all first-year students
Public Interest Law Requirement? No
Academic Journals: *Nova Law Review, Journal of International/Comparative Law, International Travel Law Journal*

STUDENT INFORMATION
Enrollment of Law School: 1,007
% Male/Female: 50/50
% Full Time: 77
% Minority: 36
Average Age of Entering Class: 27

RESEARCH FACILITIES
Research Resources Available: Almost 30,000 electonic databases
School-Supported Research Centers: Environmental and Land Use Law Center, Inter-American Center for Human Rights

EXPENSES/FINANCIAL AID
Annual Tuition: $21,312
Room and Board (On/Off Campus): $7,730/$9,203
Books and Supplies: $1,200
Financial Aid Application Deadline: 4/1
Average Grant: $21,312
Average Loan: $23,500
% Receiving Some Sort of Aid: 90
Average Total Aid Package: $39,442

ADMISSIONS INFORMATION
Application Fee: $50
Regular Application Deadline: 3/1
Regular Notification: 3/1
LSDAS Accepted? Yes
Average GPA: 2.9
Range of GPA: 2.7–3.3
Average LSAT: 149
Range of LSAT: 146–152
Transfer Students Accepted? Yes
Other Schools to Which Students Applied: Florida Coastal School of Law, Florida State University, St. Thomas University, Stetson University, University of Florida, University of Miami
Other Admissions Factors Considered: Trend of grades; hardships overcome; distinctive cultural point of view; life, socioeconomic, educational, or personal experiences; other factors indicating motivation and discipline
Number of Applications Received: 1,888
Number of Applicants Accepted: 709
Number of Applicants Enrolled: 324

INTERNATIONAL STUDENTS
TOEFL Required of International Students? Yes
Minimum TOEFL: 550 (213 computer)

EMPLOYMENT INFORMATION

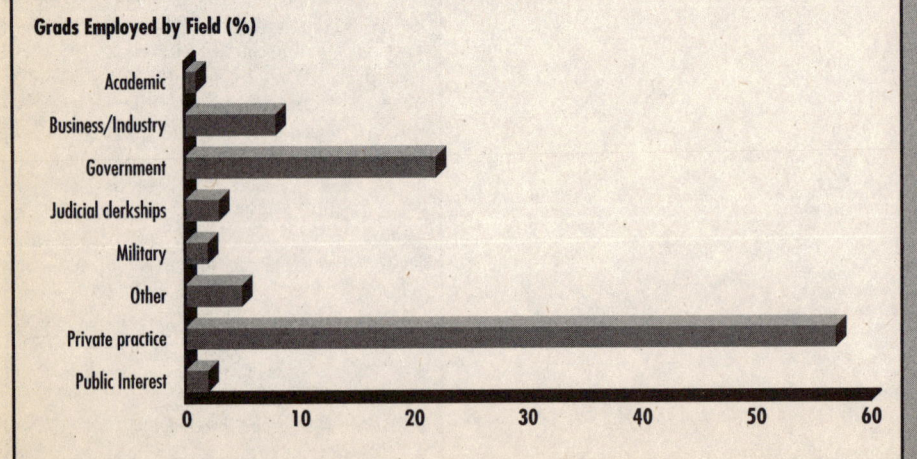

Grads Employed by Field (%)

Rate of Placement: 87%
Average Starting Salary: $50,189
Employers Who Frequently Hire Grads: Private law firms, local and state agencies, state attorney's and public defender's offices
State for Bar Exam: FL, NY, GA
Pass Rate for First-Time Bar: 80%

OHIO NORTHERN UNIVERSITY
Claude W. Pettit College of Law

Admissions Contact: Assistant Dean and Director of Law Admissions, Linda K. English
Pettit College, Ada, OH 45810-1599
Admissions Phone: 419-772-2211 • Admissions Fax: 419-772-1487
Admissions E-mail: l-english@onu.edu • Web Address: www.law.onu.edu

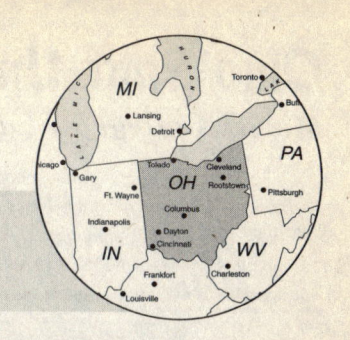

INSTITUTIONAL INFORMATION
Public/Private: Private
Affiliation: Methodist
Student/Faculty Ratio: 12:1
Total Faculty: 22
% Part Time: 30
% Female: 36
% Minority: 5

PROGRAMS
Academic Specialties: Ohio Northern's faculty brings expertise in a wide variety of legal fields. Particularly noteworthy is our faculty's expertise in Criminal Law, Federal Income Taxation, International Law, Civil Procedure, Commercial Law, Constitutional Law, Corporation Securities Law, Environmental Law, Human Rights Law, Labor Law, Legal History, Legal Philosophy, and Property.
Grading System: 4.0 scale
Clinical Program Required? No
Clinical Program Description: Criminal (Prosecution and Defense), Civil, Bankruptcy, Legal Aid, Environmental, Governmental, Legislative, Transactional, Guardian Ad Litem, ADR, Education Seminar, Judicial Externships
Legal Writing Course Requirements? Yes
Legal Writing Description: All first-year students must pass 2 semesters of Legal Research and Writing with a grade of at least C–.
Legal Methods Course Requirements? Yes
Legal Methods Description: First-year year-long course in Legal Research and Writing. Throughout the course, students are required to complete a number of research and drafting assignments, including client memos, motions, discovery materials, an appellate brief, and an oral argument.
Legal Research Course Requirements? Yes
Legal Research Description: See Legal Methods.
Moot Court Requirement? No
Moot Court Description: All students are eligible to compete in both intra- and interscholastic competitions. Recent competitions where Ohio Northern teams have fared well include the Jessup International Moot Court Competition, National Administrative Law Competition, Fall National Appellate Advocacy Competition, and National Tax Moot Court Competition.
Public Interest Law Requirement? No
Academic Journals: *Ohio Northern University Law Review*

STUDENT INFORMATION
Enrollment of Law School: 272
% Out of State: 65
% Male/Female: 60/40
% Full Time: 100
% Full Time That Are International: 1
% Minority: 10
Average Age of Entering Class: 25

RESEARCH FACILITIES
Research Resources Available: Lexis/Nexis, Westlaw

EXPENSES/FINANCIAL AID
Annual Tuition: $21,480
Room and Board (On/Off Campus): $9,100/$10,530
Books and Supplies: $900
Average Grant: $12,223
Average Loan: $23,270
% of Aid That Is Merit-Based: 30
% Receiving Some Sort of Aid: 95
Average Total Aid Package: $32,910
Average Debt: $67,877

ADMISSIONS INFORMATION
Application Fee: $40
Regular Application Deadline: Rolling
Regular Notification: Rolling
LSDAS Accepted? Yes
Average GPA: 3.1
Range of GPA: 2.7–3.4
Average LSAT: 148
Range of LSAT: 146–153
Transfer Students Accepted? Yes
Other Schools to Which Students Applied: Capital, Case Western, Ohio State, U. of Cincinnati, U. of Dayton, U. of Pittsburgh, U. of Toledo
Other Admissions Factors Considered: Quality of undergraduate/graduate school(s), degree(s) earned, diversity of background and heritage, transcript, degree interpretation (international students)
Number of Applications Received: 970
Number of Applicants Accepted: 417
Number of Applicants Enrolled: 120

INTERNATIONAL STUDENTS
TOEFL Required of International Students? Yes
Minimum TOEFL: 550

EMPLOYMENT INFORMATION

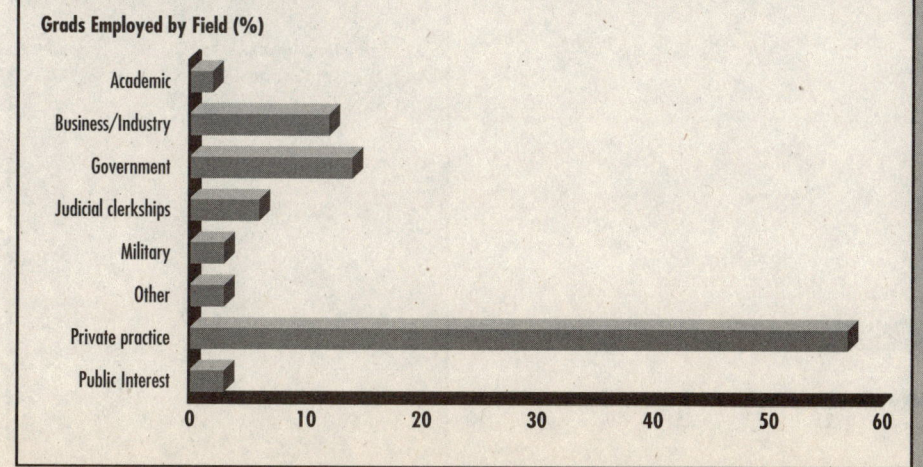

Grads Employed by Field (%)

Field	%
Academic	~2
Business/Industry	~13
Government	~14
Judicial clerkships	~7
Military	~3
Other	~3
Private practice	~58
Public Interest	~2

Rate of Placement: 95%
Average Starting Salary: $50,084
Prominent Alumni: Michael DeWine, U.S. Senator; Gregory Frost, U.S. District Judge, Southern Ohio; Benjamin Brafman, Senior Partner, Brafman & Ross; Greg Miller, U.S. Attorney for Northwest Florida
State for Bar Exam: OH, FL, PA, NC, MD
Pass Rate for First-Time Bar: 93%

OHIO STATE UNIVERSITY
Moritz College of Law

Admissions Contact: Assistant Director, Sarbeth J. Fleming
55 West 12th Avenue, Columbus, OH 43210
Admissions Phone: 614-292-8810 • Admissions Fax: 614-292-1492
Admissions E-mail: lawadmit@osu.edu • Web Address: moritzlaw.osu.edu

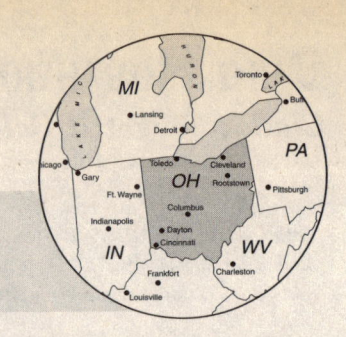

INSTITUTIONAL INFORMATION
Public/Private: Public
Student/Faculty Ratio: 14:1
Total Faculty: 67
% Part Time: 18
% Female: 37
% Minority: 16

PROGRAMS
Academic Specialties: Alternative Dispute Resolution, Labor/Employment, Health Care, Criminal Law Procedure, International Law, International Trade, Civil Rights/Civil Liberties, Constitutional Law, Commercial Law, Environmental Law, Legal Philosophy
Combined Degrees Offered: JD/MBA, JD/MHA, JD/MPA, JD/MD (all 4 years)
Clinical Program Required? No
Clinical Program Description: Civil Practicum, Student Housing Legal Clinic, Mediation Practicum and Seminar, Mulitparty Mediation Practicum, Criminal Defense Practicum, Criminal Prosecution Practicum, Justice for Children Practicum, Legal Negotiations, Trial Practice
Legal Writing Course Requirements? Yes
Legal Writing Description: Students must take Legal Research during the fall semester of the first year, Legal Writing and Analysis during the spring semester of the first year, and Appellate Advocacy I during the fall semester of the second year. Legal Writing and Analysis is a prerequisite for Appellate Advocacy I.

Legal Methods Course Requirements? Yes
Legal Methods Description: 1 semester
Legal Research Course Requirements? Yes
Legal Research Description: See Legal Writing.
Moot Court Requirement? No
Moot Court Description: We currently participate in the following national moot court competitions: Frederick Douglass, Environmental Law, ABA National Appellate Advocacy, National Moot Court, Health Law, Jessup International Law, Wagner Labor Law, Civil Rights, Criminal Law, Juvenile Law, Rendigs Products Liability Competition, and First Amendment.
Public Interest Law Requirement? No
Academic Journals: *Ohio State Law Journal, The Ohio State Journal on Dispute Resolution, Ohio State Criminal Law Journal*

STUDENT INFORMATION
Enrollment of Law School: 660
% Out of State: 33
% Male/Female: 49/51
% Full Time: 100
% Full Time That Are International: 2
% Minority: 19
Average Age of Entering Class: 23

RESEARCH FACILITIES
School-Supported Research Centers: Center for Law, Policy, and Social Science

EXPENSES/FINANCIAL AID
Annual Tuition (Residents/Nonresidents): $11,880/$23,300
Room and Board: $8,184
Books and Supplies: $1,588
Financial Aid Application Deadline: 3/1
Average Grant: $2,135
% of Aid That Is Merit-Based: 2
% Receiving Some Sort of Aid: 70
Average Debt: $50,000

ADMISSIONS INFORMATION
Application Fee: $30
Regular Application Deadline: 3/1
Regular Notification: Rolling
LSDAS Accepted? Yes
Average GPA: 3.6
Range of GPA: 3.3–3.8
Average LSAT: 160
Range of LSAT: 156–163
Transfer Students Accepted? Yes
Other Admissions Factors Considered: Résumé, personal statement
Number of Applications Received: 2,386
Number of Applicants Accepted: 645
Number of Applicants Enrolled: 246

INTERNATIONAL STUDENTS
TOEFL Required of International Students? Yes
Minimum TOEFL: 600

EMPLOYMENT INFORMATION

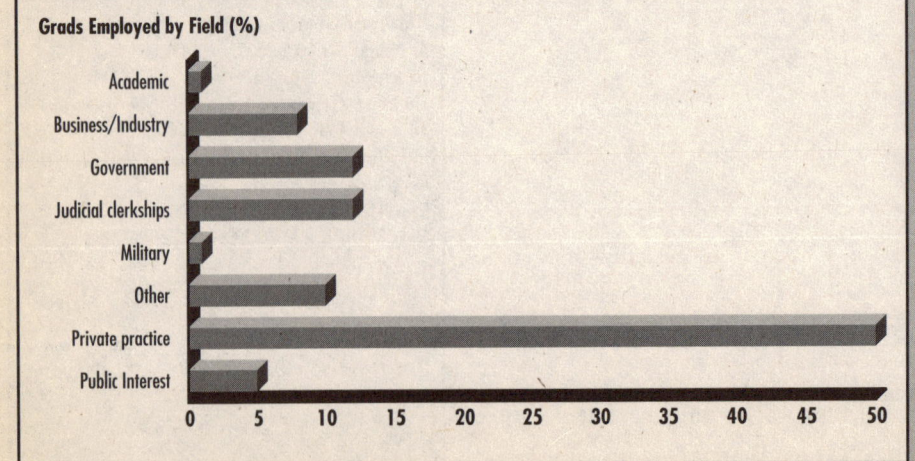

Grads Employed by Field (%)

Field	%
Academic	~1
Business/Industry	~8
Government	~12
Judicial clerkships	~12
Military	~1
Other	~9
Private practice	~50
Public Interest	~5

Rate of Placement: 94%
Average Starting Salary: $63,700
State for Bar Exam: OH
Pass Rate for First-Time Bar: 90%

OKLAHOMA CITY UNIVERSITY
School of Law

Admissions Contact: Director of Admission, Peter Storandt
PO Box 61310, Oklahoma City, OK 73146-1310
Admissions Phone: 405-521-5354 • Admissions Fax: 405-521-5814
Admissions E-mail: lawadmit@okcu.edu • Web Address: www.okcu.edu/law

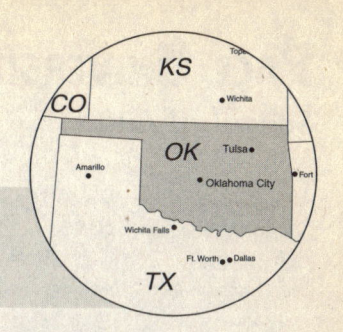

INSTITUTIONAL INFORMATION
Public/Private: Private
Affiliation: Methodist
Student/Faculty Ratio: 18:1
Total Faculty: 44
% Part Time: 30
% Female: 32
% Minority: 9

PROGRAMS
Combined Degrees Offered: JD/MBA (3 years)
Clinical Program Required? No
Legal Writing Course Requirements? Yes
Legal Writing Description: Combined with Legal Research, our program is 2 semesters and is taught in small classes by full-time faculty.
Legal Methods Course Requirements? No
Legal Research Course Requirements? Yes
Legal Research Description: See Legal Writing.
Moot Court Requirement? No
Public Interest Law Requirement? No
Academic Journals: *Law Review*

STUDENT INFORMATION
Enrollment of Law School: 537
% Out of State: 46
% Male/Female: 60/40
% Full Time: 74
% Full Time That Are International: 1
% Minority: 23
Average Age of Entering Class: 29

RESEARCH FACILITIES
Research Resources Available: All state and county libraries and libraries at other universities in the area
School-Supported Research Centers: Center for the Study of State Constitutional Law and Government, Center on Alternative Dispute Resolution, Early Settlement Central Mediation, Native American Legal Resource Center

EXPENSES/FINANCIAL AID
Annual Tuition: $15,120
Room and Board (On/Off Campus): $6,509/$8,791
Books and Supplies: $750
Average Grant: $4,297
% of Aid That Is Merit-Based: 5
% Receiving Some Sort of Aid: 88
Average Debt: $42,042
Fees Per Credit: $504

ADMISSIONS INFORMATION
Application Fee: $35
Regular Application Deadline: Rolling
Regular Notification: Rolling
LSDAS Accepted? Yes
Average GPA: 2.9
Range of GPA: 2.5–4.0
Average LSAT: 149
Transfer Students Accepted? Yes
Other Admissions Factors Considered: personal statement, letters of recommendation
Number of Applications Received: 1,445
Number of Applicants Accepted: 796
Number of Applicants Enrolled: 220

INTERNATIONAL STUDENTS
TOEFL Required of International Students? Yes
Minimum TOEFL: 560

EMPLOYMENT INFORMATION

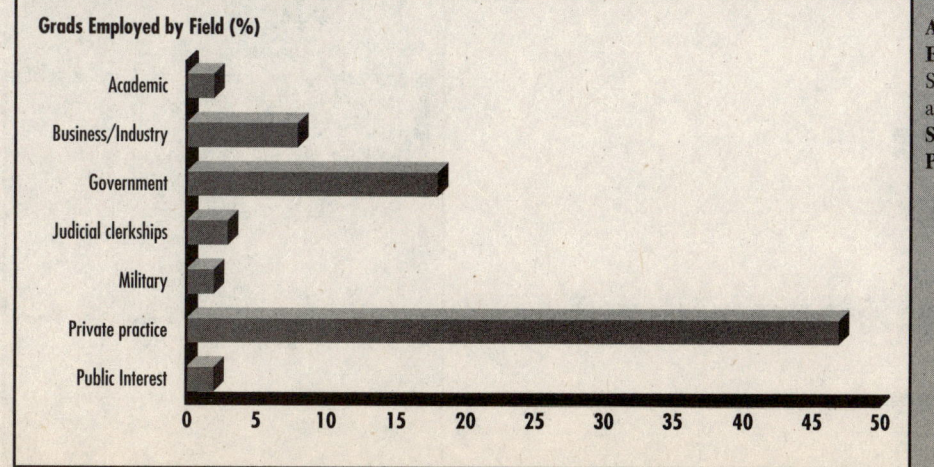

Grads Employed by Field (%)
- Academic
- Business/Industry
- Government
- Judicial clerkships
- Military
- Private practice
- Public Interest

Average Starting Salary: $48,166
Employers Who Frequently Hire Grads: Small to medium-size law firms, government agencies
State for Bar Exam: OK, TX, FL, KA, MO
Pass Rate for First-Time Bar: 76%

PACE UNIVERSITY
School of Law

Admissions Contact: Director of Admissions, Cathy M. Alexander
78 North Broadway, White Plains, NY 10603
Admissions Phone: 914-422-4210 • Admissions Fax: 914-989-8714
Admissions E-mail: admissions@law.pace.edu • Web Address: www.law.pace.edu

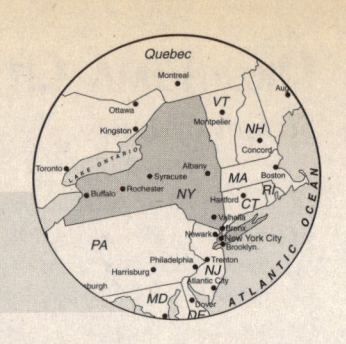

INSTITUTIONAL INFORMATION
Public/Private: Private
Student/Faculty Ratio: 16:1
Total Faculty: 75
% Part Time: 52
% Female: 37
% Minority: 5

PROGRAMS
Academic Specialties: Environmental Law, Health Law, International Law, Legal Analysis and Writing, Clinical Education, Civil Procedure, Commercial Law, Constitutional Law, Corporation Securities Law, Criminal Law, Government Services, Human Rights Law, Intellectual Property Law, Labor Law, Legal History, Property, Taxation
Advanced Degrees Offered: SJD (1 year), LLM (1 to 2 years)
Combined Degrees Offered: JD/MBA, JD/MPA, JD/MEM, JD/MS (all 4 to 6 years)
Grading System: A+, A, A–, B+, B, B–, C+, C, C–, D, F. Some courses are Pass/Fail. The A+ is an honorary and is not calculated in the GPA.
Clinical Program Required? No
Clinical Program Description: Criminal Defense Clinic, Equal Justice American Disability Rights Clinic, Environmental Litigation Clinic, Prosecution of Domestic Violence Clinic, Securities Arbitration Clinic
Legal Writing Course Requirements? Yes
Legal Writing Description: Criminal Law Analysis and Writing I and II are an integrated 2-semester, 6-credit offering that explores the substantive aspects of criminal law through legal analysis and writing. Students learn about the criminalization decision, goals of punishment, elements of criminal conduct, and defenses to criminal charges by reading statutes and using and distinguishing cases. Students also learn about legal research and the legislative process and complete numerous writing exercises in criminal law. Students write an appellate brief and argue before a moot court.
Legal Methods Course Requirements? Yes
Legal Methods Description: See Legal Writing
Legal Research Course Requirements? No
Moot Court Requirement? Yes
Moot Court Description: See Legal Writing.
Public Interest Law Requirement? No
Academic Journals: *Pace Law Review, Pace Environmental Law Review, Pace International Law Review*

STUDENT INFORMATION
Enrollment of Law School: 716
% Out of State: 60
% Male/Female: 40/60
% Full Time: 62
% Full Time That Are International: 2
% Minority: 16
Average Age of Entering Class: 26

RESEARCH FACILITIES
Research Resources Available: Westlaw, Lexis/Nexis, Dialog
School-Supported Research Centers: Pace Women's Justice Center, Pace Land Use Law Center, Pace Social Justice Center, Pace Energy Project, Pace Institute of International Commercial Law, Virtual Law Library

EXPENSES/FINANCIAL AID
Annual Tuition: $25,294
Room and Board (On/Off Campus): $9,600/$10,200
Books and Supplies: $1,000
Financial Aid Application Deadline: 2/1
Average Grant: $10,800
Average Loan: $22,390
% of Aid That Is Merit-Based: 65
% Receiving Some Sort of Aid: 84
Average Total Aid Package: $24,220
Average Debt: $66,330

ADMISSIONS INFORMATION
Application Fee: $60
Regular Application Deadline: 2/15
Regular Notification: Rolling
LSDAS Accepted? Yes
Average GPA: 3.3
Range of GPA: 3.0–3.5
Average LSAT: 153
Range of LSAT: 151–156
Transfer Students Accepted? Yes
Other Schools to Which Students Applied: Brooklyn Law School, Fordham, Hofstra, New York Law, Seton Hall, St. John's, Touro
Other Admissions Factors Considered: Undergraduate course work, community service
Number of Applications Received: 1,936
Number of Applicants Accepted: 686
Number of Applicants Enrolled: 182

INTERNATIONAL STUDENTS
TOEFL Required of International Students? Yes
Minimum TOEFL: 600 (250 computer)

EMPLOYMENT INFORMATION

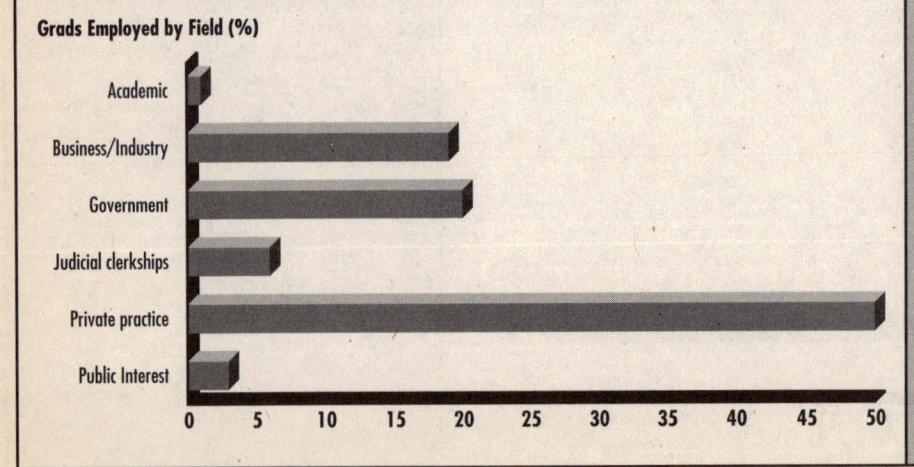

Grads Employed by Field (%)
- Academic: ~1
- Business/Industry: ~20
- Government: ~20
- Judicial clerkships: ~6
- Private practice: ~50
- Public Interest: ~3

Rate of Placement: 90%
Average Starting Salary: $60,552
Employers Who Frequently Hire Grads: Large law firms, large corporations, government and public interest offices
Prominent Alumni: Michael Finnegan, JP Morgan; John Cahill, General Counsel, NY Department of Environmental Conservation; Dan Ruben, Executive Director and Founder, Equal Justice America; John O'Connor, Partner, Milbaugh, Tweed, Hadley & McCoy; Hon. Terry Jane Ruderman, Judge, NY State Supreme Court
State for Bar Exam: NY, CT, NJ, PA, DC

PENNSYLVANIA STATE UNIVERSITY
The Dickinson School of Law

Admissions Contact: Director of Law Admissions, Barbara Guillaume
150 South College Street, Carlisle, PA 17013
Admissions Phone: 717-240-5207 • Admissions Fax: 717-241-3503
Admissions E-mail: dsladmit@psu.edu • Web Address: www.dsl.psu.edu

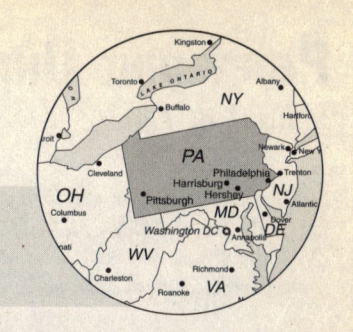

INSTITUTIONAL INFORMATION
Public/Private: Public
Student/Faculty Ratio: 20:1
Total Faculty: 89
% Part Time: 57
% Female: 24
% Minority: 3

PROGRAMS
Academic Specialties: Comparative and International Law, Advocacy, Clinical Education, Civil Procedure, Commercial Law, Constitutional Law, Corporation Securities Law, Criminal Law, Environmental Law, Government Services, Human Rights Law, Intellectual Property Law, Labor Law, Legal History, Property, Taxation
Advanced Degrees Offered: JD (3 years), LLM (1 year)
Combined Degrees Offered: JD/MBA, JD/MPA, JD/3 Environmental Pollution Control degrees, JD/MSIS, all with Penn State; JD/5 Counseling degrees with Shippensburg
Grading System: Distinguished (90+), Excellent (85–89), Good (80–84), Satisfactory (75–79), Passing (70–74), Conditional Failure (65–69), Failure (below 65)
Clinical Program Required? No
Clinical Program Description: Family Law; Disability Law; Elder Law; Art, Sports and Entertainment Law; externships in judges' chambers, district attorney's and public defender's offices, government agencies, legal services offices
Legal Writing Course Requirements? Yes
Legal Writing Description: First year, 2 semesters. Lawyering Skills involves teaching skills such as research, analysis of cases and statutes, writing of legal memoranda and briefs, and oral argument.
Legal Methods Course Requirements? Yes
Legal Methods Description: 2 semesters. Involves small-group instruction on legal research and prescriptive and persuasive writing. Third semester centers on appellate advocacy.
Legal Research Course Requirements? Yes
Legal Research Description: See Legal Writing.
Moot Court Requirement? Yes
Moot Court Description: Second year, fall semester; classroom meetings and submission of brief and presentation of oral argument, both for a grade
Public Interest Law Requirement? No
Academic Journals: *Dickinson Law Review, Penn State Environmental Law Review, Penn State International Law Review*

STUDENT INFORMATION
Enrollment of Law School: 595
% Male/Female: 52/48
% Full Time: 100
% Minority: 6
Average Age of Entering Class: 24

RESEARCH FACILITIES
Research Resources Available: Penn State libraries; libraries of Big Ten; Lexis, Westlaw, Loislaw; member libraries of the Association of College Libraries of Central Pennsylvania Consortium
School-Supported Research Centers: Agricultural Law Research and Education Center, Miller Center for Public Interest Advocacy, Center for Dispute Resolution, Center for International and Comparative Law

EXPENSES/FINANCIAL AID
Annual Tuition: $22,300
Room and Board (On/Off Campus): $6,450/$8,200
Books and Supplies: $4,800
Financial Aid Application Deadline: 2/15
Average Grant: $11,447
Average Loan: $23,407
% of Aid That Is Merit-Based: 16
% Receiving Some Sort of Aid: 88
Average Total Aid Package: $28,900
Average Debt: $63,250

ADMISSIONS INFORMATION
Application Fee: $50
Regular Application Deadline: 3/1
Regular Notification: Rolling
LSDAS Accepted? Yes
Average GPA: 3.3
Range of GPA: 3.1–3.5
Average LSAT: 154
Range of LSAT: 151–157
Transfer Students Accepted? Yes
Other Schools to Which Students Applied: American University, Temple University, University of Maryland, University of Pittsburgh, Villanova University
Other Admissions Factors Considered: Evidence of maturity, leadership, and initiative
Number of Applications Received: 1,655
Number of Applicants Accepted: 710
Number of Applicants Enrolled: 256

INTERNATIONAL STUDENTS
TOEFL Recommended for International Students? Yes

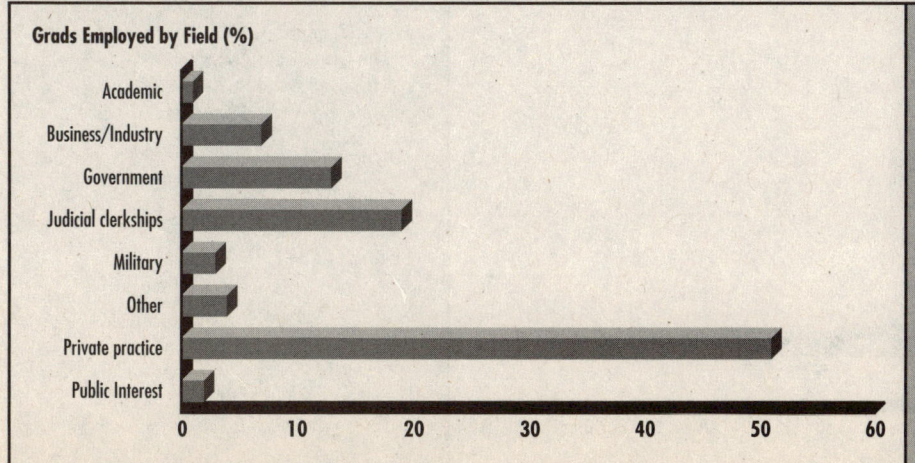

EMPLOYMENT INFORMATION

Grads Employed by Field (%)
- Academic
- Business/Industry
- Government
- Judicial clerkships
- Military
- Other
- Private practice
- Public Interest

Rate of Placement: 93%
Average Starting Salary: $54,773
Employers Who Frequently Hire Grads: National law firms, small firms, federal and state judges, government agencies, public interest organizations
Prominent Alumni: Hon. Thomas Ridge, Secretary, Homeland Security; Hon. Richard Santorum, U.S. Senator; Hon. Sylvia Rambo, Federal District Court, Middle District of PA; Lisa A. Hook, Vice President, AOL–Time Warner; Hon. J. Michael Eakin, PA Supreme Court
State for Bar Exam: PA, NJ, NY, CA, MD
Pass Rate for First-Time Bar: 82%

PEPPERDINE UNIVERSITY
School of Law

Admissions Contact: Director of Admissions, Shannon Phillips
24255 Pacific Coast Highway, Malibu, CA 90263
Admissions Phone: 310-506-4631 • Admissions Fax: 310-506-7668
Admissions E-mail: soladmis@pepperdine.edu • Web Address: law.pepperdine.edu

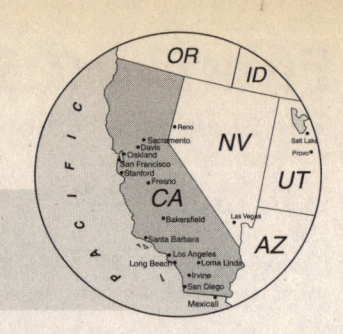

INSTITUTIONAL INFORMATION
Public/Private: Private
Student/Faculty Ratio: 18:1

PROGRAMS
Academic Specialties: Straus Institute for Dispute Resolution, Center for Entrepreneurship and Technology Law, London Program, Commercial Law, Corporation Securities Law, Intellectual Property Law, International Law, Taxation
Advanced Degrees Offered: LLM Dispute Resolution
Combined Degrees Offered: JD/MBA (4 years), JD/MDR (3 to 4 years), JD/MPP (4 years)
Grading System: Numerical system (55–100)
Clinical Program Required? No
Legal Writing Course Requirements? Yes
Legal Writing Description: Identification, description, and use of source materials for the solution of legal problems; introduction to the law library and its use. Each student will be required to produce one or more papers dealing with approved legal subjects and to engage in oral argument thereon.
Legal Methods Course Requirements? No
Legal Research Course Requirements? Yes
Legal Research Description: See Legal Writing.
Moot Court Requirement? Yes
Moot Court Description: First-year moot court
Public Interest Law Requirement? No
Academic Journals: *Law Review, Alternative Dispute Resolution Journal, Administration Law Journal*

STUDENT INFORMATION
Enrollment of Law School: 662
% Out of State: 40
% Male/Female: 52/48
% Full Time: 100
% Full Time That Are International: 1
% Minority: 18
Average Age of Entering Class: 23

EXPENSES/FINANCIAL AID
Annual Tuition: $24,820
Room and Board: $10,100
Books and Supplies: $700
Financial Aid Application Deadline: 4/1
Average Grant: $9,000
Average Loan: $24,500
% of Aid That Is Merit-Based: 60
% Receiving Some Sort of Aid: 84
Average Total Aid Package: $38,000
Average Debt: $75,000
Tuition Per Credit: $915

ADMISSIONS INFORMATION
Application Fee: $50
Regular Application Deadline: 3/1
Regular Notification: Rolling
LSDAS Accepted? Yes
Average GPA: 3.4
Range of GPA: 3.1–3.6
Average LSAT: 157
Range of LSAT: 155–160
Transfer Students Accepted? Yes
Other Schools to Which Students Applied: Loyola Marymount University, University of San Diego
Other Admissions Factors Considered: Employment experience, extracurricular activites, community involvement, commitement to high standards of ethics and morality, initiative, competence in writing and speaking, maturity
Number of Applications Received: 2,794
Number of Applicants Accepted: 984
Number of Applicants Enrolled: 270

EMPLOYMENT INFORMATION

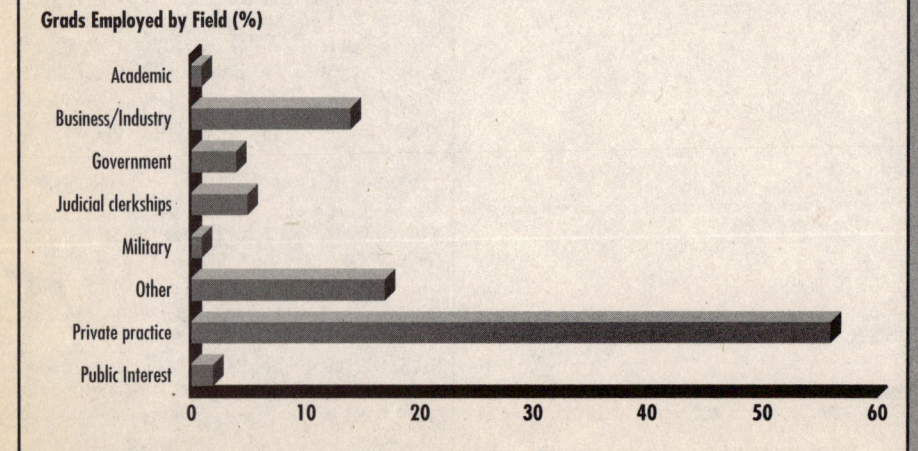

Grads Employed by Field (%)

Field	%
Academic	~1
Business/Industry	~14
Government	~4
Judicial clerkships	~5
Military	~1
Other	~17
Private practice	~57
Public Interest	~1

Rate of Placement: 86%
Average Starting Salary: $82,721
State for Bar Exam: CA
Pass Rate for First-Time Bar: 61%

QUEEN'S UNIVERSITY
Faculty of Law

Admissions Contact: Registrar of Law, Jane Emrich
Macdonald Hall, Union Street, Kingston, ON K7L 3N6
Admissions Phone: 613-533-2220 • Admissions Fax: 613-533-6611
Admissions E-mail: llb@qsilver.queensu.ca • Web Address: llb@qsilver.queensu.ca/law

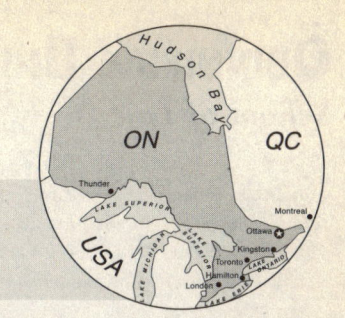

INSTITUTIONAL INFORMATION
Public/Private: Public
Student/Faculty Ratio: 6:1
Total Faculty: 78
% Part Time: 69
% Female: 36

PROGRAMS
Academic Specialties: Civil Procedure, Commercial Law, Constitutional Law, Corporation Securities Law, Criminal Law, Environmental Law, Government Services, Human Rights Law, Intellectual Property Law, International Law, Labor Law, Legal History, Legal Philosophy, Property, Taxation
Advanced Degrees Offered: LLM (1 to 5 years)
Combined Degrees Offered: MIR/LLB (4 years full time), MPA/LLB (4 years full time)
Grading System: A, Exceptional; A–, Excellent; B+, Very Good; B, Good; B–, Satisfactory; C+, Fair; C, Adequate; D, Marginal; F, Failure; PA, Pass; ED, Exam Deferred; IP, In Progress
Clinical Program Required? Yes
Clinical Program Description: Clinical Correctional Law, Clinical Litigation, Clinical Family
Legal Writing Course Requirements? Yes
Legal Writing Description: First year, Skills Introduction is a primer on legal education and skills, with a particular emphasis on legal research and writing. Sometime during their upper years, students must complete a minimum of 1 substantial term paper.
Legal Methods Course Requirements? Yes
Legal Methods Description: Practice Skills Requirement: A Legal Methods course, or Practice Skills course, is one that gives students significant opportunity to undertake legal research and to develop skills of drafting, client interaction, oral advocacy, negotiation, and mediation or that offers students a clinical legal experience.
Legal Research Course Requirements? No
Moot Court Requirement? Yes
Moot Court Description: Each student must satisfy the Moot Court Requirement in the second year, taking full responsibility as counsel in the preparation and argument of a moot case. In order to satisfy the Moot Court Requirement, a student must successfully complete a Faculty Moot, a Competitive Moot, or an upper-year course certified by the instructor as satisfying the Moot Court Requirement.
Public Interest Law Requirement? Yes
Public Interest Law Description: Each student must complete an upper-year course (in addition to Civil Procedure) in which legal ethics is certified as constituting a significant element of the course.
Academic Journals: *Queen's Law Journal*

STUDENT INFORMATION
Enrollment of Law School: 484
% Male/Female: 48/52
% Full Time: 95
Average Age of Entering Class: 25

RESEARCH FACILITIES
Research Resources Available: Queen's provides opportunities for students to enrich their LLB studies by attending other universities for a semester. Students can also spend a spring semester enrolled in the International Study Centre in East Sussex, UK.
School-Supported Research Centers: William R. Lederman Law Library; Electronic Law Library; Internet connections at every student bench in some classrooms

EXPENSES/FINANCIAL AID
Annual Tuition: $7,792
Books and Supplies: $1,850
Financial Aid Application Deadline: 10/31
Average Grant: $4,650
Average Loan: $6,500
% Receiving Some Sort of Aid: 63

ADMISSIONS INFORMATION
Application Fee: $150
Regular Application Deadline: 11/1
Regular Notification: Rolling
LSDAS Accepted? No
Average LSAT: 160
Range of LSAT: 155–169
Transfer Students Accepted? Yes
Other Schools to Which Students Applied: Dalhousie, McGill University, University of British Columbia, University of Calgary, University of Toronto, University of Windsor, York University
Other Admissions Factors Considered: Interview
Number of Applications Received: 2,170
Number of Applicants Accepted: 618
Number of Applicants Enrolled: 161

INTERNATIONAL STUDENTS
TOEFL Required of International Students? Yes
Minimum TOEFL: 600 (250 computer)

EMPLOYMENT INFORMATION
Grads Employed by Field (%)
- Business/Industry
- Government
- Judicial clerkships
- Private practice
- Public Interest

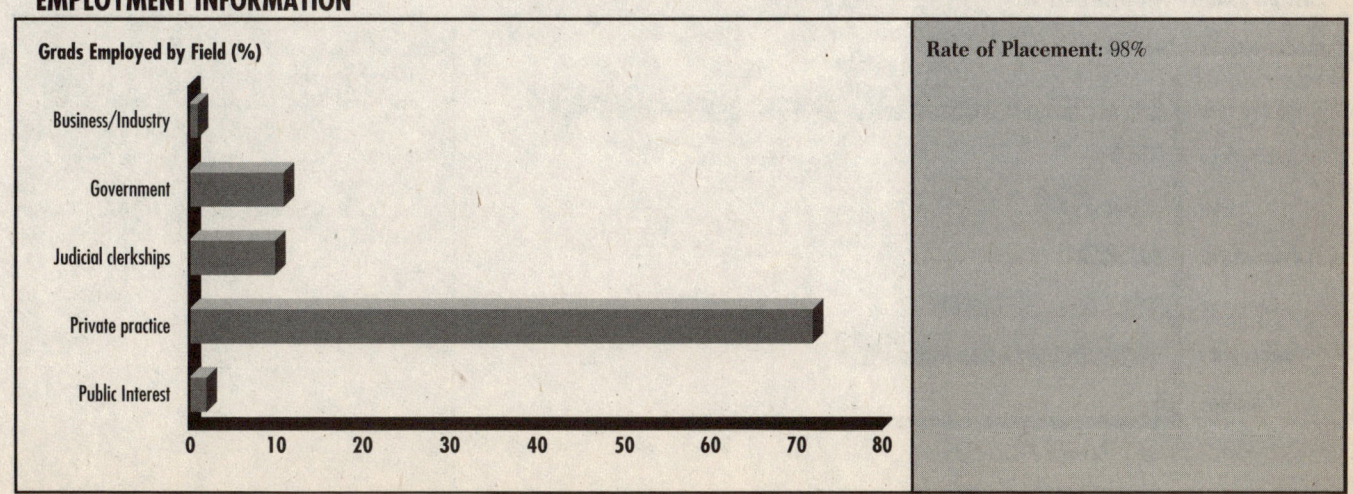

Rate of Placement: 98%

QUINNIPIAC UNIVERSITY
School of Law

Admissions Contact: Dean of Law School Admissions, John J. Noonan
275 Mount Carmel Avenue, Hamden, CT 06518-1950
Admissions Phone: 203-582-3400 • *Admissions Fax:* 203-582-3339
Admissions E-mail: ladm@quinnipiac.edu • *Web Address:* law.quinnipiac.edu

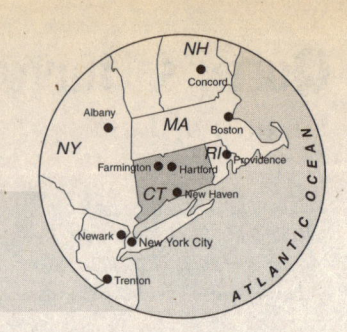

INSTITUTIONAL INFORMATION
Public/Private: Private
Student/Faculty Ratio: 16:1
Total Faculty: 90
% Part Time: 51
% Female: 32
% Minority: 5

PROGRAMS
Academic Specialties: We offer a rich curriculum, an outstanding teaching faculty, and exceptional facilities. The programs offer specialized practice courses, skills training, and hands-on experience in such areas as Civil Procedure, Commercial Law, Corporation Securities Law, Criminal Law, International Law, and Taxation.
Advanced Degrees Offered: JD (3 years full time, 4 years part time)
Combined Degrees Offered: JD/MBA (4 years), JD/MHA (4 years)
Grading System: Letter system on a 4.0 scale
Clinical Program Required? No
Clinical Program Description: Civic Clinic, Appellate Clinic, Health Law Clinic, Tax Clinic
Legal Writing Course Requirements? Yes
Legal Writing Description: This year-long course trains students in the fundamentals of legal writing, analysis, and research.
Legal Methods Course Requirements? No
Legal Research Course Requirements? No
Moot Court Requirement? No
Public Interest Law Requirement? No
Academic Journals: *Quinnipiac Law Review, Health Law Journal, Probate Law Journal*

STUDENT INFORMATION
Enrollment of Law School: 219
% Out of State: 47
% Male/Female: 55/45
% Full Time: 71
% Minority: 10
Average Age of Entering Class: 26

RESEARCH FACILITIES
Research Resources Available: Lexis, Westlaw, CALI
School-Supported Research Centers: Digital video production and editing

EXPENSES/FINANCIAL AID
Annual Tuition: $26,980
Room and Board (Off Campus): $10,715
Books and Supplies: $1,200
Average Grant: $7,500
Average Loan: $19,265
% of Aid That Is Merit-Based: 40
% Receiving Some Sort of Aid: 87
Average Total Aid Package: $20,000
Average Debt: $65,100
Tuition Per Credit: $930

ADMISSIONS INFORMATION
Application Fee: $40
Regular Application Deadline: Rolling
Regular Notification: Rolling
LSDAS Accepted? Yes
Average GPA: 2.9
Range of GPA: 2.7–3.3
Average LSAT: 151
Range of LSAT: 148–153
Transfer Students Accepted? Yes
Other Admissions Factors Considered: Personal statement, recommendations, interview
Number of Applications Received: 2,042
Number of Applicants Accepted: 702
Number of Applicants Enrolled: 219

INTERNATIONAL STUDENTS
TOEFL Recommended for International Students? Yes

EMPLOYMENT INFORMATION

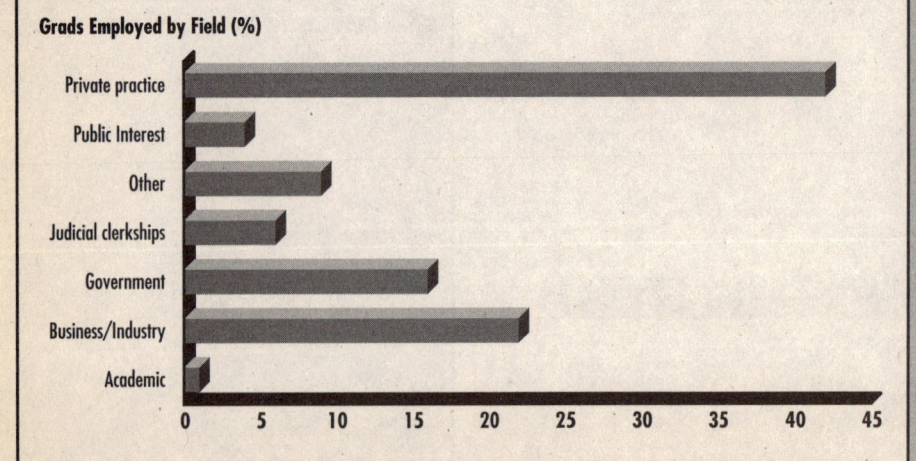

Grads Employed by Field (%)

Field	%
Private practice	~43
Public Interest	~2
Other	~8
Judicial clerkships	~4
Government	~16
Business/Industry	~22
Academic	~1

Rate of Placement: 95%
Average Starting Salary: $50,655
Employers Who Frequently Hire Grads: Law firms, corporations, public defender's offices, prosecutor's offices, various government and public interest organizations
State for Bar Exam: CT, NY, NJ, MA, RI
Pass Rate for First-Time Bar: 78%

REGENT UNIVERSITY
School of Law

Admissions Contact: Assistant to the Director of Admissions and Financial Aid, Marie Markham
1000 Regent University Drive, Virginia Beach, VA 23464
Admissions Phone: 757-226-4584 • Admissions Fax: 757-226-4139
Admissions E-mail: lawschool@regent.edu • Web Address: www.regent.edu/acad/schlaw/admit/home.html

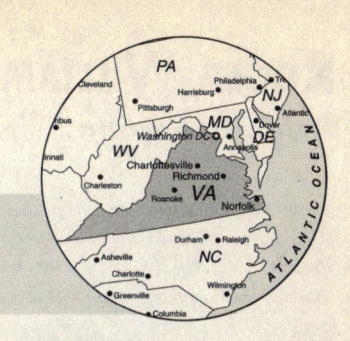

INSTITUTIONAL INFORMATION
Public/Private: Private
Student/Faculty Ratio: 22:1
Total Faculty: 27
% Part Time: 0
% Female: 22
% Minority: 19

PROGRAMS
Academic Specialties: The opportunity to work alongside attorneys for the American Center for Law and Justice, one of the nation's foremost public interest law firms, in developing legal strategies to defend life, liberty, and family; the opportunity for selected third-year students to meet regularly with federal and state judges, leading attorneys, and law faculty in the James Kent American Inn of Court to discuss ethical and practical concerns related to the practice of law; a spacious facility equipped with the latest technology, featuring computer-oriented classroom instruction; a national reputation for equipping students with the fundamental skills necessary to the effective practice of law
Combined Degrees Offered: JD/MBA, JD/MPA, JD/MPP, JD/MPM, JD/MDiv, JD/MA Management, Counseling, or Communication (all 4 years)
Grading System: A+ (4.00), through F (0.00)
Clinical Program Required? No
Clinical Program Description: Litigation Clinic, Family Mediation Clinic
Legal Writing Course Requirements? Yes
Legal Writing Description: Legal Research and Writing Program prepares students in legal reasoning, research, and brief writing. The spring semester is dedicated exclusively to persuasive writing and advocacy. Students receive a total of 6 hours of legal research and writing during their first year. These additional hours will primarily be used as a lab to supplement class lectures with in-class practice problems.
Legal Methods Course Requirements? Yes
Legal Methods Description: See Legal Writing.
Legal Research Course Requirements? Yes
Legal Research Description: The Legal Research component of the Legal Research and Writing Program includes information on the state and federal court systems, reporters, finding tools, and basic jurisdictional issues. It also includes intensive lectures in secondary sources, finding common law, researching state statutes, researching federal statutes, and researching administrative law. During the second semester, students write a trial brief and an appellate brief.
Moot Court Requirement? Yes
Moot Court Description: The annual Moot Court Competition is an integral component of the first-year Legal Writing curriculum. To receive a grade, students are required to argue 2 rounds of the competition, and may proceed to later rounds if the quality of the argument warrants.
Public Interest Law Requirement? No
Academic Journals: *Regent Law Review, Journal of Maritime Law and International Trade, Regent Journal of International Law, Journal of Entertainment, Sports and Intellectual Property*

STUDENT INFORMATION
Enrollment of Law School: 504
% Male/Female: 61/39
% Full Time: 77
% Full Time That Are International: 1
% Minority: 11
Average Age of Entering Class: 27

EXPENSES/FINANCIAL AID
Annual Tuition: $18,445
Room and Board (Off Campus): $6,111
Books and Supplies: $1,268
Financial Aid Application Deadline: 6/3
Average Grant: $7,656
Average Loan: $20,961
% of Aid That Is Merit-Based: 25
% Receiving Some Sort of Aid: 99
Average Total Aid Package: $26,141
Average Debt: $58,729
Tuition Per Credit: $595
Fees Per Credit: $226

ADMISSIONS INFORMATION
Application Fee: $40
Regular Application Deadline: 6/1
Regular Notification: Rolling
LSDAS Accepted? Yes
Average GPA: 3.1
Range of GPA: 2.8–3.6
Average LSAT: 152
Range of LSAT: 147–154
Transfer Students Accepted? Yes
Other Admissions Factors Considered: Harmony with the mission of the law school
Number of Applications Received: 446
Number of Applicants Accepted: 317
Number of Applicants Enrolled: 190

INTERNATIONAL STUDENTS
TOEFL Required of International Students? Yes
Minimum TOEFL: 600 (250 computer)

EMPLOYMENT INFORMATION

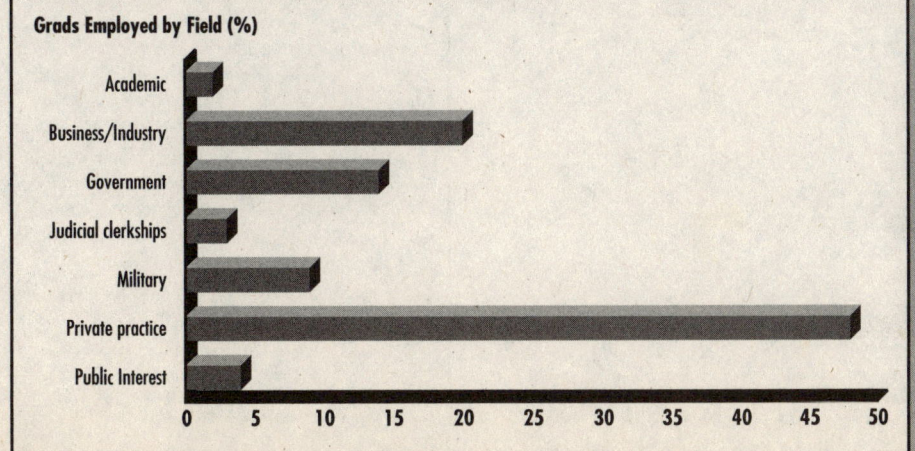

Grads Employed by Field (%)

Field	%
Academic	~1
Business/Industry	~20
Government	~15
Judicial clerkships	~5
Military	~15
Private practice	~48
Public Interest	~3

Rate of Placement: 87%
Average Starting Salary: $42,750
Employers Who Frequently Hire Grads: American Center for Law and Justice; Bopp, Coleson & Bostrom; U.S. Air Force JAG Corps; U.S. Army JAG Corps; law office of David McCormick; Portsmouth Commonwealth's Attorney; Virginia Beach Public Defender; Lexis/Nexis; Winters, King & Associates, Inc.; Smink, Thomas & Associates
Prominent Alumni: Robert F. McDonnell, Virginia House of Delegates; David J. Klarich, Missouri Senator; Ron Pahl, Judge, Oregon Circuit Court; Mary F. Covington, Judge, North Carolina District Court
State for Bar Exam: VA, NC, TX, CA, FL
Pass Rate for First-Time Bar: 56%

ROGER WILLIAMS UNIVERSITY
Ralph R. Papitto School of Law

Admissions Contact: Director of Admissions, Michael Boylen
10 Metacom Avenue, Bristol, RI 02809
Admissions Phone: 401-254-4555 • Admissions Fax: 401-254-4516
Admissions E-mail: admissions@law.rwu.edu • Web Address: law.rwu.edu

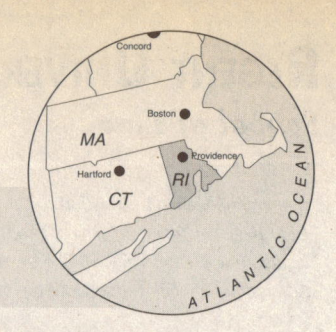

INSTITUTIONAL INFORMATION
Public/Private: Private
Student/Faculty Ratio: 17:1
Total Faculty: 62
% Part Time: 45
% Female: 33
% Minority: 7

PROGRAMS
Academic Specialties: Extensive Maritime Law Program; special emphasis on Intellectual Property and Labor Law; summer study-abroad programs in London, England, and Lisbon, Portugal; Commercial Law; Constitutional Law; Corporation Securities Law; Criminal Law; Environmental Law; International Law; Legal History
Advanced Degrees Offered: JD (3 years full time, 4 years part time)
Combined Degrees Offered: JD/MCP (4 years), JD/MMA (3.5 years), JD/MS Labor Relations and Human Resources (4 years), JD/MCJ (3.5 years)
Grading System: Letter system on a 4.0 scale
Clinical Program Required? No
Clinical Program Description: Disability Law Clinic, Criminal Defense Clinic
Legal Writing Course Requirements? No
Legal Methods Course Requirements? Yes
Legal Methods Description: 4 courses in the first 2 years: Analysis, Research and Writing; Appellate Advocacy; Interviewing and Client Counseling; Trial Advocacy
Legal Research Course Requirements? No
Moot Court Requirement? No
Public Interest Law Requirement? Yes
Public Interest Law Description: 20 hours of community service
Academic Journals: *Roger Williams University Law Review*, *The Docket* (published by the Student Bar Association)

STUDENT INFORMATION
Enrollment of Law School: 525
% Out of State: 30
% Male/Female: 46/54
% Full Time: 76
% Full Time That Are International: 2
% Minority: 13
Average Age of Entering Class: 26

RESEARCH FACILITIES
Research Resources Available: The Law Library offers the largest legal collection in Rhode Island and is a member of the New England Law Library Consortium, the Consortium of Rhode Island Academic and Research Libraries, and a number of other prestigious consortia.
School-Supported Research Centers: Marine Affairs Institute, Feinstein Institute for Legal Services, Portuguese-American Comparative Law Center

EXPENSES/FINANCIAL AID
Annual Tuition: $23,400
Books and Supplies: $1,100
Financial Aid Application Deadline: 3/15
Average Grant: $9,287
Average Loan: $28,866
% of Aid That Is Merit-Based: 16
% Receiving Some Sort of Aid: 97
Average Total Aid Package: $38,372
Average Debt: $62,612
Tuition Per Credit: $820
Fees Per Credit: $150

ADMISSIONS INFORMATION
Application Fee: $60
Regular Application Deadline: Rolling
Regular Notification: Rolling
LSDAS Accepted? Yes
Average GPA: 3.1
Range of GPA: 2.8–3.4
Average LSAT: 150
Range of LSAT: 147–154
Transfer Students Accepted? Yes
Other Schools to Which Students Applied: New England School of Law, Quinnipiac University, Suffolk University, Western New England College
Other Admissions Factors Considered: Graduate work
Number of Applications Received: 1,271
Number of Applicants Accepted: 732
Number of Applicants Enrolled: 212

INTERNATIONAL STUDENTS
TOEFL Required of International Students? Yes
Minimum TOEFL: 600 (250 computer).

EMPLOYMENT INFORMATION

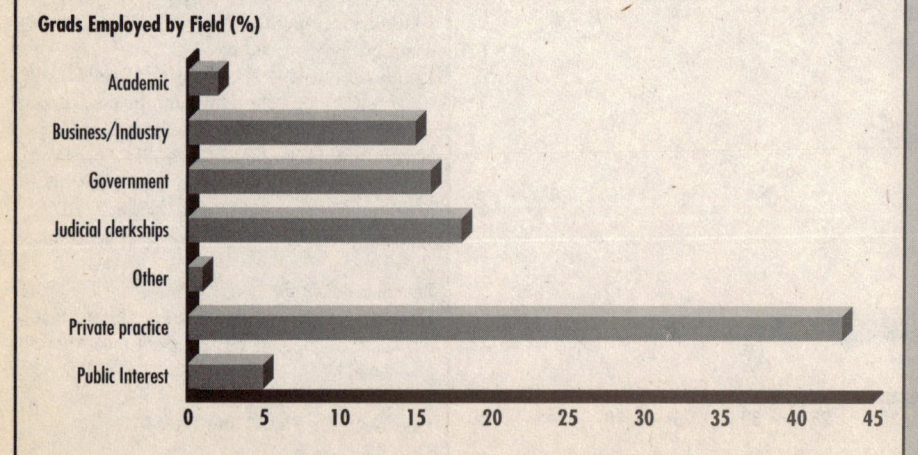

Grads Employed by Field (%)
- Academic
- Business/Industry
- Government
- Judicial clerkships
- Other
- Private practice
- Public Interest

Rate of Placement: 63%
Average Starting Salary: $44,348
Employers Who Frequently Hire Grads: Rhode Island courts
Prominent Alumni: Kenneth K. McKay, Chief of Staff of Rhode Island Governor Carcieri; John M. Sutherland III, VP of Finance and CFO, Women's and Infants Hospital; David Habich, FBI; Betty Ann Waters, attorney who freed her wrongly accused brother after 18 years
State for Bar Exam: RI, CT, MA, PA, NJ
Pass Rate for First-Time Bar: 70%

RUTGERS UNIVERSITY—CAMDEN
Rutgers School of Law at Camden

Admissions Contact: Assistant Director of Admissions, Maureen O'Boyle
406 Penn Street, 3rd floor, Camden, NJ 08102
Admissions Phone: 800-466-7561 • Admissions Fax: 856-225-6537
Admissions E-mail: admissions@camlaw.rutgers.edu • Web Address: www-camden.rutgers.edu

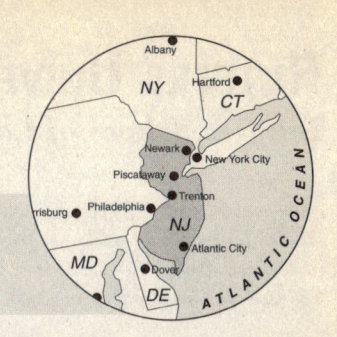

INSTITUTIONAL INFORMATION
Public/Private: Public
Student/Faculty Ratio: 6:1
Total Faculty: 128
% Part Time: 58
% Female: 31
% Minority: 9

PROGRAMS
Academic Specialties: Health Law, International Law, Sex Discrimination Law, Commercial Law, State Constitutional Law, Criminal Law, Civil Procedure, Admiralty, Legal History, Jurisprudence, Comparative Law, Commercial Law, Family Law and Domestic Violence, Health Law, Lawyering Skills and Advocacy, Constitutional Law, Corporation Securities Law, Environmental Law, Labor Law, Taxation
Advanced Degrees Offered: JD (3 years full time, 4 years part time)
Combined Degrees Offered: JD/MPP (3.5 years); JD/MBA (4 years); JD/MSW (4 years); JD/MCRP (4 years); JD/MPA Health Care Management and Policy (4 years); JD/MD, JD/DO with University of Medicine and Dentistry of New Jersey
Grading System: Letter system
Clinical Program Required? No
Clinical Program Description: Live-client clinic representing elderly and disabled clients, clinic at the LEAP Charter School for children and their families, as well as domestic violence, mediation, bankruptcy, legal education, and income tax assistance pro bono programs.
Legal Writing Course Requirements? Yes
Legal Writing Description: All students must complete Legal Writing credits in each year, starting with the first semester. Upper-class courses offer a variety of credits to supplement these studies.
Legal Methods Course Requirements? Yes
Legal Methods Description: First-year required year-long graded course covering research, analysis, writing, and oral advocacy. The school also has a unique upper-level writing requirement.
Legal Research Course Requirements? No
Legal Research Description: First-year students are required to take Legal Research and Writing in the first semester.
Moot Court Requirement? Yes
Moot Court Description: First year, spring semester. Students prepare a brief and are teamed with a partner for purposes of oral argument.
Public Interest Law Requirement? No
Academic Journals: *Rutgers Law Journal, Rutgers Journal of Law and Religion*

STUDENT INFORMATION
Enrollment of Law School: 757
% Out of State: 40
% Male/Female: 57/43
% Full Time: 75
% Full Time That Are International: 1
% Minority: 18
Average Age of Entering Class: 26

EXPENSES/FINANCIAL AID
Annual Tuition (Residents/Nonresidents): $12,522/$18,244
Room and Board (On/Off Campus): $5,334/$8,990
Books and Supplies: $1,000
Financial Aid Application Deadline: 4/1
Average Grant: $5,000
Average Loan: $19,000
% of Aid That Is Merit-Based: 20
% Receiving Some Sort of Aid: 85
Average Total Aid Package: $19,000
Average Debt: $50,000
Tuition Per Credit (Residents/Nonresidents): $518/$759
Fees Per Credit: $30

ADMISSIONS INFORMATION
Application Fee: $50
Regular Application Deadline: 4/1
Regular Notification: Rolling
LSDAS Accepted? Yes
Average GPA: 3.2
Range of GPA: 2.9–3.5
Average LSAT: 161
Range of LSAT: 158–163
Transfer Students Accepted? Yes
Other Schools to Which Students Applied: Fordham, George Washington, Rutgers, Temple, UCLA, U. of Maryland, U. of Pennsylvania
Other Admissions Factors Considered: Quality of undergraduate and graduate institutions, undergraduate major, graduate schools and GPA, life and work experiences, general background
Number of Applications Received: 2,255
Number of Applicants Accepted: 510
Number of Applicants Enrolled: 226

INTERNATIONAL STUDENTS
TOEFL Required of International Students? Yes
Minimum TOEFL: 600 (250 computer)

EMPLOYMENT INFORMATION

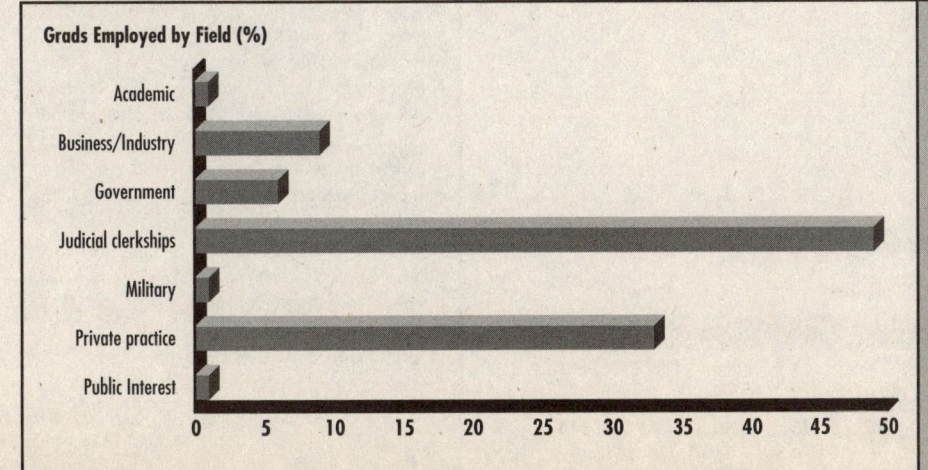

Grads Employed by Field (%)
- Academic: ~2
- Business/Industry: ~8
- Government: ~9
- Judicial clerkships: ~49
- Military: ~1
- Private practice: ~33
- Public Interest: ~1

Rate of Placement: 97%
Average Starting Salary: $76,000
Employers Who Frequently Hire Grads: All major Philadelphia, New Jersey, and Delaware law firms; numerous prestigious firms from New York City, DC, California, and other major metropolitan areas; Rutgers ranks second in the country in placing its law graduates in highly desirable judicial clerkships.
Prominent Alumni: Hon. James Florio, former Governor and U.S. Congressman; Hon. Joseph Rodriguez, U.S. Federal District Judge; Hon. Stephen Orlofsky, U.S. Federal District Judge; Hon. William Hughes, former Ambassador and U.S. Congressman
State for Bar Exam: NJ, NY, PA, CA, TX
Pass Rate for First-Time Bar: 81%

RUTGERS UNIVERSITY — NEWARK
Rutgers School of Law at Newark

Admissions Contact: Director of Admissions, Anita Walton
Center for Law and Justice, 123 Washington Street, Newark, NJ 07102
Admissions Phone: 973-353-5554 • Admissions Fax: 973-353-3459
Admissions E-mail: geddis@andromeda.rutgers.edu • Web Address: www.rutgers-newark.rutgers.edu/law

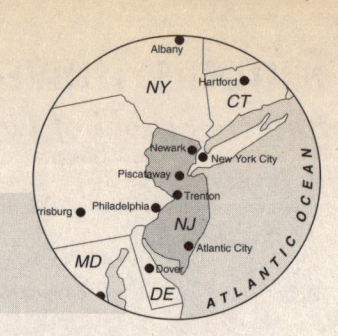

INSTITUTIONAL INFORMATION
Public/Private: Public
Student/Faculty Ratio: 20:1
Total Faculty: 62
% Part Time: 56
% Female: 31
% Minority: 21

PROGRAMS
Academic Specialties: Our diverse faculty specializes in a broad range of topics, including International Law, Human Rights and Civil Liberties, Corporate Law, and Intellectual Property. Many faculty are involved in major cases that impact both the public and private sectors. The Center for Law and Justice is a new facility that enables faculty to use new technology that is at the cutting edge. Specialties include Civil Procedure, Commercial Law, Constitutional Law, Corporation Securities Law, Criminal Law, Environmental Law, Labor Law, Legal History, Legal Philosophy, Property, and Taxation.
Combined Degrees Offered: JD/MBA (4 years), JD/MD (6 years), JD/PhD Jurisprudence (5 years), JD/MA Criminal Justice (4 years), JD/MCRP (4 years), JD/MSW (4 years)
Grading System: 4.0 scale; mandatory curve in first year
Clinical Program Required? No
Clinical Program Description: Constitutional Litigation Clinic, Environmental Law Clinic, Federal Tax Clinic, Urban Legal Clinic, Women's Rights Litigation Clinic, Child Advocacy Clinic, Women and AIDS, Special Education Clinic, Domestic Violence Project
Legal Writing Course Requirements? Yes
Legal Writing Description: First-year, 2 semesters. The first semester focuses on legal research and requires the completion of a series of legal writing assignments. The second semester focuses on oral advocacy and the completion of a legal brief.
Legal Methods Course Requirements? Yes
Legal Methods Description: 3 credits in the first year as part of Legal Research and Writing
Legal Research Course Requirements? Yes
Legal Research Description: Part of Legal Research and Writing
Moot Court Requirement? Yes
Moot Court Description: Part of Legal Research and Writing
Public Interest Law Requirement? No
Academic Journals: Rutgers Law Review, Rutgers Computer and Technology Law Journal, Women's Rights Law Reporter, Rutgers Race and the Law Journal

STUDENT INFORMATION
Enrollment of Law School: 760
% Male/Female: 49/51
% Full Time: 74
% Minority: 36
Average Age of Entering Class: 27

EXPENSES/FINANCIAL AID
Annual Tuition (Residents/Nonresidents): $10,612/$15,570
Room and Board (On/Off Campus): $7,967/$9,107
Books and Supplies: $3,962
Financial Aid Application Deadline: 3/1
Average Grant: $3,220
Average Loan: $19,350
% of Aid That Is Merit-Based: 74
% Receiving Some Sort of Aid: 81
Average Total Aid Package: $18,073
Average Debt: $39,174
Tuition Per Credit (Residents/Nonresidents): $518/$759
Fees Per Credit: $484

ADMISSIONS INFORMATION
Application Fee: $50
Regular Application Deadline: 3/15
Regular Notification: Rolling
LSDAS Accepted? Yes
Average GPA: 3.3
Range of GPA: 3.0–3.5
Average LSAT: 159
Range of LSAT: 154–160
Transfer Students Accepted? Yes
Other Schools to Which Students Applied: Fordham University, Rutgers University—Camden, American University, George Washington University, Seton Hall University, Yeshiva University, Boston University
Other Admissions Factors Considered: Graduate degree, work experience, background, socioeconomic factors, community activities, personal essay, letters of recommendation
Number of Applications Received: 3,216
Number of Applicants Accepted: 701
Number of Applicants Enrolled: 240

EMPLOYMENT INFORMATION

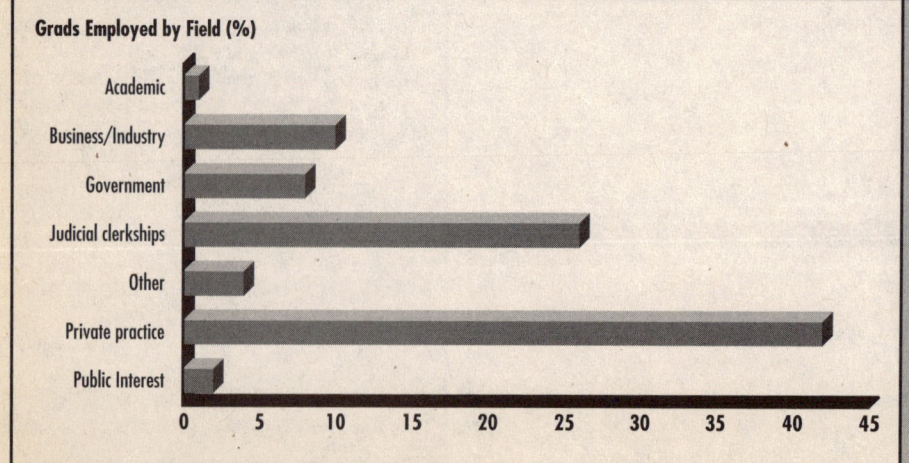

Grads Employed by Field (%)

Field	%
Academic	~1
Business/Industry	~10
Government	~8
Judicial clerkships	~26
Other	~3
Private practice	~43
Public Interest	~2

Rate of Placement: 96%
Average Starting Salary: $71,300
Employers Who Frequently Hire Grads: Federal judges, New Jersey Court judges, large NJ and NY law firms, medium-size NJ firms, NY and NJ corporations, Legal Services
Prominent Alumni: Robert Menendez, U.S. Congressman; Jaynee LaVecchia, Justice, New Jersey Supreme Court; Ida Castro, Commissioner of Personnel, New Jersey; Virginia Long, Justice, New Jersey Supreme Court
State for Bar Exam: NJ, NY, PA
Pass Rate for First-Time Bar: 82%

St. John's University
School of Law

Admissions Contact: Assistant Dean for Admissions, Robert M. Harrison
8000 Utopia Parkway, Jamaica, NY 11439
Admissions Phone: 718-990-6474 • Admissions Fax: 718-990-2526
Admissions E-mail: rsvp@stjohns.edu • Web Address: www.stjohns.edu/law

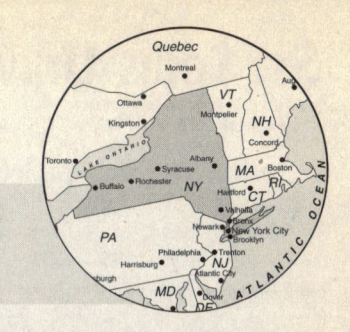

INSTITUTIONAL INFORMATION
Public/Private: Private
Student/Faculty Ratio: 19:1

PROGRAMS
Academic Specialties: Securities Law, Government Service, Labor Law, Real Estate, Bankruptcy, Criminal Law, Taxation, Environmental, Domestic and International Commercial, Legal Philosophy
Advanced Degrees Offered: JD (3 years day, 2.5 years day, 4 years evening), LLM Bankruptcy (1 year full time, 2 to 3 years part time)
Combined Degrees Offered: JD/MBA, JD/MA, JD/MS, BA/JD, BS/JD
Grading System: Letter system
Clinical Program Required? No
Clinical Program Description: Elder Law, Civil, Criminal, Judicial, and Domestic Violence Clinics
Legal Writing Course Requirements? Yes
Legal Writing Description: First-year required course
Legal Methods Course Requirements? Yes
Legal Methods Description: First-year required course
Legal Research Course Requirements? Yes
Legal Research Description: First-year required course

Moot Court Requirement? Yes
Moot Court Description: Part of the first-year research and writing program
Public Interest Law Requirement? No
Academic Journals: Law Review, Journal of Legal Commentary, N.Y. International Law Review, N.Y. Real Property Law Journal, Bankruptcy Law Review, Catholic Lawyer

STUDENT INFORMATION
Enrollment of Law School: 259
% Male/Female: 55/45
% Full Time: 80
% Minority: 18

EXPENSES/FINANCIAL AID
Annual Tuition: $22,000
Room and Board: $8,500
Average Grant: $6,904
Average Loan: $16,911
% of Aid That Is Merit-Based: 17
% Receiving Some Sort of Aid: 89
Average Total Aid Package: $18,496
Average Debt: $53,619
Tuition Per Credit: $800

ADMISSIONS INFORMATION
Application Fee: $60
Regular Application Deadline: Rolling
Regular Notification: Rolling
LSDAS Accepted? Yes
Average GPA: 3.2
Range of GPA: 2.9–3.5
Average LSAT: 156
Range of LSAT: 153–160
Transfer Students Accepted? Yes
Other Admissions Factors Considered: Undergraduate major, undergraduate educational institution, graduate work, work experience, extracurricular activities, community activities
Number of Applications Received: 2,617
Number of Applicants Accepted: 1,186
Number of Applicants Enrolled: 259

EMPLOYMENT INFORMATION

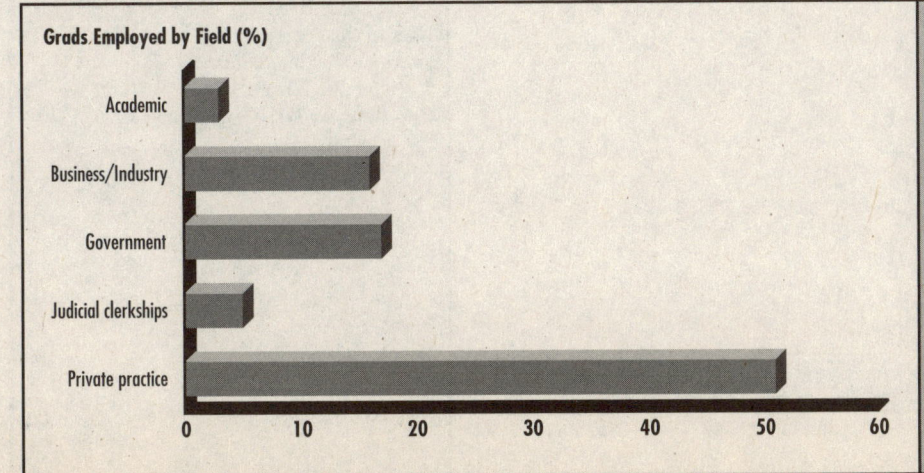

Grads Employed by Field (%)
- Academic
- Business/Industry
- Government
- Judicial clerkships
- Private practice

Rate of Placement: 98%
Average Starting Salary: $75,000
Employers Who Frequently Hire Grads: Private law firms, corporations, governmental agencies
State for Bar Exam: NY
Pass Rate for First-Time Bar: 78%

ST. LOUIS UNIVERSITY
School of Law

Admissions Contact: Assistant Dean and Director of Admissions, Michael J. Kolnik
3700 Lindell Boulevard, St. Louis, MO 63108
Admissions Phone: 314-977-2800 • Admissions Fax: 314-977-1464
Admissions E-mail: admissions@law.slu.edu • Web Address: law.slu.edu

INSTITUTIONAL INFORMATION
Public/Private: Private
Affiliation: Roman Catholic
Student/Faculty Ratio: 17:1
Total Faculty: 46
% Part Time: 0
% Female: 35
% Minority: 4

PROGRAMS
Academic Specialties: Certificate programs in Employment Law, Health Law, and International and Comparative Law, Clinic programs, Civil Procedure, Commercial Law, Constitutional Law, Corporation Securities Law, Criminal Law, Environmental Law, Government Services, Human Rights Law, Intellectual Property Law, Legal History, Legal Philosophy, Property, Taxation
Advanced Degrees Offered: LLM Health (1 year full time, 2 years part time), LLM for Foreign Lawyers (1 year full time)
Combined Degrees Offered: JD/MBA (3.5 to 4 years), JD/MHA (4 years), JD/MAPA, JD/MAUA (3.5 to 4 years), JD/MPH (4 years)
Grading System: Letter and numerical system on a 4.0 scale

Clinical Program Required? No
Clinical Program Description: In-House Clinic, Externship Program, Judicial Process Clinic, Criminal Public Defender Clinic, Corporate Counsel Externship Clinic, Immigration Law Project
Legal Writing Course Requirements? Yes
Legal Methods Course Requirements? No
Legal Methods Description: 1 year
Legal Research Course Requirements? Yes
Moot Court Requirement? No
Public Interest Law Requirement? No
Academic Journals: *Saint Louis University Law Journal, Public Law Review, The Journal of Health Law*

STUDENT INFORMATION
Enrollment of Law School: 810
% Male/Female: 51/49
% Full Time: 72
% Full Time That Are International: 0
% Minority: 11
Average Age of Entering Class: 25

EXPENSES/FINANCIAL AID
Annual Tuition: $24,510
Room and Board (Off Campus): $11,528
Books and Supplies: $1,040
Financial Aid Application Deadline: 6/2
Average Grant: $8,968
Average Loan: $21,582

% of Aid That Is Merit-Based: 19
% Receiving Some Sort of Aid: 92
Average Total Aid Package: $24,799
Average Debt: $54,981
Tuition Per Credit: $17,880
Fees Per Credit: $110

ADMISSIONS INFORMATION
Application Fee: $55
Regular Application Deadline: 3/3
Regular Notification: Rolling
LSDAS Accepted? Yes
Average GPA: 3.4
Range of GPA: 3.1–3.6
Average LSAT: 154
Range of LSAT: 151–158
Transfer Students Accepted? Yes
Other Admissions Factors Considered: Graduate degrees earned, undergraduate institution, major, academic achievement, leadership positions, motivation, work experience, service
Number of Applications Received: 1,360
Number of Applicants Accepted: 713
Number of Applicants Enrolled: 319

INTERNATIONAL STUDENTS
TOEFL Recommended for International Students? Yes
Minimum TOEFL: 232 computer

EMPLOYMENT INFORMATION

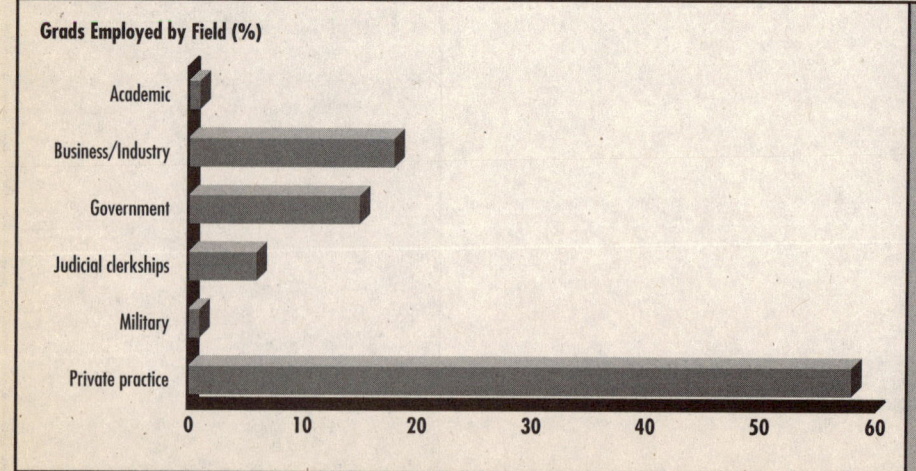

Grads Employed by Field (%)
- Academic
- Business/Industry
- Government
- Judicial clerkships
- Military
- Private practice

Rate of Placement: 90%
Average Starting Salary: $57,831
State for Bar Exam: MO
Pass Rate for First-Time Bar: 83%

St. Mary's University
School of Law

Admissions Contact: Assistant Dean and Director of Admissions
One Camino Santa Maria, San Antonio, TX 78228-8601
Admissions Phone: 866-639-5831 • Admissions Fax: 210-431-4202
Admissions E-mail: admissions@law.stmarytx.edu • Web Address: www.stmarylaw.stmarytx.edu

INSTITUTIONAL INFORMATION
Public/Private: Private
Affiliation: Roman Catholic
Student/Faculty Ratio: 18:1
Total Faculty: 95
% Part Time: 53
% Female: 35
% Minority: 22

PROGRAMS
Academic Specialties: International Law, Criminal Law, clinical offerings
Advanced Degrees Offered: LLM International and Comparative Law for U.S.-educated students, LLM American Legal Studies for foreign-educated students
Combined Degrees Offered: JD/MBA Accounting, JD/MA Economics, JD/MA International Relations with concentration in Justice Administration, JD/MA Public Administration, JD/MA English Communications-Arts, JD/MA Theology, JD/MS Computer Science, JD/MS Engineering, JD/MBA (all 3.5 to 4 years)
Grading System: Letter system on a 4.0 scale with 10 tiers
Clinical Program Required? No
Clinical Programs Description: Civil Justice Clinic, Community Development Clinic, Criminal Justice Clinic, Immigration Clinic, Human Rights Clinic
Legal Writing Course Requirements? Yes
Legal Writing Description: Part of first-year, 2-semester course
Legal Methods Course Requirements? Yes
Legal Methods Description: Part of first-year, 2-semester course
Legal Research Course Requirements? Yes
Legal Research Description: Part of first-year, 2-semester course
Moot Court Requirement? No
Moot Court Description: First-year moot court is basically a requirement.
Public Interest Law Requirement? No
Academic Journals: St. Mary's Law Journal, St. Mary's Law Review on Minority Issues

STUDENT INFORMATION
Enrollment of Law School: 705
% Out of State: 10
% Male/Female: 52/48
% Full Time: 100
% Full Time That Are International: 2
% Minority: 46
Average Age of Entering Class: 28

EXPENSES/FINANCIAL AID
Annual Tuition: $17,970
Room and Board (On/Off Campus): $5,535/$7,055
Books and Supplies: $1,100
Financial Aid Application Deadline: 4/1
Average Grant: $2,861
Average Loan: $26,984
% of Aid That Is Merit-Based: 4
% Receiving Some Sort of Aid: 90
Average Total Aid Package: $27,673
Average Debt: $78,936
Tuition Per Credit: $599

ADMISSIONS INFORMATION
Application Fee: $45
Regular Application Deadline: 3/1
Regular Notification: 5/1
LSDAS Accepted? Yes
Average GPA: 3.0
Range of GPA: 2.7–3.2
Average LSAT: 149
Range of LSAT: 146–152
Transfer Students Accepted? Yes
Other Schools to Which Students Applied: Baylor University, Oklahoma City University, Southern Methodist University, Texas A&M University, Texas Southern University, Texas Tech University, Texas Wesleyan University
Other Admissions Factors Considered: Evidence of having overcome hardships or obstacles in attaining education
Number of Applications Received: 1,066
Number of Applicants Accepted: 692
Number of Applicants Enrolled: 240

INTERNATIONAL STUDENTS
TOEFL Required of International Students? Yes

EMPLOYMENT INFORMATION

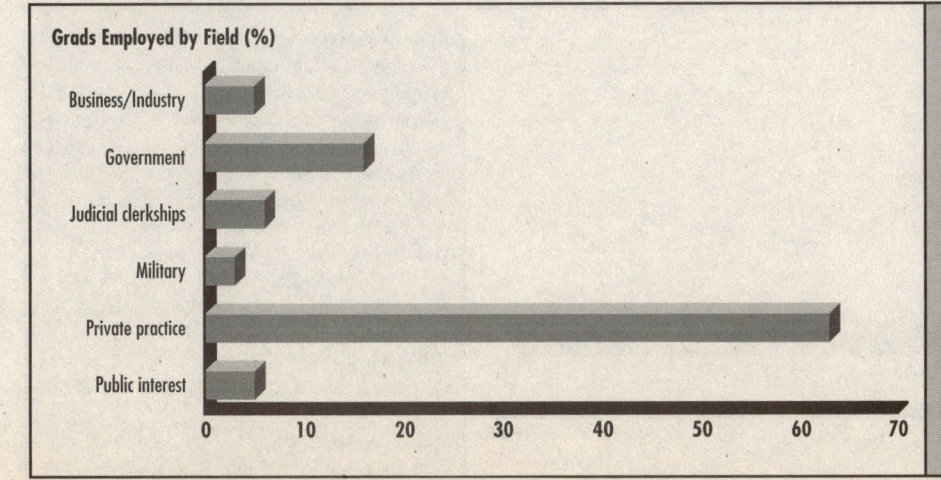

Grads Employed by Field (%)
- Business/Industry
- Government
- Judicial clerkships
- Military
- Private practice
- Public interest

Rate of Placement: 74%
Average Starting Salary: $55,000
Employers Who Frequently Hire Grads: Small and medium-sized firms, government agencies, business (banking/financial)
State for Bar Exam: TX, FL, MO, OK, NM
Pass Rate for First-Time Bar: 59%

St. Thomas University
School of Law

Admissions Contact: Assistant Director for Admissions
16400 Northwest 32nd Avenue, Miami, FL 33054
Admissions Phone: 305-623-2310 • Admissions Fax: 305-623-2357
Admissions E-mail: admitme@stu.edu • Web Address: www.stu.edu

INSTITUTIONAL INFORMATION
Public/Private: Private
Affiliation: Roman Catholic
Student/Faculty Ratio: 22:1
Total Faculty: 24
% Part Time: 39
% Female: 46
% Minority: 21

PROGRAMS
Academic Specialties: Broad curriculum, faculty that is published prolifically and in well-regarded law reviews, Human Rights Law, International Law, Taxation
Advanced Degrees Offered: Online LLM International Tax (2 years), LLM Intercultural Human Rights (1 year)
Combined Degrees Offered: JD/MS Marriage and Family Counseling (3 years), JD/MS Sports Administration (3 years), JD/MAcc (3 years), JD/MBA International Business (3 years), JD/BA (6 years)
Grading System: A, B+, B, C+, C, C–, D, F, P/NP
Clinical Program Required? No
Clinical Program Description: Immigration Clinic; Family Court Clinic; Tax Clinic; Bankruptcy Clinic; Public Defender, State's Attorney, and Legal Services externships
Legal Writing Course Requirements? Yes
Legal Writing Description: Legal Analysis, Writing and Research, first semester, 3 credits; Advanced Legal Research, fourth semester, 2 credits; Senior Writing Requirement
Legal Methods Course Requirements? Yes
Legal Methods Description: See Legal Writing.
Legal Research Course Requirements? Yes
Legal Research Description: See Legal Writing.
Moot Court Requirement? Yes
Moot Court Description: Brief written and oral argument presented in Appellate Advocacy in the spring semester of the first year
Public Interest Law Requirement? Yes
Public Interest Law Description: 20 hours of pro bono work in both the second and third years
Academic Journals: *St. Thomas Law Review*

STUDENT INFORMATION
Enrollment of Law School: 487
% Out of State: 24
% Male/Female: 50/50
% Full Time: 100
% Full Time That Are International: 1
% Minority: 47
Average Age of Entering Class: 25

RESEARCH FACILITIES
Research Resources Available: Off-campus housing with wireless Internet access
School-Supported Research Centers: St. Thomas University Human Rights Institute

EXPENSES/FINANCIAL AID
Annual Tuition: $23,100
Room and Board (On/Off Campus): $8,610/$9,675
Books and Supplies: $1,000
Financial Aid Application Deadline: 5/1
Average Grant: $11,550
Average Loan: $28,500
% of Aid That Is Merit-Based: 14
% Receiving Some Sort of Aid: 94
Average Total Aid Package: $22,262
Average Debt: $85,500

ADMISSIONS INFORMATION
Application Fee: $45
Regular Application Deadline: Rolling
Regular Notification: Rolling
LSDAS Accepted? Yes
Average GPA: 2.9
Range of GPA: 2.7–3.2
Average LSAT: 148
Range of LSAT: 146–151
Transfer Students Accepted? Yes
Other Schools to Which Students Applied: Nova Southeastern University, University of Miami
Number of Applications Received: 1,571
Number of Applicants Accepted: 719
Number of Applicants Enrolled: 179

INTERNATIONAL STUDENTS
TOEFL Recommended for International Students? Yes
Minimum TOEFL: 550

EMPLOYMENT INFORMATION

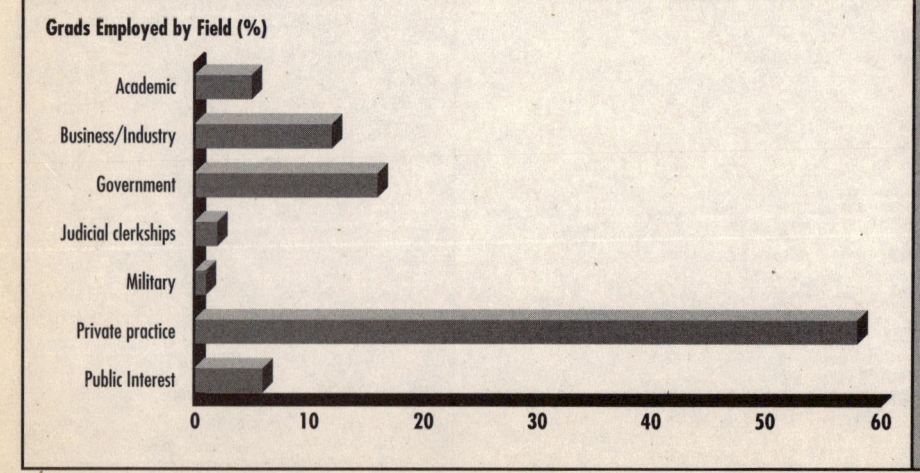

Grads Employed by Field (%)
- Academic: ~1
- Business/Industry: ~12
- Government: ~17
- Judicial clerkships: ~2
- Military: 0
- Private practice: ~58
- Public Interest: ~5

Rate of Placement: 89%
Average Starting Salary: $46,400
Employers Who Frequently Hire Grads: Private law firms of all sizes; government agencies, including the U.S. Department of Justice, the Florida State Attorney's Office, and Prosecutor's and Public Defender's Offices; public interest organizations; corporations
Prominent Alumni: Mikki Canton, Esq., Partner, Holland & Knight LLP; Hon. Samuel J. Slom, 11th Judicial Circuit, Florida; Hon. Don Thomas Hall, Judge, DeSoto County Court; Ralph G. Patino, Esq., Patino & Associates; Gaston Cantens, Esq., Florida House of Representatives
State for Bar Exam: FL, NY, GA
Pass Rate for First-Time Bar: 50%

SAMFORD UNIVERSITY
Cumberland School of Law

Admissions Contact: Director of Admissions, M. Giselle Gauthier
800 Lakeshore Drive, Birmingham, AL 35229
Admissions Phone: 205-726-2702 • Admissions Fax: 205-726-2057
Admissions E-mail: law.admissions@samford.edu • Web Address: cumberland.samford.edu

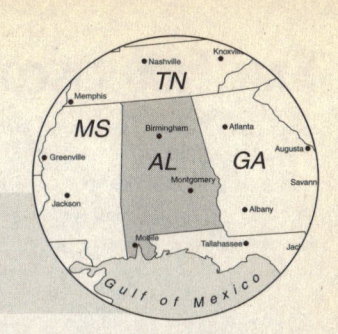

INSTITUTIONAL INFORMATION
Public/Private: Private
Affiliation: Southern Baptist
Student/Faculty Ratio: 19:1
Total Faculty: 53
% Part Time: 41
% Female: 24
% Minority: 13

PROGRAMS
Academic Specialties: Our strengths include the six-credit Lawyering and Legal Reasoning courses. All first-year law students receive intensive instructions in prelitigation skills, such as client interviewing, counseling, memorandum preperation, and negotiation; pretrial litigation skills, including summary judgement motions and making compelling oral arguments; and appellate litigation skills.
Advanced Degrees Offered: Master of Comparative Law
Combined Degrees Offered: JD/MAcc, JD/MBA, JD/MPA, JD/MPH, JD/MS Environmental Management (all 3.5 to 4 years); JD/MDiv (5 years)
Grading System: Letter system
Clinical Program Required? No
Clinical Program Description: State Court Judges, Federal Court Judges, Corporate, U.S. Attorney's Office, IRS Legal Internship, District Attorney's Office—Adult Prosecution or Juvenile Prosecution, Public Defender's Office, Legal Services, Legal Aid Society—Criminal Defense, Juvenile Defense—Family Court

Legal Writing Course Requirements? Yes
Legal Methods Course Requirements? Yes
Legal Methods Description: 1 full year, graded
Legal Research Course Requirements? Yes
Moot Court Requirement? No
Public Interest Law Requirement? No
Academic Journals: *Cumberland Law Review, The American Journal of Trial Advocacy*

STUDENT INFORMATION
Enrollment of Law School: 507
% Out of State: 44
% Male/Female: 58/42
% Full Time: 100
% Full Time That Are International: 0
% Minority: 6
Average Age of Entering Class: 25

EXPENSES/FINANCIAL AID
Annual Tuition: $21,350
Room and Board (Off Campus): $10,300
Books and Supplies: $1,250
Financial Aid Application Deadline: 3/1
Average Grant: $3,031
Average Loan: $29,074
% of Aid That Is Merit-Based: 4
% Receiving Some Sort of Aid: 87
Average Total Aid Package: $30,807
Average Debt: $72,150
Tuition Per Credit: $712
Fees Per Credit: $20

ADMISSIONS INFORMATION
Application Fee: $50
Regular Application Deadline: Rolling
Regular Notification: Rolling
LSDAS Accepted? Yes
Average GPA: 3.1
Range of GPA: 2.8–3.4
Average LSAT: 153
Range of LSAT: 151–155
Transfer Students Accepted? Yes
Other Admissions Factors Considered: Undergraduate major, grade trend, graduate studies, cultural or ethnic diversity, clarity and content of personal statement
Number of Applications Received: 1,032
Number of Applicants Accepted: 446

INTERNATIONAL STUDENTS
TOEFL Required of International Students? Yes
Minimum TOEFL: 550 (213 computer)

EMPLOYMENT INFORMATION

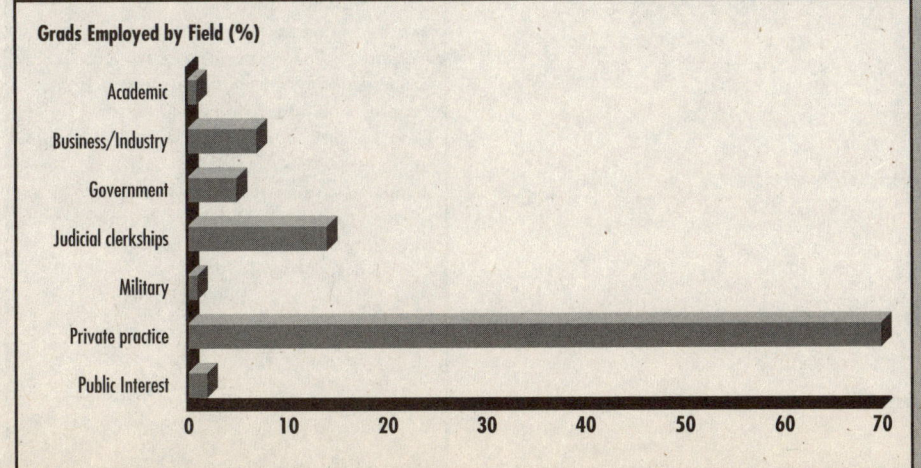

Grads Employed by Field (%)

Field	%
Academic	~1
Business/Industry	~7
Government	~5
Judicial clerkships	~14
Military	~1
Private practice	~70
Public Interest	~2

Rate of Placement: 91%
Average Starting Salary: $53,940
Employers Who Frequently Hire Grads: Bradley, Arant, Rose & White; Burr & Forman; Balch & Bingham; Lange, Simpson, Robinson & Somerville; Carbaniss, Johnston, Gardner, Dumas & O'Neal; Sirote & Permutt; Montgomery Attorney General's Office; Hand & Arendall, Lyons, Pipes, & Cook Leitner, Williams, Dooley & Neopolitan; Watkins & Ludlam; Winter and Stennis
Prominent Alumni: Cordell Hull, Founder, United Nations; Howell E. Jackson, U.S. Supreme Court; Horace H. Lurton, U.S. Supreme Court
State for Bar Exam: AL, FL, TN, GA, VA
Pass Rate for First-Time Bar: 93%

SAN FRANCISCO LAW SCHOOL

Admissions Contact: Director of Admissions
20 Haight Street, San Francisco, CA 94102
Admissions Phone: 415-626-5550 • Admissions Fax: 415-626-5584
Admissions E-mail: admin@sfls.edu • Web Address: www.sfls.edu

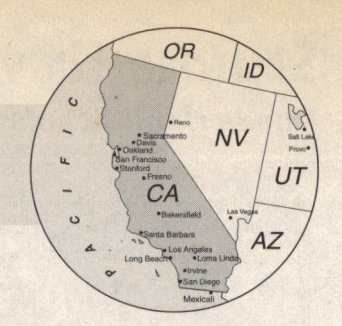

INSTITUTIONAL INFORMATION
Public/Private: Private
Student/Faculty Ratio: 20:1
Total Faculty: 32
% Part Time: 100
% Female: 20
% Minority: 1

PROGRAMS
Academic Specialties: All faculty are adjunct and are practicing judges and attorneys who teach in their field.
Advanced Degrees Offered: JD (4 to 4.5 years)
Grading System: Numerical system up to 100
Clinical Program Required? No
Clinical Program Description: Private practice, judges
Legal Writing Course Requirements? Yes
Legal Writing Description: Advanced Legal Writing, 1 semester
Legal Methods Course Requirements? No
Legal Research Course Requirements? Yes
Legal Research Description: 2 semesters; covers the use of law books as well as legal research on the Internet
Moot Court Requirement? Yes
Moot Court Description: Teams in a workshop setting, 1 semester
Public Interest Law Requirement? No
Academic Journals: *San Francisco Law Review*

STUDENT INFORMATION
Enrollment of Law School: 125
% Out of State: 0
% Male/Female: 50/50
% Full Time That Are International: 0
% Minority: 50
Average Age of Entering Class: 36

EXPENSES/FINANCIAL AID
Annual Tuition: $6,500
Room and Board (Off Campus): $25,000
Books and Supplies: $250
% of Aid That Is Merit-Based: 40
Tuition Per Credit: $325

ADMISSIONS INFORMATION
Application Fee: $50
Regular Application Deadline: 6/15
Regular Notification: Rolling
LSDAS Accepted? No
Average GPA: 2.8
Range of GPA: 2.0–3.8
Average LSAT: 140
Transfer Students Accepted? Yes
Number of Applications Received: 51
Number of Applicants Enrolled: 31

EMPLOYMENT INFORMATION

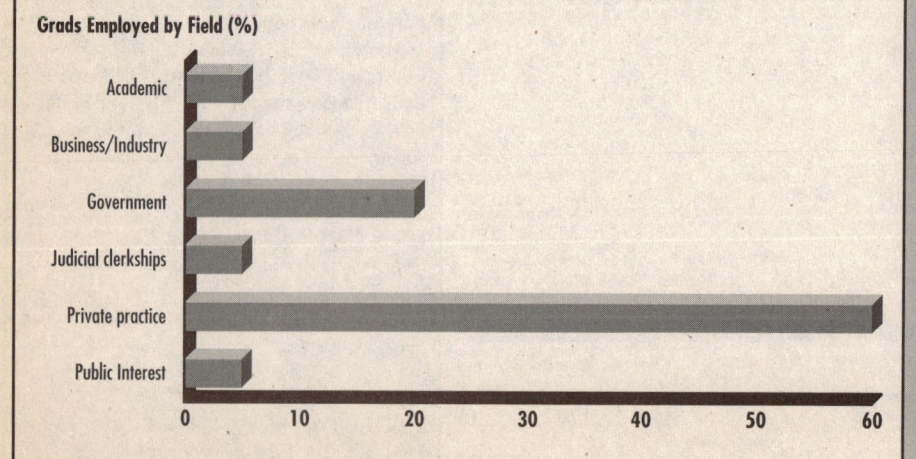

Grads Employed by Field (%)
- Academic: ~2
- Business/Industry: ~3
- Government: ~20
- Judicial clerkships: ~3
- Private practice: ~60
- Public Interest: ~3

Average Starting Salary: $40,000
Employers Who Frequently Hire Grads: Public Defender, District Attorney, private firms
Prominent Alumni: Edmund G. Brown, former Governor of California; Milton Marks Jr. former California Senator; Leo T. McCarthy, Lt. Governor of California; Hon. Lynn O'Malley Taylor, Judge, Superior Court; Hon. Henry Needham, Judge, Superior Court
State for Bar Exam: CA
Pass Rate for First-Time Bar: 30%

SAN JOAQUIN COLLEGE OF LAW

Admissions Contact: Admissions Officer
901 Fifth Street, Clovis, CA 93612-1312
Admissions Phone: 559-323-2100 • Admissions Fax: 559-323-5566
Admissions E-mail: jcanalin@sjcl.org • Web Address: www.sjcl.org

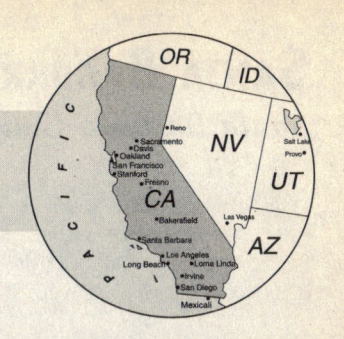

INSTITUTIONAL INFORMATION
Public/Private: Private
Student/Faculty Ratio: 16:1
Total Faculty: 36
% Part Time: 83
% Female: 45
% Minority: 14

PROGRAMS
Academic Specialties: Practice-orientated curriculum with many skills classes; law review devoted to issues surrounding agriculture; specialties include Commercial Law, Corporation Securities Law, Criminal Law, Environmental Law, International Law, Labor Law, and Taxation
Advanced Degrees Offered: JD (3 to 5 years), MS Taxation (2 years)
Grading System: A (100–85), B (84–75), C (74–65), D (64–55), F (54–0)
Clinical Program Required? Yes
Clinical Programs Description: Alternative Dispute Resolution, Small Claims
Legal Methods Course Requirements? Yes
Legal Methods Description: Legal analysis/research writing

STUDENT INFORMATION
Enrollment of Law School: 185
% Male/Female: 54/46
% Full Time: 13
% Minority: 26
Average Age of Entering Class: 33

EXPENSES/FINANCIAL AID
Annual Tuition: $10,212
Books and Supplies: $550
Average Grant: $1,600
Average Loan: $14,500
% of Aid That Is Merit-Based: 12
% Receiving Some Sort of Aid: 75
Average Total Aid Package: $18,500
Average Debt: $62,500
Fees Per Credit: $475

ADMISSIONS INFORMATION
Application Fee: $40
Regular Application Deadline: 6/30
Regular Notification: Rolling
LSDAS Accepted? No
Average GPA: 2.9
Range of GPA: 1.8–3.9
Average LSAT: 148
Range of LSAT: 139–174
Transfer Students Accepted? Yes
Number of Applications Received: 135
Number of Applicants Accepted: 108
Number of Applicants Enrolled: 91

EMPLOYMENT INFORMATION

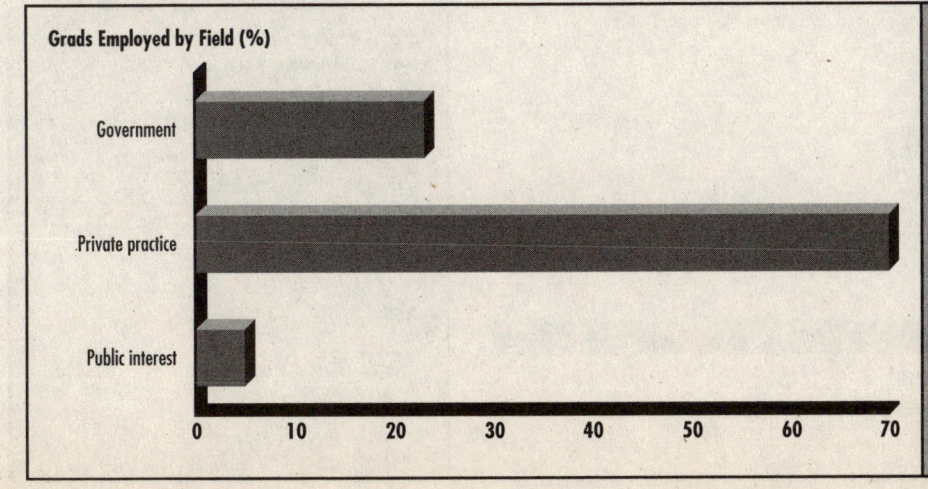

Grads Employed by Field (%)
- Government: ~23
- Private practice: ~70
- Public interest: ~5

Rate of Placement: 70%
Employers Who Frequently Hire Grads: Local District Attorney and District Defender's Offices and various small firms
State for Bar Exam: CA
Pass Rate for First-Time Bar: 56%

Santa Barbara and Ventura Colleges of Law
Santa Barbara College of Law

Admissions Contact: Assistant Dean, Mary Osborne
20 East Victoria Street, Santa Barbara, CA 93101
Admissions Phone: 805-966-0010 • Admissions Fax: 805-966-7181
Admissions E-mail: sbcl@santabarbaralaw.edu • Web Address: www.santabarbaralaw.edu

INSTITUTIONAL INFORMATION
Public/Private: Private
Student/Faculty Ratio: 11:1
Total Faculty: 19
% Part Time: 100
% Female: 26
% Minority: 5

PROGRAMS
Academic Specialties: All faculty are practicing attorneys or judges.
Grading System: Letter system
Clinical Program Required? Yes
Clinical Program Description: Government, private pro bono
Legal Writing Course Requirements? Yes
Legal Writing Description: Basic Legal Writing (30 hours), Advanced Legal Writing (30 hours)
Legal Methods Course Requirements? No
Legal Research Course Requirements? Yes
Legal Research Description: 30 hours
Moot Court Requirement? No
Public Interest Law Requirement? No

STUDENT INFORMATION
Enrollment of Law School: 917
% Male/Female: 51/49
% Full Time: 100

EXPENSES/FINANCIAL AID
Annual Tuition: $22,000
Room and Board: $9,787
Books and Supplies: $903
Average Grant: $8,071
% of Aid That Is Merit-Based: 7
% Receiving Some Sort of Aid: 85
Average Debt: $60,379

ADMISSIONS INFORMATION
Application Fee: $40
Regular Application Deadline: Rolling
Regular Notification: Rolling
LSDAS Accepted? No
Average GPA: 3.2
Range of GPA: 3.0–3.5
Average LSAT: 156
Range of LSAT: 153–158
Transfer Students Accepted? No
Other Schools to Which Students Applied: Syracuse University
Number of Applications Received: 2,528
Number of Applicants Accepted: 1,265
Number of Applicants Enrolled: 291

EMPLOYMENT INFORMATION

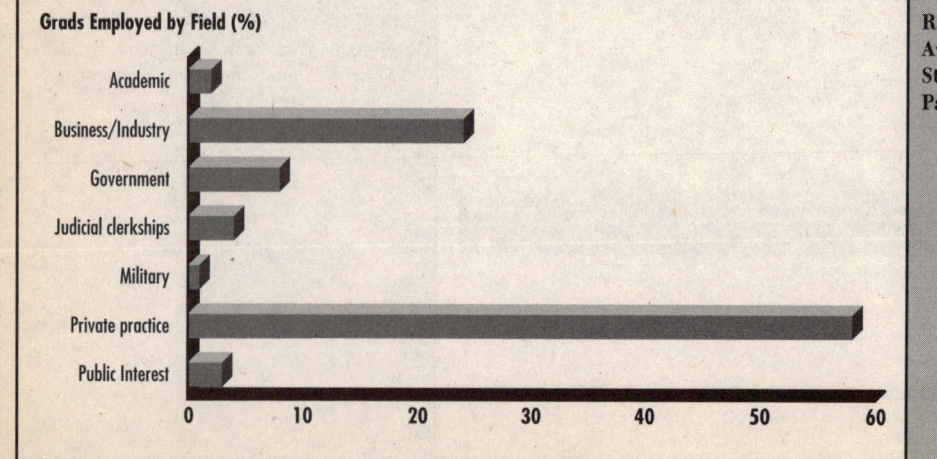

Grads Employed by Field (%)

Field	%
Academic	~1
Business/Industry	~25
Government	~5
Judicial clerkships	~3
Military	~1
Private practice	~58
Public Interest	~2

Rate of Placement: 96%
Average Starting Salary: $58,000
State for Bar Exam: CA
Pass Rate for First-Time Bar: 71%

SANTA BARBARA AND VENTURA COLLEGES OF LAW
Ventura College of Law

Admissions Contact: Assistant Dean, Barbara Doyle
4475 Market Street, Ventura, CA 93003
Admissions Phone: 805-658-0511 • Admissions Fax: 805-658-0529
Admissions E-mail: vcl@venturalaw.edu • Web Address: www.venturalaw.edu

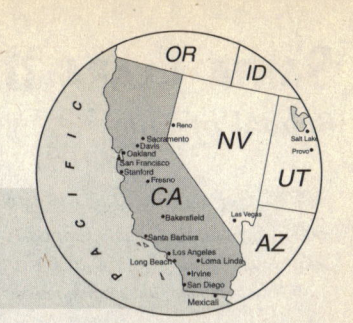

INSTITUTIONAL INFORMATION
Public/Private: Private
Student/Faculty Ratio: 6:1
Total Faculty: 18
% Part Time: 100
% Female: 22
% Minority: 22

PROGRAMS
Academic Specialties: All faculty are practicing attorneys or judges.
Advanced Degrees Offered: JD (4 years part time evening)
Grading System: Letter system on a 4.0 scale
Clinical Program Required? Yes
Clinical Program Description: Off-campus internships
Legal Writing Course Requirements? Yes
Legal Writing Description: 2 separate 2-unit courses
Legal Methods Course Requirements? No
Legal Research Course Requirements? Yes
Legal Research Description: 2-unit course
Moot Court Requirement? No
Public Interest Law Requirement? Yes
Public Interest Law Description: 65-hour (1-unit) internship

STUDENT INFORMATION
Enrollment of Law School: 115
% Male/Female: 100/0
Average Age of Entering Class: 36

EXPENSES/FINANCIAL AID
Annual Tuition: $5,565
Books and Supplies: $400
Average Grant: $1,000
Average Loan: $10,000
Tuition Per Credit: $265

ADMISSIONS INFORMATION
Application Fee: $45
Regular Application Deadline: 8/1
Regular Notification: Rolling
LSDAS Accepted? No
Average GPA: 3.2
Average LSAT: 150
Transfer Students Accepted? Yes
Number of Applications Received: 2,528
Number of Applicants Accepted: 1,265
Number of Applicants Enrolled: 291

INTERNATIONAL STUDENTS
TOEFL Recommended for International Students? Yes

EMPLOYMENT INFORMATION

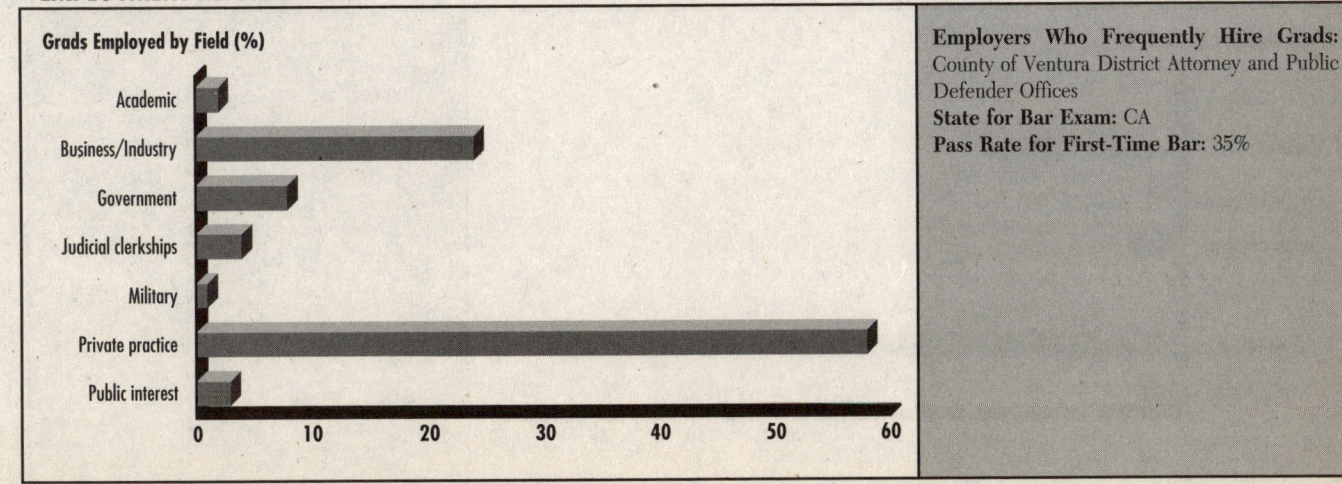

Grads Employed by Field (%)
- Academic: ~1
- Business/Industry: ~24
- Government: ~5
- Judicial clerkships: ~2
- Military: 0
- Private practice: ~58
- Public interest: ~3

Employers Who Frequently Hire Grads: County of Ventura District Attorney and Public Defender Offices
State for Bar Exam: CA
Pass Rate for First-Time Bar: 35%

SANTA CLARA UNIVERSITY
School of Law

Admissions Contact: Assistant Dean for Admissions and Diversity Services, Jeanette J. Leach
500 El Camino Real, Santa Clara, CA 95053
Admissions Phone: 408-554-4800 • Admissions Fax: 408-554-7897
Admissions E-mail: lawadmissions@scu.edu • Web Address: www.scu.edu/law

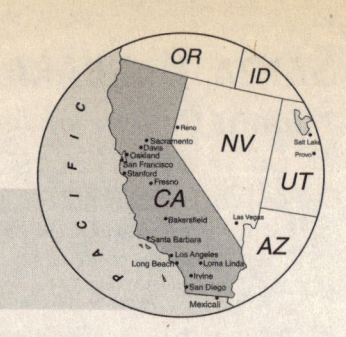

INSTITUTIONAL INFORMATION
Public/Private: Private
Affiliation: Roman Catholic
Student/Faculty Ratio: 19:1
Total Faculty: 112
% Part Time: 43
% Female: 41
% Minority: 12

PROGRAMS
Academic Specialties: Intellectual Property and High Technology—rich curriculum, law lournal, specialty certificate; International and Comparative Law—extensive summer programs in 13 nations, specialty certificate; Public Interest Law—certification, centers, financial support
Advanced Degrees Offered: LLM
Combined Degrees Offered: JD/MBA (3.5 to 4 years)
Grading System: Letter system on a 4.33 scale; minimum 2.33 required for graduation
Clinical Program Required? No
Clinical Program Description: Criminal Defense Law Clinic (Northern California Innocence Project), East San Jose Community Law Center
Legal Writing Course Requirements? Yes
Legal Writing Description: All first-year students must take Legal Analysis, Research, and Writing for 3 units over 2 semesters.
Legal Methods Course Requirements? No
Legal Research Course Requirements? Yes
Legal Research Description: See Legal Writing.

Moot Court Requirement? Yes
Moot Court Description: First-year students are required to write a brief and present oral argument as part of Legal Analysis, Research and Writing.
Public Interest Law Requirement? No
Academic Journals: *Santa Clara Law Review, Computer and High Technology Law Journal*

STUDENT INFORMATION
Enrollment of Law School: 891
% Male/Female: 46/54
% Full Time: 76
% Minority: 37
Average Age of Entering Class: 26

RESEARCH FACILITIES
Research Resources Available: Lexis, Westlaw, Loislaw, and many other electronic legal databases
School-Supported Research Centers: A good portion of the carrels in the Law Library are wired for full access to the university's network. The Law Library contains 3 computer labs, and the university has 2 large labs that the law students may access, as well as a large multimedia department.

EXPENSES/FINANCIAL AID
Annual Tuition: $25,560
Room and Board: $11,822
Books and Supplies: $1,304
Financial Aid Application Deadline: 3/1
Average Grant: $11,025
Average Loan: $26,202
% of Aid That Is Merit-Based: 15

% Receiving Some Sort of Aid: 84
Average Total Aid Package: $28,331
Average Debt: $73,738
Tuition Per Credit: $958
Fees Per Credit: $852

ADMISSIONS INFORMATION
Application Fee: $60
Regular Application Deadline: 3/1
Regular Notification: Rolling
LSDAS Accepted? Yes
Average GPA: 3.2
Range of GPA: 3.0–3.5
Average LSAT: 156
Range of LSAT: 152–159
Transfer Students Accepted? Yes
Other Schools to Which Students Applied: University of San Diego; University of San Francisco; University of California, Hastings; Pepperdine University
Other Admissions Factors Considered: Academic record, course of study, quality of institution, graduate work, employment history, maturity, community activities, extracurricular achievments, honors and awards, personal statement
Number of Applications Received: 2,371
Number of Applicants Accepted: 1,173
Number of Applicants Enrolled: 233

INTERNATIONAL STUDENTS
TOEFL Recommended for International Students? Yes

EMPLOYMENT INFORMATION

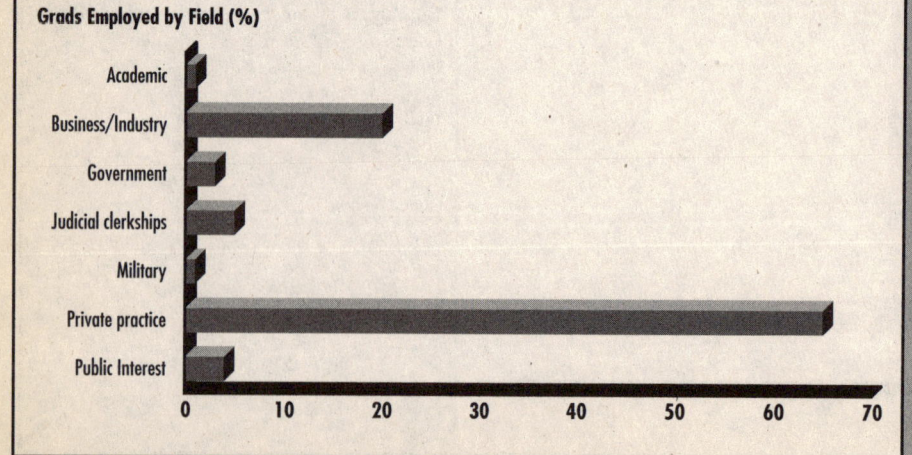

Grads Employed by Field (%)
- Academic: ~2
- Business/Industry: ~20
- Government: ~3
- Judicial clerkships: ~5
- Military: ~1
- Private practice: ~65
- Public Interest: ~3

Rate of Placement: 96%
Average Starting Salary: $96,086
Employers Who Frequently Hire Grads: Cooley, Godward; McCutchen Doyle; Crosby Heafey; Morrison & Foerster; Skjerven Morrill; Brobeck, Phleger & Harrison; Ropers Majeski; Fenwick & West; Wilson Sonsini
State for Bar Exam: CA
Pass Rate for First-Time Bar: 69%

SEATTLE UNIVERSITY
School of Law

Admissions Contact: Director of Admission, Carol Cochran
900 Broadway, Seattle, WA 98122-4340
Admissions Phone: 206-398-4200 • Admissions Fax: 206-398-4058
Admissions E-mail: lawadmis@seattleu.edu • Web Address: www.law.seattleu.edu

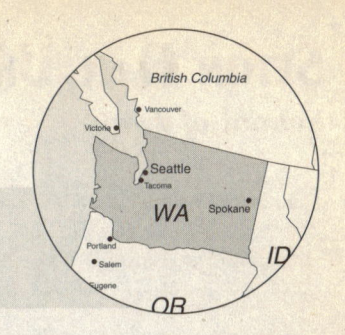

INSTITUTIONAL INFORMATION
Public/Private: Private
Affiliation: Roman Catholic
Student/Faculty Ratio: 17:1
Total Faculty: 84
% Part Time: 39
% Female: 43
% Minority: 14

PROGRAMS
Academic Specialties: Business, Civil Advocacy, Criminal Practice, Environmental Law, Estate Planning, Labor and Employment Law, Poverty Law, Real Estate, Commercial Law, Constitutional Law, Corporation Securities Law, Human Rights Law, Intellectual Property Law, International Law, Property, Taxation
Advanced Degrees Offered: JD (3 to 3.5 years)
Combined Degrees Offered: JD/MBA, JD/M International Business, JD/MS Finance (all 4 years)
Grading System: Letter system on a 4.33 scale; mandatory curve in first year, presumptive curve in upper years; some classes are Pass/Fail
Clinical Program Required? No
Clinical Program Description: Law Practice Clinic, Bankruptcy Clinic, Immigration, Health, Law and Psychology, Housing Law, Ethics, Environmental Law, Intellectual Property; Administrative Law, Trust and Estates
Legal Writing Course Requirements? Yes
Legal Writing Description: 3 semesters; Legal Writing I and II, with Legal Research element
Legal Methods Course Requirements? No
Legal Research Course Requirements? Yes

Legal Research Description: See Legal Writing.
Moot Court Requirement? No
Moot Court Description: The Moot Court Board hosts all moot court events at the law school. Board membership is selected on the basis of superior leadership, organizational skills, and moot court participation. Membership is limited to 35 members, with a minimum of 5 students from each of the 3 law school classes. The Board facilitates several competitions every year, including Environmental Law, Civil Rights, Mock Trial, Intellectual Property, Tausend Competition, Administrative Law, Reasonable Doubts, and the Jessup International. Winners are allowed to advance to regional competitions.
Public Interest Law Requirement? No
Academic Journals: Seattle University Law Review, Seattle Journal of Social Justice

STUDENT INFORMATION
Enrollment of Law School: 1,041
% Out of State: 21
% Male/Female: 45/55
% Full Time: 78
% Full Time That Are International: 2
% Minority: 22
Average Age of Entering Class: 28

RESEARCH FACILITIES
School-Supported Research Centers: West Education Network

EXPENSES/FINANCIAL AID
Annual Tuition: $22,260
Room and Board (Off Campus): $14,497
Books and Supplies: $903
Financial Aid Application Deadline: 3/1

Average Grant: $6,247
Average Loan: $24,791
% of Aid That Is Merit-Based: 9
% Receiving Some Sort of Aid: 97
Average Total Aid Package: $27,233
Average Debt: $69,000
Tuition Per Credit: $742
Fees Per Credit: $116

ADMISSIONS INFORMATION
Application Fee: $50
Regular Application Deadline: 4/1
Regular Notification: Rolling
LSDAS Accepted? Yes
Average GPA: 3.3
Range of GPA: 2.9–3.5
Average LSAT: 156
Range of LSAT: 151–158
Transfer Students Accepted? Yes
Other Schools to Which Students Applied: Gonzaga University, Lewis and Clark College, Santa Clara University, University of Oregon, University of San Francisco, University of Washington, Willamette University
Other Admissions Factors Considered: Personal accomplishments, professional achievement, community service, outstanding performance in a rigorous program of study, unique talent
Number of Applications Received: 1,817
Number of Applicants Accepted: 813
Number of Applicants Enrolled: 342

INTERNATIONAL STUDENTS
TOEFL Recommended for International Students? Yes
Minimum TOEFL: 250 computer

EMPLOYMENT INFORMATION

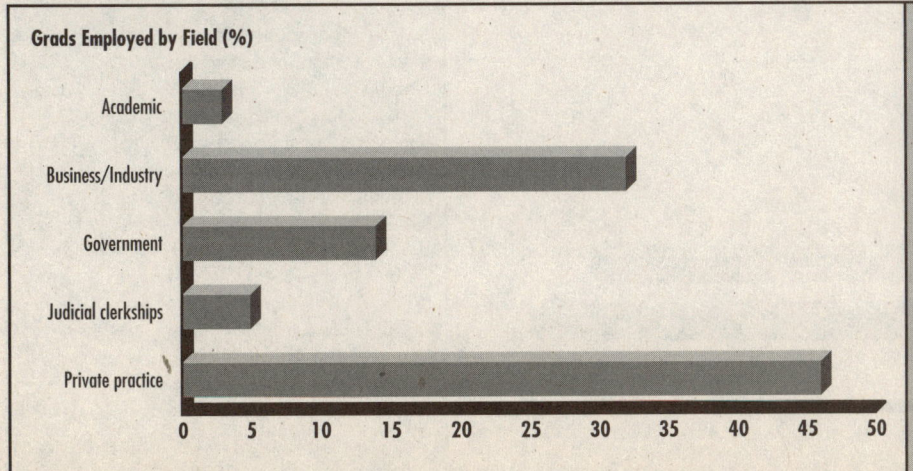

Grads Employed by Field (%)
- Academic: ~2
- Business/Industry: ~32
- Government: ~15
- Judicial clerkships: ~5
- Private practice: ~47

Rate of Placement: 99%
Employers Who Frequently Hire Grads: Perkins Coie, Lane Powell Spears Lubersky, King County Prosecuting Attorney, Washington State Attorney General, Williams Kastner & Gibbs, Foster Pepper Shefelman, Preston Gates & Ellis, Lee Smart Cook, Davis Wright Tremaine, Dorsey & Whitney, Seattle City Attorney
State for Bar Exam: WA, CA, OR, TX, IL

Seton Hall University
School of Law

Admissions Contact: Dean of Admissions/Financial Resource Management, William Perez
One Newark Center, Newark, NJ 07102
Admissions Phone: 973-642-8747 • Admissions Fax: 973-642-8876
Admissions E-mail: admitme@shu.edu • Web Address: www.law.shu.edu

INSTITUTIONAL INFORMATION
Public/Private: Private
Affiliation: Roman Catholic
Student/Faculty Ratio: 22:1
Total Faculty: 60
% Female: 40
% Minority: 20

PROGRAMS
Academic Specialties: Criminal Law, Environmental Law, International Law, Labor Law, Health Law, Commercial Law, Corporation Securities Law, Government Services, Human Rights Law, Intellectual Property Law, Legal History, Legal Philosophy, Property, Taxation
Advanced Degrees Offered: JD (3 years full time, 4 years part time), LLM (2 years part time), MSJ (1 year full time, 2 years part time)
Combined Degreees Offered: JD/MBA (4 years full time), JD/MA International Relations (4 years plus 1 summer full time), JD/MD (6 years), MSJ (1 to 2 years)
Grading System: A+ to F (4.5–0.0)
Clinical Program Required? No
Clinical Program Description: Housing Law Clinic, Immigration Law/Human Rights Clinic, Juvenile Justice Clinic, Civil Litigation Clinic, Family Law Clinic, Appellate Litigation Clinic, Pro Bono Service Program

Legal Writing Course Requirements? Yes
Legal Writing Description: Full year, 3 credits
Legal Methods Course Requirements? No
Legal Research Course Requirements? Yes
Legal Research Description: Part of Legal Research and Writing
Moot Court Requirement? No
Public Interest Law Requirement? No
Academic Journals: *Seton Hall Law Journal, Seton Hall Legislative Bureau*

STUDENT INFORMATION
Enrollment of Law School: 1,305
% Out of State: 25
% Male/Female: 52/48
% Full Time: 70
% Minority: 22
Average Age of Entering Class: 25

RESEARCH FACILITIES
Research Resources Available: Lexis, Westlaw, Findlaw, Lawcrawler, Loislaw
School-Supported Research Centers: Institute of Law, Science and Technology; Center for Social Justice; Health Law and Policy Program; Institute for Law and Mental Health

EXPENSES/FINANCIAL AID
Annual Tuition: $26,610
Room and Board: $9,000
Books and Supplies: $850
Financial Aid Application Deadline: 4/1
Average Grant: $8,755
Average Loan: $17,000
% of Aid That Is Merit-Based: 21
% Receiving Some Sort of Aid: 85
Average Total Aid Package: $21,000
Average Debt: $68,279
Tuition Per Credit: $887
Fees Per Credit: $90

ADMISSIONS INFORMATION
Application Fee: $50
Regular Application Deadline: 4/1
Regular Notification: 1/1
LSDAS Accepted? Yes
Average GPA: 3.2
Range of GPA: 2.9–3.4
Average LSAT: 155
Range of LSAT: 154–158
Transfer Students Accepted? Yes
Other Admissions Factors Considered: Life experiences
Number of Applications Received: 2,719
Number of Applicants Accepted: 1,086
Number of Applicants Enrolled: 502

INTERNATIONAL STUDENTS
TOEFL Recommended for International Students? Yes

EMPLOYMENT INFORMATION

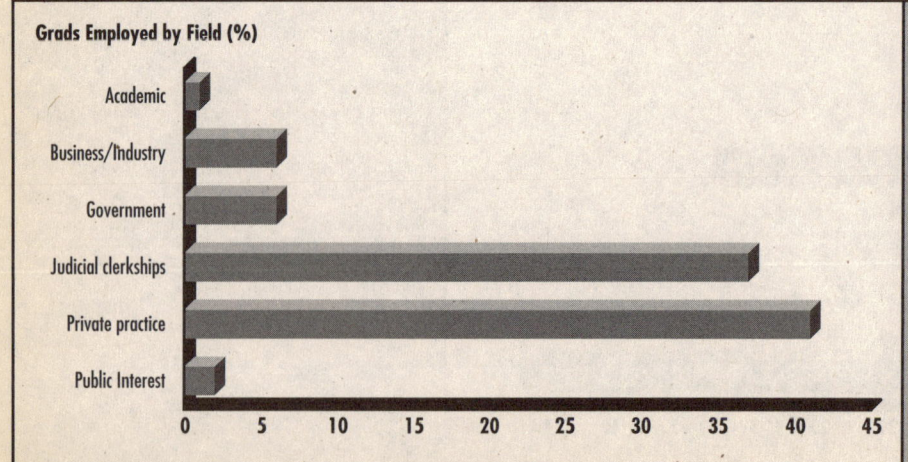

Grads Employed by Field (%)
- Academic: ~1
- Business/Industry: ~6
- Government: ~6
- Judicial clerkships: ~37
- Private practice: ~42
- Public Interest: ~2

Rate of Placement: 96%
Average Starting Salary: $61,000
Employers Who Frequently Hire Grads: Nation's most prestigious firms, all national and state government agencies, public interest organizations, state federal judges nationwide
Prominent Alumni: Anthony Principi, Secretary of Veterans Affairs; Christopher Christie, U.S. Attorney, New Jersey; Kathryn P. Duva, CEO, Main Events; Robert Dubill, Executive Editor, *USA Today*; Donald DeFranceso, former Acting Governor of New Jersey
State for Bar Exam: NJ, NY
Pass Rate for First Time Bar: 83%

SOUTH TEXAS COLLEGE OF LAW

Admissions Contact: Assistant Dean of Admissions, Alicia K. Cramer
1303 San Jacinto Street, Houston, TX 77002-7000
Admissions Phone: 713-646-1810 • Admissions Fax: 713-646-2906
Admissions E-mail: admissions@stcl.edu • Web Address: www.stcl.edu

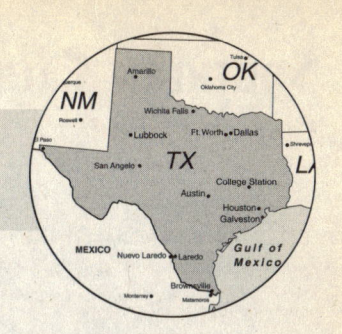

INSTITUTIONAL INFORMATION
Public/Private: Private
Student/Faculty Ratio: 19:1
Total Faculty: 95
% Part Time: 41
% Female: 27

PROGRAMS
Academic Specialties: We offer emerging programs in International Law, Environmental Law, and Dispute Resolution, as well as a nationally recognized program in advocacy. The college is a recognized leader for its Legal Research and Writing program. Hands-on live client clinics and extensive externship opportunities provide both a community service and valuable practical experience to students.
Grading System: Letter system, Honors Pass/Fail, Pass/Fail
Clinical Program Required? No
Clinical Program Description: General Civil Clinic, Criminal Process Clinic, Judicial Process Clinic, Public and Governmental Interest Clinic, Mediation Clinic
Legal Writing Course Requirements? Yes
Legal Writing Description: Students are required to take a semester each of Legal Research and Writing I and II (4 semester hours total). The courses cover the fundamentals of research and writing techniques and advance to the research and writing of an appellate brief. Students are also required to present an oral argument based on their brief.
Legal Methods Course Requirements? Yes
Legal Methods Description: Part of the Legal Research and Writing courses
Legal Research Course Requirements? No
Moot Court Requirement? No
Public Interest Law Requirement? No
Academic Journals: *Corporate Counsel Review, CURRENTS: International Trade Law Journal, South Texas Law Review*

STUDENT INFORMATION
Enrollment of Law School: 1,240
% Out of State: 7
% Male/Female: 51/49
% Full Time: 72
% Minority: 24
Average Age of Entering Class: 27

RESEARCH FACILITIES
School-Supported Research Centers: Law Institute for Medical Studies, Center for Legal Responsibility

EXPENSES/FINANCIAL AID
Annual Tuition: $17,100
Room and Board (Off Campus): $7,418
Books and Supplies: $912
Financial Aid Application Deadline: 5/1
Average Grant: $2,473
Average Loan: $23,666
% of Aid That Is Merit-Based: 2
% Receiving Some Sort of Aid: 85
Average Total Aid Package: $23,315
Average Debt: $66,222
Tuition Per Credit: $11,400
Fees Per Credit: $600

ADMISSIONS INFORMATION
Application Fee: $50
Regular Application Deadline: 2/25
Regular Notification: 5/25
LSDAS Accepted? Yes
Average GPA: 3.0
Range of GPA: 2.7–3.3
Average LSAT: 151
Range of LSAT: 147–154
Transfer Students Accepted? Yes
Other Schools to Which Students Applied: Southern Methodist University, St. Mary's University, Texas Tech University, University of Texas at Austin, University of Houston
Other Admissions Factors Considered: Personal background, accomplishments and/or achievements, letters of recommendation, LSAT score, upward grade trend
Number of Applications Received: 1,837
Number of Applicants Accepted: 917
Number of Applicants Enrolled: 369

EMPLOYMENT INFORMATION

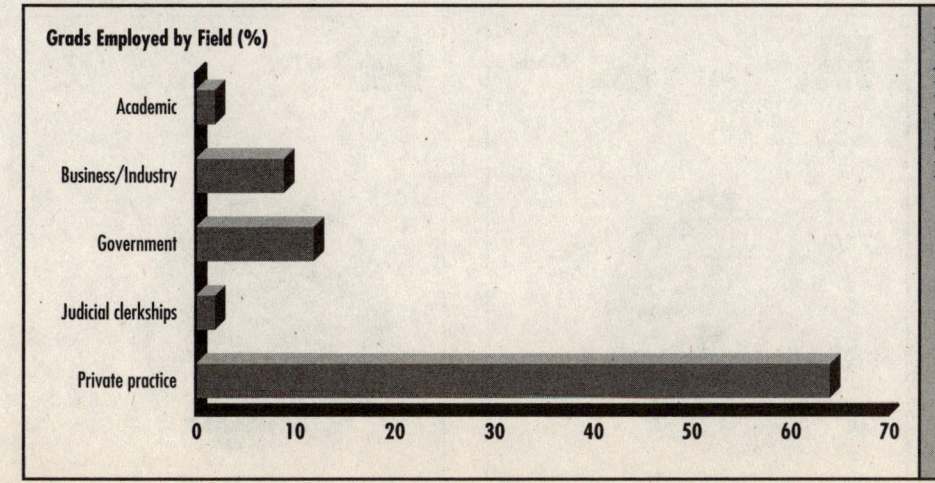

Grads Employed by Field (%)

Field	%
Academic	~2
Business/Industry	~10
Government	~13
Judicial clerkships	~3
Private practice	~65

Rate of Placement: 80%
Average Starting Salary: $70,606
Employers Who Frequently Hire Grads: Private law firms, corporations, government entities
State for Bar Exam: TX
Pass Rate for First-Time Bar: 78%

SOUTHERN CALIFORNIA INSTITUTE OF LAW
College of Law

Admissions Contact: Dean, Dr. Stanislaus Pulle
877 S. Victoria, Ventura, CA 93003
Admissions Phone: 805-644-2327 • Admissions Fax: 805-644-2367
Web Address: www.lawdegree.com

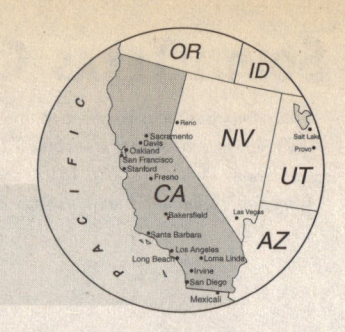

INSTITUTIONAL INFORMATION
Public/Private: Private
Affiliation: Conservative
Academic Calendar: Semester
Student/Faculty Ratio: 5:1
% Part Time: 75
% Female: 50
% Minority: 10

PROGRAMS
Academic Specialties: Strong emphasis on legal writing. Professors teach in subjects in which they have a specialized practice.

STUDENT INFORMATION
Enrollment of Law School: 50
% Male/Female: 60/40
% Full Time: 0
% Minority: 15
Average Age of Entering Class: 32

RESEARCH FACILITIES
School-Supported Research Centers: Local courthouse library

EXPENSES/FINANCIAL AID
Annual Tuition: $6,480
Books and Supplies: $500
% of Aid That Is Merit-Based: 100
Tuition Per Credit: $200
Fees Per Credit: $200

ADMISSIONS INFORMATION
LSDAS Accepted? No
Transfer Students Accepted? No
Other Schools to Which Students Applied: Ventura College of Law, San Francisco Law School, Santa Barbara College of Law, Western State University
Other Admissions Factors Considered: Working professionals

INTERNATIONAL STUDENTS
TOEFL Required of International Students? Yes

EMPLOYMENT INFORMATION
Average Starting Salary: $30,000
Employers Who Frequently Hire Grads: Local law firms, government and state agencies
Prominent Alumni: Dr. Michael Clare, vice president, HCIA; Sally La Macchia, associate general counsel, National Association of Government Employees; Dr. Jim Forrest, senior scientist, P.E. Muger Base

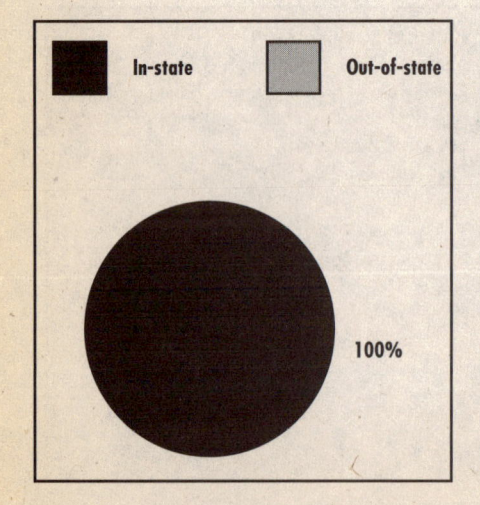

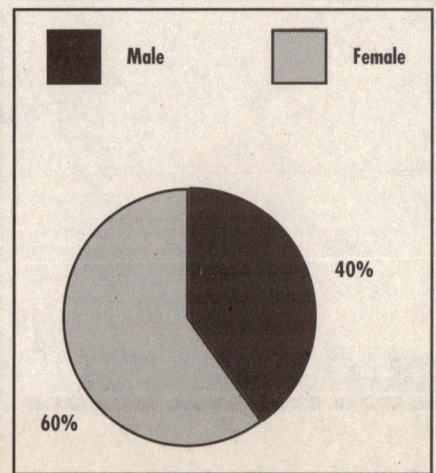

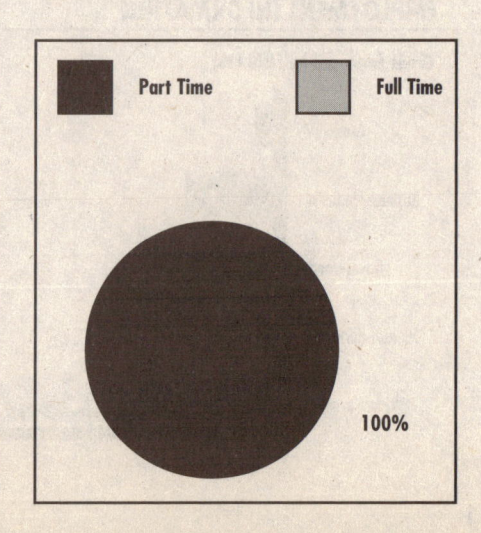

SOUTHERN ILLINOIS UNIVERSITY
School of Law

Admissions Contact: Assistant Dean, Michael Ruiz
SIU School of Law, Carbondale, IL 62901-6804
Admissions Phone: 618-453-8858 • Admissions Fax: 618-453-8769
Admissions E-mail: lawadmit@siu.edu • Web Address: www.law.siu.edu

INSTITUTIONAL INFORMATION
Public/Private: Public
Student/Faculty Ratio: 13:1
Total Faculty: 45
% Part Time: 23
% Female: 46
% Minority: 1

PROGRAMS
Academic Specialties: Health Law, Alternative Dispute Resolution, Clinical Programs (Elderly Law, Domestic Violence, ADR, Self-Help Legal Center, Agricultural Mediation)
Advanced Degrees Offered: JD (3 years)
Combined Degrees Offered: JD/MD (6 years), JD/MBA (4 years), JD/MPA (4 years), JD/Macc (4 years), JD/MSW, JD/PhD
Grading System: 4.0 scale
Clinical Program Required? No
Clinical Program Description: Elderly Law, Domestic Violence, Alternative Dispute Resolution, Self-Help Legal Center, Agricultural Mediation
Legal Writing Course Requirements? No
Legal Methods Course Requirements? Yes
Legal Methods Description: Lawyering Skills includes legal research, writing, argumentation, negotiation, and client counseling.
Legal Research Course Requirements? No
Moot Court Requirement? No
Public Interest Law Requirement? No
Academic Journals: *Southern Illinois University Law Journal, Journal of Legal Medicine*

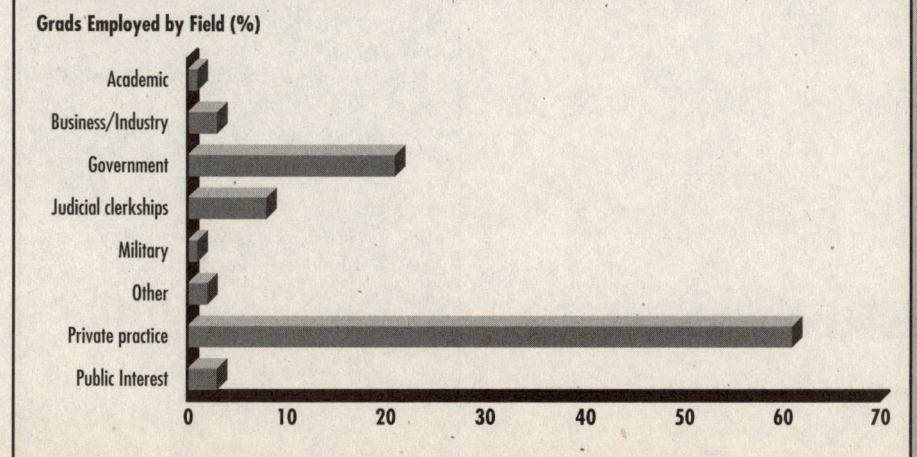

STUDENT INFORMATION
Enrollment of Law School: 363
% Male/Female: 58/42
% Full Time: 99
% Full Time That Are International: 1
% Minority: 8
Average Age of Entering Class: 25

RESEARCH FACILITIES
Research Resources Available: Lexis, Westlaw
School-Supported Research Centers: 1 computer lab in the law school, 4 computer labs on campus outside the law school

EXPENSES/FINANCIAL AID
Annual Tuition (Residents/Nonresidents): $6,120/$18,360
Room and Board: $8,951
Books and Supplies: $870
Financial Aid Application Deadline: 4/1
Average Grant: $1,500
Average Loan: $17,140
% of Aid That Is Merit-Based: 0
% Receiving Some Sort of Aid: 95
Average Total Aid Package: $17,140
Average Debt: $42,900

ADMISSIONS INFORMATION
Application Fee: $40
Regular Application Deadline: 3/1
Regular Notification: Rolling
LSDAS Accepted? Yes
Average GPA: 3.3
Range of GPA: 3.0–3.6
Average LSAT: 152
Range of LSAT: 149–154
Transfer Students Accepted? Yes
Other Schools to Which Students Applied: Northern Illinois University
Other Admissions Factors Considered: Personal statement, letters of recommendation, résumé
Number of Applications Received: 700
Number of Applicants Accepted: 363
Number of Applicants Enrolled: 152

INTERNATIONAL STUDENTS
TOEFL Required of International Students? Yes
Minimum TOEFL: 600

EMPLOYMENT INFORMATION

Grads Employed by Field (%)

Field	%
Academic	~1
Business/Industry	~3
Government	~22
Judicial clerkships	~7
Military	~1
Other	~3
Private practice	~62
Public Interest	~2

Rate of Placement: 92%
Average Starting Salary: $45,802
Employers Who Frequently Hire Grads: Various Illinois State's Attorney's Offices, large and many small law firms, public interest organizations
Prominent Alumni: Timothy Eaton, Illinois State Bar Association President, 2001; John Stuakemeyer, Corporate Counsel, State Farm of Tallahassee; William Birkett, Associate General Counsel, INS, Washington, DC
State for Bar Exam: IL, MO, KY, TN, IN
Pass Rate for First-Time Bar: 84%

SOUTHERN METHODIST UNIVERSITY
Dedman School of Law

Admissions Contact: Assistant Dean and Director of Admissions, Lynn Bozalis
PO Box 750110, Dallas, TX 75275
Admissions Phone: 214-768-2550 • Admissions Fax: 214-768-2549
Admissions E-mail: lawadmit@mail.smu.edu • Web Address: www.law.smu.edu

INSTITUTIONAL INFORMATION
Public/Private: Private
Affiliation: Methodist
Student/Faculty Ratio: 18:1
Total Faculty: 36
% Part Time: 0
% Female: 30
% Minority: 14

PROGRAMS
Academic Specialties: Business, Taxation, Securities, International Law, Litigation, Environmental Law, Health Care, Internet, Dispute Resolution
Advanced Degrees Offered: LLM (1 year)
Combined Degrees Offered: JD/MBA (4.5 years), JD/MA (4 years)
Grading System: Letter and numerical system on a 4.0 scale; no C–, D+, or D–
Clinical Program Required? Yes
Clinical Program Description: Civil, Criminal Defense, Tax, Domestic Violence, Criminal Prosecution, Poverty Law
Legal Writing Course Requirements? No
Legal Methods Course Requirements? Yes
Legal Methods Description: 1 year, 2 hours in fall, 4 hours in spring
Legal Research Course Requirements? No
Moot Court Requirement? No
Public Interest Law Requirement? No

STUDENT INFORMATION
Enrollment of Law School: 741
% Out of State: 35
% Male/Female: 56/44
% Full Time: 98
% Full Time That Are International: 1
% Minority: 11
Average Age of Entering Class: 25

EXPENSES/FINANCIAL AID
Annual Tuition: $22,550
Room and Board: $8,400
Books and Supplies: $1,300
Financial Aid Application Deadline: 6/1
Average Grant: $8,000
Average Loan: $22,500
% of Aid That Is Merit-Based: 100
% Receiving Some Sort of Aid: 80
Average Total Aid Package: $35,000
Average Debt: $70,000
Tuition Per Credit: $770
Fees Per Credit: $99

ADMISSIONS INFORMATION
Application Fee: $50
Regular Application Deadline: 2/15
Regular Notification: 4/30
LSDAS Accepted? Yes
Average GPA: 3.5
Range of GPA: 3.1–3.7
Average LSAT: 159
Range of LSAT: 156–161
Transfer Students Accepted? Yes
Other Schools to Which Students Applied: University of Texas at Austin, Tulane University, University of Houston, Baylor University
Number of Applications Received: 1,582
Number of Applicants Accepted: 595
Number of Applicants Enrolled: 262

EMPLOYMENT INFORMATION

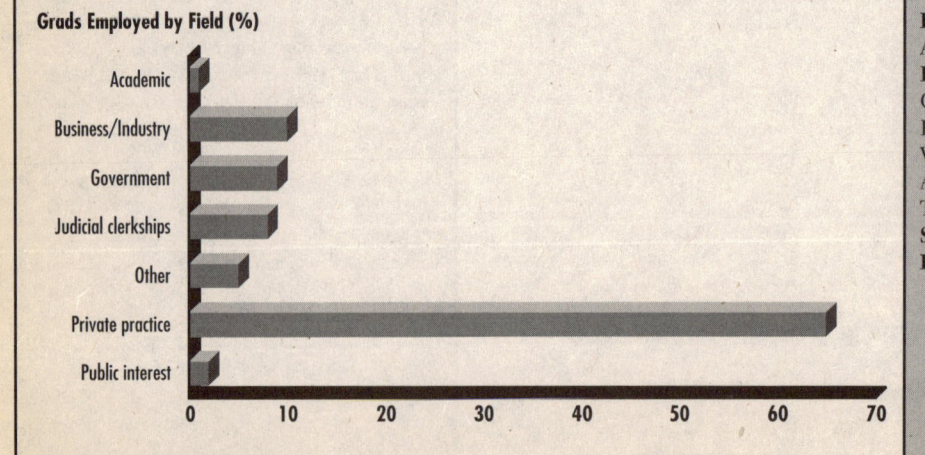

Grads Employed by Field (%)
- Academic
- Business/Industry
- Government
- Judicial clerkships
- Other
- Private practice
- Public interest

Rate of Placement: 98%
Average Starting Salary: $74,000
Employers Who Frequently Hire Grads: Akin Gump Strauss Hauer & Feld; Baker Botts; Haynes and Boone; Jones Day Reavis & Pogue; Vinson & Elkins; Dallas County District Attorney's Office
Texas Supreme Court
State for Bar Exam: TX
Pass Rate for First-Time Bar: 84%

SOUTHERN UNIVERSITY
Law Center

Admissions Contact: Gloria Simon
PO Box 9294, Baton Rouge, LA 70813
Admissions Phone: 225-771-5340 • Admissions Fax: 225-771-7424
Web Address: www.sus.edu

INSTITUTIONAL INFORMATION
Public/Private: Public
Environment: Urban
Academic Calendar: Semester
Schedule: Full time only
Student/Faculty Ratio: 12:1
Total Faculty: 44
% Female: 30
% Minority: 64

PROGRAMS
Academic Specialties: Law and Technology (Artificial Intelligence)
Grading System: 4.0 grade point scale; A (90–100), B+ (85–89), B (84–80), C+ (79–75), C (74–70), D+ (69–65), D (64–60), F (59–0)
Clinical Program Required? No
Clinical Program Description: 4 Clinics: Criminal, Juvenile, Elder Law, Administrative/Civil. Clinical Education Program is restricted to third-year law students in good standing.
Legal Writing/Methods Course Requirements: First year: Legal Writing, 2 hours/semester; second year: Advanced Legal Writing 1 hour/semester

STUDENT INFORMATION
Enrollment of Law School: 311
% Male/Female: 50/50
% Full Time: 100
% Minority: 66
Average Age of Entering Class: 27

RESEARCH FACILITIES
School-Supported Research Centers: Through a cooperative aggreement with Paul M. Herbert Law Center at Louisiana State University, students at both institutions have unlimited and free access to each institution's facilities and materials.

EXPENSES/FINANCIAL AID
Annual Tuition (Residents/Nonresidents): $3,128/$7,728

ADMISSIONS INFORMATION
Regular Application Deadline: 3/1
Regular Notification: January–May
Average GPA: 3.6
Average LSAT: 145
Other Schools to Which Students Applied: Loyola University Chicago, Howard University, Tulane University, Texas Southern University, Georgia State University, Florida State University, George Mason University, Georgetown University

EMPLOYMENT INFORMATION

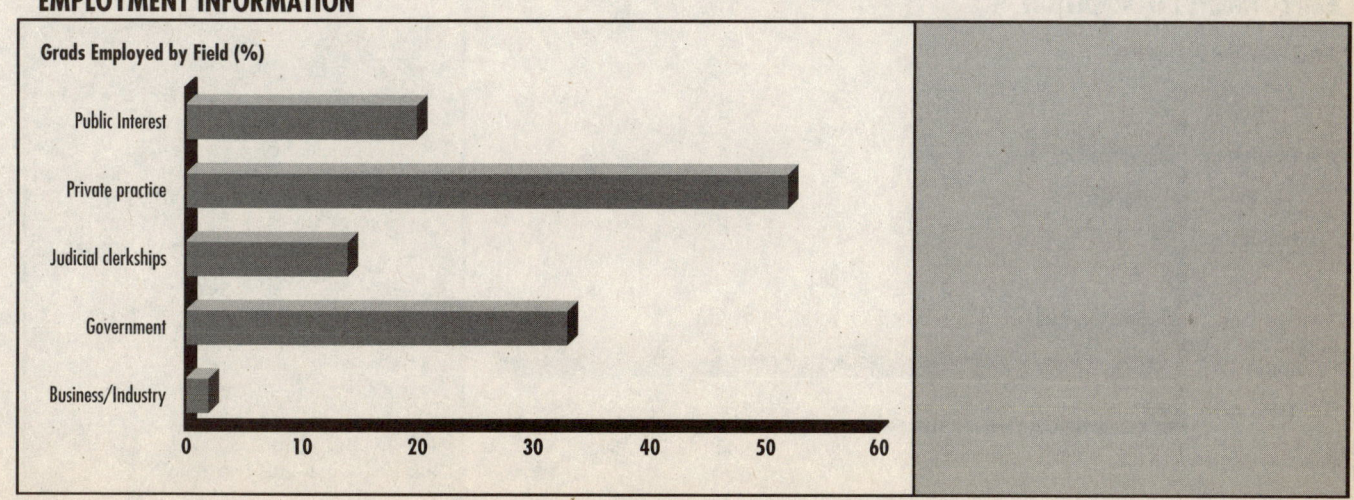

Grads Employed by Field (%)
- Public Interest: ~20
- Private practice: ~52
- Judicial clerkships: ~15
- Government: ~33
- Business/Industry: ~2

SOUTHWESTERN UNIVERSITY SCHOOL OF LAW

Admissions Contact: Director of Admissions, Anne Wilson
675 South Westmoreland Avenue, Los Angeles, CA 90005
Admissions Phone: 213-738-6717 • Admissions Fax: 213-383-1688
Admissions E-mail: admissions@swlaw.edu • Web Address: www.swlaw.edu

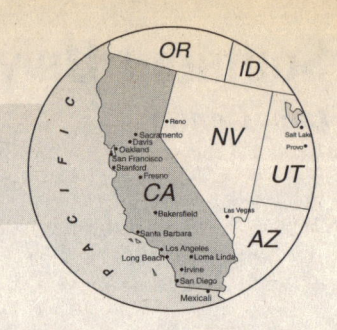

INSTITUTIONAL INFORMATION

Public/Private: Private
Student/Faculty Ratio: 16:1
Total Faculty: 73
% Part Time: 27
% Female: 36
% Minority: 20

PROGRAMS

Academic Specialties: Nationally recognized experts in Antitrust, Criminal, Environmental, Family, Housing and Urban Development, Intellectual Property, Entertainment, International, and Taxation Law; Civil Procedure, Commercial Law, Constitutional Law, Corporation Securities Law, Government Services, Human Rights Law, Labor Law, Legal History, Legal Philosophy, Property
Advanced Degrees Offered: Besides the JD, we offer the only LLM in Entertainment and Media Law (1 year full time, 2 years part time).
Grading System: Letter system on a 4.0 scale; some courses are Pass/Fail
Clinical Program Required? No
Clinical Program Description: Externships in more than 100 legal settings in judicial, public interest, federal/state/local government, or entertainment entities; clinical/simulation courses
Legal Writing Course Requirements? Yes
Legal Writing Description: Legal Reasoning, Analysis and Writing Skills includes organization, rhetorical strategies, style, and mechanics and culminates in the Moot Court Intramural Competition.
Legal Methods Course Requirements? Yes
Legal Methods Description: Required courses include an overview of the legal system, the process of litigation, the structure of court opinions, case analysis, and case briefing. Other topics include the lawyer's individual and professional obligations in addition to defining the professional role, including codes of conduct, traditions and history, and ethical philosophy.
Legal Research Course Requirements? Yes
Legal Research Description: Taught by law librarians; research sources and strategies are covered in preparation for the Moot Court Intramural Competition
Moot Court Requirement? Yes
Moot Court Description: Each first-year student prepares a written appellate brief in the Legal Research and Writing course and participates in 2 mandatory rounds of oral argument. 16 students are selected to compete in 4 final rounds judged by members of the bench and bar.
Public Interest Law Requirement? No
Academic Journals: Southwestern University Law Review, Southwestern Journal of Law and Trade in the Americas

STUDENT INFORMATION

Enrollment of Law School: 954
% Out of State: 15
% Male/Female: 49/51
% Full Time: 70
% Full Time That Are International: 1
% Minority: 34
Average Age of Entering Class: 27

RESEARCH FACILITIES

Research Resources Available: Career Development Consortium, Library and Career Service reciprocities with law schools from around the country
School-Supported Research Centers: National Entertainment and Media Law Institute, second-largest law library facility in California, new Julia Dixon Courtroom and Advocacy Center, new 10,000-square-foot state-of-the-art Fitness Center, student support program, alumni mentor programs

EXPENSES/FINANCIAL AID

Annual Tuition: $26,100
Room and Board (Off Campus): $14,400
Books and Supplies: $1,200
Financial Aid Application Deadline: 6/2
Average Grant: $6,528
Average Loan: $27,967
% Receiving Some Sort of Aid: 93
Average Total Aid Package: $30,610
Average Debt: $73,042
Tuition Per Credit: $870

ADMISSIONS INFORMATION

Application Fee: $50
Regular Application Deadline: 6/30
Regular Notification: Rolling
LSDAS Accepted? Yes
Range of GPA: 3.0–3.5
Range of LSAT: 152–158
Transfer Students Accepted? Yes
Other Schools to Which Students Applied: Loyola Marymount University; Pepperdine University; University of California, Hastings; University of California, Los Angeles; University of San Diego; University of Southern California
Number of Applications Received: 2,578
Number of Applicants Accepted: 1,029
Number of Applicants Enrolled: 316

EMPLOYMENT INFORMATION

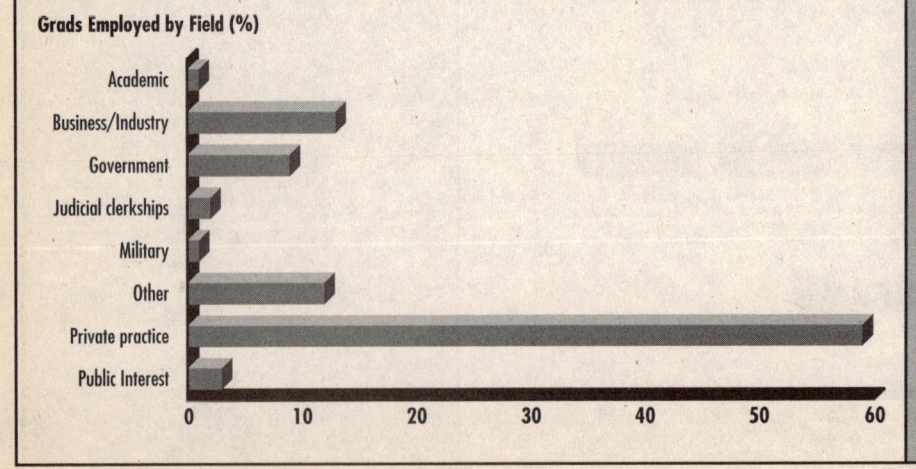

Grads Employed by Field (%)

Field	%
Academic	~1
Business/Industry	~13
Government	~12
Judicial clerkships	~2
Military	~1
Other	~11
Private practice	~59
Public Interest	~2

Rate of Placement: 98%
Average Starting Salary: $70,000
Employers Who Frequently Hire Grads: Private firms; corporations; entertainment entities; federal, state, and local courts; government agencies; public interest organizations; Barger & Wolen; Deloitte Touche LLP; Foley & Lardner; Gibson, Dunn & Crutcher LLP; Heller Ehrman White & McAuliffe LLP; Howrey Simon Arnold & White, LLP; McKenna Long & Aldridge LLP
Prominent Alumni: Hon. Tom Bradley, Los Angeles Mayor for 20 years; Hon. Stanley Mosk, longest-serving Supreme Court Justice in CA; Hon. Vaino Spencer, first African-American female Judge in CA and third in the U.S.
State for Bar Exam: CA, NY, NV, WA, FL
Pass Rate for First-Time Bar: 71%

STANFORD UNIVERSITY
School of Law

Admissions Contact: Associate Dean for Admissions and Financial Aid, Faye K. Deal
559 Nathan Abbott Way, Stanford, CA 94305-8610
Admissions Phone: 650-723-4985 • Admissions Fax: 650-723-0838
Admissions E-mail: law.admissions@forsythe.stanford.edu • Web Address: www.law.stanford.edu

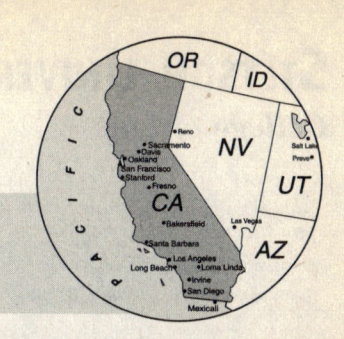

INSTITUTIONAL INFORMATION
Public/Private: Private
Student/Faculty Ratio: 13:1
Total Faculty: 38
% Female: 24
% Minority: 15

PROGRAMS
Academic Specialties: Civil Procedure, Commercial Law, Constitutional Law, Corporation Securities Law, Criminal Law, Environmental Law, Government Services, Human Rights Law, Intellectual Property Law, International Law, Labor Law, Legal History, Legal Philosophy, Property, Taxation; see lawschool.stanford.edu/faculty
Advanced Degrees Offered: MLS (1 year) JSM (1 year), LLM (1 year), JSD (2 years)
Combined Degrees Offered: JD/MBA (4 years), JD/MA (4 years)
Grading System: Letter system
Clinical Program Required? No
Legal Writing Course Requirements? Yes
Legal Writing Description: 1 year
Legal Methods Course Requirements? No
Legal Research Course Requirements? Yes
Legal Research Description: 1 year
Moot Court Requirement? No
Public Interest Law Requirement? No

Academic Journals: *Stanford Agora: An Online Journal of Legal Perspectives, Stanford Environmental Law Journal, Stanford Law Review, Stanford Journal of International Law, Stanford Law and Public Policy Review, Stanford Technology and Law Review, Stanford Journal of Law, Business and Finance*

STUDENT INFORMATION
Enrollment of Law School: 559
% Male/Female: 52/48
% Full Time: 100
% Full Time That Are International: 2
% Minority: 32
Average Age of Entering Class: 25

EXPENSES/FINANCIAL AID
Annual Tuition: $29,398
Room and Board (On/Off Campus): $12,040/$18,535
Books and Supplies: $1,360
Financial Aid Application Deadline: 3/15
Average Grant: $11,147
Average Loan: $34,727
% of Aid That Is Merit-Based: 0
% Receiving Some Sort of Aid: 84
Average Total Aid Package: $39,550
Average Debt: $74,000

ADMISSIONS INFORMATION
Application Fee: $65
Regular Application Deadline: Rolling
Regular Notification: 4/30
LSDAS Accepted? Yes
Average GPA: 3.7
Range of GPA: 3.7–3.9
Average LSAT: 168
Range of LSAT: 165–170
Transfer Students Accepted? Yes
Number of Applications Received: 4,273
Number of Applicants Accepted: 478
Number of Applicants Enrolled: 178

INTERNATIONAL STUDENTS
TOEFL Recommended for International Students? Yes

EMPLOYMENT INFORMATION

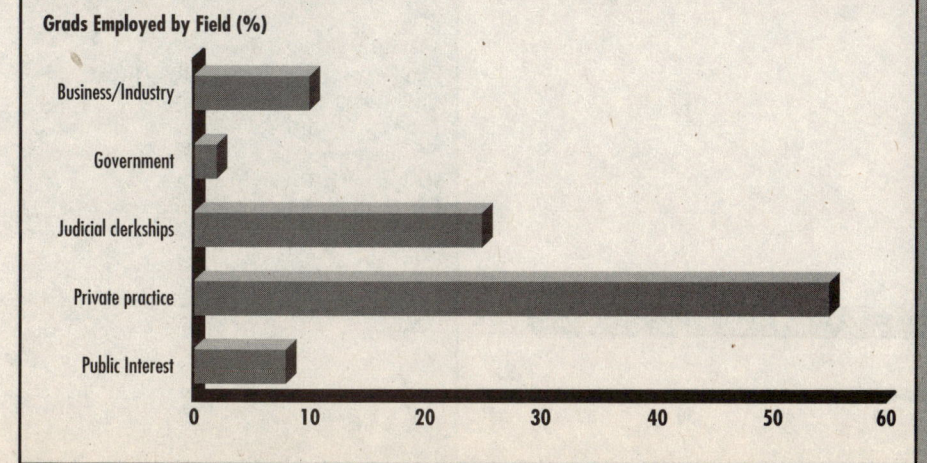

Grads Employed by Field (%)

Field	%
Business/Industry	~10
Government	~3
Judicial clerkships	~25
Private practice	~55
Public Interest	~7

Rate of Placement: 100%
Average Starting Salary: $89,876
Prominent Alumni: Sandra Day O'Connor, Justice, U.S. Supreme Court; William Rehnquist, Justice, U.S. Supreme Court; Warren Christopher, former Secretary of State; Cheryl D. Mills, former Deputy Counsel to President Clinton
State for Bar Exam: CA
Pass Rate for First-Time Bar: 85%

STETSON UNIVERSITY
College of Law

Admissions Contact: Assistant Dean of Admissions, Pamela B. Coleman
1401 61st Street South, Gulfport, FL 33707
Admissions Phone: 727-562-7802 • Admissions Fax: 727-343-0136
Admissions E-mail: lawadmit@law.stetson.edu • Web Address: www.law.stetson.edu

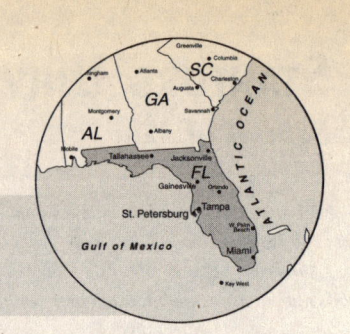

INSTITUTIONAL INFORMATION
Public/Private: Private
Student/Faculty Ratio: 17:1
Total Faculty: 86
% Part Time: 49
% Female: 40
% Minority: 14

PROGRAMS
Academic Specialties: Nationally ranked Stetson Advocacy Program; award-winning Moot Court Program; Centers for Excellence in Advocacy, Health Law, Elder Law, and Alternative Dispute Resolution; honors program for students who earn a 3.5 GPA after the first or second full academic semester; comprehensive academic success program; International Law
Advanced Degrees Offered: JD (3 years full time, 4 years part time), LLM (1 year full time)
Combined Degrees Offered: JD/MBA (3 years full time)
Grading System: 4.0 scale
Clinical Program Required? No
Clinical Program Description: Local Government (ADR) Clinic, Civil Poverty Clinic, Elder Law Clinic, Labor Law Clinic, Public Defender (Prosecution) Clinic, EEOC Clinic
Legal Writing Course Requirements? Yes
Legal Writing Description: 2-semester, graded course focuses on legal research, objective and persuasive writing, and oral advocacy.
Legal Methods Course Requirements? No
Legal Research Course Requirements? Yes
Legal Research Description: Legal research is taught as part of the Research and Writing course. We focus on print and computer-assisted research. Students have the opportunity to participate in small-group lab sessions.
Moot Court Requirement? Yes
Moot Court Description: First-year students are taught oral advocacy in the second semester of Research and Writing II. Students give 4 oral presentations. Top oralists compete in a first-year appellate advocacy competition for cash prizes and positions on the Moot Court Board.
Public Interest Law Requirement? Yes
Public Interest Law Description: 20 hours of pro bono work
Academic Journals: Stetson Law Review, Stetson Law Forum (online), Journal of International Law: Aging and Policy

STUDENT INFORMATION
Enrollment of Law School: 770
% Out of State: 27
% Male/Female: 45/55
% Full Time: 91
% Full Time That Are International: 1
% Minority: 18
Average Age of Entering Class: 23

RESEARCH FACILITIES
Research Resources Available: A satellite campus will be built in Tampa in August 2003. This facility will have computer labs and a library for all students and alumni to use. The facility will offer some of the part-time evening courses and will include courtrooms set up with advanced technologies, as well as fully wired classrooms.

EXPENSES/FINANCIAL AID
Annual Tuition: $22,785
Room and Board (On/Off Campus): $7,500/$10,000
Books and Supplies: $1,200
Average Grant: $15,495
Average Loan: $30,000
% of Aid That Is Merit-Based: 68
% Receiving Some Sort of Aid: 96
Average Total Aid Package: $38,000
Average Debt: $96,000

ADMISSIONS INFORMATION
Application Fee: $55
Regular Application Deadline: Rolling
Regular Notification: Rolling
LSDAS Accepted? Yes
Average GPA: 3.2
Range of GPA: 2.9–3.5
Average LSAT: 152
Range of LSAT: 149–155
Transfer Students Accepted? Yes
Other Schools to Which Students Applied: Florida State University, Mercer University, University of Florida, University of Miami
Other Admissions Factors Considered: Personal statements, grade trends, letters of recommendation, campus activities, work experience, diversity
Number of Applications Received: 1,644
Number of Applicants Accepted: 577
Number of Applicants Enrolled: 201

INTERNATIONAL STUDENTS
TOEFL Required of International Students? Yes
Minimum TOEFL: 600 (250 computer)

EMPLOYMENT INFORMATION

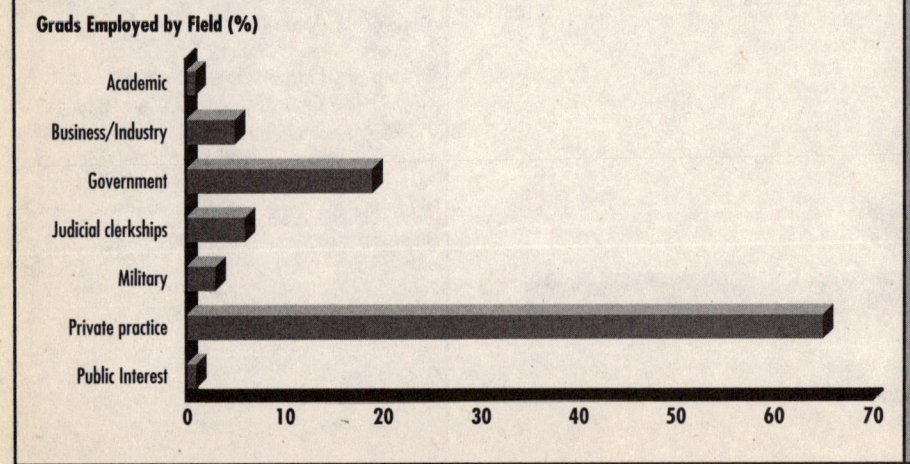

Rate of Placement: 96%
Average Starting Salary: $49,070
Employers Who Frequently Hire Grads: Small, medium, and large firms in the greater Tampa Bay area, state attorney's and public defender's offices
State for Bar Exam: FL
Pass Rate for First-Time Bar: 85%

Suffolk University
Law School

Admissions Contact: Dean of Admissions, Gail Ellis
120 Tremont Street, Boston, MA 02108-4977
Admissions Phone: 617-573-8144 • Admissions Fax: 617-523-1367
Admissions E-mail: lawadm@suffolk.edu • Web Address: www.law.suffolk.edu

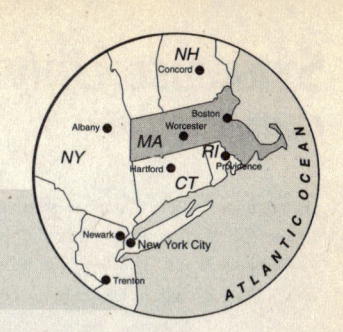

INSTITUTIONAL INFORMATION
Public/Private: Private
Student/Faculty Ratio: 20:1
Total Faculty: 160
% Part Time: 60
% Female: 17
% Minority: 5

PROGRAMS
Academic Specialties: High Tech/Intellectual Property, Health Care/Biomedical Law, Financial Services, Civil Litigation, International Law, Human Rights/Civil Rights, Labor and Employment Law, Juvenile Law, Commercial Law, Constitutional Law, Corporation Securities Law, Criminal Law, Environmental Law, Government Services, Legal History, Legal Philosophy, Property, Taxation; study-abroad program at University of Lund, Sweden
Advanced Degrees Offered: JD (3 years full time, 4 years part time)
Combined Degrees Offered: JD/MBA, JD/MPA, JD/MSIE, JD/MSF, JD/MSCJ (all 3 years full time, 5 years part time)
Grading System: Letter and numerical system from A+ to F (4.3–0.0)
Clinical Program Required? Yes
Clinical Program Description: Voluntary Defenders, Prosecutor Program, Battered Women's Advocacy Program, Center for Juvenile Justice, Civil Clinic, Landlord/Tenant Clinic, Housing Clinic, Suffolk University Legal Assistance Bureau, Macaronis Institute for Trial and Appellate Advocacy

Legal Writing Course Requirements? No
Legal Methods Course Requirements? Yes
Legal Methods Description: 2 semesters
Legal Research Course Requirements? No
Moot Court Requirement? No
Public Interest Law Requirement? No
Academic Journals: *Suffolk University Law Review, Transnational Law Review, Suffolk Journal of Trial and Appellate Advocacy, Journal of High Technology Law*

STUDENT INFORMATION
Enrollment of Law School: 1,690
% Out of State: 46
% Male/Female: 46/54
% Full Time: 67
% Full Time That Are International: 5
% Minority: 12
Average Age of Entering Class: 25

RESEARCH FACILITIES
Research Resources Available: The school is located in the heart of downtown Boston, across the street from the Boston Common and Public Gardens, and within walking distance to the Massachusetts State House and federal and state courts.
School-Supported Research Centers: 3,000 data ports in the new law school facility; laptop accessibility at all classroom desktops, library study carrels, and tables; access to high-speed Internet connections at all student lounges and in cafeteria

EXPENSES/FINANCIAL AID
Annual Tuition: $26,540
Room and Board (Off Campus): $14,775
Books and Supplies: $900
Financial Aid Application Deadline: 3/3
Average Grant: $4,042
Average Loan: $27,452
% of Aid That Is Merit-Based: 39
% Receiving Some Sort of Aid: 75
Average Total Aid Package: $25,000
Average Debt: $72,886
Tuition Per Credit: $900

ADMISSIONS INFORMATION
Application Fee: $50
Regular Application Deadline: 3/1
Regular Notification: Rolling
LSDAS Accepted? Yes
Average GPA: 3.2
Range of GPA: 2.9–3.4
Average LSAT: 153
Range of LSAT: 150–155
Transfer Students Accepted? Yes
Other Admissions Factors Considered: Community service
Number of Applications Received: 3,088
Number of Applicants Enrolled: 530

INTERNATIONAL STUDENTS
TOEFL Required of International Students? Yes
Minimum TOEFL: 600 (250 computer)

EMPLOYMENT INFORMATION

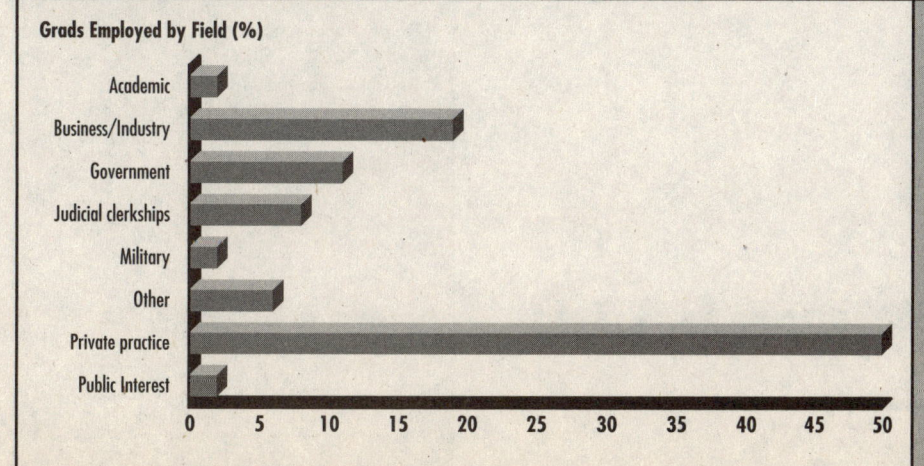

Grads Employed by Field (%)

Field	%
Academic	~1
Business/Industry	~20
Government	~12
Judicial clerkships	~7
Military	~2
Other	~5
Private practice	~50
Public Interest	~2

Rate of Placement: 91%
Average Starting Salary: $64,532
Employers Who Frequently Hire Grads: Testa, Hurwitz & Thibeault, LLP; Navy J.A.G.; Massachusetts Superior Court; Suffolk County District Attorney's Office
State for Bar Exam: MA
Pass Rate for First-Time Bar: 84%

Syracuse University
College of Law

Admissions Contact: Director of Admissions, Nikki S. Laubenstein
Office of Admissions and Financial Aid, Suite 340, Syracuse, NY 13244
Admissions Phone: 315-443-1962 • *Admissions Fax:* 315-443-9568
Admissions E-mail: admissions.law.syr.edu • *Web Address:* www.law.syr.edu

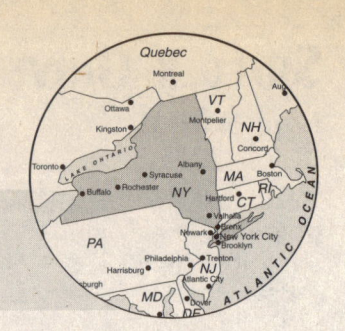

INSTITUTIONAL INFORMATION
Public/Private: Private
Student/Faculty Ratio: 16:1
Total Faculty: 49
% Female: 41
% Minority: 16

PROGRAMS
Academic Specialties: We have developed programs that emphasize the intergration of theory and practical training. These applied learning opportunities provide hands-on experience in a variety of fields. We offer many joint degree programs with other colleges and departments on campus. We also offer Trial Practice; Law, Technology, and Management; Law and Economics; and Clinical Training as specializations. Specialties include Commercial Law, Constitutional Law, Corporation Securities Law, Criminal Law, Environmental Law, Government Services, Human Rights Law, Intellectual Property Law, International Law, Labor Law, and Taxation.
Combined Degrees Offered: JD/MS, JD/MBA, JD/MA, JD/PhD, JD/MSW, JD/MPA
Grading System: A, A–, B+, B, B–, C+, C, C–, D, F, Pass/Fail
Clinical Program Required? No
Clinical Program Description: Community Development, Criminal Law, Public Interest Law, Children's Rights and Family Law, Low Income Taxpayer Clinic; externships in Judicial, Advocacy, Public Interest, and Washington, DC
Legal Writing Course Requirements? Yes
Legal Writing Description: Law Firm, first year, 2 semesters
Legal Methods Course Requirements? Yes
Legal Methods Description: See Legal Writing.
Legal Research Course Requirements? Yes
Legal Research Description: See Legal Writing.
Moot Court Requirement? No
Public Interest Law Requirement? No
Academic Journals: *Law Review, Syracuse Journal of International Law and Commerce, The Digest, The Labor Lawyer, The Journal of Law and Technology*

STUDENT INFORMATION
Enrollment of Law School: 782
% Male/Female: 50/50
% Full Time: 99
% Full Time That Are International: 4
% Minority: 19
Average Age of Entering Class: 25

RESEARCH FACILITIES
School-Supported Research Centers: 84 PCs available in dedicated computer clusters

EXPENSES/FINANCIAL AID
Annual Tuition: $27,500
Room and Board: $10,240
Books and Supplies: $1,100
Financial Aid Application Deadline: 2/10
Average Grant: $7,640
Average Loan: $24,900
Average Debt: $66,998
Tuition Per Credit: $1,203
Fees Per Credit: $189

ADMISSIONS INFORMATION
Application Fee: $50
Regular Application Deadline: Rolling
Regular Notification: Rolling
LSDAS Accepted? Yes
Average GPA: 3.3
Range of GPA: 3.0–3.5
Average LSAT: 151
Range of LSAT: 148–154
Transfer Students Accepted? Yes
Other Admissions Factors Considered: Trend of undergraduate performance and course selection; graduate course work and degree; writing ability; overcoming personal hardship, including such burdens as poverty or disability; age; race/ethnicity; gender; community activities
Number of Applications Received: 1,910
Number of Applicants Accepted: 795
Number of Applicants Enrolled: 295

INTERNATIONAL STUDENTS
TOEFL Required of International Students? Yes
Minimum TOEFL: 600 (250 computer)

EMPLOYMENT INFORMATION

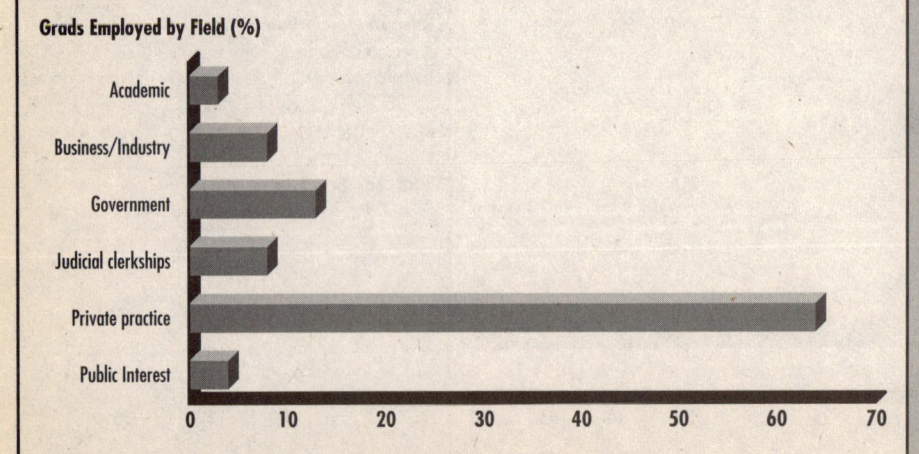

Grads Employed by Field (%)
- Academic: ~2
- Business/Industry: ~8
- Government: ~13
- Judicial clerkships: ~10
- Private practice: ~64
- Public Interest: ~3

Rate of Placement: 84%
Average Starting Salary: $61,532
Prominent Alumni: Joseph R. Biden Jr., U.S. Senator; Theodore A. McKee, Federal Appeals Court Judge; Donald T. MacNaughton, Partner, White & Case

TEMPLE UNIVERSITY
Beasley School of Law

Admissions Contact: Director of Admissions and Financial Aid, Johanne L. Johnston
1719 North Broad Street, Philadelphia, PA 19122
Admissions Phone: 800-560-1428 • Admissions Fax: 215-204-9319
Admissions E-mail: lawadmis@blue.temple.edu • Web Address: www.temple.edu/lawschool

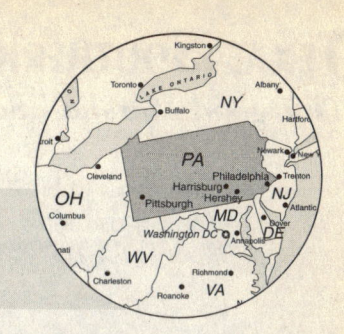

INSTITUTIONAL INFORMATION
Public/Private: Public
Student/Faculty Ratio: 16:1
Total Faculty: 61
% Female: 33
% Minority: 25

PROGRAMS
Academic Specialties: Trial Advocacy, Business and Tax Law, International Law, Public Interest Law, Criminal Law, Transactional Law, Technology Law/Intellectual Property
Advanced Degrees Offered: JD (3 years full time, 4 years part time); LLM (1 year)
Combined Degrees Offered: JD/MBA (4 years), JD/LLM Taxation or Transnational Law (3.5 years)
Grading System: 4.0 scale
Clinical Program Required? No
Clinical Program Description: Clinical offerings in 25 areas
Legal Writing Course Requirements? Yes
Legal Writing Description: 1-year intensive program that includes drafting briefs and memos and conducting an oral argument
Legal Methods Course Requirements? Yes
Legal Methods Description: 1-semester course that includes an introduction to legal methods and legal reasoning and analysis
Legal Research Course Requirements? Yes
Legal Research Description: See Legal Writing.
Moot Court Requirement? No
Public Interest Law Requirement? No

Academic Journals: Temple Law Review, Temple International and Comparative Law Review, Temple Political and Civil Rights Law Review, Temple Environmental Law and Technology Journal

STUDENT INFORMATION
Enrollment of Law School: 1,074
% Male/Female: 51/49
% Full Time: 73
% Full Time That Are International: 1
% Minority: 19
Average Age of Entering Class: 26

RESEARCH FACILITIES
Research Resources Available: Brand-new recreational and exercise facilities, including a student field house
School-Supported Research Centers: Shusterman Hall—brand-new state-of-the-art conference center devoted entirely to law school activities

EXPENSES/FINANCIAL AID
Annual Tuition (Residents/Nonresidents): $10,308/$17,864
Room and Board: $6,720
Books and Supplies: $1,500
Financial Aid Application Deadline: 3/1
Average Grant: $2,749
Average Loan: $19,238
% of Aid That Is Merit-Based: 83
% Receiving Some Sort of Aid: 80
Average Total Aid Package: $20,606
Average Debt: $53,524
Tuition Per Credit (Residents/Nonresidents): $398/$729

ADMISSIONS INFORMATION
Application Fee: $50
Regular Application Deadline: 3/1
Regular Notification: Rolling
LSDAS Accepted? Yes
Average GPA: 3.3
Range of GPA: 3.0–3.6
Average LSAT: 157
Range of LSAT: 154–160
Transfer Students Accepted? Yes
Other Schools to Which Students Applied: American University, George Washington University, Rutgers University—Camden, Villanova University, Widener University
Other Admissions Factors Considered: Graduate course work; demonstrated leadership ability in college, community, or career activities; economic disadvantage; academic honors; committment to service (Peace Corps, VISTA, military); serious disabilities
Number of Applications Received: 3,226
Number of Applicants Accepted: 1,276
Number of Applicants Enrolled: 345

INTERNATIONAL STUDENTS
TOEFL Required of International Students? Yes

EMPLOYMENT INFORMATION

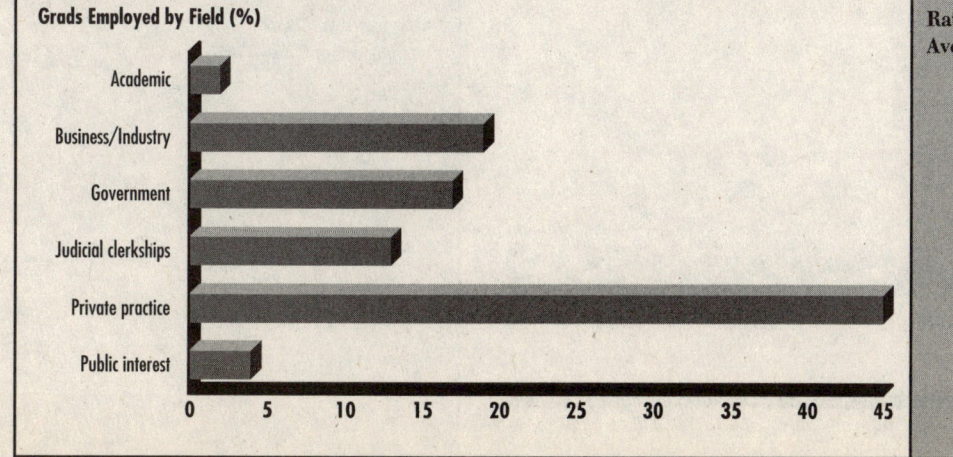

Grads Employed by Field (%)

Field	%
Academic	~1
Business/Industry	~18
Government	~14
Judicial clerkships	~14
Private practice	~45
Public interest	~3

Rate of Placement: 93%
Average Starting Salary: $65,450

TEXAS SOUTHERN UNIVERSITY
Thurgood Marshall School of Law

Admissions Contact: Dean of Admissions
3100 Cleburne Avenue, Houston, TX 77004
Admissions Phone: 713-313-7114 • Web Address: www.tsulaw.edu

INSTITUTIONAL INFORMATION
Public/Private: Public
Student/Faculty Ratio: 17:1
Total Faculty: 35
% Female: 20
% Minority: 83

PROGRAMS
Academic Specialties: Commercial Law, Corporation Securities Law
Clinical Program Required? No
Legal Methods Course Requirements? No

STUDENT INFORMATION
Enrollment of Law School: 541
% Male/Female: 57/43
% Full Time: 100
% Minority: 77

EXPENSES/FINANCIAL AID
Annual Tuition (Residents/Nonresidents): $4,466/$7,562
Room and Board (Off Campus): $6,000
Books and Supplies: $700

ADMISSIONS INFORMATION
Application Fee: $40
Regular Application Deadline: 4/1
Regular Notification: Rolling
LSDAS Accepted? No
Average GPA: 3.0
Transfer Students Accepted? Yes
Number of Applications Received: 1,460
Number of Applicants Accepted: 540
Number of Applicants Enrolled: 265

EMPLOYMENT INFORMATION

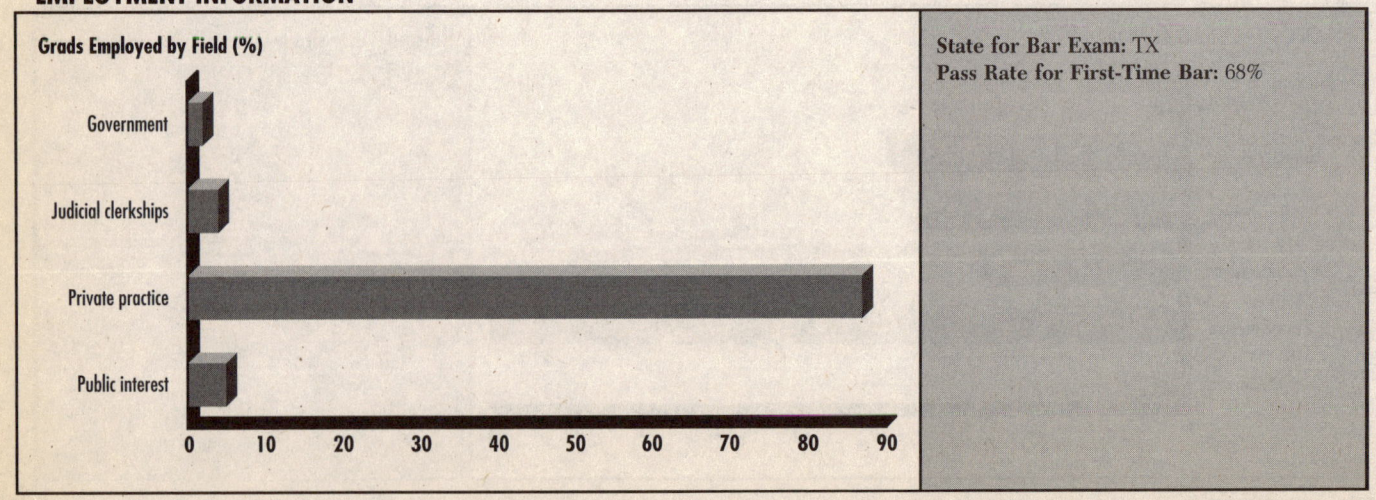

Grads Employed by Field (%)
- Government
- Judicial clerkships
- Private practice
- Public interest

State for Bar Exam: TX
Pass Rate for First-Time Bar: 68%

TEXAS TECH UNIVERSITY
School of Law

Admissions Contact: Admissions Counselor, Donna Williams
1802 Hartford Avenue, Lubbock, TX 79409
Admissions Phone: 806-742-3990 • Admissions Fax: 806-742-1629
Admissions E-mail: donna.williams@ttu.edu • Web Address: www.law.ttu.edu

INSTITUTIONAL INFORMATION
Public/Private: Public
Student/Faculty Ratio: 20:1
Total Faculty: 48
% Part Time: 35
% Female: 27
% Minority: 25

PROGRAMS
Academic Specialties: Litigation Skills, Civil Procedure, Commercial Law, Constitutional Law, Corporation Securities Law, Criminal Law, Environmental Law, Government Services, Human Rights Law, Intellectual Property Law, International Law, Labor Law, Legal History, Legal Philosophy, Property, Taxation
Combined Degrees Offered: JD/MBA (3 years); JD/MPA (3.5 years); JD/MS Agriculture and Applied Science, Taxation, or Environmental Toxicology (3 to 3.5 years); JD/FFP (3 to 3.5 years)
Grading System: A (4.0), B+ (3.5), B (3.0), C+ (2.5), c (2.0), D+ (1.5), D (1.0), F (0.0)
Clinical Program Required? No
Clinical Program Description: Tax Clinic, Civil Litigation Clinic, Criminal Prosecution Clinic, Family Law Counseling Clinic
Legal Writing Course Requirements? No
Legal Methods Course Requirements? Yes
Legal Methods Description: 2 semesters, 6 credits, approximately 22 students per class
Legal Research Course Requirements? No
Moot Court Requirement? No
Public Interest Law Requirement? No

Academic Journals: Texas Tech Law Review, Texas Tech Journal of Texas Administrative Law Journal, The Texas Bank Lawyer, Texas Judges Bench Book

STUDENT INFORMATION
Enrollment of Law School: 698
% Out of State: 9
% Male/Female: 52/48
% Full Time: 100
% Full Time That Are International: 1
% Minority: 14
Average Age of Entering Class: 25

RESEARCH FACILITIES
Research Resources Available: Access to virtually all publically funded library resources in the state
School-Supported Research Centers: Wireless network; laptop computers for student checkout; more than 250 computers in library

EXPENSES/FINANCIAL AID
Annual Tuition (Residents/Nonresidents): $7,952/$13,048
Room and Board: $10,418
Books and Supplies: $883
Average Grant: $3,300
Average Loan: $14,515
% of Aid That Is Merit-Based: 14
% Receiving Some Sort of Aid: 87
Average Total Aid Package: $17,429
Average Debt: $40,481

ADMISSIONS INFORMATION
Application Fee: $50
Regular Application Deadline: 2/1
Regular Notification: Rolling
LSDAS Accepted? Yes
Average GPA: 3.4
Range of GPA: 3.1–3.6
Average LSAT: 154
Range of LSAT: 150–157
Transfer Students Accepted? Yes
Other Schools to Which Students Applied: Baylor University, Southern Methodist University, University of Houston, University of Texas at Austin
Other Admissions Factors Considered: Socioeconomic background, household income, parents' level of education
Number of Applications Received: 1,299
Number of Applicants Accepted: 534
Number of Applicants Enrolled: 247

INTERNATIONAL STUDENTS
TOEFL Required of International Students? Yes
Minimum TOEFL: 550 (213 computer)

EMPLOYMENT INFORMATION

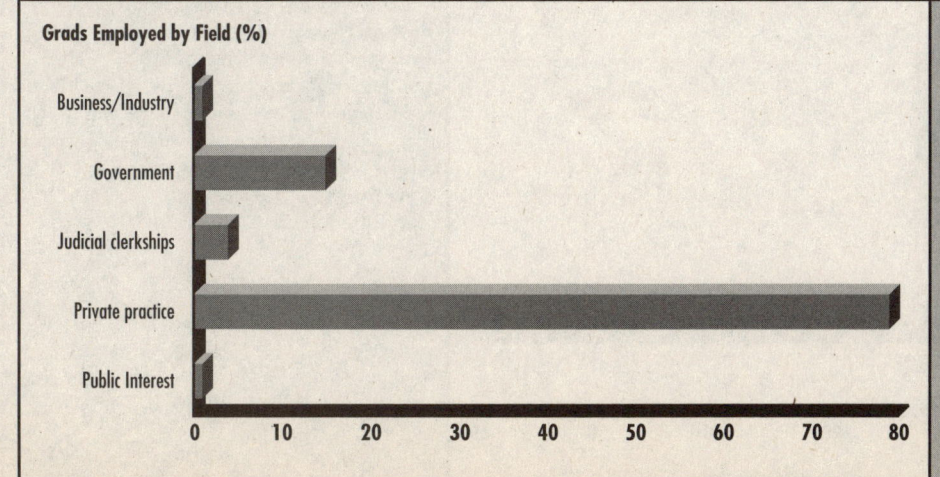

Grads Employed by Field (%)
- Business/Industry
- Government
- Judicial clerkships
- Private practice
- Public Interest

Rate of Placement: 98%
Average Starting Salary: $49,700
Employers Who Frequently Hire Grads: Jones, Day, Reavis & Pogue; Thompson & Knight; Haynes & Boone; Thompson & Coe; Cousins & Irons; Strasburger & Price; Cooper & Aldous; Kemp, Smith, Duncan & Hammond; Mehaffy & Weber; Orgain, Bell & Tucker; Akin, Gump; Baker, Botts; Gibson, Ochsner & Adkins; State and Federal Judiciary
Prominent Alumni: Jeff Wentworth, Texas Senator, District 25; Sue Walker, Court of Appeals; Robert L. Duncan, Texas Senator, District 28; Wayne Reaud, Litigator; Rob Junell, Federal Judge
State for Bar Exam: TX, NM
Pass Rate for First-Time Bar: 88%

TEXAS WESLEYAN UNIVERSITY
School of Law

Admissions Contact: Director of Admissions Operations, Lynda L. Culver
1515 Commerce Street, Fort Worth, TX 76102
Admissions Phone: 800-733-9529 • Admissions Fax: 817-212-4002
Admissions E-mail: lawadmissions@law.txwes.edu • Web Address: law.txwes.edu

INSTITUTIONAL INFORMATION
Public/Private: Private
Affiliation: Methodist
Student/Faculty Ratio: 20:1
Total Faculty: 29
% Part Time: 36
% Female: 38
% Minority: 10

PROGRAMS
Academic Specialties: Innovative program of skills courses called Practicum Courses—a course of study designed especially for the preparation of practitioners that involves the supervised practical application of previously studied theory
Advanced Degrees Offered: JD (3 years full time, 4 years part time)
Grading System: Numerical system
Clinical Program Required? No
Legal Writing Course Requirements? Yes
Legal Writing Description: 2-semester course that includes briefing
Legal Methods Course Requirements? Yes
Legal Methods Description: See Legal Writing.
Legal Research Course Requirements? Yes
Legal Research Description: See Legal Writing.
Moot Court Requirement? No
Public Interest Law Requirement? Yes
Public Interest Law Description: 30 hours of pro bono work

STUDENT INFORMATION
% Out of State: 0
% Male/Female: 100/0
% Full Time: 100
% Full Time That Are International: 0
% Minority: 0
Average Age of Entering Class: 29

RESEARCH FACILITIES
Research Resources Available: Lexis/Nexis, Westlaw
School-Supported Research Centers: Various city and state bar associations; legal and judicial internship program

EXPENSES/FINANCIAL AID
Annual Tuition: $17,800
Room and Board (Off Campus): $8,500
Books and Supplies: $1,500
Average Grant: $2,500
Average Loan: $17,800
Average Total Aid Package: $20,000
Average Debt: $56,500
Tuition Per Credit: $600

ADMISSIONS INFORMATION
Application Fee: $50
Regular Application Deadline: 3/31
Regular Notification: Rolling
LSDAS Accepted? Yes
Average GPA: 3.0
Range of GPA: 2.7–3.4
Average LSAT: 151
Range of LSAT: 148–154
Transfer Students Accepted? Yes
Other Schools to Which Students Applied: Baylor University, Southern Methodist University, Texas Tech University, Texas A&M University
Number of Applications Received: 1,307
Number of Applicants Accepted: 582
Number of Applicants Enrolled: 254

EMPLOYMENT INFORMATION

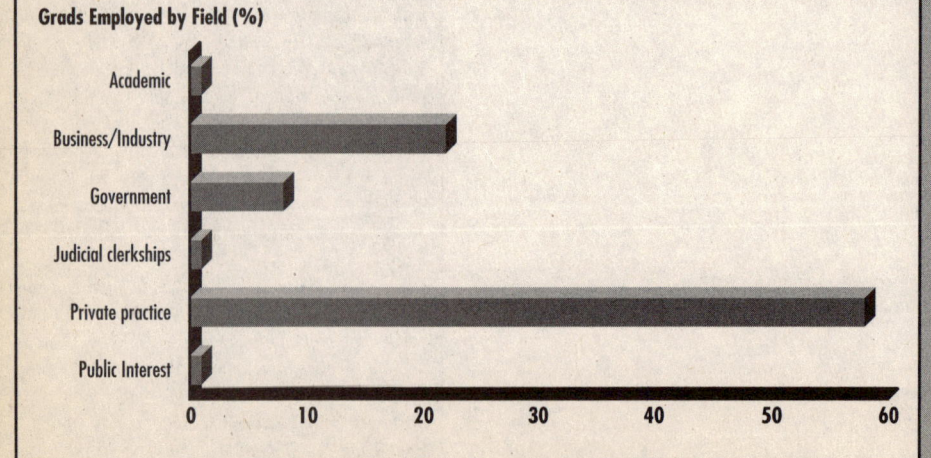

Grads Employed by Field (%)
- Academic: ~1
- Business/Industry: ~22
- Government: ~8
- Judicial clerkships: ~1
- Private practice: ~58
- Public Interest: ~1

Rate of Placement: 91%
Average Starting Salary: $45,000
Employers Who Frequently Hire Grads: Small to medium-size private practice firms, District Attorney's Offices, government agencies, various corporations and businesses
State for Bar Exam: TX
Pass Rate for First-Time Bar: 82%

THOMAS JEFFERSON SCHOOL OF LAW

Admissions Contact: Assistant Dean, Jennifer Keller
2121 San Diego Avenue, San Diego, CA 92110
Admissions Phone: 619-297-9700 • Admissions Fax: 619-294-4713
Admissions E-mail: adm@tjsl.edu • Web Address: www.tjsl.edu

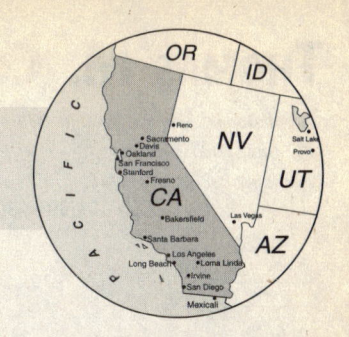

INSTITUTIONAL INFORMATION
Public/Private: Private
Student/Faculty Ratio: 10:1
Total Faculty: 74
% Part Time: 61
% Female: 32
% Minority: 6

PROGRAMS
Academic Specialties: Faculty members specialize in a wide variety of areas, with some emphasis on International Law; curriculum emphasizes professional skills; Constitutional Law, Criminal Law, Environmental Law, Government Services, and Taxation.
Advanced Degrees Offered: JD (3 years full time, 4 years part time)
Grading System: 4.0 scale
Clinical Program Required? No
Legal Writing Course Requirements? Yes
Legal Writing Description: 2 semesters; second semester is upper-level.
Legal Methods Course Requirements? No
Legal Research Course Requirements? No
Moot Court Requirement? No
Public Interest Law Requirement? No
Academic Journals: *Thomas Jefferson Law Review*

STUDENT INFORMATION
Enrollment of Law School: 691
% Out of State: 68
% Male/Female: 58/42
% Full Time: 72
% Full Time That Are International: 16
% Minority: 17
Average Age of Entering Class: 26

EXPENSES/FINANCIAL AID
Annual Tuition: $23,450
Room and Board (Off Campus): $11,502
Books and Supplies: $1,616
Financial Aid Application Deadline: 4/20
Average Grant: $8,864
Average Loan: $28,396
% Receiving Some Sort of Aid: 93
Average Total Aid Package: $24,755
Average Debt: $99,000
Tuition Per Credit: $14,750
Fees Per Credit: $150

ADMISSIONS INFORMATION
Application Fee: $35
Regular Application Deadline: Rolling
Regular Notification: Rolling
LSDAS Accepted? Yes
Average GPA: 2.9
Range of GPA: 2.6–3.2
Average LSAT: 151
Range of LSAT: 148–155
Transfer Students Accepted? Yes
Other Schools to Which Students Applied: California Western, Southwestern University School of Law, University of San Diego, University of the Pacific, Whittier College
Number of Applications Received: 2,174
Number of Applicants Accepted: 1,201
Number of Applicants Enrolled: 249

INTERNATIONAL STUDENTS
TOEFL Required of International Students? Yes

EMPLOYMENT INFORMATION

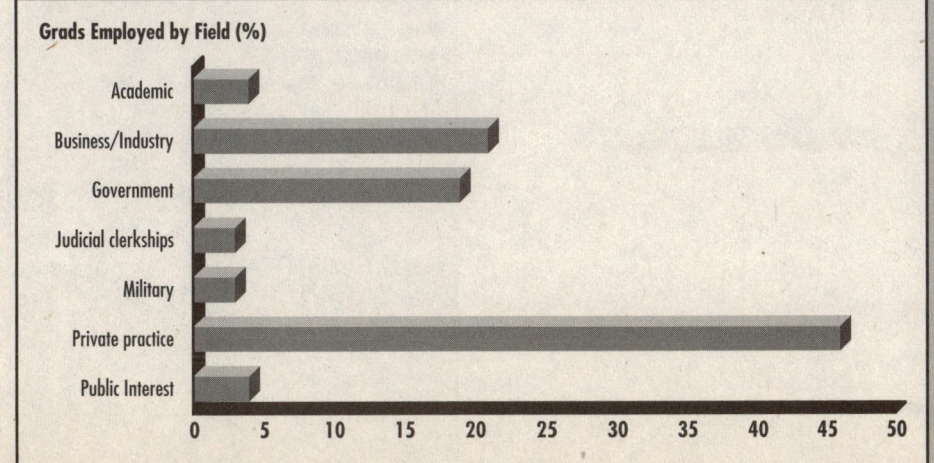

Grads Employed by Field (%)
- Academic: ~1
- Business/Industry: ~22
- Government: ~20
- Judicial clerkships: ~2
- Military: ~2
- Private practice: ~47
- Public Interest: ~3

Rate of Placement: 65%
Average Starting Salary: $56,287
Employers Who Frequently Hire Grads: District Attorney's, Attorney General's, and Public Defender's Offices; numerous small firms; medium-size local firms
State for Bar Exam: CA, NV, AZ, CO, UT
Pass Rate for First-Time Bar: 59%

THOMAS M. COOLEY LAW SCHOOL

Admissions Contact: Assistant Dean of Admissions, Stephanie Gregg
PO Box 13038, Lansing, MI 48901
Admissions Phone: 517-371-5140 • Admissions Fax: 517-334-5718
Admissions E-mail: admissions@cooley.edu • Web Address: www.cooley.edu

INSTITUTIONAL INFORMATION
Public/Private: Private
Student/Faculty Ratio: 24:1
Total Faculty: 144
% Part Time: 67
% Female: 37
% Minority: 8

PROGRAMS
Academic Specialties: Constitutional Law, Environmental Law, Government Services, International Law, Business Transactions, General Practice, Litigation, Administrative Law
Advanced Degrees Offered: JD (2 to 4 years)
Combined Degrees Offered: JD/MPA with Western Michigan University (3 to 6 years)
Grading System: In most courses, grades are based on written final exams. Professors adhere to established grade definitions.
Clinical Program Required? Yes
Clinical Programs Description: 4 clinical options: 1) an extensive third-year externship program which places senior students in real work situations throughout the U.S.; 2) Sixty Plus, an award-winning in-house clinical program, providing representation to senior citizens in mid-Michigan; 3) Estate Planning Clinic, an evening or weekend clinic with students providing estate planning services to seniors; and 4) Innocence Project, where students use forensic science to aid innocent persons wrongfully convicted of crimes.
Legal Writing Course Requirements? Yes
Legal Writing Description: Research and Writing (first year) and Advanced Research and Writing (third year) are required of all students.
Legal Methods Course Requirements? Yes
Legal Methods Description: Introduction to Law I is required of all students, exposing them to law school briefing, examinations, and jurisprudence.
Legal Research Course Requirements? Yes
Legal Research Description: In 2 sequenced courses, students learn both traditional book research and efficient and effective computer research. Additional instruction is available in Advanced Computer Research elective.
Moot Court Requirement? No
Moot Court Description: We offer a first-year moot court competition to all interested students, a second-year class, and several invitation-only teams that compete in national programs.
Public Interest Law Requirement? No
Academic Journals: *The Thomas M. Cooley Law Review, The Thomas M. Cooley Journal of Practical and Clinical Law*

STUDENT INFORMATION
Enrollment of Law School: 1,819
% Out of State: 75
% Male/Female: 51/49
% Full Time: 21
% Full Time That Are International: 1
% Minority: 27
Average Age of Entering Class: 30

RESEARCH FACILITIES
Research Resources Available: 2 computer labs; Academic Resource Center provides access to a variety of CALI instruction materials; clinical programs are networked to assist interns and their clients

EXPENSES/FINANCIAL AID
Annual Tuition: $20,460
Room and Board (Off Campus): $6,860
Books and Supplies: $800
Financial Aid Application Deadline: 9/1
Average Grant: $3,251
Average Loan: $18,500
% of Aid That Is Merit-Based: 5
% Receiving Some Sort of Aid: 97
Average Total Aid Package: $18,500
Average Debt: $82,330
Tuition Per Credit: $682

ADMISSIONS INFORMATION
Regular Application Deadline: Rolling
Regular Notification: Rolling
LSDAS Accepted? Yes
Average GPA: 2.9
Range of GPA: 2.4–3.2
Average LSAT: 142
Range of LSAT: 138–146
Transfer Students Accepted? Yes
Other Schools to Which Students Applied: Michigan State, New England School of Law, Ohio Northern, Florida Coastal, Thomas Jefferson School of Law, Widener, The John Marshall Law School
Other Admissions Factors Considered: None other than character and fitness
Number of Applications Received: 2,061
Number of Applicants Accepted: 1,513
Number of Applicants Enrolled: 273

EMPLOYMENT INFORMATION

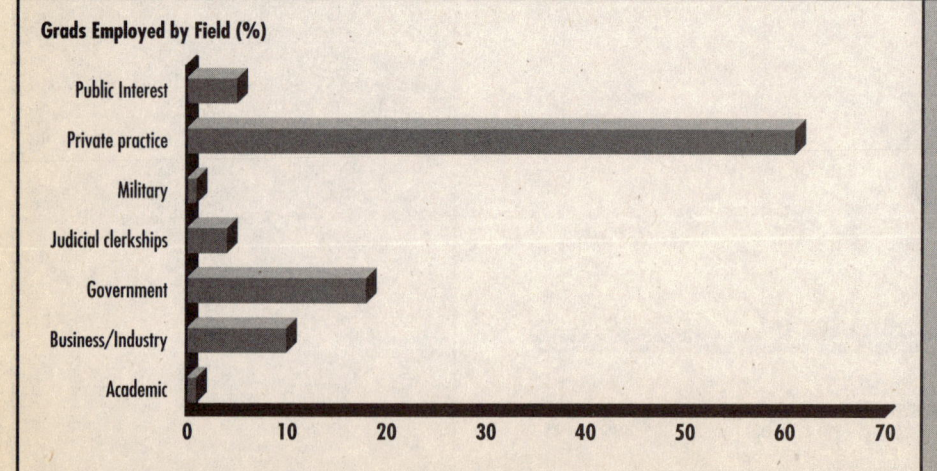

Grads Employed by Field (%)
- Public Interest
- Private practice
- Military
- Judicial clerkships
- Government
- Business/Industry
- Academic

Rate of Placement: 96%
Average Starting Salary: $41,895
Employers Who Frequently Hire Grads: Michigan Court of Appeals, prosecutors, Legal Services programs, Michigan law firms
State for Bar Exam: MI, NY, NJ, FL, IN
Pass Rate for First-Time Bar: 63%

TOURO COLLEGE
Jacob D. Fuchsberg Law Center

Admissions Contact: Director of Admissions, Grant Keener
300 Nassau Road, Huntington, NY 11743
Admissions Phone: 631-421-2244 • Admissions Fax: 631-421-9708
Admissions E-mail: admissions@tourolaw.edu • Web Address: www.tourolaw.edu

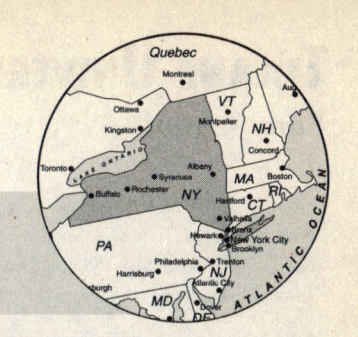

INSTITUTIONAL INFORMATION
Public/Private: Private
Student/Faculty Ratio: 17:1
Total Faculty: 50
% Part Time: 28
% Female: 35
% Minority: 7

PROGRAMS
Academic Specialties: Business Law, Criminal Law, Family Law, Health Law, Intellectual Property Law, International Law, Public Interest Law, Commercial Law, Human Rights Law
Advanced Degrees Offered: JD (3 years full time, 4 years part time), LLM (1 year full time, 3 semesters part time)
Combined Degrees Offered: JD/MBA, JD/MPA, JD/MSW (all add 1 year to regular programs)
Grading System: Clinics and courses are graded; pro bono work is Pass/Fail
Clinical Program Required? No
Clinical Program Description: Civil Rights Litigation Clinic, Elder Law Clinic, International Human Rights Litigation Clinic, Family Law Clinic, Judicial Clerkship Clinic, Not-for-Profit Corporation Law, Criminal Law Clinic
Legal Writing Course Requirements? Yes
Legal Writing Description: Part of Legal Methods
Legal Methods Course Requirements? Yes
Legal Methods Description: 2 semesters, 4 credits
Legal Research Course Requirements? Yes
Legal Research Description: Part of Legal Methods
Moot Court Requirement? No
Moot Court Description: Membership is by competition (combination of brief and oral argument). Members must serve for 4 consecutive semesters.
Public Interest Law Requirement? Yes
Public Interest Law Description: Successful completion of a clinic, a course plus 20 hours of pro bono work, or 40 hours of pro bono work
Academic Journals: *Touro Law Review*, *Journal of the Suffolk Academy of Law*

STUDENT INFORMATION
Enrollment of Law School: 667
% Male/Female: 53/47
% Full Time: 59
% Minority: 27
Average Age of Entering Class: 28

EXPENSES/FINANCIAL AID
Annual Tuition: $23,310
Room and Board: $15,000
Books and Supplies: $750
Average Grant: $7,500
Average Loan: $38,500
% of Aid That Is Merit-Based: 53
% Receiving Some Sort of Aid: 90
Average Total Aid Package: $30,000
Average Debt: $65,000
Tuition Per Credit: $850

ADMISSIONS INFORMATION
Application Fee: $50
Regular Application Deadline: Rolling
Regular Notification: Rolling
LSDAS Accepted? Yes
Range of GPA: 2.6–3.3
Range of LSAT: 145–151
Transfer Students Accepted? Yes
Other Admissions Factors Considered: Personal statement, work experience, graduate degree
Number of Applications Received: 1,609
Number of Applicants Accepted: 677
Number of Applicants Enrolled: 273

INTERNATIONAL STUDENTS
TOEFL Recommended for International Students? Yes
Minimum TOEFL: 600 (250 computer)

EMPLOYMENT INFORMATION

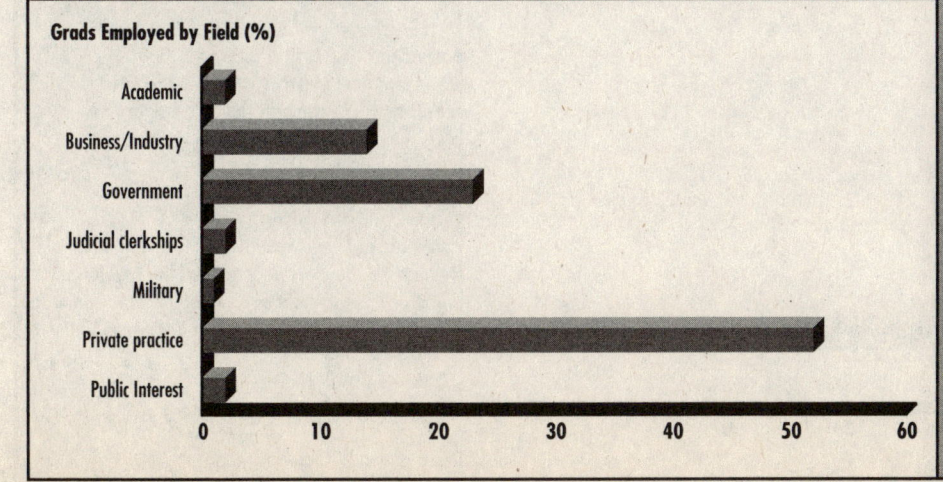

Grads Employed by Field (%)
- Academic: ~1
- Business/Industry: ~14
- Government: ~23
- Judicial clerkships: ~2
- Military: ~1
- Private practice: ~53
- Public Interest: ~2

Rate of Placement: 89%
Average Starting Salary: $45,000
Employers Who Frequently Hire Grads: District attorney's offices, public interest employers, small and medium-size law firms
State for Bar Exam: NY
Pass Rate for First-Time Bar: 63%

TULANE UNIVERSITY
Law School

Admissions Contact: Admission Coordinator
Weinmann Hall, New Orleans, LA 70118
Admissions Phone: 504-865-5930 • Admissions Fax: 504-865-6710
Admissions E-mail: admissions@law.tulane.edu • Web Address: www.law.tulane.edu

INSTITUTIONAL INFORMATION
Public/Private: Private
Student/Faculty Ratio: 20:1
Total Faculty: 50
% Female: 24
% Minority: 12

PROGRAMS
Academic Specialties: International and Comparative Law, Maritime Law, Environmental Law, Intellectual Property, Sports Law, Civil Law
Advanced Degrees Offered: SLD (1 to 3 years), LLM (1 year full time, 2 years part time)
Combined Degrees Offered: JD/BA or BS (6 years), JD/MBA (4 to 4.5 years), JD/MHA (4 to 4.5 years), JD/MSPH (4 to 4.5 years), LLM/MSPH (2 years), JD/MSW (4 to 4.5 years), JD/MA (3 to 3.5 years), JD/Macc (3.5 to 4 years)
Grading System: Letter and numerical system on a 4.0 scale
Clinical Program Required? No
Clinical Program Description: Criminal Defense Clinic, Civil Litigation Clinic, Juvenile Litigation Clinic, Domestic Violence Clinic, Environmental Law Clinic, Legislative Advocacy Clinic, State Agency Rulemaking and Drafting Clinic, Trial Advocacy
Legal Writing Course Requirements? Yes
Legal Writing Description: Year-long course during the first year; 10 sections led by an instructor and senior fellow. Instructors are experienced lawyers who are hired as full-time Legal Research and Writing instructors.
Legal Methods Course Requirements? No
Legal Research Course Requirements? Yes
Legal Research Description: See Legal Writing.
Moot Court Requirement? Yes
Moot Court Description: Required as part of the first-year Legal Research and Writing course; thereafter, Moot Court is optional, with both inter- and intraschool programs offered at trial and appellate levels and in the ADR area.
Public Interest Law Requirement? Yes
Public Interest Law Description: 20 hours of community legal service
Academic Journals: Tulane Law Review, Tulane Maritime Law Journal, Tulane Environmental Law Journal, Tulane Journal of International and Comparative Law, Journal of Law and Sexuality, Sports Law Journal, European and Civil Law Forum

STUDENT INFORMATION
Enrollment of Law School: 1,015
% Out of State: 84
% Male/Female: 50/50
% Full Time: 100
% Full Time That Are International: 3
% Minority: 23
Average Age of Entering Class: 24

RESEARCH FACILITIES
School-Supported Research Centers: Maritime Law Center, Environmental Law and Policy Institute, Eason-Weinmann Center for Comparative Law

EXPENSES/FINANCIAL AID
Annual Tuition: $26,100
Room and Board (Off Campus): $7,650
Books and Supplies: $1,270
Financial Aid Application Deadline: 4/15
Average Grant: $14,000
Average Loan: $26,837
% of Aid That Is Merit-Based: 90
% Receiving Some Sort of Aid: 86
Average Total Aid Package: $28,000
Average Debt: $75,000

ADMISSIONS INFORMATION
Application Fee: $60
Regular Application Deadline: Rolling
Regular Notification: Rolling
LSDAS Accepted? Yes
Average GPA: 3.4
Range of GPA: 3.2–3.7
Average LSAT: 160
Range of LSAT: 156–161
Transfer Students Accepted? Yes
Other Schools to Which Students Applied: George Washington University, American University, Emory University, Boston University, Georgetown University, University of Miami, Boston College
Other Admissions Factors Considered: Life experience, qualities or characteristics that may be underrepresented and/or that indicate special motivation, leadership skills, industriousness, seriousness of purpose
Number of Applications Received: 3,859
Number of Applicants Accepted: 1,194
Number of Applicants Enrolled: 358

EMPLOYMENT INFORMATION

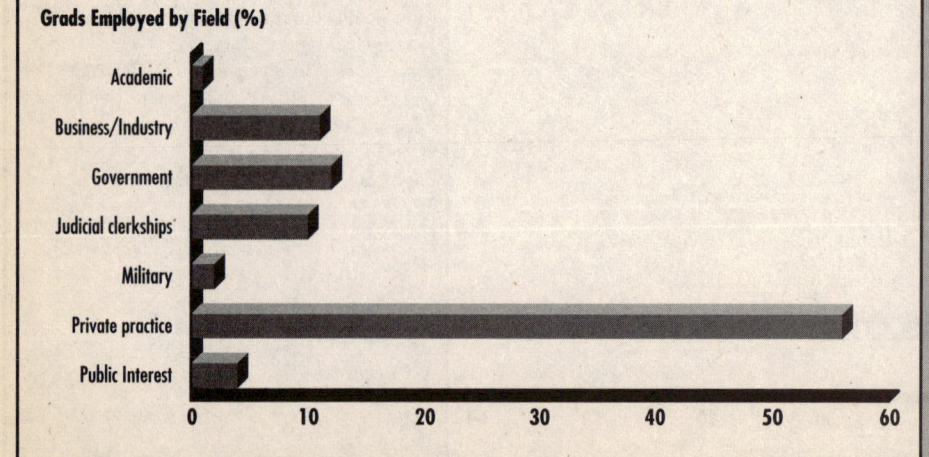

Grads Employed by Field (%)

Field	%
Academic	~1
Business/Industry	~12
Government	~12
Judicial clerkships	~8
Military	~1
Private practice	~57
Public Interest	~4

Rate of Placement: 95%
Average Starting Salary: $87,000
Employers Who Frequently Hire Grads: Fulbright & Jaworski; Skadden Arps; Arnold & Porter; White & Case; Mayer Brown & Platt; Cleary Gottlieb; Winthrop Stimson; McGlinchey; Adams & Reese; Exxon Co.; U.S. Army; U.S. Department of Justice
Prominent Alumni: Robert Livingston, U.S. politician; David Vitter, U.S. politician; John Minor Wisdom, judiciary; William Suter, Clerk, U.S. Supreme Court; William Pryor, Alabama Attorney General
State for Bar Exam: TX, NY, LA, FL, DC
Pass Rate for First-Time Bar: 93%

UNIVERSITY AT BUFFALO, STATE UNIVERSITY OF NY
Law School

Admissions Contact: Associate Dean for Admissions and Financial Aid, Lillie V. Wiley-Upshaw
309 O'Brian Hall, Buffalo, NY 14260
Admissions Phone: 716-645-2907 • Admissions Fax: 716-645-6676
Admissions E-mail: law-admissions@buffalo.edu • Web Address: www.law.buffalo.edu

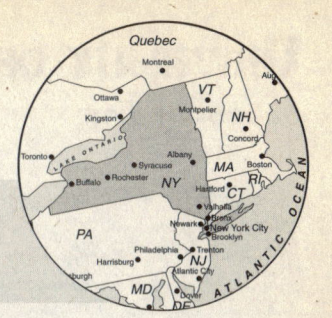

INSTITUTIONAL INFORMATION
Public/Private: Public
Student/Faculty Ratio: 14:1
Total Faculty: 85
% Part Time: 50
% Female: 33
% Minority: 11

PROGRAMS
Academic Specialties: Law and Society, Law and Gender, Litigation, Family Violence, Corporate Finances, International Human Rights, Family Law, Affordable Housing, Labor and Employment Law, Health Law and Management, Community Economic Development, Environmental Law, State and Local Government Law, Business Transactions, Commercial Law, Corporation Securities Law, Criminal Law, Intellectual Property Law, International Law, Property
Advanced Degrees Offered: LLM Criminal Law (1 year)
Combined Degrees Offered: JD/MSW (4 years), JD/MBA (4 years), JD/MPH (4 years), JD/MLS (4 years), JD/MA Applied Economics (3.5 years), JD/PhD (5 to 6 years)
Grading System: A, B+, B, C, D, F
Clinical Program Required? No
Clinical Program Description: Clinics for Affordable Housing, Community Economic Development, Family Violence, Education Law, Health Related Legal Concerns of the Elderly, Criminal Law, Securities Law, Environment and Development, Judicial and Legislative Externships
Legal Writing Course Requirements? Yes
Legal Writing Description: 7 credits, 2 semesters, combined with Legal Research during the first year
Legal Methods Course Requirements? No
Legal Research Course Requirements? Yes
Legal Research Description: See Legal Writing.
Moot Court Requirement? No
Moot Court Description: Students participate in moot court competitions: intramural for first-years, regional and international for second- and third-years.
Public Interest Law Requirement? No
Academic Journals: *Buffalo Law Review, Buffalo Criminal Law Review, Buffalo Environmental Law Review,* and several others

STUDENT INFORMATION
Enrollment of Law School: 728
% Out of State: 4
% Male/Female: 46/54
% Full Time: 99
% Full Time That Are International: 1
% Minority: 17
Average Age of Entering Class: 25

RESEARCH FACILITIES
Research Resources Available: Lexis/Nexis; city, state, and federal courthouses with legal libraries
School-Supported Research Centers: Charles B. Sears Law Library, Baldy Center for Law and Social Policy, Criminal Law Center, Human Rights Center, Ewin F. Jaeckle Center for State and Local Government, Center for the Study of Business Transactions, Environment and Society Institute, Institute for Research and Education on Women and Gender

EXPENSES/FINANCIAL AID
Annual Tuition (Residents/Nonresidents): $10,500/$16,050
Room and Board: $7,433
Books and Supplies: $1,323
Financial Aid Application Deadline: 3/1
Average Grant: $4,550
Average Loan: $18,500
% of Aid That Is Merit-Based: 45
% Receiving Some Sort of Aid: 60
Average Total Aid Package: $18,500
Average Debt: $42,591
Tuition Per Credit (Res./Nonres.): $438/$669
Fees Per Credit: $39

ADMISSIONS INFORMATION
Application Fee: $50
Regular Application Deadline: 3/15
Regular Notification: Rolling
LSDAS Accepted? Yes
Range of GPA: 3.0–3.6
Range of LSAT: 152–158
Transfer Students Accepted? Yes
Other Schools to Which Students Applied: Albany Law, American, Brooklyn Law, Fordham, Hofstra, New York Law, Syracuse
Other Admissions Factors Considered: Achievements or activities that suggest a high probability of scholastic excellence or distinctive intellectual contribution while in law school
Number of Applications Received: 1,463
Number of Applicants Accepted: 535
Number of Applicants Enrolled: 243

INTERNATIONAL STUDENTS
TOEFL Required of International Students? Yes
Minimum TOEFL: 650 (280 computer)

EMPLOYMENT INFORMATION

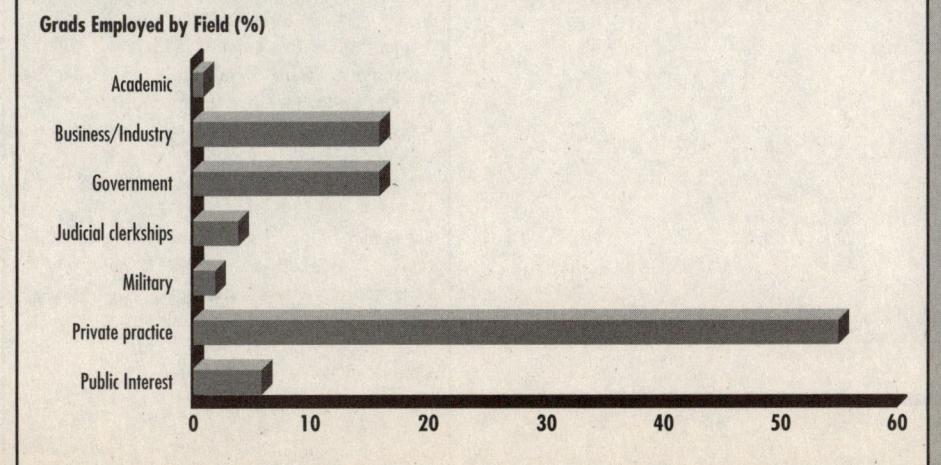

Grads Employed by Field (%): Academic, Business/Industry, Government, Judicial clerkships, Military, Private practice, Public Interest

Rate of Placement: 99%
Average Starting Salary: $52,855
Employers Who Frequently Hire Grads: LeBoeuf Lamb; Hodgson Russ; New York Appellate Division, 4th Department; Dewey Ballantine; Nixon Peabody; Phillips Lytle; Harris Beach & Wilcox; New York County District Attorney's Office; National Labor Relations Board; White & Case; Bond, Schoeneck, Schulte, Roth & Zabel
Prominent Alumni: Hon. Julio Fuentes, U.S. 3rd Circuit Court of Appeals; Herald Price Fahringer, Constitutional Lawyer; Susan Horwitz, MacArthur Foundation; Theodore Hess, Marine Brigadier General; Julia Hall, Human Rights Watch
State for Bar Exam: NY, PA, NJ, IL, MD
Pass Rate for First-Time Bar: 74%

UNIVERSITY OF AKRON
School of Law

Admissions Contact: Assistant Dean of Admission and Financial Aid, Lauri S. File
Akron, OH 44325-2901
Admissions Phone: 800-425-7668 • Admissions Fax: 330-258-2343
Admissions E-mail: lawadmissions@uakron.edu • Web Address: www.uakron.edu/law

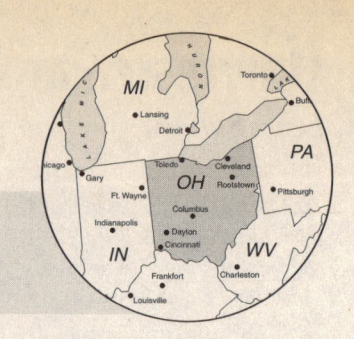

INSTITUTIONAL INFORMATION
Public/Private: Public
Student/Faculty Ratio: 18:1
Total Faculty: 58
% Part Time: 47
% Female: 45
% Minority: 7

PROGRAMS
Academic Specialties: Small class sizes, nationally recognized Intellectual Property and Trial Advocacy Programs, Litigation, Corporation Securities Law, Criminal Law, Intellectual Property Law, International Law, Taxation
Combined Degrees Offered: JD/MBA, JD/M Science and Management in Human Resources, JD/M Taxation, JD/MPA (all add 1 semester to regular programs)
Grading System: 4.0 scale; minimum 2.0 required for good standing
Clinical Program Required? No
Clinical Program Description: Legal Clinic, Appellate Review, Trial Litigation Clinic, Clinical Seminar, Inmate Assistance Program, New Business Legal Clinic
Legal Writing Course Requirements? Yes
Legal Writing Description: Legal Analysis Research and Writing I (1 semester, 3 credits); Legal Analysis Research and Writing II (1 semester, 2 credits); Legal Drafting (1 semester, 1 credit)
Legal Methods Course Requirements? Yes
Legal Methods Description: Introduction to Law and Legal Systems is a week-long intensive course held before the first semester.
Legal Research Course Requirements? Yes
Legal Research Description: Basic legal research, part of the Legal Analysis Research and Writing courses, is 1 credit and includes manual research as well as Westlaw and Lexis training. Advanced Legal Research is a 1-credit upper-class course that includes 8 hours of required modules and 6 hours of elective specialty research modules.
Moot Court Requirement? No
Moot Court Description: 1-semester, 2-credit course with 2 briefs and an oral argument
Public Interest Law Requirement? No
Academic Journals: Akron Law Review, Akron Tax Journal

STUDENT INFORMATION
Enrollment of Law School: 611
% Male/Female: 55/45
% Full Time: 63
% Full Time That Are International: 0
% Minority: 9
Average Age of Entering Class: 25

RESEARCH FACILITIES
School-Supported Research Centers: Wireless laptop program; Microsoft Licensing Agreement, which provides Microsoft products to students for $20; Road Runner high-speed online access for $22.50 per month

EXPENSES/FINANCIAL AID
Annual Tuition (Residents/Nonresidents): $8,471/$14,157
Room and Board: $12,262
Books and Supplies: $860
Financial Aid Application Deadline: 3/15
Average Grant: $8,068
Average Loan: $12,600
% of Aid That Is Merit-Based: 99
% Receiving Some Sort of Aid: 91
Average Total Aid Package: $13,950
Average Debt: $32,850
Tuition Per Credit (Residents/Nonresidents): $282/$472
Fees Per Credit: $10

ADMISSIONS INFORMATION
Application Fee: $0
Regular Application Deadline: Rolling
Regular Notification: Rolling
LSDAS Accepted? Yes
Average GPA: 3.2
Range of GPA: 2.8–3.6
Average LSAT: 155
Range of LSAT: 153–157
Transfer Students Accepted? Yes
Other Schools to Which Students Applied: Case Western, Cleveland State, Ohio State, U. of Toledo, U. of Cincinnati, U. of Dayton, Capital
Other Admissions Factors Considered: Economic hardship, educational deprivation, physical disability, discrimination, or assimilation to a different culture/society
Number of Applications Received: 1,569
Number of Applicants Accepted: 472
Number of Applicants Enrolled: 219

INTERNATIONAL STUDENTS
TOEFL Required of International Students? Yes
Minimum TOEFL: 600

EMPLOYMENT INFORMATION

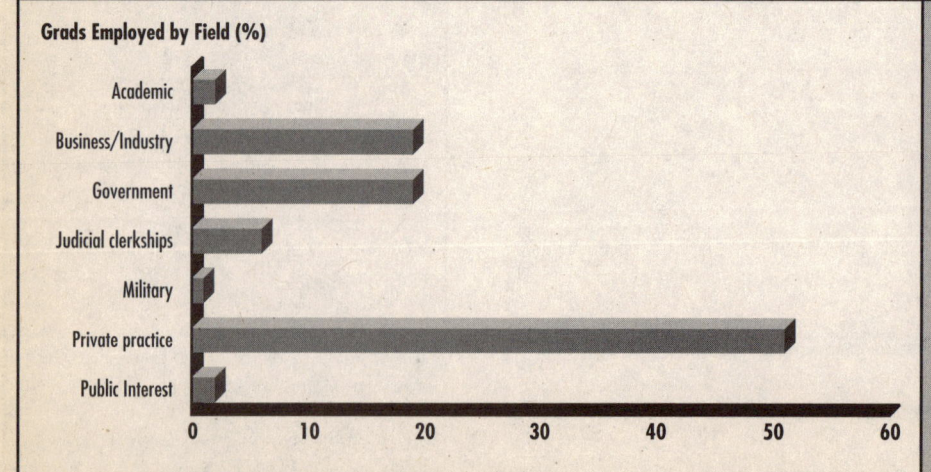

Grads Employed by Field (%)

Field	%
Academic	~1
Business/Industry	~19
Government	~18
Judicial clerkships	~5
Military	~1
Private practice	~52
Public Interest	~2

Rate of Placement: 86%
Average Starting Salary: $51,900
Employers Who Frequently Hire Grads: Buckingham, Doolittle, & Burroughs; Brouse & McDowell; Roetzel & Andress; County Prosecutor Offices; Stark & Summit; Courts of Common Pleas; 9th District Court of Appeals; U.S. Army JAG Corps; CSFA; City of Akron Law Deparment; Jones, Day, Reavis & Pogue; Hahn Loeser; 11th District Court of Appeals
Prominent Alumni: Deborah Cook, Justice, Ohio Supreme Court; Rochelle Seide, Partner, Baker Botts; James Troxell, Partner, Squire, Sanders & Dempsey
State for Bar Exam: OH
Pass Rate for First-Time Bar: 79%

UNIVERSITY OF ALABAMA
School of Law

Admissions Contact: Assistant Dean, Ms. Claude Beers
Box 870382, Tuscaloosa, AL 35487
Admissions Phone: 205-348-5440 • Admissions Fax: 205-348-3917
Admissions E-mail: admissions@law.ua.edu • Web Address: www.law.ua.edu

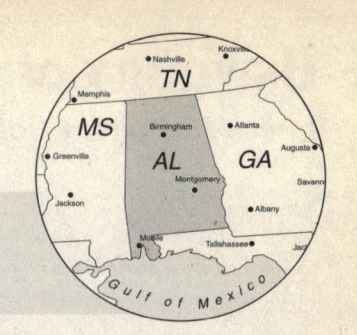

INSTITUTIONAL INFORMATION
Public/Private: Public
Student/Faculty Ratio: 11:1
Total Faculty: 94
% Part Time: 49
% Female: 14
% Minority: 4

PROGRAMS
Academic Specialties: Business and Tax Law, Criminal Law, Commercial Law, Bankruptcy Law, Intellectual Property, Environmental Law, Trial Advocacy, International Law
Advanced Degrees Offered: LLM Taxation (2 years part time), LLM (1 year)
Combined Degrees Offered: JD/MBA (4 years)
Grading System: Letter and numerical system on a 4.0 scale
Clinical Program Required? No
Clinical Program Description: Summer and academic-year externship programs, 6 in-house clinics
Legal Writing Course Requirements? Yes
Legal Writing Description: First year, 2 semesters
Legal Methods Course Requirements? No
Legal Research Course Requirements? Yes
Legal Research Description: First year, 2 semesters
Moot Court Requirement? Yes
Moot Court Description: Legal Writing/Research II in the second semester of the first year

Public Interest Law Requirement? No
Public Interest Law Description: The Public Interest Institute encourages students to participate in legal and nonlegal service. Awards are presented to students who participate.
Academic Journals: Alabama Law Review, The Journal of the Legal Profession, Law and Psychology Review

STUDENT INFORMATION
Enrollment of Law School: 541
% Male/Female: 62/38
% Full Time: 100
% Minority: 9
Average Age of Entering Class: 25

RESEARCH FACILITIES
School-Supported Research Centers: John Payne Special Collections Room, which houses Alabama historical legal materials; Howell Heflin Papers; Hugo Black Special Collection

EXPENSES/FINANCIAL AID
Annual Tuition (Residents/Nonresidents): $6,144/$12,850
Room and Board (On Campus): $5,776
Books and Supplies: $1,068
Average Grant: $4,871

ADMISSIONS INFORMATION
Application Fee: $25
Regular Application Deadline: 3/1
Regular Notification: Rolling
LSDAS Accepted? Yes
Average GPA: 3.4
Range of GPA: 3.1–3.6
Average LSAT: 160
Range of LSAT: 157–162
Transfer Students Accepted? Yes
Other Admissions Factors Considered: Difficulty of undergraduate course work, graduate study, writing ability, trends in academic performance, leadership qualities, unique work or service experience, career achievement, history of overcoming adversity
Number of Applications Received: 1,019
Number of Applicants Accepted: 336
Number of Applicants Enrolled: 194

INTERNATIONAL STUDENTS
TOEFL Required of International Students? Yes

EMPLOYMENT INFORMATION

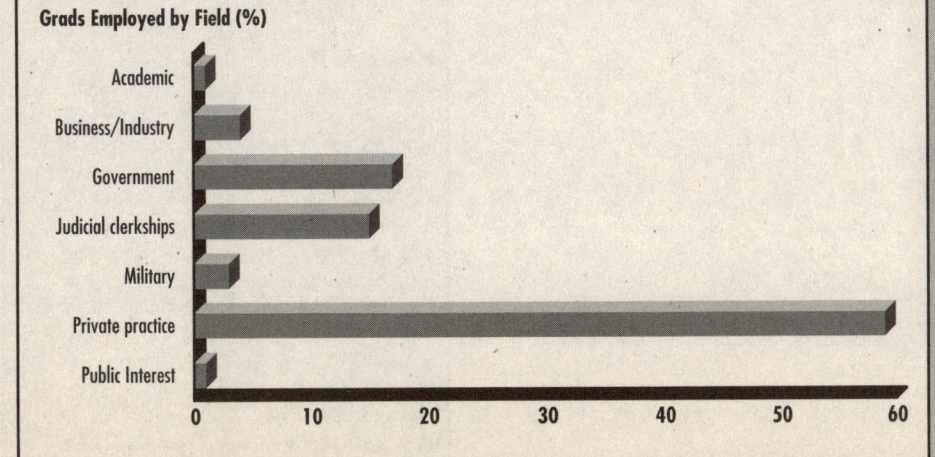

Grads Employed by Field (%)
- Academic: ~2
- Business/Industry: ~3
- Government: ~17
- Judicial clerkships: ~15
- Military: ~3
- Private practice: ~59
- Public Interest: ~1

Rate of Placement: 99%
Average Starting Salary: $57,248
Employers Who Frequently Hire Grads: Private practices, government agencies, public interest agencies
State for Bar Exam: AL, GA, MS, TN, FL
Pass Rate for First-Time Bar: 90%

UNIVERSITY OF ARIZONA
James E. Rogers College of Law

Admissions Contact: Assistant Dean for Admissions, Terry Sue Holpert
PO Box 210176, Tucson, AZ 85721-0176
Admissions Phone: 520-621-3477 • Admissions Fax: 520-621-9140
Admissions E-mail: admissions@law.arizona.edu • Web Address: www.law.arizona.edu

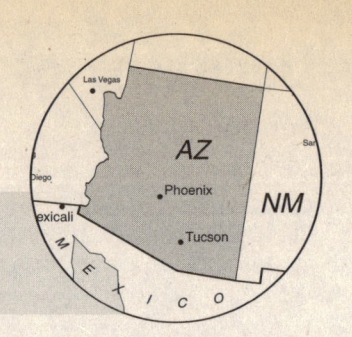

INSTITUTIONAL INFORMATION
Public/Private: Public
Student/Faculty Ratio: 15:1
Total Faculty: 85
% Part Time: 60
% Female: 42
% Minority: 20

PROGRAMS
Academic Specialties: Outstanding faculty with extraordinary strength in all first-year classes; particular strength in Torts, Tax, Corporations, Indian Law, Water Law, Intellectual Property, Constitutional Law, Employment Law, Trial Advocacy, Family Law, Legal History, International Trade, International Human Rights, Criminal Law, Mental Health Law, Commercial Law, Environmental Law, International Law, Legal Philosophy, Property
Advanced Degrees Offered: JD (85 units, 3 years), LLM International Trade Law or in International Indigenous Peoples Law and Policy (24 units, 1 year)
Combined Degrees Offered: JD/PhD (6 years.), JD/MBA (4 years), JD/MPA (4 years), JD/MA (4 years)
Grading System: For all courses with 21 or more students, there is a curve of 25% A; 55% B; and 20% C, D, and E. For classes with 20 or fewer students, the mean GPA shall not exceed 3.5.
Clinical Program Required? No
Clinical Program Description: Criminal Prosecution and Defense Clinic, Immigration Law Clinic, Domestic Violence Clinic, Child Advocacy Clinic, Indian/Tribal Law Clinic
Legal Writing Course Requirements? Yes

Legal Writing Description: First-year Practice Labs and required graded legal writing class. Before graduation, all students must produce a paper of publishable quality or participate in an Advanced Writing Seminar.
Legal Methods Course Requirements? No
Legal Research Course Requirements? Yes
Legal Research Description: Part of the Legal Analysis, Writing and Research class required in the second semester of the first year
Moot Court Requirement? No
Moot Court Description: Presenting an oral argument is an integral part of the first-year Legal Writing program. Optional Moot Court Program offered in the second year and advanced course work in Moot Court in the third year, and additional competitions open to all students.
Public Interest Law Requirement? No
Academic Journals: *Arizona Law Review, Arizona Journal of International and Comparative Law, Journal of Law, Psychology and Public Policy*

STUDENT INFORMATION
Enrollment of Law School: 480
% Out of State: 25
% Male/Female: 48/52
% Full Time: 100
% Full Time That Are International: 1
% Minority: 27
Average Age of Entering Class: 26

RESEARCH FACILITIES
School-Supported Research Centers: National Center for Inter-American Trade, Morris K. Udall Center for Environment and Public Policy, the Native Nations Institute

EXPENSES/FINANCIAL AID
Annual Tuition (Residents/Nonresidents): $5,840/$14,364
Room and Board (On/Off Campus): $8,864/$12,688
Books and Supplies: $750
Financial Aid Application Deadline: 3/1
Average Grant: $3,250
Average Loan: $13,500
% of Aid That Is Merit-Based: 43
% Receiving Some Sort of Aid: 78
Average Total Aid Package: $15,000
Average Debt: $40,022

ADMISSIONS INFORMATION
Application Fee: $50
Regular Application Deadline: 2/15
Regular Notification: Rolling
LSDAS Accepted? Yes
Average GPA: 3.5
Range of GPA: 2.4–4.0
Average LSAT: 161
Range of LSAT: 148–177
Transfer Students Accepted? Yes
Other Schools to Which Students Applied: Arizona State, UC Hastings, UCLA, U. of Colorado, U. of San Diego, U. of Southern California, UT Austin
Other Admissions Factors Considered: Background, work experience, community and public service
Number of Applications Received: 2,210
Number of Applicants Accepted: 406
Number of Applicants Enrolled: 152

INTERNATIONAL STUDENTS
TOEFL Required of International Students? Yes

EMPLOYMENT INFORMATION

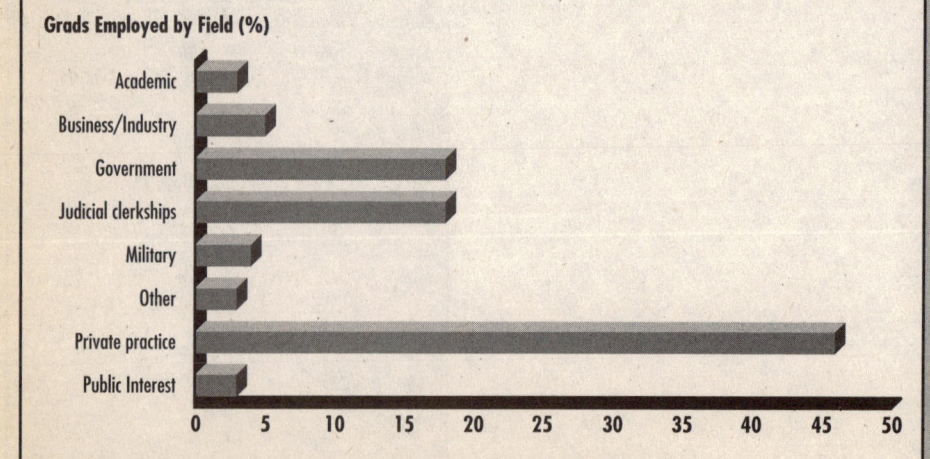

Grads Employed by Field (%)

Field	%
Academic	~2
Business/Industry	~6
Government	~18
Judicial clerkships	~18
Military	~2
Other	~3
Private practice	~47
Public Interest	~4

Rate of Placement: 93%
Average Starting Salary: $60,590
Employers Who Frequently Hire Grads: Snell & Wilmer; Quarles & Brady Streich Lang; Bryan Cave; Gibson Dunn & Crutcher; Squire Sanders; Jennings Strouss & Salmon; O'Melveny & Myers; Arizona Supreme Court and Court of Appeals; U.S. District Courts; U.S. Circuit Courts; Department of Justice; State Attorney General's Office; District Attorney's, Public Defender's, and City Attorney's offices in AZ, CA, and NV
Prominent Alumni: Morris K. Udall, former Congressman; Stewart Udall, former Congressman and Secretary of the Interior; Dennis DeConcini, former Senator
State for Bar Exam: AZ, CA, WA, NV, DC
Pass Rate for First-Time Bar: 95%

UNIVERSITY OF ARKANSAS — FAYETTEVILLE
School of Law

Admissions Contact: Associate Dean for Students, James K. Miller
Leflar Law Center, Fayetteville, AR 72701
Admissions Phone: 479-575-3102 • Admissions Fax: 479-575-3320
Admissions E-mail: jkmiller@uark.edu • Web Address: law.uark.edu

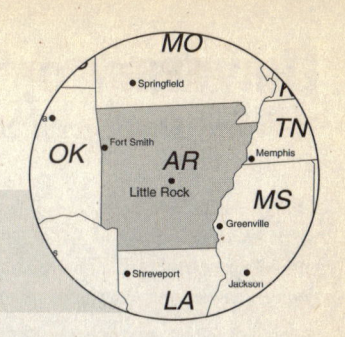

INSTITUTIONAL INFORMATION
Public/Private: Public
Student/Faculty Ratio: 12:1
Total Faculty: 49
% Part Time: 31
% Female: 33
% Minority: 16

PROGRAMS
Academic Specialties: Only LLM in Agricultural Law program in the United States; specialized Agricultural Law courses generally open to JD students; comprehensive Legal Research and Writing Program staffed by five full-time faculty members whose primary or exclusive focus is on the three required courses
Advanced Degrees Offered: LLM Agricultural Law (1 year)
Combined Degrees Offered: JD/MBA (1.5 to 3 years), JD/MPA (1 to 3 years), LLM/MS (1 to 1.5 years)
Grading System: A (4.00), A– (3.67), B+ (3.33), B (3.00), B– (2.67), C+ (2.33), C (2.00), C– (1.67), D+ (1.33), D (1.00), D– (0.67), F (0.00)
Clinical Program Required? No
Clinical Program Description: Civil Litigation Clinic, Criminal Prosecution Clinic, Criminal Defense Clinic, Federal Practice Clinic, Tobacco Clinic
Legal Writing Course Requirements? Yes
Legal Writing Description: Legal Research and Writing I (3 credits) is required in the first semester, Legal Research and Writing II (2 credits) in the second semester, and Legal Research and Writing III (2 credits) by the end of the second year. All students must complete 1 skills course before graduation. The skills requirement fosters widespread student interest in various skills competitions, with approximately half of the students each year participating in the intramural competitions in Moot Court, Trial Advocacy, Negotiations, and Client Counseling.
Legal Methods Course Requirements? No
Legal Research Course Requirements? No
Legal Research Description: While legal research is not a separate course, it is an intrinsic part of the Legal Research and Writing sequence.
Moot Court Requirement? Yes
Moot Court Description: First-year students participate in a moot court exercise as part of Legal Research and Writing. In addition, second-year students are invited to participate in an intraschool competition, which is a feeder program for our interschool competition program. Selected students compete in interschool competitions each year.
Public Interest Law Requirement? No
Academic Journals: *Arkansas Law Review*

STUDENT INFORMATION
Enrollment of Law School: 409
% Male/Female: 56/44
% Full Time: 100
% Full Time That Are International: 1
% Minority: 17
Average Age of Entering Class: 26

RESEARCH FACILITIES
School-Supported Research Centers: National Center for Agricultural Law Research and Information

EXPENSES/FINANCIAL AID
Annual Tuition (Residents/Nonresidents): $6,146/$13,230
Room and Board: $5,312
Books and Supplies: $6,188
Financial Aid Application Deadline: 7/2
Average Grant: $4,680
Average Loan: $13,840
% of Aid That Is Merit-Based: 48
Average Debt: $42,458

ADMISSIONS INFORMATION
Regular Application Deadline: Rolling
Regular Notification: Rolling
LSDAS Accepted? Yes
Average GPA: 3.3
Range of GPA: 3.0–3.6
Average LSAT: 152
Range of LSAT: 149–156
Transfer Students Accepted? Yes
Other Schools to Which Students Applied: University of Arkansas—Little Rock
Other Admissions Factors Considered: Geographic, age, gender, cultural, ethnic, and racial background
Number of Applications Received: 865
Number of Applicants Accepted: 374
Number of Applicants Enrolled: 179

INTERNATIONAL STUDENTS
TOEFL Required of International Students? Yes
Minimum TOEFL: 550

EMPLOYMENT INFORMATION

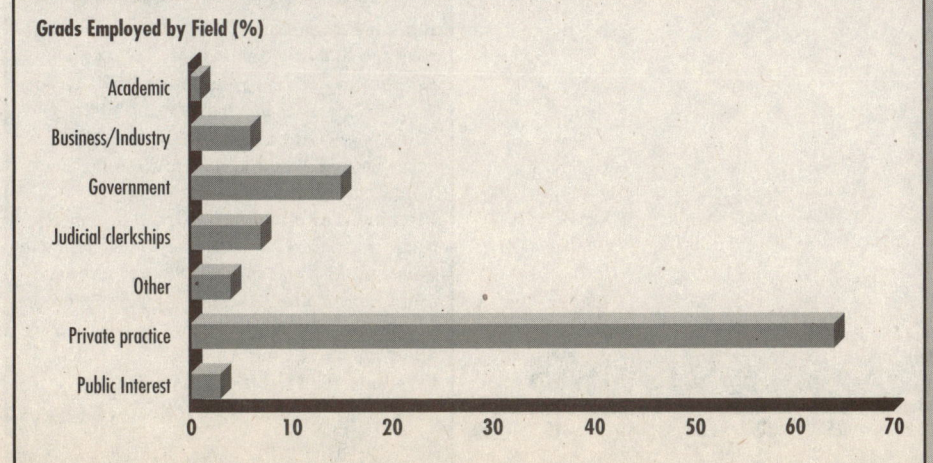

Grads Employed by Field (%)
- Academic: ~1
- Business/Industry: ~4
- Government: ~15
- Judicial clerkships: ~8
- Other: ~5
- Private practice: ~65
- Public Interest: ~2

Rate of Placement: 88%
Employers Who Frequently Hire Grads: Majority of graduates go into small firms
Prominent Alumni: George W. Haley, former Ambassador to Gambia; Philip S. Anderson, former President, American Bar Association; Morris S. Arnold, Judge, U.S. 8th Circuit Court of Appeals; Rodney Slater, former U.S. Secretary of Transportation; Thomas A. Mars Sr., VP, General Counsel, and Secretary, Wal-Mart, Inc.
State for Bar Exam: AR, TN, MO, OK, TX
Pass Rate for First-Time Bar: 85%

UNIVERSITY OF ARKANSAS — LITTLE ROCK
William H. Bowen School of Law

Admissions Contact: Director of Admissions, Jean Probasco
1201 McMath, Little Rock, AR 72202-5142
Admissions Phone: 501-324-9903 • Admissions Fax: 501-324-9433
Admissions E-mail: lawadm@ualr.edu • Web Address: www.ualr.edu/~lawschool

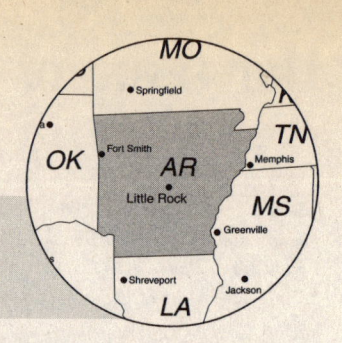

INSTITUTIONAL INFORMATION
Public/Private: Public
Student/Faculty Ratio: 17:1
Total Faculty: 48
% Part Time: 38
% Female: 38
% Minority: 8

PROGRAMS
Academic Specialties: Faculty publish articles and books in a number of areas. Our curriculum offers a strong foundation in traditional areas as well as requiring all students to take Trial Advocacy. Specialties include Civil Procedure, Commercial Law, Constitutional Law, Corporation Securities Law, Criminal Law, Environmental Law, International Law, Labor Law, Legal History, Property, and Taxation.
Combined Degrees Offered: JD/MBA, JD/MPA (3.5 years)
Grading System: Letter system on a 4.0 scale
Clinical Program Required? No
Clinical Program Description: Litigation Clinic, Mediation Clinic
Legal Writing Course Requirements? Yes
Legal Methods Course Requirements? Yes
Legal Methods Description: First-year and upper-level requirement
Legal Research Course Requirements? Yes
Moot Court Requirement? No
Public Interest Law Requirement? No

STUDENT INFORMATION
Enrollment of Law School: 385
% Out of State: 13
% Male/Female: 52/48
% Full Time: 65
% Minority: 11
Average Age of Entering Class: 27

EXPENSES/FINANCIAL AID
Annual Tuition (Residents/Nonresidents): $6,600/$13,200
Room and Board (Off Campus): $9,200
Books and Supplies: $800
Average Grant: $6,019
Average Loan: $15,369
% of Aid That Is Merit-Based: 13
% Receiving Some Sort of Aid: 68
Average Total Aid Package: $14,590
Average Debt: $26,000
Tuition Per Credit (Residents/Nonresidents): $220/$440
Fees Per Credit: $18

ADMISSIONS INFORMATION
Application Fee: $40
Regular Application Deadline: 4/15
Regular Notification: Rolling
LSDAS Accepted? Yes
Average GPA: 3.3
Range of GPA: 2.9–3.6
Average LSAT: 153
Range of LSAT: 149–156
Transfer Students Accepted? Yes
Other Schools to Which Students Applied: Mercer University, University of Tulsa, University of Arkansas—Fayetteville
Other Admissions Factors Considered: Background and experience relevant to success in law school, diversity of student body
Number of Applications Received: 430
Number of Applicants Accepted: 253
Number of Applicants Enrolled: 135

INTERNATIONAL STUDENTS
TOEFL Recommended for International Students? Yes

EMPLOYMENT INFORMATION

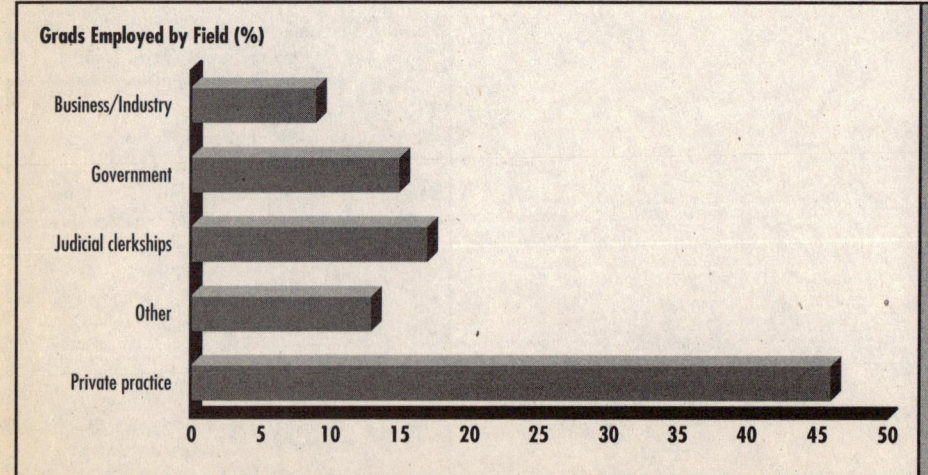

Grads Employed by Field (%)
- Business/Industry: ~10
- Government: ~15
- Judicial clerkships: ~17
- Other: ~13
- Private practice: ~46

Rate of Placement: 91%
Average Starting Salary: $46,206
Employers Who Frequently Hire Grads: Wright, Lindsey & Jennings; Friday, Eldredge & Clark; prosecuting attorneys; Mitchell, Williams, Selig, Gates & Woodyard; State Supreme Court; State Court of Appeals
Prominent Alumni: Vic Snyder, U.S. Congressman; Annabelle Clinton-Imber, State Supreme Court; Andrea Layton Roaf, State Court of Appeals; H.E. "Bud" Cummins, U.S. Attorney; Charles W. "Bill" Burton, Attorney, Jones Day
State for Bar Exam: AR, TN, TX, GA, FL
Pass Rate for First-Time Bar: 82%

UNIVERSITY OF BALTIMORE
School of Law

Admissions Contact: Assistant Director of Admissions, Lisa Lawler
1420 North Charles Street, Baltimore, MD 21201
Admissions Phone: 410-837-4459 • Admissions Fax: 410-837-4450
Admissions E-mail: lwadmiss@ubmail.ubalt.edu • Web Address: www.law.ubalt.edu

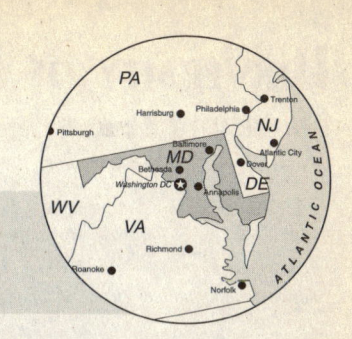

INSTITUTIONAL INFORMATION
Public/Private: Public
Student/Faculty Ratio: 18:1
Total Faculty: 104
% Part Time: 58
% Female: 32
% Minority: 11

PROGRAMS
Academic Specialties: 12 concentrations as well as an LLM in Taxation. Specialities include Family Law, Intellectual Property, Evidence, Antitrust, Environmental, Commercial Law, Corporation Securities Law, Criminal Law, Government Services, International Law, Labor Law, Legal History, Legal Philosophy, Property, and Taxation.
Advanced Degrees Offered: LLM Taxation
Combined Degrees Offered: JD/MBA, JD/MS Criminal Justice, JD/MPA, JD/PhD Policy Science in conjunction with University of Maryland at Baltimore, JD/LLM Taxation, JD/MS Negotiation and Conflict Management. Most combined degrees add 1 year of study.
Grading System: 4.0 quality scale from A to F
Clinical Program Required? No
Clinical Program Description: Family Law Clinic, Criminal Practice Clinic, Community Development Clinic, Appellate Advocacy Clinic, Civil Clinic, Disability Law Clinic
Legal Writing Course Requirements? Yes
Legal Writing Description: 3 semesters of legal writing and an upper-level writing requirement
Legal Methods Course Requirements? Yes
Legal Methods Description: Part of 3-semester program encompassing legal writing and research
Legal Research Course Requirements? Yes
Legal Research Description: Part of 3-semester writing program
Moot Court Requirement? No
Public Interest Law Requirement? No
Academic Journals: *Law Review, Law Forum, Environmental Law Journal, Intellectual Property Law Journal*

STUDENT INFORMATION
Enrollment of Law School: 889
% Out of State: 15
% Male/Female: 51/49
% Full Time: 66
% Full Time That Are International: 1
% Minority: 21
Average Age of Entering Class: 27

EXPENSES/FINANCIAL AID
Annual Tuition (Residents/Nonresidents): $10,116/$17,552
Room and Board (Off Campus): $10,000
Books and Supplies: $850
Financial Aid Application Deadline: 4/1
Average Grant: $4,000
Average Loan: $12,500
% Receiving Some Sort of Aid: 68
Average Debt: $38,300
Tuition Per Credit (Residents/Nonresidents): $392/$662
Fees Per Credit: $22

ADMISSIONS INFORMATION
Application Fee: $35
Regular Application Deadline: Rolling
Regular Notification: Rolling
LSDAS Accepted? Yes
Average GPA: 2.9
Range of GPA: 2.7–3.3
Average LSAT: 149
Range of LSAT: 147–152
Transfer Students Accepted? Yes
Other Schools to Which Students Applied: Widener University, Catholic University of America, American University, University of Maryland, College Park
Other Admissions Factors Considered: Difficulty of the undergraduate major, graduate degrees, work experience, ability to overcome adversity, individual achievement, motivation, character
Number of Applications Received: 1,463
Number of Applicants Accepted: 684
Number of Applicants Enrolled: 269

EMPLOYMENT INFORMATION

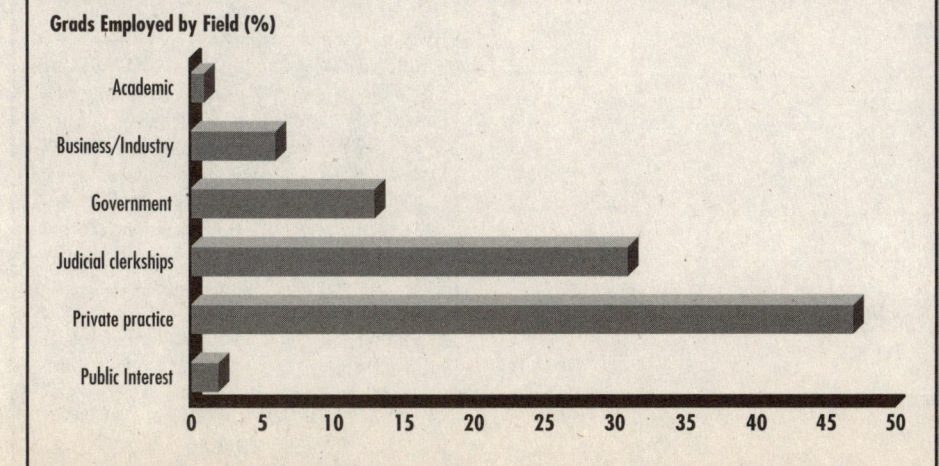

Grads Employed by Field (%)

Field	%
Academic	~1
Business/Industry	~6
Government	~13
Judicial clerkships	~31
Private practice	~47
Public Interest	~2

Rate of Placement: 92%
Average Starting Salary: $39,391
Employers Who Frequently Hire Grads: Law firms, judges, government agencies, corporations
State for Bar Exam: MD
Pass Rate for First-Time Bar: 72%

UNIVERSITY OF BRITISH COLUMBIA
Faculty of Law

Admissions Contact: Admissions Officer, Elaine L. Borthwick
1822 East Mall, Vancouver, BC V6T 1Z1
Admissions Phone: 604-822-6303 • Admissions Fax: 604-822-8108
Admissions E-mail: borthwick@law.ubc.ca • Web Address: www.law.ubc.ca

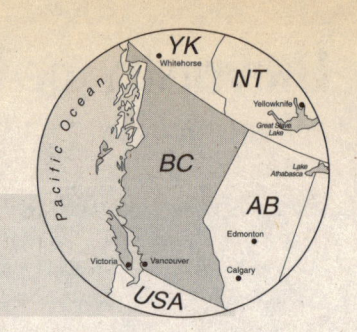

INSTITUTIONAL INFORMATION
Public/Private: Public
Student/Faculty Ratio: 5:1
Total Faculty: 118
% Part Time: 67
% Female: 45

PROGRAMS
Academic Specialties: We do not have specialization programs that are reflected on the graduate's degree; however, it is possible for students to concentrate their electives in certain areas of study due to the very large choice of courses offered. We offer formal programs that provide focus for research and teaching in specific areas of law: the Centre for Asian Legal Studies; the Centre for Feminist Legal Studies; the First Nations Legal Studies Program; the Environment, Sustainable Development and the Law; the International Centre for Criminal Law Reform and Criminal Justice Policy; Legal History; Law and Computers; and the new Alternate Dispute Resolution Program.
Advanced Degrees Offered: LLB (3 years full time), LLM (12 months), PhD (1 to 2 years)
Combined Degrees Offered: LLB/MBA (4 years), LLB/MAPPS (3 years)
Grading System: Grades are given in percentages.
Clinical Program Required? No
Clinical Program Description: Law Students Legal Advice Program, Women's Clinic, Persons with AIDS Clinic, Street Youth Clinic, Chinese Clinic, First Nations Clinic
Legal Writing Course Requirements? Yes
Legal Writing Description: The Legal Research and Writing Program is 1 full year during the first year. Students learn proper legal research and writing formatting and where to find the legal tools they require to complete memos and serve clients.
Legal Methods Course Requirements? No
Legal Research Course Requirements? Yes
Legal Research Description: See Legal Writing.
Moot Court Requirement? No
Moot Court Description: All first-year students are required to participate in a moot court program. Each student must write an appeal factum and participate as an advocate in the mock appeal in front of a bench of legal practitioners acting as judges.
Public Interest Law Requirement? No
Academic Journals: *Law Review*, *Journal of Family Law*

STUDENT INFORMATION
Enrollment of Law School: 688
% Out of State: 19
% Male/Female: 42/58
% Full Time: 90
% Full Time That Are International: 1
% Minority: 10
Average Age of Entering Class: 26

RESEARCH FACILITIES
Research Resources Available: Quicklaw, Westlaw, Lexis/Nexis, Canadian Bar Association
School-Supported Research Centers: Centre for Asian Legal Studies; Chinese Legal Studies; Southeast Asian Legal Studies; Centre for Feminist Legal Studies; First Nations Legal Studies Program; Environment, Sustainable Development and Law; International Centre for Criminal Law Reform and Criminal Justice Policy; Alternate Dispute Resolution Program; Legal History, Law and Computers

EXPENSES/FINANCIAL AID
Annual Tuition (Residents/Nonresidents): $7,000/$15,000
Room and Board (On/Off Campus): $27,018/$15,000
Books and Supplies: $1,300
Financial Aid Application Deadline: 5/15
Average Loan: $5,350
% of Aid That Is Merit-Based: 50
% Receiving Some Sort of Aid: 70
Average Total Aid Package: $5,500
Average Debt: $25,000

ADMISSIONS INFORMATION
Application Fee: $45
Regular Application Deadline: 2/1
Regular Notification: Rolling
LSDAS Accepted? No
Average GPA: 3.7
Range of GPA: 3.2–4.0
Average LSAT: 163
Range of LSAT: 152–173
Transfer Students Accepted? Yes
Other Schools to Which Students Applied: U. of Calgary, U. of Toronto, U. of Victoria, York
Number of Applications Received: 1,826
Number of Applicants Accepted: 468
Number of Applicants Enrolled: 208

EMPLOYMENT INFORMATION

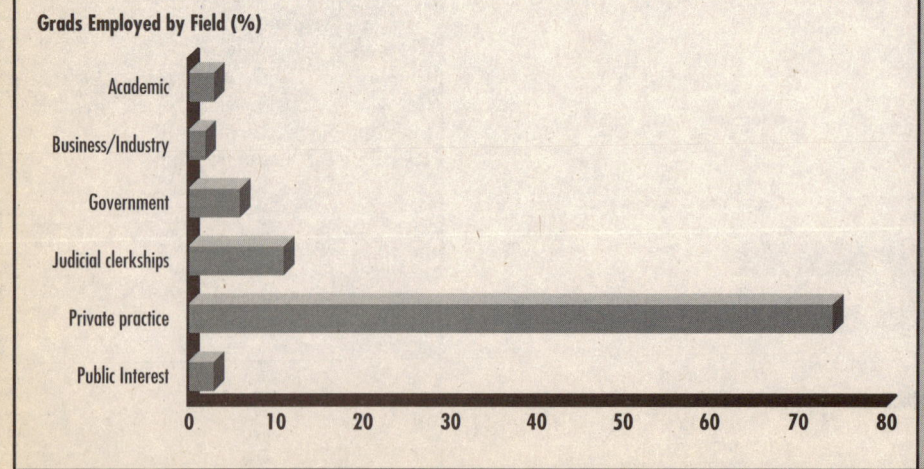

Grads Employed by Field (%)
- Academic: ~1
- Business/Industry: ~2
- Government: ~5
- Judicial clerkships: ~12
- Private practice: ~75
- Public Interest: ~3

Rate of Placement: 99%
Average Starting Salary: $51,000
Employers Who Frequently Hire Grads: British Columbia law firms and government Agencies, Ontario law firms and government agencies, Alberta law firms and government agencies, New York law firms, Canadian public interest groups, Canadian courts (federal and provincial), corporate legal departments, Canadian crown corporations, Boston firms, California firms, Nova Scotia firms, Yukon/Northwest Territories firms
Prominent Alumni: Frank Iacobucci, Justice, Supreme Court of Canada; Lance Finch, Chief Justice, British Columbia; Kim Campbell, former Prime Minister of Canada
State for Bar Exam: BC, AB, NY, MA, ON
Pass Rate for First-Time Bar: 99%

UNIVERSITY OF CALGARY
Faculty of Law

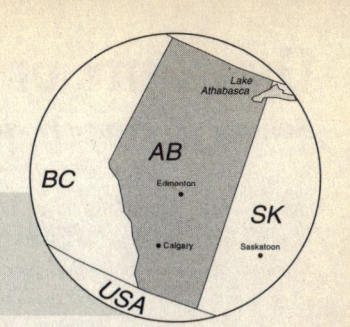

Admissions Contact: Admissions/Student Services Officer, Susan Marks
Room 4380A, Murray Fraser Hall, 2500 University Drive NW, Calgary, AB T2N 1N4
Admissions Phone: 403-220-8154 • Admissions Fax: 403-282-8325
Admissions E-mail: law@ucalgary.ca • Web Address: www.ucalgary.ca/faculties/law

INSTITUTIONAL INFORMATION
Public/Private: Public
Student/Faculty Ratio: 15:1
Total Faculty: 17
% Female: 47

PROGRAMS
Academic Specialties: We believe that experimental learning is an important part of a sound legal education, and we offer many opportunities including classroom exercises, mooting, and debating programs and use of our microcomputer faculty. This, coupled with our special strengths in the areas of Skills Training, Natural Resources Law, Environmental Law, and Social Responsibility, provide students with a strong, well-rounded education.
Advanced Degrees Offered: LLB (3 years), LLM (15 to 18 months)
Combined Degrees Offered: LLB/MBA (4 years), LLB/MED
Grading System: 4.0 scale
Clinical Program Required? No
Clinical Program Description: Criminal Seminar, Family Seminar, Naural Resources Seminar, Business Seminar
Legal Methods Course Requirements? Yes

STUDENT INFORMATION
Enrollment of Law School: 229
% Male/Female: 43/57
% Full Time: 100
Average Age of Entering Class: 29

RESEARCH FACILITIES
Research Resources Available: Canadian Institute for Resources Law, Canadian Research Institute for Law and the Family, Alberta Civil Liberties Research Centre

EXPENSES/FINANCIAL AID
Annual Tuition: $4,944
Room and Board (On/Off Campus): $5,000/$8,000
Books and Supplies: $1,600

ADMISSIONS INFORMATION
Application Fee: $60
Regular Application Deadline: 2/1
Regular Notification: Rolling
LSDAS Accepted? No
Average GPA: 4.0
Range of GPA: 3.0–4.0
Average LSAT: 67
Range of LSAT: 22–97
Transfer Students Accepted? Yes
Number of Applications Received: 761
Number of Applicants Accepted: 70
Number of Applicants Enrolled: 70

INTERNATIONAL STUDENTS
TOEFL Required of International Students? Yes
Minimum TOEFL: 600 (250 computer)

EMPLOYMENT INFORMATION
Rate of Placement: 90%
State for Bar Exam: AB
Pass Rate for First-Time Bar: 98%

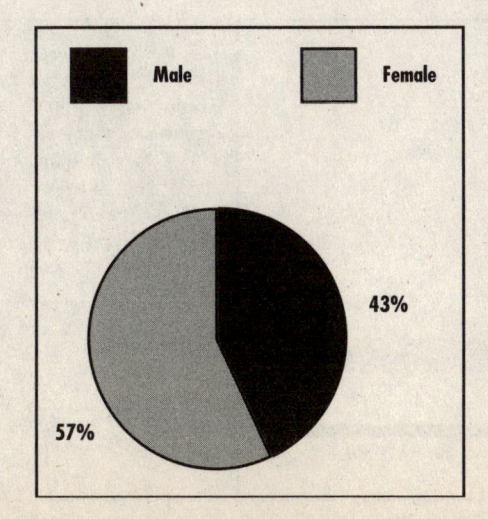

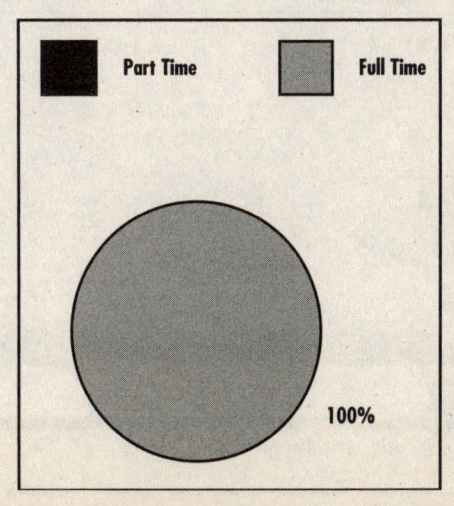

UNIVERSITY OF CALIFORNIA, BERKELEY
School of Law (Boalt Hall)

Admissions Contact: Director of Admissions, Edward Tom
5 Boalt Hall, Berkeley, CA 94720-7200
Admissions Phone: 510-642-2274 • Admissions Fax: 510-643-6222
Admissions E-mail: admissions@law.berkeley.edu • Web Address: www.law.berkeley.edu

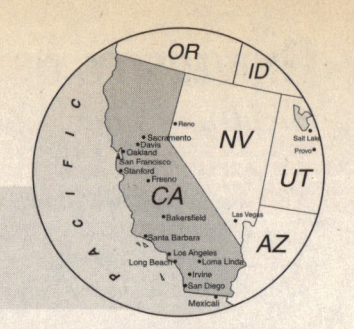

INSTITUTIONAL INFORMATION
Public/Private: Public
Student/Faculty Ratio: 12:1
Total Faculty: 166
% Part Time: 54
% Female: 34
% Minority: 8

PROGRAMS
Academic Specialties: Please see www.law.berkeley.edu/faculty/index.html for more information on Boalt Hall's faculty. For information regarding our curriculum, please see www.law.berkeley.edu/prospectives/academics.html. Specialties include Corporation Securities Law, Environmental Law, Intellectual Property Law, and International Law.
Advanced Degrees Offered: LLM (1 year), JSD, PhD Jurisprudence and Social Policy (6 years)
Combined Degrees Offered: JD/MA, JD/MS, JD/MBA, JD/MCP, JD/MJ, JD/MPP, JD/MSW (4 years); JD/PhD
Grading System: High Honors is assigned to the top 10% of the first-year class and the top 10–15% of the second- and third-year classes; Honors to the next 30% of the first-year class and 30–35% of the second- and third-year classes; and Pass to the remainder. Substandard Pass or No Credit is used when work is unsatisfactory and are not governed by a curve.
Clinical Program Required? No
Clinical Program Description: Death Penalty Clinic, International Human Rights Law Clinic, Samuelson Law, Technology and Public Policy Clinic, East Bay Community Law Center, Faculty-Supervised Clinics, Field Placement Program, Professional Lawyering Skills Courses, Central American Refugee Clinic, East Bay Workers' Rights Clinic, HIV Outreach Program, Homeless Outreach Program, Migrant Legal Services, Street Law Clinic
Legal Writing Course Requirements? Yes
Legal Writing Description: First-year course
Legal Methods Course Requirements? Yes
Legal Methods Description: First-year course
Legal Research Course Requirements? Yes
Legal Research Description: First-year course
Moot Court Requirement? Yes
Moot Court Description: First year spring
Public Interest Law Requirement? No
Academic Journals: *African-American Law and Policy Report, Asian Law Journal, Berkeley Journal of Employment and Labor Law, Berkeley Journal of International Law, Berkeley La Raza Law Journal, Berkeley Technology Law Journal, Berkeley Women's Law Journal, California Criminal Law Review, California Law Review, Ecology Law Quarterly*

STUDENT INFORMATION
Enrollment of Law School: 909
% Out of State: 11
% Male/Female: 39/61
% Full Time: 100
% Minority: 35
Average Age of Entering Class: 24

RESEARCH FACILITIES
School-Supported Research Centers: Student Computing Labs, network access from Library Reading Rooms, Disabled Students Program on the Berkeley campus, expanding wireless access

EXPENSES/FINANCIAL AID
Annual Tuition (Residents/Nonresidents): $11,561/$22,694
Room and Board: $12,408
Books and Supplies: $1,170
Financial Aid Application Deadline: 3/2
Average Grant: $6,600
Average Loan: $17,562
% of Aid That Is Merit-Based: 1
% Receiving Some Sort of Aid: 87
Average Total Aid Package: $26,276
Average Debt: $51,155

ADMISSIONS INFORMATION
Application Fee: $70
Regular Application Deadline: 2/1
Regular Notification: Rolling
LSDAS Accepted? Yes
Average GPA: 3.8
Range of GPA: 3.7–3.9
Average LSAT: 164
Range of LSAT: 161–168
Transfer Students Accepted? Yes
Other Schools to Which Students Applied: Harvard University; New York University; Stanford University; University of California, Los Angeles
Number of Applications Received: 6,897
Number of Applicants Accepted: 790
Number of Applicants Enrolled: 277

INTERNATIONAL STUDENTS
TOEFL Required of International Students? Yes
Minimum TOEFL: 570 (230 computer)

EMPLOYMENT INFORMATION

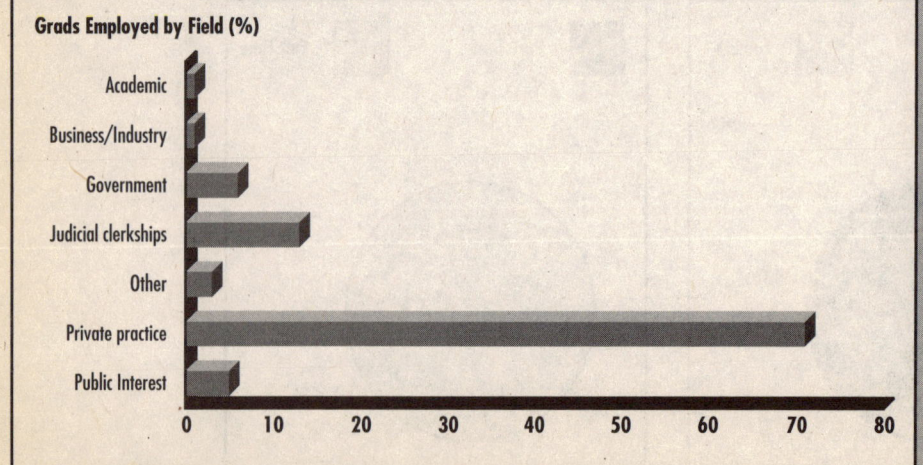

Grads Employed by Field (%)
- Academic
- Business/Industry
- Government
- Judicial clerkships
- Other
- Private practice
- Public Interest

Rate of Placement: 96%
Average Starting Salary: $100,743
Employers Who Frequently Hire Grads: 450 employers recruit at Boalt Hall each fall, including national firms, multinational corporations, public interest groups, and governmental agencies.
State for Bar Exam: CA
Pass Rate for First-Time Bar: 90%

UNIVERSITY OF CALIFORNIA, DAVIS
School of Law

Admissions Contact: Director of Admission, Sharon L. Pinkney
King Hall, 400 Mrak Hall Drive, Davis, CA 95616-5201
Admissions Phone: 530-752-6477
Admissions E-mail: lawadmissions@ucdavis.edu • Web Address: www.law.ucdavis.edu

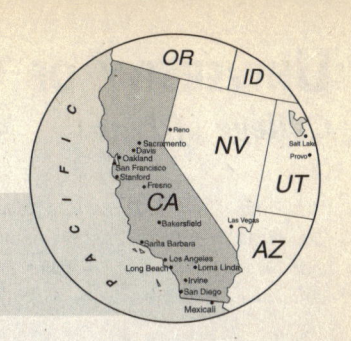

INSTITUTIONAL INFORMATION
Public/Private: Public
Student/Faculty Ratio: 16:1
Total Faculty: 45
% Part Time: 31
% Female: 31
% Minority: 27

PROGRAMS
Academic Specialties: Immigration, Public Interest, Skills Training, Civil Rights, Clinical Programs, Criminal Law, Environmental Law, Human Rights Law, Intellectual Property Law, International Law, Taxation
Advanced Degrees Offered: LLM (1 year)
Combined Degrees Offered: JD/MBA, JD/MA, JD/MS (all 4 years)
Grading System: A to F, Satisfactory/Unsatisfactory, Pass/Fail. All Clinicals are Pass/Fail.
Clinical Program Required? No
Clinical Program Description: Prison Law; Civil Rights; Immigration and Family Protection; Tax, Labor, Criminal, Public Interest, Judicial, and Environmental Externships
Legal Writing Course Requirements? Yes
Legal Writing Description: 1-semester instruction in the form and substance of writing. A variety of law-related documents are discussed and drafted. An experience in oral advocacy is included.
Legal Methods Course Requirements? Yes
Legal Methods Description: 2-hour lecture in the form and substance of writing. A variety of law-related documents are discussed and drafted.
Legal Research Course Requirements? Yes
Legal Research Description: A description of the evolution and use of sources of law and secondary authority
Moot Court Requirement? No
Moot Court Description: Appellate Advocacy (Moot Court) teaches basic appellate practice and procedure. The course also provides beginning instruction in oral advocacy skills and an opportunity to practice these skills in front of a moot court. At the end of the semester, students compete in 2 rounds of oral arguments, which, combined with the second semester, determine the rankings for participants in the annual Neumiller Competition and other interschool competition teams.
Public Interest Law Requirement? No
Academic Journals: Environs, UC Davis Journal of International Law and Policy, UC Davis Law Review, UC Davis Journal of Juvenile Law and Policy

STUDENT INFORMATION
Enrollment of Law School: 551
% Male/Female: 44/56
% Full Time: 100
% Full Time That Are International: 1
% Minority: 33
Average Age of Entering Class: 25

RESEARCH FACILITIES
Research Resources Available: Access to all computer labs on the campus outside the law school
School-Supported Research Centers: Wireless network in upper reading room and main reading room of the library, wireless access to some student carrels

EXPENSES/FINANCIAL AID
Annual Tuition (Residents/Nonresidents): $11,425/$22,557
Room and Board (Off Campus): $9,479
Books and Supplies: $973
Financial Aid Application Deadline: 3/2
Average Grant: $5,673
Average Loan: $16,220
% of Aid That Is Merit-Based: 1
% Receiving Some Sort of Aid: 92
Average Total Aid Package: $21,543
Average Debt: $46,477

ADMISSIONS INFORMATION
Application Fee: $70
Regular Application Deadline: 2/1
Regular Notification: Rolling
LSDAS Accepted? Yes
Average GPA: 3.5
Range of GPA: 3.3–3.7
Average LSAT: 160
Range of LSAT: 157–163
Transfer Students Accepted? Yes
Other Admissions Factors Considered: Undergraduate course of study, and school attended, advanced degrees or course work, diversity of background and experiences, significant work experience
Number of Applications Received: 3,276
Number of Applicants Accepted: 757
Number of Applicants Enrolled: 190

INTERNATIONAL STUDENTS
TOEFL Required of International Students? Yes
Minimum TOEFL: 600 (250 computer)

EMPLOYMENT INFORMATION

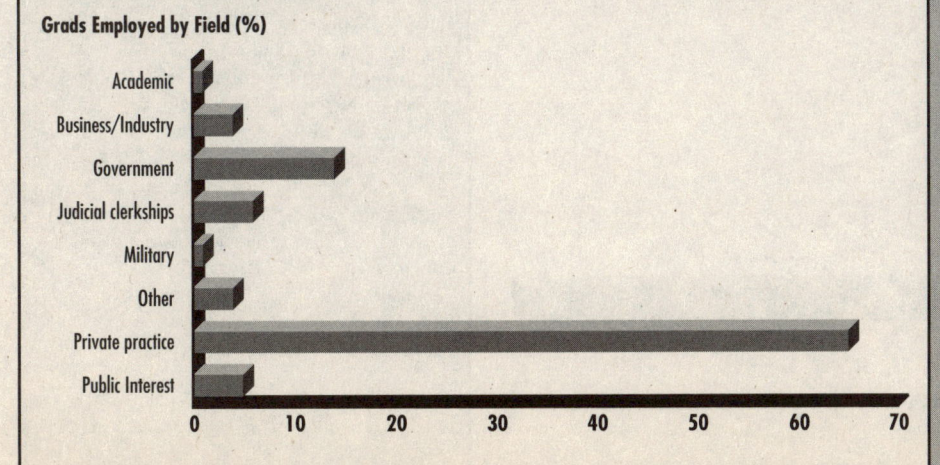

Grads Employed by Field (%)
- Academic
- Business/Industry
- Government
- Judicial clerkships
- Military
- Other
- Private practice
- Public Interest

Rate of Placement: 95%
Average Starting Salary: $78,184
Employers Who Frequently Hire Grads: State of california, private law firms, district attorneys, public defenders, public interest entities
State for Bar Exam: CA
Pass Rate for First-Time Bar: 77%

UNIVERSITY OF CALIFORNIA, HASTINGS
College of Law

Admissions Contact: Director of Admissions, Akira Shiroma
200 McAllister Street #214, San Francisco, CA 94102
Admissions Phone: 415-565-4623 • Admissions Fax: 415-565-4863
Admissions E-mail: admiss@uchastings.edu • Web Address: www.uchastings.edu

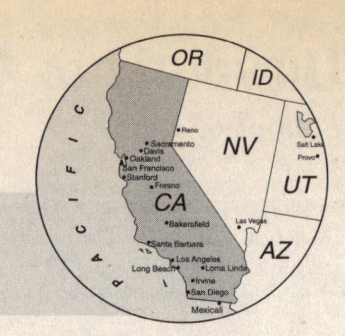

INSTITUTIONAL INFORMATION
Public/Private: Public
Student/Faculty Ratio: 21:1
Total Faculty: 137
% Part Time: 60
% Female: 11
% Minority: 10

PROGRAMS
Academic Specialties: Civil Litigation, International Law, Public Interest Law, Taxation
Advanced Degrees Offered: JD (3 years)
Combined Degrees Offered: JD/MBA, JD/MA (4 to 5 years)
Grading System: 4.0 scale; no D+ or D–
Clinical Program Required? No
Clinical Program Description: Civil Justice Clinic, Criminal Practice Clinic, Environmental Law, Immigrants' Rights, Local Government, Workers' Rights
Legal Writing Course Requirements? Yes
Legal Methods Course Requirements? No
Legal Research Course Requirements? Yes
Moot Court Requirement? Yes
Moot Court Description: 1 semester, introduces students to oral and written appellate advocacy
Public Interest Law Requirement? No
Academic Journals: Hastings Communications and Entertainment Law Journal, Hastings Constitutional Law Quarterly, Hastings International and Comparative Law Review, Hastings Law Journal, Hastings West-Northwest Journal of Environmental Law and Policy, Hastings Women's Law Journal

STUDENT INFORMATION
Enrollment of Law School: 1,252
% Out of State: 12
% Male/Female: 47/53
% Full Time: 100
% Full Time That Are International: 1
% Minority: 33
Average Age of Entering Class: 24

RESEARCH FACILITIES
Research Resources Available: Land Conservation Institute
School-Supported Research Centers: Public Law Research Institute, Civil Justice Clinic

EXPENSES/FINANCIAL AID
Annual Tuition (Residents/Nonresidents): $10,175/$20,182
Room and Board (Off Campus): $18,826
Books and Supplies: $863
Financial Aid Application Deadline: 3/1
Average Grant: $4,625
Average Loan: $21,709
% of Aid That Is Merit-Based: 1
% Receiving Some Sort of Aid: 96
Average Total Aid Package: $25,852
Average Debt: $53,198

ADMISSIONS INFORMATION
Application Fee: $60
Regular Application Deadline: 3/1
Regular Notification: 5/1
LSDAS Accepted? Yes
Average GPA: 3.5
Range of GPA: 3.3–3.7
Average LSAT: 161
Range of LSAT: 159–164
Transfer Students Accepted? Yes
Other Admissions Factors Considered: Writing ability, obstacles overcome
Number of Applications Received: 4,800
Number of Applicants Accepted: 1,496
Number of Applicants Enrolled: 420

EMPLOYMENT INFORMATION

Grads Employed by Field (%)
- Business/Industry
- Government
- Judicial clerkships
- Private practice
- Public Interest

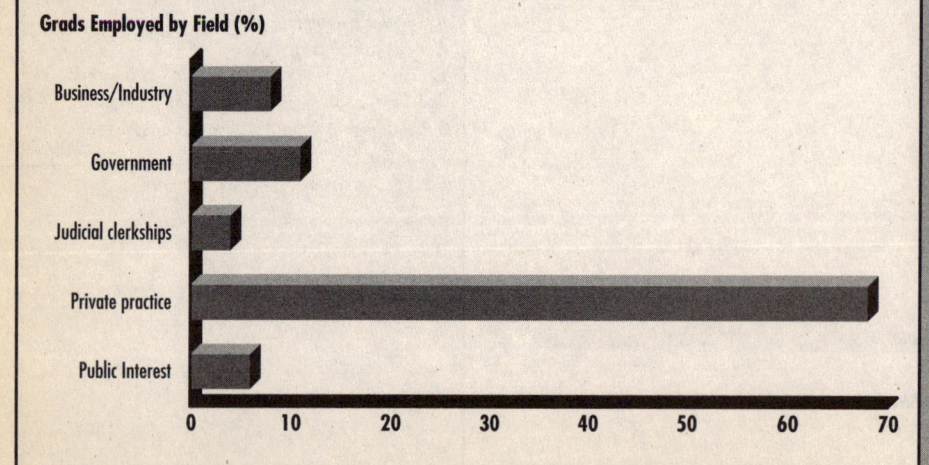

Rate of Placement: 93%
Average Starting Salary: $88,741
Employers Who Frequently Hire Grads: Major San Francisco and Los Angeles large and medium-size law firms
Prominent Alumni: Marvin Baxter, Associate Justice, CA Supreme Court; Willie Brown, Mayor, San Francisco; Joseph Cotchett, Founding Partner, Cotchett Pitre & Simon; Robert Matsui, U.S. Congressman, Fifth District of CA; Ann M. Veneman, Secretary, U.S. Agriculture
State for Bar Exam: CA
Pass Rate for First-Time Bar: 84%

UNIVERSITY OF CALIFORNIA, LOS ANGELES
School of Law

Admissions Contact: Assistant Dean and Director of Admissions, Andrea Sossin-Bergman
Box 951445, Los Angeles, CA 90095-1445
Admissions Phone: 310-825-4041 • Admissions Fax: 310-825-9450
Admissions E-mail: admissions@law.ucla.edu • Web Address: www.law.ucla.edu

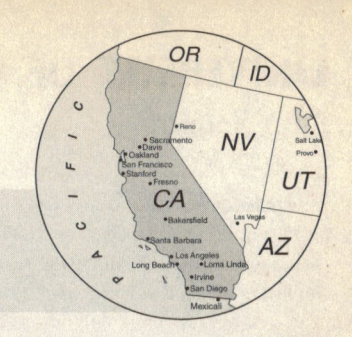

INSTITUTIONAL INFORMATION
Public/Private: Public
Student/Faculty Ratio: 15:1
Total Faculty: 110
% Part Time: 25
% Female: 30
% Minority: 7

PROGRAMS
Academic Specialties: Public Law (Constitutional and Criminal Law), Intellectual Property (including Entertainment Law), Legal and Moral Philosophy, Communications and Cyber Law, Business Law, Public Interest Law and Policy, International Law, Environmental Law, Civil Procedure, Commercial Law, Corporation Securities Law, Government Services, Human Rights Law, Labor Law, Legal History, Property, Taxation
Advanced Degrees Offered: JD, LLM
Combined Degrees Offered: JD/MA, JD/MBA, JD/MPH, JD/MAPPS, JD/MSW (all 4 years)
Grading System: Letter system from A+ to F (4.3–0.0); mandatory curve in all first-year classes and in advanced courses of 40 or more students; recommended, discretionary distribution of pluses and minuses within each letter grade
Clinical Program Required? Yes
Clinical Program Description: The required first-year Lawyering Skills course has a clinical component; working mediation clinic
Legal Writing Course Requirements? Yes
Legal Writing Description: Introduction to critical writing
Legal Methods Course Requirements? Yes
Legal Methods Description: Introduction to fundamentals of legal research, reasoning, client counseling, and fact investigation using clinical methods
Legal Research Course Requirements? No
Moot Court Requirement? No
Public Interest Law Requirement? No
Academic Journals: Asian Pacific American Law Journal, Journal of Law and Technology, Chicano/Latino Law Review, Entertainment Law Review, Journal of Environmental Law and Policy, Journal of International Law and Foreign Policy, Pacific Basin Law Journal, UCLA Law Review, Women's Law Journal

STUDENT INFORMATION
Enrollment of Law School: 951
% Out of State: 26
% Male/Female: 48/52
% Full Time: 100
% Full Time That Are International: 0
% Minority: 28
Average Age of Entering Class: 25

RESEARCH FACILITIES
Research Resources Available: Public Counsel, the pro bono arm of the Los Angeles County and Beverly Hills bar associations; Environmental Law Clinic; program in public interest law and policy
School-Supported Research Centers: A number of extensive libraries, Center for 17th- and 18th-Century Studies, Mental Retardation Research Center, Coleman African Studies Center, Center for European and Russian Studies, Latin American Center, Von Grunebaum Center for Near East Studies, Center for International Relations, Center for Pacific Rim Studies, Center for Chinese Studies, Joint Center in East Asian Studies, Center for Japanese Studies, Center for Korean Studies, Center for the Study of Women, Institute of American Cultures, Institute of Archaeology, Institute for Social Science

EXPENSES/FINANCIAL AID
Annual Tuition (Residents/Nonresidents): $12,248/$22,836
Room and Board (Off Campus): $13,575
Books and Supplies: $1,425
Financial Aid Application Deadline: 3/2
Average Grant: $6,250
Average Loan: $16,824
% of Aid That Is Merit-Based: 5
% Receiving Some Sort of Aid: 87
Average Total Aid Package: $26,156
Average Debt: $52,701

ADMISSIONS INFORMATION
Application Fee: $70
Regular Application Deadline: 2/1
Regular Notification: 5/1
LSDAS Accepted? Yes
Average GPA: 3.6
Range of GPA: 3.5–3.8
Average LSAT: 164
Range of LSAT: 161–166
Transfer Students Accepted? Yes
Other Schools to Which Students Applied: University of Southern California, UC Berkeley, UC Hastings, Georgetown, NYU
Other Admissions Factors Considered: Undergraduate program, graduate study, awards or publications, unusual or exceptional career or personal achievements, diversity characteristics, challenges overcome
Number of Applications Received: 5,091
Number of Applicants Accepted: 967
Number of Applicants Enrolled: 304

EMPLOYMENT INFORMATION

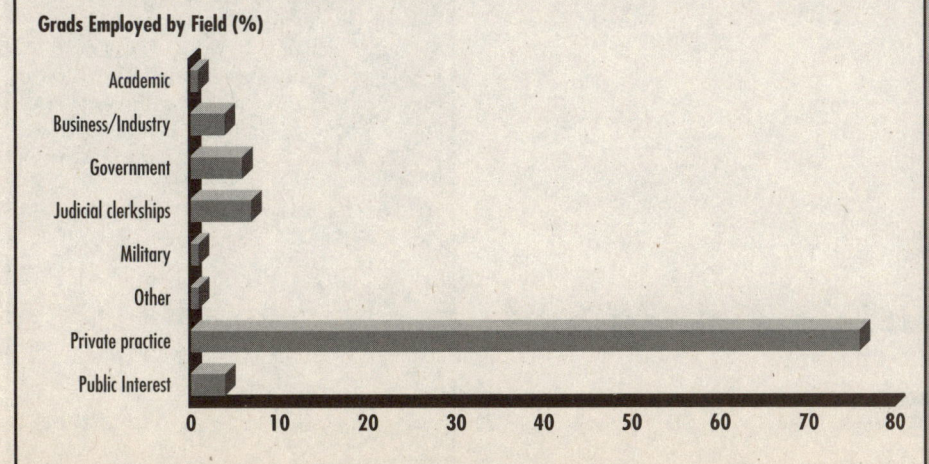

Grads Employed by Field (%)

Field	%
Academic	~1
Business/Industry	~3
Government	~5
Judicial clerkships	~5
Military	0
Other	~1
Private practice	~77
Public Interest	~3

Rate of Placement: 97%
Average Starting Salary: $101,570
Employers Who Frequently Hire Grads: Latham & Watkins; O'Melveny & Myers; Irell & Manella; Gibson, Dunn & Crutcher; Morrison & Foerster; Skadden, Arps et al.; Foley & Lardner; Gray, Cary, et al.; Kirkland & Ellis; Arnold & Porter; Cox, Castle & Nicholson; Gunderson, Dettmer et al.; Knobbe, Martens et al.
Prominent Alumni: Hon. Henry Waxman, U.S. House of Representatives, 29th District; Antonia Hernandez, Director, Mexican American Legal Defense and Education Fund; Hon. Howard L. Berman, U.S. House of Representatives, 26th District
State for Bar Exam: CA
Pass Rate for First-Time Bar: 90%

UNIVERSITY OF CHICAGO
Law School

Admissions Contact: Deans of Admissions
1111 East 60th Street, Chicago, IL 60637
Admissions Phone: 773-702-9484 • Admissions Fax: 773-834-0942
Admissions E-mail: admissions@law.uchicago.edu • Web Address: www.law.uchicago.edu

INSTITUTIONAL INFORMATION
Public/Private: Private
Student/Faculty Ratio: 19:1
Total Faculty: 30
% Female: 17
% Minority: 13

PROGRAMS
Academic Specialties: Interdisciplinary Studies, International Law, Law and Technology, Law and Economics, Constitutional Law, Antitrust, Corporate Law, Entrepreneurship
Advanced Degrees Offered: LLM (1 year), JSD (up to 5 years)
Combined Degrees Offered: JD/MBA (4 years), JD/PhD
Grading System: A (80+), B (74–79), C (68–73), D (60–67), F (55–59)
Clinical Program Required? Yes
Clinical Program Description: Employment Discrimination, Criminal Justice, Mental Health, Clinic on Entrepreneurship, Death Penalty, Civil Rights, Fair Housing, Public Guardian
Legal Methods Course Requirements? Yes
Legal Methods Description: 1 year during the first year; students are divided into 6 sections of 30 and taught by full-time fellows

STUDENT INFORMATION
Enrollment of Law School: 565
% Out of State: 74
% Male/Female: 59/41
% Full Time: 100
% Full Time That Are International: 1
% Minority: 18
Average Age of Entering Class: 24

RESEARCH FACILITIES
School-Supported Research Centers: Program in Law and Economics, Program in Legal History, Center for Studies in Criminal Justice, Program in Law and Government

EXPENSES/FINANCIAL AID
Annual Tuition: $27,276
Room and Board (On/Off Campus): $10,100/$10,575
Books and Supplies: $1,500
Average Grant: $8,000
% Receiving Some Sort of Aid: 82

ADMISSIONS INFORMATION
Application Fee: $60
Regular Application Deadline: 2/1
Regular Notification: 3/30
LSDAS Accepted? Yes
Average GPA: 3.7
Range of GPA: 3.5–3.8
Average LSAT: 170
Range of LSAT: 165–172
Transfer Students Accepted? Yes
Other Admissions Factors Considered: Quality of undergraduate school, quality of academic record, interview

INTERNATIONAL STUDENTS
TOEFL Required of International Students? Yes
Minimum TOEFL: 600

EMPLOYMENT INFORMATION

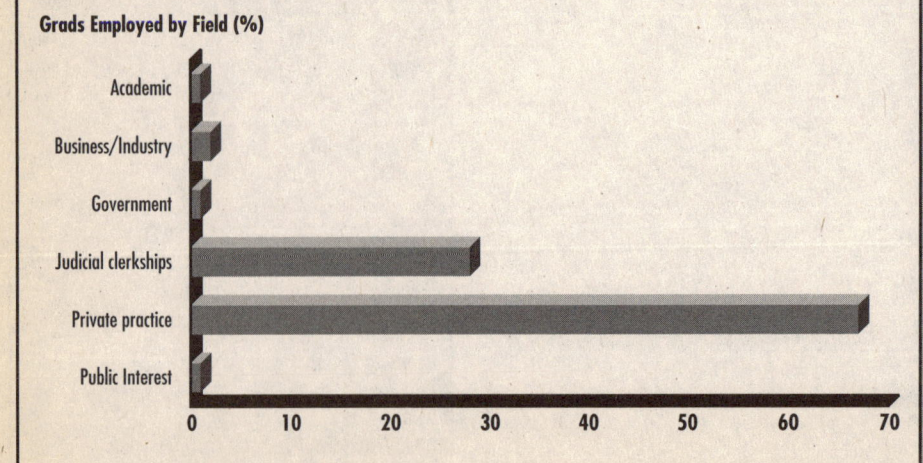

Grads Employed by Field (%)

Field	%
Academic	~1
Business/Industry	~2
Government	~2
Judicial clerkships	~28
Private practice	~67
Public Interest	~1

Rate of Placement: 99%
Average Starting Salary: $125,000
Employers Who Frequently Hire Grads: Cravath Swain & Moore, Mayer Brown & Platt, Gibson Dunn & Crutcher, Sidley & Austin, Kirkland & Ellis, Skadden Arps Slate Meagher & Flom
State for Bar Exam: IL
Pass Rate for First-Time Bar: 94%

UNIVERSITY OF CINCINNATI
College of Law

Admissions Contact: Assistant Dean and Director of Admission and Financial Aid, Al Watson
PO Box 210040, Cincinnati, OH 45221
Admissions Phone: 513-556-6805 • Admissions Fax: 513-556-2391
Admissions E-mail: admissions@law.uc.edu • Web Address: www.law.uc.edu

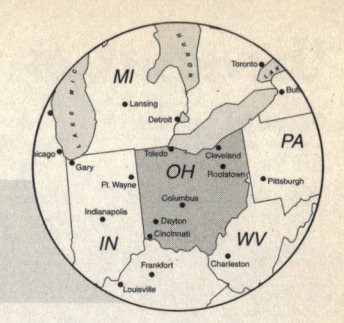

INSTITUTIONAL INFORMATION
Public/Private: Public
Student/Faculty Ratio: 13:1
Total Faculty: 54
% Part Time: 46
% Female: 30
% Minority: 13

PROGRAMS
Academic Specialties: National program with experienced and dedicated faculty to help advocate a selective and diverse student body; Human Rights Law
Advanced Degrees Offered: JD (3 years)
Combined Degrees Offered: JD/MBA (4 years), JD/Master of Community Planning (4.5 years), JD/MA Women's Studies (4 years)
Grading System: 4.0 scale; first-year courses graded on a B curve; no mandatory curve after the first year
Clinical Program Required? No
Clinical Program Description: We offer a very wide range of internships and externships, including judicial.
Legal Writing Course Requirements? Yes
Legal Writing Description: Full-time instructors teach small sections of legal research and writing.
Legal Methods Course Requirements? Yes
Legal Research Course Requirements? Yes
Moot Court Requirement? No
Moot Court Description: Moot court teams participate in all national competitions and host the annual Product Liability Competition.

Public Interest Law Requirement? No
Public Interest Law Description: The program is optional, but a full-time director supervises externship programs and public interest externships and programs.
Academic Journals: UC Law Review, Immigration and Nationality Law Review, Human Rights Quarterly, Freedom Center Journal

STUDENT INFORMATION
Enrollment of Law School: 366
% Out of State: 35
% Male/Female: 47/53
% Full Time: 100
% Full Time That Are International: 1
% Minority: 20
Average Age of Entering Class: 25

RESEARCH FACILITIES
School-Supported Research Centers: International Human Rights, Corporate Law, and Law and Psychiatry centers; Practice in Negotiation and Problem Solving; Urban Justice Institute; Ohio Innocence Project

EXPENSES/FINANCIAL AID
Annual Tuition (Residents/Nonresidents): $12,111/$22,902
Room and Board: $11,949
Books and Supplies: $4,500
Financial Aid Application Deadline: 4/1
Average Grant: $5,000
% Receiving Some Sort of Aid: 75
Average Debt: $38,500

ADMISSIONS INFORMATION
Application Fee: $35
Regular Application Deadline: 4/1
Regular Notification: Rolling
LSDAS Accepted? Yes
Average GPA: 3.5
Range of GPA: 3.2–3.7
Average LSAT: 160
Range of LSAT: 156–162
Transfer Students Accepted? Yes
Other Schools to Which Students Applied: Indiana University, Ohio State University, University of Dayton, University of Pittsburgh
Other Admissions Factors Considered: Quality of applicant's previous education, trend of academic performance, community service, graduate work
Number of Applications Received: 1,170
Number of Applicants Accepted: 372
Number of Applicants Enrolled: 126

INTERNATIONAL STUDENTS
TOEFL Required of International Students? Yes

EMPLOYMENT INFORMATION

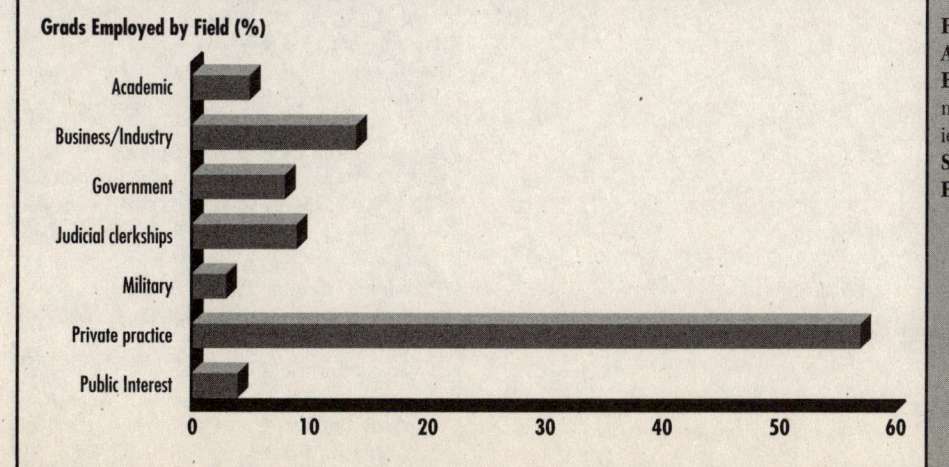

Grads Employed by Field (%)

Field	%
Academic	~2
Business/Industry	~15
Government	~10
Judicial clerkships	~10
Military	~1
Private practice	~58
Public Interest	~4

Rate of Placement: 94%
Average Starting Salary: $57,086
Employers Who Frequently Hire Grads: All major law firms in Cincinnati and other Ohio cities as well as other midwestern cities
State for Bar Exam: OH
Pass Rate for First-Time Bar: 93%

UNIVERSITY OF COLORADO
School of Law

Admissions Contact: Assistant Dean for Admissions and Financial Aid, Carol Nelson-Douglas
403 UCB, Boulder, CO 80309-0403
Admissions Phone: 303-492-7203 • *Admissions Fax:* 303-492-2542
Admissions E-mail: lawadmin@colorado.edu • *Web Address:* www.colorado.edu/law

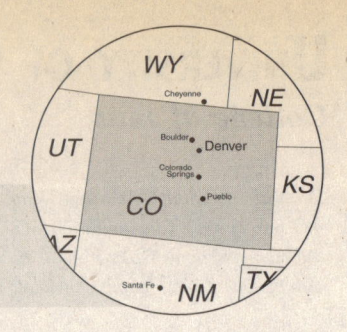

INSTITUTIONAL INFORMATION
Public/Private: Public
Student/Faculty Ratio: 14:1
Total Faculty: 76
% Part Time: 28
% Female: 23
% Minority: 15

PROGRAMS
Academic Specialties: Natural Resources and Environmental Law, Constitutional Law, Legal Theory, Corporate Law, International Law, Alternative Dispute Resolution, Taxation, American Indian Law, Telecommunications Law
Advanced Degrees Offered: JD, Tax Certificate, Environmental Policy Certificate (all 3 years)
Combined Degrees Offered: JD/MBA (4 years), JD/MPA (4 years)
Grading System: Letter and numerical system on a 4.0/50–99 scale
Clinical Program Required? No
Clinical Program Description: Entrepreneurial Law, Indian Law, Legal Aid and Defender Program, Natural Resources Litigation
Legal Writing Course Requirements? Yes
Legal Writing Description: First-year courses in Legal Writing and Appellate Court Advocacy. We also require a seminar with a major research paper, as well as requiring writing in many second- and third-year courses.
Legal Methods Course Requirements? Yes
Legal Methods Description: The first-year courses in Legal Writing and Appellate Court Advocacy include the study of legal methods.

Legal Research Course Requirements? Yes
Legal Research Description: The first-year courses in Legal Writing and Appellate Court Advocacy include the study of legal research, both traditional and electronic.
Moot Court Requirement? No
Moot Court Description: Moot court competitions. Students may earn academic credit.
Public Interest Law Requirement? No
Academic Journals: *University of Colorado Law Review, Colorado Journal of International Environmental Law and Policy, Journal on Telecommunications and High Technology Law*

STUDENT INFORMATION
Enrollment of Law School: 485
% Out of State: 13
% Male/Female: 46/54
% Full Time: 100
% Full Time That Are International: 0
% Minority: 19
Average Age of Entering Class: 26

RESEARCH FACILITIES
Research Resources Available: Native American Rights Fund, Law and Water Fund, Natural Resources Litigation Clinic, National Center for Atmospheric Research, National Oceanographic and Atmospheric Administration
School-Supported Research Centers: Natural Resources Law Center, Byron R. White Center for the Study of American Constitutional Law, National Wildlife Federation, Center for the Study of Race and Ethnicity, Center of the American West, Environmental Center, Center for Entrepreneurial Law, Silicon Flatirons Telecommunications Program

EXPENSES/FINANCIAL AID
Annual Tuition (Residents/Nonresidents): $5,920/$20,418
Room and Board (On/Off Campus): $7,875/$10,992
Books and Supplies: $1,142
Financial Aid Application Deadline: 4/1
Average Grant: $2,531
Average Loan: $14,969
% of Aid That Is Merit-Based: 5
% Receiving Some Sort of Aid: 91
Average Total Aid Package: $16,966
Average Debt: $51,668
Tuition Per Credit (Residents/Nonresidents): $5,920/$20,418

ADMISSIONS INFORMATION
Application Fee: $55
Regular Application Deadline: 2/15
Regular Notification: Rolling
LSDAS Accepted? Yes
Average GPA: 3.5
Range of GPA: 3.3–3.7
Average LSAT: 161
Range of LSAT: 158–163
Transfer Students Accepted? Yes
Other Schools to Which Students Applied: U. of Denver, George Washington, UT Austin, UC Hastings, Georgetown, Boston College, U. of Arizona
Other Admissions Factors Considered: Geographic, economic, social, or cultural background; variation in undergraduate or graduate program; unusual employment or other experience
Number of Applications Received: 2,239
Number of Applicants Accepted: 601
Number of Applicants Enrolled: 165

EMPLOYMENT INFORMATION

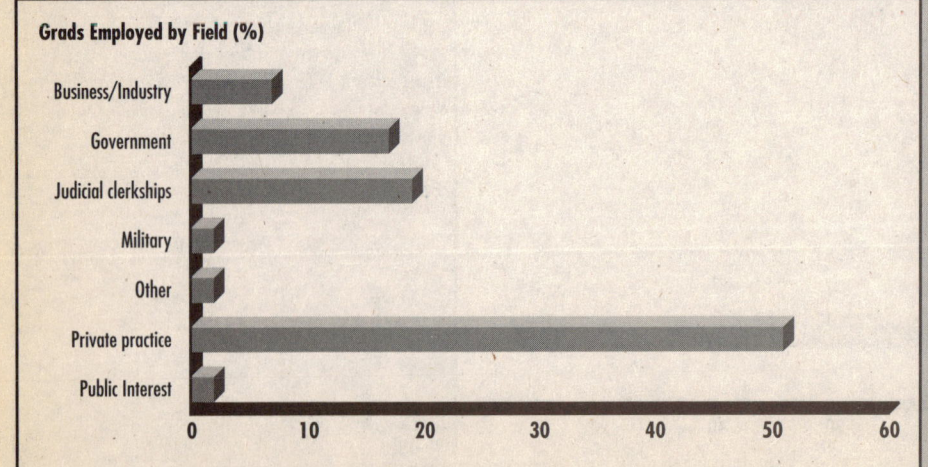

Grads Employed by Field (%)
- Business/Industry
- Government
- Judicial clerkships
- Military
- Other
- Private practice
- Public Interest

Rate of Placement: 91%
Average Starting Salary: $56,553
Employers Who Frequently Hire Grads: Arnold & Porter; Baker & Hostetler; Ballard Spahr; Blackwell, Sanders; Blakely, Sokoloff; Brobeck; Brownstein Hyatt; Bullivant Houser; Campbell Carr; Caplan & Earnest; Cooley Godward; Cornish & Dell'Olio; Davis Graham & Stubbs LLP; Dorsey & Whitney, Eastham Johnson; Faegre & Benson; Featherstone & Shea
Prominent Alumni: Wiley B. Rutledge, Associate Justice, U.S. Supreme Court; Luis D. Rovira, Chief Justice (retired), Colorado Supreme Court; Roy Romer, former Governor of Colorado; Glenn R. Jones, Chairman and CEO, Jones International
State for Bar Exam: CO
Pass Rate for First-Time Bar: 93%

UNIVERSITY OF CONNECTICUT
School of Law

Admissions Contact: Director of Admission, Karen DeMeola
45 Elizabeth Street, Hartford, CT 06105
Admissions Phone: 860-570-5159 • Admissions Fax: 860-570-5153
Admissions E-mail: admit@law.uconn.edu • Web Address: www.law.uconn.edu

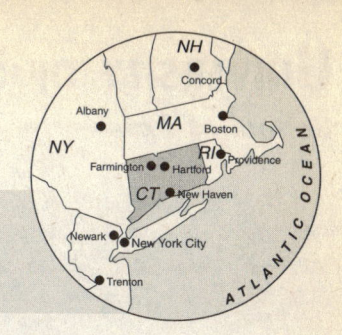

INSTITUTIONAL INFORMATION
Public/Private: Public
Student/Faculty Ratio: 11:1
Total Faculty: 126
% Part Time: 59
% Female: 29
% Minority: 11

PROGRAMS
Academic Specialties: Commercial Law, Constitutional Law, Corporation Securities Law, Criminal Law, Environmental Law, Government Services, Human Rights Law, Intellectual Property Law, International Law, Labor Law, Legal History, Legal Philosophy, Property, Taxation
Advanced Degrees Offered: LLM (1 year), JD (3 to 4 years)
Combined Degrees Offered: JD/MAPPS, JD/MBA, JD/MLS, JD/MPA, JD/MSW, JD/MPH, JD/LLM
Grading System: Letter system; some courses are Pass/Fail
Clinical Program Required? No
Clinical Program Description: Administrative Law, Civil Rights, Disability Law, Criminal Law, Tax Law, Street Law, Judicial Clerkship, Women's Rights, Children's Rights, Labor Relations, Mediation, Poverty Law, Health Law, Legslative Process
Legal Writing Course Requirements? No
Legal Methods Course Requirements? Yes
Legal Methods Description: 1-year Lawyering Process course; writing and lawyering skills
Legal Research Course Requirements? Yes
Legal Research Description: Part of Lawyering Process course
Moot Court Requirement? Yes
Moot Court Description: First year, 6 weeks; intensive brief writing and appellate arguments
Public Interest Law Requirement? No
Academic Journals: Connecticut Law Review, Connecticut Journal of International Law, Connecticut Insurance Law Journal, Connecticut Public Interest law Journal

STUDENT INFORMATION
Enrollment of Law School: 571
% Out of State: 33
% Male/Female: 50/50
% Full Time: 67
% Full Time That Are International: 1
% Minority: 18
Average Age of Entering Class: 25

RESEARCH FACILITIES
Research Resources Available: Center for Children's Advocacy, Connecticut Urban Legal Initiative

EXPENSES/FINANCIAL AID
Annual Tuition (Residents/Nonresidents): $11,374/$23,992
Room and Board (Off Campus): $8,152
Books and Supplies: $964
Financial Aid Application Deadline: 3/15
Average Grant: $7,172
Average Loan: $15,555
% of Aid That Is Merit-Based: 19
% Receiving Some Sort of Aid: 76
Average Total Aid Package: $19,075
Average Debt: $43,439
Tuition Per Credit (Residents/Nonresidents): $397/$837
Fees Per Credit: $527

ADMISSIONS INFORMATION
Application Fee: $30
Regular Application Deadline: 3/15
Regular Notification: Rolling
LSDAS Accepted? Yes
Average GPA: 3.3
Range of GPA: 3.1–3.5
Average LSAT: 160
Range of LSAT: 158–161
Transfer Students Accepted? Yes
Other Admissions Factors Considered: Quality and maturity of written essays, undergraduate/graduate curriculum, achievement of academic awards and honors
Number of Applications Received: 1,465
Number of Applicants Accepted: 505
Number of Applicants Enrolled: 118

INTERNATIONAL STUDENTS
TOEFL Required of International Students? Yes

EMPLOYMENT INFORMATION

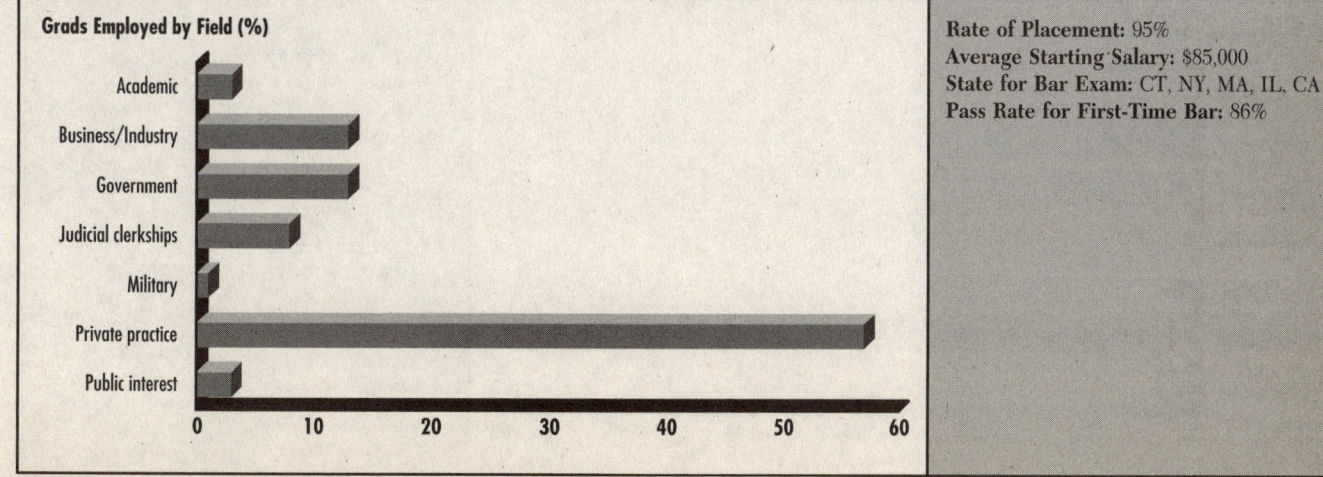

Grads Employed by Field (%)
- Academic
- Business/Industry
- Government
- Judicial clerkships
- Military
- Private practice
- Public interest

Rate of Placement: 95%
Average Starting Salary: $85,000
State for Bar Exam: CT, NY, MA, IL, CA
Pass Rate for First-Time Bar: 86%

UNIVERSITY OF DAYTON
School of Law

Admissions Contact: Assistant Dean/Director of Admissions and Financial Aid, Janet L. Hein
300 College Park, Dayton, OH 45469-2760
Admissions Phone: 937-229-3555 • Admissions Fax: 937-229-4194
Admissions E-mail: lawinfo@notes.udayton.edu • Web Address: www.law.udayton.edu

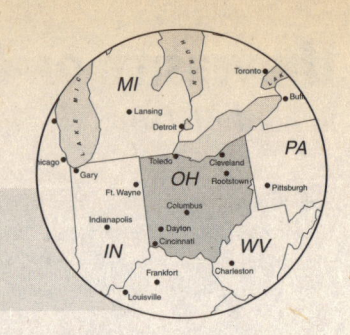

INSTITUTIONAL INFORMATION
Public/Private: Private
Affiliation: Roman Catholic
Student/Faculty Ratio: 17:1
Total Faculty: 28
% Part Time: 0
% Female: 36
% Minority: 11

PROGRAMS
Academic Specialties: One of the top Law and Technology programs in the country, with approximately 15 courses offered in Intellectual Property, Copyright, and Trademark, Computer-Related Law, Cyberspace Law and Electronic Commerce, and Entertainment Law. Our strong Legal Profession Program is a unique three-semester, 8-credit series of required legal writing, analysis, and research training. Specialties include Civil Procedure, Commercial Law, Constitutional Law, Corporation Securities Law, Criminal Law, and Taxation.
Advanced Degrees Offered: JD (3 years)
Combined Degrees Offered: JD/MBA (4 years)
Grading System: 4.0 scale
Clinical Program Required? No
Clinical Program Description: Students are responsible for assisting low-income clients in real legal disputes.
Legal Writing Course Requirements? Yes
Legal Writing Description: 3 required semesters of legal research, writing, and analysis in Legal Profession I, II, and III (8 credits total). The courses are client simulation–driven and introduce students to research in several media, objective writing, and persuasive writing and oral argument at the trial and appellate levels.
Legal Methods Course Requirements? Yes
Legal Methods Description: See Legal Writing.
Legal Research Course Requirements? Yes
Legal Research Description: See Legal Writing.
Moot Court Requirement? No
Moot Court Description: Second- and third-year students represent the school in interschool and national competitions. The course is designed to provide students with an opportunity to develop both written and oral appellate advocacy skills.
Public Interest Law Requirement? No
Academic Journals: *University of Dayton Law Review*

STUDENT INFORMATION
Enrollment of Law School: 464
% Out of State: 48
% Male/Female: 59/41
% Full Time: 100
% Full Time That Are International: 1
% Minority: 14
Average Age of Entering Class: 24

RESEARCH FACILITIES
Research Resources Available: Lexis/Nexis, Westlaw, Index master
School-Supported Research Centers: Separate law school server

EXPENSES/FINANCIAL AID
Annual Tuition: $22,420
Room and Board: $9,000
Books and Supplies: $900
Financial Aid Application Deadline: 3/1
Average Grant: $10,000
Average Loan: $23,222
% Receiving Some Sort of Aid: 90
Average Total Aid Package: $33,005
Average Debt: $60,856

ADMISSIONS INFORMATION
Application Fee: $50
Regular Application Deadline: 5/1
Regular Notification: Rolling
LSDAS Accepted? Yes
Average GPA: 3.2
Range of GPA: 2.8–3.4
Average LSAT: 151
Range of LSAT: 147–154
Transfer Students Accepted? Yes
Other Schools to Which Students Applied: Capital, Cleveland State, Ohio Northern, Ohio State, U. of Akron, U. of Cincinnati, U. of Toledo
Other Admissions Factors Considered: Diversity of experiences, leadership, motivation, abillity to overcome hardships, breadth and depth of skills and interests
Number of Applications Received: 1,395
Number of Applicants Accepted: 792
Number of Applicants Enrolled: 204

INTERNATIONAL STUDENTS
TOEFL Recommended for International Students? Yes
Minimum TOEFL: 600 (250 computer)

EMPLOYMENT INFORMATION

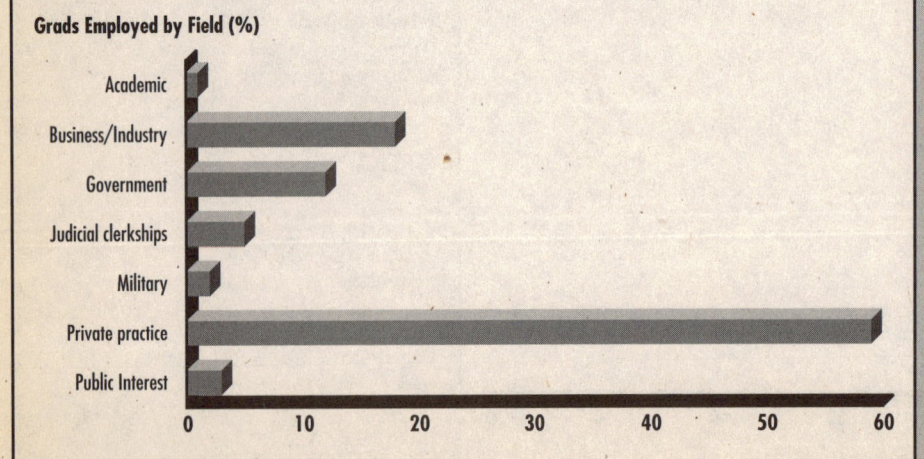

Grads Employed by Field (%)
- Academic: ~1
- Business/Industry: ~18
- Government: ~12
- Judicial clerkships: ~5
- Military: ~2
- Private practice: ~60
- Public Interest: ~3

Rate of Placement: 91%
Average Starting Salary: $50,100
Prominent Alumni: Barbara Gorman, Judge, Common Pleas Court; Ron Brown, CEO, Milacron Inc.; Nancy Michaud, VP and General Counsel, Huffy Inc.; Steve Powell, Judge, Appellate Court, 12th District; Michael Coleman, Mayor, Columbus, Ohio
State for Bar Exam: OH, FL, GA, KY, IN
Pass Rate for First-Time Bar: 70%

UNIVERSITY OF DENVER
College of Law

Admissions Contact: Assistant Director of Admissions
7039 East 18th Avenue, Denver, CO 80220
Admissions Phone: 303-871-6135 • Admissions Fax: 303-871-6100
Admissions E-mail: admissions@law.du.edu • Web Address: www.law.du.edu

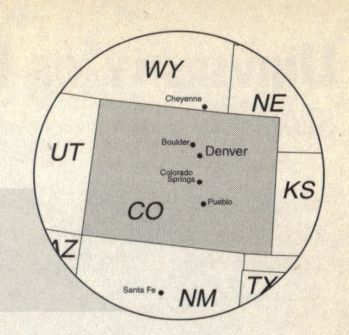

INSTITUTIONAL INFORMATION
Public/Private: Private
Student/Faculty Ratio: 17:1
Total Faculty: 61
% Female: 30
% Minority: 16

PROGRAMS
Academic Specialties: Civil Procedure, Corporation Securities Law, Environmental Law, Human Rights Law, International Law, Taxation
Clinical Program Required? No
Clinical Program Description: Natural Resources and Environmental Law Program, Public Interest, Transportation, Litigation, Child Advocacy, Metro Volunteer Lawyers, Low-Income Taxpayer Representation Clinic, Domestic Violence Clinic, Civil Justice Project, EarthJustice, MACLAW, MSLA, Spanish for Lawyers
Legal Writing Course Requirements? Yes
Legal Methods Course Requirements? Yes
Legal Methods Description: 2 semesters
Legal Research Course Requirements? No
Moot Court Requirement? No
Public Interest Law Requirement? No
Academic Journals: *Law Journal, Trans Law Journal, Water Law*

STUDENT INFORMATION
Enrollment of Law School: 1,182
% Out of State: 48
% Male/Female: 48/52
% Full Time: 72
% Full Time That Are International: 2
% Minority: 13
Average Age of Entering Class: 25

EXPENSES/FINANCIAL AID
Annual Tuition: $21,960
Room and Board (On Campus): $7,984
Books and Supplies: $900
Financial Aid Application Deadline: 3/30
Average Grant: $10,000
Average Loan: $18,500
% of Aid That Is Merit-Based: 33
% Receiving Some Sort of Aid: 80
Average Total Aid Package: $36,000
Average Debt: $60,000
Tuition Per Credit: $732

ADMISSIONS INFORMATION
Application Fee: $45
Regular Application Deadline: 5/30
Regular Notification: Rolling
LSDAS Accepted? Yes
Average GPA: 3.1
Range of GPA: 2.8–3.4
Average LSAT: 155
Range of LSAT: 150–157
Transfer Students Accepted? Yes
Other Admissions Factors Considered: Résumé (required)
Number of Applications Received: 2,054
Number of Applicants Accepted: 1,041
Number of Applicants Enrolled: 375

INTERNATIONAL STUDENTS
TOEFL Required of International Students? Yes
Minimum TOEFL: 580

EMPLOYMENT INFORMATION

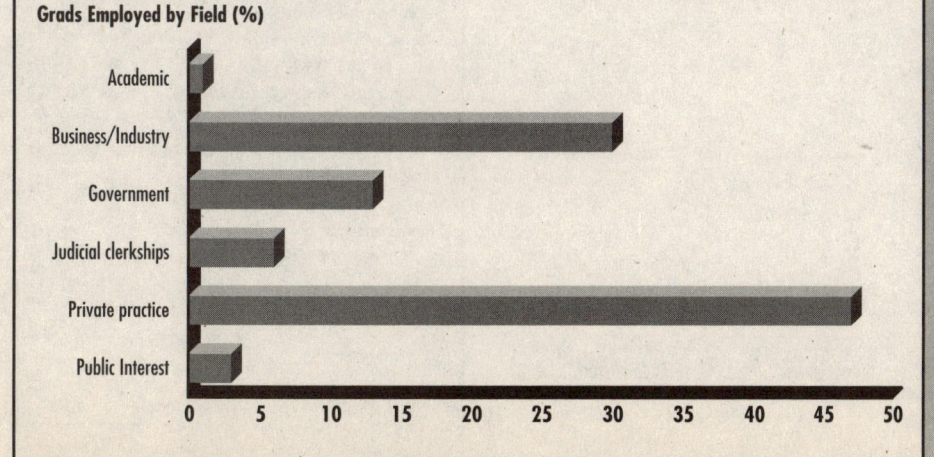

Grads Employed by Field (%)
- Academic: ~1
- Business/Industry: ~30
- Government: ~13
- Judicial clerkships: ~6
- Private practice: ~47
- Public Interest: ~3

Rate of Placement: 94%
Average Starting Salary: $50,000
Employers Who Frequently Hire Grads: Law firms, government agencies (DA's office, Attorney General's office, etc.), corporations
State for Bar Exam: CO
Pass Rate for First-Time Bar: 81%

UNIVERSITY OF DETROIT MERCY
School of Law

Admissions Contact: Assistant Dean, Kathleen H. Caprio
651 East Jefferson Avenue, Detroit, MI 48226
Admissions Phone: 313-596-0264 • Admissions Fax: 313-596-0280
Admissions E-mail: udmlawao@udmercy.edu • Web Address: www.law.udmercy.edu

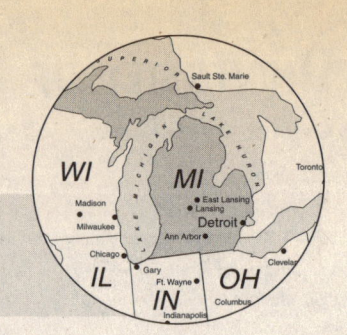

INSTITUTIONAL INFORMATION
Public/Private: Private
Affiliation: Roman Catholic
Student/Faculty Ratio: 19:1

PROGRAMS
Academic Specialties: Writing and ethics across the curriculum, clinical programs, global issues
Advanced Degrees Offered: JD (3 years full time)
Combined Degrees Offered: JD/MBA (4 years full time), JD/LLB (3 years full time)
Grading System: 4.0 scale
Clinical Program Required? No
Clinical Program Description: Urban Law Clinic, Immigration Law Clinic, Externship Program
Legal Writing Course Requirements? Yes
Legal Writing Description: Applied Legal Theory and Analysis is a first-year, 6-credit, 2-semester course.
Legal Methods Course Requirements? Yes
Legal Methods Description: See Legal Writing.
Legal Research Course Requirements? Yes
Legal Research Description: See Legal Writing.
Moot Court Requirement? Yes
Moot Court Description: First-year moot court program arguing in appellate court
Public Interest Law Requirement? No
Academic Journals: *University of Detroit Mercy School of Law, Law Review*

STUDENT INFORMATION
Enrollment of Law School: 408
% Male/Female: 55/45
% Full Time: 64
% Full Time That Are International: 11
% Minority: 8
Average Age of Entering Class: 28

EXPENSES/FINANCIAL AID
Annual Tuition: $21,240
Room and Board (Off Campus): $14,327
Books and Supplies: $1,020
Financial Aid Application Deadline: 4/1
Average Grant: $10,000
Average Loan: $19,300
Average Debt: $69,678
Tuition Per Credit: $715

ADMISSIONS INFORMATION
Application Fee: $50
Regular Application Deadline: 4/15
Regular Notification: Rolling
LSDAS Accepted? Yes
Average GPA: 3.1
Range of GPA: 2.9–3.4
Average LSAT: 148
Range of LSAT: 145–152
Transfer Students Accepted? Yes
Other Schools to Which Students Applied: Michigan State University, Wayne State University
Other Admissions Factors Considered: Strong writing skills, undergraduate course work
Number of Applications Received: 543
Number of Applicants Accepted: 255
Number of Applicants Enrolled: 91

INTERNATIONAL STUDENTS
TOEFL Required of International Students? Yes

EMPLOYMENT INFORMATION

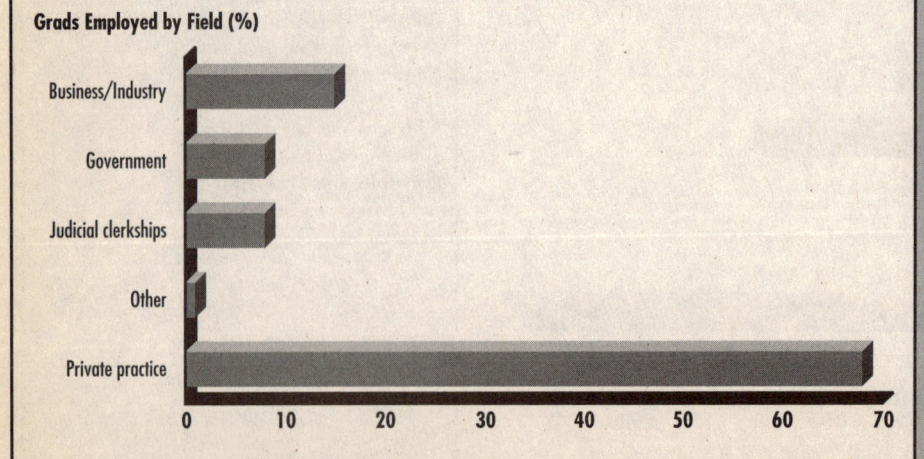

Grads Employed by Field (%)
- Business/Industry: ~15
- Government: ~8
- Judicial clerkships: ~8
- Other: ~1
- Private practice: ~68

Rate of Placement: 93%
Average Starting Salary: $55,500
Employers Who Frequently Hire Grads: County Prosecutors; Dickinson Wright PLLC; Dykema Gossett PLLC; Michigan Court of Appeals; Butzel Long; Bodman Longley; Howard & Howard; Michigan Supreme Court
State for Bar Exam: MI
Pass Rate for First-Time Bar: 81%

UNIVERSITY OF FLORIDA
Levin College of Law

Admissions Contact: Assistant Dean for Admissions, J. Michael Patrick
Box 117622, Gainesville, FL 32611
Admissions Phone: 352-392-2087 • Admissions Fax: 352-392-4087
Admissions E-mail: admissions@law.ufl.edu • Web Address: www.law.ufl.edu

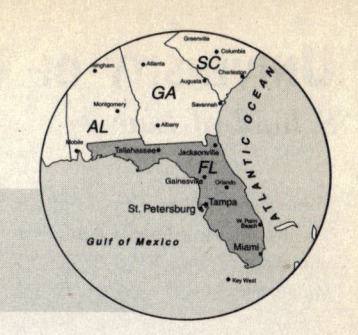

INSTITUTIONAL INFORMATION
Public/Private: Public
Student/Faculty Ratio: 15:1
Total Faculty: 74
% Female: 35
% Minority: 9

PROGRAMS
Academic Specialties: Centers or degree programs in Taxation, International and Comparative Law, Environmental and Land Use Law, Intellectual Property, Dispute Resolution, and Race and Race Relations; Center for Estate and Elder Law Planning; Center for Government Responsibility; Center on Children and the Law; Estates and Trusts practice; Family Law Certificate; Civil Procedure; Commercial Law; Constitutional Law; Corporation Securities Law; Criminal Law; Government Services; Human Rights Law; Labor Law; Legal History; Legal Philosophy; Property
Advanced Degrees Offered: LLM Taxation or Comparative Law (1 year), SJD Taxation.
Combined Degrees Offered: JD/MA, JD/MBA, JD/MA/PhD, JD/PhD, JD/MD
Grading System: Letter and numerical system on a 4.0 scale; minimum 2.0 required for good academic standing and graduation
Clinical Program Required? Yes
Clinical Program Description: Civil Clinic, Criminal Clinic, Mediation Clinic, Juvenile Clinic, Pro Se Clinic, Conservation Clinic

Legal Writing Course Requirements? Yes
Legal Methods Course Requirements? Yes
Legal Methods Description: Legal Research and Writing, first year, first semester; Appellate Advocacy, first year, second semester; Legal Drafting, second year
Legal Research Course Requirements? No
Moot Court Requirement? No
Public Interest Law Requirement? No

STUDENT INFORMATION
Enrollment of Law School: 1,186
% Out of State: 10
% Male/Female: 52/48
% Full Time: 100
% Full Time That Are International: 2
% Minority: 28
Average Age of Entering Class: 25

RESEARCH FACILITIES
School-Supported Research Centers: Center for Governmental Responsibility (public policy and law research center) Legal Technology Institute

EXPENSES/FINANCIAL AID
Annual Tuition (Residents/Nonresidents): $6,014/$21,282
Room and Board (On/Off Campus): $6,330/$6,740
Books and Supplies: $3,685
Financial Aid Application Deadline: 3/15
Average Grant: $6,200
Average Loan: $14,500
% of Aid That Is Merit-Based: 11
% Receiving Some Sort of Aid: 83
Average Total Aid Package: $16,000
Average Debt: $42,421
Tuition Per Credit (Residents/Nonresidents): $200/$709

ADMISSIONS INFORMATION
Application Fee: $20
Regular Application Deadline: 2/1
Regular Notification: 4/1
LSDAS Accepted? Yes
Average GPA: 3.5
Range of GPA: 3.3–3.7
Average LSAT: 159
Range of LSAT: 154–162
Transfer Students Accepted? Yes
Other Admissions Factors Considered: Undergraduate or other academic performance, undergraduate institution, post-bachelor's degree course work, leadership or other relevant activities, maturing experiences, economic background
Number of Applications Received: 2,558
Number of Applicants Accepted: 450
Number of Applicants Enrolled: 190

INTERNATIONAL STUDENTS
TOEFL Required of International Students? Yes
Minimum TOEFL: 550 (213 computer)

EMPLOYMENT INFORMATION

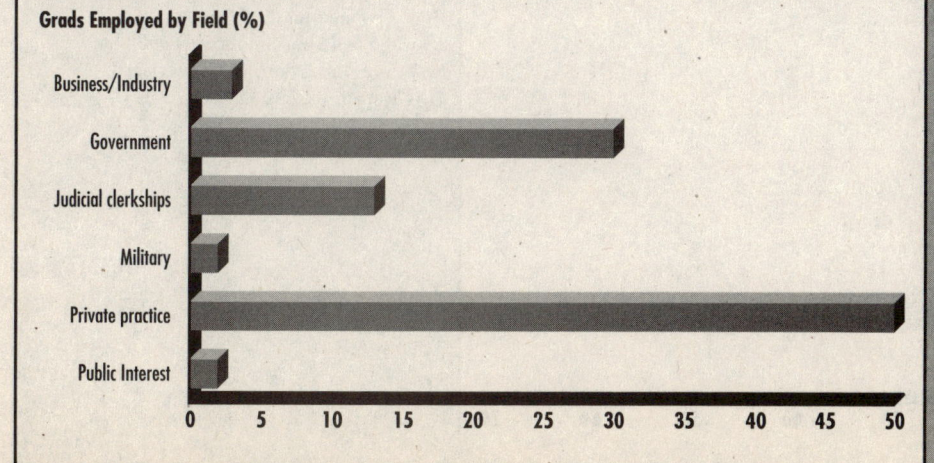

Grads Employed by Field (%)
- Business/Industry: ~2
- Government: ~30
- Judicial clerkships: ~13
- Military: ~1
- Private practice: ~50
- Public Interest: ~3

Rate of Placement: 90%
Average Starting Salary: $55,218
Employers Who Frequently Hire Grads: Foley & Lardner; King & Spalding; Holland & Knight; Troutman Sanders; Steel Hector & Davis; Gunster Yoakley; Powell Goldstein; Lowndes Drosdick; Kilpatrick Stockton; federal and state judges; State Attorney's Offices; Public Defender's Offices; Legal Services
State for Bar Exam: FL
Pass Rate for First-Time Bar: 91%

UNIVERSITY OF GEORGIA
School of Law

Admissions Contact: Director of Law Admissions, Dr. Giles Kennedy
225 Herty Drive, Athens, GA 30602-6012
Admissions Phone: 706-542-7060 • Admissions Fax: 706-542-5556
Admissions E-mail: ugajd@jd.lawsch.uga.edu • Web Address: www.lawsch.uga.edu

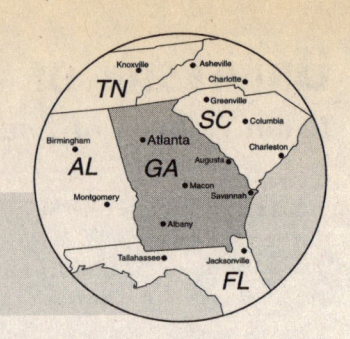

INSTITUTIONAL INFORMATION
Public/Private: Public
Student/Faculty Ratio: 17:1
Total Faculty: 84
% Part Time: 26
% Female: 17
% Minority: 2

PROGRAMS
Academic Specialties: Commercial/Corporate Law, Constitutional Law, Criminal Law, Environmental Law, Government Services, International Law, Labor Law, Taxation
Advanced Degrees Offered: LLM (1 year)
Combined Degrees Offered: JD/MBA, JD/MHP, JD/MPA, JD/MA (all 4 years)
Grading System: 0.0–4.33 on a curve
Clinical Program Required? No
Clinical Program Description: Legal Aid Clinic, Prosecutorial Clinic, Civil Clinic, Public Interest Practicum, Civil Externships, Family Violence Clinic
Legal Writing Course Requirements? No
Legal Writing Description: 2 semesters, combined with Legal Research
Legal Methods Course Requirements? No
Legal Research Course Requirements? Yes
Legal Research Description: See Legal Writing.
Moot Court Requirement? No
Public Interest Law Requirement? No
Academic Journals: Georgia Law Review, Journal of Intellectual Property Law, Georgia Journal of International Law

STUDENT INFORMATION
Enrollment of Law School: 632
% Out of State: 22
% Male/Female: 53/47
% Full Time: 100
% Full Time That Are International: 1
% Minority: 12
Average Age of Entering Class: 25

EXPENSES/FINANCIAL AID
Annual Tuition (Residents/Nonresidents): $4,657/$17,473
Room and Board (On/Off Campus): $6,762/$8,888
Books and Supplies: $1,000
Financial Aid Application Deadline: 3/1
Average Grant: $2,000
Average Loan: $12,500
% of Aid That Is Merit-Based: 10
% Receiving Some Sort of Aid: 85
Average Debt: $34,000

ADMISSIONS INFORMATION
Application Fee: $30
Regular Application Deadline: 3/1
Regular Notification: Rolling
LSDAS Accepted? Yes
Average GPA: 3.6
Range of GPA: 3.3–3.8
Average LSAT: 162
Range of LSAT: 156–164
Transfer Students Accepted? Yes
Other Schools to Which Students Applied: Georgia State University, Emory University, Mercer University, University of Virginia, Vanderbilt University, Duke University, University of Tennessee
Number of Applications Received: 1,826
Number of Applicants Accepted: 490
Number of Applicants Enrolled: 201

EMPLOYMENT INFORMATION

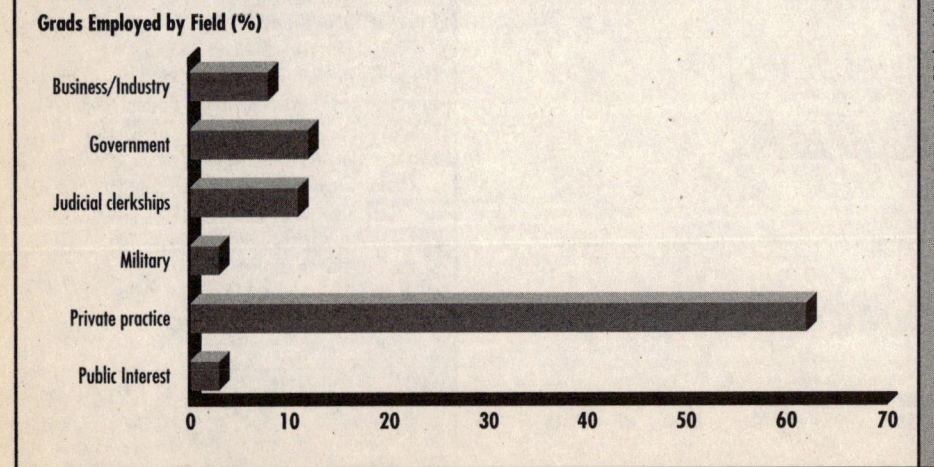

Grads Employed by Field (%)

Field	%
Business/Industry	~8
Government	~12
Judicial clerkships	~12
Military	~2
Private practice	~62
Public Interest	~3

Rate of Placement: 99%
Average Starting Salary: $54,799
State for Bar Exam: GA
Pass Rate for First-Time Bar: 92%

UNIVERSITY OF HAWAII — MANOA
William S. Richardson School of Law

Admissions Contact: Assistant Dean, Laurie Tochiki
2515 Dole Street, Honolulu, HI 96822
Admissions Phone: 808-956-3000 • Admissions Fax: 808-956-3813
Admissions E-mail: lawadm@hawaii.edu • Web Address: www.hawaii.edu/law

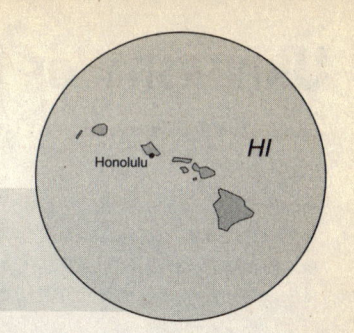

INSTITUTIONAL INFORMATION
Public/Private: Public
Student/Faculty Ratio: 13:1
Total Faculty: 18
% Female: 50
% Minority: 22

PROGRAMS
Academic Specialties: Pacific Asian Legal Studies with emphasis on China, Japan, and Pacific Rim; Environmental Law Studies with emphasis on ocean and water resources; International Law
Advanced Degrees Offered: JD (3 years)
Combined Degrees Offered: JD Environmental Law (3 years), JD Pacific-Asian Legal Studies (3 years), JD/Grad. Ocean Policy (varies), JD/MA (varies), JD/MBA (varies), JD/MS (varies), JD/MSW (varies), JD/PhD (varies)
Grading System: Grades are on a C+/B− curve, and this standard is in effect for all classes except writing classes. Median GPA is 2.60. Grading allowances within curve are: A (0–15 percent), B (25–45 percent), C (40–65 percent), D (0–20 percent), and F (0–10 percent).
Clinical Program Required? Yes
Clinical Program Description: Elder Law, Family, Prosecution, Mediation, Native Hawaiian Rights, Estate Planning, Defense, Trial Practice
Legal Writing Course Requirements? Yes
Legal Writing Description: Appellate Advocacy, first year, second semester (2 credits); Second Year Seminar (4 credits)
Legal Methods Course Requirements? Yes
Legal Methods Description: First semester, 3 credits
Legal Research Course Requirements? Yes
Legal Research Description: 1 credit
Moot Court Requirement? No
Public Interest Law Requirement? Yes
Public Interest Law Description: 60 hours of pro bono work
Academic Journals: Law Review, Asian-Pacific Law and Policy Journal

STUDENT INFORMATION
Enrollment of Law School: 241
% Out of State: 22
% Male/Female: 46/54
% Full Time: 100
% Full Time That Are International: 2
% Minority: 68
Average Age of Entering Class: 27

RESEARCH FACILITIES
% of JD Classrooms Wired: 100

EXPENSES/FINANCIAL AID
Annual Tuition (Residents/Nonresidents): $9,624/$16,344
Room and Board (On/Off Campus): $7,550/$8,900
Books and Supplies: $2,800
Financial Aid Application Deadline: 3/1
Average Grant: $3,951
Average Loan: $13,332
% of Aid That Is Merit-Based: 31
% Receiving Some Sort of Aid: 65
Average Total Aid Package: $16,642
Average Debt: $41,265

ADMISSIONS INFORMATION
Application Fee: $45
Regular Application Deadline: 3/1
Regular Notification: 4/15
LSDAS Accepted? Yes
Average GPA: 3.3
Range of GPA: 3.1–3.6
Average LSAT: 157
Range of LSAT: 153–160
Transfer Students Accepted? Yes
Other Schools to Which Students Applied: Santa Clara University, University of California—Los Angeles, University of California—Berkeley, University of California Hastings, University of San Diego
Other Admissions Factors Considered: Personal factors such as writing ability, work experience, volunteer or community involvement, letters of recommendation, honors, and awards as well as a history of overcoming adversity
Number of Applications Received: 594
Number of Applicants Accepted: 189
Number of Applicants Enrolled: 74

EMPLOYMENT INFORMATION

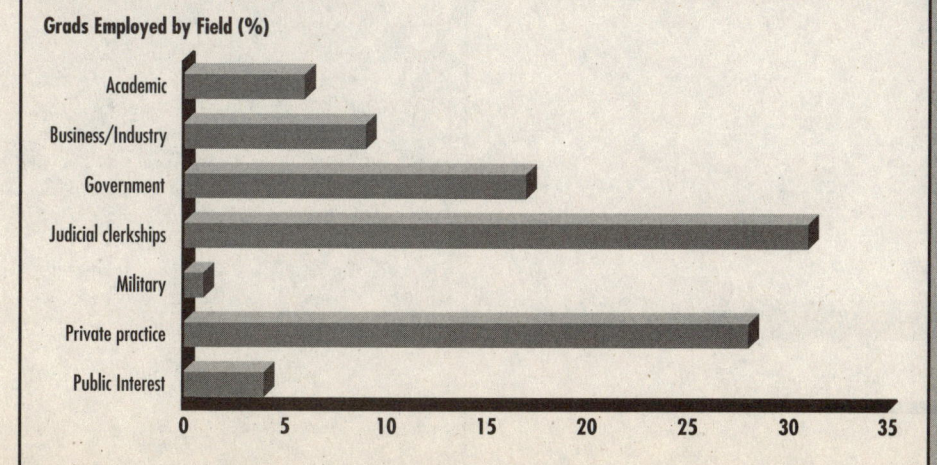

Grads Employed by Field (%)

Field	%
Academic	~6
Business/Industry	~9
Government	~17
Judicial clerkships	~31
Military	~1
Private practice	~28
Public Interest	~4

Rate of Placement: 96%
Average Starting Salary: $43,900
Employers Who Frequently Hire Grads: Office of the prosecuting attorney; public defender's office; Ashford & Wriston; Carlsmith Ball; Goodsill Anderson Quinn & Stifel; Cades Schutte Fleming & Wright; Bays Deaver et al.; Dwyer Imanaka, et al.
State for Bar Exam: HI
Pass Rate for First-Time Bar: 85%

UNIVERSITY OF HOUSTON
Law Center

Admissions Contact: Assistant Dean for Admissions, Sondra R. Tennessee
100 Law Center, Houston, TX 77204-6060
Admissions Phone: 713-743-2280 • Admissions Fax: 713-743-2194
Admissions E-mail: admissions@www.law.uh.edu • Web Address: www.law.uh.edu

INSTITUTIONAL INFORMATION
Public/Private: Public
Student/Faculty Ratio: 16:1
Total Faculty: 124
% Part Time: 45
% Female: 32
% Minority: 9

PROGRAMS
Academic Specialties: Health Law, Corporate and Taxation, Energy Law and Enterprise, Trial Advocacy, Commercial Law, Environmental Law, Intellectual Property Law, International Law, Legal History
Advanced Degrees Offered: LLM (24 credits)
Combined Degrees Offered: JD/MBA (4 years), JD/MPH (3.5 years), JD/MA (4 years), JD/PhD (5 years), JD/MSW (4 years)
Grading System: A (4.00), A– (3.67), B+ (3.33), B (3.00), B– (2.67), C+ (2.33), C (2.00), C– (1.67), D+ (1.33), D (1.00), D– (0.67), F (0.00)
Clinical Program Required? No
Clinical Program Description: Family and Poverty Law Clinic, Criminal Defense, Criminal Prosecution, Health, Judicial, Environmental, Mediation Clinic, Transactional Clinic, Immigration Clinic
Legal Writing Course Requirements? Yes
Legal Writing Description: First-year, year-long course on legal research and writing includes small groups.
Legal Methods Course Requirements? Yes
Legal Methods Description: See Legal Writing.
Legal Research Course Requirements? Yes
Legal Research Description: See Legal Writing.
Moot Court Requirement? Yes
Moot Court Description: First-year students have a moot court competition.
Public Interest Law Requirement? No
Academic Journals: *Houston Law Review, Houston Business and Tax Law Journal, Houston Journal of Health Law and Policy, Houston Journal of International Law, Journal of Texas Consumer Law*

STUDENT INFORMATION
Enrollment of Law School: 1,028
% Out of State: 17
% Male/Female: 49/51
% Full Time: 80
% Full Time That Are International: 1
% Minority: 16
Average Age of Entering Class: 25

EXPENSES/FINANCIAL AID
Annual Tuition (Residents/Nonresidents): $7,440/$10,540
Room and Board (On/Off Campus): $5,538/$6,642
Books and Supplies: $900
Financial Aid Application Deadline: 4/1
Average Grant: $2,550
Average Loan: $14,493
% of Aid That Is Merit-Based: 18
% Receiving Some Sort of Aid: 73
Average Total Aid Package: $14,208
Average Debt: $43,481
Tuition Per Credit (Residents/Nonresidents): $240/$340
Fees Per Credit: $589

ADMISSIONS INFORMATION
Application Fee: $50
Regular Application Deadline: 2/15
Regular Notification: 5/15
LSDAS Accepted? Yes
Average GPA: 3.4
Range of GPA: 3.2–3.6
Average LSAT: 157
Range of LSAT: 154–160
Transfer Students Accepted? Yes
Other Schools to Which Students Applied: Baylor University, Southern Methodist University, Texas A&M University, Texas Tech University, University of Texas at Austin
Number of Applications Received: 3,040
Number of Applicants Accepted: 971
Number of Applicants Enrolled: 338

INTERNATIONAL STUDENTS
TOEFL Required of International Students? Yes
Minimum TOEFL: 600 (250 computer)

EMPLOYMENT INFORMATION

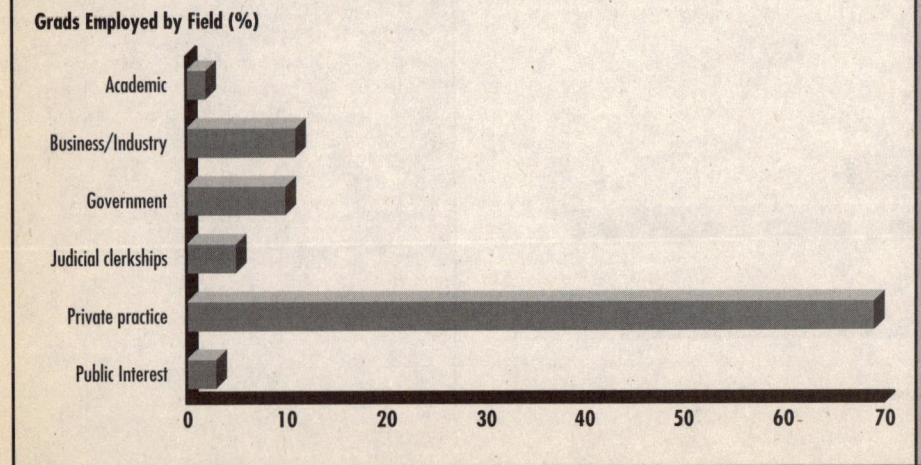

Grads Employed by Field (%):
- Academic: ~0
- Business/Industry: ~10
- Government: ~10
- Judicial clerkships: ~3
- Private practice: ~70
- Public Interest: ~3

Rate of Placement: 91%
Average Starting Salary: $76,418
Employers Who Frequently Hire Grads: Baker & Botts; Locke Liddel & Sapp; Fulbright & Jaworski; Vinson & Elkins; Bracewell & Patterson; Harris Co. D.A.; Weil Gotshal & Manges
Prominent Alumni: Richard Haynes, Litigation; John O'Quinn, Litigation; Clarence Bradford, Houston Police Chief; Star Jones, television personality; Charles Matthews, Vice President and General Counsel, ExxonMobil
State for Bar Exam: TX
Pass Rate for First-Time Bar: 90%

UNIVERSITY OF IDAHO
College of Law

Admissions Contact: Admissions Coordinator, Erick J. Larson
Sixth and Rayburn, Moscow, ID 83844-2321
Admissions Phone: 208-885-2300 • Admissions Fax: 208-885-5709
Admissions E-mail: lawadmit@uidaho.edu • Web Address: www.uidaho.edu/law

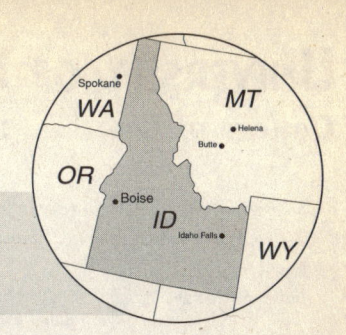

INSTITUTIONAL INFORMATION
Public/Private: Public
Student/Faculty Ratio: 16:1
Total Faculty: 26
% Female: 9

PROGRAMS
Academic Specialties: Business Law, Environmental and Natural Resource Law, Professional and Litigation Skills, Environmental Law
Combined Degrees Offered: JD/MS Environmental Science, JD/MA Business and Economics, JD/MBA with Washington State (all 4 years)
Grading System: Letter system on a 4.0 scale
Clinical Program Required? No
Clinical Program Description: Tax Clinic, Tribal Clinic, Appellate Clinic, General Clinic
Legal Writing Course Requirements? Yes
Legal Writing Description: 1 year for all first-year students
Legal Methods Course Requirements? Yes
Legal Methods Description: 1 year for all first-year students
Legal Research Course Requirements? Yes
Legal Research Description: 1 year for all first-year students
Moot Court Requirement? No
Public Interest Law Requirement? No
Academic Journals: *Law Review*

STUDENT INFORMATION
Enrollment of Law School: 320
% Out of State: 17
% Male/Female: 63/37
% Full Time: 100
% Full Time That Are International: 0
% Minority: 7
Average Age of Entering Class: 28

RESEARCH FACILITIES
School-Supported Research Centers: Legal Aid Clinic; External Program Office in Boise, Idaho

EXPENSES/FINANCIAL AID
Annual Tuition (Residents/Nonresidents): $5,984/$12,704
Room and Board (On/Off Campus): $6,550/$7,150
Books and Supplies: $1,188
Financial Aid Application Deadline: 2/15
Average Grant: $2,200
Average Loan: $10,000
% of Aid That Is Merit-Based: 20
% Receiving Some Sort of Aid: 99
Average Total Aid Package: $18,500
Average Debt: $42,000

ADMISSIONS INFORMATION
Application Fee: $40
Regular Application Deadline: 2/1
Regular Notification: 4/1
LSDAS Accepted? Yes
Average GPA: 3.4
Range of GPA: 3.2–3.7
Average LSAT: 153
Range of LSAT: 149–156
Transfer Students Accepted? Yes
Other Schools to Which Students Applied: Brigham Young University, Gonzaga University, University of Utah, Willamette University, Lewis and Clark College
Other Admissions Factors Considered: Personal statement, résumé, letters of recommendation, work experience
Number of Applications Received: 604
Number of Applicants Accepted: 286
Number of Applicants Enrolled: 114

INTERNATIONAL STUDENTS
TOEFL Required of International Students? Yes
Minimum TOEFL: 560 (280 computer)

EMPLOYMENT INFORMATION

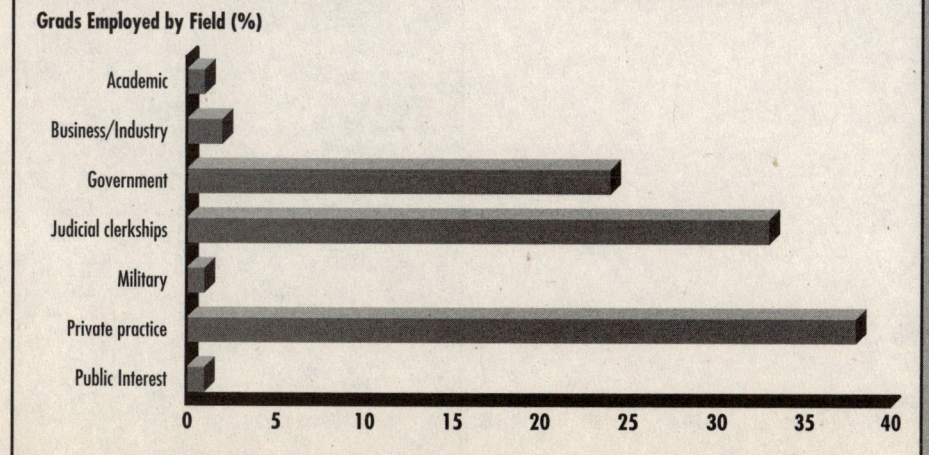

Grads Employed by Field (%)
- Academic
- Business/Industry
- Government
- Judicial clerkships
- Military
- Private practice
- Public Interest

Rate of Placement: 96%
Average Starting Salary: $42,301
Employers Who Frequently Hire Grads: Employers in Idaho, Washington, Oregon, and Utah
Prominent Alumni: Linda Copple Trout, Chief Justice, Idaho Supreme Court; Frank A. Shrontz, former CEO, Boeing Co.; Dennis E. Wheeler, President, Coeur: The Precious Metals Co.; James A. McClure, former U.S. Senator; James M. English, President, Idaho Forest Industries
State for Bar Exam: ID, WA, UT, OR, NV
Pass Rate for First-Time Bar: 70%

UNIVERSITY OF ILLINOIS
College of Law

Admissions Contact: Assistant Dean for Admissions and Financial Aid, Maggie D. Austin
504 East Pennsylvania Avenue, Champaign, IL 61820
Admissions Phone: 217-244-6415 • Admissions Fax: 217-244-1478
Admissions E-mail: admissions@law.uiuc.edu • Web Address: www.law.uiuc.edu

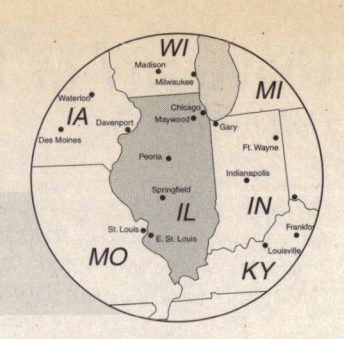

INSTITUTIONAL INFORMATION
Public/Private: Public
Student/Faculty Ratio: 14:1
Total Faculty: 75
% Part Time: 32
% Female: 36
% Minority: 12

PROGRAMS
Academic Specialties: Constitutional Law, Criminal Law, Intellectual Property, Professional Responsibility, International Law, Environmental Law, Property Law, Family Law, Civil Procedure, Commercial Law, Corporation Securities Law, Government Services, Human Rights Law, Labor Law, Legal History, Legal Philosophy, Taxation
Advanced Degrees Offered: JD (3 years), LLM (1 year)
Combined Degrees Offered: JD/MBA (4 years), JD/MA (4 years), JD/PhD, JD/DVM (6 years), JD/MD (6 years), JD/MUP (4 years), JD/MHRIR (4 years)
Grading System: Letter and numerical system on a 4.0 scale
Clinical Program Required? No
Clinical Program Description: Civil Clinic, International Human Rights Clinic, Appellate Defender Clinic
Legal Writing Course Requirements? Yes
Legal Writing Description: First-year students learn legal writing from full-time faculty. In the first semester, students learn objective writing; in the second semester, students learn to write as advocates. Both classes focus on research skills.

Legal Methods Course Requirements? No
Legal Research Course Requirements? Yes
Legal Research Description: Students learn research skills throughout their first year through hands-on training offered by full-time faculty and librarians. This is taught as a part of both the Legal Research and Writing and Introduction to Advocacy courses.
Moot Court Requirement? No
Moot Court Description: Second-year students can participate in and receive credit for many different internal moot court competitions, from constitutional law to intellectual property. Those who advance internally represent the college in regional and national competitions.
Public Interest Law Requirement? No
Academic Journals: *University of Illinois Law Review; The Elder Law Journal; Journal of Law, Techonology, and Policy; Illinois Law Update*

STUDENT INFORMATION
Enrollment of Law School: 674
% Out of State: 24
% Male/Female: 58/42
% Full Time: 100
% Minority: 26
Average Age of Entering Class: 24

RESEARCH FACILITIES
School-Supported Research Centers: Secure wireless access in the library

EXPENSES/FINANCIAL AID
Annual Tuition (Residents/Nonresidents): $11,310/$24,398
Room and Board: $8,200
Books and Supplies: $3,390
Financial Aid Application Deadline: 3/15
Average Grant: $4,300
Average Loan: $18,500
% of Aid That Is Merit-Based: 100
% Receiving Some Sort of Aid: 95
Average Total Aid Package: $24,412
Average Debt: $51,591

ADMISSIONS INFORMATION
Application Fee: $50
Regular Application Deadline: 3/15
Regular Notification: 1/1
LSDAS Accepted? Yes
Average GPA: 3.4
Range of GPA: 2.1–4.0
Average LSAT: 160
Range of LSAT: 144–178
Transfer Students Accepted? Yes
Other Schools to Which Students Applied: Northwestern, U. of Chicago, U. of Iowa, U. of Michigan, U. of Wisconsin, Washington University
Other Admissions Factors Considered: Graduate work in other fields, demonstrated leadership
Number of Applications Received: 2,418
Number of Applicants Accepted: 618
Number of Applicants Enrolled: 239

INTERNATIONAL STUDENTS
TOEFL Required of International Students? Yes
Minimum TOEFL: 600 (250 computer)

EMPLOYMENT INFORMATION

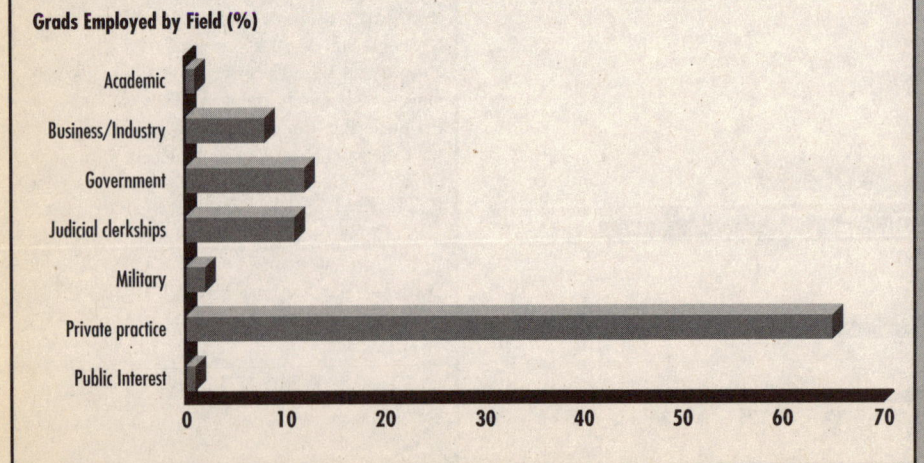

Grads Employed by Field (%)
- Academic
- Business/Industry
- Government
- Judicial clerkships
- Military
- Private practice
- Public Interest

Rate of Placement: 100%
Average Starting Salary: $78,529
Employers Who Frequently Hire Grads: Baker & McKenzie; Bell Boyd & Lloyd; Foley & Lardner; Gardner Carton & Douglas; Jenner & Block; Jones Day; Lord Bissell & Brook; Mayer Brown Rowe & Mau; Piper Rudnick; Sidley Austin Brown & Wood; Skadden Arps Slate Meagher & Flom; Sonnenschein Nath & Rosenthal; Winston & Strawn
State for Bar Exam: IL, CA, DC, NY, MO
Pass Rate for First-Time Bar: 94%

UNIVERSITY OF IOWA
College of Law

Admissions Contact: Admissions Coordinator, Jan Barnes
Melrose at Byington Streets, Iowa City, IA 52242
Admissions Phone: 319-335-9095 • Admissions Fax: 319-335-9019
Admissions E-mail: law-admissions@uiowa.edu • Web Address: www.law.uiowa.edu

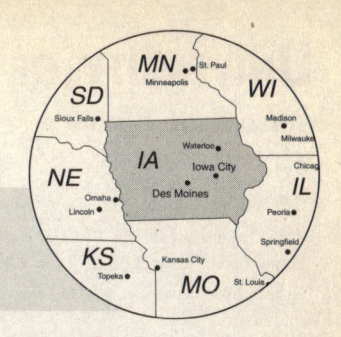

INSTITUTIONAL INFORMATION
Public/Private: Public
Student/Faculty Ratio: 11:1
Total Faculty: 50
% Part Time: 2
% Female: 26
% Minority: 15

PROGRAMS
Academic Specialties: We are renowned for our writing program, International Law, and other strengths. For a more complete description of our curriculum and to learn more about the academic specialties of our faculty, please visit our website.
Advanced Degrees Offered: LLM International and Comparative Law (24 credits plus thesis)
Combined Degrees Offered: JD/MBA, JD/MA, JD/MHA, JD/MSW (all 4 years)
Grading System: Letter and numerical system (55–90)
Clinical Program Required? No
Legal Writing Course Requirements? Yes
Legal Writing Description: In addition to 2 first-year small-section classes (during which students earn a total of 3 credits for research and writing under the direct supervision of a regular faculty member), all students must complete 5 upper-class writing credits, 2 of which must be faculty-supervised.
Legal Methods Course Requirements? Yes
Legal Research Course Requirements? Yes
Legal Research Description: At the beginning of the first year, our Legal Research training initiates students by means of 4 hourly sessions evenly divided between lecture and library exercises. Each student also completes a series of research and writing assignments and is trained in Westlaw and Lexis. An advanced Legal Research class is offered for credit.
Moot Court Requirement? Yes
Moot Court Description: All students participate in a for-credit appellate advocacy course, in which they write a brief and do an oral argument that is supervised and graded by a faculty member.
Public Interest Law Requirement? No
Academic Journals: Journal of Gender, Race and Justice; Journal of Corporation Law; Law Review; Transnational Law and Contemporary Problems Journal

STUDENT INFORMATION
Enrollment of Law School: 707
% Out of State: 37
% Male/Female: 53/47
% Full Time: 100
% Full Time That Are International: 2
% Minority: 15
Average Age of Entering Class: 24

RESEARCH FACILITIES
Research Resources Available: Iowa State Bar Association, Iowa Attorney General's Prosecution Intern Program, Iowa Bar Review School
School-Supported Research Centers: Iowa International and Comparative Law Program, Iowa Non-Profit Center, Disability Law and Policy Institute, Maternal and Child Health Resource Center, Iowa Center for Human Rights

EXPENSES/FINANCIAL AID
Annual Tuition (Residents/Nonresidents): $10,000/$23,758
Room and Board (Off Campus): $5,760
Books and Supplies: $1,440
Financial Aid Application Deadline: 1/1
Average Grant: $9,910
Average Loan: $19,065
% of Aid That Is Merit-Based: 6
% Receiving Some Sort of Aid: 97
Average Total Aid Package: $21,039
Average Debt: $51,436

ADMISSIONS INFORMATION
Application Fee: $30
Regular Application Deadline: 2/3
Regular Notification: Rolling
LSDAS Accepted? Yes
Average GPA: 3.5
Range of GPA: 3.3–3.8
Average LSAT: 159
Range of LSAT: 157–163
Transfer Students Accepted? Yes
Other Schools to Which Students Applied: George Washington, Indiana, UT Austin, U. of Illinois, U. of Minnesota, U. of Wisconsin, Washington University
Other Admissions Factors Considered: Letters of recommendation, extracurricular activities
Number of Applications Received: 1,832
Number of Applicants Accepted: 523
Number of Applicants Enrolled: 225

INTERNATIONAL STUDENTS
TOEFL Required of International Students? Yes
Minimum TOEFL: 580 (237 computer)

EMPLOYMENT INFORMATION

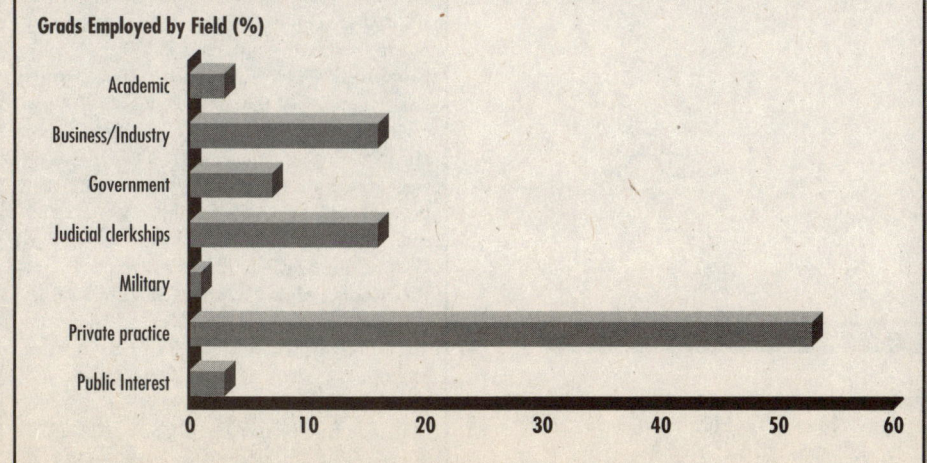

Grads Employed by Field (%)
- Academic
- Business/Industry
- Government
- Judicial clerkships
- Military
- Private practice
- Public Interest

Rate of Placement: 99%
Average Starting Salary: $53,000
Employers Who Frequently Hire Grads: National law firms, government agencies, state and federal judges
Prominent Alumni: Donald P. Lay, former Chief Judge, U.S. 8th Circuit Court of Appeals; James D. Ericson, President, Northwestern Mutual Life; John J. Bouma, Chairman, Snell & Wilmer; Ronald T. Moon, Chief Justice, Hawaii Supreme Court; Carol Havermann Lynch, Senior Tax Counsel, Exxon Co. USA
State for Bar Exam: IA
Pass Rate for First-Time Bar: 88%

UNIVERSITY OF KANSAS
School of Law

Admissions Contact: Assistant Dean of Admissions, Rachel Smith
1535 West 15th Street, Lawrence, KS 66045-7577
Admissions Phone: 785-864-4378 • Admissions Fax: 785-864-5054
Admissions E-mail: admitlaw@ku.edu • Web Address: www.law.ku.edu

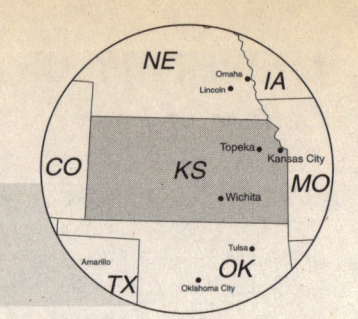

INSTITUTIONAL INFORMATION
Public/Private: Public
Student/Faculty Ratio: 16:1
Total Faculty: 70
% Part Time: 47
% Female: 38
% Minority: 14

PROGRAMS
Academic Specialties: Tax and Business Law, Family Law, Environmental/ Natural Resource Law, International Law, Agriculture Law, Media Law, Public Law, Litigation, Constitutional Law, Commercial Law, Corporation Securities Law, Criminal Law, Intellectual Property Law, Property
Advanced Degrees Offered: JD (26 months to 3 years)
Combined Degrees Offered: JD/MBA, JD/MA Economics or Philosophy, JD/MPA, JD/MSW, JD/MUP, JD/MHSA (all 4 years)
Grading System: Letter system, Credit/No Credit, Credit/F
Clinical Program Required? No
Clinical Program Description: Legal Aid Clinic, Judicial Clerkship Clinic, Criminal Justice Clinic, Defender Project, Elder Law Clinic, Public Policy Clinic, Legislative Clinic, Media Law Clinic
Legal Writing Course Requirements? Yes
Legal Writing Description: Lawyering is a 2-semester course required of all first-year students that teaches legal writing, motions drafting, and other practical skills. There is also an upper-level writing requirement.
Legal Methods Course Requirements? Yes
Legal Methods Description: See Legal Writing.
Legal Research Course Requirements? Yes
Legal Research Description: See Legal Writing.
Moot Court Requirement? No
Public Interest Law Requirement? No
Academic Journals: *Kansas Law Review, Kansas Journal of Law and Public Policy*

STUDENT INFORMATION
Enrollment of Law School: 539
% Out of State: 27
% Male/Female: 57/43
% Full Time: 100
% Full Time That Are International: 0
% Minority: 14
Average Age of Entering Class: 25

RESEARCH FACILITIES
School-Supported Research Centers: Wireless network

EXPENSES/FINANCIAL AID
Annual Tuition (Residents/Nonresidents): $7,630/$15,761
Room and Board: $6,546
Books and Supplies: $650
Financial Aid Application Deadline: 3/15
Average Grant: $8,500
Average Loan: $8,500
% of Aid That Is Merit-Based: 85
% Receiving Some Sort of Aid: 80
Average Total Aid Package: $18,500
Average Debt: $40,000

ADMISSIONS INFORMATION
Application Fee: $50
Regular Application Deadline: 3/15
Regular Notification: Rolling
LSDAS Accepted? Yes
Average GPA: 3.4
Range of GPA: 3.1–3.7
Average LSAT: 157
Range of LSAT: 154–160
Transfer Students Accepted? Yes
Other Schools to Which Students Applied: University of Texas at Austin, Tulane University, University of Denver, University of Missouri—Columbia, University of Missouri—Kansas City, University of Nebraska—Lincoln, Washburn University
Other Admissions Factors Considered: Ability to overcome cultural, financial, or other disadvantages; preference to Kansas residents
Number of Applications Received: 1,087
Number of Applicants Accepted: 428
Number of Applicants Enrolled: 201

INTERNATIONAL STUDENTS
TOEFL Required of International Students? Yes
Minimum TOEFL: 550

EMPLOYMENT INFORMATION

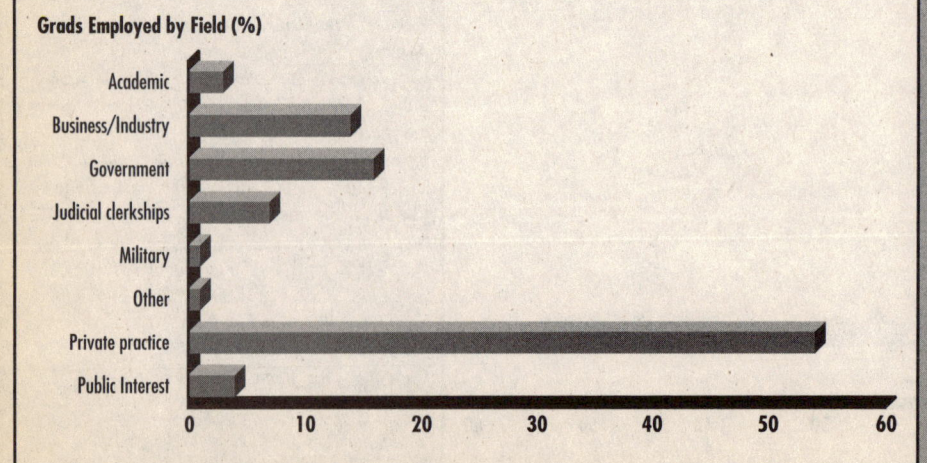

Grads Employed by Field (%)

Field	%
Academic	~2
Business/Industry	~15
Government	~16
Judicial clerkships	~5
Military	~1
Other	~2
Private practice	~55
Public Interest	~3

Rate of Placement: 95%
Average Starting Salary: $58,225
Employers Who Frequently Hire Grads: Baker Sterchi Cowden & Rice, Blackwell Sanders Peper Martin, Bryan Cave, Hinkle Elkouri, Husch & Eppenberger, Kutak Rock, Lathrop & Gage, Lewis Ric & Fingersh, McDonald Tinker, Polsinelli Shalton & Welte, Shook Hardy & Bacon, Shughart Thomson & Kilroy, Snell & Wilmer, Spencer Fane Britt & Browne
Prominent Alumni: Carla Stovall, Attorney General, Kansas; Sam Brownback, U.S. Senate; Mary Beck Briscoe, Judge, 10th Circuit; Jerry Moran, U.S. House of Representatives; Bill Hines, Dean, Iowa Law School
State for Bar Exam: KS, MO, CA, CO, TX

UNIVERSITY OF KENTUCKY
College of Law

Admissions Contact: Associate Dean, Drusilla V. Bakert
209 Law Building, Lexington, KY 40506-0048
Admissions Phone: 859-257-6770 • Admissions Fax: 859-323-1061
Admissions E-mail: dbakert@uky.edu • Web Address: www.uky.edu/law

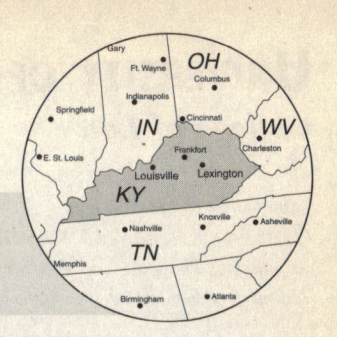

INSTITUTIONAL INFORMATION
Public/Private: Public
Student/Faculty Ratio: 14:1
Total Faculty: 29
% Part Time: 0
% Female: 30
% Minority: 7

PROGRAMS
Academic Specialties: Family Law, Fair Housing Law, Bankruptcy Law, White Collar Crime, Professional Responsibility, Civil Procedure, Commercial Law, Constitutional Law, Corporation Securities Law, Criminal Law, Environmental Law, Human Rights Law, Intellectual Property Law, International Law, Labor Law, Property, Taxation
Advanced Degrees Offered: JD
Combined Degrees Offered: JD/MPA, JD/MBA, JD/M Diplomacy and International Commerce (all 4 years)
Grading System: A to E (4.3–0.0); typical curve is 2.7 median for first-years, 2.8 for second- and third-years
Clinical Program Required? No
Clinical Program Description: UK Law Legal Clinic, Judicial Clerkship, Kentucky Innocence Project externship, prosecutorial externship, prison externship
Legal Writing Course Requirements? Yes
Legal Writing Description: Year-long, first-year course legal research and writing is taught in small groups of 10 to 12 students.
Legal Methods Course Requirements? No
Legal Research Course Requirements? Yes
Legal Research Description: See Legal Writing.
Moot Court Requirement? Yes
Moot Court Description: First-year legal research and writing. All students write and argue a brief before an appellate panel. Second- and third-year programs in moot court and trial advocacy are optional.
Public Interest Law Requirement? No
Academic Journals: Kentucky Law Journal, Journal of Natural Resources and Environmental Law

STUDENT INFORMATION
Enrollment of Law School: 398
% Out of State: 15
% Male/Female: 53/47
% Full Time: 100
% Full Time That Are International: 1
% Minority: 8
Average Age of Entering Class: 23

RESEARCH FACILITIES
Research Resources Available: Member of national law library consortium; access to state loan library and state library system
School-Supported Research Centers: New library has state-of-the-art resources available to law students and faculty; half of classrooms have wireless Internet access and laptop use; Law Library includes computer lab and laptops.

EXPENSES/FINANCIAL AID
Annual Tuition (Residents/Nonresidents): $6,580/$16,080
Room and Board: $8,100
Books and Supplies: $650
Financial Aid Application Deadline: 4/1
Average Grant: $3,000
Average Loan: $17,000
% of Aid That Is Merit-Based: 85
% Receiving Some Sort of Aid: 75
Average Total Aid Package: $20,000
Average Debt: $43,000

ADMISSIONS INFORMATION
Application Fee: $35
Regular Application Deadline: 3/1
Regular Notification: Rolling
LSDAS Accepted? Yes
Average GPA: 3.5
Range of GPA: 3.3–3.7
Average LSAT: 159
Range of LSAT: 156–161
Transfer Students Accepted? Yes
Other Schools to Which Students Applied: Indiana University, Northern Kentucky University, University of Cincinnati, University of Georgia, University of Louisville, University of Tennessee, Vanderbilt University
Other Admissions Factors Considered: Geographic, racial, or ethnic diversity; diversity of experience; success in career prior to law school
Number of Applications Received: 1,035
Number of Applicants Accepted: 349
Number of Applicants Enrolled: 141

INTERNATIONAL STUDENTS
TOEFL Required of International Students? Yes
Minimum TOEFL: 650 (280 computer)

EMPLOYMENT INFORMATION

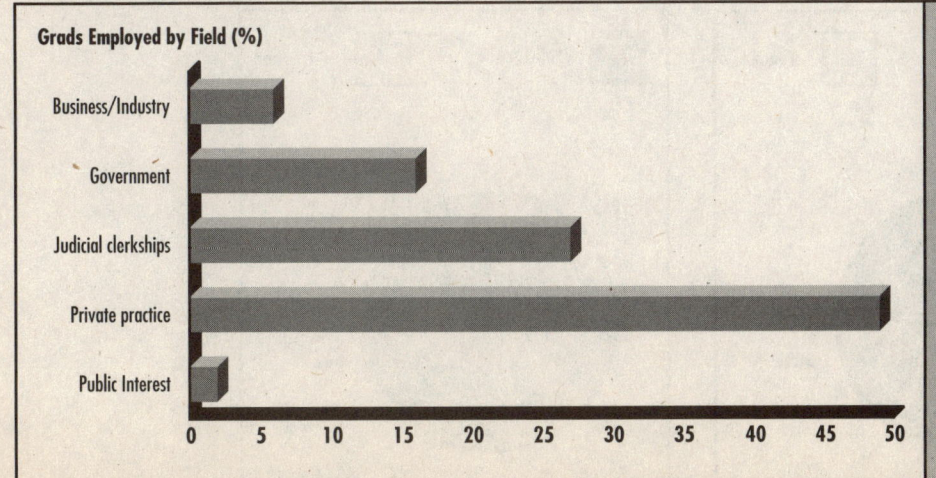

Grads Employed by Field (%)
- Business/Industry: ~6
- Government: ~16
- Judicial clerkships: ~27
- Private practice: ~48
- Public Interest: ~2

Rate of Placement: 99%
Average Starting Salary: $50,500
Employers Who Frequently Hire Grads: All Kentucky legal employers; major firms in Cincinnati, Nashville, West Virginia, DC, and Atlanta. Through job fairs, students also have access to employers nationwide, with the most popular locations being New York City, Chicago, California, Florida, Texas, and Arizona.
Prominent Alumni: Mitch McConnell, U.S. Senator; Hal Rodgers, U.S. Representative; Jim Rogers, CEO, Cinergy Corp; Steve Bright, National Public Interest Attorney; Ben Chandler, Kentucky Attorney General
State for Bar Exam: KY
Pass Rate for First-Time Bar: 92%

UNIVERSITY OF LA VERNE
College of Law

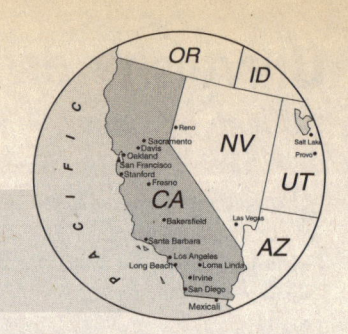

Admissions Contact: Director of Admissions, John Osborne
1950 3rd Street, La Verne, CA 91715
Admissions Phone: 909-596-1848 • Admissions Fax: 909-392-2707
Admissions E-mail: osborne@ulv.edu • Web Address: www.ulv.edu

INSTITUTIONAL INFORMATION
Public/Private: Private
Academic Calendar: Semester
Schedule: Full time or part time
Student/Faculty Ratio: 25:1

PROGRAMS
Advanced Degrees Offered: JD (3 years full time, 4 years part time)
Grading System: A to F
Clinical Program Required? No
Legal Writing/Methods Course Requirements: Legal Analysis, 2-unit class

STUDENT INFORMATION
Enrollment of Law School: 160
% Male/Female: 50/50
% Full Time: 50

EXPENSES/FINANCIAL AID
Books and Supplies: $1,500
Tuition Per Credit: $575

ADMISSIONS INFORMATION
Regular Application Deadline: 8/1
Transfer Students Accepted? Yes

EMPLOYMENT INFORMATION
Employers Who Frequently Hire Grads: County government and law firms

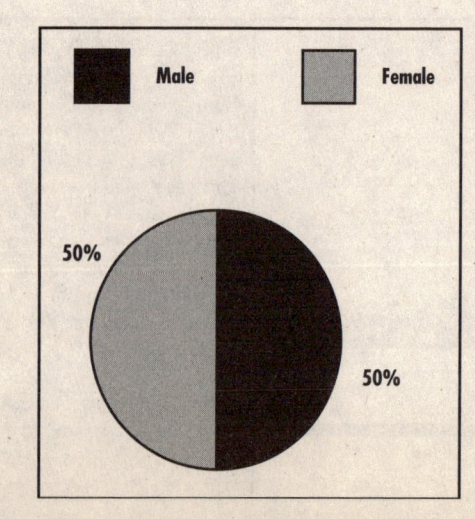

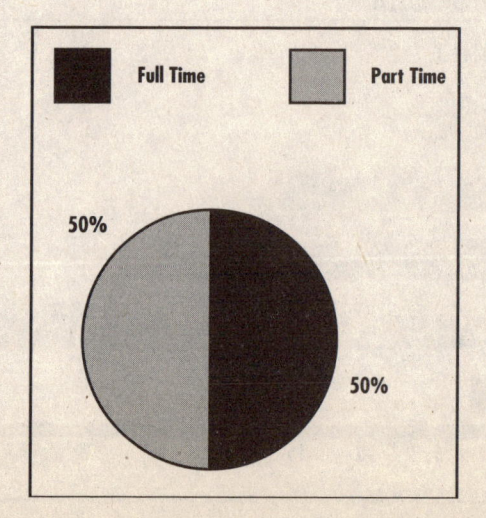

UNIVERSITY OF LOUISVILLE
Louis D. Brandeis School of Law

Admissions Contact: Assistant Dean for Admissions, Connie Shumake
Louisville, KY 40292
Admissions Phone: 502-852-6364 • Admissions Fax: 502-852-0862
Admissions E-mail: lawadmissions@louisville.edu • Web Address: www.louisville.edu/brandeislaw

INSTITUTIONAL INFORMATION
Public/Private: Public
Student/Faculty Ratio: 12:1
Total Faculty: 33
% Part Time: 19
% Female: 36
% Minority: 15

PROGRAMS
Academic Specialties: Commercial Law, Corporation Securities Law, Criminal Law, Government Services, International Law, Labor Law, Taxation
Advanced Degrees Offered: JD (3 years full time, 4 years part time)
Combined Degrees Offered: JD/MBA, JD/MSW, JD/MDiv, JD/MA Humanities (4 to 5 years)
Grading System: 4.0 scale
Clinical Program Required? Yes
Clinical Program Description: Public Service Program, 6 externship programs
Legal Writing Course Requirements? Yes
Legal Writing Description: Basic Legal Skill Writing (3 credits in the first year)
Legal Methods Course Requirements? Yes
Legal Methods Description: See Legal Writing.
Legal Research Course Requirements? Yes
Legal Research Description: Research and Writing (1 credit in the first semester)
Moot Court Requirement? Yes
Moot Court Description: Basic Legal Skills, second semester, oral arguments

Public Interest Law Requirement? Yes
Public Interest Law Description: 30 hours of public service
Academic Journals: Brandeis Law Journal, Journal of Law and Education

STUDENT INFORMATION
Enrollment of Law School: 383
% Out of State: 18
% Male/Female: 52/48
% Full Time: 73
% Full Time That Are International: 2
% Minority: 9

RESEARCH FACILITIES
Research Resources Available: Westlaw, Lexis/Nexis, CALI, Kentucky Commonwealth Virtual University

EXPENSES/FINANCIAL AID
Annual Tuition (Residents/Nonresidents): $6,882/$17,710
Room and Board: $10,030
Books and Supplies: $854
Financial Aid Application Deadline: 6/1
Average Grant: $3,000
Average Loan: $15,000
% of Aid That Is Merit-Based: 20
% Receiving Some Sort of Aid: 79
Average Total Aid Package: $18,000
Average Debt: $42,000
Tuition Per Credit (Residents/Nonresidents): $292/$744

ADMISSIONS INFORMATION
Application Fee: $40
Regular Application Deadline: 5/15
Regular Notification: Rolling
LSDAS Accepted? Yes
Average GPA: 3.3
Range of GPA: 3.0–3.7
Average LSAT: 156
Range of LSAT: 152–159
Transfer Students Accepted? Yes
Other Schools to Which Students Applied: University of Cincinnati, Northern Kentucky University, University of Memphis, University of Dayton, University of Kentucky, University of Tennessee, Vanderbilt University
Other Admissions Factors Considered: Academic improvement, overcoming adversity, diversity factors, community service
Number of Applications Received: 796
Number of Applicants Accepted: 271
Number of Applicants Enrolled: 129

EMPLOYMENT INFORMATION

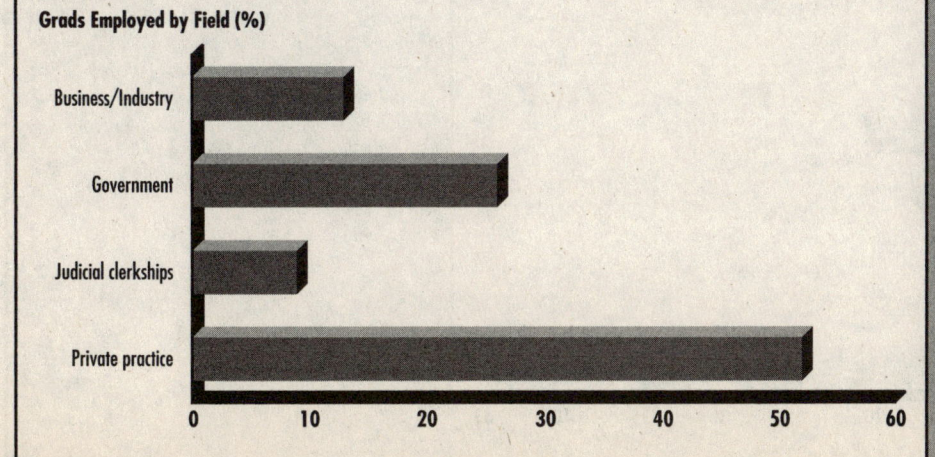

Grads Employed by Field (%)

Field	%
Business/Industry	~13
Government	~27
Judicial clerkships	~8
Private practice	~52

Rate of Placement: 95%
Average Starting Salary: $40,000
Employers Who Frequently Hire Grads: Frost, Brown & Todd; Dinsmore & Shohl; Greenebaum, Doll & McDonald; Wyatt, Tarrant & Combs
Prominent Alumni: Chris Dodd, U.S. Senator; Ron Mazzoli, former U.S. Congressman; Joseph Lambert, Chief Justice, Kentucky; Stanley Chauvin, former President, ABA; Ernie Allen, Director, National Center for Missing and Exploited Children
State for Bar Exam: KY, IN, FL, TN, DC
Pass Rate for First-Time Bar: 83%

UNIVERSITY OF MAINE
School of Law

Admissions Contact: Admissions Coordinator, Rebecca Warsinsky
246 Deering Avenue, Portland, ME 04102
Admissions Phone: 207-780-4341 • Admissions Fax: 207-780-4239
Admissions E-mail: mainelaw@usm.maine.edu • Web Address: www.law.usm.maine.edu

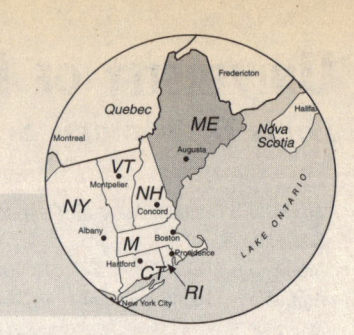

INSTITUTIONAL INFORMATION
Public/Private: Public
Student/Faculty Ratio: 15:1
Total Faculty: 16
% Female: 38
% Minority: 0

PROGRAMS
Advanced Degrees Offered: JD (3 years)
Combined Degrees Offered: JD/MA Community Planning and Development, Health Policy Management, or Public Policy and Management
Grading System: Letter system
Clinical Program Required? No
Clinical Program Description: General Practice Clinic, Criminal Law Clinic, Family Law Clinic, Environmental Law Clinic
Legal Writing Course Requirements? Yes
Legal Writing Description: First-year research and writing course
Legal Methods Course Requirements? Yes
Legal Methods Description: 3 credits in the first semester, 2 credits in the second semester
Legal Research Course Requirements? No
Legal Research Description: Includes research, writing, and moot court
Moot Court Requirement? Yes
Moot Court Description: All students do a moot court brief and oral argument as part of the first-year legal writing course.
Public Interest Law Requirement? No
Academic Journals: *Maine Law Review, Ocean and Coastal Law Journal*

STUDENT INFORMATION
Enrollment of Law School: 243
% Out of State: 27
% Male/Female: 54/46
% Full Time: 97
% Minority: 4
Average Age of Entering Class: 29

RESEARCH FACILITIES
Research Resources Available: Westlaw, Lexis
School-Supported Research Centers: Computer lab

EXPENSES/FINANCIAL AID
Annual Tuition (Residents/Nonresidents): $9,900/$17,790
Room and Board: $8,670
Books and Supplies: $1,050
Average Grant: $3,412
Average Loan: $17,932
% of Aid That Is Merit-Based: 20
% Receiving Some Sort of Aid: 85
Average Debt: $53,598
Tuition Per Credit (Residents/Nonresidents): $333/$593

ADMISSIONS INFORMATION
Application Fee: $50
Regular Application Deadline: 3/1
Regular Notification: Rolling
LSDAS Accepted? Yes
Average GPA: 3.1
Range of GPA: 2.9–3.5
Average LSAT: 155
Range of LSAT: 150–158
Transfer Students Accepted? Yes
Other Admissions Factors Considered: Academic record, difficulty of courses taken, undergraduate institution, professional background
Number of Applications Received: 568
Number of Applicants Accepted: 280
Number of Applicants Enrolled: 80

INTERNATIONAL STUDENTS
TOEFL Required of International Students? Yes

EMPLOYMENT INFORMATION

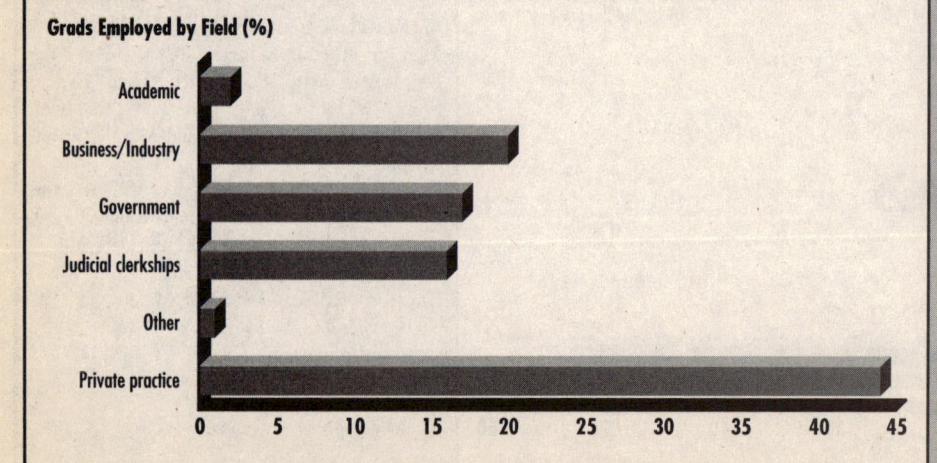

Grads Employed by Field (%)
- Academic: ~1
- Business/Industry: ~20
- Government: ~17
- Judicial clerkships: ~17
- Other: ~1
- Private practice: ~44

Rate of Placement: 84%
Average Starting Salary: $48,263
Employers Who Frequently Hire Grads: Maine/New England law firms and corporations; federal/state government; federal/state courts
State for Bar Exam: ME, MA
Pass Rate for First-Time Bar: 80%

UNIVERSITY OF MARYLAND
School of Law

Admissions Contact: Director of Admissions, Patricia Scott
500 West Baltimore Street, Baltimore, MD 21201
Admissions Phone: 410-706-3492 • Admissions Fax: 410-706-1793
Admissions E-mail: admissions@law.umaryland.edu • Web Address: www.law.umaryland.edu

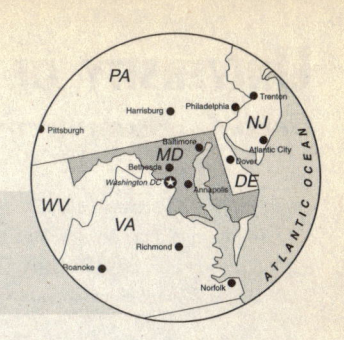

INSTITUTIONAL INFORMATION
Public/Private: Public
Student/Faculty Ratio: 12:1
Total Faculty: 150
% Part Time: 63
% Female: 37
% Minority: 15

PROGRAMS
Academic Specialties: Health Care Law, Environmental Law, International and Comparative Law, Business and Intellectual Property Law, Trial and Appellate Advocacy, Alternative Dispute Resolution, Constitutional Law, Corporation Securities Law, Criminal Law, Environmental Law, Taxation
Advanced Degrees Offered: JD (3 years full time, 4 years part time)
Combined Degrees Offered: JD/PhD Policy Sciences (7 years), JD/MA Policy Sciences (4 years), JD/MBA (4 years), JD/MA Public Management (4 years), JD/MA Criminal Justice (3.5 to 4 years), JD/MSW (3.5 to 4 years), JD/MA Liberal Education (4 years), JD/MA Applied and Professional Ethics (4 years), JD/MA Community Planning (4 years), JD/PharmD (7 years)
Grading System: Letter and numerical system on a 4.3 scale, Credit/No Credit
Clinical Program Required? Yes
Clinical Program Description: Access to Justice; Appellate Advocacy; Civil Rights of Persons with Disabilities; Civil Rights—Racial and Ethnic Discrimination; Community Law in Action; Drug Policy; Economic, Housing, and Community Development; Environmental Law; General Practice Clinic; and several others.

EMPLOYMENT INFORMATION

Grads Employed by Field (%)

Legal Writing Description: 3 semesters of Legal Analysis, Research, and Writing (LAWR) and Advanced Legal Research are required.
Legal Methods Description: See Legal Writing.
Legal Research Description: See Legal Writing.
Moot Court Description: The Moot Court requirement is met in LAWR III. Students are selected for Moot Court Board in second or third year.
Public Interest Law Description: Students enrolling in the first-year full-time day program must take and pass one of the designated Cardin Program courses.
Academic Journals: *The Business Lawyer, The Journal of Health Care Law and Policy, MARGINS, Maryland Law Review*

STUDENT INFORMATION
Enrollment of Law School: 841
% Out of State: 33
% Male/Female: 43/57
% Full Time: 74
% Full Time That Are International: 1
% Minority: 21
Average Age of Entering Class: 28

RESEARCH FACILITIES
Research Resources Available: Civil Justice Network; Community Law in Action
School-Supported Research Centers: Legal Resource Center for Tobacco Regulation, Litigation, and Advocacy; Maryland Intellectual Property Legal Resource Center; Center for Dispute Resolution; Women, Leadership and Equality Program; Technology Assisted Learning Center; Writing Center

EXPENSES/FINANCIAL AID
Annual Tuition (Residents/Nonresidents): $11,547/$22,289

Room and Board (On/Off Campus): $13,210/$17,216
Books and Supplies: $1,500
Financial Aid Application Deadline: 3/1
Average Grant: $4,300
Average Loan: $19,593
% of Aid That Is Merit-Based: 1
% Receiving Some Sort of Aid: 75
Average Total Aid Package: $21,500
Average Debt: $67,179
Tuition Per Credit (Res./Nonres.): $429/$832
Fees Per Credit: $216

ADMISSIONS INFORMATION
Application Fee: $60
Regular Application Deadline: Rolling
Regular Notification: Rolling
LSDAS Accepted? Yes
Average GPA: 3.5
Average LSAT: 159
Transfer Students Accepted? Yes
Other Schools to Which Students Applied: American, George Mason, George Washington, Georgetown, U. of Baltimore
Other Admissions Factors Considered: Geographic origin; language, cultural, social, disability, and economic barriers overcome; interpersonal skills; extracurricular activities; work or service experience; leadership record; potential for service to the institution
Number of Applications Received: 4,916
Number of Applicants Accepted: 619
Number of Applicants Enrolled: 221

INTERNATIONAL STUDENTS
Minimum TOEFL: 600 (250 computer)

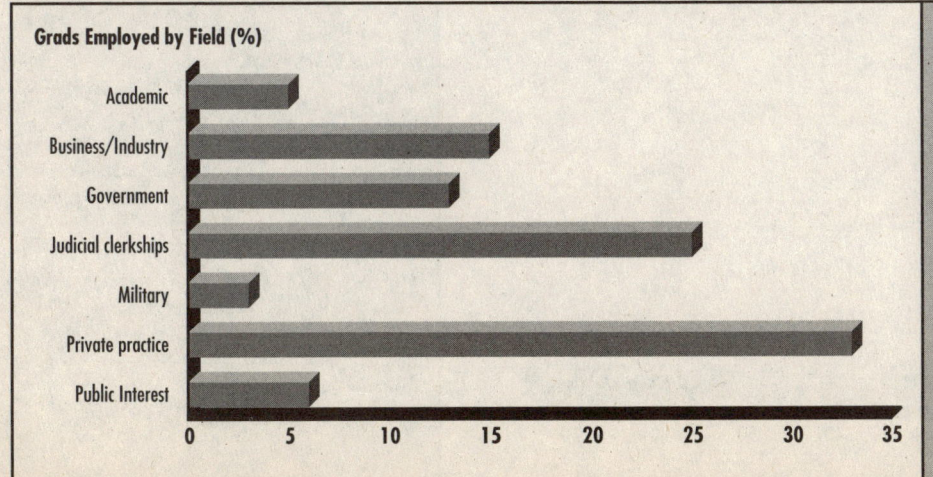

Rate of Placement: 97%
Average Starting Salary: $54,708
Employers Who Frequently Hire Grads: U.S. Department of Justice; Dickstein, Shapiro & Morin, LLP; Environmental Protection Agency; Miles & Stockbridge; Ober, Kaler, Grimes & Shriver; Piper, Marbury, Rudnick & Wolfe, LLP; Public Defender's Office; State of Maryland, Attorney General's Office; Venable, Baetjer and Howard, LLP; Whiteford, Taylor & Preston, LLP
Prominent Alumni: Christine A. Edwards, Chief Legal Officer and Secretary, Bank One Corp.; Benjamin R. Civiletti, former U.S. Attorney General; Alvin Krongard, Executive Director, CIA
State for Bar Exam: MD
Pass Rate for First-Time Bar: 86%

UNIVERSITY OF MEMPHIS
Cecil C. Humphreys School of Law

Admissions Contact: Assistant Dean for Admissions, Dr. Sue Ann McClellan
207 Humphreys Law School, Memphis, TN 38152–3140
Admissions Phone: 901-678-5403 • Admissions Fax: 901-678-5210
Admissions E-mail: lawadmissions@mail.law.memphis.edu • Web Address: www.law.memphis.edu

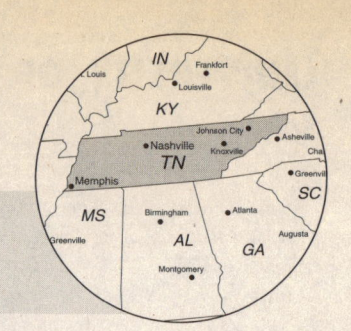

INSTITUTIONAL INFORMATION
Public/Private: Public
Student/Faculty Ratio: 23:1
Total Faculty: 57
% Part Time: 54
% Female: 32
% Minority: 9

PROGRAMS
Academic Specialties: The curriculum is designed to prepare students for general practice in civil and criminal matters, and contains numerous required courses that expose students to all major facets of the practice of law. Specialties include Civil Procedure, Commercial Law, Constitutional Law, Corporation Securities Law, Criminal Law, Environmental Law, Intellectual Property Law, International Law, Labor Law, Legal History, Property, and Taxation.
Advanced Degrees Offered: JD (6 semesters)
Combined Degrees Offered: JD/MBA (4 years)
Grading System: Letter system, Excellent, Satisfactory, Unsatisfactory. A grade of D or better is passing; below D is failing; below C is unsatisfactory.
Clinical Program Required? No
Clinical Program Description: Civil Litigation, Child Advocacy, Elder Law, Domestic Violence, General Sessions
Legal Writing Course Requirements? No
Legal Methods Course Requirements? Yes
Legal Methods Description: 3 credits in the first year
Legal Research Course Requirements? Yes
Legal Research Description: Upper-class research requirement
Moot Court Requirement? No
Public Interest Law Requirement? No
Academic Journals: The University of Memphis Law Review, The Tennessee Journal of Practice and Procedure

STUDENT INFORMATION
Enrollment of Law School: 480
% Out of State: 14
% Male/Female: 54/46
% Full Time: 93
% Full Time That Are International: 6
% Minority: 13
Average Age of Entering Class: 25

RESEARCH FACILITIES
Research Resources Available: Interlibrary loan programs with other law schools
School-Supported Research Centers: Law Library, Student Computer Lab; all Tiger LAN labs located on the university campus

EXPENSES/FINANCIAL AID
Annual Tuition (Residents/Nonresidents): $6,740/$18,840
Room and Board: $6,570
Books and Supplies: $1,300
Financial Aid Application Deadline: 4/1
Average Grant: $6,069
Average Loan: $16,543
% of Aid That Is Merit-Based: 38
% Receiving Some Sort of Aid: 72
Average Total Aid Package: $18,424
Average Debt: $47,797
Tuition Per Credit (Residents/Nonresidents): $331/$881

ADMISSIONS INFORMATION
Application Fee: $25
Regular Application Deadline: 2/15
Regular Notification: 4/15
LSDAS Accepted? Yes
Average GPA: 3.3
Range of GPA: 3.0–3.6
Average LSAT: 153
Range of LSAT: 151–156
Transfer Students Accepted? Yes
Other Schools to Which Students Applied: Florida State University, Georgia State University, Mercer University, Samford University, University of Mississippi, University of Tennessee, Vanderbilt University
Number of Applications Received: 984
Number of Applicants Accepted: 355
Number of Applicants Enrolled: 184

INTERNATIONAL STUDENTS
TOEFL Required of International Students? Yes
Minimum TOEFL: 600 (263 computer)

EMPLOYMENT INFORMATION

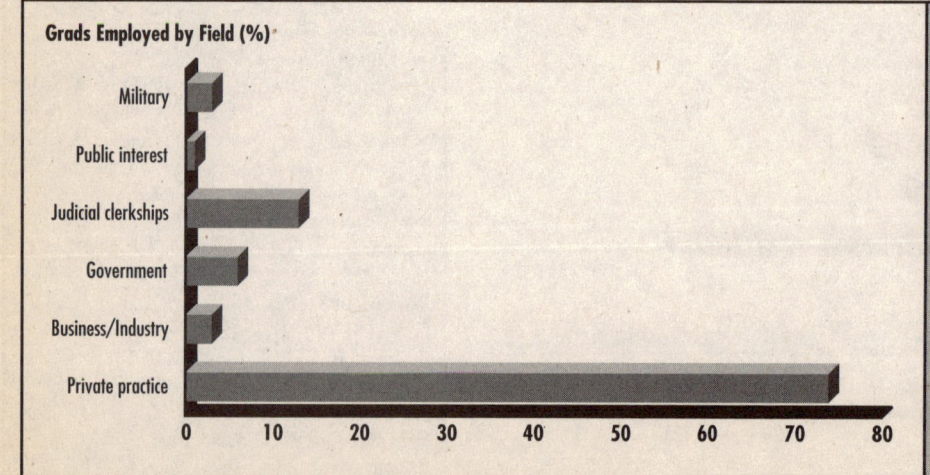

Grads Employed by Field (%)
- Military
- Public interest
- Judicial clerkships
- Government
- Business/Industry
- Private practice

Rate of Placement: 95%
Average Starting Salary: $42,000
Employers Who Frequently Hire Grads: Major area and regional law firms, Tennessee Attorney General, Public Defender's office, Tennessee Supreme Court and Court of Appeals, major area corporate legal departments, city and county government
Prominent Alumni: John Wilder, Speaker of the Tennessee House, State of Tennessee; Bernice Donald, Judge, U.S. District Court; Jere Glover, Chief Counsel, U.S. Small Business Administration
State for Bar Exam: TN
Pass Rate for First-Time Bar: 92%

UNIVERSITY OF MIAMI
School of Law

Admissions Contact: Director of Student Recruiting, Therese Lambert
PO Box 248087, Coral Gables, FL 33124-8087
Admissions Phone: 305-284-6746 • Admissions Fax: 305-284-3084
Admissions E-mail: admissions@law.miami.edu • Web Address: www.law.miami.edu

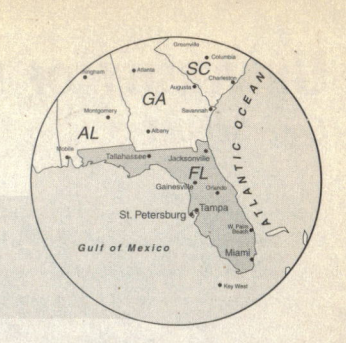

INSTITUTIONAL INFORMATION
Public/Private: Private
Student/Faculty Ratio: 16:1
Total Faculty: 76
% Part Time: 24
% Female: 38
% Minority: 16

PROGRAMS
Academic Specialties: Known for being exceptionally strong in International Law (we currently offer three courses taught in Spanish), Entertainment and Sports Law, Computer Law, Estate Planning, Public Interest, Taxation and Litigation Skills, Civil Procedure, Commercial Law, Constitutional Law, Corporation Securities Law, Criminal Law, Environmental Law, Human Rights Law, Labor Law, Legal History, Legal Philosophy, Property
Advanced Degrees Offered: LLM (1 year full time)
Combined Degrees Offered: JD/MBA, JD/MPH, JD/MS Marine Affairs (all 3.5 years)
Grading System: Letter system; some courses are Pass/Fail
Clinical Program Required? No
Clinical Program Description: Clinical Placement Program
Legal Writing Course Requirements? Yes
Legal Writing Description: Legal Research and Writing is a required first-year course in both the fall and spring semesters. Students are assigned to writing instructors who work with students in small groups of approximately 20 students. The instructors guide the students in developing a strong grounding in legal writing, analysis, research, and oral advocacy.
Legal Methods Course Requirements? Yes
Legal Methods Description: In addition to the required first-year course, we offer an advanced legal writing course and several sections of advanced legal research.
Legal Research Course Requirements? Yes
Legal Research Description: See Legal Writing.
Moot Court Requirement? Yes
Moot Court Description: In the second semester of Legal Research and Writing, students concentrate on brief writing and preparing for a moot court argument. Optional moot court is offered through competitions sponsored by the Moot Court Board, which hosts competitions in moot court, mock trial, client counseling, and negotiation.
Public Interest Law Requirement? No
Academic Journals: *University of Miami Law Review, University of Miami Inter-American Law Review, Business Law Journal, International and Comparative Law Review, Tax Law Chronicle, Amicus Curiae, The Hearsay*

STUDENT INFORMATION
Enrollment of Law School: 1,168
% Male/Female: 51/49
% Full Time: 94
% Full Time That Are International: 6
% Minority: 26
Average Age of Entering Class: 24

EXPENSES/FINANCIAL AID
Annual Tuition: $26,070
Room and Board: $9,547
Books and Supplies: $1,000
Financial Aid Application Deadline: 3/1
Average Grant: $14,630
Average Loan: $27,439
% of Aid That Is Merit-Based: 19
% Receiving Some Sort of Aid: 80
Average Total Aid Package: $31,053
Average Debt: $73,915
Tuition Per Credit: $1,138

ADMISSIONS INFORMATION
Application Fee: $50
Regular Application Deadline: 7/31
Regular Notification: Rolling
LSDAS Accepted? Yes
Average GPA: 3.4
Range of GPA: 3.2–3.6
Average LSAT: 155
Range of LSAT: 153–158
Transfer Students Accepted? Yes
Other Schools to Which Students Applied: Nova Southeastern University, Stetson University, Tulane University, University of Florida, American University, Florida State University, George Washington University
Other Admissions Factors Considered: Undergraduate institution and major, LSAT writing sample, pattern and trend of grades, work and internship experience, graduate work, diversity
Number of Applications Received: 4,170
Number of Applicants Accepted: 1,597
Number of Applicants Enrolled: 435

INTERNATIONAL STUDENTS
TOEFL Required of International Students? Yes
Minimum TOEFL: 600 (250 computer)

EMPLOYMENT INFORMATION

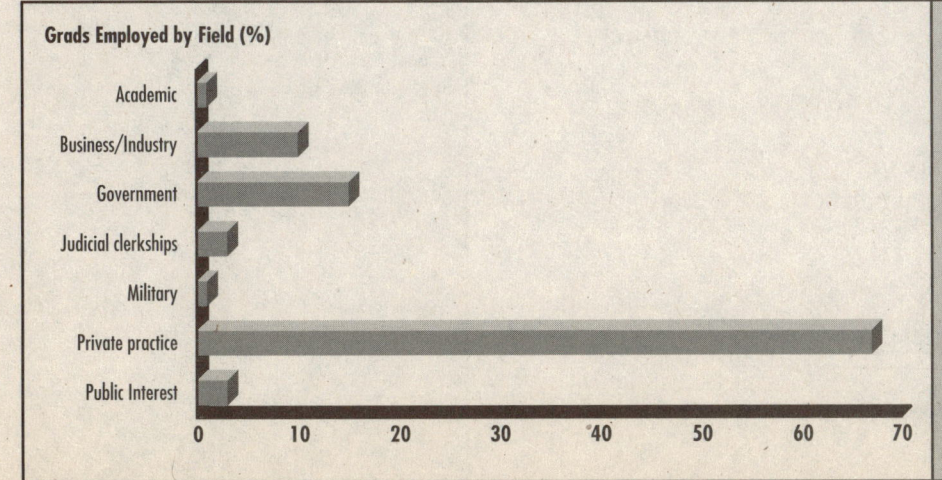

Grads Employed by Field (%)

Field	%
Academic	~1
Business/Industry	~10
Government	~15
Judicial clerkships	~3
Military	~1
Private practice	~68
Public Interest	~2

Rate of Placement: 90%
Average Starting Salary: $72,277
Employers Who Frequently Hire Grads: Holland & Knight; Greenberg Traurig; Hunton & Williams; Steel, Hector and Davis; White & Case; Weil, Gotshal & Manges; Morgan Lewis & Bockius; Carlton, Fields; Shutts & Bowen; Ruden McClosky; Gunster Yoakley; McDermott, Will & Emery; Stearns Weaver
Prominent Alumni: Patricia Ireland, former President of NOW; Alex Pinelas, Mayor of Miami Dade County; Roy Black, prominent criminal defense attorney and legal expert; Joseph P. Klock, managing partner and noted trial attorney; Hon. Gerald Kogan, former Florida Supreme Court Justice, legal scholar
State for Bar Exam: FL, NY, GA, IL, NC
Pass Rate for First-Time Bar: 85%

UNIVERSITY OF MICHIGAN
Law School

Admissions Contact: Assistant Dean and Director of Admissions, Sarah C. Zearfoss
726 Oakland Avenue, Ann Arbor, MI 48104-3031
Admissions Phone: 734-764-0537 • Admissions Fax: 734-647-3218
Admissions E-mail: law.jd.admissions@umich.edu • Web Address: www.law.umich.edu

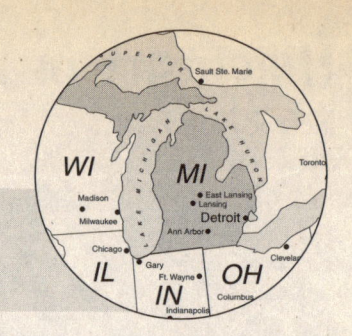

INSTITUTIONAL INFORMATION
Public/Private: Public
Student/Faculty Ratio: 14:1
Total Faculty: 127
% Part Time: 28
% Female: 30
% Minority: 7

PROGRAMS
Academic Specialties: Strong interdisciplinary legal scholarship and teaching; diverse clinical offerings, including several litigation clinics, an appellate clinic, and a transactional clinic; Civil Procedure; Commercial Law; Constitutional Law; Corporation Securities Law; Criminal Law; Environmental Law; Government Services; Human Rights Law; Intellectual Property Law; International Law; Labor Law; Legal History; Legal Philosophy; Property; Taxation
Advanced Degrees Offered: LLM, MCL, SJD
Combined Degrees Offered: JD/MBA (4 years), JD/PhD Economics (5 years), JD/MA Modern Middle Eastern and North African Studies (3.5 to 4 years), JD/MPP (4 years), JD/MS Natural Resources (4 years), JD/MHSA (9 semesters), JD/MA Russian and East European Studies (3.5 years), JD/MA World Politics (3.5 years), JD/MSW (8 semesters), JD/MSI (8 semesters), JD/MPH (8 semesters), JD/MA Japanese Studies (3.5 years), JD/MUP (8 semesters)
Clinical Program Required? No
Clinical Program Description: General Clinic (civil or criminal concentration), Child Advocacy Law Clinic, Legal Assistance for Urban Communities Program, Environmental Law Clinic, Criminal Appellate Practice Clinic, student-run advocacy programs
Legal Writing Course Requirements? Yes
Legal Writing Description: Legal Practice Program provides first-year students with individual instruction in legal research and analysis, persuasive legal writing, and oral advocacy. Students are assigned to a full-time Legal Practice professor.
Legal Methods Course Requirements? Yes
Legal Methods Description: See Legal Writing.
Legal Research Course Requirements? Yes
Legal Research Description: See Legal Writing.
Moot Court Requirement? No
Public Interest Law Requirement? No
Academic Journals: *Michigan Law Review, Michigan Journal of Law Reform, Michigan Journal of International Law, Michigan Journal of Gender and Law, Michigan Journal of Race and Law, Michigan Telecommunications and Technology Law Review*

STUDENT INFORMATION
Enrollment of Law School: 1,109
% Male/Female: 58/42
% Full Time: 100
% Full Time That Are International: 0
% Minority: 22
Average Age of Entering Class: 23

RESEARCH FACILITIES
School-Supported Research Centers: The Law School has one of the largest wireless Ethernet networks on campus, supporting Law School students, faculty, and staff with network access through multiple stationary access. Power outlets are available throughout the Law School's classrooms. Internet services are provided during exams and as special teaching aids when requested by the professor.

EXPENSES/FINANCIAL AID
Annual Tuition (Residents/Nonresidents): $24,806/$30,806
Room and Board: $8,500
Books and Supplies: $846
Average Grant: $9,899
Average Loan: $23,560
% of Aid That Is Merit-Based: 25
% Receiving Some Sort of Aid: 93
Average Total Aid Package: $32,504
Average Debt: $75,744

ADMISSIONS INFORMATION
Application Fee: $60
Regular Application Deadline: 2/15
Regular Notification: Rolling
LSDAS Accepted? Yes
Average GPA: 3.6
Range of GPA: 3.4–3.8
Average LSAT: 166
Range of LSAT: 163–168
Transfer Students Accepted? Yes
Other Schools to Which Students Applied: Columbia University; Georgetown University; Harvard University; New York University; University of California, Berkeley; University of Chicago; Yale University
Number of Applications Received: 5,243
Number of Applicants Accepted: 1,122
Number of Applicants Enrolled: 352

EMPLOYMENT INFORMATION

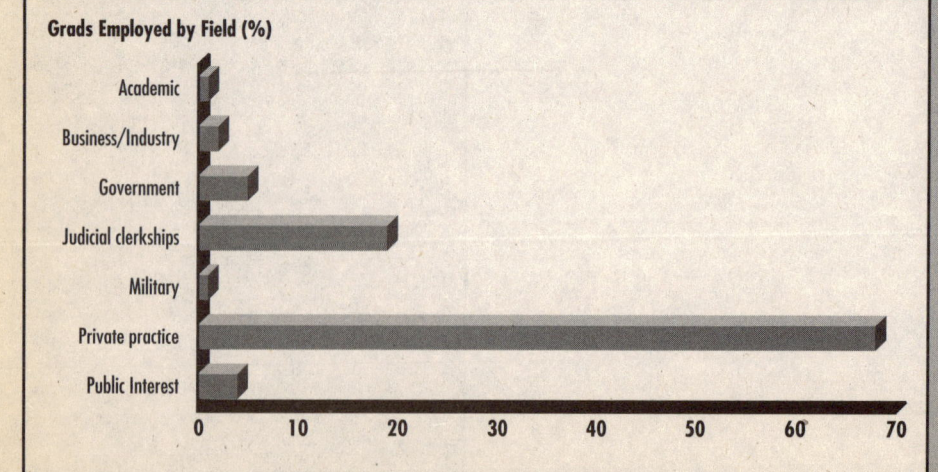

Grads Employed by Field (%)

Field	%
Academic	~2
Business/Industry	~2
Government	~3
Judicial clerkships	~18
Military	~0
Private practice	~68
Public Interest	~3

Rate of Placement: 98%
Average Starting Salary: $125,000
State for Bar Exam: NY, IL, CA, MI, MA

UNIVERSITY OF MINNESOTA
Law School

Admissions Contact: Director of Admissions, Collins B. Byrd, Jr.
229 19th Avenue South, Minneapolis, MN 55455
Admissions Phone: 612-625-5005 • Admissions Fax: 612-625-2011
Admissions E-mail: umnlsadm@tc.umn.edu • Web Address: www.law.umn.edu

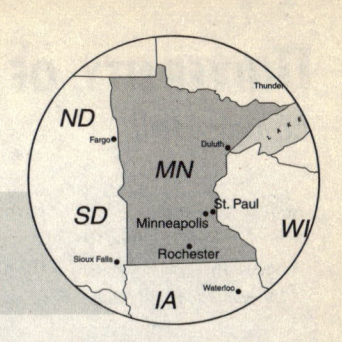

INSTITUTIONAL INFORMATION
Public/Private: Public
Environment: Urban
Academic Calendar: Semester
Schedule: Full time only
Student/Faculty Ratio: 16:1
Total Faculty: 44
% Part Time: 100
% Female: 30
% Minority: 11

PROGRAMS
Academic Specialties: Public Law, Public and Private International Law, Constitutional Law, Criminal Law, Corporate and Business Law, Regulatory Law, Legislation, Human Rights Law, Legal Philosophy, Law Clinic
Advanced Degrees Offered: LLM for foreign lawyers (1 year)
Combined Degrees Offered: JD/MBA, JD/MPA, joint degrees available with most graduate programs (all are 4 years)
Grading System: Numerical system on a 4 to 16 scale
Clinical Program Required? No
Clinical Program Description: 16 separate clinics, including Bankruptcy, Child Advocacy, Civil Litigation, Criminal Appeals, Disability, Domestic Abuse, Federal Prosecution, Federal Taxation, Housing, Immigration, Indian Child Welfare, Law and Violence Against Women, Legal Assistance
Legal Writing/Methods Course Requirements: 3 years of writing requirements

STUDENT INFORMATION
Enrollment of Law School: 744
% Male/Female: 53/47
% Full Time: 100
% Full Time That Are International: 2
% Minority: 17
Average Age of Entering Class: 24

RESEARCH FACILITIES
School-Supported Research Centers: 6 international exchanges programs in France, Germany, Ireland, the Netherlands, Spain, and Sweden

EXPENSES/FINANCIAL AID
Annual Tuition (Residents/Nonresidents): $9,000/$15,300
Average Grant: $6,300
Average Loan: $17,500
% Receiving Some Sort of Aid: 91
Average Debt: $38,000

ADMISSIONS INFORMATION
Application Fee: $40
Regular Application Deadline: 3/1
Regular Notification: Rolling
LSDAS Accepted? Yes
Average GPA: 3.6
Range of GPA: 3.3–3.8
Average LSAT: 162
Range of LSAT: 158–164
Transfer Students Accepted? Yes
Other Schools to Which Students Applied: University of Wisconsin, University of Michigan, William Mitchell College of Law, Hamline University, Yale University, Harvard University, Georgetown University, University of Iowa
Number of Applications Received: 1,467

INTERNATIONAL STUDENTS
TOEFL Required of International Students? Yes

EMPLOYMENT INFORMATION

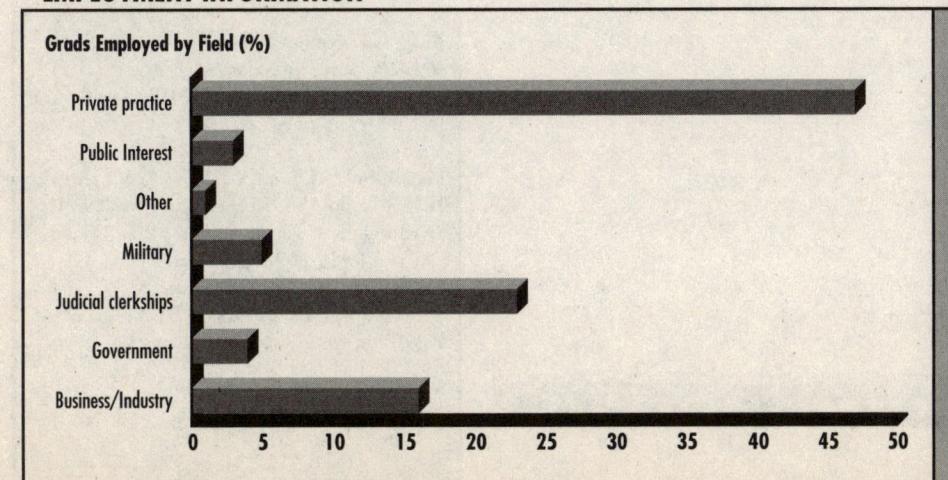

Grads Employed by Field (%)

Field	%
Private practice	~48
Public Interest	~2
Other	~1
Military	~3
Judicial clerkships	~23
Government	~5
Business/Industry	~16

Rate of Placement: 99%
Average Starting Salary: $60,000
Prominent Alumni: Walter Mondale, former vice president and ambassador to Japan; James Blanchard, former governor of Michigan and ambassador to Canada; Constance Barry Newman, director of the U.S. Office of Personnel Management; Robert Stein, executive director of the American Bar Association; A. W. Clausen, former president of the World Bank, and CEO of Bank America; Michael Sullivan, president of International Dairy Queen; Michael Wright, President of SUPERVALU Inc.; over 250 federal and state court judges nationwide

SCHOOL PROFILES • 249

UNIVERSITY OF MISSISSIPPI
Lamar Hall

Admissions Contact: Director of Admissions, Barbara Vinson
School of Law, Room 310, University, MS 38677
Admissions Phone: 662-915-6910 • Admissions Fax: 662-915-1289
Admissions E-mail: lawmiss@olemiss.edu • Web Address: www.olemiss.edu/depts/law_school

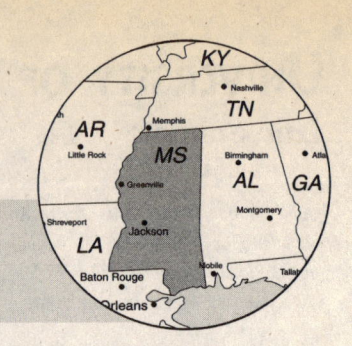

INSTITUTIONAL INFORMATION
Public/Private: Public
Student/Faculty Ratio: 21:1
Total Faculty: 35
% Part Time: 11
% Female: 28
% Minority: 8

PROGRAMS
Academic Specialties: Business Law, Space Law, Commercial Law, Corporation Securities Law, Criminal Law, Environmental Law, International Law, Taxation
Grading System: A (4.0), B+ (3.5), B (3.0), C+ (2.5), C (2.0), D+ (1.5), D (1.0), F (0.0), Z (Pass), X (Audit), W (Withdrew), I (Incomplete)
Clinical Program Required? No
Clinical Program Description: Prosecutorial Externship, Criminal Appeals Clinic, Public Service Internships
Legal Writing Course Requirements? Yes
Legal Writing Description: First-year course. First semester (3 credits) includes the study and practice of basic legal research and legal writing skills, primarily using state materials and focusing on objective legal writing. Second semester (3 credits) continues with more complex legal problems, primarily federal materials, and focuses on persuasive legal writing with an oral argument component.
Legal Methods Course Requirements? Yes
Legal Methods Description: 1 year; Legal Research and Writing—advanced skills writing requirement
Legal Research Course Requirements? Yes
Legal Research Description: See Legal Writing.
Moot Court Requirement? Yes
Moot Court Description: First year—oral arguments; second/third year—appellate and trial requirement
Public Interest Law Requirement? No
Academic Journals: *Mississippi Law Journal*, *The Journal of Space Law*

STUDENT INFORMATION
Enrollment of Law School: 531
% Out of State: 16
% Male/Female: 58/42
% Full Time: 100
% Full Time That Are International: 0
% Minority: 10
Average Age of Entering Class: 23

RESEARCH FACILITIES
School-Supported Research Centers: Sea Grant Legal Program, Mississippi Law Research Institute, National Center for Justice and the Rule of Law, National Center for Remote Sensing and Space Law

EXPENSES/FINANCIAL AID
Annual Tuition (Residents/Nonresidents): $6,215/$12,142
Room and Board: $11,228
Books and Supplies: $1,200
Average Grant: $4,063
Average Loan: $15,334
% of Aid That Is Merit-Based: 90
Average Debt: $40,947

ADMISSIONS INFORMATION
Application Fee: $25
Regular Application Deadline: 3/1
Regular Notification: 4/15
LSDAS Accepted? Yes
Average GPA: 3.5
Range of GPA: 3.3–3.7
Average LSAT: 153
Range of LSAT: 150–156
Transfer Students Accepted? Yes
Other Schools to Which Students Applied: Mississippi College, University of Alabama, University of Tennessee
Other Admissions Factors Considered: Grade patterns and progression, difficulty of major, field of study, job experience, social or economic circumstances, nonacademic achievements, letters of recommendation, residency
Number of Applications Received: 1,295
Number of Applicants Accepted: 440
Number of Applicants Enrolled: 229

INTERNATIONAL STUDENTS
TOEFL Required of International Students? Yes
Minimum TOEFL: 625 (263 computer)

EMPLOYMENT INFORMATION

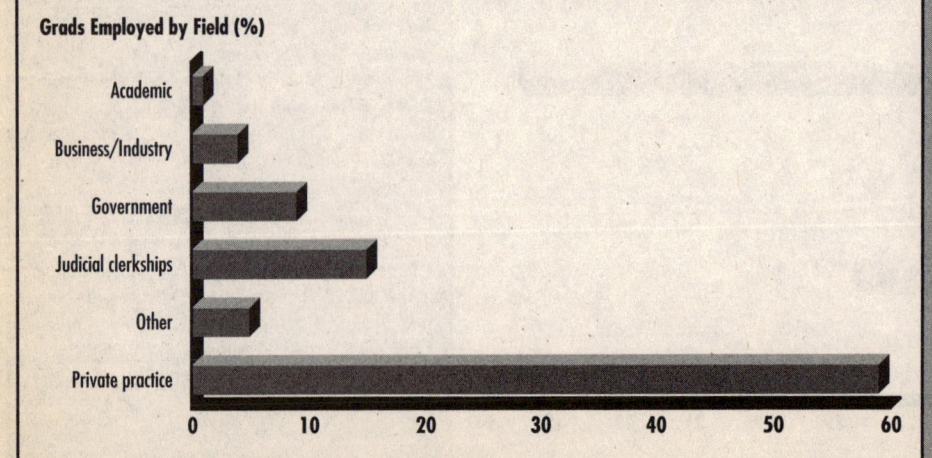

Grads Employed by Field (%)
- Academic
- Business/Industry
- Government
- Judicial clerkships
- Other
- Private practice

Rate of Placement: 98%
Average Starting Salary: $58,000
Employers Who Frequently Hire Grads: Top regional employers from across the South and Southeast
Prominent Alumni: C. Trent Lott, Minority Leader of the U.S. Senate; Thad Cochran, U.S. Senator; John Grisham, Author; Richard Scruggs, Attorney for first tobacco case; Robert C. Khayat, Chancellor, University of Mississippi
State for Bar Exam: MS, TN, GA, FL, TX
Pass Rate for First-Time Bar: 88%

UNIVERSITY OF MISSOURI—COLUMBIA
School of Law

Admissions Contact: Assistant Dean, Donna Pavlick
103 Hulston Hall, Columbia, MO 65211
Admissions Phone: 573-882-6042 • Admissions Fax: 573-882-9625
Admissions E-mail: umclawadmissions@missouri.edu • Web Address: www.law.missouri.edu

INSTITUTIONAL INFORMATION
Public/Private: Public
Student/Faculty Ratio: 16:1
Total Faculty: 41
% Female: 27
% Minority: 1

PROGRAMS
Academic Specialties: Dispute Resolution, Criminal Law, Environmental Law, Intellectual Property Law, International Law, Labor Law, Property, Taxation
Advanced Degrees Offered: LLM Dispute Resolution (1 year)
Combined Degrees Offered: JD/MBA, JD/MPA, JD/MA (all 4 years); JD/PhD Journalism (5 years)
Grading System: Numerical system (55–100); minimum 70 required for graduation
Clinical Program Required? No
Clinical Program Description: Family Violence Clinic, Criminal Clinic, Mediation Clinic, Child Advocacy Clinic
Legal Writing Course Requirements? No
Legal Methods Course Requirements? Yes
Legal Methods Description: First year, 2 hours, fall and winter; research, writing, and oral advocacy
Legal Research Course Requirements? No
Moot Court Requirement? Yes
Moot Court Description: Second- and third-year students selected by participation in previous competitions and GPA; credit for each competition; 1 year

Public Interest Law Requirement? No
Academic Journals: *Missouri Law Review, Journal of Dispute Resolution, Missouri Environmental Law and Policy Review*

STUDENT INFORMATION
Enrollment of Law School: 513
% Out of State: 20
% Male/Female: 60/40
% Full Time: 99
% Full Time That Are International: 1
% Minority: 20
Average Age of Entering Class: 24

RESEARCH FACILITIES
School-Supported Research Centers: Center for the Study of Dispute Resolution

EXPENSES/FINANCIAL AID
Annual Tuition (Residents/Nonresidents): $11,264/$21,845
Room and Board: $7,710
Books and Supplies: $1,240
Financial Aid Application Deadline: 3/1
Average Grant: $4,000
Average Loan: $16,500
% Receiving Some Sort of Aid: 90
Average Debt: $48,442

ADMISSIONS INFORMATION
Application Fee: $50
Regular Application Deadline: Rolling
Regular Notification: Rolling
LSDAS Accepted? Yes
Average GPA: 3.4
Range of GPA: 3.1–3.7
Average LSAT: 157
Range of LSAT: 154–160
Transfer Students Accepted? Yes
Other Schools to Which Students Applied: Saint Louis University, University of Missouri—Kansas City, Washington University
Other Admissions Factors Considered: Suitability for career
Number of Applications Received: 908
Number of Applicants Accepted: 323
Number of Applicants Enrolled: 150

INTERNATIONAL STUDENTS
TOEFL Required of International Students? Yes
Minimum TOEFL: 600 (250 computer)

EMPLOYMENT INFORMATION

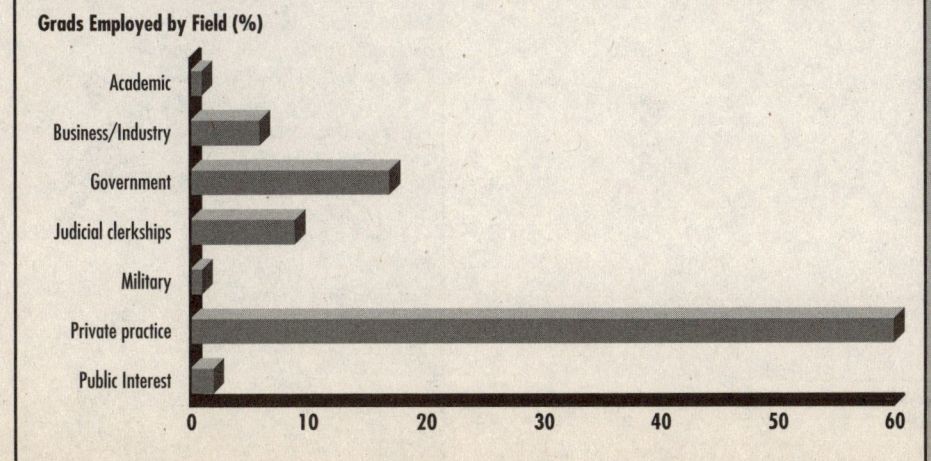

Grads Employed by Field (%)
- Academic
- Business/Industry
- Government
- Judicial clerkships
- Military
- Private practice
- Public Interest

Rate of Placement: 97%
Average Starting Salary: $51,644
Employers Who Frequently Hire Grads: Missouri law firms of all sizes; Missouri, federal, and governmental agencies; business, accounting, and insurance industries; federal and state judges inside and outside the state of Missouri
State for Bar Exam: MO, IL, TX, KS, CA
Pass Rate for First-Time Bar: 90%

UNIVERSITY OF MISSOURI—KANSAS CITY
School of Law

Admissions Contact: Director of Admissions, Jean Klosterman
5100 Rockhill Road, Kansas City, MO 64110
Admissions Phone: 816-235-1644 • Admissions Fax: 816-235-5276
Admissions E-mail: klostermanm@umkc.edu • Web Address: www.law.umkc.edu

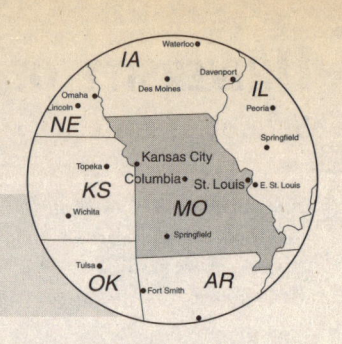

INSTITUTIONAL INFORMATION
Public/Private: Public
Student/Faculty Ratio: 18:1
Total Faculty: 34
% Part Time: 6
% Female: 30
% Minority: 6

PROGRAMS
Academic Specialties: Law students do not have a formal major, but many students desire to take a concentration of courses in one of the many practice areas, including Advocacy and Litigation, Business and Tax Law, Commercial Law, Estate Planning and Administration, Criminal Law and Procedure, Domestic Relations, Labor and Employment, International Law, Property and Real Estate, Civil Liberties and Civil Rights, and Environmental Law. In addition, through participation in the mentor program, externships, competitions, journals, and student organizations, students are able to develop skills and contacts in specialized areas of the law. Other specialties include Taxation.
Advanced Degrees Offered: LLM (1 to 3 years)
Combined Degrees Offered: JD/MBA (3 to 4 years), JD/LLM (3.5 to 4 years)
Grading System: A, B, C, D, F (with plus and minus)
Clinical Program Required? No
Clinical Programs: Students counsel clients in federal, state, and local tax controversy matters in the Kansas City Tax Clinic under the supervision and direction of tax faculty, clinic director, and volunteer attorneys.

Legal Writing Course Requirements? No
Legal Methods Course Requirements? Yes
Legal Methods Description: 5-hour course split between a student's first 2 semesters. First semester consists of an introduction to legal reasoning; case analysis and synthesis; case research; and structure and style in legal writing with emphasis on expository writing, including office memoranda. Second semester includes introduction to advocacy; introduction to interviewing, counseling, and negotiation; statutory and computerized research; writing to and on behalf of a client, including a trial or appellate brief; and oral advocacy.
Legal Research Course Requirements? No
Moot Court Requirement? Yes
Moot Court Description: Students write and argue an appellate brief in their Introduction to Law and Lawyering Processes class.
Public Interest Law Requirement? No
Academic Journals: Law Review, Urban Lawyer, Journal of the American Academy of Matrimonial Lawyers

STUDENT INFORMATION
Enrollment of Law School: 485
% Male/Female: 51/49
% Full Time: 94
% Full Time That Are International: 1
% Minority: 16
Average Age of Entering Class: 27

EXPENSES/FINANCIAL AID
Annual Tuition (Residents/Nonresidents): $8,814/$17,624
Room and Board (On/Off Campus): $9,740/$11,690
Books and Supplies: $1,520
Financial Aid Application Deadline: 3/1
Average Grant: $4,500
Average Loan: $18,512
% Receiving Some Sort of Aid: 33
Tuition Per Credit (Residents/Nonresidents): $315/$630
Fees Per Credit: $26

ADMISSIONS INFORMATION
Application Fee: $25
Regular Application Deadline: Rolling
Regular Notification: Rolling
LSDAS Accepted? Yes
Average GPA: 3.2
Range of GPA: 2.1–4.0
Average LSAT: 154
Range of LSAT: 150–156
Transfer Students Accepted? Yes
Other Admissions Factors Considered: Extracurricular activities, work experience, advanced degrees, efforts to overcome societally imposed disadvantages
Number of Applications Received: 646
Number of Applicants Accepted: 401
Number of Applicants Enrolled: 165

EMPLOYMENT INFORMATION

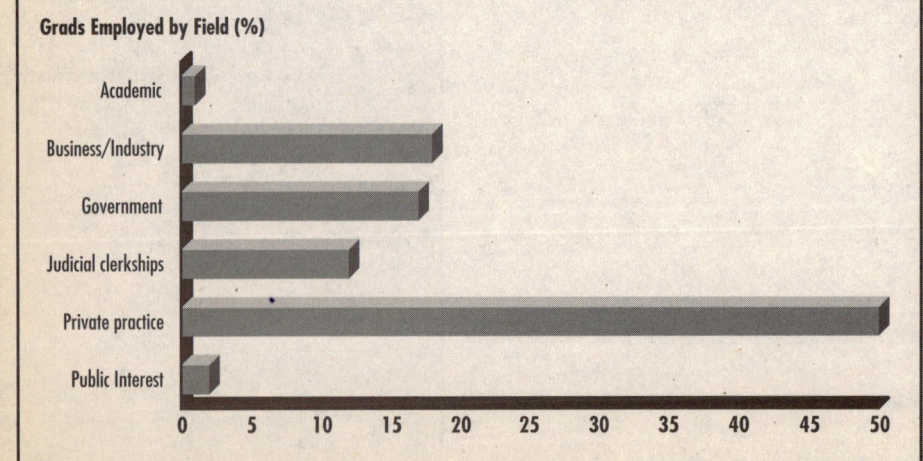

Grads Employed by Field (%)
- Academic
- Business/Industry
- Government
- Judicial clerkships
- Private practice
- Public Interest

Rate of Placement: 92%
Average Starting Salary: $46,088
Employers Who Frequently Hire Grads: Jackson County, Missouri, Prosecutor; Shook, Hardy & Bacon; Blackwell, Sanders, Peper, Martin, LLP; Bryan Cave, LLP; United Missouri Bank; Shughart, Thomson & Kilroy, PC; Lathrop & Gage, LC; Stinson, Mag & Fizzell, PC; Morrison & Hecker, LLP; Husch & Eppenberger, LLC
State for Bar Exam: MO
Pass Rate for First-Time Bar: 76%

UNIVERSITY OF MONTANA
School of Law

Admissions Contact: Director of Admissions, Heidi Fanslow
Admissions Office, Missoula, MT 59812
Admissions Phone: 406-243-2698 • *Admissions Fax:* 406-243-2576
Admissions E-mail: lawadmis@selway.umt.edu • *Web Address:* www.umt.edu/law

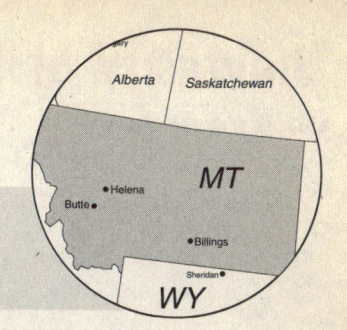

INSTITUTIONAL INFORMATION
Public/Private: Public
Student/Faculty Ratio: 19:1
Total Faculty: 22
% Part Time: 18
% Female: 32
% Minority: 5

PROGRAMS
Academic Specialties: Competency-based curriculum, Indian Law, Trial Advocacy Law, Environmental Law, Taxation
Advanced Degrees Offered: JD (3 years)
Combined Degrees Offered: JD/MPA (3 years), JD/MBA (3 years), JD/MS Environmental Studies (4 years)
Grading System: No mandatory curve
Clinical Program Required? Yes
Clinical Program Description: Criminal Defense, Indian, Prosecution, Legal Aid, Disability, Judicial, Environmental, Mediation, Land Use and Planning
Legal Writing Course Requirements? Yes
Legal Writing Description: Legal writing and an advanced writing project are required.
Legal Methods Course Requirements? Yes
Legal Methods Description: The first year begins with the basics of legal research, analysis, and writing. Students complete several legal memoranda; draft contract provisions, legal pleadings, and 2 briefs to a court; and argue their motions for summary judgment. All second-year students enroll in Business Transactions, in which they negotiate and draft business agreements. All students must fulfill our Advanced Writing Requirement by completing a major written piece (and presenting and defending it orally) during their second or third year. To further underscore the inportance of legal writing, roughly half of our elective courses involve writing papers or legal memoranda.
Legal Research Course Requirements? Yes
Moot Court Requirement? No
Public Interest Law Requirement? No
Academic Journals: *Montana Law Review, Public Land and Natural Resource Law Review*

STUDENT INFORMATION
Enrollment of Law School: 240
% Out of State: 29
% Male/Female: 58/42
% Full Time: 100
% Full Time That Are International: 1
% Minority: 7
Average Age of Entering Class: 28

EXPENSES/FINANCIAL AID
Annual Tuition (Residents/Nonresidents): $8,000/$15,000
Room and Board: $7,900
Books and Supplies: $1,010
Financial Aid Application Deadline: 3/1
Average Grant: $1,457
Average Loan: $14,350
% of Aid That Is Merit-Based: 3
% Receiving Some Sort of Aid: 88
Average Total Aid Package: $14,619
Average Debt: $45,000

ADMISSIONS INFORMATION
Application Fee: $60
Regular Application Deadline: 3/1
Regular Notification: Rolling
LSDAS Accepted? Yes
Average GPA: 3.3
Range of GPA: 3.1–3.6
Average LSAT: 154
Range of LSAT: 151–157
Transfer Students Accepted? Yes
Other Schools to Which Students Applied: University of Oregon, University of Wyoming, University of Colorado, Lewis and Clark College, University of Denver, Gonzaga University, University of Idaho
Other Admissions Factors Considered: Ability to overcome economic or other disadvantage, writing ability
Number of Applications Received: 484
Number of Applicants Accepted: 204
Number of Applicants Enrolled: 81

INTERNATIONAL STUDENTS
TOEFL Required of International Students? Yes
Minimum TOEFL: 600

EMPLOYMENT INFORMATION

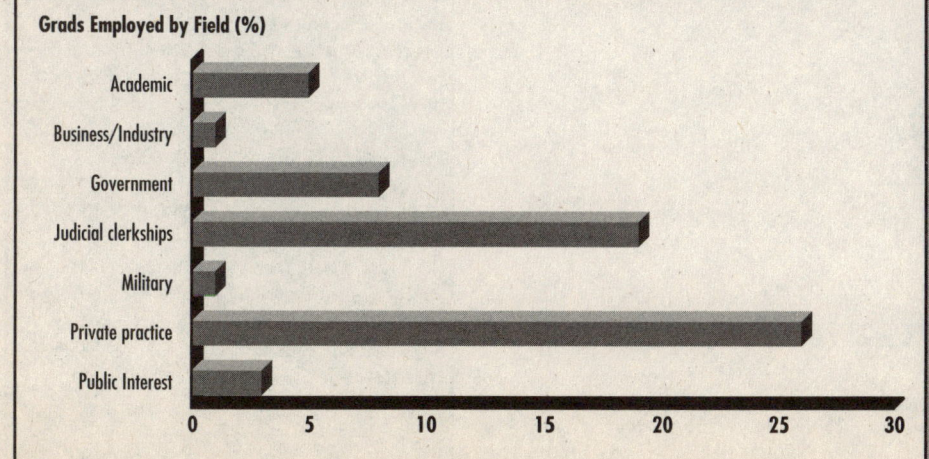

Grads Employed by Field (%)

Field	%
Academic	~5
Business/Industry	~2
Government	~8
Judicial clerkships	~19
Military	~1
Private practice	~26
Public Interest	~3

Rate of Placement: 89%
Average Starting Salary: $39,086
Employers Who Frequently Hire Grads: Church, Harris, Johnson and Williams; Moulton, Bellingham, Longo and Mather; Crowley, Haughy, Hanson, Toole and Dietrich
Prominent Alumni: Sid Thomas, Judge, 9th Circuit Court of Appeals
State for Bar Exam: MT
Pass Rate for First-Time Bar: 80%

UNIVERSITY OF NEBRASKA — LINCOLN
College of Law

Admissions Contact: Associate Dean, Glenda J. Pierce
PO Box 830902, Lincoln, NE 68583-0902
Admissions Phone: 402-472-2161 • Admissions Fax: 402-472-5185
Admissions E-mail: lawadm@unl.edu • Web Address: law.unl.edu

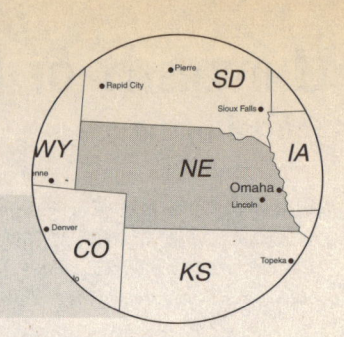

INSTITUTIONAL INFORMATION
Public/Private: Public
Student/Faculty Ratio: 14:1
Total Faculty: 58
% Part Time: 40
% Female: 29
% Minority: 5

PROGRAMS
Academic Specialties: The faculty have national/international reputations in Tort Law, Intellectual Property Law, and Labor and Employment Law. Clinical programs are supervised by in-house faculty. Eight faculty members have published case books that are used as teaching materials in law schools throughout the country. We offer a Civil Clinic and a Criminal Prosecution Clinic. Students may work with professors to develop individual programs of concentrated studies. Specialties include Commercial Law, Corporation Securities Law, Environmental Law, International Law, and Taxation.
Advanced Degrees Offered: JD (3 years), MLS (1 year)
Combined Degrees Offered: JD/PhD Psychology (6 years); JD/MA Economics, Community of Regional Planning, Political Science, or International Affairs (4 years); JD/MBA (4 years); JD/MPA (4 years); JD/PhD Education Administration (5 years)
Grading System: Letter system
Clinical Program Required? No
Clinical Program Description: Criminal Prosecution Clinic, Civil Clinic
Legal Writing Course Requirements? Yes
Legal Writing Description: Legal Research and Writing—6 credits, 2 semesters, first year
Legal Methods Course Requirements? No
Legal Research Course Requirements? Yes
Legal Research Description: See Legal Writing.
Moot Court Requirement? No
Moot Court Description: The Nebraska Moot Court Board is composed of students selected on the basis of either their class rank or their performance in an annual writing competition.
Public Interest Law Requirement? No
Academic Journals: *The Nebraska Law Journal*

STUDENT INFORMATION
Enrollment of Law School: 415
% Out of State: 26
% Male/Female: 52/48
% Full Time: 100
% Full Time That Are International: 1
% Minority: 8
Average Age of Entering Class: 24

RESEARCH FACILITIES
Research Resources Available: Access to government offices, state legislature, and courts
School-Supported Research Centers: Center for Children, Families and the Law; Center for the Teaching and Study of Applied Ethics

EXPENSES/FINANCIAL AID
Annual Tuition (Residents/Nonresidents): $5,220/$14,625
Room and Board (On/Off Campus): $8,306/$9,132
Books and Supplies: $1,098
Financial Aid Application Deadline: 3/1
Average Grant: $6,553
Average Loan: $14,382
% of Aid That Is Merit-Based: 38
% Receiving Some Sort of Aid: 85
Average Total Aid Package: $15,000
Average Debt: $37,146

ADMISSIONS INFORMATION
Application Fee: $25
Regular Application Deadline: 3/1
Regular Notification: Rolling
LSDAS Accepted? Yes
Average GPA: 3.7
Range of GPA: 3.3–3.9
Average LSAT: 154
Range of LSAT: 153–158
Transfer Students Accepted? Yes
Other Schools to Which Students Applied: Creighton University, Drake University, University of Iowa, University of Kansas, University of Minnesota, Washburn University
Other Admissions Factors Considered: Major, courses taken and level of difficulty, upward or downward trend in undergraduate GPA, graduate study, work experience, extracurricular activities
Number of Applications Received: 787
Number of Applicants Accepted: 370
Number of Applicants Enrolled: 154

INTERNATIONAL STUDENTS
TOEFL Required of International Students? Yes
Minimum TOEFL: 600 (250 computer)

EMPLOYMENT INFORMATION

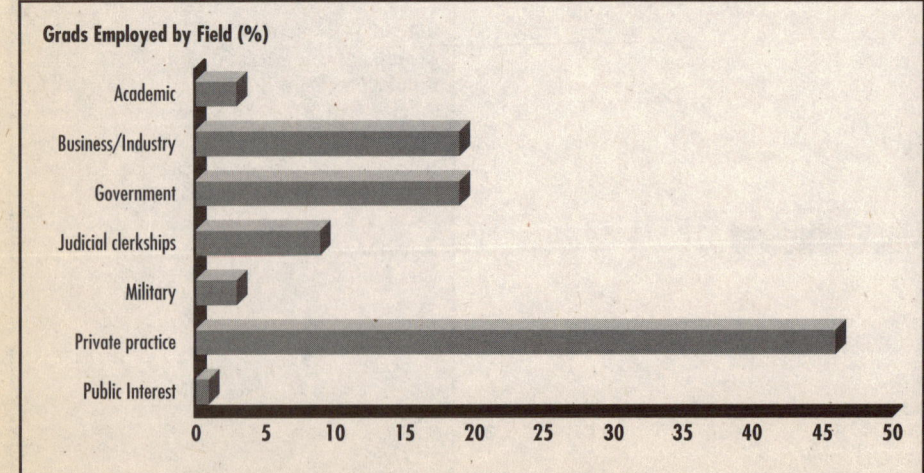

Grads Employed by Field (%)

Field	%
Academic	~2
Business/Industry	~19
Government	~19
Judicial clerkships	~9
Military	~1
Private practice	~46
Public Interest	~1

Rate of Placement: 90%
Average Starting Salary: $48,000
Employers Who Frequently Hire Grads: Very small law firms (2–10 attorneys), small law firms (11–25 attorneys), state government
Prominent Alumni: Ted Sorensen, Special Counsel to President John F. Kennedy; Harvey Perlman, Chancellor, University of Nebraska—Lincoln; Ben Nelson, U.S. Senator and former Governor of Nebraska; Lee Rankin, former Solicitor General of the United States; John Hendry, Chief Justice, Nebraska Supreme Court
State for Bar Exam: NE, AZ, CA, IL, MO
Pass Rate for First-Time Bar: 85%

UNIVERSITY OF NEVADA — LAS VEGAS
William S. Boyd School of Law

Admissions Contact: Assistant Dean of Admissions and Financial Aid, Frank Durand
4505 Maryland Parkway, Box 451003, Las Vegas, NV 89154–1003
Admissions Phone: 702-895-2440 • Admissions Fax: 702-895-2414
Admissions E-mail: request@law.unlv.edu • Web Address: www.law.unlv.edu

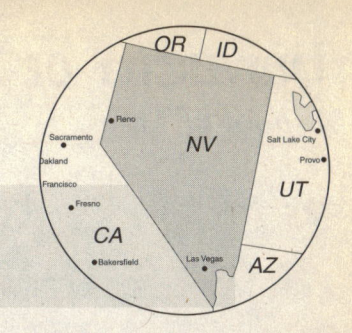

INSTITUTIONAL INFORMATION
Public/Private: Public
Student/Faculty Ratio: 13:1
Total Faculty: 52
% Part Time: 31
% Female: 40
% Minority: 15

PROGRAMS
Academic Specialties: We offer, and encourage our students to undertake, a broad curriculum.
Grading System: Letter system on a 4.0 scale; Pass, Satisfactory, Unsatisfactory, Incomplete, Audit, Withdrawal, Not Reported
Clinical Program Required? No
Clinical Program Description: Child Welfare, Juvenile Justice
Legal Writing Course Requirements? Yes
Legal Writing Description: Lawyering Process I (3 credits) provides students, through course work and simulated cases, with the opportunity to examine the relationship between legal analysis and lawyering tasks such as effective legal research strategies, legal writing, oral advocacy, and client interviewing and counseling, with an emphasis on professionalism and ethnics. Lawyering Process II (3 credits) continues Lawyering Process I. Lawyering Process III (4 credits) teaches legal writing, legal research, and professionalism and introduces other lawyering skills, focusing on appellate advocacy. Students complete a complex, multi-issue brief. Assignments are staged to allow intervention and instruction during the writing process. Additionally, students engage in oral argument before a panel of judges.
Legal Methods Course Requirements? Yes
Legal Methods Description: See Legal Writing.
Legal Research Course Requirements? Yes
Legal Research Description: See Legal Writing.
Moot Court Requirement? No
Public Interest Law Requirement? Yes
Public Interest Law Description: First-year students must participate in a community service program. Working with Clark County Legal Services and Nevada Legal Services, teams of students prepare and conduct weekly workshops for unrepresented people on basic procedure in family or small claims court and on paternity, custody, guardianship, and bankruptcy matters. This program offers students the chance to educate groups of people in a general way without giving specifc legal advice. Students are required to attend approximately 5 hours of training and to conduct weekly 2-hour workshops.
Academic Journals: *Nevada Law Journal*

STUDENT INFORMATION
Enrollment of Law School: 454
% Male/Female: 51/49
% Full Time: 59
% Minority: 20
Average Age of Entering Class: 29

RESEARCH FACILITIES
Research Resources Available: Lexis/Nexis, Westlaw

EXPENSES/FINANCIAL AID
Annual Tuition (Residents/Nonresidents): $7,000/$14,000
Room and Board (Off Campus): $6,910
Books and Supplies: $850
Average Grant: $3,700
Average Loan: $13,900
% Receiving Some Sort of Aid: 71
Average Total Aid Package: $14,500
Average Debt: $28,000
Tuition Per Credit (Residents/Nonresidents): $250/$500
Fees Per Credit: $262

ADMISSIONS INFORMATION
Application Fee: $40
Regular Application Deadline: 3/17
Regular Notification: 4/1
LSDAS Accepted? Yes
Average GPA: 3.3
Range of GPA: 3.0–3.6
Average LSAT: 154
Range of LSAT: 151–158
Transfer Students Accepted? Yes
Other Schools to Which Students Applied: Arizona State University, California Western, University of San Diego, University of the Pacific, University of Denver, University of Arizona
Other Admissions Factors Considered: Undergraduate and/or graduate academic record; career; community service; meeting challenges of race, ethnicity, gender, economic status, or disability
Number of Applications Received: 1,106
Number of Applicants Accepted: 267
Number of Applicants Enrolled: 141

EMPLOYMENT INFORMATION

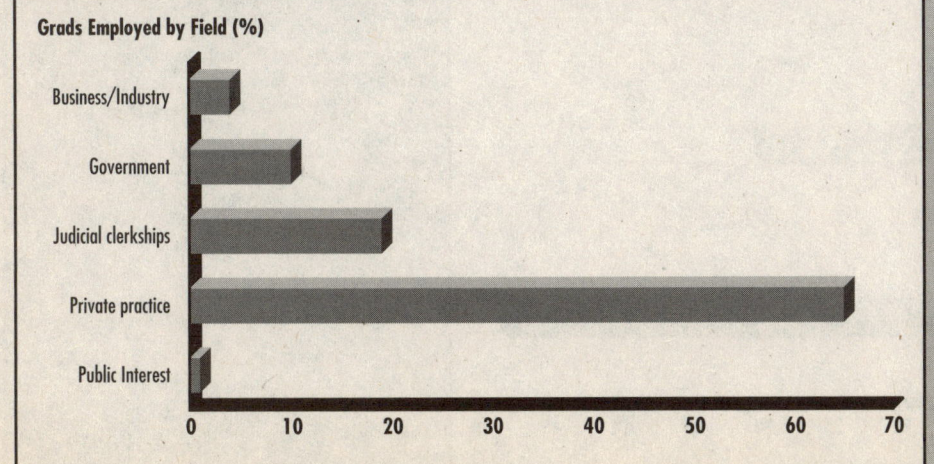

Grads Employed by Field (%):
- Business/Industry: ~3
- Government: ~10
- Judicial clerkships: ~18
- Private practice: ~65
- Public Interest: ~2

Rate of Placement: 96%
Average Starting Salary: $45,000
Employers Who Frequently Hire Grads: Local private firms, governmental agencies, and judiciary
State for Bar Exam: NV
Pass Rate for First-Time Bar: 64%

UNIVERSITY OF NEW MEXICO
School of Law

Admissions Contact: Director of Admissions, Susan Mitchell
1117 Stanford, NE, Albuquerque, NM 87131
Admissions Phone: 505-277-0158 • Admissions Fax: 505-277-9958
Admissions E-mail: mitchell@law.unm.edu • Web Address: lawschool.unm.edu

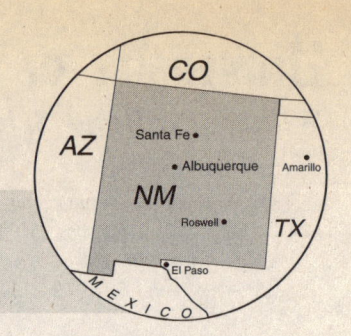

INSTITUTIONAL INFORMATION
Public/Private: Public
Student/Faculty Ratio: 12:1
Total Faculty: 34
% Female: 44
% Minority: 27

PROGRAMS
Advanced Degrees Offered: JD (3 years)
Combined Degrees Offered: JD/MA, JD/MS, JD/PhD, JD/MAPA (all 4 years)
Grading System: 4.0 scale; minimum 2.0 required
Clinical Program Required? Yes
Clinical Program Description: Southwest Indian Law Clinic, District Attorney Clinic, Law Practice Clinic, Community Lawyering Clinic
Legal Writing Course Requirements? Yes
Legal Writing Description: First-year Legal Research/Writing
Legal Methods Course Requirements? No
Legal Research Course Requirements? Yes
Legal Research Description: See Legal Writing.
Moot Court Requirement? No
Public Interest Law Requirement? No
Academic Journals: *Natural Resources Journal, New Mexico Law Review, Tribal Law Journal (online), US-Mexico Law Journal*

STUDENT INFORMATION
Enrollment of Law School: 324
% Male/Female: 40/60
% Full Time: 100
% Full Time That Are International: 0
% Minority: 35
Average Age of Entering Class: 29

EXPENSES/FINANCIAL AID
Annual Tuition (Residents/Nonresidents): $6,098/$18,560
Room and Board (Off Campus): $6,710
Books and Supplies: $1,188
Financial Aid Application Deadline: 3/1
Average Grant: $4,600
Average Loan: $13,900

ADMISSIONS INFORMATION
Application Fee: $40
Regular Application Deadline: 2/15
Regular Notification: Rolling
LSDAS Accepted? Yes
Average GPA: 3.4
Range of GPA: 3.0–3.7
Average LSAT: 157
Range of LSAT: 151–160
Transfer Students Accepted? Yes
Other Admissions Factors Considered: Preference to New Mexico residents
Number of Applications Received: 781
Number of Applicants Accepted: 248
Number of Applicants Enrolled: 113

INTERNATIONAL STUDENTS
TOEFL Required of International Students? Yes

EMPLOYMENT INFORMATION

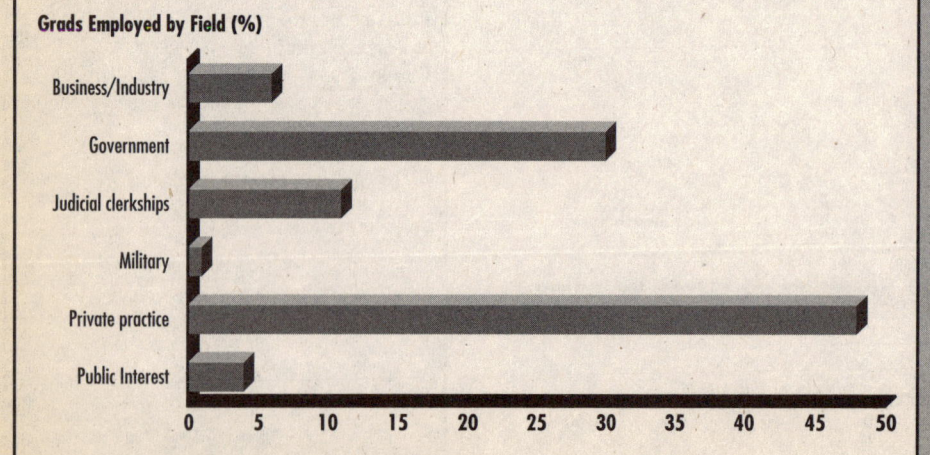

Grads Employed by Field (%)
- Business/Industry: ~5
- Government: ~30
- Judicial clerkships: ~10
- Military: ~1
- Private practice: ~48
- Public Interest: ~3

Rate of Placement: 87%
Average Starting Salary: $44,075
State for Bar Exam: NM
Pass Rate for First-Time Bar: 82%

UNIVERSITY OF NORTH CAROLINA — CHAPEL HILL
School of Law

Admissions Contact: Assistant Dean for Admissions, Victoria Taylor Carter
Campus Box 3380, Chapel Hill, NC 27599
Admissions Phone: 919-962-5109 • Admissions Fax: 919-843-7939
Admissions E-mail: law_admission@unc.edu • Web Address: www.law.unc.edu

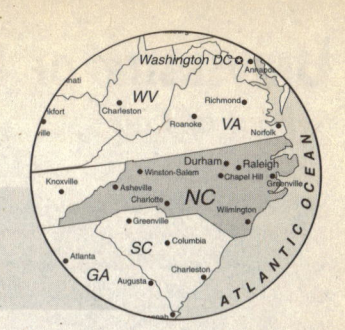

INSTITUTIONAL INFORMATION
Public/Private: Public
Student/Faculty Ratio: 15:1
Total Faculty: 84
% Part Time: 47
% Female: 32
% Minority: 6

PROGRAMS
Academic Specialties: Civil Procedure, Commercial Law, Constitutional Law, Corporation Securities Law, Criminal Law, Environmental Law, Government Services, Human Rights Law, International Law, Labor Law, Legal History, Legal Philosophy, Property, Taxation
Combined Degrees Offered: JD/MBA (4 years), JD/MPA (4 years), JD/MPPS (4 years), JD/MPH (4 years), JD/MRP (4 years), JD/MSW (4 years)
Grading System: Numerical system ranging from 4.3 to 0.0
Clinical Program Required? No
Clinical Program Description: Live Client Clinics in criminal and civil law, simulation programs in trial advocacy, dispute resolution
Legal Writing Course Requirements? Yes
Legal Writing Description: Research, Reasoning, Writing and Advocacy (RRWA) is a required first-year course that provides intensive instruction in the basics of legal reasoning and in communicating accurate legal analysis clearly, both orally and in writing.
Legal Methods Course Requirements? No
Legal Research Course Requirements? Yes
Legal Research Description: See Legal Writing.
Moot Court Requirement? No
Public Interest Law Requirement? No
Academic Journals: *North Carolina Banking Institute Journal, North Carolina Law Review, North Carolina Journal of International Law and Commercial Regulation, North Carolina Journal of Law and Technology*

STUDENT INFORMATION
Enrollment of Law School: 780
% Out of State: 25
% Male/Female: 48/52
% Full Time: 100
% Full Time That Are International: 1
% Minority: 14

EXPENSES/FINANCIAL AID
Annual Tuition (Residents/Nonresidents): $5,031/$17,131
Room and Board (On Campus): $7,695
Books and Supplies: $800
Average Grant: $2,800
Average Debt: $33,982

ADMISSIONS INFORMATION
Application Fee: $60
Regular Application Deadline: Rolling
Regular Notification: Rolling
LSDAS Accepted? Yes
Average GPA: 3.6
Range of GPA: 3.4–3.8
Average LSAT: 159
Range of LSAT: 156–164
Transfer Students Accepted? Yes
Other Schools to Which Students Applied: Villanova University
Number of Applications Received: 2,649
Number of Applicants Accepted: 718
Number of Applicants Enrolled: 325

EMPLOYMENT INFORMATION

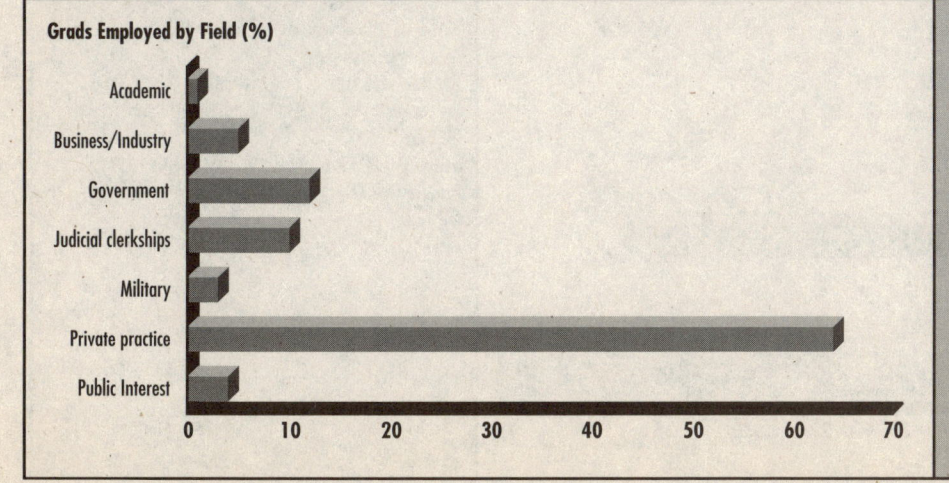

Grads Employed by Field (%)
- Academic: ~1
- Business/Industry: ~5
- Government: ~12
- Judicial clerkships: ~10
- Military: ~2
- Private practice: ~65
- Public Interest: ~3

Rate of Placement: 99%
Average Starting Salary: $53,781
State for Bar Exam: NC
Pass Rate for First-Time Bar: 81%

UNIVERSITY OF NORTH DAKOTA
School of Law

Admissions Contact: Admissions and Records Associate, Linda D. Kohoutek
Centennial Drive, PO Box 9003, Grand Forks, ND 58202
Admissions Phone: 701-777-2260 • Admissions Fax: 701-777-2217
Admissions E-mail: mark.brickson@thor.law.und.nodak.edu • Web Address: www.law.und.nodak.edu

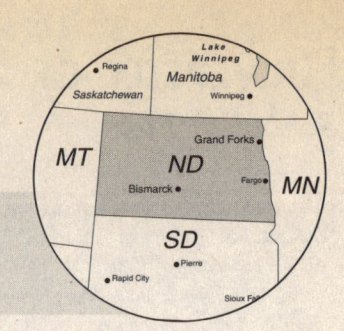

INSTITUTIONAL INFORMATION
Public/Private: Public
Student/Faculty Ratio: 9:1
Total Faculty: 26
% Part Time: 46
% Female: 54
% Minority: 1

PROGRAMS
Advanced Degrees Offered: JD (3 years)
Combined Degrees Offered: JD/MPA (4 years)
Grading System: Letter system
Clinical Program Required? No
Legal Writing Course Requirements? Yes
Legal Writing Description: Fall and spring of first year
Legal Methods Course Requirements? Yes
Legal Methods Description: Fall and spring of first year
Legal Research Course Requirements? Yes
Legal Research Description: Fall and spring of first year
Moot Court Requirement? No
Public Interest Law Requirement? No
Academic Journals: *North Dakota Law Review*

STUDENT INFORMATION
Enrollment of Law School: 211
% Male/Female: 49/51
% Full Time: 100
% Full Time That Are International: 3
% Minority: 8

EXPENSES/FINANCIAL AID
Annual Tuition (Residents/Nonresidents): $3,472/$9,270
Room and Board: $7,200
Books and Supplies: $800
Financial Aid Application Deadline: 4/15
Average Grant: $500
Average Loan: $16,300
% of Aid That Is Merit-Based: 1
% Receiving Some Sort of Aid: 83
Average Total Aid Package: $17,480
Average Debt: $40,800
Tuition Per Credit (Residents/Nonresidents): $145/$386
Fees Per Credit: $50

ADMISSIONS INFORMATION
Application Fee: $35
Regular Application Deadline: 4/1
Regular Notification: Rolling
LSDAS Accepted? Yes
Average GPA: 3.3
Range of GPA: 3.1–3.7
Average LSAT: 151
Range of LSAT: 148–155
Transfer Students Accepted? Yes
Number of Applications Received: 280
Number of Applicants Accepted: 154
Number of Applicants Enrolled: 81

EMPLOYMENT INFORMATION

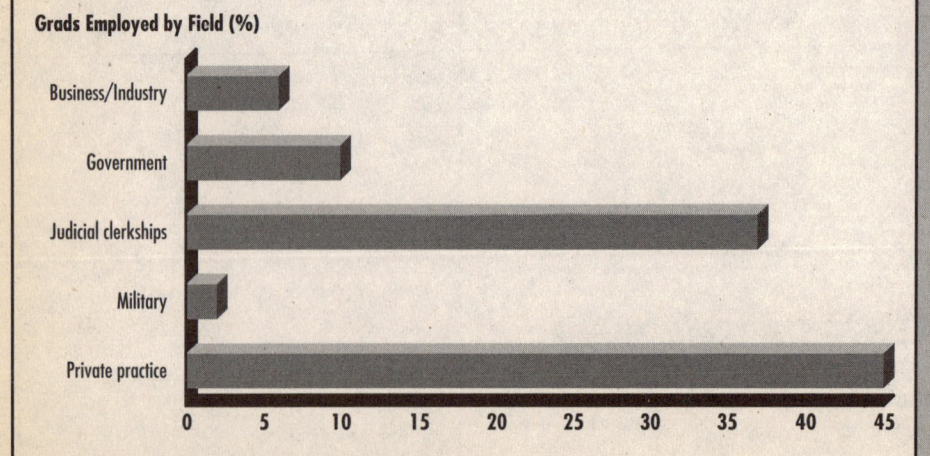

Grads Employed by Field (%)

Field	%
Business/Industry	~6
Government	~10
Judicial clerkships	~37
Military	~2
Private practice	~45

Rate of Placement: 88%
Average Starting Salary: $40,900
Employers Who Frequently Hire Grads: Judicial systems of ND and MN; private firms in ND and MN
State for Bar Exam: ND, MN, AZ, MT, IL
Pass Rate for First-Time Bar: 90%

UNIVERSITY OF NOTRE DAME
Law School

Admissions Contact: Director of Admissions, Charles W. Roboski
PO Box 959, Notre Dame, IN 46556-0959
Admissions Phone: 574-631-6626 • Admissions Fax: 574-631-5474
Admissions E-mail: lawadmit@nd.edu • Web Address: www.law.nd.edu

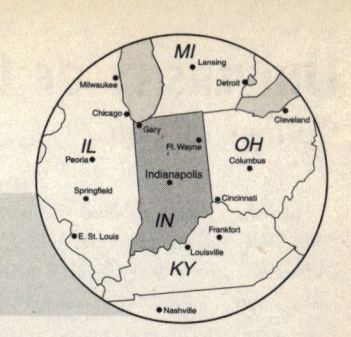

INSTITUTIONAL INFORMATION
Public/Private: Private
Affiliation: Roman Catholic
Student/Faculty Ratio: 17:1
Total Faculty: 60
% Part Time: 45
% Female: 22
% Minority: 4

PROGRAMS
Academic Specialties: Trial Advocacy, International Human Rights Law, Comparative Law, Law and Religion, Professionalism and Ethics, International Law
Advanced Degrees Offered: LLM International Human Rights (1 year), JSD International Human Rights (3 to 5 years, including 1 year of residency), LLM International Comparative Law—London campus only (1 year)
Combined Degrees Offered: JD/MBA (4 years), JD/ME (4 years), JD/MA English or Peace Studies (3 to 4 years)
Grading System: Letter system on a 4.0 scale; no mandatory curve; median grades are 3.0 for first year, 3.1 second, 3.3 third
Clinical Program Required? No
Clinical Program Description: Immigration Law, General Civil Practice
Legal Writing Course Requirements? Yes
Legal Writing Description: First-year, year-long course
Legal Methods Course Requirements? Yes
Legal Methods Description: 2-credit legal writing course in the first semester, 2-credit Legal Research and Writing program (moot court) in the second semester
Legal Research Course Requirements? Yes
Legal Research Description: First semester of first year
Moot Court Requirement? Yes
Moot Court Description: First year, second semester
Public Interest Law Requirement? No
Academic Journals: *Notre Dame Law Review*; *Journal of College and University Law*; *Journal of Law, Ethics and Public Policy*; *Journal of Legislation*

STUDENT INFORMATION
Enrollment of Law School: 550
% Male/Female: 57/43
% Full Time: 100
% Minority: 19
Average Age of Entering Class: 24

RESEARCH FACILITIES
School-Supported Research Centers: Center for Civil and Human Rights, London Law Centre

EXPENSES/FINANCIAL AID
Annual Tuition: $26,110
Room and Board: $10,965
Books and Supplies: $1,080
Financial Aid Application Deadline: 3/1
Average Grant: $7,500
Average Loan: $23,900
% of Aid That Is Merit-Based: 95
Average Debt: $65,750

ADMISSIONS INFORMATION
Application Fee: $55
Regular Application Deadline: 3/1
Regular Notification: Rolling
LSDAS Accepted? Yes
Average GPA: 3.6
Range of GPA: 3.3–3.8
Average LSAT: 163
Range of LSAT: 160–165
Transfer Students Accepted? Yes
Other Schools to Which Students Applied: Boston College, George Washington University, Georgetown University, Boston University, Northwestern University, Vanderbilt University
Other Admissions Factors Considered: Leadership, extracurricular activities, work experience, community service personal statement
Number of Applications Received: 2,894
Number of Applicants Accepted: 566
Number of Applicants Enrolled: 203

INTERNATIONAL STUDENTS
TOEFL Required of International Students? Yes

EMPLOYMENT INFORMATION

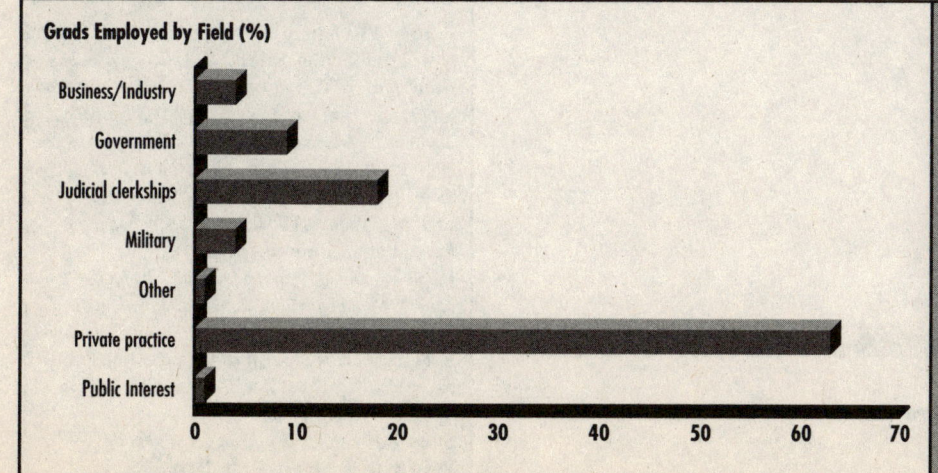

Grads Employed by Field (%)
- Business/Industry: ~3
- Government: ~10
- Judicial clerkships: ~18
- Military: ~2
- Other: ~1
- Private practice: ~64
- Public Interest: ~2

Rate of Placement: 97%
Average Starting Salary: $85,000
Employers Who Frequently Hire Grads: Major law firms in locations throughout the country and abroad, judges at all levels, government agencies, corporations, public interest organizations
State for Bar Exam: IL
Pass Rate for First-Time Bar: 97%

UNIVERSITY OF OKLAHOMA
College of Law

Admissions Contact: Admissions Coordinator, Kathie G. Madden
300 Timberdell Road, Norman, OK 73019
Admissions Phone: 405-325-4726 • Admissions Fax: 405-325-0502
Admissions E-mail: kmadden@ou.edu • Web Address: www.law.ou.edu

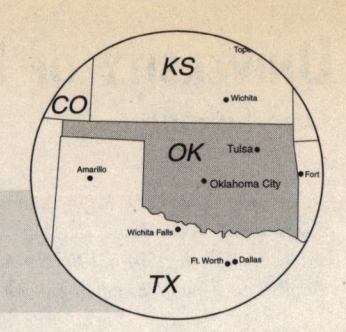

INSTITUTIONAL INFORMATION
Public/Private: Public
Student/Faculty Ratio: 15:1
Total Faculty: 67
% Part Time: 33
% Female: 18
% Minority: 6

PROGRAMS
Academic Specialties: Oil and Gas, Criminal Law, International Law, Taxation, Indian Law, Products Liability, Constitutional Law, Professional Responsibility, Environmental Law, Family Law, Commercial Law, Corporation Securities Law, Intellectual Property Law, Labor Law
Combined Degrees Offered: JD/MBA (4 years), JD/MPH (4 years)
Grading System: Letter system
Clinical Program Required? No
Clinical Program Description: Judicial Clinic, Civil Clinic, Criminal Defense Clinic
Legal Writing Course Requirements? Yes
Legal Writing Description: First year, fall and spring semesters
Legal Methods Course Requirements? No
Legal Research Course Requirements? Yes
Legal Research Description: First year, fall and spring semesters
Moot Court Requirement? No
Public Interest Law Requirement? No
Academic Journals: Oklahoma Law Review, American Indian Law Review

STUDENT INFORMATION
Enrollment of Law School: 524
% Out of State: 13
% Male/Female: 53/47
% Full Time: 100
% Full Time That Are International: 0
% Minority: 13
Average Age of Entering Class: 24

RESEARCH FACILITIES
Research Resources Available: Westlaw, Lexis/Nexis, Wilsonweb, CCH, LegalTrac

EXPENSES/FINANCIAL AID
Annual Tuition (Residents/Nonresidents): $5,784/$15,713
Room and Board (On/Off Campus): $7,088/$7,930
Books and Supplies: $913
Financial Aid Application Deadline: 3/1
Average Grant: $2,000
Average Loan: $16,176
% of Aid That Is Merit-Based: 16
% Receiving Some Sort of Aid: 89
Average Total Aid Package: $16,860
Average Debt: $56,819
Tuition Per Credit (Residents/Nonresidents): $193/$524

ADMISSIONS INFORMATION
Application Fee: $50
Regular Application Deadline: 3/15
Regular Notification: Rolling
LSDAS Accepted? Yes
Average GPA: 3.5
Range of GPA: 3.2–3.8
Average LSAT: 157
Range of LSAT: 153–160
Transfer Students Accepted? Yes
Other Admissions Factors Considered: LSAT; undergraduate GPA; cultural, economic, and educational background grade trends; extracurricular activities; work experience; military achievements; graduate studies; adjustments to personal difficulties
Number of Applications Received: 1,009
Number of Applicants Accepted: 281
Number of Applicants Enrolled: 172

EMPLOYMENT INFORMATION

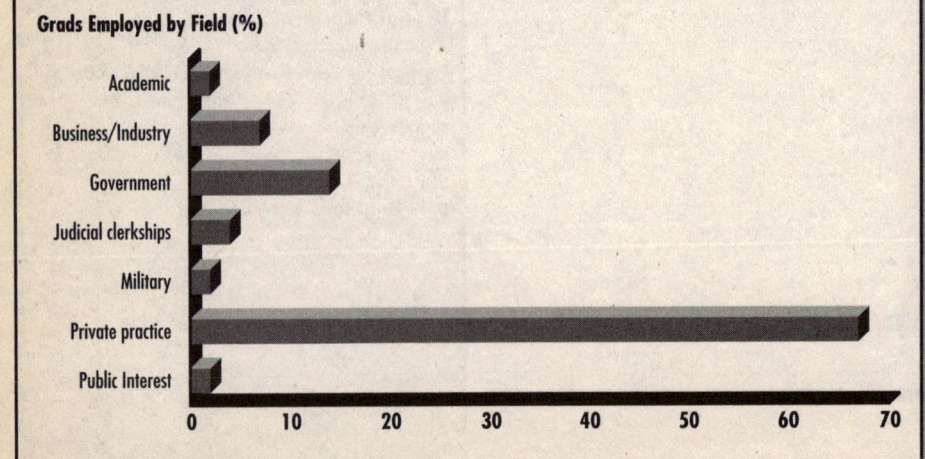

Grads Employed by Field (%):
- Academic: ~2
- Business/Industry: ~7
- Government: ~15
- Judicial clerkships: ~3
- Military: ~1
- Private practice: ~68
- Public Interest: ~2

Rate of Placement: 95%
Average Starting Salary: $53,023
Employers Who Frequently Hire Grads: McAfee & Taft; Crowe & Dunlevy; McKinney & Stringer; Conner & Winters; Gable & Gotwals; Hall, Estill, Hardwick, Gable & Nelson; Phillips, McFall, McCaffrey, McVay & Murray; U.S. Government; State of Oklahoma
Prominent Alumni: Frank Keating, former Governor of Oklahoma; David L. Boren, President, OU, and former U.S. Senator; William T. Comfort, President, CitiCorp Venture Capital; Robert Henry, Judge, 10th Circuit Court of Appeals; Andrew M. Coats, Dean, OU Law, and former Mayor, Oklahoma City
State for Bar Exam: OK, TX, CO, NM, VA
Pass Rate for First-Time Bar: 88%

UNIVERSITY OF OREGON
School of Law

Admissions Contact: Admissions Director
1221 University of Oregon, Eugene, OR 97403-1221
Admissions Phone: 541-346-3846 • Admissions Fax: 541-346-3984
Admissions E-mail: admissions@law.uoregon.edu • Web Address: www.law.uoregon.edu

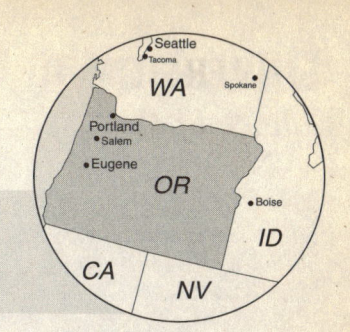

INSTITUTIONAL INFORMATION
Public/Private: Public
Student/Faculty Ratio: 18:1
Total Faculty: 42
% Female: 38
% Minority: 13

PROGRAMS
Academic Specialties: Commercial Law, Constitutional Law, Corporation Securities Law, Criminal Law, Environmental Law, Government Services, Human Rights Law, International Law, Labor Law, Legal History, Property, Taxation
Clinical Program Required? No
Legal Writing Course Requirements? Yes
Legal Methods Course Requirements? Yes
Legal Research Course Requirements? Yes
Moot Court Requirement? No
Public Interest Law Requirement? No

STUDENT INFORMATION
Enrollment of Law School: 503
% Out of State: 55
% Male/Female: 57/43
% Full Time: 100
% Full Time That Are International: 1
% Minority: 15
Average Age of Entering Class: 27

EXPENSES/FINANCIAL AID
Annual Tuition (Residents/Nonresidents): $11,500/$15,600
Books and Supplies: $800
Financial Aid Application Deadline: 2/1
Average Grant: $3,000
Average Loan: $18,500
% Receiving Some Sort of Aid: 90
Average Total Aid Package: $18,500
Average Debt: $43,000

ADMISSIONS INFORMATION
Application Fee: $50
Regular Application Deadline: 2/15
Regular Notification: 4/1
LSDAS Accepted? Yes
Average GPA: 3.4
Average LSAT: 159
Range of LSAT: 156–161
Transfer Students Accepted? Yes
Other Admissions Factors Considered: Personal statement, work experience, résumé, letters of recommendation
Number of Applications Received: 1,734
Number of Applicants Accepted: 655
Number of Applicants Enrolled: 183

INTERNATIONAL STUDENTS
TOEFL Required of International Students? Yes
Minimum TOEFL: 650

EMPLOYMENT INFORMATION
Rate of Placement: 92%
Average Starting Salary: $52,000
State for Bar Exam: OR
Pass Rate for First-Time Bar: 82%

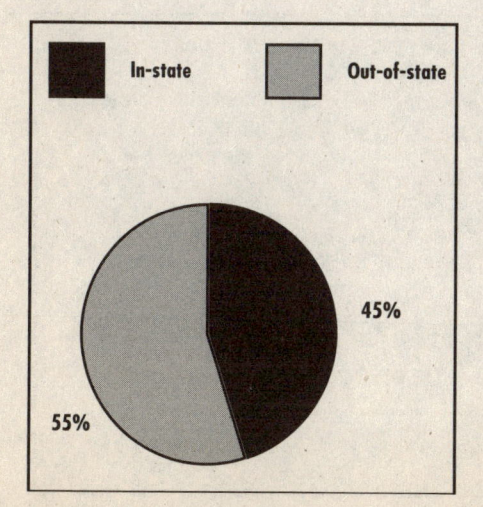

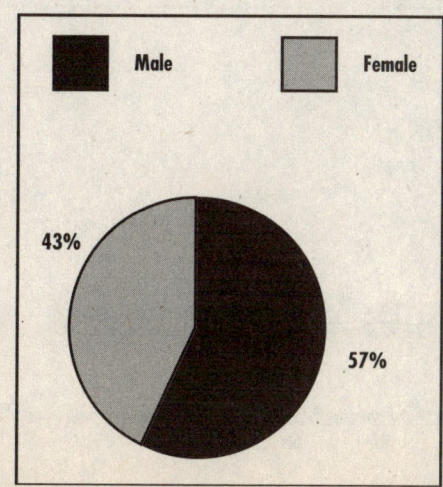

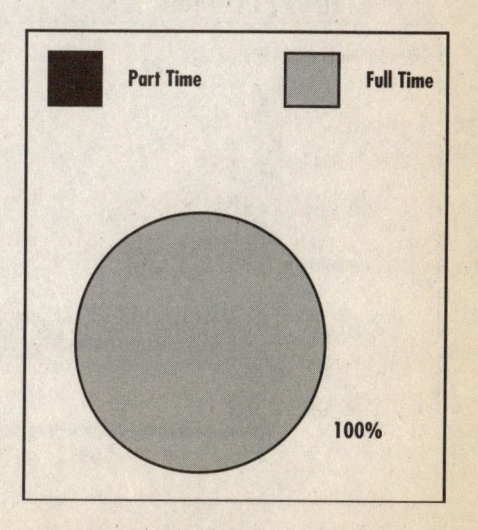

In-state 45% / Out-of-state 55%

Male 57% / Female 43%

Full Time 100%

UNIVERSITY OF PENNSYLVANIA
Law School

Admissions Contact: Assistant Dean of Admissions and Financial Aid, Derek E. Meeker
3400 Chestnut Street, Philadelphia, PA 19104-6204
Admissions Phone: 215-898-7400 • Admissions Fax: 215-573-2025
Admissions E-mail: admissions@law.upenn.edu • Web Address: www.law.upenn.edu

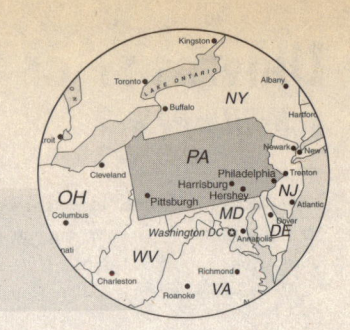

INSTITUTIONAL INFORMATION
Public/Private: Private
Student/Faculty Ratio: 13:1
Total Faculty: 123
% Part Time: 48
% Female: 31
% Minority: 13

PROGRAMS
Academic Specialties: Administrative Law, Health Law, Jurisprudence, Law and Economics, Civil Procedure, Commercial Law, Constitutional Law, Corporation Securities Law, Criminal Law, Environmental Law, Government Services, Human Rights Law, Intellectual Property Law, International Law, Labor Law, Legal History, Legal Philosophy, Property, Taxation
Advanced Degrees Offered: JD (3 years), LLM (1 year), SJD (1 year minimum), LLCM (1 year)
Combined Degrees Offered: JD/MBA (4 years), JD/MA or PhD Economics (4 years minimum), JD/MA or PhD Public Policy and Management (4 years minimum), JD/MA or PhD Philosophy (6 years), JD/MA Islamic Studies, (3 years minimum), JD/MCP (4 years), JD/MSW (4 years), JD/MD
Grading System: Letter system; mandatory distribution in first year
Clinical Program Required? No
Clinical Program Description: Civil Practice Clinic, Advanced Civil Practice Clinic, Small Business Clinic, Mediation Clinic, Criminal Defense Clinic, Legislative Clinic, Child Advocacy Clinic

Legal Writing Course Requirements? Yes
Legal Writing Description: A year-long course, taught in small groups by third-year students under the supervision of the Legal Writing instructor that covers legal research, basic legal analysis, objective and persuasive writing, and oral advocacy
Legal Methods Course Requirements? Yes
Legal Methods Description: See Legal Writing.
Legal Research Course Requirements? Yes
Legal Research Description: See Legal Writing.
Moot Court Requirement? No
Public Interest Law Requirement? Yes
Public Interest Law Description: 70 hours of public service
Academic Journals: Law Review, Journal of Constitutional Law, Journal of Labor and Employment Law, Journal of International Economic Law

STUDENT INFORMATION
Enrollment of Law School: 823
% Male/Female: 52/48
% Full Time: 100
% Full Time That Are International: 3
% Minority: 28
Average Age of Entering Class: 24

EXPENSES/FINANCIAL AID
Annual Tuition: $29,310
Room and Board: $14,412
Books and Supplies: $850
Financial Aid Application Deadline: 3/1
Average Grant: $12,400
Average Loan: $30,000
% of Aid That Is Merit-Based: 12

ADMISSIONS INFORMATION
Application Fee: $70
Regular Application Deadline: 3/1
Regular Notification: Rolling
LSDAS Accepted? Yes
Average GPA: 3.6
Range of GPA: 3.4–3.8
Average LSAT: 167
Range of LSAT: 165–169
Transfer Students Accepted? Yes
Other Schools to Which Students Applied: Columbia University, Georgetown University, Harvard University, New York University
Other Admissions Factors Considered: Pprofessional and personal accomplishments, interest in interdisciplinary academic curricula or joint degrees, leadership, service, advanced degree or course work
Number of Applications Received: 5,232
Number of Applicants Accepted: 856
Number of Applicants Enrolled: 335

EMPLOYMENT INFORMATION

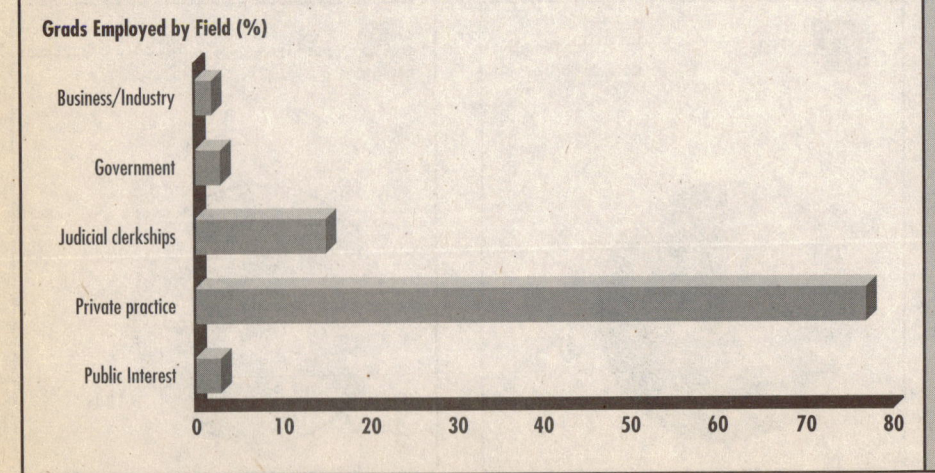

Grads Employed by Field (%)

Field	%
Business/Industry	~2
Government	~3
Judicial clerkships	~16
Private practice	~77
Public Interest	~3

Rate of Placement: 98%
Average Starting Salary: $125,000
Employers Who Frequently Hire Grads: Variety of major corporate law firms nationwide; prestigious national fellowship organizations and public interest organizations; federal and state judges
State for Bar Exam: NY
Pass Rate for First-Time Bar: 94%

UNIVERSITY OF PITTSBURGH
School of Law

Admissions Contact: Assistant Dean for Admissions and Financial Aid, Fredi G. Miller
3900 Forbes Avenue, Pittsburgh, PA 15260
Admissions Phone: 412-648-1413 • Admissions Fax: 412-648-2647
Admissions E-mail: admissions@law.pitt.edu • Web Address: www.law.pitt.edu

INSTITUTIONAL INFORMATION
Public/Private: Public
Student/Faculty Ratio: 13:1
Total Faculty: 98
% Part Time: 55
% Female: 29
% Minority: 12

PROGRAMS
Academic Specialties: New Certificate programs offered include Health Law, Environmental Law, International and Comparative Law, and Civil Litigation. Specialties include Civil Procedure, Corporation Securities Law, and Intellectual Property Law.
Advanced Degrees Offered: LLM (2 semesters)
Combined Degrees Offered: JD/MPA (4 years), JD/MPIA (4 years), JD/MBA (3.5 years), JD/MPH (3.5 years), JD/MA Medical Ethics (3.5 years), JD/MSIA (4 years), JD/MS Public Management with Carnegie Mellon (4 years), JD/MBA with Carnegie Mellon (4 years)
Grading System: Letter system; some seminars and clinics are Honors/Pass/Fail
Clinical Program Required? No
Clinical Program Description: Civil Practice Clinic (Health Law, Elder Law, Disability Law, Discrimination Law), Tax Clinic, Enviromental Law Clinic

Legal Writing Course Requirements? Yes
Legal Writing Description: The first-year class is divided into 3 small sections for Legal Writing. There is also an upper-level writing requirement.
Legal Methods Course Requirements? No
Legal Research Course Requirements? Yes
Legal Research Description: 2-semester course combined with Legal Writing
Moot Court Requirement? No
Public Interest Law Requirement? No
Academic Journals: University of Pittsburgh Law Review, University of Pittsburgh Journal of Law and Commerce, The Pittsburgh Journal of Technology Law and Policy

STUDENT INFORMATION
Enrollment of Law School: 744
% Out of State: 30
% Male/Female: 55/45
% Full Time: 100
% Full Time That Are International: 0
% Minority: 10
Average Age of Entering Class: 24

EXPENSES/FINANCIAL AID
Annual Tuition (Residents/Nonresidents): $15,936/$24,038
Room and Board: $11,530
Books and Supplies: $1,210
Financial Aid Application Deadline: 3/1
Average Grant: $8,000
Average Loan: $18,500
% of Aid That Is Merit-Based: 67
% Receiving Some Sort of Aid: 87
Average Debt: $65,000

ADMISSIONS INFORMATION
Application Fee: $55
Regular Application Deadline: 3/1
Regular Notification: Rolling
LSDAS Accepted? Yes
Average GPA: 3.3
Range of GPA: 3.1–3.6
Average LSAT: 158
Range of LSAT: 154–161
Transfer Students Accepted? Yes
Other Schools to Which Students Applied: American University, Boston University, Case Western Reserve University, George Washington University, Temple University, Pennsylvania State University, Villanova University
Other Admissions Factors Considered: Undergraduate institution, curriculum, campus activities
Number of Applications Received: 1,952
Number of Applicants Accepted: 683
Number of Applicants Enrolled: 264

INTERNATIONAL STUDENTS
TOEFL Required of International Students? Yes
Minimum TOEFL: 600

EMPLOYMENT INFORMATION

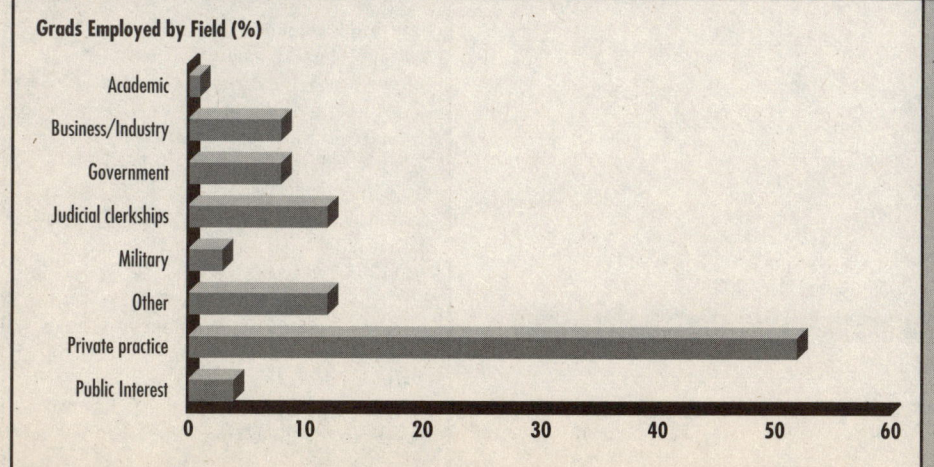

Grads Employed by Field (%)
- Academic: ~1
- Business/Industry: ~8
- Government: ~10
- Judicial clerkships: ~13
- Military: ~1
- Other: ~13
- Private practice: ~53
- Public Interest: ~3

Rate of Placement: 92%
Average Starting Salary: $71,943
Employers Who Frequently Hire Grads: Buchanan Ingersoll; Kirkpatrick & Lockhart; Reed, Smith, Shaw & McClay; Morgan, Lewis & Bockius; Jones, Day, Reavis & Pogue; Pepper Hamilton; Milbank Tweed
Prominent Alumni: Richard Thornburg, former U.S. Attorney General; Orrin Hatch, Utah Senator; Joseph Weis, Senior Judge, Third Circut; Ruggerio Aldisert, Senior Judge, Ninth Circuit; William Lerach, Litigator, Plantif Security
State for Bar Exam: PA, VA, MD, NY, CA
Pass Rate for First-Time Bar: 84%

UNIVERSITY OF RICHMOND
School of Law

Admissions Contact: Director of Admissions, Michelle Rahman
Richmond, VA 23173
Admissions Phone: 804-289-8189 • Admissions Fax: 804-287-6516
Admissions E-mail: admissions@uofrlaw.richmond.edu • Web Address: law.richmond.edu

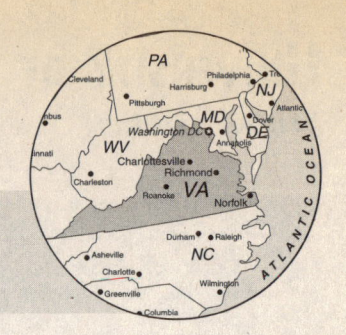

INSTITUTIONAL INFORMATION
Public/Private: Private
Student/Faculty Ratio: 18:1
Total Faculty: 105
% Part Time: 54
% Female: 32
% Minority: 4

PROGRAMS
Academic Specialties: First law school in the country to require all students to have a laptop computer, numerous International and Comparative Law courses, several courses that focus on lawyering skills (advanced trial practice, interviewing, counseling, negotiations, business transactions), Civil Procedure, Commercial Law, Constitutional Law, Corporation Securities Law, Criminal Law, Environmental Law, Intellectual Property Law, Labor Law, Legal History, Property, Taxation
Advanced Degrees Offered: JD (3 years)
Combined Degrees Offered: JD/MBA, JD/MURP, JD/MHA, JD/MSW, JD/MPA (all 4 years)
Grading System: 4.0 scale
Clinical Program Required? No
Clinical Program Description: Clinical Placement Program (judicial, criminal, and civil externships), Juvenile Delinquency Clinic, Mental Disabilities Law Clinic
Legal Writing Course Requirements? Yes
Legal Writing Description: First year, Lawyering Skills; third year, Writing Requirement seminar or Independent Study course
Legal Methods Course Requirements? Yes
Legal Methods Description: 4 semesters, Lawyering Skills
Legal Research Course Requirements? Yes
Legal Research Description: 4 semesters, Lawyering Skills
Moot Court Requirement? Yes
Moot Court Description: In the second year of a required 2-year Lawyering Skills course, the fall semester is devoted to trial advocacy skills, the spring semester to appellate advocacy skills.
Public Interest Law Requirement? No
Academic Journals: *Law Review, Journal of Law and Technology, Journal of Law and Public Interest, Journal of Global Law and Business*

STUDENT INFORMATION
Enrollment of Law School: 486
% Out of State: 47
% Male/Female: 52/48
% Full Time: 100
% Full Time That Are International: 3
% Minority: 7
Average Age of Entering Class: 24

EXPENSES/FINANCIAL AID
Annual Tuition: $22,860
Room and Board (On/Off Campus): $5,214/$7,920
Books and Supplies: $1,100
Financial Aid Application Deadline: 2/25
Average Grant: $5,050
Average Loan: $24,630
% of Aid That Is Merit-Based: 25
% Receiving Some Sort of Aid: 95
Average Total Aid Package: $27,365
Average Debt: $63,480
Tuition Per Credit: $1,145

ADMISSIONS INFORMATION
Application Fee: $35
Regular Application Deadline: 1/15
Regular Notification: 4/15
LSDAS Accepted? Yes
Average GPA: 3.3
Range of GPA: 2.9–4.0
Average LSAT: 159
Range of LSAT: 157–160
Transfer Students Accepted? Yes
Other Schools to Which Students Applied: American University, College of William and Mary, George Washington University, University of Virginia, Wake Forest University, Washington and Lee University, George Mason University
Other Admissions Factors Considered: Community service, letters of recommendation, extracurricular activities
Number of Applications Received: 1,864
Number of Applicants Accepted: 573
Number of Applicants Enrolled: 178

INTERNATIONAL STUDENTS
TOEFL Recommended for International Students? Yes
Minimum TOEFL: 650

EMPLOYMENT INFORMATION

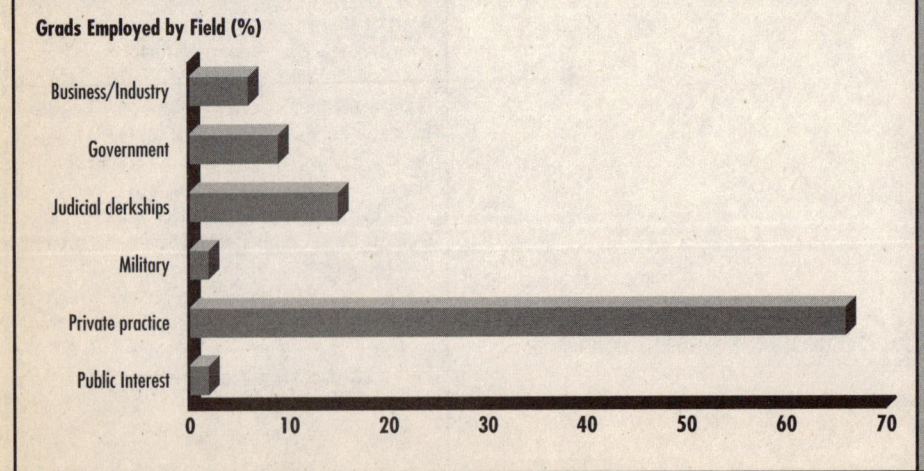

Grads Employed by Field (%)

- Business/Industry: ~7
- Government: ~10
- Judicial clerkships: ~15
- Military: ~2
- Private practice: ~65
- Public Interest: ~2

Rate of Placement: 97%
Average Starting Salary: $57,208
Employers Who Frequently Hire Grads: Bowman & Brooke, Cooper Spong, Gentry Locke, Holland & Knight, Hunton & Williams, Jackson & Kelly, Kaufman & Canoles, LeClair Ryan, McGuire Woods, Odin Feldman, Reed Smith, Troutman Sanders, Venable Willcox & Savage, Williams Mullen, Woods Rogers & Hazlegrove
Prominent Alumni: Lawrence L. Koontz, Justice, VA Supreme Court; Harvey E. Schlesinger, Judge, U.S. District Court, Middle District of FL; Frederick P. Stamp Jr., Judge, U.S. District Court, Northern District of WV
State for Bar Exam: NC, NY, FL, VA, DC
Pass Rate for First-Time Bar: 95%

UNIVERSITY OF SAN DIEGO
School of Law

Admissions Contact: Director of Admissions and Financial Aid, Carl Eging
5998 Alcala Park, San Diego, CA 92110
Admissions Phone: 619-260-4528 • Admissions Fax: 619-260-2218
Admissions E-mail: jdinfo@sandiego.edu • Web Address: www.sandiego.edu/usdlaw

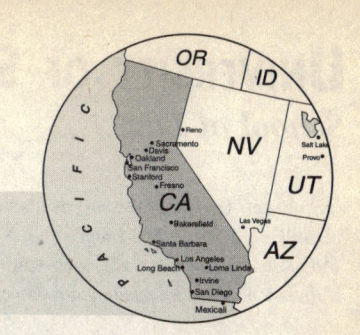

INSTITUTIONAL INFORMATION
Public/Private: Private
Affiliation: Roman Catholic
Student/Faculty Ratio: 18:1
Total Faculty: 173
% Part Time: 36
% Female: 24
% Minority: 10

PROGRAMS
Academic Specialties: Our large faculty contains experts in virtually every field of law, as well as authors of leading case books, treatises, and scholarly monographs published by the best university presses. Specialties include Civil Procedure, Commercial Law, Constitutional Law, Criminal Law, Environmental Law, Human Rights Law, International Law, Labor Law, and Taxation.
Advanced Degrees Offered: JD (3 years day, 4 years evening), LLM (1 year)
Combined Degrees Offered: JD/MBA, JD/MA International Relations (4 to 4.5 years), JD/IMBA
Grading System: Letter and numerical system (65–93); some courses are Pass/Low Pass/Fail, Honors
Clinical Program Required? No
Clinical Program Description: Children's Advocacy, Civil, Criminal, Environmental, Immigration, Mental Health, Public Interest, Judicial Internship, Land Development, Tax, Small Claims Clinic
Legal Writing Course Requirements? Yes
Legal Writing Description: Lawyering Skills—1 semester, small sections, small student/faculty ratio
Legal Methods Course Requirements? No
Legal Research Course Requirements? No
Moot Court Requirement? No
Moot Court Description: Students simulate the appellate advocacy process by researching and writing an appellate brief, then arguing the case before a distinguished panel of judges.
Public Interest Law Requirement? No
Academic Journals: *San Diego Law Review, Journal of Contemporary Legal Issues, San Diego International Law Journal, California Regulatory Law Reporter, Children's Regulatory Law Reporter, California Children's Budget, Legal Theory, Motions*

STUDENT INFORMATION
Enrollment of Law School: 990
% Out of State: 33
% Male/Female: 52/48
% Full Time: 76
% Full Time That Are International: 4
% Minority: 26
Average Age of Entering Class: 24

RESEARCH FACILITIES
School-Supported Research Centers: Academic Support Program, Legal Research and Writing Programs, Alumni Advisor Program, clinical and internship opportunities, Children's Advocacy Institute, Center for Public Interest Law

EXPENSES/FINANCIAL AID
Annual Tuition: $26,070
Room and Board: $13,454
Books and Supplies: $750
Financial Aid Application Deadline: 3/1
Average Grant: $14,378
Average Loan: $22,744
% Receiving Some Sort of Aid: 80
Average Total Aid Package: $40,324
Average Debt: $73,000
Tuition Per Credit: $905
Fees Per Credit: $40

ADMISSIONS INFORMATION
Application Fee: $50
Regular Application Deadline: Rolling
Regular Notification: Rolling
LSDAS Accepted? Yes
Average GPA: 3.4
Range of GPA: 3.1–3.6
Average LSAT: 162
Range of LSAT: 160–164
Transfer Students Accepted? Yes
Number of Applications Received: 4,475

INTERNATIONAL STUDENTS
TOEFL Required of International Students? Yes
Minimum TOEFL: 600 (250 computer)

EMPLOYMENT INFORMATION

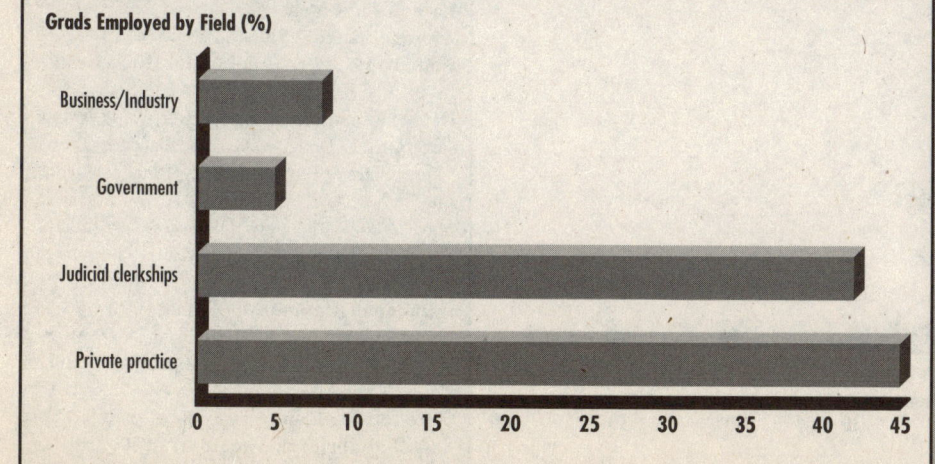

Grads Employed by Field (%)
- Business/Industry: ~8
- Government: ~5
- Judicial clerkships: ~42
- Private practice: ~45

Rate of Placement: 90%
Average Starting Salary: $74,500
Employers Who Frequently Hire Grads: Gibson Dunn & Crutcher; Cooley Godward; Gray Cary; Littler Mendelson; Pillsbury Winthrop; Department Of Justice; Luce Forward; Heller Ehrman; Shell & Wilmer; Knobbe Martins Olson & Bear; Foley Lardner Howrey
Prominent Alumni: Nancy Ely-Raphel, U.S. Ambassador to Slovenia; Michael Thorsness, Thorsness, Bartolotta and Mcguire; Michael Ferrara, Ferrara, Rosetti & Devoto; Michael Streit, Justice, Iowa State Supreme Court; Hon. Lynn Schenk, Chief of Staff for Governor Gray Davis
State for Bar Exam: CA
Pass Rate for First-Time Bar: 73%

UNIVERSITY OF SAN FRANCISCO
School of Law

Admissions Contact: Director of Admissions, Alan Guerrero
2130 Fulton Street, San Francisco, CA 94117
Admissions Phone: 415-422-6586 • Admissions Fax: 415-422-6433
Admissions E-mail: lawadmissions@usfca.edu • Web Address: www.law.usfca.edu

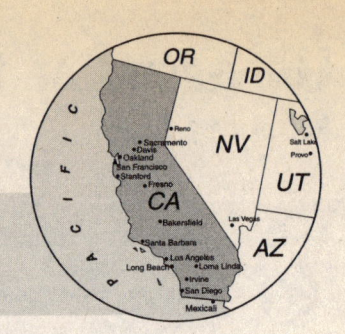

INSTITUTIONAL INFORMATION
Public/Private: Private
Affiliation: Roman Catholic
Student/Faculty Ratio: 17:1
Total Faculty: 88
% Part Time: 65
% Female: 33
% Minority: 20

PROGRAMS
Academic Specialties: Trial Advocacy and Dispute Resolution, Intellectual Property Law, International Law, Maritime Law
Advanced Degrees Offered: LLM (1 year)
Combined Degrees Offered: JD/MBA (4 years)
Grading System: Letter and numerical system on a 4.0 scale, Credit/No Credit
Clinical Program Required? No
Clinical Program Description: Criminal Law Clinic, Civil Law Clinic, Mediation Clinic, International Human Rights Clinic, Investigation Law Clinic, Judicial Externships
Legal Writing Course Requirements? Yes
Legal Writing Description: An intensive 6-unit, year-long Legal Research, Writing, and Analysis course is required for all first-year students, taught by experienced teachers and practitioners.
Legal Methods Course Requirements? No
Legal Research Course Requirements? Yes
Legal Research Description: See Legal Writing.
Moot Court Requirement? Yes
Moot Court Description: Moot Court is a required part of the first-year curriculum (second year for part-time students). During the spring semester, students are assigned to prepare a brief for either an appellant or a respondent in one of several Moot Court problems and then argue before a panel of local judges and attorneys. There is an advanced Moot Court program for upper-level students who participate in numerous intra- and interschool competitions.
Public Interest Law Requirement? No
Public Interest Law Description: Numerous students pursue an elective Public Interest Certificate Program, requiring significant pro bono activity.
Academic Journals: *University of San Francisco Law Review, USF Maritime Law Journal, USF Intellectual Property Law Bulletin*

STUDENT INFORMATION
Enrollment of Law School: 670
% Male/Female: 44/56
% Full Time: 82
% Full Time That Are International: 0
% Minority: 31
Average Age of Entering Class: 25

RESEARCH FACILITIES
Research Resources Available: Consortium arrangement with other ABA-approved law schools in the San Francisco Bay Area
School-Supported Research Centers: USF Law Library, Gleeson Library/Geschke Learning Center, USF Center for Law and Global Justice, McCarthy Institute for Intellectual Property and Technology, Center for Applied Legal Ethics

EXPENSES/FINANCIAL AID
Annual Tuition: $26,282
Room and Board (On/Off Campus): $9,120/$12,000
Books and Supplies: $800
Financial Aid Application Deadline: 2/15
Average Grant: $10,991
Average Loan: $26,112
% Receiving Some Sort of Aid: 88
Average Total Aid Package: $24,000
Average Debt: $68,772
Tuition Per Credit: $941
Fees Per Credit: $2

ADMISSIONS INFORMATION
Application Fee: $60
Regular Application Deadline: 2/3
Regular Notification: Rolling
LSDAS Accepted? Yes
Average GPA: 3.2
Range of GPA: 3.0–3.4
Average LSAT: 156
Range of LSAT: 154–159
Transfer Students Accepted? Yes
Other Schools to Which Students Applied: UC Berkeley, Santa Clara, Golden Gate, Loyola Marymount, UC Davis, UC Hastings, University of San Diego
Number of Applications Received: 3,107
Number of Applicants Accepted: 1,011
Number of Applicants Enrolled: 249

INTERNATIONAL STUDENTS
TOEFL Required of International Students? Yes
Minimum TOEFL: 600 (250 computer)

EMPLOYMENT INFORMATION

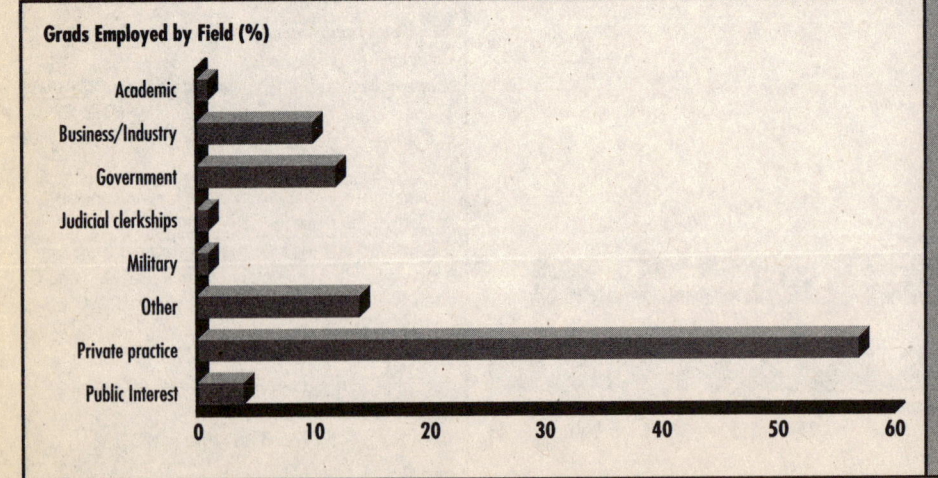

Grads Employed by Field (%)
- Academic: ~1
- Business/Industry: ~10
- Government: ~12
- Judicial clerkships: ~2
- Military: ~1
- Other: ~14
- Private practice: ~58
- Public Interest: ~3

Rate of Placement: 92%
Average Starting Salary: $85,000
Employers Who Frequently Hire Grads: Brobeck, Phleger & Harrison; Sedgewick, Detert, Moran & Arnold; Keesel, Young & Logan; Hanson, Bridgett, Marcus, Vlahos & Rudy; Miller, Starr & Regalia; Shook, Hardy & Bacon; Bingham McCutchen; Crosby, Heafy, Roach & May; Alameda County District Attorney and Public Defenders; Townshend, Townshend & Crew; Hancock, Rothert, & Burnshaft LLP
Prominent Alumni: Ming Chin, Justice, California Supreme Court; Kevin Ryan, U.S. Attorney; Saundra B. Armstrong, Judge, U.S. District Court, Northern California
State for Bar Exam: CA
Pass Rate for First-Time Bar: 73%

UNIVERSITY OF SOUTH CAROLINA
School of Law

Admissions Contact: Assistant Dean for Admissions
Main and Greene Streets, Columbia, SC 29208
Admissions Phone: 803-777-6605 • Admissions Fax: 803-777-7751
Admissions E-mail: usclaw@law.law.sc.edu • Web Address: www.law.sc.edu

INSTITUTIONAL INFORMATION
Public/Private: Public
Student/Faculty Ratio: 21:1
Total Faculty: 43
% Female: 4
% Minority: 2

PROGRAMS
Academic Specialties: Corporation Securities Law, Environmental Law, International Law, Property, Taxation, Criminal Law, Constitutional Law, Clinical Legal Education. Clinical Legal Education programs afford students the opportunity to gain practical experience while enrolled in the School of Law.
Advanced Degrees Offered: JD (3 years)
Combined Degrees Offered: JD/MIB (4 years), JD/MBA (4 years), JD/MPA (4 years), JD/Masters in Criminal Justice (4 years), JD/Masters in Economics (4 years), JD/Masters in Accounting (4 years), JD/Masters in Social Work (4 years), JD/Masters in Environmental Sciences (4 years), JD/Masters in Earth and Environmental Resource Management
Grading System: A to F (4.0 scale)

Clinical Program Required? No
Legal Writing Course Requirements? Yes
Legal Writing Description: 1 year
Legal Methods Course Requirements? Yes
Legal Methods Description: First year, 2 semesters
Legal Research Course Requirements? No
Moot Court Requirement? No
Public Interest Law Requirement? No
Public Interest Law Description: Outstanding pro bono program
Academic Journals: S.C. Law Review, ABA Real Property Trust and Probate

STUDENT INFORMATION
Enrollment of Law School: 669
% Out of State: 15
% Male/Female: 55/45
% Full Time: 100
% Full Time That Are International: 0
% Minority: 11
Average Age of Entering Class: 24

RESEARCH FACILITIES
% of JD Classrooms Wired: 40

EXPENSES/FINANCIAL AID
Annual Tuition (Residents/Nonresidents): $7,990/$16,530
Room and Board: $10,000
Books and Supplies: $500
Financial Aid Application Deadline: 4/15
Average Grant: $1,200
Average Loan: $18,000
% of Aid That Is Merit-Based: 15
% Receiving Some Sort of Aid: 69
Average Total Aid Package: $19,226
Average Debt: $42,000

ADMISSIONS INFORMATION
Application Fee: $40
Regular Application Deadline: 2/15
Regular Notification: Rolling
LSDAS Accepted? Yes
Average GPA: 3.2
Average LSAT: 156
Range of LSAT: 152–159
Transfer Students Accepted? Yes
Other Admissions Factors Considered: Undergraduate institution, undergraduate major, graduate work, diversity, joint degree candidacy, maturity
Number of Applications Received: 1,179
Number of Applicants Enrolled: 223

EMPLOYMENT INFORMATION

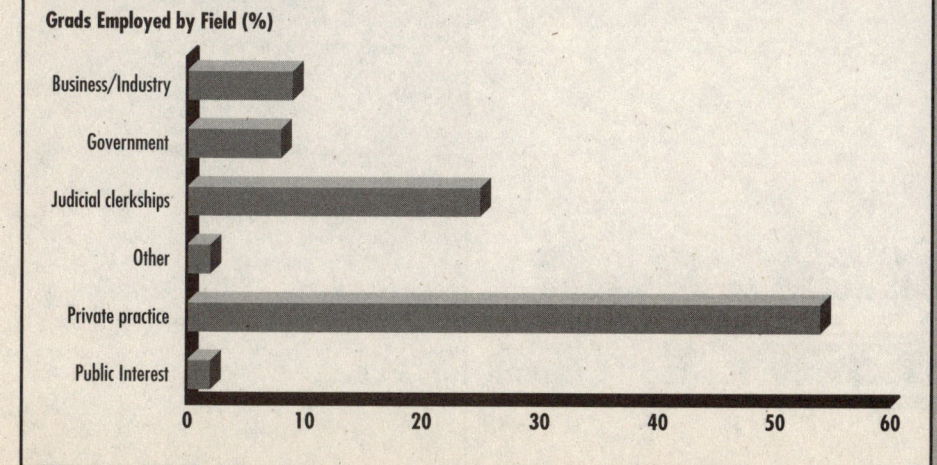

Grads Employed by Field (%)
- Business/Industry
- Government
- Judicial clerkships
- Other
- Private practice
- Public Interest

Rate of Placement: 90%
Average Starting Salary: $46,956
Employers Who Frequently Hire Grads: Nelson Mullins Riley & Scarborough; Kennedy, Covington, Labdell, & Hickman; Alston and Bird
State for Bar Exam: SC, NC, GA, TX, PA
Pass Rate for First-Time Bar: 82%

UNIVERSITY OF SOUTH DAKOTA
School of Law

Admissions Contact: Admission Officer/Registrar, Jean Henriques
414 East Clark Street, Vermillion, SD 57069-2390
Admissions Phone: 605-677-5443 • Admissions Fax: 605-677-5417
Admissions E-mail: lawreq@usd.edu • Web Address: www.usd.edu/law

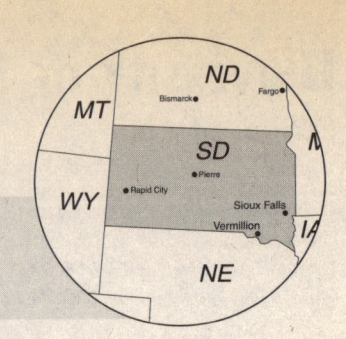

INSTITUTIONAL INFORMATION
Public/Private: Public
Student/Faculty Ratio: 13:1
Total Faculty: 17
% Part Time: 1
% Female: 17
% Minority: 5

PROGRAMS
Academic Specialties: Indian Law, Environmental Law, opportunity to write for *Great Plains Natural Resources Journal*
Combined Degrees Offered: JD/MBA, JD/MPA, JD/MA
Grading System: A (90–99), B (80–89), C (70–79), D (60–69), F (50–59)
Clinical Program Required? No
Legal Writing Course Requirements? Yes
Legal Writing Description: First year, fall semester
Legal Methods Course Requirements? Yes
Legal Methods Description: Legal Research and Writing, first year, first semester; Appellate Advocacy, first year, second semester
Legal Research Course Requirements? Yes
Legal Research Description: First year, fall semester
Moot Court Requirement? No
Public Interest Law Requirement? No
Academic Journals: *Law Review, Great Plains Natural Resources Journal*

STUDENT INFORMATION
Enrollment of Law School: 233
% Out of State: 30
% Male/Female: 55/45
% Full Time: 97
% Full Time That Are International: 1
% Minority: 11
Average Age of Entering Class: 27

EXPENSES/FINANCIAL AID
Annual Tuition (Residents/Nonresidents): $3,573/$10,356
Room and Board (On/Off Campus): $3,523/$5,703
Books and Supplies: $800
Average Grant: $1,000
Average Loan: $16,500
% of Aid That Is Merit-Based: 90
Average Total Aid Package: $17,500
Average Debt: $27,000
Tuition Per Credit (Residents/Nonresidents): $119/$345
Fees Per Credit: $100

ADMISSIONS INFORMATION
Application Fee: $35
Regular Application Deadline: Rolling
Regular Notification: Rolling
LSDAS Accepted? Yes
Average GPA: 3.1
Range of GPA: 2.8–3.5
Average LSAT: 150
Range of LSAT: 146–154
Transfer Students Accepted? Yes
Other Schools to Which Students Applied: University of Wyoming, Creighton University, University of Tulsa, University of Nebraska—Lincoln, Drake University, University of North Dakota, University of Denver
Number of Applications Received: 344
Number of Applicants Accepted: 173
Number of Applicants Enrolled: 91

INTERNATIONAL STUDENTS
TOEFL Required of International Students? Yes
Minimum TOEFL: 600 (250 computer)

EMPLOYMENT INFORMATION

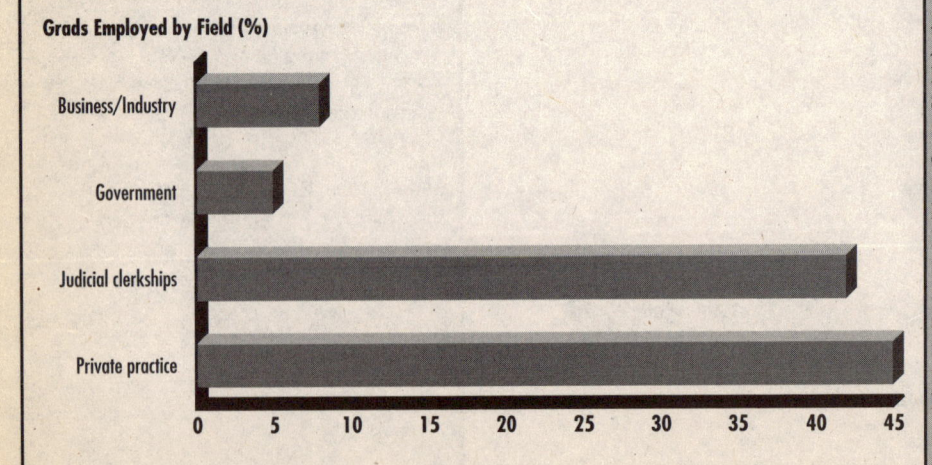

Grads Employed by Field (%)
- Business/Industry
- Government
- Judicial clerkships
- Private practice

Rate of Placement: 90%
Average Starting Salary: $39,633
Employers Who Frequently Hire Grads: U.S. 8th Circuit Court of Appeals; U.S. District Court; South Dakota Supreme Court; South Dakota Circuit Court; Minnehaha Public Defender; law firms; Minnesota District Courts
Prominent Alumni: Tim Johnson, U.S. Senator; David Gilbertson, Chief Justice, South Dakota Supreme Court; Bill Janklow, U.S. Congressman, South Dakota; Thomas J. Erickson, Commissioner, U.S. Commodity Futures Trading Commission
State for Bar Exam: SD, MN, IA, NE, NY
Pass Rate for First-Time Bar: 90%

UNIVERSITY OF SOUTHERN CALIFORNIA
The Law School

Admissions Contact: Associate Dean, William Hoye
Los Angeles, CA 90089-0074
Admissions Phone: 213-740-2523 • Admissions Fax: 213-740-4570
Admissions E-mail: admissions@law.usc.edu • Web Address: www.law.usc.edu

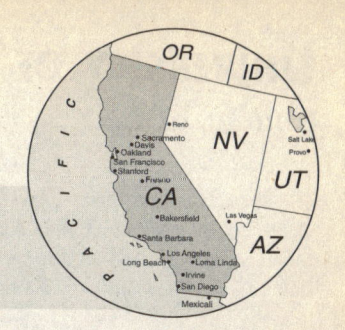

INSTITUTIONAL INFORMATION
Public/Private: Private
Student/Faculty Ratio: 14:1
Total Faculty: 64
% Part Time: 42
% Female: 28
% Minority: 17

PROGRAMS
Academic Specialties: Corporate and Business Law, Bioethics, International Law, Civil Rights and Liberties, Taxation, Intellectual Property, and Environmental Law, Civil Procedure, Commercial Law, Constitutional Law, Criminal Law, Government Services, Human Rights Law, Labor Law, Legal History, Legal Philosophy, Property
Advanced Degrees Offered: JD (3 years), LLM (1 year)
Combined Degrees Offered: JD/MBA (3.5 to 4 years); JD/MPA (3 years); JD/PhD Economics (5 years); JD/MA Economics, International Relations, Communications Management, Philosophy, or Religion (3 years); JD/MSW (4 years); JD/M Real Estate Development (3.5 years); JD/M Business Taxation (3.5 to 4 years); JD/MS Gerontology (4 years); JD/MPP (3 years); JD/PhD (5 years); JD/MA Political Science (4 years)
Grading System: A+ (4.1–4.4), A (3.8–4.0), A– (3.5–3.7), B+ (3.3–3.4), B (3.0–3.2), C+ (2.7–2.9), C (2.5–2.6), C– (2.4), D (2.0–2.3), F (1.9), CR (satisfactory)
Clinical Program Required? No
Clinical Program Description: Post-Conviction Justice Project, Children's Legal Issues, Externship/Internship Program, Trial Advocacy, Pre-Trial Advocacy, Negotiations, Employment Law Advice Clinic, Family Violence Clinic, Immigration Clinic
Legal Writing Course Requirements? Yes
Legal Writing Description: Introduction to Lawyering Skills is a 2-semester course that focuses on developing analytic and communication skills.
Legal Methods Course Requirements? Yes
Legal Methods Description: In Introduction to Lawyering Skills, students also develop oral advocacy skills through oral argument.
Legal Research Course Requirements? Yes
Legal Research Description: Legal Research examines the basic sources of law for federal and California jurisdictions utilizing a vast array of sources.
Moot Court Requirement? Yes
Moot Court Description: All students participate in moot court as part of Introduction to Lawyering Skills. Forty students participate during their second year.
Public Interest Law Requirement? No
Academic Journals: *Southern California Law Review, Southern California Interdisciplinary Law Journal, Southern California Review of Law and Women's Studies*

STUDENT INFORMATION
Enrollment of Law School: 636
% Out of State: 46
% Male/Female: 52/48
% Full Time: 100
% Full Time That Are International: 2
% Minority: 43
Average Age of Entering Class: 25

RESEARCH FACILITIES
Research Resources Available: CalTech, extensive alumni network, externship, One Institute
School-Supported Research Centers: Pacific Center for Health Policy and Ethics; Public Interest Law Foundation; Center for the Study of Law and Politics; Center for Law, Economics, and Organization; Center for Communication Law and Policy; Center for Feminist Research; Center for Law, History and Culture

EXPENSES/FINANCIAL AID
Annual Tuition: $31,074
Room and Board: $9,632
Books and Supplies: $3,779
Financial Aid Application Deadline: 2/15
Average Grant: $9,550
Average Loan: $30,270
% Receiving Some Sort of Aid: 87
Average Total Aid Package: $45,556
Average Debt: $80,985

ADMISSIONS INFORMATION
Application Fee: $70
Regular Application Deadline: 2/1
Regular Notification: Rolling
LSDAS Accepted? Yes
Average GPA: 3.5
Average LSAT: 165
Transfer Students Accepted? Yes
Other Schools to Which Students Applied: Georgetown, NYU, Stanford, UC Berkeley, UCLA
Other Admissions Factors Considered: Academic and professional promise, diverse background and experience
Number of Applications Received: 5,744
Number of Applicants Accepted: 1,198
Number of Applicants Enrolled: 208

INTERNATIONAL STUDENTS
TOEFL Recommended for International Students? Yes

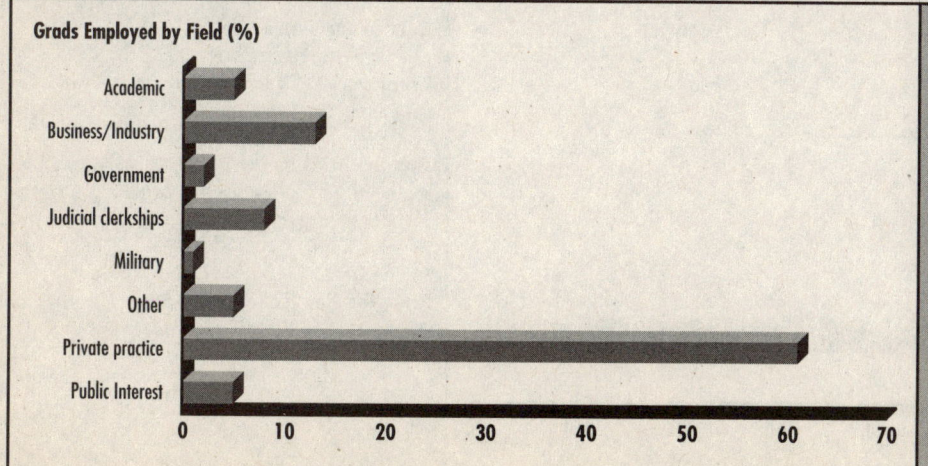

Rate of Placement: 96%
Average Starting Salary: $104,688
Employers Who Frequently Hire Grads: Private firms, corporations, federal judges, government, public interest nonprofits
Prominent Alumni: Joyce Kennard, Justice, California Supreme Court; Larry Flax, Founder, California Pizza Kitchen; Dorothy Nelson, Judge, 9th Circuit Court of Appeals; Walter Zifkin, CEO, William Morris Agency; Carlos Moorehead, U.S. Congressman
State for Bar Exam: CA, NY, DC, WA, TX
Pass Rate for First-Time Bar: 90%

EMPLOYMENT INFORMATION

Grads Employed by Field (%)

Field	%
Academic	~1
Business/Industry	~13
Government	~3
Judicial clerkships	~7
Military	~0
Other	~3
Private practice	~62
Public Interest	~5

UNIVERSITY OF TENNESSEE
College of Law

Admissions Contact: Director of Admissions and Career Services, Karen R. Britton
1505 West Cumberland Avenue, Knoxville, TN 37996-1810
Admissions Phone: 865-974-4131 • Admissions Fax: 865-974-1572
Admissions E-mail: lawadmit@libra.law.utk.edu • Web Address: www.law.utk.edu

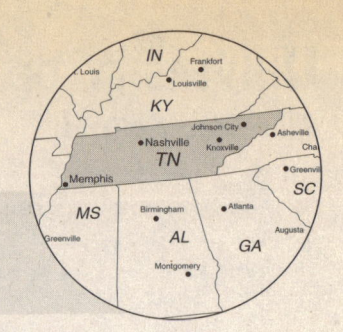

INSTITUTIONAL INFORMATION
Public/Private: Public
Student/Faculty Ratio: 13:1
Total Faculty: 57
% Part Time: 49
% Female: 37
% Minority: 5

PROGRAMS
Academic Specialties: Business Transactions, Advocacy and Dispute Resolution, Commercial Law
Advanced Degrees Offered: JD (3 years)
Combined Degrees Offered: JD/MBA (4 years)
Grading System: Letter system; some courses are Pass/Fail
Clinical Program Required? No
Legal Writing Course Requirements? No
Legal Methods Course Requirements? Yes
Legal Methods Description: Legal Process I and II, required in the first year, are an introduction to formal legal writing, appellate procedure, and oral advocacy.
Legal Research Course Requirements? No
Moot Court Requirement? No
Public Interest Law Requirement? No
Academic Journals: Tennessee Law Review

STUDENT INFORMATION
Enrollment of Law School: 475
% Out of State: 20
% Male/Female: 53/47
% Full Time: 100
% Full Time That Are International: 0
% Minority: 16
Average Age of Entering Class: 25

EXPENSES/FINANCIAL AID
Annual Tuition (Residents/Nonresidents): $6,576/$18,382
Room and Board: $6,456
Books and Supplies: $1,282
Financial Aid Application Deadline: 3/1
Average Grant: $6,200
Average Loan: $16,051
% Receiving Some Sort of Aid: 83
Average Total Aid Package: $17,425
Average Debt: $43,224
Tuition Per Credit (Residents/Nonresidents): $366/$1,022
Fees Per Credit (Residents/Nonresidents): $26/$43

ADMISSIONS INFORMATION
Application Fee: $35
Regular Application Deadline: 2/15
Regular Notification: 3/15
LSDAS Accepted? No
Average GPA: 3.4
Range of GPA: 3.2–3.7
Average LSAT: 157
Range of LSAT: 155–160
Transfer Students Accepted? Yes
Other Schools to Which Students Applied: Mercer University, Samford University, University of Memphis, University of Georgia, University of Kentucky, University of North Carolina—Chapel Hill, Vanderbilt University
Other Admissions Factors Considered: Academic factors; employment; activities and service; economic, social, or cultural background; evidence of maturity, responsibility, and motivation; circumstances that may have affected an applicant's undergraduate GPA
Number of Applications Received: 1,334
Number of Applicants Accepted: 374
Number of Applicants Enrolled: 160

INTERNATIONAL STUDENTS
TOEFL Required of International Students? Yes
Minimum TOEFL: 213 computer

EMPLOYMENT INFORMATION

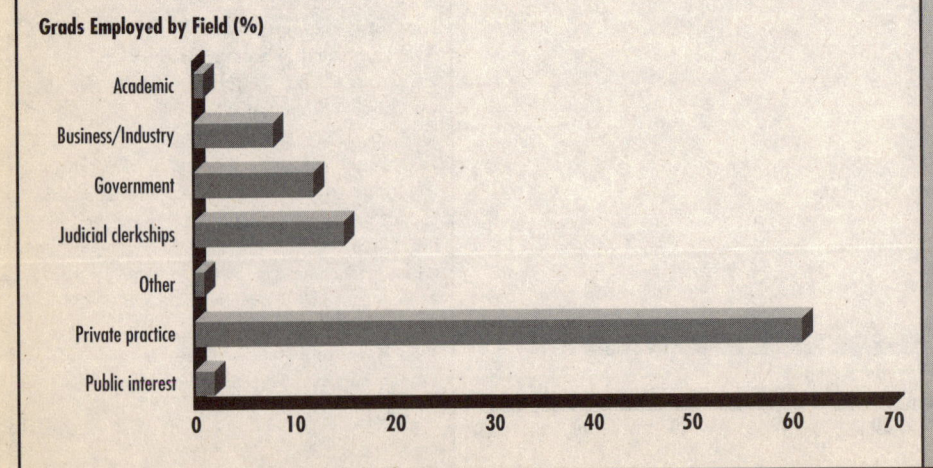

Grads Employed by Field (%)
- Academic: ~1
- Business/Industry: ~8
- Government: ~15
- Judicial clerkships: ~16
- Other: ~1
- Private practice: ~62
- Public interest: ~2

Rate of Placement: 96%
Average Starting Salary: $56,512
Employers Who Frequently Hire Grads: Legal employers, law firms, and judges across the southeast and the United States
Prominent Alumni: Howard H. Baker Jr., Government/Public Service; Joel A. Katz, Entertainment Lawyer; Jim Hall, former Chair, NTSB; Art Stolnitz, former VP, Warner Bros.; Penny White, former Justice, Tennessee Supreme Court
State for Bar Exam: TN
Pass Rate for First-Time Bar: 88%

UNIVERSITY OF TEXAS — AUSTIN
School of Law

Admissions Contact: Assistant Dean for Admissions, Monica Ingram
727 East Dean Keeton Street, Austin, TX 78705-3299
Admissions Phone: 512-232-1200 • Admissions Fax: 512-471-2765
Admissions E-mail: admissions@mail.law.utexas.edu • Web Address: www.utexas.edu/law

INSTITUTIONAL INFORMATION

Public/Private: Public
Student/Faculty Ratio: 18:1
Total Faculty: 176
% Part Time: 59
% Female: 26
% Minority: 9

PROGRAMS

Academic Specialties: Very prestigious, multitalented, published faculty world-reknowned for legal expertise and excellence in classroom teaching, very broad and diverse curriculum, Commercial Law, Constitutional Law, Criminal Law, Environmental Law, International Law, Labor Law, Property
Advanced Degrees Offered: LLM (1 year)
Combined Degrees Offered: JD/MBA, JD/MPA, JD/MS Community and Regional Planning, JD/MA
Grading System: A+ (4.3), A (4.0), A– (3.7), B+ (3.3), B (3.0), B– (2.7), C+ (2.3), C (2.0), D (1.7), F (1.3)
Clinical Program Required? No
Clinical Program Description: Mediation Clinic, Housing Law Clinic, Domestic Violence Clinic, Capital Punishment Clinic, Children's Rights Clinic, Criminal Defense Clinic, Juvenile Justice Clinic, Mental Health Clinic, Immigration Law Clinic
Legal Writing Course Requirements? Yes
Legal Writing Description: First year, second semester
Legal Methods Course Requirements? No
Legal Research Course Requirements? Yes
Legal Research Description: See Legal Writing.
Moot Court Requirement? Yes
Moot Court Description: Part of Legal Writing
Public Interest Law Requirement? No
Academic Journals: *American Journal of Criminal Law, Texas Environmental Law Journal, Texas Forum on Civil Liberties and Civil Rights, Texas Hispanic Journal of Law and Policy, Texas Intellectual Property Law Journal, Texas International Law Journal, Texas Journal of Business Law, Texas Journal of Women and the Law, Texas Law Review, Texas Review of Entertainment and Sports Law, Texas Review of Law and Politics, The Review of Litigation*

STUDENT INFORMATION

Enrollment of Law School: 1,525
% Out of State: 16
% Male/Female: 53/47
% Full Time: 100
% Full Time That Are International: 1
% Minority: 20
Average Age of Entering Class: 25

EXPENSES/FINANCIAL AID

Annual Tuition (Residents/Nonresidents): $8,520/$16,680
Room and Board (On/Off Campus): $7,088/$7,478
Books and Supplies: $916
Average Grant: $3,000
Average Loan: $18,500
% of Aid That Is Merit-Based: 25
% Receiving Some Sort of Aid: 93
Average Total Aid Package: $27,792
Average Debt: $52,000
Tuition Per Credit (Residents/Nonresidents): $284/$556

ADMISSIONS INFORMATION

Application Fee: $65
Regular Application Deadline: 2/1
Regular Notification: 4/30
LSDAS Accepted? Yes
Average GPA: 3.6
Range of GPA: 3.3–3.8
Average LSAT: 163
Range of LSAT: 160–165
Transfer Students Accepted? Yes
Other Schools to Which Students Applied: Southern Methodist University; George Washington University; University of California, Los Angeles; University of Houston; Vanderbilt University
Number of Applications Received: 5,448
Number of Applicants Accepted: 1,138
Number of Applicants Enrolled: 543

INTERNATIONAL STUDENTS

TOEFL Required of International Students? Yes
Minimum TOEFL: 213 computer

EMPLOYMENT INFORMATION

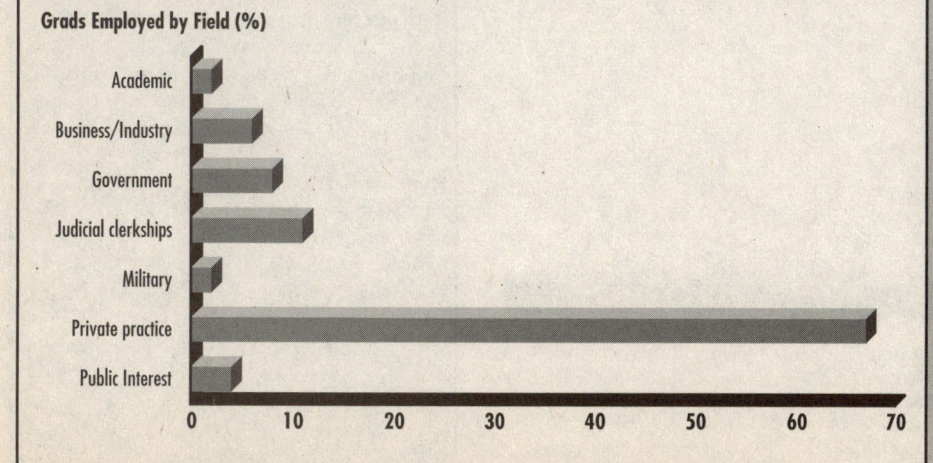

Grads Employed by Field (%)

Field	%
Academic	~1
Business/Industry	~8
Government	~10
Judicial clerkships	~11
Military	~1
Private practice	~68
Public Interest	~3

Rate of Placement: 99%
Average Starting Salary: $90,971
Employers Who Frequently Hire Grads: Baker Botts, LLP; Fulbright & Jaworski, LLP; Vinson & Elkins, LLP; Haynes & Boone, LLP; Bracewell & Patterson, LLP; Skadden, Arps, Slate, Meagher & Flom, LLP; U.S. District Courts; U.S. Court of Appeals; Texas Court of Appeals
Prominent Alumni: Joseph D. Jamail Jr., Owner, Jamail & Kolius; Kay Bailey Hutchison, U.S. Senator; Frederico Pena, former Secretary of Transportation; Rodney G. Ellis, Texas State Senator
State for Bar Exam: TX
Pass Rate for First-Time Bar: 93%

UNIVERSITY OF THE DISTRICT OF COLUMBIA
David A. Clarke School of Law

Admissions Contact: Director of Admissions, Vivian Canty
4200 Connecticut Avenue, NW, Washington, DC 20008
Admissions Phone: 202-274-7336 • Admissions Fax: 202-274-5583
Admissions E-mail: vcanty@udc.edu • Web Address: www.law.udc.edu

INSTITUTIONAL INFORMATION
Public/Private: Public
Student/Faculty Ratio: 9:1
Total Faculty: 23
% Female: 43
% Minority: 39

PROGRAMS
Academic Specialties: Public Interest and Civil Rights Law emphasis, 14 required credits in clinics that serve indigent DC residents
Advanced Degrees Offered: JD (3 years)
Grading System: A (4.0), B (3.0), C (2.0), D (1.0)
Clinical Program Required? Yes
Clinical Program Description: Legislation, Juvenile/Special Education, HIV/AIDS, Housing and Consumer, Community Development, Small Business
Legal Writing Course Requirements? Yes
Legal Writing Description: Lawyering Process I and II are required first-year courses that carry 5 credits and are taught in small sections of approximately 12 students.
Legal Methods Course Requirements? No
Legal Research Course Requirements? No
Moot Court Requirement? Yes
Moot Court Description: 2 credits, part of the Legal Writing curriculum
Public Interest Law Requirement? Yes
Public Interest Law Description: Law and Justice is a required course offered in the first year, which includes 40 hours of law-related community service.

Academic Journals: *University of the District of Columbia Law Review*

STUDENT INFORMATION
Enrollment of Law School: 126
% Out of State: 55
% Male/Female: 36/64
% Full Time: 100
% Minority: 74
Average Age of Entering Class: 30

RESEARCH FACILITIES
Research Resources Available: Library of Congress, five area law schools

EXPENSES/FINANCIAL AID
Annual Tuition (Residents/Nonresidents): $7,000/$14,000
Room and Board (Off Campus): $19,900
Books and Supplies: $2,000
Financial Aid Application Deadline: 5/1
Average Grant: $5,033
Average Loan: $21,000
% of Aid That Is Merit-Based: 12
% Receiving Some Sort of Aid: 96
Average Total Aid Package: $34,000
Average Debt: $63,000
Fees Per Credit (Residents/Nonresidents): $250/$500

ADMISSIONS INFORMATION
Application Fee: $35
Regular Application Deadline: 4/1
Regular Notification: Rolling
LSDAS Accepted? Yes
Average GPA: 2.7
Range of GPA: 2.3–3.0
Average LSAT: 148
Range of LSAT: 145–150
Transfer Students Accepted? Yes
Other Schools to Which Students Applied: American University, City University of New York, George Mason University, Howard University, Catholic University of America, University of Baltimore, University of Maryland
Other Admissions Factors Considered: Goals; family background; community involvment; graduate work, if applicable; college attended; college major
Number of Applications Received: 427
Number of Applicants Accepted: 94
Number of Applicants Enrolled: 40

INTERNATIONAL STUDENTS
TOEFL Required of International Students? Yes

EMPLOYMENT INFORMATION

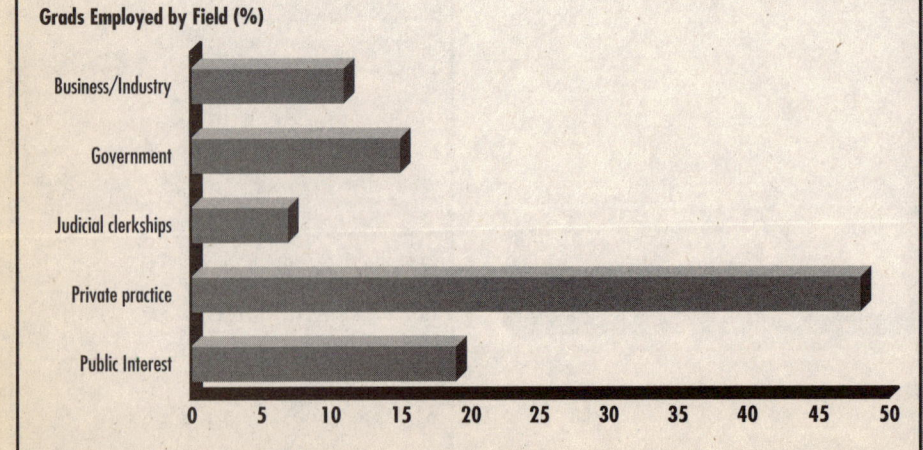

Grads Employed by Field (%)

Field	%
Business/Industry	~12
Government	~16
Judicial clerkships	~7
Private practice	~48
Public Interest	~19

Rate of Placement: 87%
Average Starting Salary: $55,200
Employers Who Frequently Hire Grads: District of Columbia Council, various U.S. agencies, legal services providers, smaller litigation-oriented law firms
State for Bar Exam: MD
Pass Rate for First-Time Bar: 55%

UNIVERSITY OF THE PACIFIC
McGeorge School of Law

Admissions Contact: Assistant Dean and Director of Admissions, Adam W. Barrett
3200 Fifth Avenue, Sacramento, CA 95817
Admissions Phone: 916-739-7105 • Admissions Fax: 916-739-7134
Admissions E-mail: admissionsmcgeorge@uop.edu • Web Address: www.mcgeorge.edu

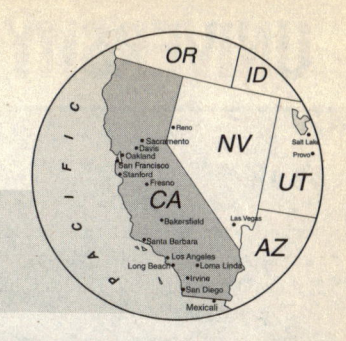

INSTITUTIONAL INFORMATION
Public/Private: Private
Student/Faculty Ratio: 22:1
Total Faculty: 108
% Part Time: 59
% Female: 27
% Minority: 6

PROGRAMS
Academic Specialties: Governmental Affairs, International Legal Studies, Trial Advocacy, Criminal Justice, Intellectual Property, and Taxation including Estate Planning, Business and Corporate Law, Environmental Law, and Family, Child, and Elder Law. Other specialties include Civil Procedure, Commercial Law, Constitutional Law, Criminal Law, Human Rights Law, Labor Law, Property
Advanced Degrees Offered: JD (3 to 4 years), LLM (1 year)
Combined Degrees Offered: JD/MBA, JD/MPPA, JD/MA or MS upon approval (all 4 years)
Grading System: Letter and numerical system on a 4.33 scale
Clinical Program Required? No
Clinical Program Description: Administrative Adjudication Clinic; Business and Community Development Clinic; Community Legal Services; Immigration Clinic; Legislative Process, Strategy, and Ethics; Parole Representation Clinic; Internships
Legal Writing Course Requirements? Yes
Legal Writing Description: First-year, 2-semester course offered in small group sessions. Students become familiar with preparation of legal documents.
Legal Methods Course Requirements? No
Legal Research Course Requirements? Yes
Legal Research Description: Offered in combination with the legal writing course. Through small-group assignments, students become familiar with the law library, and paper- and computer-based research.
Moot Court Requirement? Yes
Moot Court Description: Appellate or International Advocacy is required for all second-year students, though if a student is a member of a law review, the course is optional. The course is year-long, culminating in oral argument before judges. Trial Advocacy is an optional elective.
Public Interest Law Requirement? No
Academic Journals: McGeorge Law Review, The Transnational Lawyer

STUDENT INFORMATION
Enrollment of Law School: 927
% Male/Female: 50/50
% Full Time: 68
% Minority: 25
Average Age of Entering Class: 25

RESEARCH FACILITIES
Research Resources Available: California State University (Sacramento) and the Eberhardt School of Business of our university for concurrent degree programs, extensive computer resources
School-Supported Research Centers: Institute for Legislative Practice

EXPENSES/FINANCIAL AID
Annual Tuition: $22,956
Room and Board: $8,883
Books and Supplies: $800
Average Grant: $7,553
Average Loan: $21,755
% of Aid That Is Merit-Based: 41
% Receiving Some Sort of Aid: 92
Average Total Aid Package: $27,500
Average Debt: $64,599
Tuition Per Credit: $739
Fees Per Credit: $38

ADMISSIONS INFORMATION
Application Fee: $40
Regular Application Deadline: 5/15
Regular Notification: Rolling
LSDAS Accepted? Yes
Average GPA: 3.0
Range of GPA: 2.7–3.3
Average LSAT: 151
Range of LSAT: 148–155
Transfer Students Accepted? Yes
Other Schools to Which Students Applied: Golden Gate, Santa Clara, UC Davis, UC Hastings
Other Admissions Factors Considered: Career experiences, graduate study, extracurricular leadership activities, recommendation letters, diversity
Number of Applications Received: 1,301
Number of Applicants Accepted: 880
Number of Applicants Enrolled: 265

INTERNATIONAL STUDENTS
TOEFL Required of International Students? Yes
Minimum TOEFL: 600

EMPLOYMENT INFORMATION

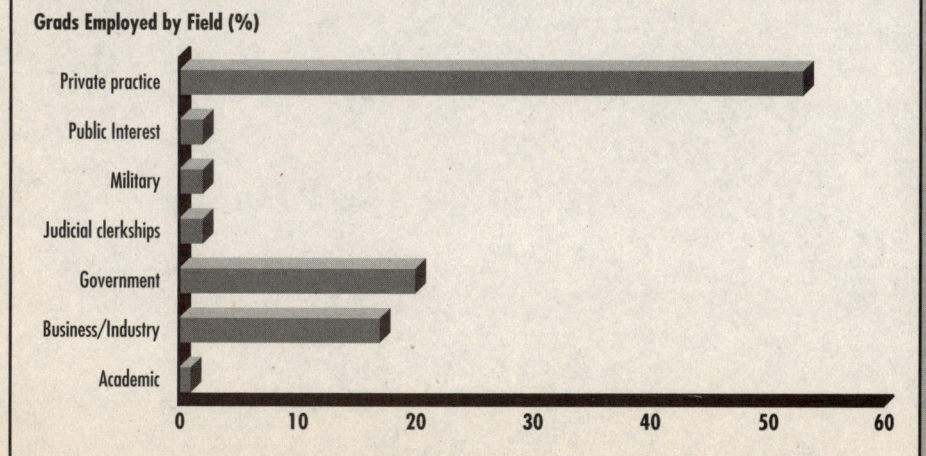

Grads Employed by Field (%)
- Private practice: ~54
- Public Interest: ~2
- Military: ~1
- Judicial clerkships: ~2
- Government: ~21
- Business/Industry: ~18
- Academic: ~1

Rate of Placement: 89%
Average Starting Salary: $56,457
Prominent Alumni: Scott Boras, Sports Agent, Baseball; Bill Lockyer, Attorney General, State of CA; Steve Martini, Novelist; Johnnie Rawlinson, 9th Circuit Court of Appeals
State for Bar Exam: CA, NV, HI, OR, DC
Pass Rate for First-Time Bar: 69%

UNIVERSITY OF THE PACIFIC

AT A GLANCE
Pacific Law is located in Sacramento, California. This beautiful 22-acre, 26-building campus is the largest law-school-only campus in the nation. It features a courtroom, a law library, a dozen technologically advanced classrooms, seven on-campus clinics (with 75 off-campus clinics) and student housing. McGeorge has six key concentrations: Advocacy, Criminal Justice, Governmental Affairs, Intellectual Property, International Law, and Tax. Pacific Law has 142 different course offerings—one of the largest selections in the nation. To learn more, visit us at www.mcgeorge.edu.

DEGREES OFFERED
McGeorge offers the JD, LLM in International Law, LLM in Transnational Business Practice, and JSD in International Water Resources.

PROGRAMS AND CURRICULUM
McGeorge has six key concentrations: Advocacy, Criminal Justice, Governmental Affairs, Intellectual Property, International Law, and Tax. With one of the largest course offerings in the nation, the School has 142 different course offerings. There are joint degree programs for JD/MBA and JD/MPPA. McGeorge also has summer abroad study programs in Salzburg, Autria; Bucerius Law School, Hamburg, Germany; Universite Catholique de Louivain, Belgium; University of Copenhagen, Denmark; and University of Parma, Italy.

CAMPUS AND LOCATION
Pacific Law features a beautiful 22-acre campus with 26 buildings, the largest law-school-only campus in the nation. The school is located in California's capitol city, Sacramento.

McGeorge School of Law

FACILITIES
With a 22-acre, 26-building law-school-only campus, McGeorge features a courtroom, law library, seven on-campus clinics (with more than 75 off-campus clinics), a dozen technologically advanced classrooms, and student housing. The campus also enjoys wireless Internet access.

EXPENSES AND FINANCIAL AID
Pacific Law is a private school. Tuition for the 2003–2004 academic year is $27,698. McGeorge has a wide variety of merit-based scholarships for first-year students. There are also endowed scholarships. More information about scholarships and financial aid can be obtained from www.mcgeorge.edu.

FACULTY
McGeorge has 43 full-time faculty members—15 women and 28 men. We also have 61 adjunct professors.

STUDENTS
McGeorge has a total enrollment of 1,007 students. There are 686 full-time students—352 men and 334 women. There are 321 part-time students—157 men and 164 women.

ADMISSIONS
McGeorge admits new students only for the fall term. For the fall 2004 entering class, McGeorge will begin accepting applications on September 1, 2003.

To learn more, visit us at www.mcgeorge.edu.

UNIVERSITY OF TOLEDO
College of Law

Admissions Contact: Assistant Dean for Admissions
2801 West Bancroft, Toledo, OH 43606
Admissions Phone: 419-530-4131 • Admissions Fax: 419-530-4345
Admissions E-mail: law.admissions@utoledo.edu • Web Address: www.utlaw.edu

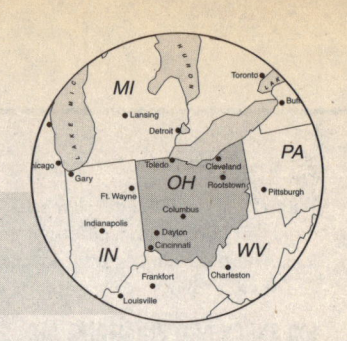

INSTITUTIONAL INFORMATION
Public/Private: Public
Student/Faculty Ratio: 12:1
Total Faculty: 54
% Part Time: 40
% Female: 37
% Minority: 4

PROGRAMS
Academic Specialties: The curriculum reflects the interest in the Great Lakes region, with numerous courses and seminars in Environmental Law, International Law, Intellectual Property Law, Civil Procedure, Commercial Law, Constitutional Law, Corporation Securities Law, Criminal Law, Government Services, Human Rights Law, Labor Law, Legal History, Legal Philosophy, Property, and Taxation.
Advanced Degrees Offered: JD (3 to 4 years)
Combined Degrees Offered: JD/MBA (3 to 3.5 years), JD/MSE (3 to 3.5 years), JD/PhD (3.5 to 4 years), JD/MPH (3 to 3.5 years), JD/M Criminal Justice (3 to 3.5 years)
Grading System: Letter system on a 4.0 scale, DR, W
Clinical Program Required? No
Clinical Program Description: Legal Clinic, Criminal Law Practice Program (Prosecutor Intern Program), Dispute Resolution Clinic, Domestic Violence Project, Human Rights Project
Legal Writing Course Requirements? No
Legal Methods Course Requirements? Yes
Legal Methods Description: 2-semester intensive study of research tools and techniques and their utilization in the preparation of memoranda of law; researching and writing a brief and presenting an oral argument to an appellate court of faculty and students; instruction through class meetings and individual conferences
Legal Research Course Requirements? Yes
Moot Court Requirement? No
Public Interest Law Requirement? No
Academic Journals: *Law Review*

STUDENT INFORMATION
Enrollment of Law School: 485
% Out of State: 32
% Male/Female: 55/45
% Full Time: 60
% Full Time That Are International: 0
% Minority: 8
Average Age of Entering Class: 27

RESEARCH FACILITIES
Research Resources Available: Toledo Lucas County Public Library, Medical College of Ohio, Toledo Museum of Art
School-Supported Research Centers: Legal Institute of the Great Lakes (LIGL)

EXPENSES/FINANCIAL AID
Annual Tuition (Residents/Nonresidents): $9,029/$18,760
Room and Board (Off Campus): $6,596
Books and Supplies: $1,056
Financial Aid Application Deadline: 8/1
Average Grant: $8,598
Average Loan: $17,055
% of Aid That Is Merit-Based: 21
% Receiving Some Sort of Aid: 93
Average Total Aid Package: $19,953
Average Debt: $44,088
Tuition Per Credit (Residents/Nonresidents): $376/$782
Fees Per Credit: $54

ADMISSIONS INFORMATION
Application Fee: $40
Regular Application Deadline: Rolling
Regular Notification: Rolling
LSDAS Accepted? Yes
Average GPA: 3.1
Range of GPA: 2.8–3.5
Average LSAT: 157
Range of LSAT: 153–158
Transfer Students Accepted? Yes
Number of Applications Received: 878
Number of Applicants Accepted: 286
Number of Applicants Enrolled: 87

EMPLOYMENT INFORMATION

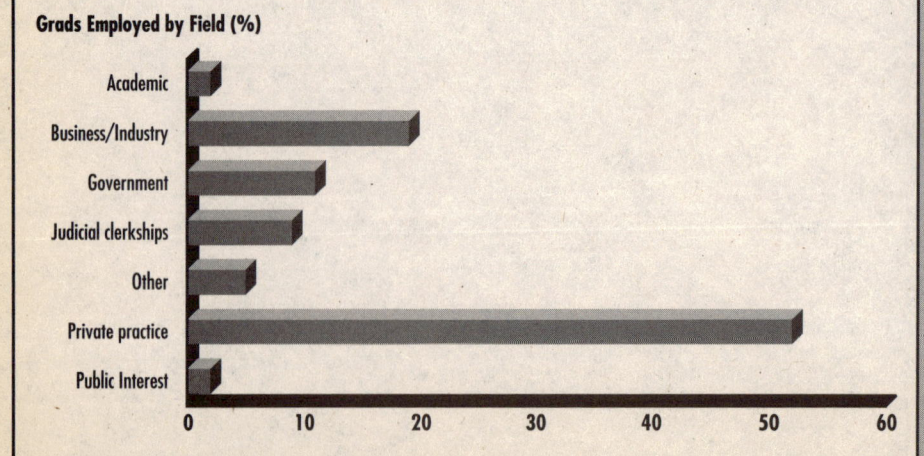

Grads Employed by Field (%)

Field	%
Academic	~1
Business/Industry	~18
Government	~11
Judicial clerkships	~6
Other	~6
Private practice	~52
Public Interest	~2

Rate of Placement: 94%
Average Starting Salary: $50,000
Employers Who Frequently Hire Grads: Spengler Nathanson; Shumaker Loop & Kendrik; Eastman & Smith; DeNune & Killam; Gallon & Takacs; Wagoner & Steinberg; Kalniz Iorio & Feldstein; Connelly Soutar & Jackson; Marshall & Melhorn; Cooper Walinski & Cramer; Fuller & Henry; Robison Curphey & O'Connell; Newcomer Shaffer & Spangler; Watkins Bates & Carey; Williams Jilek Lafferty & Gallagher
Prominent Alumni: Hon. Andrew Douglas, Justice, Ohio Supreme Court; Hon. Deborah Agosti, Chief Justice, State of Nevada; Alan G. Lance Sr., Attorney General, State of Idaho
State for Bar Exam: OH, MI, FL, IN, IL
Pass Rate for First-Time Bar: 77%

UNIVERSITY OF TORONTO
Faculty of Law

Admissions Contact: Admissions Officer, Judy Finlay
84 Queens Park, Toronto, ON M5S 2C5
Admissions Phone: 416-978-3716 • Admissions Fax: 416-978-7899
Admissions E-mail: law.admissions@utoronto.ca • Web Address: www.law.utoronto.ca

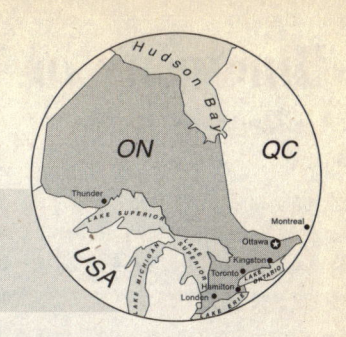

INSTITUTIONAL INFORMATION
Public/Private: Public
Student/Faculty Ratio: 9:1
Total Faculty: 54
% Female: 30

PROGRAMS
Academic Specialties: Administrative Law and Regulation Business Law, including Corporations, Commercial Law, and Taxation; Constitutional Law; Crime and Criminology; Family Law; Intellectual Property and Technology Law; International and Comparative Law; Labor Law and Social Justice Law; Law and Economics; Legal Research and Writing; Legal Theory; Litigation and Dispute Settlement; Women's Studies
Advanced Degrees Offered: LLM (1 year), SJD (1 year plus thesis), MSL (1 year)
Combined Degrees Offered: JD/MBA (4 years), JD/MSW (4 years), JD/MA (3 to 4 years), JD/PhD Economics or Philosophy (4 years)
Grading System: A, B+, B, C, C+, D, F; students in the top 10% each year are awarded A Honours Standing
Clinical Program Required? No
Clinical Program Description: Centre for Spanish-Speaking People, Advocates for Injured Workers, Downtown Legal Services, Enterprise Legal Services
Legal Writing Course Requirements? Yes
Legal Writing Description: Students must complete writing assignments as part of their first-year program in their small group (see Legal Methods).
Legal Methods Course Requirements? Yes
Legal Methods Description: The cornerstone of the first-year curriculum is the small group, which permits students to study one of the first-year subjects with a member of the faculty and 15 classmates. The small group introduces students to the techniques of legal research and writing in a personal and direct setting.
Legal Research Course Requirements? Yes
Legal Research Description: As part of the small group in the first year (see Legal Methods), students are introduced the many elements of legal research.
Moot Court Requirement? Yes
Moot Court Description: Students complete a compulsory moot in the first semester of the second year, and can participate for credit in competitive moots in the second semester of the second year.
Public Interest Law Requirement? No
Public Interest Law Description: Many students participate in our Pro Bono Students Canada program, which offers students volunteer placements and summer internships abroad or domestically.
Academic Journals: *University of Toronto Faculty of Law Review, Journal of Law and Equality, Indigenous Law Journal*

STUDENT INFORMATION
Enrollment of Law School: 530
% Male/Female: 48/52
% Full Time: 100
% Minority: 28
Average Age of Entering Class: 25

EXPENSES/FINANCIAL AID
Annual Tuition (Residents/Nonresidents): $14,000/$21,192
Room and Board (On/Off Campus): $10,250/$8,900
Books and Supplies: $1,100
Financial Aid Application Deadline: 9/16
Average Grant: $5,000
Average Loan: $8,692
% of Aid That Is Merit-Based: 3
% Receiving Some Sort of Aid: 42
Average Total Aid Package: $5,844
Average Debt: $26,604
Tuition Per Credit (Residents/Nonresidents): $7,000/$10,596
Fees Per Credit (Residents/Nonresidents): $7,405/$11,739

ADMISSIONS INFORMATION
Application Fee: $50
Regular Application Deadline: 11/1
Regular Notification: 1/4
LSDAS Accepted? No
Average GPA: 3.8
Range of GPA: 3.7–4.0
Average LSAT: 165
Range of LSAT: 157–180
Transfer Students Accepted? Yes
Other Schools to Which Students Applied: Harvard, Columbia, York, Queen's
Other Admissions Factors Considered: Nonacademic achievement, response to disadvantage, barriers faced by cultural (including racial or ethnic) or linguistic minorities, motivation and involvement in academic and nonacademic activities, impact of temporary or permanent physical disabilities
Number of Applications Received: 1,822
Number of Applicants Accepted: 283
Number of Applicants Enrolled: 179

EMPLOYMENT INFORMATION

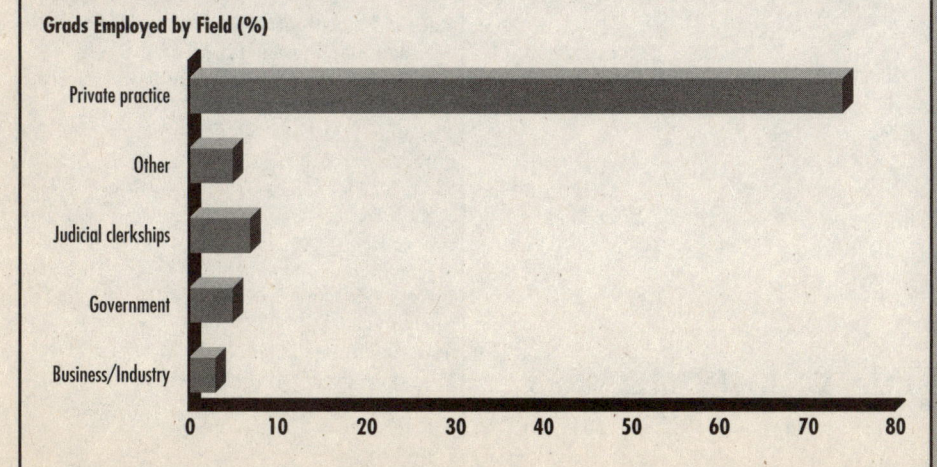

Grads Employed by Field (%)

Field	%
Private practice	~75
Other	~5
Judicial clerkships	~5
Government	~5
Business/Industry	~3

Rate of Placement: 95%
Average Starting Salary: $50,000
Employers Who Frequently Hire Grads: All major Toronto law firms, all provincial and federal government departments, many large New York and Boston law firms, large and midsize Vancouver, Halifax, and Calgary law firms
Prominent Alumni: Frank Iacobucci, Justice, Supreme Court of Canada; Rosalie Abella, Justice, Ontario Court of Appeal; Bonnie Croll, Justice, Ontario Superior Court; Hon. Paul Martin, Member, Parliament
State for Bar Exam: NY, MA, CA

UNIVERSITY OF TULSA
College of Law

Admissions Contact: Assistant Dean of Admissions and Financial Aid, George Justice
3120 East Fourth Place, Tulsa, OK 74104-3189
Admissions Phone: 918-631-2709 • Admissions Fax: 918-631-3630
Admissions E-mail: george-justice@utulsa.edu • Web Address: www.utulsa.edu/law

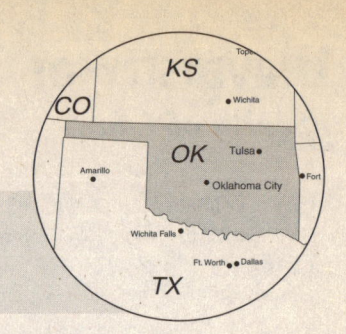

INSTITUTIONAL INFORMATION
Public/Private: Private
Affiliation: Presbyterian
Student/Faculty Ratio: 14:1
Total Faculty: 69
% Part Time: 41
% Female: 36
% Minority: 12

PROGRAMS
Academic Specialties: The law school offers certificate programs in Alternative Methods of Dispute Resolution; Comparative and International Law; Health Law; Native American Public Policy and Regulation; Resources, Energy and Environmental Law; and Entrepreneurial Law and Practical Skills. Our Legal Clinic offers clinical programs—the Older Americans Law Project, the Indian Law Clinic, and the Health Law Project—that provide students with an opportunity to handle actual cases and develop professional skills under the close supervision of faculty supervisors. Students may gain valuable hands-on experience in the Judicial and Legal Internship programs. Also offered is Government Services.
Advanced Degrees Offered: LLM American Indian and Indigenous Law (1 to 2 years)
Combined Degrees Offered: History, Industrial/Organizational Psychology, Geosciences, Biological Sciences, Anthropology, Accounting, Taxation, Business Administration, Clinical Psychology, English (all 4 years)

Grading System: A (4.0), B+ (3.5), B (3.0), C+ (2.5), C (2.0), D+ (1.5), D (1.0), F (0.0)
Clinical Program Required? No
Clinical Program Description: Older Americans Law Project, Health Law Project, Muscogee (Creek) National Indian Law Clinic
Legal Writing Course Requirements? Yes
Legal Methods Course Requirements? Yes
Legal Methods Description: 1 year, 6 credits; teaches students to research and analyze the law and to communicate that analysis effectively in writing
Legal Research Course Requirements? Yes
Legal Research Description: Year-long, first-year course
Moot Court Requirement? No
Moot Court Description: Regional, national, and international competitions
Public Interest Law Requirement? No
Academic Journals: Law Review, International Law Journal, Energy Law Journal

STUDENT INFORMATION
Enrollment of Law School: 558
% Out of State: 53
% Male/Female: 56/44
% Full Time: 81
% Full Time That Are International: 1
% Minority: 20
Average Age of Entering Class: 27

EXPENSES/FINANCIAL AID
Annual Tuition: $21,425
Room and Board (On/Off Campus): $6,000/$7,210
Books and Supplies: $1,500
Financial Aid Application Deadline: 4/1
Average Grant: $6,500
Average Loan: $25,290
% of Aid That Is Merit-Based: 25
% Receiving Some Sort of Aid: 89
Average Total Aid Package: $22,550
Average Debt: $67,952
Tuition Per Credit: $800

ADMISSIONS INFORMATION
Application Fee: $30
Regular Application Deadline: Rolling
Regular Notification: Rolling
LSDAS Accepted? Yes
Average GPA: 3.2
Range of GPA: 2.8–3.5
Average LSAT: 148
Range of LSAT: 145–153
Transfer Students Accepted? Yes
Number of Applications Received: 1,096
Number of Applicants Accepted: 580
Number of Applicants Enrolled: 216

INTERNATIONAL STUDENTS
TOEFL Required of International Students? Yes

EMPLOYMENT INFORMATION

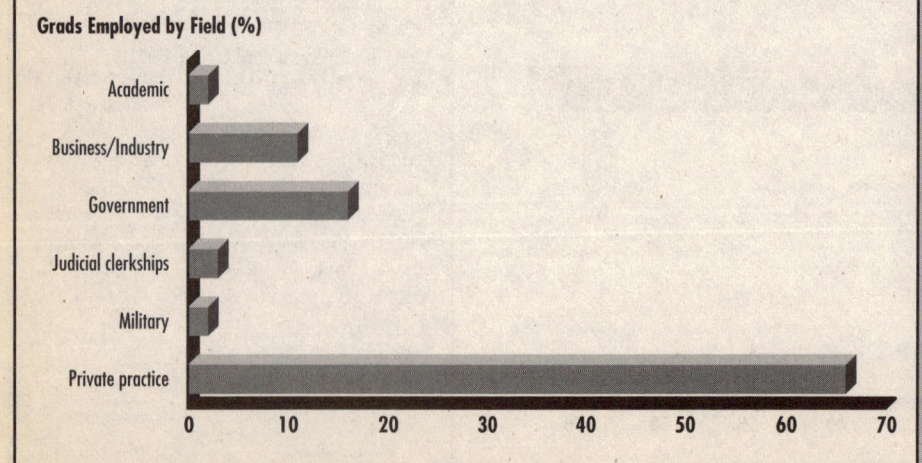

Grads Employed by Field (%)

Field	%
Academic	~1
Business/Industry	~12
Government	~17
Judicial clerkships	~3
Military	~1
Private practice	~67

Rate of Placement: 87%
Average Starting Salary: $51,960
Employers Who Frequently Hire Grads: Shook Hardy & Bacon; Williams; Tulsa law firms
Prominent Alumni: Chadwick Smith, Chief of the Cherokee Nation; Hon. David Leonard Levy, Third District Court of Appeals; David Barclay Waller, Deputy Director General, International Atomic Energy Agency; Daniel J. Boudreau, Justice, Oklahoma Supreme Court; R. Michelle Beale, Vice President of HR/Public Affairs, Minute Maid
State for Bar Exam: OK, TX, MO, FL, GA
Pass Rate for First-Time Bar: 81%

UNIVERSITY OF UTAH
S.J. Quinney College of Law

Admissions Contact: Coordinator for Admissions, Gwen Spotted Elk
332 South 1400 East, Room 101, Salt Lake City, UT 84112
Admissions Phone: 801-581-7479 • Admissions Fax: 801-581-6897
Admissions E-mail: admission@law.utah.edu • Web Address: www.law.utah.edu

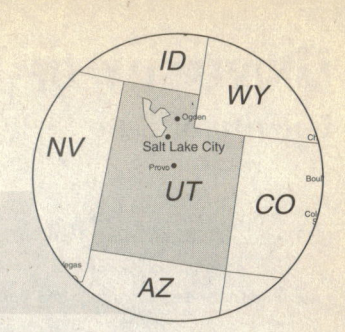

INSTITUTIONAL INFORMATION
Public/Private: Public
Student/Faculty Ratio: 13:1
Total Faculty: 65
% Part Time: 51
% Female: 30
% Minority: 13

PROGRAMS
Academic Specialties: Environmental, Resource, and Energy Law, Business and Commercial Law, Constitutional Law, Criminal Law, International Law
Advanced Degrees Offered: LLM Environmental Law (1 year)
Combined Degrees Offered: JD/MPA (4 years), JD/MBA (4 years)
Grading System: 4.0 scale
Clinical Program Required? No
Clinical Program Description: Mediation Clinic, Health Law Clinic, Legislative Clinic, Criminal Law Clinic, Civil Clinic
Legal Writing Course Requirements? Yes
Legal Writing Description: Legal Methods (2 semesters, 4 credits) consists of legal writing and research.
Legal Methods Course Requirements? Yes
Legal Methods Description: See Legal Writing.
Legal Research Course Requirements? Yes
Legal Research Description: See Legal Writing.
Moot Court Requirement? No
Moot Court Description: In the 1-year intramural program, Traynor Moot Court Competition, a finalist is invited to serve on the National Moot Court Competition team.
Public Interest Law Requirement? No
Public Interest Law Description: The Pro Bono Project facilitates volunteerism and public service.
Academic Journals: *Utah Law Review*; *Journal of Land, Resources and Evvironmental Law*; *Journal of Law and Family Studies*

STUDENT INFORMATION
Enrollment of Law School: 388
% Out of State: 20
% Male/Female: 59/41
% Full Time: 100
% Full Time That Are International: 1
% Minority: 14
Average Age of Entering Class: 28

EXPENSES/FINANCIAL AID
Annual Tuition (Residents/Nonresidents): $6,213/$13,952
Room and Board: $6,264
Books and Supplies: $1,156
Financial Aid Application Deadline: 3/15
Average Grant: $4,340
Average Loan: $14,000
% of Aid That Is Merit-Based: 15
% Receiving Some Sort of Aid: 81
Average Total Aid Package: $16,400
Average Debt: $39,000

ADMISSIONS INFORMATION
Application Fee: $50
Regular Application Deadline: 2/1
Regular Notification: Rolling
LSDAS Accepted? Yes
Average GPA: 3.5
Range of GPA: 3.3–3.7
Average LSAT: 158
Range of LSAT: 154–162
Transfer Students Accepted? Yes
Other Schools to Which Students Applied: Arizona State University, Brigham Young University, George Washington University, University of Arizona, University of Colorado, University of Oregon, University of San Diego
Other Admissions Factors Considered: Personal statement; letter of recommendation; résumé; leadership; diverse educational, cultural, economic, and/or ethnic background
Number of Applications Received: 908
Number of Applicants Accepted: 344
Number of Applicants Enrolled: 138

INTERNATIONAL STUDENTS
TOEFL Required of International Students? Yes
Minimum TOEFL: 600 (250 computer)

EMPLOYMENT INFORMATION

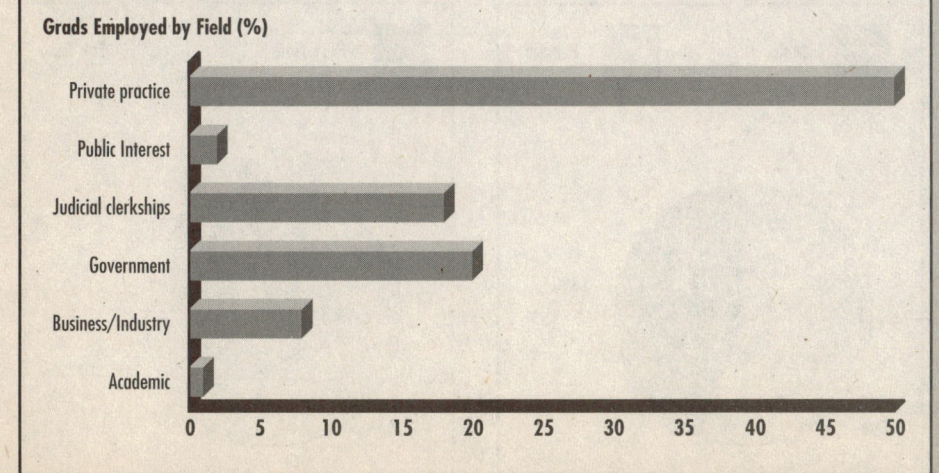

Grads Employed by Field (%)

Field	%
Private practice	~50
Public Interest	~2
Judicial clerkships	~14
Government	~20
Business/Industry	~9
Academic	~1

Rate of Placement: 96%
Average Starting Salary: $55,377
Employers Who Frequently Hire Grads: Utah Attorney General's office, Van Cott Bagley Cornwall & McCarthy, Ray Quinney & Nebeker, Jones Waldo Holbrook & Mconough
Prominent Alumni: Jimmy Gurule, Undersecretary for Enforcement, U.S. Treasury; Hon. Stephen Anderson, 10th Circuit Court of Appeals; Hon. Richard Howe, Chief Justice, Utah Supreme Court; Tom Green Sr., VP for Law and Administraton, Dell Computers; Hon. Nancy Rice, Colorado Supreme Court
State for Bar Exam: UT, CA, NV, AZ, ID
Pass Rate for First-Time Bar: 90%

UNIVERSITY OF VICTORIA
Faculty of Law

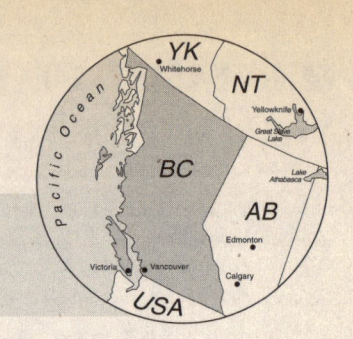

Admissions Contact: Admissions Assistant, Neela Paige
PO Box 2400, Victoria, BC V8W 3H7
Admissions Phone: 250-721-8151 • Admissions Fax: 250-721-6390
Admissions E-mail: lawadmss@uvic.ca • Web Address: www.law.uvic.ca

INSTITUTIONAL INFORMATION
Public/Private: Public
Student/Faculty Ratio: 7:1
Total Faculty: 57
% Part Time: 54
% Female: 20
% Minority: 5

PROGRAMS
Academic Specialties: Environmental Law, Intellectual Property Law, Aboriginal Law, Asia-Pacific Law, Dispute Resolution, International Law, Legal History, Property
Combined Degrees Offered: LLB/MPA (4 years), LLB/MBA (4 years), LLB/MIA (3.5 years), LLB/BCL (4.5 years), LLB/MAIG (4 years)
Grading System: 9-point system: 9 (A+), 8 (A), 7 (A–), 6 (B+), 5 (B), 4 (B–), 3 (C+), 2 (C), 1(D), 0 (F)
Clinical Program Required? No
Clinical Program Description: Business Law Clinic, Clinical Law Term, Environmental Law Centre Clinic
Legal Writing Course Requirements? Yes
Legal Writing Description: Legal Research and Writing (8 months) acquaints first-year students with the variety of materials in the Law Library and provides a knowledge of basic legal research techniques. Through a variety of written assignments, students become familiar with accepted principles pertaining to proper citation in legal writing and develop a degree of proficiency in legal writing and research.
Legal Methods Course Requirements? Yes
Legal Methods Description: The Law, Legislation and Policy (8 months in the first year) considers the development and interpretation of legislation.
Legal Research Course Requirements? Yes
Legal Research Description: See Legal Writing.
Moot Court Requirement? Yes
Moot Court Description: All first-year students must complete a moot court exercise as part of Legal Research and Writing. In upper years, there are optional competitive mooting programs in which students can take part for credit.
Public Interest Law Requirement? No
Academic Journals: APPEAL: Review of Current Law and Law Reform

STUDENT INFORMATION
Enrollment of Law School: 365
% Out of State: 50
% Male/Female: 44/56
% Full Time: 96
% Minority: 20
Average Age of Entering Class: 26

EXPENSES/FINANCIAL AID
Annual Tuition: $16,948
Room and Board (On/Off Campus): $8,000/$11,000
Books and Supplies: $1,600
Average Grant: $2,500
Average Loan: $10,000
% of Aid That Is Merit-Based: 60
% Receiving Some Sort of Aid: 54
Average Total Aid Package: $1,500
Average Debt: $30,000

ADMISSIONS INFORMATION
Application Fee: $50
Regular Application Deadline: 2/1
Regular Notification: 5/31
LSDAS Accepted? No
Average GPA: 3.8
Range of GPA: 3.3–4.0
Average LSAT: 162
Range of LSAT: 157–179
Transfer Students Accepted? Yes
Other Schools to Which Students Applied: University of British Columbia, University of Toronto
Other Admissions Factors Considered: Academically related extracurricular activities, community involvement, work experience, personal characterisitics
Number of Applications Received: 1,171
Number of Applicants Accepted: 227
Number of Applicants Enrolled: 108

INTERNATIONAL STUDENTS
TOEFL Required of International Students? Yes
Minimum TOEFL: 600 (250 computer)

EMPLOYMENT INFORMATION
Rate of Placement: 93%

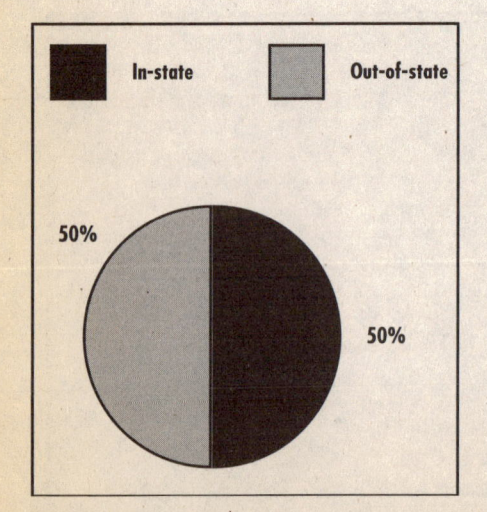

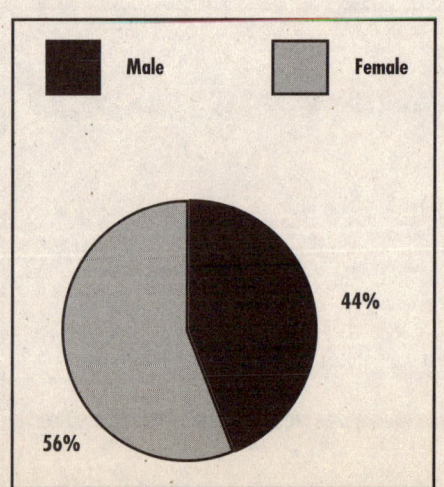

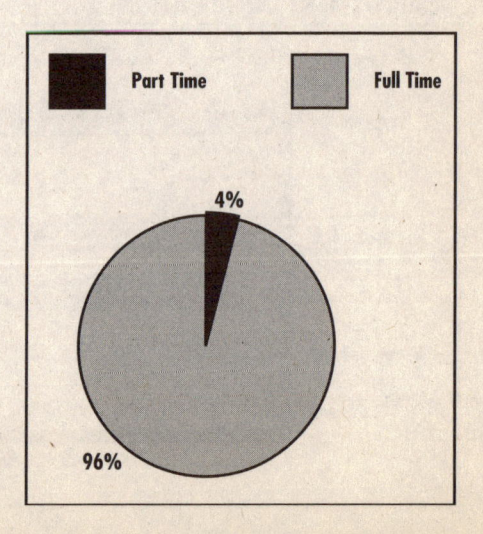

280 • COMPLETE BOOK OF LAW SCHOOLS

UNIVERSITY OF VIRGINIA
School of Law

Admissions Contact: Associate Dean for Admissions, Susan Palmer
580 Massie Road, Charlottesville, VA 22903-1789
Admissions Phone: 434-924-7351 • Admissions Fax: 434-982-2128
Admissions E-mail: lawadmit@virginia.edu • Web Address: www.law.virginia.edu

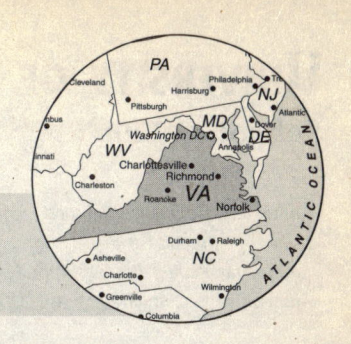

INSTITUTIONAL INFORMATION
Public/Private: Public
Student/Faculty Ratio: 14:1
Total Faculty: 122
% Part Time: 44
% Female: 20
% Minority: 6

PROGRAMS
Academic Specialties: Commercial Law, Constitutional Law, Corporation Securities Law, Criminal Law, Environmental Law, Government Services, Human Rights Law, Intellectual Property Law, International Law, Labor Law, Legal History, Taxation
Advanced Degrees Offered: SJD, LLM (1 year full time) JD (3 years full time)
Combined Degrees Offered: JD/PhD Government; JD/MA History, Government, Economics, English, Philosophy, Sociology, or Marine Affairs; JD/MBA (4 years full time), JD/MPP; JD/MS Accounting
Grading System: Letter and numerical system; most classes adhere to a mean grade of B+
Clinical Program Required? No
Clinical Program Description: Appellate Litigation, Child Advocacy, Criminal Defense, Criminal Prosecution, Employment Discrimination, Environmental Practice, First Amendment, Public Practice, Psychiatry and Civil Practice, Housing Law, Post-Conviction Capital Representation, Patents and Licensing

Legal Writing Course Requirements? No
Legal Methods Course Requirements? Yes
Legal Methods Description: 2 semesters; small sections; research, writing, and oral argument
Legal Research Course Requirements? No
Moot Court Requirement? No
Moot Court Description: More than 200 second-year students, in 2-person teams, hone their oral argument skills in the annual William Minor Lile Moot Court Competition. Winners receive a cash prize, and their names are inscribed on a plaque located outside the moot courtrooms. Teams of students chosen from among those entered in the competition may represent the school in the national Moot Court Competition and other extramural competitions nationwide.
Public Interest Law Requirement? No
Academic Journals: *Journal of Law and Politics, Virginia Environmental Law Journal, Virginia Journal of International Law, Virginia Journal of Law and Technology, Virginia Journal of Social Policy and the Law, Virginia Journal of Sports and the Law, Virginia Law Review, Virginia Tax Review*

STUDENT INFORMATION
Enrollment of Law School: 1,066
% Out of State: 56
% Male/Female: 58/42
% Full Time: 100
% Minority: 16
Average Age of Entering Class: 24

EXPENSES/FINANCIAL AID
Annual Tuition (Residents/Nonresidents): $19,319/$25,659
Room and Board: $11,565
Books and Supplies: $800
Financial Aid Application Deadline: 2/28
Average Grant: $9,825
Average Loan: $21,160
% of Aid That Is Merit-Based: 30
% Receiving Some Sort of Aid: 80
Average Total Aid Package: $26,708
Average Debt: $61,830

ADMISSIONS INFORMATION
Application Fee: $65
Regular Application Deadline: 1/15
Regular Notification: 4/15
LSDAS Accepted? Yes
Average GPA: 3.6
Range of GPA: 3.5–3.8
Average LSAT: 166
Range of LSAT: 164–168
Transfer Students Accepted? Yes
Other Schools to Which Students Applied: Columbia University, Duke University, George Washington University, Georgetown University, Harvard University, New York University, Stanford University
Other Admissions Factors Considered: Maturing effect of some years away from formal education, rising trend in academic performance, financial pressure requiring undergraduate employment, significant personal achievement
Number of Applications Received: 4,417
Number of Applicants Accepted: 985
Number of Applicants Enrolled: 350

INTERNATIONAL STUDENTS
TOEFL Required of International Students? Yes

EMPLOYMENT INFORMATION

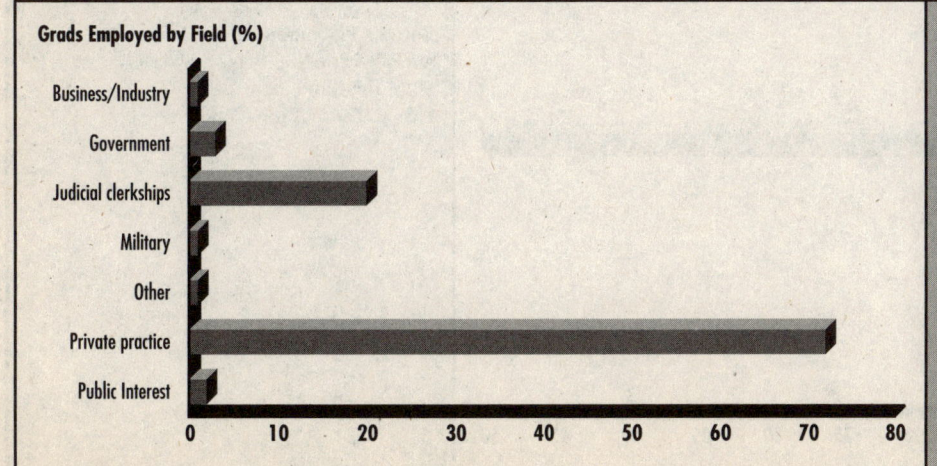

Grads Employed by Field (%)
- Business/Industry: ~2
- Government: ~2
- Judicial clerkships: ~20
- Military: ~1
- Other: ~2
- Private practice: ~73
- Public Interest: ~2

Rate of Placement: 100%
Average Starting Salary: $100,000
Employers Who Frequently Hire Grads: Top 100 firms in the country
State for Bar Exam: NY, VA
Pass Rate for First-Time Bar: 93%

UNIVERSITY OF WASHINGTON
School of Law

Admissions Contact: Admissions Supervisor, Kathy Swinehart
1100 NE Campus Parkway, Seattle, WA 98105-6617
Admissions Phone: 206-543-4078 • Admissions Fax: 206-543-5671
Admissions E-mail: admissions@law.washington.edu • Web Address: www.law.washington.edu

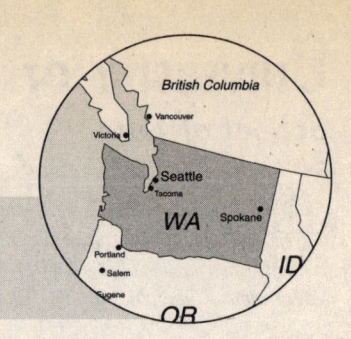

INSTITUTIONAL INFORMATION
Public/Private: Public
Student/Faculty Ratio: 13:1
Total Faculty: 47
% Female: 31
% Minority: 8

PROGRAMS
Academic Specialties: Civil Procedure, Commercial Law, Constitutional Law, Corporation Securities Law, Criminal Law, Environmental Law, Government Services, Human Rights Law, Intellectual Property Law, International Law, Labor Law, Legal History, Legal Philosophy, Property, Taxation
Advanced Degrees Offered: LLM Asian Law or Law of Sustainable International Development (1 year full time), LLM Taxation (1 year evening)
Combined Degrees Offered: 90 programs as approved
Grading System: Letter system
Clinical Program Required? No
Clinical Program Description: 9 clinical programs
Legal Writing Course Requirements? Yes
Legal Writing Description: Analytic Writing—first year
Legal Methods Course Requirements? Yes
Legal Methods Description: 1 year
Legal Research Course Requirements? No
Moot Court Requirement? No
Public Interest Law Requirement? Yes
Public Interest Law Description: 60 hours (2 credits)
Academic Journals: *Washington Law Review, Pacific Rim Law and Policy Journal*

STUDENT INFORMATION
Enrollment of Law School: 485
% Out of State: 20
% Male/Female: 49/51
% Full Time: 100
% Full Time That Are International: 1
% Minority: 6
Average Age of Entering Class: 25

EXPENSES/FINANCIAL AID
Annual Tuition (Residents/Nonresidents): $6,521/$16,724
Room and Board: $8,640
Books and Supplies: $1,000
Financial Aid Application Deadline: 2/28
Average Grant: $5,200
Average Loan: $12,881
% of Aid That Is Merit-Based: 4
% Receiving Some Sort of Aid: 70
Average Debt: $42,260

ADMISSIONS INFORMATION
Application Fee: $50
Regular Application Deadline: 1/15
Regular Notification: 4/1
LSDAS Accepted? Yes
Average GPA: 3.6
Range of GPA: 3.4–3.8
Average LSAT: 162
Range of LSAT: 159–165
Transfer Students Accepted? Yes
Other Schools to Which Students Applied: University of California, Berkeley; University of California, Hastings; Georgetown University; University of California, Los Angeles; George Washington University, Seattle University, University of Southern California
Number of Applications Received: 1,954
Number of Applicants Accepted: 468
Number of Applicants Enrolled: 177

EMPLOYMENT INFORMATION

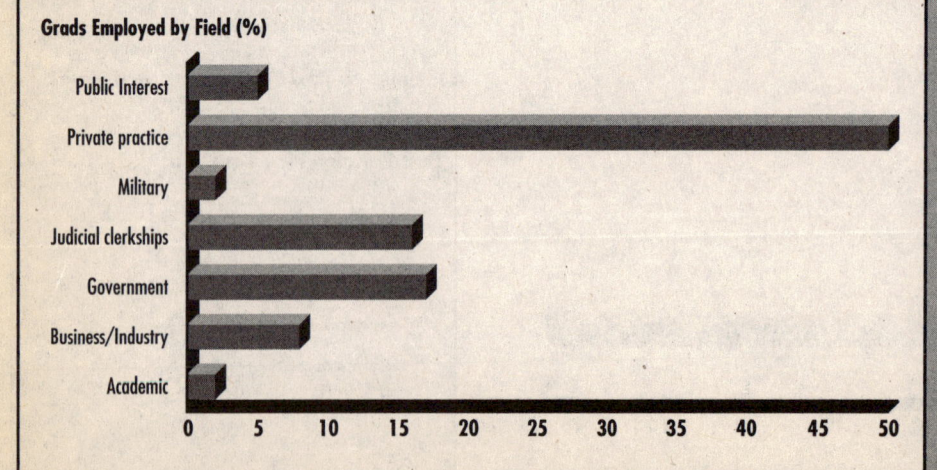

Grads Employed by Field (%)

Field	%
Public Interest	~2
Private practice	~50
Military	~2
Judicial clerkships	~15
Government	~17
Business/Industry	~10
Academic	~1

Rate of Placement: 98%
Average Starting Salary: $65,000
State for Bar Exam: WA
Pass Rate for First-Time Bar: 90%

UNIVERSITY OF WEST LOS ANGELES
School of Law

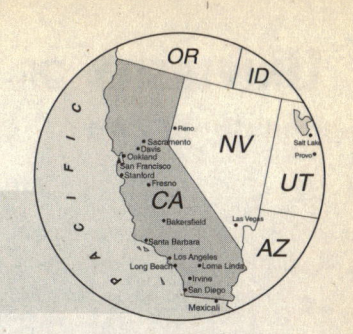

Admissions Contact: Director of Admissions, Lynda Freeman
1155 West Arbor Vitae Street, Inglewood, CA 90301-2902
Admissions Phone: 310-342-5254 • Admissions Fax: 310-342-5295
Admissions E-mail: lfreeman@uwla.edu • Web Address: www.uwla.edu

INSTITUTIONAL INFORMATION
Public/Private: Private
Student/Faculty Ratio: 30:1
Total Faculty: 36
% Part Time: 81
% Female: 19
% Minority: 17

PROGRAMS
Academic Specialties: Emphasis is on practicum. Adjunct professors are specialists in their fields.
Advanced Degrees Offered: JD (3 years full time, 4 years part time)
Grading System: Letter system on a 4.0 scale
Clinical Program Required? No
Clinical Program Description: Judicial and public agency externships (such as Legal Aid)
Legal Writing Course Requirements? Yes
Legal Writing Description: 3 courses: basic research and writing after the first year, advanced writing in the second year, moot court
Legal Methods Course Requirements? Yes
Legal Methods Description: First semester
Legal Research Course Requirements? Yes
Legal Research Description: Students learn how to use print and online research tools after the first year.
Moot Court Requirement? Yes
Moot Court Description: 15 weeks
Public Interest Law Requirement? No
Academic Journals: *UWLA Law Review*

STUDENT INFORMATION
Enrollment of Law School: 294
% Male/Female: 55/45
% Full Time: 14
% Minority: 32
Average Age of Entering Class: 35

EXPENSES/FINANCIAL AID
Annual Tuition: $14,980
Books and Supplies: $1,000
Financial Aid Application Deadline: 3/1
Average Grant: $18,500
Average Loan: $18,500
% Receiving Some Sort of Aid: 90
Average Total Aid Package: $18,500
Average Debt: $70,000
Tuition Per Credit: $535

ADMISSIONS INFORMATION
Application Fee: $55
Regular Application Deadline: Rolling
Regular Notification: Rolling
LSDAS Accepted? No
Range of GPA: 2.0–3.9
Average LSAT: 31
Range of LSAT: 31–75
Transfer Students Accepted? Yes
Other Admissions Factors Considered: If an applicant has completed less than 60 academic units, 3 general CLEP exams are required.
Number of Applications Received: 79
Number of Applicants Accepted: 59
Number of Applicants Enrolled: 17

INTERNATIONAL STUDENTS
TOEFL Required of International Students? Yes
Minimum TOEFL: 550 (213 computer)

EMPLOYMENT INFORMATION
Prominent Alumni: Paula Zinneman, California Real Estate Commissioner; Gail Margolis, Director, Mental Health Services, State of CA; Hon. Ron Skyers, L.A. Superior Court Judge; Lael Rubin, District Attorney's Office
State for Bar Exam: CA
Pass Rate for First-Time Bar: 30%

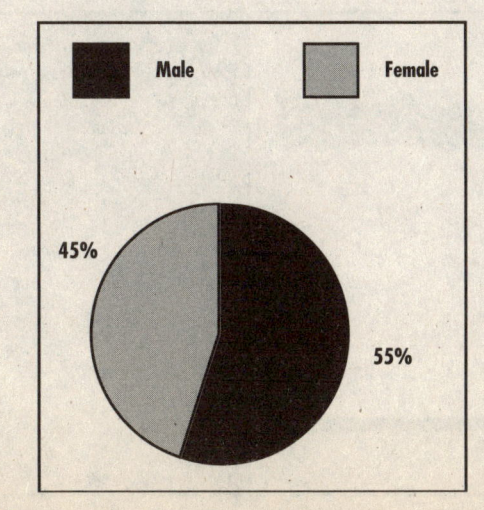

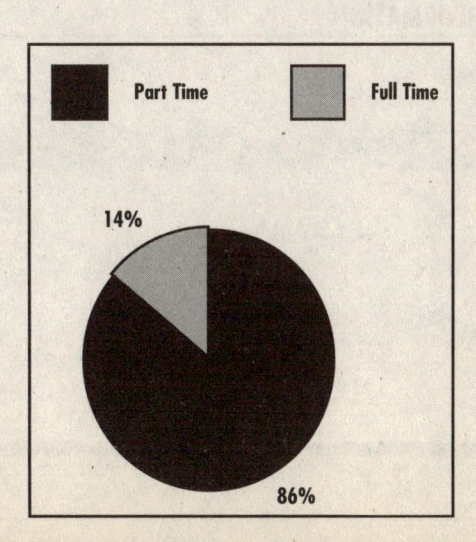

UNIVERSITY OF WINDSOR
Faculty of Law

Admissions Contact: Assistant to the Dean/Director of Admissions, Michelle Pilutti
401 Sunset, Windsor, ON N9B 3P4
Admissions Phone: 519-253-3000 • Admissions Fax: 519-973-7064
Admissions E-mail: lawadmit@uwindsor.ca • Web Address: www.uwindsor.ca/law

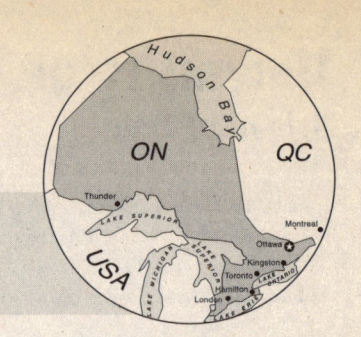

INSTITUTIONAL INFORMATION
Public/Private: Public
Student/Faculty Ratio: 20:1
Total Faculty: 23
% Part Time: 24
% Female: 30
% Minority: 10

PROGRAMS
Academic Specialties: Canada–U.S. Relations, Environmental Law, Access to Justice, Civil Procedure, Commercial Law, Constitutional Law, Corporation Securities Law, Criminal Law, Human Rights Law, Intellectual Property Law, International Law, Labor Law, Legal History, Legal Philosophy, Property, Taxation
Combined Degrees Offered: MBA/LLB (3 to 4 years), JD/LLB (3 years)
Clinical Program Required? No
Clinical Program Description: Legal Assistance of Windsor, Community Legal Aid, University of Windsor Mediation Service, Pro Bono Students of Canada
Legal Writing Course Requirements? Yes
Legal Writing Description: Law I is a 1-year series of legal research and writing assignments, culminating in moot court.
Legal Methods Course Requirements? Yes
Legal Methods Description: See Legal Writing.
Legal Research Course Requirements? Yes
Legal Research Description: See Legal Writing.
Moot Court Requirement? Yes
Moot Court Description: Part of Law I
Public Interest Law Requirement? No
Academic Journals: *Windsor Review of Legal and Social Issues*

STUDENT INFORMATION
Enrollment of Law School: 469
% Out of State: 22
% Male/Female: 42/58
% Full Time: 98
% Full Time That Are International: 0
% Minority: 0
Average Age of Entering Class: 26

RESEARCH FACILITIES
School-Supported Research Centers: CARC (Canadian-American Research Centre for Law and Policy), IPLI (Intellectual Property Law Institute)

EXPENSES/FINANCIAL AID
Annual Tuition (Residents/Nonresidents): $8,203/$11,565
Room and Board (On Campus): $4,218
Books and Supplies: $1,315
Average Grant: $750
Average Loan: $9,350
% of Aid That Is Merit-Based: 60
Tuition Per Credit (Residents/Nonresidents): $1,948/$2,941

ADMISSIONS INFORMATION
Application Fee: $50
Regular Application Deadline: 1/11
Regular Notification: Rolling
LSDAS Accepted? No
Transfer Students Accepted? Yes
Other Admissions Factors Considered: Work experience, community involvement, personal accomplishments, career objectives
Number of Applications Received: 1,682
Number of Applicants Accepted: 164
Number of Applicants Enrolled: 164

INTERNATIONAL STUDENTS
TOEFL Recommended for International Students? Yes

EMPLOYMENT INFORMATION

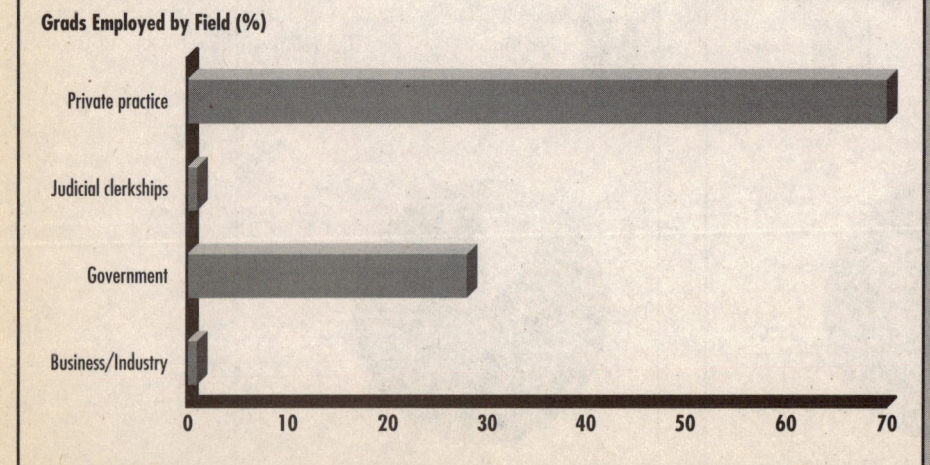

Grads Employed by Field (%)

Field	%
Private practice	~70
Judicial clerkships	~1
Government	~28
Business/Industry	~1

Rate of Placement: 98%
Employers Who Frequently Hire Grads: Law firms
State for Bar Exam: ON, AB, BC, NS, NF
Pass Rate for First-Time Bar: 99%

UNIVERSITY OF WISCONSIN
Law School

Admissions Contact: Assistant Dean for Admissions and Financial Aid, M. Elizabeth Kransberger
975 Bascom Mall, Madison, WI 53706
Admissions Phone: 608-262-5914 • Admissions Fax: 608-263-3190
Admissions E-mail: admissions@law.wisc.edu • Web Address: www.law.wisc.edu

INSTITUTIONAL INFORMATION
Public/Private: Public
Student/Faculty Ratio: 20:1
Total Faculty: 49
% Female: 20
% Minority: 15

PROGRAMS
Academic Specialties: We are well known for a number of academic specialties, from International Law to Criminal Law, but it is our law-in-action philosophy, interdisciplinary opportunities, and clinical programs that differentiate us from other law schools. The law-in-action approach, for which we are known internationally, is a unique brand of scholarship that shapes the way people around the world think about law. Wisconsin scholars have established an enduring reputation for using the insights of a variety of disciplines to study and explain how law works in fact rather than in theory, and this approach has consistently put our scholars at the cutting edge. Many of today's principal trends in legal scholarship can trace their origins, in whole or in part, to work first done at Wisconsin. Specialties include Corporation Securities Law, Environmental Law, Government Services, Intellectual Property Law, Labor Law, Legal History, and Legal Philosophy.
Advanced Degrees Offered: JD, LLM, SJD
Combined Degrees Offered: JD/MBA, Environmental Studies, Ibero-American Studies, Sociology
Grading System: Letter and numerical system (65–95)

Clinical Program Required? No
Legal Writing Course Requirements? Yes
Legal Writing Description: First year
Legal Methods Course Requirements? Yes
Legal Methods Description: 3-credit legal process course
Legal Research Course Requirements? Yes
Legal Research Description: First year
Moot Court Requirement? No
Public Interest Law Requirement? No
Academic Journals: Wisconsin Law Review, Wisconsin International Law Journal, Wisconsin Women's Law Journal

STUDENT INFORMATION
Enrollment of Law School: 830
% Male/Female: 52/48
% Full Time: 93
% Minority: 21
Average Age of Entering Class: 26

RESEARCH FACILITIES
School-Supported Research Centers: 15 campus computer labs, campus-wide wireless Ethernet

EXPENSES/FINANCIAL AID
Annual Tuition (Residents/Nonresidents): $8,930/$24,520
Room and Board: $6,550
Books and Supplies: $1,820
Financial Aid Application Deadline: 2/15
Average Grant: $1,000
Average Loan: $12,797

% of Aid That Is Merit-Based: 10
% Receiving Some Sort of Aid: 90
Average Total Aid Package: $18,500
Average Debt: $47,796

ADMISSIONS INFORMATION
Application Fee: $45
Regular Application Deadline: 2/1
Regular Notification: Rolling
LSDAS Accepted? Yes
Average GPA: 3.3
Range of GPA: 3.0–3.6
Average LSAT: 160
Range of LSAT: 156–162
Transfer Students Accepted? Yes
Other Admissions Factors Considered: Trend of college grades, letters of recommendation, graduate study, time between college graduation and application to law school, undergraduate institution, college grading and course selection patterns, work while in college, writing sample, unusual cultural background, geographical diversity, residency, acceptance in a prior year, diversity of experience or background, diversity of stated professional goals
Number of Applications Received: 2,300
Number of Applicants Accepted: 730
Number of Applicants Enrolled: 301

INTERNATIONAL STUDENTS
TOEFL Required of International Students? Yes

EMPLOYMENT INFORMATION

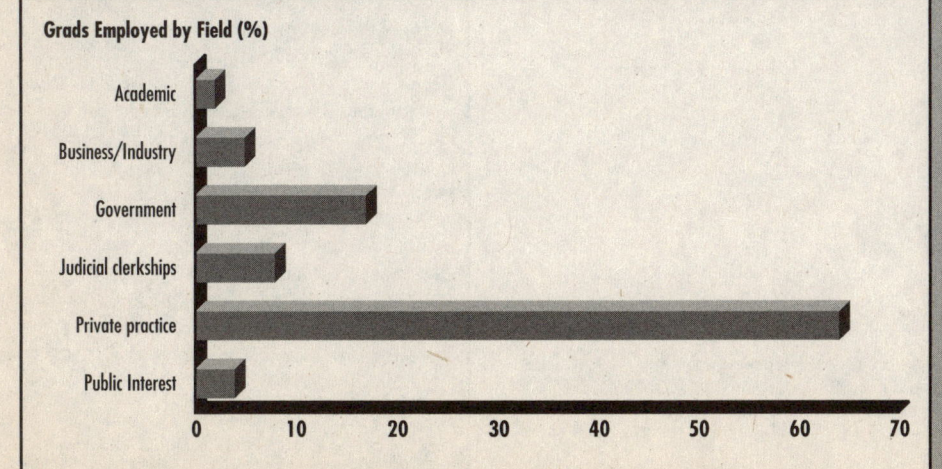

Grads Employed by Field (%)
- Academic
- Business/Industry
- Government
- Judicial clerkships
- Private practice
- Public Interest

Rate of Placement: 98%
Average Starting Salary: $69,406
Employers Who Frequently Hire Grads: Gibson Dunn & Crutcher; Morrison & Forester; Foley & Lardner; Sidley & Austin; Mayer Brown Rowe & Maw; Jenner & Block; Dewey Ballantine
Prominent Alumni: Tommy Thompson, Secretary, U.S. Dept. of Health and Human Services; Tammy Baldwin, U.S. House of Representatives; Gaylord Nelson, Director, Wilderness Society, founder of Earth Day; John Rowe, CEO, Exelon Corp. in Chicago; Francis Ulmer, Lt. Governor of Alaska, 1995–2003
State for Bar Exam: WI
Pass Rate for First-Time Bar: 100%

UNIVERSITY OF WYOMING
College of Law

Admissions Contact: Coordinator of Admissions, Carol Persson
PO Box 3035, Laramie, WY 82071
Admissions Phone: 307-766-6416 • Admissions Fax: 307-766-6417
Admissions E-mail: lawadmis@uwyo.edu • Web Address: www.uwyo.edu/law

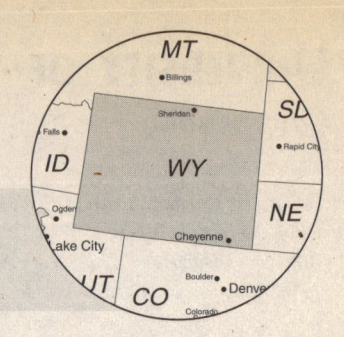

INSTITUTIONAL INFORMATION
Public/Private: Public
Student/Faculty Ratio: 17:1
Total Faculty: 30
% Part Time: 47
% Female: 53
% Minority: 7

PROGRAMS
Academic Specialties: We offer a general curriculum designed to equip students for the general practice of law, with sufficient course work to develop specializations (such as Environmental Law or Natural Resources Law). We also offer three clinical programs, which give third-year students the opportunity to make court appearances, write appellate briefs, and appear before the Wyoming Supreme Court.
Advanced Degrees Offered: JD (3 years)
Combined Degrees Offered: JD/MPA (3.5 years), JD/MBA (3.5 to 4 years)
Grading System: Letter system; Incomplete (X) and Withdrawn (W) are disregarded. Satisfactory/Unsatisfactory may be granted if the student so requests at registration. An S/U course does not count toward hours required for graduation unless it is offered for the S/U grade only or it is a nonlaw UW graduate course preapproved for credit toward the law degree (up to 6 credits).
Clinical Program Required? No
Clinical Program Description: Defender Aid, Legal Services/Domestic Violence, Prosecution Assistance

Legal Writing Course Requirements? Yes
Legal Writing Description: 2 credits, first semester
Legal Methods Course Requirements? No
Legal Research Course Requirements? Yes
Legal Research Description: 1 credit, the first semester
Moot Court Requirement? Yes
Moot Court Description: In the spring semester of the first year, all students take a 1-credit course called Appellate Advocacy, which includes brief writing and a moot appellate argument.
Public Interest Law Requirement? No
Academic Journals: *Wyoming Law Review*

STUDENT INFORMATION
Enrollment of Law School: 220
% Out of State: 45
% Male/Female: 56/44
% Full Time: 100
% Full Time That Are International: 1
% Minority: 7
Average Age of Entering Class: 26

RESEARCH FACILITIES
School-Supported Research Centers: Wireless Internet access available throughout the facility

EXPENSES/FINANCIAL AID
Annual Tuition (Residents/Nonresidents): $4,512/$10,176
Room and Board: $5,120
Books and Supplies: $800

Financial Aid Application Deadline: 3/1
Average Grant: $1,691
Average Loan: $12,580
% of Aid That Is Merit-Based: 14
% Receiving Some Sort of Aid: 85
Average Total Aid Package: $14,271
Average Debt: $34,000

ADMISSIONS INFORMATION
Application Fee: $35
Regular Application Deadline: 3/15
Regular Notification: 4/15
LSDAS Accepted? Yes
Average GPA: 3.3
Range of GPA: 3.1–3.6
Average LSAT: 153
Range of LSAT: 150–156
Transfer Students Accepted? Yes
Other Schools to Which Students Applied: Gonzaga University, University of Colorado, University of Denver, University of Idaho, University of Montana, University of Oregon, University of Utah
Other Admissions Factors Considered: Grade progression
Number of Applications Received: 686
Number of Applicants Accepted: 205
Number of Applicants Enrolled: 82

INTERNATIONAL STUDENTS
TOEFL Required of International Students? Yes
Minimum TOEFL: 525 (195 computer)

EMPLOYMENT INFORMATION

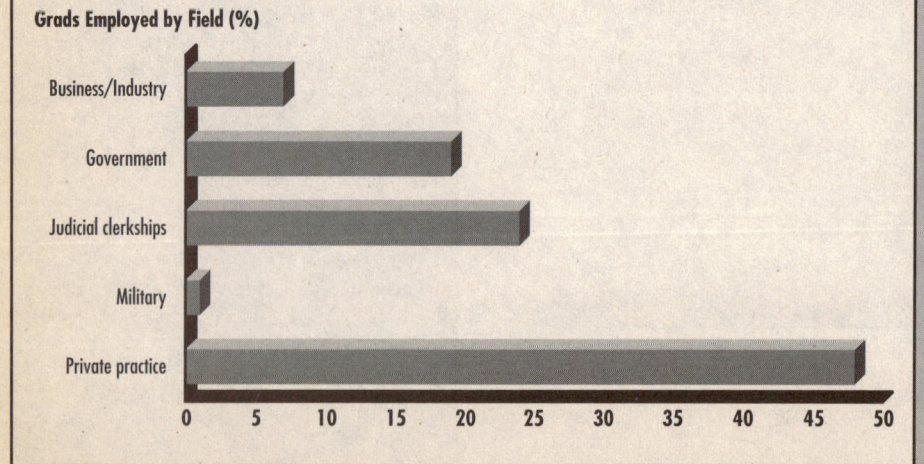

Grads Employed by Field (%)

Field	%
Business/Industry	~7
Government	~20
Judicial clerkships	~24
Military	~1
Private practice	~48

Rate of Placement: 93%
Average Starting Salary: $40,317
Employers Who Frequently Hire Grads: Government (Attorney General, District and Federal Courts, Public Defender, County Attorney); general practice firms
Prominent Alumni: Gerry Spence, Trial Lawyer, Author, and Television Commentator; Mike Sullivan, former U.S. Ambassador to Ireland and Governor of Wyoming; Alan K. Simpson, former U.S. Senator of Wyoming, Political Commentator; David Freudenthal, Governor of Wyoming
State for Bar Exam: WY, CO, CA, UT, MT

VALPARAISO UNIVERSITY
School of Law

Admissions Contact: Assistant Dean of Admissions and Student Services, Marilyn Olson
Wesemann Hall, Valparaiso, IN 46383
Admissions Phone: 888-825-7652 • Admissions Fax: 219-465-7808
Admissions E-mail: valpolaw@valpo.edu • Web Address: www.valpo.edu/law

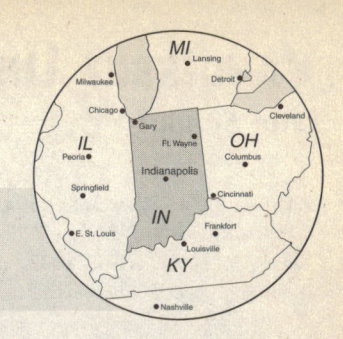

INSTITUTIONAL INFORMATION
Public/Private: Private
Affiliation: Lutheran
Student/Faculty Ratio: 17:1
Total Faculty: 72
% Part Time: 51
% Female: 38
% Minority: 4

PROGRAMS
Academic Specialties: Opportunity to select a minor or concentration area; each includes course work, practical experience, and a scholarly paper. Specialties include Civil Procedure, Criminal Law, Environmental Law, International Law, and Labor Law.
Advanced Degrees Offered: JD (3 years full time, 5 years part time), LLM (1 year full time, 2 years part time)
Combined Degrees Offered: JD/MA Psychology (4 years), JD/MBA (4 years)
Grading System: Numerical and letter system, A (4.0) to F (0.0)
Clinical Program Required? No
Clinical Program Description: 6 clinical options: Civil, Criminal, Domestic Violence, Tax, Mediation, and Juvenile.
Legal Writing Course Requirements? Yes
Legal Writing Description: Legal writing required each of the 3 years
Legal Methods Course Requirements? Yes
Legal Research Course Requirements? Yes
Legal Research Description: Legal research is a first-year course taught by the law librarians.
Moot Court Requirement? No
Public Interest Law Requirement? No

STUDENT INFORMATION
Enrollment of Law School: 420
% Out of State: 41
% Male/Female: 54/46
% Full Time: 87
% Full Time That Are International: 1
% Minority: 13
Average Age of Entering Class: 26

RESEARCH FACILITIES
% of JD Classrooms Wired: 90

EXPENSES/FINANCIAL AID
Annual Tuition: $19,950
Room and Board: $6,600
Books and Supplies: $750
Average Grant: $11,502
Average Loan: $20,200
% Receiving Some Sort of Aid: 90
Average Total Aid Package: $23,210
Average Debt: $56,916
Tuition Per Credit: $740
Fees Per Credit: $18

ADMISSIONS INFORMATION
Application Fee: $30
Regular Application Deadline: 4/15
Regular Notification: Rolling
LSDAS Accepted? Yes
Average GPA: 3.2
Range of GPA: 2.9–3.6
Average LSAT: 152
Range of LSAT: 148–157
Transfer Students Accepted? Yes
Other Admissions Factors Considered: Undergraduate institution, undergraduate major, graduate work, life/work experience
Number of Applications Received: 692
Number of Applicants Accepted: 491
Number of Applicants Enrolled: 167

EMPLOYMENT INFORMATION

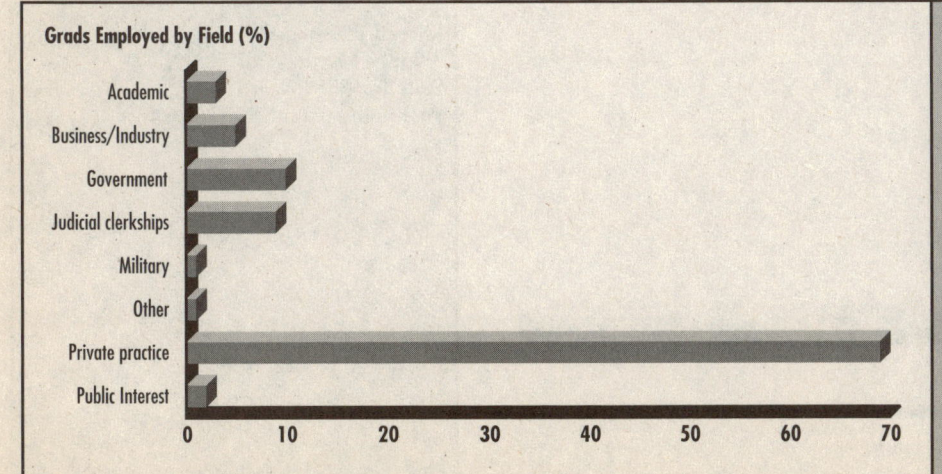

Grads Employed by Field (%)

Field	%
Academic	~2
Business/Industry	~5
Government	~10
Judicial clerkships	~10
Military	~1
Other	~2
Private practice	~70
Public Interest	~2

Rate of Placement: 96%
Average Starting Salary: $50,000
Employers Who Frequently Hire Grads: Jenner & Block; Sidley & Austin; Foley & Lardner; Hinshaw & Culbertson; Querrey & Harrow; Ungaaretti & Harris; Thacher, Proffitt & Wood; Beckman Lawson; Bose, McKinney & Evans; Barnes & Thornburg; Baker & Daniels; Ice, Miller, Donadio & Ryan; Locke Reynolds; May, Oberfell & Lorber; Hoeppner, Wagner & Evans; Ruman, Clements, Tobin & Holub; Kightlinger & Gray; Lucas, Holcomb, & Medrea; Warner, Norcross & Judd; Briggs and Morgan
State for Bar Exam: IN
Pass Rate for First-Time Bar: 88%

VANDERBILT UNIVERSITY
Law School

Admissions Contact: Assistant Dean, Sonya G. Smith
131 21st Avenue South, Nashville, TN 37203
Admissions Phone: 615-322-6452 • Admissions Fax: 615-322-1531
Admissions E-mail: admissions@law.vanderbilt.edu • Web Address: www.law.vanderbilt.edu

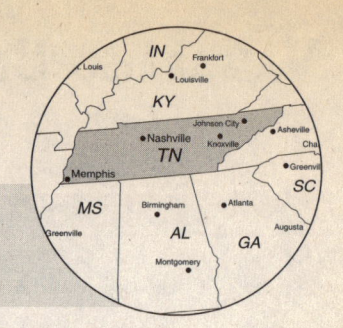

INSTITUTIONAL INFORMATION
Public/Private: Private
Student/Faculty Ratio: 13:1
Total Faculty: 69
% Part Time: 52
% Female: 30
% Minority: 10

PROGRAMS
Academic Specialties: Public and Constitutional Law, Corporate Law, Entertainment Law and Practice, Cyberspace and Technology Law, Civil Procedure, Commercial Law, Criminal Law, Environmental Law, Government Services, Human Rights Law, Intellectual Property Law, International Law, Labor Law, Legal History, Legal Philosophy, Property, Taxation
Advanced Degrees Offered: LLM (1 year)
Combined Degrees Offered: JD/MBA (4 years), JD/MA (5 years), JD/PhD (7 years), JD/MDiv (5 years), JD/MTS (4 years), JD/MD (6 years)
Grading System: Letter system
Clinical Program Required? No
Clinical Program Description: Civil Practice Clinic, Criminal Practice Clinic, Juvenile Practice Clinic, Child and Family Practice Clinic
Legal Writing Course Requirements? Yes
Legal Writing Description: First year
Legal Methods Course Requirements? Yes
Legal Methods Description: 2 semesters, first year
Legal Research Course Requirements? No
Moot Court Requirement? No
Public Interest Law Requirement? No
Academic Journals: *The Vanderbilt Law Review, Journal of Transnational Law, Journal of Sports and Entertainment Law*

STUDENT INFORMATION
Enrollment of Law School: 564
% Out of State: 84
% Male/Female: 52/48
% Full Time: 100
% Full Time That Are International: 5
% Minority: 28
Average Age of Entering Class: 24

EXPENSES/FINANCIAL AID
Annual Tuition: $28,350
Room and Board (On/Off Campus): $14,225/$15,585
Books and Supplies: $1,255
Financial Aid Application Deadline: 2/15
Average Grant: $10,000
Average Loan: $15,500
% of Aid That Is Merit-Based: 40
% Receiving Some Sort of Aid: 80
Average Total Aid Package: $44,184
Average Debt: $82,000

ADMISSIONS INFORMATION
Application Fee: $50
Regular Application Deadline: 3/15
Regular Notification: 4/15
LSDAS Accepted? Yes
Average GPA: 3.6
Range of GPA: 3.4–3.8
Average LSAT: 164
Range of LSAT: 161–165
Transfer Students Accepted? Yes
Other Schools to Which Students Applied: Duke University, Emory University, Georgetown University, Harvard University, Stanford University, University of Texas at Austin, University of Virginia
Other Admissions Factors Considered: Letters of recommendation, personal statements, rigor of academic courses, extracurricular activities, work experience, diverse background
Number of Applications Received: 3,535
Number of Applicants Accepted: 509
Number of Applicants Enrolled: 194

INTERNATIONAL STUDENTS
TOEFL Required of International Students? Yes

EMPLOYMENT INFORMATION

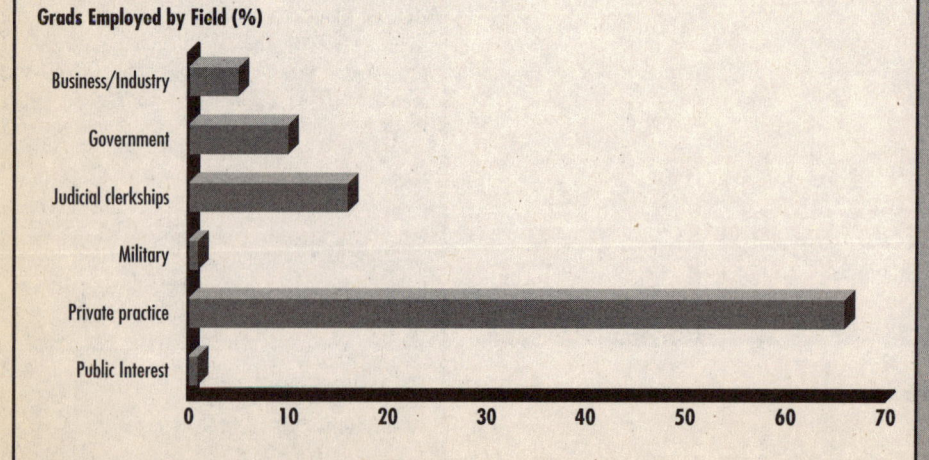

Grads Employed by Field (%)

Field	%
Business/Industry	~3
Government	~10
Judicial clerkships	~17
Military	~1
Private practice	~67
Public Interest	~1

Rate of Placement: 99%
Average Starting Salary: $107,000
State for Bar Exam: TN
Pass Rate for First-Time Bar: 93%

Vermont Law School

Admissions Contact: Assistant Dean for Admissions and Financial Aid, Kathy Hartman
Chelsea Street, South Royalton, VT 05068-0096
Admissions Phone: 888-277-5985 • Admissions Fax: 802-763-7071
Admissions E-mail: admiss@vermontlaw.edu • Web Address: www.vermontlaw.edu

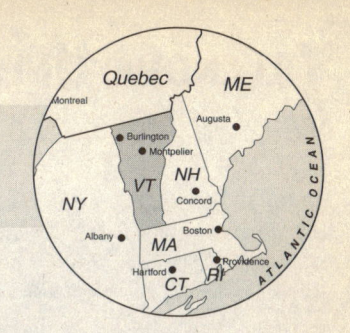

INSTITUTIONAL INFORMATION

Public/Private: Private
Student/Faculty Ratio: 18:1
Total Faculty: 36
% Part Time: 0
% Female: 38
% Minority: 1

PROGRAMS

Academic Specialties: Clinical/experiential programs, General Practice Program certificate, Canadian Studies Program, First Nations Environmental Law Program, Public Interest Law, Civil Procedure, Commercial Law, Constitutional Law, Corporation Securities Law, Criminal Law, Government Services, Human Rights Law, International Law, Labor Law, Legal History, Legal Philosophy, Property, Taxation
Advanced Degrees Offered: JD (3 years), MSEL (1 year), LLM Environmental Law (1 year)
Combined Degrees Offered: JD/MSEL (6 semesters, 2 summers)
Grading System: Letter system
Clinical Program Required? No
Clinical Program Description: South Royalton Legal Clinic, Semester in Practice, Environmental Semester in Washington, Legislation Clinic, Environmental Law Clinic
Legal Writing Course Requirements? Yes
Legal Writing Description: 2 courses over 3 years
Legal Methods Course Requirements? Yes
Legal Methods Description: 4 courses over 3 years
Legal Research Course Requirements? Yes
Legal Research Description: 2 courses over 1 year
Moot Court Requirement? Yes
Moot Court Description: 1 semester
Public Interest Law Requirement? No
Academic Journals: *Vermont Law Review, Res Communes*

STUDENT INFORMATION

Enrollment of Law School: 511
% Out of State: 90
% Male/Female: 51/49
% Full Time: 100
% Full Time That Are International: 2
% Minority: 11
Average Age of Entering Class: 27

EXPENSES/FINANCIAL AID

Annual Tuition: $23,494
Room and Board (Off Campus): $8,636
Books and Supplies: $900
Financial Aid Application Deadline: 3/1
Average Grant: $6,000
Average Loan: $18,500
% of Aid That Is Merit-Based: 17
% Receiving Some Sort of Aid: 90
Average Total Aid Package: $27,500
Average Debt: $72,000

ADMISSIONS INFORMATION

Application Fee: $50
Regular Application Deadline: 3/15
Regular Notification: 4/1
LSDAS Accepted? Yes
Average GPA: 3.1
Range of GPA: 2.8–3.3
Average LSAT: 153
Range of LSAT: 149–156
Transfer Students Accepted? Yes
Other Schools to Which Students Applied: Albany Law School, Franklin Pierce Law Center, Lewis and Clark College, Pace University, Suffolk University, University of Colorado, University of Denver
Number of Applications Received: 826
Number of Applicants Accepted: 500
Number of Applicants Enrolled: 190

INTERNATIONAL STUDENTS

TOEFL Required of International Students? Yes
Minimum TOEFL: 600

EMPLOYMENT INFORMATION

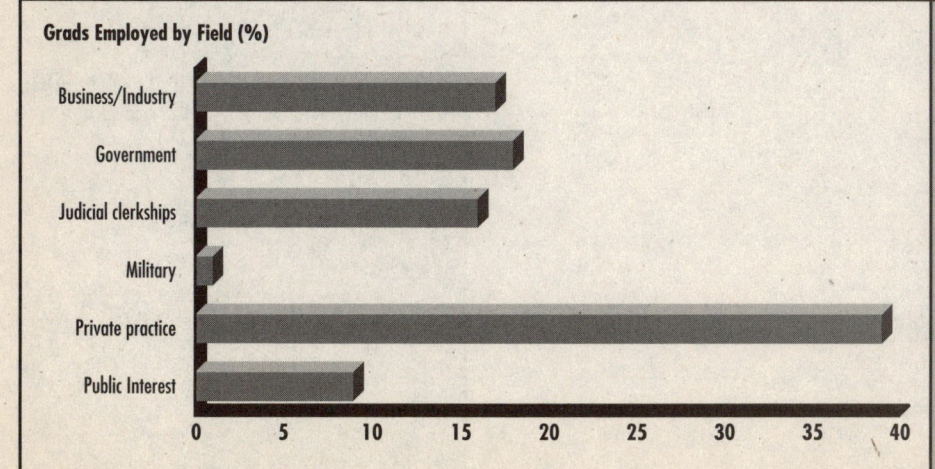

Grads Employed by Field (%)
- Business/Industry: ~17
- Government: ~17
- Judicial clerkships: ~17
- Military: ~1
- Private practice: ~40
- Public Interest: ~9

Rate of Placement: 85%
Average Starting Salary: $40,000
Employers Who Frequently Hire Grads: Various federal agencies including Environmental Protection Agency, Department of Justice, and nonprofit legal aid organizations and advocacy groups; various state and federal appellate and trial court systems
State for Bar Exam: VT, MA, NY
Pass Rate for First-Time Bar: 65%

VILLANOVA UNIVERSITY
School of Law

Admissions Contact: Director of Admissions
299 North Spring Mill Road, Villanova, PA 19085
Admissions Phone: 610-519-7010 • Admissions Fax: 610-519-6291
Admissions E-mail: admissions@law.villanova.edu • Web Address: www.law.villanova.edu

INSTITUTIONAL INFORMATION
Public/Private: Private
Affiliation: Roman Catholic
Student/Faculty Ratio: 16:1
Total Faculty: 84
% Part Time: 46
% Female: 32
% Minority: 8

PROGRAMS
Academic Specialties: Law and Technology (policy and applications), International Law, Corporation Securities Law
Advanced Degrees Offered: JD (3 years), LLM Taxation (24 credits)
Combined Degrees Offered: JD/MBA (3 to 4.5 years), JD/PhD Psychology (7 to 8 years)
Grading System: 4.0 scale
Clinical Program Required? No
Clinical Program Description: Tax Clinic, Information Law Clinic, Juvenile Justice Clinic, Villanova Community Legal Services, Externships, Law and Entrepreneurship, Immigration Law Clinic
Legal Writing Course Requirements? No
Legal Methods Course Requirements? Yes
Legal Methods Description: 1 year, small group, hands-on process
Legal Research Course Requirements? No
Moot Court Requirement? Yes
Moot Court Description: Reimel Moot Court Competition participants prepare briefs and present appellate arguments before lawyers and judges in a round-robin tournament. Finalists argue before a distinguished bench. Students also participate in the National Moot Court Competition, the Benton International Moot Court Competition, the Frederick Douglas Moot Court Competition, and the Jessup International Law Competition.
Public Interest Law Requirement? No
Academic Journals: The Villanova Law Review, The Villanova Environmental Law Journal, The Villanova Sports and Entertainment Law Journal

STUDENT INFORMATION
Enrollment of Law School: 710
% Out of State: 54
% Male/Female: 53/47
% Full Time: 100
% Full Time That Are International: 2
% Minority: 15
Average Age of Entering Class: 24

RESEARCH FACILITIES
Research Resources Available: Full Internet access
School-Supported Research Centers: Center for Information Law and Policy (CILP)

EXPENSES/FINANCIAL AID
Annual Tuition: $20,000
Room and Board (Off Campus): $10,990
Books and Supplies: $1,000
Average Grant: $6,414
Average Loan: $26,169
% Receiving Some Sort of Aid: 77
Average Total Aid Package: $27,278
Average Debt: $73,076

ADMISSIONS INFORMATION
Application Fee: $75
Regular Application Deadline: 3/1
Regular Notification: Rolling
LSDAS Accepted? Yes
Average GPA: 3.3
Range of GPA: 3.0–3.5
Average LSAT: 157
Range of LSAT: 153–158
Transfer Students Accepted? Yes

INTERNATIONAL STUDENTS
TOEFL Recommended for International Students? Yes

EMPLOYMENT INFORMATION

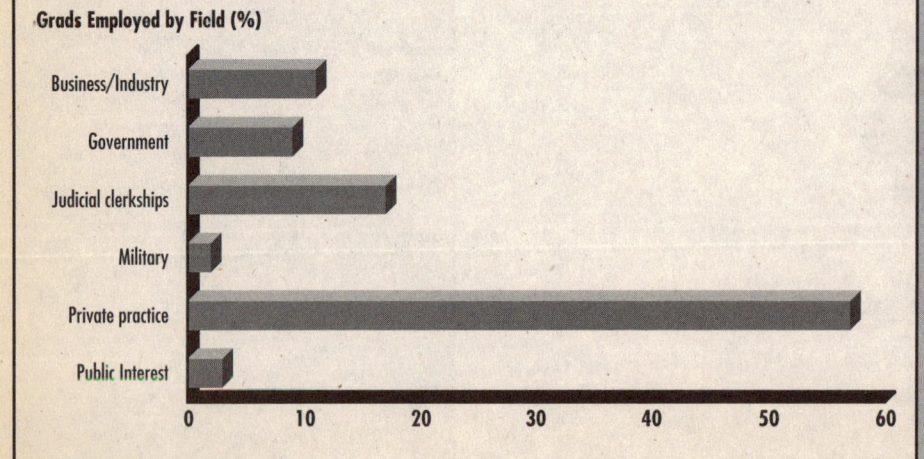

Grads Employed by Field (%)

Field	%
Business/Industry	~12
Government	~10
Judicial clerkships	~18
Military	~2
Private practice	~58
Public Interest	~2

Rate of Placement: 97%
Average Starting Salary: $71,975
Employers Who Frequently Hire Grads: State judges and government; law firms in Philadelphia, New York, New Jersey, DC, and Delaware
State for Bar Exam: PA
Pass Rate for First-Time Bar: 75%

WAKE FOREST UNIVERSITY
School of Law

Admissions Contact: Director of Admissions and Financial Aid, Melanie E. Nutt
PO Box 7206, Winston-Salem, NC 27109
Admissions Phone: 336-758-5437 • Admissions Fax: 336-758-4632
Admissions E-mail: admissions@law.wfu.edu • Web Address: www.law.wfu.edu

INSTITUTIONAL INFORMATION
Public/Private: Private
Student/Faculty Ratio: 13:1
Total Faculty: 30
% Part Time: 18
% Female: 32
% Minority: 4

PROGRAMS
Academic Specialties: Commercial Law, Constitutional Law, Corporation Securities Law, Criminal Law, International Law, Taxation
Advanced Degrees Offered: LLM (foreign lawyers only)
Combined Degrees Offered: JD/MBA
Grading System: A (91–100), B (81–90), C (71–80), D (66–70), F (59–65)
Clinical Program Required? No
Clinical Program Description: Litigation Clinic, Elder Care Clinic, Domestic Advocacy
Legal Writing Course Requirements? Yes
Legal Writing Description: 3 semesters
Legal Methods Course Requirements? Yes
Legal Methods Description: 3 semesters; begins with instruction in legal methods and ethics
Legal Research Course Requirements? Yes
Legal Research Description: See Legal Methods.
Moot Court Requirement? No
Public Interest Law Requirement? Yes

Public Interest Law Description: Entering students are assigned a pro bono project in the first week to encourage them to become involved throughout their career.
Academic Journals: *Wake Forest Law Review, On-Line Virtual Intellectual Property Journal*

STUDENT INFORMATION
Enrollment of Law School: 474
% Out of State: 60
% Male/Female: 53/47
% Full Time: 95
% Full Time That Are International: 1
% Minority: 10
Average Age of Entering Class: 25

RESEARCH FACILITIES
Research Resources Available: Lexis; Westlaw; library resources available electronically and via CD
School-Supported Research Centers: We have 53 computers in our student computer lab and another 28 dedicated PCs in the library. Every student organization office has at least one computer, and all the library carrels are wired so that students can plug in their laptops and get network and Internet access.

EXPENSES/FINANCIAL AID
Annual Tuition: $23,950
Room and Board (Off Campus): $11,000
Books and Supplies: $700
Financial Aid Application Deadline: 5/1
Average Grant: $17,212
Average Loan: $18,500

% of Aid That Is Merit-Based: 40
% Receiving Some Sort of Aid: 80
Average Total Aid Package: $33,940
Average Debt: $66,600

ADMISSIONS INFORMATION
Application Fee: $60
Regular Application Deadline: 3/15
Regular Notification: Rolling
LSDAS Accepted? Yes
Average GPA: 3.4
Range of GPA: 2.4–4.0
Average LSAT: 159
Range of LSAT: 158–163
Transfer Students Accepted? Yes
Other Schools to Which Students Applied: University of North Carolina—Chapel Hill, George Washington University, College of William and Mary, Emory University, American University, Tulane University, Vanderbilt University
Other Admissions Factors Considered: Undergraduate institution; undergraduate course work; maturity; trend in academic performance; employment during undergraduate years; military service; experience acquired in business, industry, or the community
Number of Applications Received: 2,175
Number of Applicants Accepted: 608
Number of Applicants Enrolled: 162

INTERNATIONAL STUDENTS
TOEFL Required of International Students? Yes
Minimum TOEFL: 600

EMPLOYMENT INFORMATION

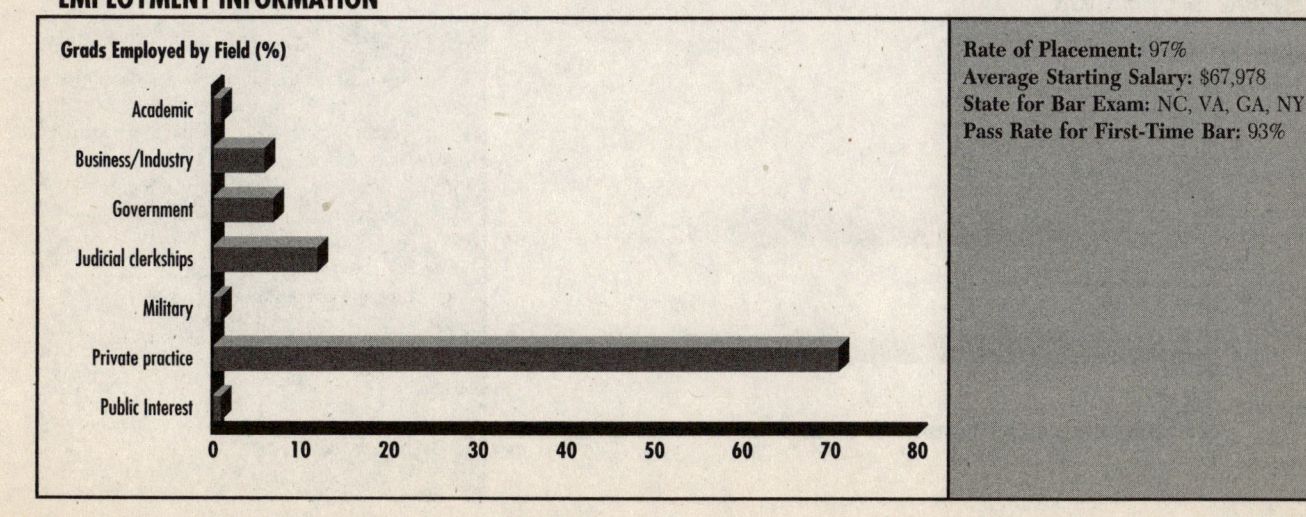

Grads Employed by Field (%)
- Academic
- Business/Industry
- Government
- Judicial clerkships
- Military
- Private practice
- Public Interest

Rate of Placement: 97%
Average Starting Salary: $67,978
State for Bar Exam: NC, VA, GA, NY
Pass Rate for First-Time Bar: 93%

WASHBURN UNIVERSITY
School of Law

Admissions Contact: Director of Admissions, James L. Nelson
1700 College, Topeka, KS 66621-1060
Admissions Phone: 785-231-1185 • Admissions Fax: 785-232-8087
Admissions E-mail: admissions@washburnlaw.edu • Web Address: washburnlaw.edu

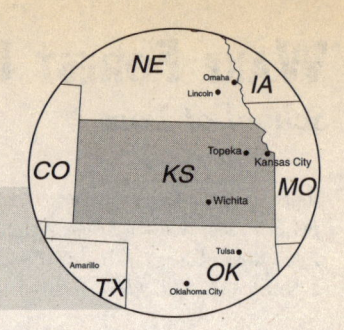

INSTITUTIONAL INFORMATION

Public/Private: Public
Student/Faculty Ratio: 9:1
Total Faculty: 47
% Part Time: 51
% Female: 32
% Minority: 15

PROGRAMS

Academic Specialties: Constitutional Law, Commercial Law, Corporation Securities Law, Criminal Law, Environmental Law, Family Law, Taxation, Oil and Gas Law, Agricultural Law, Administrative Law; the summer program in London team-taught by Washburn and British professors presents International Comparative Tort Law seminars that are taught by professors from around the world.
Advanced Degrees Offered: JD (90 credit hours, 3 years)
Combined Degrees Offered: JD/MBA (3 to 4 years), JD/MCJ (3 to 4 years)
Grading System: A (4.0), B+ (3.5), B (3.0), C+ (2.5), C (2.0), D+ (1.5), D (1.0), F (0.0); minimum 2.0 required for graduation. Some courses may be designated as Outstanding, Credit, or No Credit rather than graded.
Clinical Program Required? Yes
Clinical Program Description: General Practice Clinic that includes a strong mediation program. Approximately half of students participate in live-client clinic during their third year.
Legal Writing Course Requirements? No
Legal Writing Description: Legal Research and Writing Seminar (3 hours required in each of the first two semesters)
Legal Methods Course Requirements? Yes
Legal Research Course Requirements? No
Moot Court Requirement? No
Public Interest Law Requirement? No
Academic Journals: Washburn Law Journal, Family Law Quarterly

STUDENT INFORMATION

Enrollment of Law School: 451
% Male/Female: 55/45
% Full Time: 100
% Full Time That Are International: 1
% Minority: 12
Average Age of Entering Class: 23

RESEARCH FACILITIES

Research Resources Available: Menninger Psychiatric Center, Information Network of Kansas (INK), Kansas Supreme Court Library, Kansas Supreme Court and Court of Appeals, Kansas State Library, Kansas Legislature and all levels of state government, Federal District Court, Bankruptcy Court, 3rd Judicial District of Kansas (14 judges)
School-Supported Research Centers: Rural Law Center, public television station and broadcast facilities, Academic Computer Center, Multi-Media Center

EXPENSES/FINANCIAL AID

Annual Tuition (Residents/Nonresidents): $9,870/$16,200
Room and Board (On/Off Campus): $3,500/$6,525
Books and Supplies: $1,325
Financial Aid Application Deadline: 4/1
Average Grant: $4,675
Average Loan: $17,687
% Receiving Some Sort of Aid: 95
Average Total Aid Package: $18,913
Tuition Per Credit (Residents/Nonresidents): $329/$540

ADMISSIONS INFORMATION

Application Fee: $40
Regular Application Deadline: 4/1
Regular Notification: 6/1
LSDAS Accepted? Yes
Average GPA: 3.2
Range of GPA: 2.9–3.5
Average LSAT: 148
Range of LSAT: 144–153
Transfer Students Accepted? Yes
Other Admissions Factors Considered: Life experiences, undergraduate course work and major, undergraduate institution, graduate work, cultural background, need for diversity in the student body, community service
Number of Applications Received: 651
Number of Applicants Accepted: 384
Number of Applicants Enrolled: 187

INTERNATIONAL STUDENTS

TOEFL Recommended for International Students? Yes

EMPLOYMENT INFORMATION

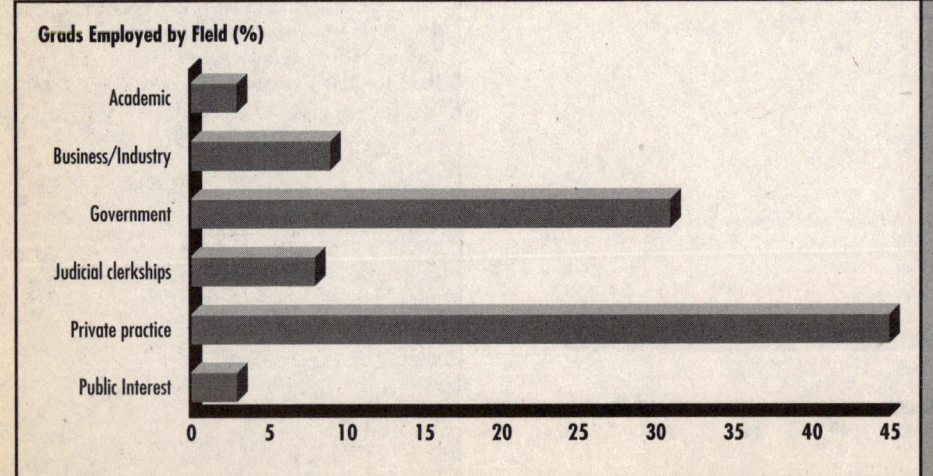

Grads Employed by Field (%):
- Academic: ~2
- Business/Industry: ~9
- Government: ~31
- Judicial clerkships: ~9
- Private practice: ~45
- Public Interest: ~3

Rate of Placement: 98%
Prominent Alumni: Lillian A. Apodaca, past President, Hispanic Bar Association; Robert J. Dole, former U.S. Senator; William H. Kurtis, Journalist/American Justice; Delano E. Lewis, former Ambassador to South Africa; Ron Richey, Chair of Executive Communications, Torchmark Corp.
State for Bar Exam: KS
Pass Rate for First-Time Bar: 83%

WASHINGTON AND LEE UNIVERSITY
School of Law

Admissions Contact: Director of Admissions, Bennie C. Rogers III
Sydney Lewis Hall, Lexington, VA 24450
Admissions Phone: 540-458-8503 • Admissions Fax: 540-458-8586
Admissions E-mail: lawadm@wlu.edu • Web Address: www.law.wlu.edu

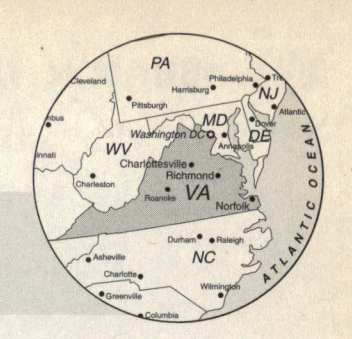

INSTITUTIONAL INFORMATION
Public/Private: Private
Student/Faculty Ratio: 11:1
Total Faculty: 57
% Part Time: 40
% Female: 19
% Minority: 9

PROGRAMS
Advanced Degrees Offered: LLM U.S. Law
Grading System: A, A–, B+, B, B–, C+, C, C–, D+, D, D–, F, I (Incomplete), CR (Credit), W/P (Work in Progress), P (Pass), NP (No Pass)
Clinical Program Required? No
Clinical Program Description: Black Lung Administrative/Labor Law Clinic, Virginia Capital Case Clearinghouse, Public Defender Service, U.S. Attorney's Prosecutorial Clinic, Legal Aid Society; judicial clerkships in a trial, juvenile and domestic relations, or federal bankruptcy court
Legal Writing Course Requirements? Yes
Legal Writing Description: Assignments are designed to sharpen students' writing and analytical skills and to familiarize students with law library resources and research methods. Instruction is coordinated with small sections in Contracts and American Public Law Process or Civil Procedure.
Legal Methods Course Requirements? No
Legal Research Course Requirements? No
Moot Court Requirement? No

Public Interest Law Requirement? No
Academic Journals: Washington and Lee Law Review, Capital Defense Journal, Washington and Lee Race and Ethnic Ancestry Law Journal, Environmental Law News

STUDENT INFORMATION
Enrollment of Law School: 378
% Out of State: 79
% Male/Female: 57/43
% Full Time: 100
% Full Time That Are International: 1
% Minority: 18
Average Age of Entering Class: 25

RESEARCH FACILITIES
School-Supported Research Centers: The Frances Lewis Law Center supports research in the area of legal reform and brings visiting scholars, lawyers, and judges to the School of Law to research, write, and teach.

EXPENSES/FINANCIAL AID
Annual Tuition: $21,320
Room and Board (Off Campus): $10,519
Books and Supplies: $1,100
Financial Aid Application Deadline: 2/15
Average Grant: $11,646
Average Loan: $21,758
% of Aid That Is Merit-Based: 100
% Receiving Some Sort of Aid: 95
Average Total Aid Package: $29,568
Average Debt: $51,719

ADMISSIONS INFORMATION
Application Fee: $50
Regular Application Deadline: 2/1
Regular Notification: 4/1
LSDAS Accepted? Yes
Average GPA: 3.5
Range of GPA: 3.3–3.8
Average LSAT: 165
Range of LSAT: 163–166
Transfer Students Accepted? Yes
Other Schools to Which Students Applied: College of William and Mary, University of Virginia, Vanderbilt University
Other Admissions Factors Considered: Trends in grades, rigor of undergraduate curriculum, length of time out of school, history of standardized test performance and how accurately tests have predicted classroom performance, obstacles overcome, alumni connection, special talents and interests
Number of Applications Received: 2,429
Number of Applicants Accepted: 510
Number of Applicants Enrolled: 138

EMPLOYMENT INFORMATION

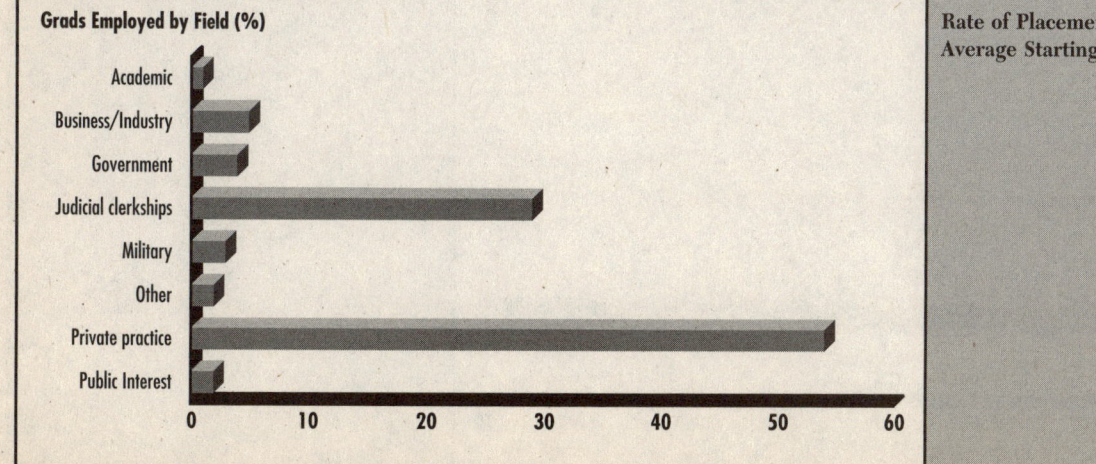

Grads Employed by Field (%)
- Academic: ~2
- Business/Industry: ~5
- Government: ~5
- Judicial clerkships: ~29
- Military: ~3
- Other: ~2
- Private practice: ~54
- Public Interest: ~1

Rate of Placement: 95%
Average Starting Salary: $70,476

WASHINGTON UNIVERSITY
School of Law

Admissions Contact: Associate Dean of Admissions and Financial Aid, Janet Bolin
1 Brookings Drive, Campus Box 1120, St. Louis, MO 63130-4899
Admissions Phone: 314-935-4525 • Admissions Fax: 314-935-8778
Admissions E-mail: admiss@wulaw.wustl.edu • Web Address: ls.wustl.edu

INSTITUTIONAL INFORMATION
Public/Private: Private
Student/Faculty Ratio: 14:1
Total Faculty: 77
% Part Time: 41
% Female: 46
% Minority: 2

PROGRAMS
Academic Specialties: Public Interest Law, Trial Advocacy and Transactional Skills Training, Clinical Programs, Interdisciplinary Offerings, Civil Procedure, Commercial Law, Constitutional Law, Corporation Securities Law, Criminal Law, Environmental Law, Government Services, Human Rights Law, Intellectual Property Law, International Law, Labor Law, Legal History, Legal Philosophy, Property, Taxation
Advanced Degrees Offered: JD (3 years), JSD, LLM
Combined Degrees Offered: JD/MA East Asian Studies, European Studies, or Islamic Studies; JD/PhD Political Science; JD/MBA; JD/MHA; JD/MSW
Grading System: 65–100; mandatory median 82–84
Clinical Program Required? No
Clinical Program Description: Civil Justice, Interdisciplinary Environmental, Employment Law, U.S. Attorney, Criminal Justice, Judicial Clerkship, Congressional and Administrative Law Clinic
Legal Writing Course Requirements? Yes
Legal Writing Description: In this year-long course taught by 6 full-time faculty, first-year students learn, through simulated lawsuits, to approach and solve problems as lawyers do and to write clear, concise, and analytical trial briefs and office memoranda. Students meet twice a week in small groups, where they discuss recent writing projects with their instructor and receive individual feedback.
Legal Methods Course Requirements? No
Legal Research Course Requirements? Yes
Legal Research Description: See Legal Writing.
Moot Court Requirement? No
Public Interest Law Requirement? No
Academic Journals: Washington University Law Quarterly, Journal of Law and Policy, Global Studies Law Review

STUDENT INFORMATION
Enrollment of Law School: 742
% Out of State: 75
% Male/Female: 56/44
% Full Time: 100
% Minority: 17
Average Age of Entering Class: 24

RESEARCH FACILITIES
School-Supported Research Centers: Center for Global Legal Studies, Center for Interdisciplinary Studies

EXPENSES/FINANCIAL AID
Annual Tuition: $28,500
Room and Board (Off Campus): $9,500
Books and Supplies: $1,500
Financial Aid Application Deadline: 3/1
Average Grant: $10,000
Average Loan: $35,000
% of Aid That Is Merit-Based: 100
% Receiving Some Sort of Aid: 75

ADMISSIONS INFORMATION
Application Fee: $60
Regular Application Deadline: 3/1
Regular Notification: 4/15
LSDAS Accepted? Yes
Average GPA: 3.5
Range of GPA: 3.2–3.6
Average LSAT: 163
Range of LSAT: 162–165
Transfer Students Accepted? Yes
Other Schools to Which Students Applied: Boston College, Boston University, Emory University, George Washington University, Georgetown University, Northwestern University, Vanderbilt University
Number of Applications Received: 3,145
Number of Applicants Accepted: 811
Number of Applicants Enrolled: 223

INTERNATIONAL STUDENTS
TOEFL Recommended for International Students? Yes
Minimum TOEFL: 600

EMPLOYMENT INFORMATION

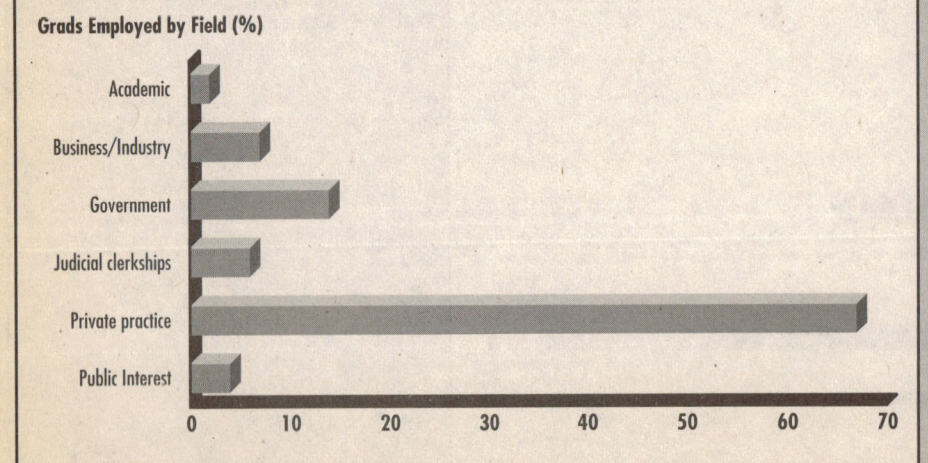

Grads Employed by Field (%)
- Academic: ~2
- Business/Industry: ~5
- Government: ~15
- Judicial clerkships: ~7
- Private practice: ~68
- Public Interest: ~3

Average Starting Salary: $50,303
State for Bar Exam: MO, IL, CA, NY
Pass Rate for First-Time Bar: 86%

WAYNE STATE UNIVERSITY
Law School

Admissions Contact: Assistant Dean for Recruitment and Admissions, Linda Fowler Sims
471 West Palmer, Detroit, MI 48202
Admissions Phone: 313-577-3937 • Admissions Fax: 313-993-8129
Admissions E-mail: law.inquire@law.wayne.edu • Web Address: www.law.wayne.edu

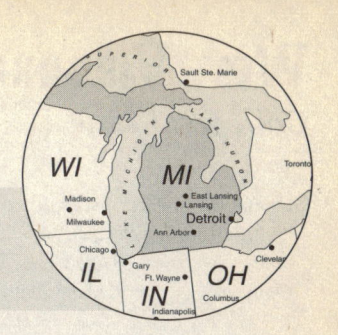

INSTITUTIONAL INFORMATION
Public/Private: Public
Student/Faculty Ratio: 23:1
Total Faculty: 33
% Part Time: 59
% Female: 39
% Minority: 12

PROGRAMS
Academic Specialties: Taxation, Labor Law, Intellectual Property Law
Advanced Degrees Offered: JD (3 years full time), LLM (1 year full time)
Combined Degrees Offered: JD/MBA, JD/MA, JD/MADR (all 4 years)
Grading System: A to E for courses and seminars; High Pass/Fail, Honors, Pass/Low Pass/Fail for Legal Writing
Clinical Program Required? No
Clinical Program Description: Free Legal Clinic, Commercial Law Clinic, Criminal Appellate Practice, Non-Profit Corporations and Urban Development Law, Civil Rights Litigation Clinic, Disability Law Clinic, Judicial Internship, Civil Law Internship, Criminal Justice Internship, numerous simulation courses
Legal Writing Course Requirements? Yes
Legal Writing Description: Drafting memos, briefs, contracts, complaints and answers, research methods, and strategy
Legal Methods Course Requirements? No
Legal Methods Description: 1 year
Legal Research Course Requirements? Yes
Legal Research Description: See Legal Writing.
Moot Court Requirement? Yes
Moot Court Description: At the end of the first-year legal writing course
Public Interest Law Requirement? No
Academic Journals: Law Review, Journal of Law and Society

STUDENT INFORMATION
Enrollment of Law School: 751
% Out of State: 2
% Male/Female: 53/47
% Full Time: 69
% Full Time That Are International: 0
% Minority: 19
Average Age of Entering Class: 25

RESEARCH FACILITIES
Research Resources Available: Lexis/Nexis printing and database, Westlaw printing

EXPENSES/FINANCIAL AID
Annual Tuition (Residents/Nonresidents): $7,829/$17,016
Room and Board: $8,970
Books and Supplies: $800
Financial Aid Application Deadline: 3/15
Average Grant: $2,881
Average Loan: $16,511
% of Aid That Is Merit-Based: 5
% Receiving Some Sort of Aid: 80
Average Total Aid Package: $17,943
Average Debt: $45,000
Tuition Per Credit (Residents/Nonresidents): $280/$608
Fees Per Credit: $89

ADMISSIONS INFORMATION
Application Fee: $20
Regular Application Deadline: Rolling
Regular Notification: Rolling
LSDAS Accepted? Yes
Average GPA: 3.3
Range of GPA: 3.1–3.5
Average LSAT: 154
Range of LSAT: 151–157
Transfer Students Accepted? Yes
Other Schools to Which Students Applied: Loyola University Chicago, Michigan State University, Thomas M. Cooley Law School, University of Detroit Mercy, University of Michigan
Number of Applications Received: 873
Number of Applicants Accepted: 531
Number of Applicants Enrolled: 250

EMPLOYMENT INFORMATION

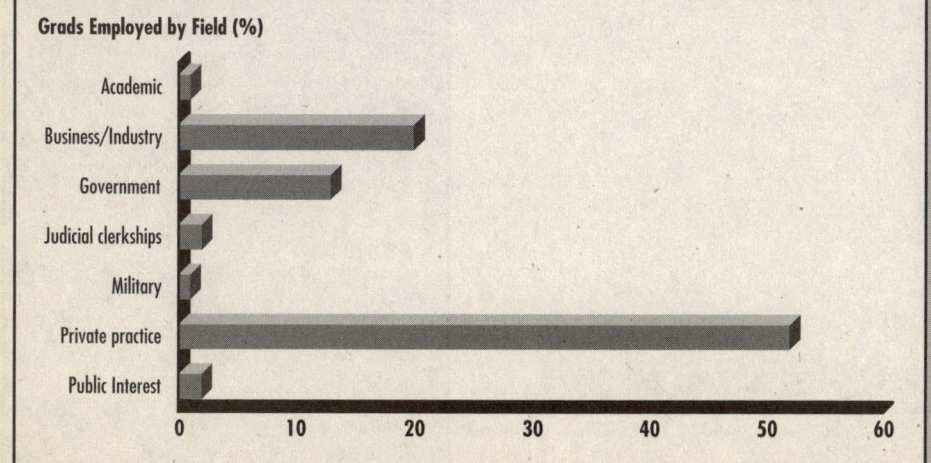

Grads Employed by Field (%)

Field	%
Academic	~0
Business/Industry	~20
Government	~13
Judicial clerkships	~2
Military	~0
Private practice	~52
Public Interest	~2

Rate of Placement: 97%
Average Starting Salary: $58,000
Employers Who Frequently Hire Grads: Leading law firms throughout Michigan; major multinational corporations based in Michigan, including the Big Three U.S. automakers; federal, state, and local courts; governmental agencies and legal service providers
State for Bar Exam: MI
Pass Rate for First-Time Bar: 81%

WEST VIRGINIA UNIVERSITY
College of Law

Admissions Contact: Assistant Dean for Admissions, Janet Armistead
PO Box 6130, Morgantown, WV 26506-6103
Admissions Phone: 304-293-5304 • Admissions Fax: 304-293-6891
Admissions E-mail: wvulaw.admissions@mail.wvu.edu • Web Address: www.wvu.edu/~law

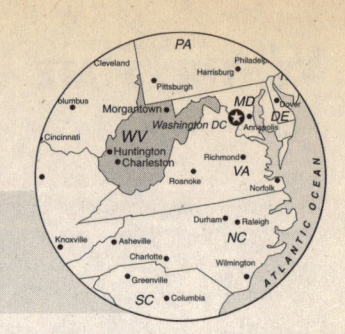

INSTITUTIONAL INFORMATION
Public/Private: Public
Affiliation: Christian Science
Student/Faculty Ratio: 16:1
Total Faculty: 37
% Part Time: 11
% Female: 11

PROGRAMS
Academic Specialties: Legal Writing Program, Civil Procedure, Commercial Law, Constitutional Law, Corporation Securities Law, Criminal Law, Environmental Law, Government Services, Human Rights Law, International Law, Labor Law, Legal History, Legal Philosophy, Property, Taxation
Advanced Degrees Offered: JD (3 years)
Combined Degrees Offered: JD/MPA (4 years), JD/MBA (4 years)
Grading System: 4.3 scale
Clinical Program Required? No
Clinical Program Description: Optional clinical programs help students learn the skills of interviewing, counseling, drafting, litigation planning, negotiation, and trial advocacy. They also confront issues of ethics and the professional role and handle cases of violence and social security disability.
Legal Writing Course Requirements? Yes
Legal Writing Description: 1 year
Legal Methods Course Requirements? Yes
Legal Research Course Requirements? No
Moot Court Requirement? No
Public Interest Law Requirement? No

STUDENT INFORMATION
Enrollment of Law School: 456
% Out of State: 18
% Male/Female: 58/42
% Full Time: 97
% Full Time That Are International: 1
% Minority: 8
Average Age of Entering Class: 26

EXPENSES/FINANCIAL AID
Annual Tuition (Residents/Nonresidents): $5,296/$12,568
Room and Board (Off Campus): $9,130
Books and Supplies: $853
Average Grant: $4,111
Average Loan: $13,945
% of Aid That Is Merit-Based: 1
% Receiving Some Sort of Aid: 88
Average Total Aid Package: $13,196
Average Debt: $36,373

ADMISSIONS INFORMATION
Application Fee: $50
Regular Application Deadline: 2/1
Regular Notification: Rolling
LSDAS Accepted? Yes
Average GPA: 3.4
Range of GPA: 3.1–3.7
Average LSAT: 154
Range of LSAT: 148–154
Transfer Students Accepted? Yes
Number of Applications Received: 668
Number of Applicants Accepted: 309
Number of Applicants Enrolled: 156

INTERNATIONAL STUDENTS
TOEFL Required of International Students? Yes
Minimum TOEFL: 600

EMPLOYMENT INFORMATION

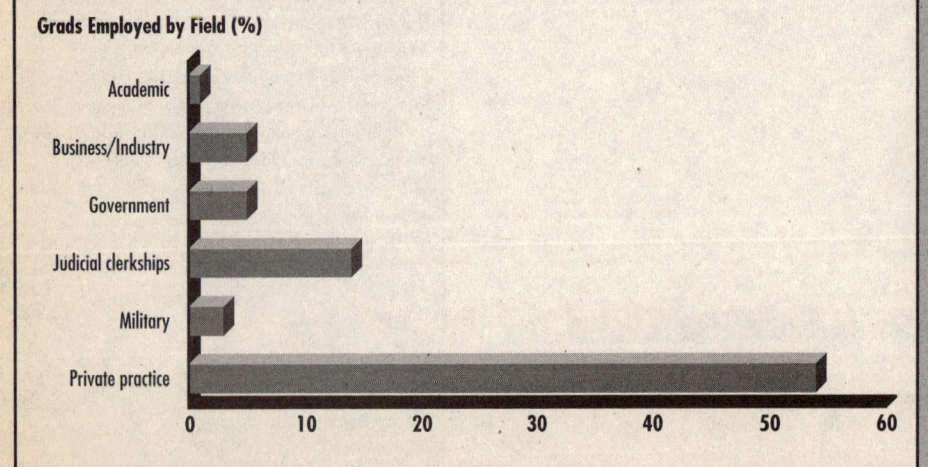

Grads Employed by Field (%)
- Academic: ~1
- Business/Industry: ~5
- Government: ~4
- Judicial clerkships: ~14
- Military: ~2
- Private practice: ~55

Rate of Placement: 96%
Average Starting Salary: $45,614
Employers Who Frequently Hire Grads: Law firms, government, judicial clerks
State for Bar Exam: WV
Pass Rate for First-Time Bar: 74%

WESTERN NEW ENGLAND COLLEGE
School of Law

Admissions Contact: Assistant Dean and Director of Admissions, Sherri J. Berendt
1215 Wilbraham Road, Springfield, MA 01119
Admissions Phone: 413-782-1406 • Admissions Fax: 413-796-2067
Admissions E-mail: lawadmis@wnec.edu • Web Address: www.law.wnec.edu

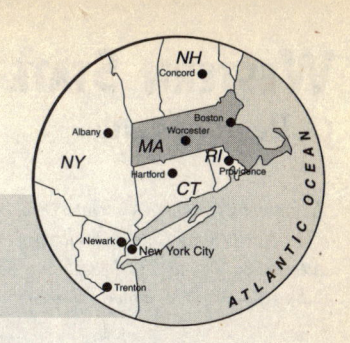

INSTITUTIONAL INFORMATION
Public/Private: Private
Student/Faculty Ratio: 9:1
Total Faculty: 60
% Part Time: 47
% Female: 40
% Minority: 7

PROGRAMS
Academic Specialties: Our faculty members teach a wide variety of legal subjects. Electives are offered in almost every area of law a student would wish to investigate. Our clinics in Criminal Law, Civil Litigation, Consumer Protection, and Legal Services offer additional opportunities for gaining practical experience.
Combined Degrees Offered: JD/MRP with University of Masssachusetts, JD/MSW with Springfield College, JD/MBA with Western New England College (all 4 years)
Grading System: Numerical system (55–99); minimum 70 required for graduation; some courses are Pass/Fail
Clinical Program Required? No
Legal Writing Course Requirements? Yes
Legal Writing Description: Full-year, 2-credit, first-year course that covers legal writing and research and introduction to oral arguments
Legal Methods Course Requirements? Yes
Legal Methods Description: See Legal Writing.
Legal Research Course Requirements? Yes
Legal Research Description: See Legal Writing.
Moot Court Requirement? No
Public Interest Law Requirement? No
Academic Journals: *Western New England Law Review*

STUDENT INFORMATION
Enrollment of Law School: 180
% Male/Female: 52/48
% Full Time: 54
% Minority: 22
Average Age of Entering Class: 27

RESEARCH FACILITIES
Research Resources Available: Criminal Law Clinic, affiliated with Hampden County District Attorney's Office; Discrimination Law Clinic, affiliated with Massachusetts Commission Against Discrimination; Legal Services Clinic, affiliated with Western Massachusettes Legal Services; Consumer Protection Clinic, affiliated with Mayor of Springfield's Office of Consumer Affairs; Colleges of Greater Springfield Consortium; New England Law Libraries Consortium
School-Supported Research Centers: Wireless technology throughout the building

EXPENSES/FINANCIAL AID
Annual Tuition: $21,866
Room and Board: $9,640
Books and Supplies: $1,155
Average Grant: $8,392
Average Loan: $20,973
% of Aid That Is Merit-Based: 12
% Receiving Some Sort of Aid: 98
Average Total Aid Package: $23,174
Average Debt: $69,013

ADMISSIONS INFORMATION
Application Fee: $45
Regular Application Deadline: Rolling
Regular Notification: Rolling
LSDAS Accepted? Yes
Average GPA: 3.1
Range of GPA: 2.9–3.5
Average LSAT: 150
Range of LSAT: 146–154
Transfer Students Accepted? Yes
Other Schools to Which Students Applied: New England School of Law, Quinnipiac University, Roger Williams University, University of Connecticut
Other Admissions Factors Considered: Writing ability as evidenced in personal statement and writing sample on LSAT; background and personal experience that will add to classroom discussions, such as racial, gender, economic, or physical obstacles
Number of Applications Received: 975
Number of Applicants Accepted: 476
Number of Applicants Enrolled: 180

INTERNATIONAL STUDENTS
TOEFL Required of International Students? Yes

EMPLOYMENT INFORMATION

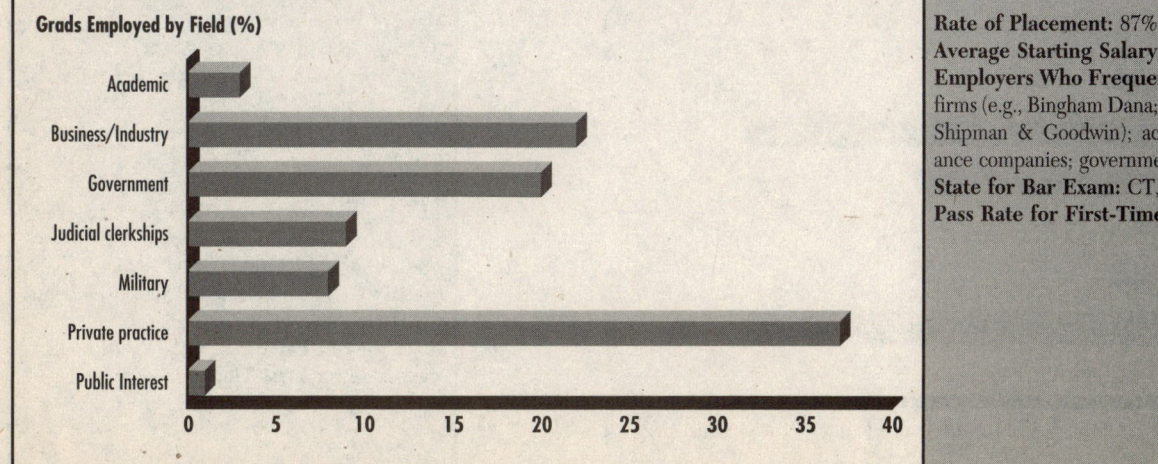

Grads Employed by Field (%)
- Academic
- Business/Industry
- Government
- Judicial clerkships
- Military
- Private practice
- Public Interest

Rate of Placement: 87%
Average Starting Salary: $50,685
Employers Who Frequently Hire Grads: Law firms (e.g., Bingham Dana; Day, Berry & Howard; Shipman & Goodwin); accounting firms; insurance companies; government agencies
State for Bar Exam: CT, MA, NY, NJ, PA
Pass Rate for First-Time Bar: 71%

WESTERN STATE UNIVERSITY
College of Law

Admissions Contact: Associate Dean of Admission, Phyllis L. Wignall, JD
1111 North State College Boulevard, Fullerton, CA 92831
Admissions Phone: 714-738-1000 • Admissions Fax: 714-441-1748
Admissions E-mail: adm@wsulaw.edu • Web Address: www.wsulaw.edu

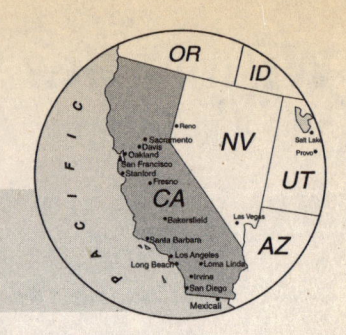

INSTITUTIONAL INFORMATION
Public/Private: Private
Student/Faculty Ratio: 9:1
Total Faculty: 54
% Part Time: 61
% Female: 35
% Minority: 19

PROGRAMS
Academic Specialties: Entrepreneurial Law Center, Professional Skills, Academic Success and Enrichment Program, Criminal Law Practice Center
Advanced Degrees Offered: JD (3 years full time, 4 years part time)
Grading System: 4.0 scale
Clinical Program Required? No
Clinical Program Description: Legal Clinic
Legal Writing Course Requirements? Yes
Legal Writing Description: Incorporated into Professional Skills I and II and Advocacy courses
Legal Methods Course Requirements? No
Legal Research Course Requirements? Yes
Legal Research Description: See Legal Writing.
Moot Court Requirement? Yes
Moot Court Description: Incorporated into the Advocacy course
Public Interest Law Requirement? No
Academic Journals: *Law Review*

STUDENT INFORMATION
Enrollment of Law School: 189
% Out of State: 31
% Male/Female: 64/36
% Full Time: 64
% Full Time That Are International: 0
% Minority: 45
Average Age of Entering Class: 28

RESEARCH FACILITIES
Research Resources Available: The resources of CSU Fullerton

EXPENSES/FINANCIAL AID
Annual Tuition: $22,168
Room and Board (Off Campus): $11,739
Books and Supplies: $810
Financial Aid Application Deadline: 4/14
% of Aid That Is Merit-Based: 14
% Receiving Some Sort of Aid: 75

ADMISSIONS INFORMATION
Application Fee: $50
Regular Application Deadline: Rolling
Regular Notification: Rolling
LSDAS Accepted? Yes
Average GPA: 2.9
Range of GPA: 2.6–3.2
Average LSAT: 146
Range of LSAT: 143–149
Transfer Students Accepted? Yes
Other Schools to Which Students Applied: Southwestern University School of Law, Whittier College, Chapman University, Thomas Jefferson School of Law, California Western, University of San Diego, University of the Pacific
Other Admissions Factors Considered: work history/experience, volunteer/community service, academic honors/awards, leadership positions held
Number of Applications Received: 789
Number of Applicants Accepted: 451
Number of Applicants Enrolled: 121

EMPLOYMENT INFORMATION

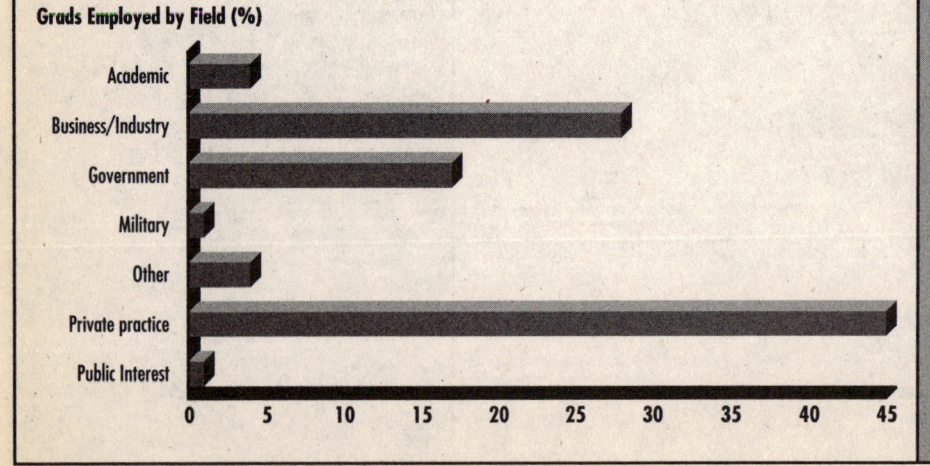

Grads Employed by Field (%)

Field	%
Academic	~1
Business/Industry	~28
Government	~17
Military	~1
Other	~3
Private practice	~45
Public Interest	~1

Rate of Placement: 93%
Average Starting Salary: $58,200
Employers Who Frequently Hire Grads: Medium-size law firms, district attorneys, public defenders, corporations, state governments, federal governments
Prominent Alumni: Ross Johnson, CA Senator; Joseph Mederow, Chief Counsel, UPS; Gary Kermott, President, First American Title; Chuck Middleton, Chief Assistant D.A., Orange County, CA; Daniel Pratt, Judge, Los Angeles Superior Court
State for Bar Exam: CA, AZ, TX, OR, CO
Pass Rate for First-Time Bar: 43%

WHITTIER COLLEGE
Law School

Admissions Contact: Director of Admissions, Patricia Abracia
3333 Harbor Boulevard, Costa Mesa, CA 92626
Admissions Phone: 714-444-4141 • Admissions Fax: 714-444-0250
Admissions E-mail: info@law.whittier.edu • Web Address: www.law.whittier.edu

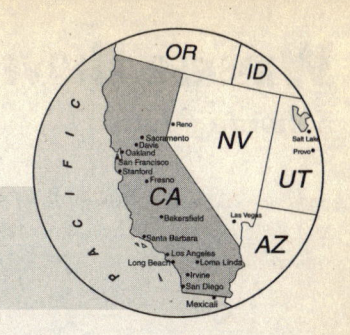

INSTITUTIONAL INFORMATION
Public/Private: Private
Student/Faculty Ratio: 23:1
Total Faculty: 71
% Part Time: 55
% Female: 42
% Minority: 8

PROGRAMS
Academic Specialties: Health Law Symposium, Center for Children's Rights, Center for International and Comparative Law, Intellectual Property Law
Advanced Degrees Offered: JD (3 years full time, 4 years part time), LLM (1 year)
Grading System: Letter and numerical system on a 100-point scale; minimum 77 required for good standing
Clinical Program Required? No
Clinical Program Description: Special Education Clinic, Guardianship and Adoption Clinic, Family Law and Domestic Violence Clinic, Street Law Program
Legal Writing Course Requirements? Yes
Legal Writing Description: 5 units of Legal Writing
Legal Methods Course Requirements? No
Legal Research Course Requirements? Yes
Legal Research Description: Part of Legal Writing
Moot Court Requirement? Yes
Moot Court Description: The Moot Court component of the first-year Legal Skills course is designed to enhance oral advocacy skills. Students pair up to argue against another pair of students before a panel of 3 "judges" who are members of the Moot Court Honors Board. Students are given written and oral feedback on their performance. The Board advances student skills in appellate advocacy. Improvement of oral advocacy and brief writing skills is accomplished through participation in national and internal appellate competitions and appellate workshops.
Public Interest Law Requirement? No
Academic Journals: *Whittier Law Review, Whittier Journal of Child and Family Advocacy*

STUDENT INFORMATION
Enrollment of Law School: 746
% Out of State: 20
% Male/Female: 45/55
% Full Time: 56
% Full Time That Are International: 0
% Minority: 40
Average Age of Entering Class: 25

RESEARCH FACILITIES
Research Resources Available: Library

EXPENSES/FINANCIAL AID
Annual Tuition: $25,230
Room and Board (Off Campus): $9,698
Books and Supplies: $5,712
Financial Aid Application Deadline: 5/1
Average Grant: $8,964
Average Loan: $25,120
% of Aid That Is Merit-Based: 97
% Receiving Some Sort of Aid: 92
Average Total Aid Package: $28,500
Average Debt: $73,626
Tuition Per Credit: $801

ADMISSIONS INFORMATION
Application Fee: $50
Regular Application Deadline: Rolling
Regular Notification: Rolling
LSDAS Accepted? Yes
Average GPA: 3.0
Range of GPA: 2.7–3.4
Average LSAT: 150
Range of LSAT: 144–154
Transfer Students Accepted? Yes
Other Schools to Which Students Applied: California Western; Loyola Marymount University; Pepperdine University; Southwestern University School of Law; University of California, Los Angeles; University of San Diego; University of Southern California
Other Admissions Factors Considered: maturity, capacity for self-discipline, work experience, year-to-year progress in college, courses completed, graduate work, participation in student organizations and/or volunteer work
Number of Applications Received: 1,213
Number of Applicants Accepted: 702
Number of Applicants Enrolled: 204

INTERNATIONAL STUDENTS
TOEFL Required of International Students? Yes
Minimum TOEFL: 550 (213 computer)

EMPLOYMENT INFORMATION

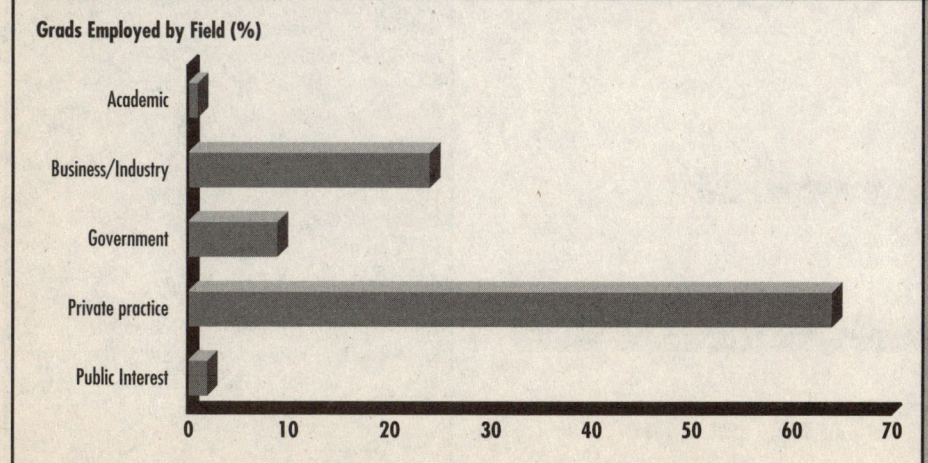

Grads Employed by Field (%)

Field	%
Academic	~1
Business/Industry	~24
Government	~10
Private practice	~64
Public Interest	~2

Rate of Placement: 94%
Average Starting Salary: $60,000
Employers Who Frequently Hire Grads: Small law firms (2–10 attorneys)
Prominent Alumni: Florence Marie Cooper, U.S. District Judge; Giaro Mardirossian, Mardirossian and Associates; Judith Ashmann-Gerst, California Court of Appeal; Blair Westlake, Corporate Executive VP, Gemstar—TV Guide International; Kathleen Strothman, Counsel to Senator Mary Landrieu
State for Bar Exam: CA
Pass Rate for First-Time Bar: 47%

WIDENER UNIVERSITY, DELAWARE
School of Law

Admissions Contact: Assistant Dean for Admissions, Barbara Ayars
PO Box 7474, 4601 Concord Pike, Wilmington, DE 19803
Admissions Phone: 302-477-2162 • Admissions Fax: 302-477-2224
Admissions E-mail: law.admissions@law.widener.edu • Web Address: www.law.widener.edu

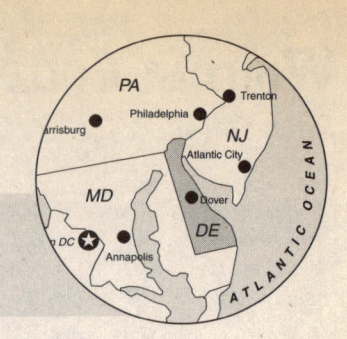

INSTITUTIONAL INFORMATION
Public/Private: Private
Student/Faculty Ratio: 21:1
Total Faculty: 143
% Part Time: 57
% Female: 47
% Minority: 5

PROGRAMS
Academic Specialties: Health Law Institute, Corporate Law and Finance, Environmental Law Clinic, Intellectual Property, Constitutional Law (H. Albert Young Fellowship), Intensive Trial Advocacy Program, International Law, Civil Procedure, Commercial Law, Corporation Securities Law, Criminal Law, Human Rights Law, Labor Law, Property
Advanced Degrees Offered: LLM (24 credits), MJ (30 credits), SJD, DL
Combined Degrees Offered: JD/PsyD (6 years), JD/MBA (4 years), JD/MMP with University of Delaware (4.5 years)
Grading System: Letter system on a 4.0 scale
Clinical Program Required? No
Clinical Program Description: Civil Law Clinic, Criminal Defense Clinic, Civil Law Clinic, Veterans Assistance Program, Environmental Law and Natural Resources Clinic
Legal Writing Course Requirements? Yes
Legal Writing Description: Legal Methods/Moot Court, 2 credits; Legal Methods/Advanced Legal Writing, third semester, 2 credits
Legal Methods Course Requirements? Yes
Legal Methods Description: See Legal Writing.
Legal Research Course Requirements? Yes
Legal Research Description: See Legal Writing.
Moot Court Requirement? No
Public Interest Law Requirement? No
Academic Journals: *Delaware Journal of Corporate Law, Widener Law Symposium Journal*

STUDENT INFORMATION
Enrollment of Law School: 1,094
% Out of State: 68
% Male/Female: 52/48
% Full Time: 60
% Full Time That Are International: 1
% Minority: 8
Average Age of Entering Class: 27

EXPENSES/FINANCIAL AID
Annual Tuition: $23,260
Room and Board: $7,500
Books and Supplies: $1,000
Financial Aid Application Deadline: 4/15
Average Grant: $5,310
Average Loan: $20,598
% of Aid That Is Merit-Based: 91
% Receiving Some Sort of Aid: 35
Average Total Aid Package: $21,288
Average Debt: $67,866
Tuition Per Credit: $775

ADMISSIONS INFORMATION
Application Fee: $60
Regular Application Deadline: 5/15
Regular Notification: Rolling
LSDAS Accepted? Yes
Average GPA: 3.0
Range of GPA: 2.7–3.3
Average LSAT: 150
Range of LSAT: 148–152
Transfer Students Accepted? Yes
Other Schools to Which Students Applied: Rutgers University—Camden, Temple University, Pennsylvania State University, University of Baltimore, Villanova University
Other Admissions Factors Considered: Personal essay, work experience, life experiences, extracurricular activities, letters of recommendation
Number of Applications Received: 1,526
Number of Applicants Accepted: 793
Number of Applicants Enrolled: 305

INTERNATIONAL STUDENTS
TOEFL Recommended for International Students? Yes
Minimum TOEFL: 550 (220 computer)

EMPLOYMENT INFORMATION

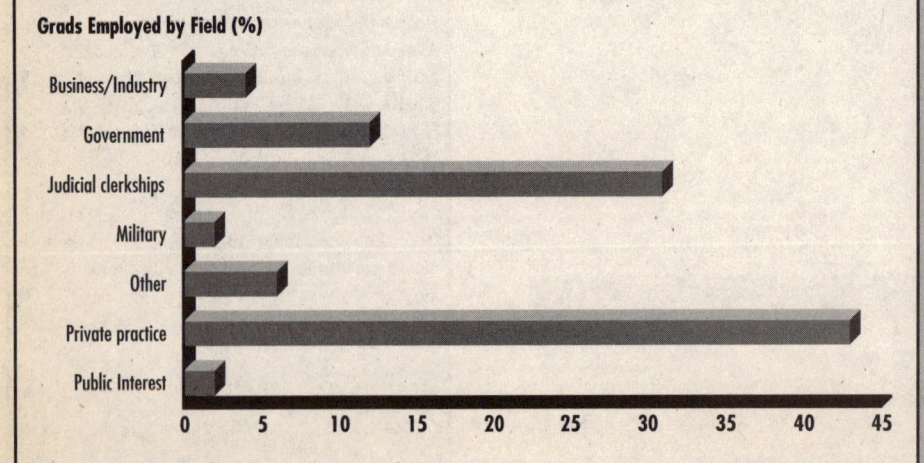

Grads Employed by Field (%)
- Business/Industry
- Government
- Judicial clerkships
- Military
- Other
- Private practice
- Public Interest

Rate of Placement: 86%
Average Starting Salary: $54,778
Employers Who Frequently Hire Grads: Law firms, judges, corporations, and other government employers.
Prominent Alumni: Steven Kram, Chief Operating Officer, William Morris Agency; Cynthia Rhoades Ryan, Chief Counsel, Drug Enforcement Administration; G. Fred DiBona, President and CEO, Independence Blue Cross; Lee A. Solomon, Deputy U.S. Attorney; Hon. Susan C. DelPesco, Superior Court of Delaware
State for Bar Exam: PA, NJ, DE, MD, NY
Pass Rate for First-Time Bar: 58%

WIDENER UNIVERSITY, HARRISBURG
School of Law

Admissions Contact: Assistant Dean of Admissions, Barbara Ayars
3800 Vartan Way, PO Box 69381, Harrisburg, PA 17106-9381
Admissions Phone: 717-541-3903 • Admissions Fax: 717-541-3999
Admissions E-mail: law.admissions@law.widener.edu • Web Address: www.law.widener.edu

INSTITUTIONAL INFORMATION
Public/Private: Private
Student/Faculty Ratio: 22:1
Total Faculty: 49
% Part Time: 55
% Female: 14
% Minority: 1

PROGRAMS
Academic Specialties: Administrative Law, Trial Advocacy, Law and Government, Public Interest Law, Legislation—Legislative Drafting, Commercial Law, Constitutional Law, Criminal Law, Environmental Law, Property, Taxation
Combined Degrees Offered: JD/MBA (4 years), JD/MSLS with Clarion University (4 years)
Grading System: Letter system on a 4.0 scale
Clinical Program Required? No
Clinical Program Description: Civil Law Clinic
Legal Writing Course Requirements? Yes
Legal Writing Description: 2- to 3-credit courses taken in the first 2 semesters
Legal Methods Course Requirements? Yes
Legal Methods Description: See Legal Writing.
Legal Research Course Requirements? Yes
Legal Research Description: See Legal Writing.
Moot Court Requirement? No
Public Interest Law Requirement? No
Academic Journals: The Widener Journal of Public Law

STUDENT INFORMATION
Enrollment of Law School: 464
% Out of State: 5
% Male/Female: 51/49
% Full Time: 60
% Full Time That Are International: 1
% Minority: 9
Average Age of Entering Class: 27

EXPENSES/FINANCIAL AID
Annual Tuition: $23,260
Room and Board (Off Campus): $7,500
Books and Supplies: $1,000
Financial Aid Application Deadline: 4/15
Average Grant: $5,245
Average Loan: $20,556
% of Aid That Is Merit-Based: 88
% Receiving Some Sort of Aid: 36
Average Total Aid Package: $22,100
Average Debt: $67,701
Tuition Per Credit: $775

ADMISSIONS INFORMATION
Application Fee: $60
Regular Application Deadline: 5/15
Regular Notification: Rolling
LSDAS Accepted? Yes
Average GPA: 3.1
Range of GPA: 2.8–3.3
Average LSAT: 148
Range of LSAT: 146–151
Transfer Students Accepted? Yes
Other Schools to Which Students Applied: Rutgers University—Camden, Temple University, Pennsylvania State University, University of Baltimore, Villanova University
Other Admissions Factors Considered: Personal essay, work experience, life experiences, extracurricular activities, letters of recommendation
Number of Applications Received: 467
Number of Applicants Accepted: 347
Number of Applicants Enrolled: 145

INTERNATIONAL STUDENTS
TOEFL Recommended for International Students? Yes
Minimum TOEFL: 550 (220 computer)

EMPLOYMENT INFORMATION

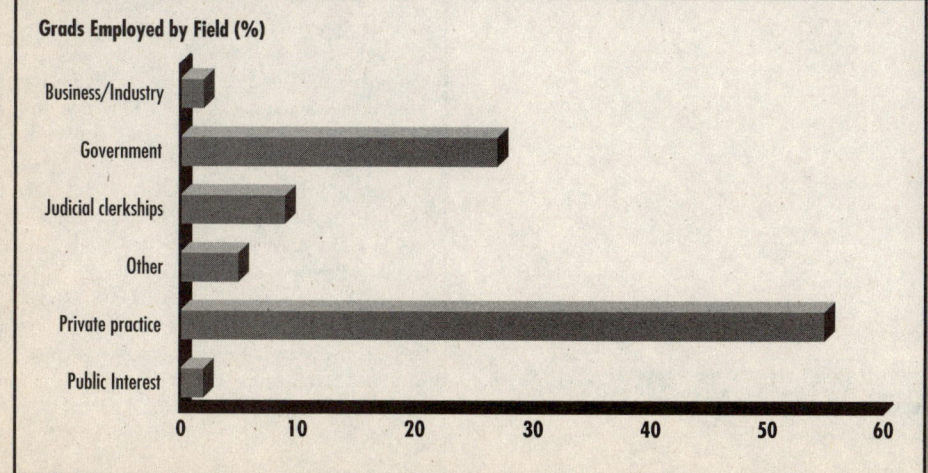

Grads Employed by Field (%)

Field	%
Business/Industry	~2
Government	~27
Judicial clerkships	~7
Other	~4
Private practice	~56
Public Interest	~2

Rate of Placement: 83%
Average Starting Salary: $46,045
Employers Who Frequently Hire Grads: Law firms, judges, corporations, and other government employers
Prominent Alumni: Hon. Mark Cohen, Member, Pennsylvania House of Representatives; Hon. David Judy, District Judge, Dauphin County, PA; Douglas Wolfberg, Esq., Partner, Page, Wolfberg & Wirth; Hon. Mary Sponaugle, District Judge, Lancaster County, PA; John Milliron, Lobbyist
State for Bar Exam: PA, NJ
Pass Rate for First-Time Bar: 63%

WILLAMETTE UNIVERSITY
College of Law

Admissions Contact: Assistant Dean of Admissions and Communications, Lawrence Seno
245 Winter Street, SE, Salem, OR 97301-3922
Admissions Phone: 503-370-6282 • Admissions Fax: 503-370-6375
Admissions E-mail: law-admission@willamette.edu • Web Address: www.willamette.edu/wucl

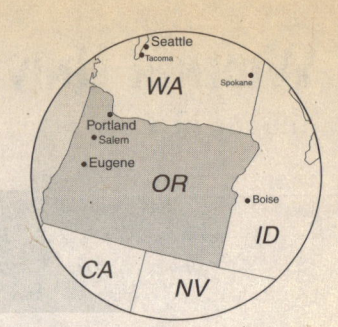

INSTITUTIONAL INFORMATION
Public/Private: Private
Student/Faculty Ratio: 15:1
Total Faculty: 30
% Part Time: 17
% Female: 20
% Minority: 1

PROGRAMS
Academic Specialties: Certificate programs in Dispute Resolution, Law and Government, International Law, Law and Business
Combined Degrees Offered: JD/MBA (4 years)
Grading System: Letter system
Clinical Program Required? No
Legal Writing Course Requirements? Yes
Legal Methods Course Requirements? Yes
Legal Methods Description: 2 semesters, 2 hours per semester
Legal Research Course Requirements? No
Moot Court Requirement? No
Public Interest Law Requirement? No
Academic Journals: *Willamette Law Review, Willamette Journal of International Law and Dispute Resolution*

STUDENT INFORMATION
Enrollment of Law School: 418
% Out of State: 42
% Male/Female: 52/48
% Full Time: 100
% Full Time That Are International: 3
% Minority: 11
Average Age of Entering Class: 26

RESEARCH FACILITIES
School-Supported Research Centers: Center for Dispute Resolution, Oregon Law Commission

EXPENSES/FINANCIAL AID
Annual Tuition: $20,850
Room and Board: $12,100
Books and Supplies: $1,250
Average Grant: $10,000
Average Loan: $21,133
Average Debt: $60,416
Fees Per Credit: $695

ADMISSIONS INFORMATION
Application Fee: $50
Regular Application Deadline: 4/1
Regular Notification: 4/15
LSDAS Accepted? Yes
Average GPA: 3.2
Range of GPA: 3.0–3.5
Average LSAT: 154
Range of LSAT: 152–157
Transfer Students Accepted? Yes
Other Schools to Which Students Applied: Lewis and Clark College, Seattle University, University of Oregon
Other Admissions Factors Considered: Some additional consideration is given to candidates who have strong ties to Oregon or to the Pacific Northwest and who intend to practice in the state or region.
Number of Applications Received: 742
Number of Applicants Accepted: 445
Number of Applicants Enrolled: 142

INTERNATIONAL STUDENTS
TOEFL Required of International Students? Yes
Minimum TOEFL: 575

EMPLOYMENT INFORMATION

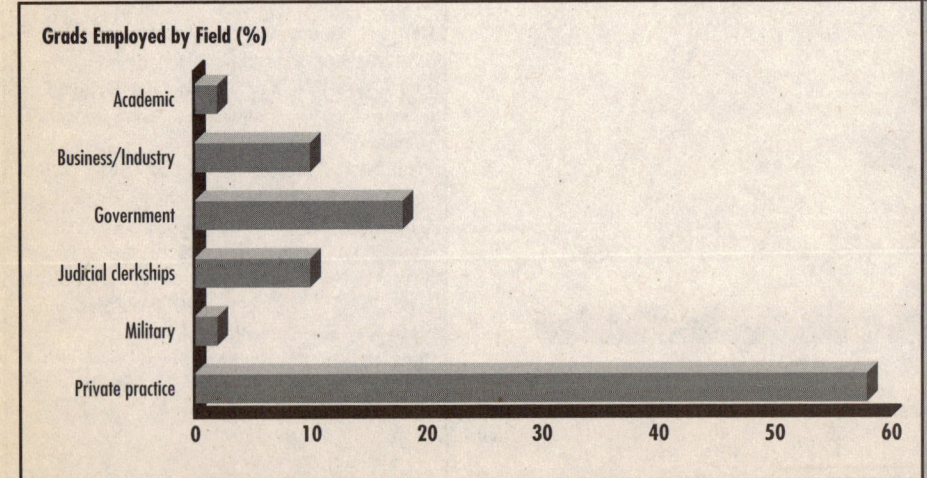

Grads Employed by Field (%)

Field	%
Academic	~2
Business/Industry	~10
Government	~18
Judicial clerkships	~10
Military	~2
Private practice	~58

Rate of Placement: 78%
Average Starting Salary: $53,354
Employers Who Frequently Hire Grads: Stoel Rives; Marion, Lane, and King counties; Schwabe, Williamson and Wyatt; Ater Wynne; Harrang Long; Miller Nash; Oregon Courts
Prominent Alumni: Lindsay D. Stewart, Vice President, Law and Corporate Affairs, Nike, Inc.; Steven E. Wynne, former President and CEO, Adidas America; Faith Ireland, Supreme Court Justice, WA Supreme Court; Wallace P. Carson, Chief Justice, Oregon Supreme Court; Mary Deitz, Chief Judge, Oregon Court of Appeals
State for Bar Exam: OR
Pass Rate for First-Time Bar: 71%

WILLIAM MITCHELL COLLEGE OF LAW

Admissions Contact: Assistant Dean and Director of Admissions, Tina Proctor
875 Summit Avenue, St. Paul, MN 55105
Admissions Phone: 651-290-6476 • Admissions Fax: 651-290-6414
Admissions E-mail: admissions@wmitchell.edu • Web Address: www.wmitchell.edu

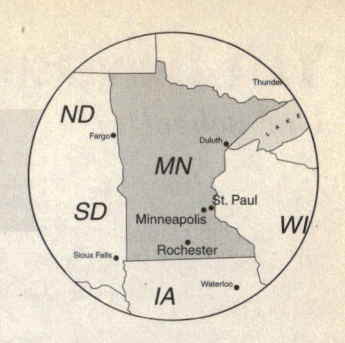

INSTITUTIONAL INFORMATION

Public/Private: Private
Student/Faculty Ratio: 22:1
Total Faculty: 195
% Part Time: 85
% Female: 38
% Minority: 13

PROGRAMS

Academic Specialties: Business/Commercial Law, Torts, Taxation, Lawyering Skills, Clinical Programs, Intellectual Property Law
Advanced Degrees Offered: JD (3 years full time, 4 years part time)
Combined Degrees Offered: JD/MPA with Minnesota State (4 to 6 years)
Grading System: Letter and numerical system on a 4.0 scale
Clinical Program Required? No
Clinical Program Description: Business Law Clinic, Civil Advocacy Clinic, Criminal Appeals Clinic, Immigration Clinic, Legal Assistance to Minnesota Prisoners, Misdemeanor Clinic, Tax Planning Clinic, Law and Psychiatry Clinic, Independent Clinic, Administrative Law Externship, Court of Appeals Externship, International Civil and Human Rights Externship, District Court Externship
Legal Writing Course Requirements? Yes
Legal Writing Description: Writing and Representation: Advice and Persuasion (first year) includes research and writing skills, client interviewing, contract negotiation, and dispute mediation. Writing and Representation: Advocacy (second or third year) introduces researching legislative process materials, examining witnesses, making opening and closing statements, and presenting appellate arguments.
Legal Methods Course Requirements? Yes
Legal Methods Description: See Legal Writing.
Legal Research Course Requirements? Yes
Legal Research Description: See Legal Writing.
Moot Court Requirement? No
Public Interest Law Requirement? No
Academic Journals: *William Mitchell Law Review*

STUDENT INFORMATION

Enrollment of Law School: 1,038
% Out of State: 25
% Male/Female: 47/53
% Full Time: 54
% Full Time That Are International: 1
% Minority: 9
Average Age of Entering Class: 25

EXPENSES/FINANCIAL AID

Annual Tuition: $21,140
Room and Board (Off Campus): $8,308
Books and Supplies: $5,132
Financial Aid Application Deadline: 3/15
Average Grant: $7,663
Average Loan: $17,795
% of Aid That Is Merit-Based: 89
% Receiving Some Sort of Aid: 98
Average Total Aid Package: $22,037
Average Debt: $65,412
Tuition Per Credit: $875

ADMISSIONS INFORMATION

Application Fee: $45
Regular Application Deadline: 6/30
Regular Notification: Rolling
LSDAS Accepted? Yes
Average GPA: 3.3
Range of GPA: 3.0–3.5
Average LSAT: 155
Range of LSAT: 152–158
Transfer Students Accepted? Yes
Other Schools to Which Students Applied: Hamline University, University of Minnesota
Other Admissions Factors Considered: difficulty of course work completed, quality of institutions attended, employment while earning degree(s), experience gained through work or volunteer activities
Number of Applications Received: 1,162
Number of Applicants Accepted: 740
Number of Applicants Enrolled: 331

INTERNATIONAL STUDENTS

TOEFL Required of International Students? Yes
Minimum TOEFL: 600 (250 computer)

EMPLOYMENT INFORMATION

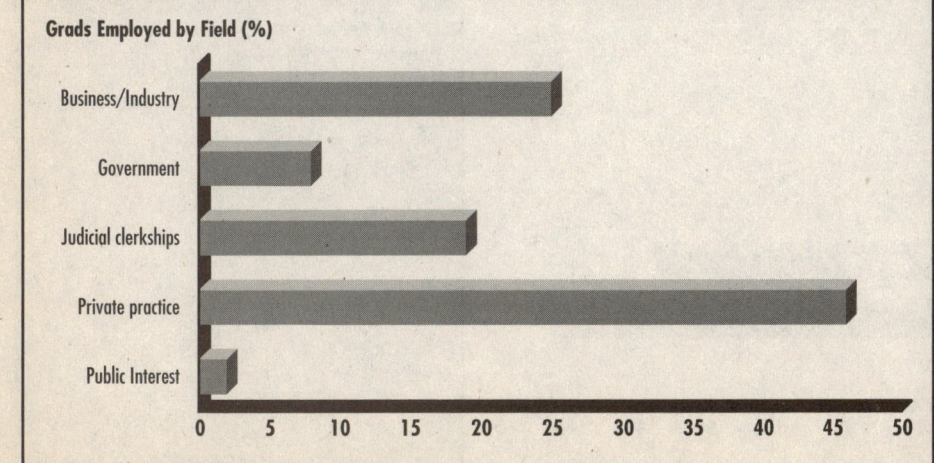

Grads Employed by Field (%)

Field	%
Business/Industry	~25
Government	~7
Judicial clerkships	~20
Private practice	~46
Public Interest	~2

Rate of Placement: 97%
Average Starting Salary: $54,500
Employers Who Frequently Hire Grads: Briggs & Morgan; Faegre & Benson; Gray, Plant, Mooty; Robins, Kaplan, Miller & Ciresi; 3M
Prominent Alumni: Warren E. Burger, Chief Justice, U.S. Supreme Court; Rosalie Wahl, Justice, Minnesota Supreme Court (retired); Douglas Amdahl, Chief Justice, Minnesota Supreme Court (retired)
State for Bar Exam: MN
Pass Rate for First-Time Bar: 87%

YALE UNIVERSITY
Law School

Admissions Contact: Associate Dean, Megan Barnett
PO Box 208329, New Haven, CT 06520-8329
Admissions Phone: 203-432-4995
Admissions E-mail: admissions.law@yale.edu • Web Address: www.law.yale.edu

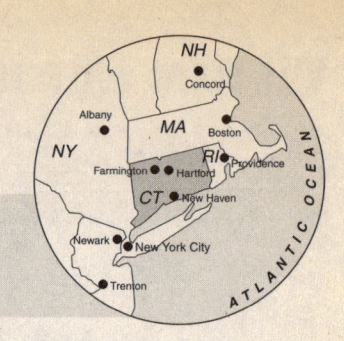

INSTITUTIONAL INFORMATION
Public/Private: Private
Student/Faculty Ratio: 7:1
Total Faculty: 66
% Female: 21
% Minority: 13

PROGRAMS
Advanced Degrees Offered: JD (3 years), LLM (1 year), MSL (1 year), JSD (up to 5 years)
Combined Degrees Offered: JD/PhD History or Political Science; JD/MS Forestry, Sociology, or Statistics; JD/MBA with Yale
Grading System: Honors, Pass, Low Pass, Credit, Failure
Clinical Program Required? No
Clinical Program Description: Advocacy for Parents and Children, Advocacy for Children and Youth, Community Legal Services, Housing and Community Development, Immigration, Landlord/Tenant, Legal Assistance, Prison Legal Services, Complex Federal Litigation, Environmental Protection Clinic, International Human Rights Law Clinic, Capital Defense Project, Domestic Violence Temporary Restraining Order Project, Greenhaven Prison Project, Street Law, Thomas Swan Barristers' Union, Morris Tyler Moot Court of Appeals
Legal Writing Course Requirements? No
Legal Methods Course Requirements? No
Legal Research Course Requirements? No
Moot Court Requirement? No
Public Interest Law Requirement? No
Academic Journals: Yale Law Journal, Yale Journal of International Law, Yale Journal of Law and Feminism, Yale Journal of Law and the Humanities, Yale Journal on Regulation, Yale Human Rights and Development Law Journal, Yale Law and Policy Review

STUDENT INFORMATION
Enrollment of Law School: 594
% Male/Female: 53/47
% Full Time: 100
% Minority: 32
Average Age of Entering Class: 24

EXPENSES/FINANCIAL AID
Annual Tuition: $31,400
Room and Board (On Campus): $10,020
Books and Supplies: $2,610
Financial Aid Application Deadline: 3/15
Average Grant: $13,035
Average Loan: $25,700
% Receiving Some Sort of Aid: 78
Average Debt: $70,300

ADMISSIONS INFORMATION
Application Fee: $55
Regular Application Deadline: 2/15
Regular Notification: Rolling
LSDAS Accepted? Yes
Average GPA: 3.8
Range of GPA: 3.7–3.9
Average LSAT: 171
Range of LSAT: 168–174
Transfer Students Accepted? Yes
Number of Applications Received: 3,610
Number of Applicants Accepted: 256
Number of Applicants Enrolled: 191

INTERNATIONAL STUDENTS
TOEFL Recommended for International Students? Yes
Minimum TOEFL: 600 (250 computer)

EMPLOYMENT INFORMATION

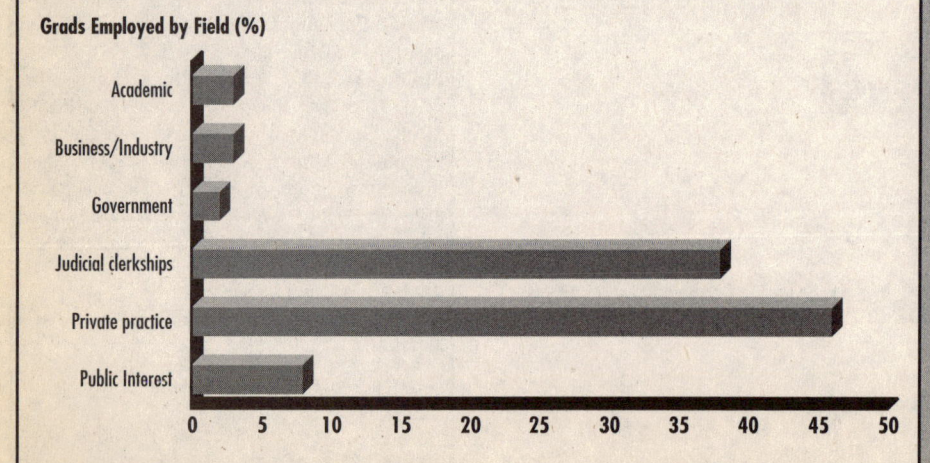

Grads Employed by Field (%)
- Academic
- Business/Industry
- Government
- Judicial clerkships
- Private practice
- Public Interest

Rate of Placement: 96%
Average Starting Salary: $76,464
State for Bar Exam: NY
Pass Rate for First-Time Bar: 98%

York University
Osgoode Hall Law School

Admissions Contact: Admissions Officer, Louise Resendes
4700 Keele Street, Toronto, ON M3J 1P3
Admissions Phone: 416-736-5712 • Admissions Fax: 416-736-5618
Admissions E-mail: ozadmit@yorku.ca • Web Address: www.osgoode.yorku.ca

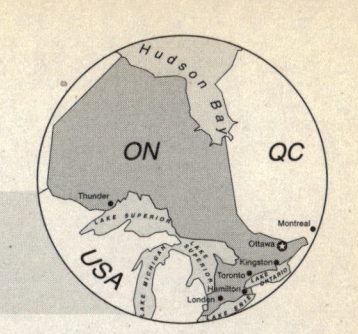

INSTITUTIONAL INFORMATION
Public/Private: Public
Student/Faculty Ratio: 18:1
Total Faculty: 48
% Female: 44

PROGRAMS
Academic Specialties: International Law, Taxation
Advanced Degrees Offered: JD, LLM
Combined Degrees Offered: LLB/MBA (4 years), LLB/MES (4 years)
Grading System: A+, A, B+, B, C+, C, D+, D, F
Clinical Program Required? No
Clinical Program Description: Immigration and Refugee, Business, Criminal, Aboriginal, Poverty Law
Legal Writing Course Requirements? Yes
Legal Writing Description: Year-long course; case comments, memos, and factum
Legal Methods Course Requirements? Yes
Legal Methods Description: Legal dimensions; 1 panel, 4 times per semester
Legal Research Course Requirements? Yes
Legal Research Description: See Legal Writing.
Moot Court Requirement? Yes
Moot Court Description: First year
Public Interest Law Requirement? No
Academic Journals: *Osgoode Hall Law Journal*

STUDENT INFORMATION
Enrollment of Law School: 825
% Male/Female: 48/52
% Full Time: 100
% Minority: 18
Average Age of Entering Class: 25

RESEARCH FACILITIES
School-Supported Research Centers: Centre for Public Law and Policy, Institute for Feminist Legal Studies, Nathanson Centre for the Study of Organized Crime and Corruption

EXPENSES/FINANCIAL AID
Annual Tuition: $8,000
Room and Board (On/Off Campus): $10,000/$7,000
Books and Supplies: $1,300
Financial Aid Application Deadline: 9/2
Average Grant: $4,000
Average Loan: $5,000
% of Aid That Is Merit-Based: 25
% Receiving Some Sort of Aid: 36
Average Total Aid Package: $2,500

ADMISSIONS INFORMATION
Application Fee: $50
Regular Application Deadline: 11/1
Regular Notification: Rolling
LSDAS Accepted? No
Average GPA: 3.7
Range of GPA: 3.3–4.0
Average LSAT: 75
Transfer Students Accepted? Yes
Number of Applications Received: 2,054
Number of Applicants Accepted: 665
Number of Applicants Enrolled: 287

INTERNATIONAL STUDENTS
TOEFL Required of International Students? Yes

EMPLOYMENT INFORMATION

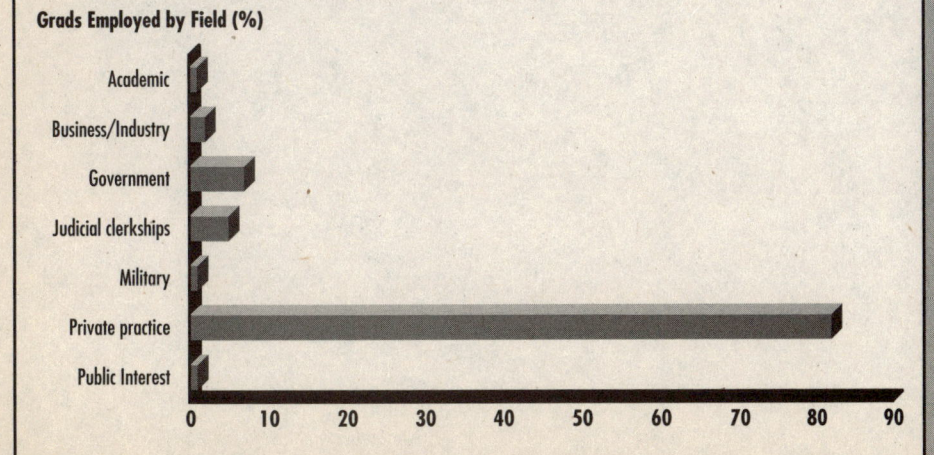

Rate of Placement: 92%
Average Starting Salary: $45,000
Employers Who Frequently Hire Grads: Blake, Cassels & Graydon; Fasken Martineau; Goodmans
State for Bar Exam: ON
Pass Rate for First-Time Bar: 98%

INDEXES

Alphabetical List of Schools

A

Albany Law School	98
American University	99
Arizona State University	100
Ave Maria College	101

B

Baylor University	102
Boston College	103
Boston University	104
Brigham Young University	105
Brooklyn Law School	106

C

Cal Northern School of Law	107
California Western	108
Campbell University	109
Capital University	110
Cardozo School of Law	111
Case Western Reserve University	112
Catholic University of America	113
Chapman University	114
City University of New York	115
Cleveland State University	116
College of William and Mary	117
Columbia University	118
Cornell University	119
Creighton University	120

D

Dalhousie University	121
DePaul University	122
Drake University	123
Duke University	124
Duquesne University	125

E

Emory University	126
Empire College	127

F

Florida Costal School of Law	128
Florida State University	129
Fordham University	130
Franklin Pierce Law Center	131

G

George Mason University	132
George Washington University	133
Georgetown University	134
Georgia State University	135
Golden Gate University	136
Gonzaga University	139

H

Hamline University	140
Harvard University	141
Hofstra University	142
Howard University	143
Humphreys College	144

I

Illinois Institute of Technology	145
Indiana University—Bloomington	146
Indiana University—Indianapolis	147

J

John F. Kennedy University	148
John Marshall Law School	149

L

Lewis and Clark College	150
Lincoln Law School of Sacramento	151
Louisiana State University	152
Loyola Marymount University	153
Loyola University Chicago	154
Loyola University New Orleans	155

M

Marquette University	156
Mercer University	157
Michigan State University	158
Mississippi College	159
Monterey College of Law	160

N

New College of California	161
New England School of Law	162
New York Law School	163
New York University	164
North Carolina Central University	165
Northeastern University	166
Northern Illinois University	167
Northern Kentucky University	168
Northwestern University	169
Nova Southeastern University	170

O

Ohio Northern University	171
Ohio State University	172
Oklahoma City University	173

P

Pace University	174
Pennsylvania State University	175
Pepperdine University	176

Q

Queen's University	177
Quinnipiac University	178

R

Regent University	179
Roger Williams University	180
Rutgers University—Camden	181
Rutgers University—Newark	182

S

St. John's University	183
St. Louis University	184
St. Mary's University	185
St. Thomas University	186
Samford University	187
San Francisco Law School	188
San Joaquin College of Law	189
Santa Barbara and Ventura Colleges of Law, Santa Barbara College of Law	190
Santa Barbara and Ventura Colleges of Law, Ventura College of Law	191
Santa Clara University	192
Seattle University	193
Seton Hall University	194
South Texas College of Law	195
Southern California Institute of Law	196
Southern Illinois University	197
Southern Methodist University	198
Southern University	199
Southwestern University School of Law	200
Stanford University	201
Stetson University	202
Suffolk University	203
Syracuse University	204

T

Temple University	205
Texas Southern University	206
Texas Tech University	207
Texas Wesleyan University	208
Thomas Jefferson School of Law	209
Thomas M. Cooley Law School	210
Touro College	211
Tulane University	212

U

University at Buffalo, State University of New York	213
University of Akron	214
University of Alabama	215
University of Arizona	216
University of Arkansas—Fayetteville	217
University of Arkansas—Little Rock	218
University of Baltimore	219
University of British Columbia	220
University of Calgary	221
University of California, Berkeley	222
University of California, Davis	223
University of California, Hastings	224
University of California, Los Angeles	225
University of Chicago	226
University of Cincinnati	227
University of Colorado	228
University of Connecticut	229
University of Dayton	230
University of Denver	231
University of Detroit Mercy	232
University of Florida	233
University of Georgia	234
University of Hawaii—Manoa	235
University of Houston	236
University of Idaho	237
University of Illinois	238
University of Iowa	239
University of Kansas	240
University of Kentucky	241
University of La Verne	242
University of Louisville	243
University of Maine	244
University of Maryland	245
University of Memphis	246
University of Miami	247
University of Michigan	248
University of Minnesota	249
University of Mississippi	250
University of Missouri—Columbia	251
University of Missouri—Kansas City	252
University of Montana	253
University of Nebraska—Lincoln	254
University of Nevada—Las Vegas	255
University of New Mexico	256
University of North Carolina—Chapel Hill	257
University of North Dakota	258
University of Notre Dame	259
University of Oklahoma	260
University of Oregon	261
University of Pennsylvania	262
University of Pittsburgh	263
University of Richmond	264
University of San Diego	265
University of San Francisco	266
University of South Carolina	267
University of South Dakota	268
University of Southern California	269
University of Tennessee	270
University of Texas—Austin	271
University of the District of Columbia	272
University of the Pacific	273
University of Toledo	276
University of Toronto	277
University of Tulsa	278
University of Utah	279
University of Victoria	280
University of Virginia	281
University of Washington	282
University of West Los Angeles	283
University of Windsor	284
University of Wisconsin	285
University of Wyoming	286

V

Valparaiso University	287
Vanderbilt University	288
Vermont Law School	289
Villanova University	290

W

Wake Forest University	291
Washburn University	292
Washington and Lee University	293
Washington University	294
Wayne State University	295
West Virginia University	296
Western New England College	297
Western State University	298
Whittier College	299
Widener University, Delaware	300
Widener University, Harrisburg	301
Willamette University	302
William Mitchell College of Law	303

Y

Yale University	304
York University	305

Law Program Name

Beasley School of Law	205
Cecil C. Humphreys School of Law	246
Chicago-Kent College of Law	145
Claude W. Pettit College of Law	171
Cleveland-Marshall College of Law	116
Columbus School of Law	113
Cumberland School of Law	187
CUNY School of Law at Queens College	115
David A. Clarke School of Law	272
Dedman School of Law	198
Detroit College of Law	158
Dickinson School of Law	175
J. Reuben Clark Law School	105
Jacob D. Fuchsberg Law Center	211
James E. Rogers College of Law	216
Lamar Hall	250
Levin College of Law	233
Louis D. Brandeis School of Law	243
McGeorge School of Law	273
Moritz College of Law	172
Norman Adrian Wiggins School of Law	109
Northwestern School of Law	150
Osgoode Hall Law School	305
Paul M. Hebert Law Center	152
Ralph R. Papitto School of Law	180
S.J. Quinney College of Law	279
Salmon P. Chase College of Law	168
School of Law (Boalt Hall)	222
Shepard Broad Law Center	170
Thurgood Marshall School of Law	206
Walter F. George School of Law	157
Washington College of Law	99
William H. Bowen School of Law	218
William S. Boyd School of Law	255
William S. Richardson School of Law	235

Location
USA

ALABAMA

Samford University	187
University of Alabama	215

ARIZONA

Arizona State University	100
University of Arizona	216

ARKANSAS

University of Arkansas—Fayetteville	217
University of Arkansas—Little Rock	218

CALIFORNIA

Cal Northern School of Law	107
California Western	108
Chapman University	114
Empire College	127
Golden Gate University	136
Humphreys College	144
John F. Kennedy University	148
Lincoln Law School of Sacramento	151
Loyola Marymount University	153
Monterey College of Law	160
New College of California	161
Pepperdine University	176
San Francisco Law School	188
San Joaquin College of Law	189
Santa Barbara and Ventura Colleges of Law, Santa Barbara College of Law	190
Santa Barbara and Ventura Colleges of Law, Ventura College of Law	191
Santa Clara University	192
Southern California Institute of Law	196
Southwestern University School of Law	200
Stanford University	201
Thomas Jefferson School of Law	209
University of California, Berkeley	222
University of California, Davis	223
University of California, Hastings	224
University of California, Los Angeles	225
University of La Verne	242
University of San Diego	265
University of San Francisco	266
University of Southern California	269
University of the Pacific	273
University of West Los Angeles	283
Western State University	298
Whittier College	299

COLORADO

University of Colorado	228
University of Denver	231

CONNECTICUT

Quinnipiac University	178
University of Connecticut	229
Yale University	304

DELAWARE

Widener University, Delaware	300

DISTRICT OF COLUMBIA

American University	99
Catholic University of America	113
George Washington University	133
Georgetown University	134
Howard University	143
University of the District of Columbia	272

FLORIDA

Florida Costal School of Law	128
Florida State University	129
Nova Southeastern University	170
St. Thomas University	186
Stetson University	202
University of Florida	233
University of Miami	247

GEORGIA

Emory University	126
Georgia State University	135
Mercer University	157
University of Georgia	234

HAWAII

University of Hawaii—Manoa	237

IDAHO

University of Idaho	237

ILLINOIS

DePaul University	122
Illinois Institute of Technology	145
John Marshall Law School	149
Loyola University Chicago	154
Northern Illinois University	167
Northwestern University	169
Southern Illinois University	197
University of Chicago	226
University of Illinois	238

INDIANA

Indiana University—Bloomington	146
Indiana University—Indianapolis	147
University of Notre Dame	259
Valparaiso University	287

LOCATION • 313

IOWA

Drake University	123
University of Iowa	239

KANSAS

University of Kansas	240
Washburn University	292

KENTUCKY

Northern Kentucky University	168
University of Kentucky	241
University of Louisville	243

LOUISIANA

Louisiana State University	152
Loyola University New Orleans	155
Southern University	199
Tulane University	212

MAINE

University of Maine	244

MARYLAND

University of Baltimore	219
University of Maryland	245

MASSACHUSETTS

Boston College	103
Boston University	104
Harvard University	141
New England School of Law	162
Northeastern University	166
Suffolk University	203
Western New England College	297

MICHIGAN

Ave Maria College	101
Michigan State University	158
Thomas M. Cooley Law School	210
University of Detroit Mercy	232
University of Michigan	248
Wayne State University	295

MINNESOTA

Hamline University	140
University of Minnesota	249
William Mitchell College of Law	303

MISSISSIPPI

Mississippi College	159
University of Mississippi	250

MISSOURI

St. Louis University	184
University of Missouri—Columbia	251
University of Missouri—Kansas City	252
Washington University	294

MONTANA

University of Montana	253

NEBRASKA

Creighton University	120
University of Nebraska—Lincoln	254

NEW HAMPSHIRE

Franklin Pierce Law Center	131

NEW JERSEY

Rutgers University—Camden	181
Rutgers University—Newark	182
Seton Hall University	194

NEW MEXICO

University of New Mexico	256

NEW YORK

Albany Law School	98
Brooklyn Law School	106
Cardozo School of Law	111
City University of New York	115
Columbia University	118
Cornell University	119
Fordham University	130
Hofstra University	142
New York Law School	163
New York University	164
Pace University	174
St. John's University	183
Syracuse University	204
Touro College	211
University at Buffalo, State University of New York	213

NORTH CAROLINA

Campbell University	109
Duke University	124
North Carolina Central University	165
University of North Carolina—Chapel Hill	257
Wake Forest University	291

NORTH DAKOTA

University of North Dakota	258

OHIO

Capital University	110
Case Western Reserve University	112
Cleveland State University	116

Ohio Northern University	171
Ohio State University	172
University of Akron	214
University of Cincinnati	227
University of Dayton	230
University of Toledo	276

OKLAHOMA

Oklahoma City University	173
University of Oklahoma	260
University of Tulsa	278

OREGON

Lewis and Clark College	150
University of Oregon	261
Willamette University	302

PENNSYLVANIA

Duquesne University	125
Pennsylvania State University	175
Temple University	205
University of Pennsylvania	262
University of Pittsburgh	263
Villanova University	290
Widener University, Harrisburg	301

RHODE ISLAND

Roger Williams University	180

SOUTH CAROLINA

University of South Carolina	267

SOUTH DAKOTA

University of South Dakota	268

TENNESSEE

University of Memphis	246
University of Tennessee	270
Vanderbilt University	288

TEXAS

Baylor University	102
St. Mary's University	185
South Texas College of Law	195
Southern Methodist University	198
Texas Southern University	206
Texas Tech University	207
Texas Wesleyan University	208
University of Houston	236
University of Texas—Austin	271

UTAH

Brigham Young University	105
University of Utah	279

VERMONT

Vermont Law School	289

VIRGINIA

College of William and Mary	117
George Mason University	132
Regent University	179
University of Richmond	264
University of Virginia	281
Washington and Lee University	293

WASHINGTON

Gonzaga University	139
Seattle University	193
University of Washington	282

WEST VIRGINIA

West Virginia University	296

WISCONSIN

Marquette University	156
University of Wisconsin	285

WYOMING

University of Wyoming	286

CANADA

Dalhousie University	121
Queen's University	177
University of British Columbia	220
University of Calgary	221
University of Toronto	277
University of Victoria	280
University of Windsor	284
York University	305

COST
(IN-STATE TUITION)

LESS THAN $10,000

Arizona State University	100
Brigham Young University	105
Cal Northern School of Law	107
City University of New York	115
Cleveland State University	116
Empire College	127
Florida State University	129
George Mason University	132
Georgia State University	135
Humphreys College	144
Indiana University—Indianapolis	147
John F. Kennedy University	148
Lincoln Law School of Sacramento	151
Louisiana State University	152
Monterey College of Law	160
North Carolina Central University	165
Northern Illinois University	167
Northern Kentucky University	168
Queen's University	177
San Francisco Law School	188
Santa Barbara and Ventura Colleges of Law, Ventura College of Law	191
Southern California Institute of Law	196
Southern Illinois University	197
Southern University	199
Texas Southern University	206
Texas Tech University	207
University of Akron	214
University of Alabama	215
University of Arizona	216
University of Arkansas—Fayetteville	217
University of Arkansas—Little Rock	218
University of British Columbia	220
University of Calgary	221
University of California, Berkeley	222
University of California, Davis	223
University of California, Los Angeles	225
University of Colorado	228
University of Florida	233
University of Georgia	234
University of Houston	236
University of Idaho	237
University of Kansas	240
University of Kentucky	241
University of Louisville	243
University of Maine	244
University of Memphis	246
University of Mississippi	250
University of Missouri—Kansas City	252
University of Montana	253
University of Nebraska—Lincoln	254
University of Nevada—Las Vegas	255
University of New Mexico	256
University of North Carolina—Chapel Hill	257
University of North Dakota	258
University of Oklahoma	260
University of South Carolina	267
University of South Dakota	268
University of Tennessee	270
University of Texas—Austin	271
University of the District of Columbia	272
University of Toledo	276
University of Utah	279
University of Victoria	280
University of Washington	282
University of Windsor	284
University of Wisconsin	285
University of Wyoming	286
Washburn University	292
Wayne State University	295
West Virginia University	296
York University	305

$10,000 TO $22,000

Ave Maria College	101
Baylor University	102
Campbell University	109
Capital University	110
College of William and Mary	117
Creighton University	120
Drake University	123
Duquesne University	125
Florida Costal School of Law	128
Franklin Pierce Law Center	131
Gonzaga University	139
Hamline University	140
Howard University	143
Indiana University—Bloomington	146
John Marshall Law School	149
Marquette University	156
Michigan State University	158
Mississippi College	159
New College of California	161
New England School of Law	162
Nova Southeastern University	170
Ohio Northern University	171
Ohio State University	172
Oklahoma City University	173
Regent University	179
Rutgers University—Camden	181
Rutgers University—Newark	182
St. Mary's University	185
Samford University	187
San Joaquin College of Law	189
South Texas College of Law	195
Temple University	205
Texas Wesleyan University	208
Thomas M. Cooley Law School	210
University at Buffalo, State University of New York	213
University of Baltimore	219
University of California, Hastings	224
University of Cincinnati	227
University of Connecticut	229
University of Denver	231
University of Detroit Mercy	232
University of Illinois	238
University of Iowa	239
University of Maryland	245
University of Minnesota	249
University of Missouri—Columbia	251
University of Oregon	261
University of Pittsburgh	263
University of Toronto	277
University of Tulsa	278
University of Virginia	281
University of West Los Angeles	283
Valparaiso University	287
Villanova University	290
Washington and Lee University	293
Western New England College	297
Willamette University	302
William Mitchell College of Law	303

MORE THAN $22,000

Albany Law School	98
American University	99
Boston College	103
Boston University	104
Brooklyn Law School	106
California Western	108
Cardozo School of Law	111
Case Western Reserve University	112
Catholic University of America	113
Chapman University	114
Columbia University	118
Cornell University	119
DePaul University	122
Duke University	124
Emory University	126
Fordham University	130
George Washington University	133
Georgetown University	134
Golden Gate University	136
Harvard University	141
Hofstra University	142
Illinois Institute of Technology	145
Lewis and Clark College	150
Loyola Marymount University	153
Loyola University Chicago	154
Loyola University New Orleans	155
Mercer University	157
New York Law School	163

New York University	164
Northeastern University	166
Northwestern University	169
Pace University	174
Pennsylvania State University	175
Pepperdine University	176
Quinnipiac University	178
Roger Williams University	180
St. John's University	183
St. Louis University	184
St. Thomas University	186
Santa Barbara and Ventura Colleges of Law, Santa Barbara College of Law	190
Santa Clara University	192
Seattle University	193
Seton Hall University	194
Southern Methodist University	198
Southwestern University School of Law	200
Stanford University	201
Stetson University	202
Suffolk University	203
Syracuse University	204
Thomas Jefferson School of Law	209
Touro College	211
Tulane University	212
University of Chicago	226
University of Dayton	230
University of Miami	247
University of Michigan	248
University of Notre Dame	259
University of Pennsylvania	262
University of Richmond	264
University of San Diego	265
University of San Francisco	266
University of Southern California	269
University of the Pacific	273
Vanderbilt University	288
Vermont Law School	289
Wake Forest University	291
Washington University	294
Western State University	298
Whittier College	299
Widener University, Delaware	300
Widener University, Harrisburg	301
Yale University	304

ENROLLMENT OF LAW SCHOOL

LESS THAN 500 STUDENTS

Ave Maria College	101
Baylor University	102
Brigham Young University	105
Cal Northern School of Law	107
Campbell University	109
Chapman University	114
City University of New York	115
Creighton University	120
Dalhousie University	121
Drake University	123
Empire College	127
Franklin Pierce Law Center	131
Golden Gate University	136
Howard University	143
Humphreys College	144
John F. Kennedy University	148
Lincoln Law School of Sacramento	151
Mercer University	157
Mississippi College	159
Monterey College of Law	160
New College of California	161
North Carolina Central University	165
Northern Illinois University	167
Northern Kentucky University	168
Ohio Northern University	171
Queen's University	177
Quinnipiac University	178
St. John's University	183
St. Thomas University	186
San Francisco Law School	188
San Joaquin College of Law	189
Santa Barbara and Ventura Colleges of Law, Ventura College of Law	191
Southern California Institute of Law	196
Southern Illinois University	197
Southern University	199
Texas Wesleyan University	208
University of Arizona	216
University of Arkansas—Fayetteville	217
University of Arkansas—Little Rock	218
University of Calgary	221
University of Cincinnati	227
University of Colorado	228
University of Dayton	230
University of Detroit Mercy	232
University of Idaho	237
University of Kentucky	241
University of La Verne	242
University of Louisville	243
University of Maine	244
University of Memphis	246
University of Missouri—Kansas City	252
University of Montana	253
University of Nebraska—Lincoln	254
University of Nevada—Las Vegas	255
University of New Mexico	256
University of North Dakota	258
University of Richmond	264
University of South Dakota	268
University of Tennessee	270
University of the District of Columbia	272
University of Toledo	276
University of Utah	279
University of Victoria	280
University of Washington	282
University of West Los Angeles	283
University of Windsor	284
University of Wyoming	286
Valparaiso University	287
Wake Forest University	291
Washburn University	292
Washington and Lee University	293
West Virginia University	296
Western New England College	297
Western State University	298
Widener University, Harrisburg	301
Willamette University	302

500 TO 800 STUDENTS

Arizona State University	100
Capital University	110
Case Western Reserve University	112
College of William and Mary	117
Cornell University	119
Duke University	124
Duquesne University	125
Emory University	126
Florida Costal School of Law	128
Florida State University	129
George Mason University	132
Georgia State University	135
Gonzaga University	139
Hamline University	140
Indiana University—Bloomington	146
Lewis and Clark College	150
Louisiana State University	152
Marquette University	156
Michigan State University	158
Northeastern University	166
Northwestern University	169
Ohio State University	172
Oklahoma City University	173
Pace University	174
Pennsylvania State University	175
Pepperdine University	176
Regent University	179
Roger Williams University	180
Rutgers University—Camden	181
Rutgers University—Newark	182
St. Mary's University	185
Samford University	187
Southern Methodist University	198
Stanford University	201
Stetson University	202
Syracuse University	204
Texas Southern University	206
Texas Tech University	207
Thomas Jefferson School of Law	209
Touro College	211
University at Buffalo, State University of New York	213
University of Akron	214
University of Alabama	215
University of British Columbia	220
University of California, Davis	223
University of Chicago	226
University of Connecticut	229
University of Georgia	234
University of Illinois	238
University of Iowa	239
University of Kansas	240
University of Minnesota	249
University of Mississippi	250
University of Missouri—Columbia	251
University of North Carolina—Chapel Hill	257
University of Notre Dame	259
University of Oklahoma	260
University of Oregon	261
University of Pittsburgh	263
University of San Francisco	266
University of South Carolina	267
University of Southern California	269
University of Toronto	277
University of Tulsa	278
Vanderbilt University	288
Vermont Law School	289
Villanova University	290
Washington University	294
Wayne State University	295
Whittier College	299
Yale University	304

MORE THAN 800 STUDENTS

Albany Law School	98
American University	99
Boston College	103
Boston University	104
Brooklyn Law School	106
California Western	108
Cardozo School of Law	111
Catholic University of America	113
Cleveland State University	116
Columbia University	118
DePaul University	122
Fordham University	130

School	Page
George Washington University	133
Georgetown University	134
Harvard University	141
Hofstra University	142
Illinois Institute of Technology	145
Indiana University—Indianapolis	147
John Marshall Law School	149
Loyola Marymount University	153
Loyola University Chicago	154
Loyola University New Orleans	155
New England School of Law	162
New York Law School	163
New York University	164
Nova Southeastern University	170
St. Louis University	184
Santa Barbara and Ventura Colleges of Law, Santa Barbara College of Law	190
Santa Clara University	192
Seattle University	193
Seton Hall University	194
South Texas College of Law	195
Southwestern University School of Law	200
Suffolk University	203
Temple University	205
Thomas M. Cooley Law School	210
Tulane University	212
University of Baltimore	219
University of California, Berkeley	222
University of California, Hastings	224
University of California, Los Angeles	225
University of Denver	231
University of Florida	233
University of Houston	236
University of Maryland	245
University of Miami	247
University of Michigan	248
University of Pennsylvania	262
University of San Diego	265
University of Texas—Austin	271
University of the Pacific	273
University of Virginia	281
University of Wisconsin	285
Widener University, Delaware	300
William Mitchell College of Law	303
York University	305

Average LSAT

LESS THAN 153

Albany Law School	98
Cal Northern School of Law	107
California Western	108
Capital University	110
City University of New York	115
Cleveland State University	116
Empire College	127
Florida Costal School of Law	128
Franklin Pierce Law Center	131
Golden Gate University	136
Gonzaga University	139
Hamline University	140
Howard University	143
Humphreys College	144
John F. Kennedy University	148
John Marshall Law School	149
Lincoln Law School of Sacramento	151
Michigan State University	158
Mississippi College	159
Monterey College of Law	160
New College of California	161
New England School of Law	162
North Carolina Central University	165
Northern Kentucky University	168
Nova Southeastern University	170
Ohio Northern University	171
Oklahoma City University	173
Quinnipiac University	178
Regent University	179
Roger Williams University	180
St. Mary's University	185
St. Thomas University	186
San Francisco Law School	188
San Joaquin College of Law	189
Santa Barbara and Ventura Colleges of Law, Ventura College of Law	191
South Texas College of Law	195
Southern Illinois University	197
Southern University	199
Southwestern University School of Law	200
Stetson University	202
Syracuse University	204
Texas Southern University	206
Texas Wesleyan University	208
Thomas Jefferson School of Law	209
Thomas M. Cooley Law School	210
University of Arkansas—Fayetteville	217
University of Baltimore	219
University of Calgary	221
University of Dayton	230
University of Detroit Mercy	232
University of North Dakota	258
University of South Dakota	268
University of the District of Columbia	272
University of the Pacific	273
University of Tulsa	278
University of West Los Angeles	283
Valparaiso University	287
Washburn University	292
Western New England College	297
Western State University	298
Whittier College	299
Widener University, Delaware	300
Widener University, Harrisburg	301
York University	305

153 TO 156

Campbell University	109
Campbell University	109
Chapman University	114
Creighton University	120
DePaul University	122
Drake University	123
Duquesne University	125
Florida State University	129
Hofstra University	142
Indiana University—Indianapolis	147
Louisiana State University	152
Loyola University New Orleans	155
Marquette University	156
Mercer University	157
New York Law School	163
Northern Illinois University	167
Pace University	174
Pennsylvania State University	175
St. John's University	183
St. Louis University	184
Samford University	187
Santa Barbara and Ventura Colleges of Law, Santa Barbara College of Law	190
Santa Clara University	192
Seattle University	193
Seton Hall University	194
Suffolk University	203
Texas Tech University	207
University at Buffalo, State University of New York	213
University of Akron	214
University of Arkansas—Little Rock	218
University of Denver	231
University of Idaho	237
University of Louisville	243
University of Maine	244
University of Memphis	246
University of Miami	247
University of Mississippi	250
University of Missouri—Kansas City	252
University of Montana	253
University of Nebraska—Lincoln	254
University of Nevada—Las Vegas	255
University of San Francisco	266
University of South Carolina	267
University of Wyoming	286
Vermont Law School	289
Wayne State University	295
West Virginia University	296
Willamette University	302
William Mitchell College of Law	303

GREATER THAN 156

American University	99
Arizona State University	100
Ave Maria College	101
Baylor University	102
Boston College	103
Boston University	104
Brigham Young University	105
Brooklyn Law School	106
Cardozo School of Law	111
Case Western Reserve University	112
Catholic University of America	113
College of William and Mary	117
Columbia University	118
Cornell University	119
Dalhousie University	121
Duke University	124
Emory University	126
Fordham University	130
George Mason University	132
George Washington University	133
Georgetown University	134
Georgia State University	135
Harvard University	141
Illinois Institute of Technology	145
Indiana University—Bloomington	146
Lewis and Clark College	150
Loyola Marymount University	153
Loyola University Chicago	154
New York University	164
Northeastern University	166
Northwestern University	169
Ohio State University	172
Pepperdine University	176
Queen's University	177
Rutgers University—Camden	181
Rutgers University—Newark	182
Southern Methodist University	198
Stanford University	201
Temple University	205
Tulane University	212
University of Alabama	215
University of Arizona	216
University of British Columbia	220
University of California, Berkeley	222
University of California, Davis	223
University of California, Hastings	224
University of California, Los Angeles	225
University of Chicago	226
University of Cincinnati	227

University of Colorado	228
University of Connecticut	229
University of Florida	233
University of Georgia	234
University of Houston	236
University of Illinois	238
University of Iowa	239
University of Kansas	240
University of Kentucky	241
University of Maryland	245
University of Michigan	248
University of Minnesota	249
University of Missouri—Columbia	251
University of New Mexico	256
University of North Carolina—Chapel Hill	257
University of Notre Dame	259
University of Oklahoma	260
University of Oregon	261
University of Pennsylvania	262
University of Pittsburgh	263
University of Richmond	264
University of San Diego	265
University of Southern California	269
University of Tennessee	270
University of Texas—Austin	271
University of Toledo	276
University of Toronto	277
University of Utah	279
University of Victoria	280
University of Virginia	281
University of Washington	282
University of Wisconsin	285
Vanderbilt University	288
Villanova University	290
Wake Forest University	291
Washington and Lee University	293
Washington University	294
Yale University	304

Average Undergrad GPA

3.1 AND LOWER

Cal Northern School of Law	107
Capital University	110
City University of New York	115
Cleveland State University	116
Empire College	127
Florida Costal School of Law	128
Golden Gate University	136
Howard University	143
Humphreys College	144
John Marshall Law School	149
Lincoln Law School of Sacramento	151
Mississippi College	159
Monterey College of Law	160
New College of California	161
New York Law School	163
North Carolina Central University	165
Nova Southeastern University	170
Ohio Northern University	171
Oklahoma City University	173
Quinnipiac University	178
Regent University	179
Roger Williams University	180
St. Mary's University	185
St. Thomas University	186
Samford University	187
San Francisco Law School	188
San Joaquin College of Law	189
South Texas College of Law	195
Southwestern University School of Law	200
Texas Southern University	206
Texas Wesleyan University	208
Thomas Jefferson School of Law	209
Thomas M. Cooley Law School	210
University of Baltimore	219
University of Denver	231
University of Detroit Mercy	232
University of Maine	244
University of South Dakota	268
University of the District of Columbia	272
University of the Pacific	273
University of Toledo	276
Vermont Law School	289
Western New England College	297
Western State University	298
Whittier College	299
Widener University, Delaware	300
Widener University, Harrisburg	301

3.2 TO 3.3

Albany Law School	98
Ave Maria College	101
California Western	108
Campbell University	109
Case Western Reserve University	112
Catholic University of America	113
Chapman University	114
Creighton University	120
Duquesne University	125
Franklin Pierce Law Center	131
Georgia State University	135
Gonzaga University	139
Hamline University	140
Hofstra University	142
Illinois Institute of Technology	145
Louisiana State University	152
Loyola Marymount University	153
Loyola University Chicago	154
Loyola University New Orleans	155
Marquette University	156
Mercer University	157
Michigan State University	158
Northeastern University	166
Northern Illinois University	167
Northern Kentucky University	168
Pace University	174
Pennsylvania State University	175
Rutgers University—Camden	181
Rutgers University—Newark	182
St. John's University	183
Santa Barbara and Ventura Colleges of Law, Santa Barbara College of Law	190
Santa Barbara and Ventura Colleges of Law, Ventura College of Law	191
Santa Clara University	192
Seattle University	193
Seton Hall University	194
Southern Illinois University	197
Stetson University	202
Suffolk University	203
Syracuse University	204
Temple University	205
University at Buffalo, State University of New York	213
University of Akron	214
University of Arkansas—Fayetteville	217
University of Arkansas—Little Rock	218
University of Connecticut	229
University of Dayton	230
University of Louisville	243
University of Memphis	246
University of Missouri—Kansas City	252
University of Montana	253
University of Nevada—Las Vegas	255
University of North Dakota	258
University of Pittsburgh	263
University of Richmond	264
University of San Francisco	266
University of South Carolina	267
University of Tulsa	278
University of Wisconsin	285
University of Wyoming	286
Valparaiso University	287
Villanova University	290
Washburn University	292
Wayne State University	295
Willamette University	302
William Mitchell College of Law	303

3.4 AND HIGHER

American University	99
Arizona State University	100
Baylor University	102
Boston College	103
Boston University	104
Brigham Young University	105
Brooklyn Law School	106
Cardozo School of Law	111
College of William and Mary	117
Columbia University	118
Cornell University	119
Dalhousie University	121
DePaul University	122
Drake University	123
Duke University	124
Emory University	126
Florida State University	129
Fordham University	130
George Mason University	132
George Washington University	133
Georgetown University	134
Harvard University	141
Indiana University—Bloomington	146
Indiana University—Indianapolis	147
Lewis and Clark College	150
New York University	164
Northwestern University	169
Ohio State University	172
Pepperdine University	176
St. Louis University	184
Southern Methodist University	198
Southern University	199
Stanford University	201
Texas Tech University	207
Tulane University	212
University of Alabama	215
University of Arizona	216
University of British Columbia	220
University of Calgary	221
University of California, Berkeley	222
University of California, Davis	223
University of California, Hastings	224
University of California, Los Angeles	225

University of Chicago	226
University of Cincinnati	227
University of Colorado	228
University of Florida	233
University of Georgia	234
University of Houston	236
University of Idaho	237
University of Illinois	238
University of Iowa	239
University of Kansas	240
University of Kentucky	241
University of Maryland	245
University of Miami	247
University of Michigan	248
University of Minnesota	249
University of Mississippi	250
University of Missouri—Columbia	251
University of Nebraska—Lincoln	254
University of New Mexico	256
University of North Carolina—Chapel Hill	257
University of Notre Dame	259
University of Oklahoma	260
University of Oregon	261
University of Pennsylvania	262
University of San Diego	265
University of Southern California	269
University of Tennessee	270
University of Texas—Austin	271
University of Toronto	277
University of Utah	279
University of Victoria	280
University of Virginia	281
University of Washington	282
Vanderbilt University	288
Wake Forest University	291
Washington and Lee University	293
Washington University	294
West Virginia University	296
Yale University	304
York University	305

Average Starting Salary

LESS THAN $47,000

Ave Maria College	101
Campbell University	109
City University of New York	115
Creighton University	120
Georgetown University	134
Gonzaga University	139
Hamline University	140
John Marshall Law School	149
Lincoln Law School of Sacramento	151
Mississippi College	159
New England School of Law	162
Regent University	179
Roger Williams University	180
St. Thomas University	186
San Francisco Law School	188
Southern California Institute of Law	196
Southern Illinois University	197
Texas Wesleyan University	208
Thomas M. Cooley Law School	210
Touro College	211
University of Arkansas—Little Rock	218
University of Baltimore	219
University of Idaho	237
University of Louisville	243
University of Memphis	246
University of Missouri—Kansas City	252
University of Montana	253
University of Nevada—Las Vegas	255
University of New Mexico	256
University of North Dakota	258
University of South Carolina	267
University of South Dakota	268
University of Wyoming	286
Vermont Law School	289
West Virginia University	296
Widener University, Harrisburg	301
York University	305

$47,000 TO $60,000

Albany Law School	98
Baylor University	102
California Western	108
Capital University	110
Chapman University	114
Cleveland State University	116
Drake University	123
Duquesne University	125
Florida Costal School of Law	128
Golden Gate University	136
Indiana University—Indianapolis	147
Lewis and Clark College	150
Louisiana State University	152
Marquette University	156
Mercer University	157
Northern Kentucky University	168
Nova Southeastern University	170
Ohio Northern University	171
Oklahoma City University	173
Pennsylvania State University	175
Quinnipiac University	178
St. Louis University	184
St. Mary's University	185
Samford University	187
Santa Barbara and Ventura Colleges of Law, Santa Barbara College of Law	190
Stetson University	202
Texas Tech University	207
Thomas Jefferson School of Law	209
University at Buffalo, State University of New York	213
University of Akron	214
University of Alabama	215
University of British Columbia	220
University of Cincinnati	227
University of Colorado	228
University of Dayton	230
University of Denver	231
University of Detroit Mercy	232
University of Florida	233
University of Georgia	234
University of Iowa	239
University of Kansas	240
University of Kentucky	241
University of Maine	244
University of Maryland	245
University of Mississippi	250
University of Missouri—Columbia	251
University of Nebraska—Lincoln	254
University of North Carolina—Chapel Hill	257
University of Oklahoma	260
University of Oregon	261
University of Richmond	264
University of Tennessee	270
University of the District of Columbia	272
University of the Pacific	273
University of Toledo	276
University of Toronto	277
University of Tulsa	278
University of Utah	279
Valparaiso University	287
Washington University	294
Wayne State University	295
Western New England College	297
Western State University	298
Widener University, Delaware	300
Willamette University	302
William Mitchell College of Law	303

MORE THAN $60,000

American University	99
Arizona State University	100
Boston University	104
Brigham Young University	105
Brooklyn Law School	106
Cardozo School of Law	111
Catholic University of America	113
College of William and Mary	117
Columbia University	118
Cornell University	119
DePaul University	122
Duke University	124
Emory University	126
Florida State University	129
Fordham University	130
Franklin Pierce Law Center	131
George Mason University	132
George Washington University	133
Georgia State University	135
Harvard University	141
Hofstra University	142
Howard University	143
Illinois Institute of Technology	145
Indiana University—Bloomington	146
Loyola Marymount University	153
Loyola University Chicago	154
Michigan State University	158
New York Law School	163
Northeastern University	166
Northwestern University	169
Ohio State University	172
Pace University	174
Pepperdine University	176
Rutgers University—Camden	181
Rutgers University—Newark	182
St. John's University	183
Santa Clara University	192
Seton Hall University	194
South Texas College of Law	195
Southern Methodist University	198
Southwestern University School of Law	200
Stanford University	201
Suffolk University	203
Syracuse University	204
Temple University	205
Tulane University	212
University of Arizona	216
University of California, Berkeley	222
University of California, Davis	223
University of California, Hastings	224
University of California, Los Angeles	225
University of Chicago	226
University of Connecticut	229
University of Houston	236
University of Illinois	238
University of Miami	247

University of Michigan	248
University of Minnesota	249
University of Notre Dame	259
University of Pennsylvania	262
University of Pittsburgh	263
University of San Diego	265
University of San Francisco	266
University of Southern California	269
University of Texas—Austin	271
University of Virginia	281
University of Washington	282
University of Wisconsin	285
Vanderbilt University	288
Villanova University	290
Wake Forest University	291
Washington and Lee University	293
Whittier College	299
Yale University	304

Pass Rate for First-Time Bar

LESS THAN 75 PERCENT

American University	99
Cal Northern School of Law	107
Capital University	110
Chapman University	114
Cleveland State University	116
Golden Gate University	136
Gonzaga University	139
Humphreys College	144
Lewis and Clark College	150
Lincoln Law School of Sacramento	151
Loyola University New Orleans	155
Monterey College of Law	160
New College of California	161
New York Law School	163
Pepperdine University	176
Regent University	179
Roger Williams University	180
St. Mary's University	185
St. Thomas University	186
San Francisco Law School	188
San Joaquin College of Law	189
Santa Barbara and Ventura Colleges of Law, Santa Barbara College of Law	190
Santa Barbara and Ventura Colleges of Law, Ventura College of Law	191
Santa Clara University	192
Southern California Institute of Law	196
Southern University	199
Southwestern University School of Law	200
Texas Southern University	206
Thomas Jefferson School of Law	209
Thomas M. Cooley Law School	210
Touro College	211
University at Buffalo, State University of New York	213
University of Baltimore	219
University of Dayton	230
University of Idaho	237
University of Nevada—Las Vegas	255
University of San Diego	265
University of San Francisco	266
University of the District of Columbia	272
University of the Pacific	273
University of West Los Angeles	283
Vermont Law School	289
West Virginia University	296
Western New England College	297
Western State University	298
Whittier College	299
Widener University, Delaware	300
Widener University, Harrisburg	301
Willamette University	302

75 PERCENT TO 89 PERCENT

Albany Law School	98
Arizona State University	100
Baylor University	102
Brooklyn Law School	106
California Western	108
Cardozo School of Law	111
Case Western Reserve University	112
City University of New York	115
College of William and Mary	117
Creighton University	120
DePaul University	122
Drake University	123
Duquesne University	125
Empire College	127
Florida Costal School of Law	128
Florida State University	129
Fordham University	130
Franklin Pierce Law Center	131
Hamline University	140
Hofstra University	142
Illinois Institute of Technology	145
Indiana University—Indianapolis	147
John Marshall Law School	149
Louisiana State University	152
Loyola University Chicago	154
Mercer University	157
Michigan State University	158
Mississippi College	159
New England School of Law	162
Northeastern University	166
Northern Illinois University	167
Northern Kentucky University	168
Nova Southeastern University	170
Oklahoma City University	173
Pennsylvania State University	175
Quinnipiac University	178
Rutgers University—Camden	181
Rutgers University—Newark	182
St. John's University	183
St. Louis University	184
Seton Hall University	194
South Texas College of Law	195
Southern Illinois University	197
Southern Methodist University	198
Stanford University	201
Stetson University	202
Suffolk University	203
Texas Tech University	207
Texas Wesleyan University	208
University of Akron	214
University of Arkansas—Fayetteville	217
University of Arkansas—Little Rock	218
University of California, Davis	223
University of California, Hastings	224
University of Connecticut	229
University of Denver	231
University of Detroit Mercy	232
University of Iowa	239
University of Louisville	243
University of Maine	244
University of Maryland	245
University of Miami	247
University of Minnesota	249
University of Mississippi	250
University of Missouri—Kansas City	252
University of Montana	253
University of Nebraska—Lincoln	254
University of North Carolina—Chapel Hill	257
University of Oklahoma	260
University of Oregon	261
University of Pittsburgh	263
University of South Carolina	267
University of Tennessee	270
University of Toledo	276
University of Tulsa	278
Villanova University	290
Washburn University	292
Washington University	294
Wayne State University	295
William Mitchell College of Law	303

90 PERCENT OR MORE

Boston College	103
Boston University	104
Brigham Young University	105
Campbell University	109
Columbia University	118
Cornell University	119
Duke University	124
Emory University	126
George Washington University	133
Georgia State University	135
Harvard University	141
Indiana University—Bloomington	146
Marquette University	156
New York University	164
Northwestern University	169
Ohio Northern University	171
Ohio State University	172
Samford University	187
Tulane University	212
University of Alabama	215
University of Arizona	216
University of British Columbia	220
University of Calgary	221
University of California, Berkeley	222
University of California, Los Angeles	225
University of Chicago	226
University of Cincinnati	227
University of Colorado	228

University of Florida	233
University of Georgia	234
University of Houston	236
University of Illinois	238
University of Kentucky	241
University of Memphis	246
University of Missouri—Columbia	251
University of New Mexico	256
University of North Dakota	258
University of Notre Dame	259
University of Pennsylvania	262
University of Richmond	264
University of South Dakota	268
University of Southern California	269
University of Texas—Austin	271
University of Utah	279
University of Virginia	281
University of Washington	282
University of Windsor	284
University of Wisconsin	285
Vanderbilt University	288
Wake Forest University	291
Yale University	304
York University	305

ABOUT THE AUTHOR

Eric Owens, Esq., lives in Chicago with his brilliant, lovely, and forgiving wife, Rachel Brown. He recently left private practice to try to convince the Foreign Service that he would make a worthwhile diplomat. It's a slow process. He is an SAT teacher, tutor, and master trainer and a GMAT teacher and tutor for The Princeton Review.

NOTES

NOTES

NOTES

NOTES

NOTES

NOTES

NOTES

NOTES

NOTES

NOTES

NOTES

A candid, entertaining look at one lawyer's journey from law school to the bar exam to the firm—and the surprising revelations he had along the way.

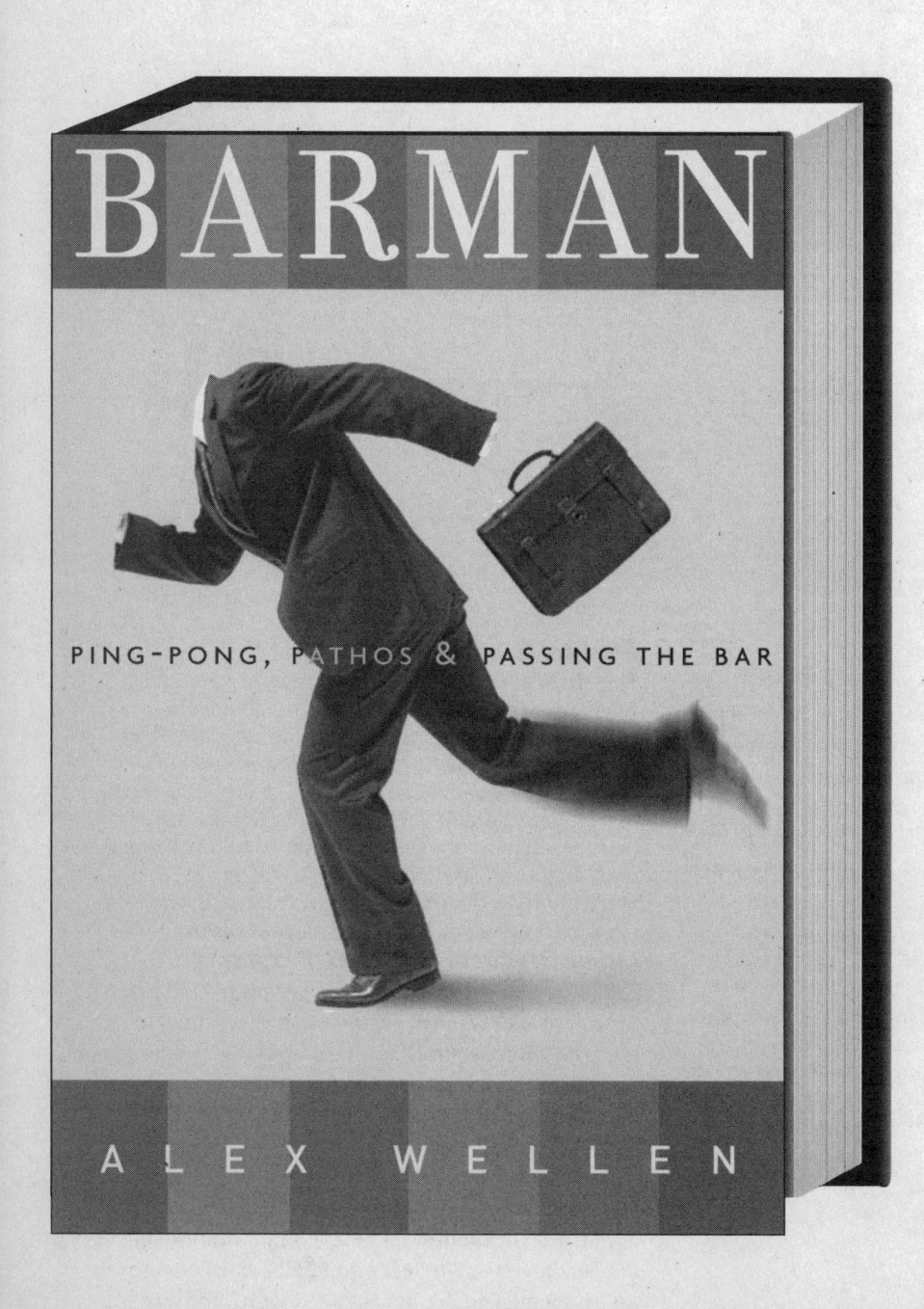

BARMAN

PING-PONG, PATHOS & PASSING THE BAR

ALEX WELLEN

Savvy, honest, and often hilarious, *Barman* is *The Paper Chase* meets *Sex and the City*. Alex Whellen's memoir of dealing with life and other distractions while in pursuit of a law career is a fresh and contemporary portrait of the lawyer as a young man.

As he moves from graduating student to licensed lawyer, Alex fantasizes about the glitzy, high-powered lifestyle of a Manhattan attorney with a top firm. But one question keeps nagging him: will overpriced ties from Barneys and cavorting with B-list celebs keep anyone from noticing that he did not go to Harvard? Barman recounts the real-life, not-so-romantic metamorphosis of an average guy into a lawyer.

"*Alex Wellen is an authentic voice.... Funny, honest, touching, Barman shows us the life that most lawyers really live.*"
— John J. Osborn Jr., author of *The Paper Chase*

HARMONY BOOKS
A MEMBER OF THE CROWN PUBLISHING GROUP

CROWNPUBLISHING.COM

Graduate School Entrance Tests

Business School
Is an MBA in your future? If so, you'll need to take the GMAT. The GMAT is a computer-based test offered year round, on most days of the week. October and November are the most popular months for testing appointments. Most business schools require you to have a few years of work experience before you apply, but that doesn't mean you should put off taking the GMAT. Scores are valid for up to five years, so you should take the test while you're still in college and in the test-taking frame of mind.

Law School
If you want to be able to call yourself an "esquire", you'll need to take the LSAT. Most students take the LSAT in the fall of their senior year—either the October or the December administration. The test is also offered in February and in June. The June test is the only afternoon administration – so if your brain doesn't start functioning until the P.M., this might be the one for you. Just make sure to take it in June of your junior year if you want to meet the application deadlines.

Medical School
The MCAT is offered twice each year, in April and in August. It's a beastly eight-hour exam, but it's a necessary evil if you want to become a doctor. Since you'll need to be familiar with the physics, chemistry, and biology tested on the exam, you'll probably want to wait until April of your junior year to take the test—that's when most students take the MCAT. If you wait until August to give it a shot, you'll still be able to meet application deadlines, but you won't have time to take it again if you're not satisfied with your results.

Other Graduate and Ph.D. Programs
For any other graduate or Ph.D. program, be it art history or biochemical engineering, you'll need to take the GRE General Test. This is another computer-based test, and, like the GMAT, it's offered year-round on most days of the week. The most popular test dates are in late summer and in the fall. Take the test no later than October or November before you plan to enter graduate school to ensure that you meet all application deadlines (and the all-important financial aid deadlines) and to leave yourself some room to take it again if you're not satisfied with your scores.

Understanding the Tests

MCAT
Structure and Format
The Medical College Admission Test (MCAT) is a six-hour paper-and-pencil exam that can take up to eight or nine hours to administer.

The MCAT consists of four scored sections that always appear in the same order:

1. Physical Sciences: 100 minutes; 77 physics and general chemistry questions
2. Verbal Reasoning: 85 minutes; 60 questions based on nine passages
3. Writing Sample: two 30-minute essays
4. Biological Sciences: 100 minutes; 77 biology and organic chemistry questions

Scoring
The Physical Sciences, Biological Sciences, and Verbal Reasoning sections are each scored on a scale of 1 to 15, with 8 as the average score. These scores will be added together to form your Total Score. The Writing Sample is scored from J (lowest) to T (highest), with O as the average score.

Test Dates
The MCAT is offered twice each year—in April and August.

Registration
The MCAT is administered and scored by the MCAT Program Office under the direction of the AAMC. To request a registration packet, you can write to the MCAT Program Office,
P.O. Box 4056, Iowa City, Iowa 52243
or call 319-337-1357.

GRE
Structure and Format
The Graduate Record Examinations (GRE) General Test is a multiple-choice test for applicants to graduate school that is taken on computer. It is a computer-adaptive test (CAT), consisting of three sections.

- One 30-minute, 30-question "Verbal Ability" (vocabulary and reading) section
- One 45-minute, 28-question "Quantitative Ability" (math) section
- An Analytical Writing Assessment, consisting of two essay tasks
  - One 45-minute "Analysis of an Issue" task
  - One 30-minute "Analysis of an Argument" task

The GRE is a computer-adaptive test, which means that it uses your performance on previous questions to determine which question you will be asked next. The software calculates your score based on the number of questions you answer correctly, the difficulty of the questions you answer, and the number of questions you complete. Questions that appear early in the test impact your score to a greater degree than do those that come toward the end of the exam.

Scoring
You will receive a Verbal score and a Math score, each ranging from 200 to 800, as well as an Analytic Writing Assessment (AWA) score ranging from 0 to 6.

Test Dates
The GRE is offered year-round in testing centers, by appointment.

Registration
To register for the GRE, call 1-800-GRE-CALL or register online at www.GRE.org.

Understanding the Tests

LSAT
Structure and Format
The Law School Admission Test (LSAT) is a four-hour exam comprised of five 35-minute multiple-choice test sections of approximately 25 questions each, plus an essay:

- Reading Comprehension (1 section)
- Analytical Reasoning (1 section)
- Logical Reasoning (2 sections)
- Experimental Section (1 section)

Scoring
- Four of the five multiple-choice sections count toward your final LSAT score
- The fifth multiple-choice section is an experimental section used solely to test new questions for future exams
- Correct responses count equally and no points are deducted for incorrect or blank responses
- Test takers get a final, scaled score between 120 and 180
- The essay is not scored, and is rarely used to evaluate your candidacy by admissions officers

Test Dates
The LSAT is offered four times each year—in February, June, October, and December.

Registration
To register for the LSAT, visit www.LSAC.org to order a registration book or to register online.

GMAT
Structure and Format
The Graduate Management Admission Test (GMAT) is a multiple-choice test for applicants to business school that is taken on computer. It is a computer-adaptive test (CAT), consisting of three sections:

- Two 30-minute essays to be written on the computer: Analysis of an Argument and Analysis of an Issue
- One 75-minute, 37-question Math section: Problem Solving and Data Sufficiency
- One 75-minute, 41-question Verbal section: Sentence Corrections, Critical Reasoning, and Reading Comprehension

The GMAT is a computer-adaptive test, which means that it uses your performance on previous questions to determine which question you will be asked next. The software calculates your score based on the number of questions you answer correctly, the difficulty of the questions you answer, and the number of questions you complete. Questions that appear early in the test impact your score to a greater degree than do those that come toward the end of the exam.

Scoring
You will receive a composite score ranging from 200 to 800 in 10-point increments, in addition to a Verbal score and a Math score, each ranging from 0 to 60. You will also receive an Analytic Writing Assessment (AWA) score ranging from 0 to 6.

Test Dates
The GMAT is offered year-round in testing centers, by appointment.

Registration
To register for the GMAT, call 1-800-GMAT-NOW or register online at www.MBA.com.

Dispelling the Myths about Test Preparation and Admissions

MYTH: If you have a solid GPA, your test score isn't as important for getting into a college or graduate school.

FACT: While it is true that admissions committees consider several factors in their admissions decisions, including test scores, GPA, work or extra-curricular experience, and letters of recommendation, it is not always true that committees will overlook your test scores if you are strong in other areas. Particularly for large programs with many applicants, standardized tests are often the first factor that admissions committees use to evaluate prospective students.

MYTH: Standardized exams test your basic skills or innate ability; therefore your score cannot be significantly improved through studying.

FACT: Nothing could be farther from the truth. You can benefit tremendously from exposure to actual tests and expert insight into the test writers' habits and the most commonly used tricks.

MYTH: There are lots of skills you can learn to help you improve your math score, but you can't really improve your verbal score.

FACT: The single best way to improve your verbal score is to improve your vocabulary. Question types in the verbal reasoning sections of standardized tests all rely upon your understanding of the words in the questions and answer choices. If you know what the words mean, you'll be able to answer the questions quickly and accurately. Improving your critical reading skills is also very important.

MYTH: Standardized exams measure your intelligence.

FACT: While test scores definitely matter, they do NOT test your intelligence. The scores you achieve reflect only how prepared you were to take that particular exam and how good a test taker you are.

800-2Review | www.PrincetonReview.com

Hyperlearning *MCAT Prep Course*

The Princeton Review Difference
Nearly 40% of all MCAT test takers take the exam twice due to inadequate preparation the first time. **Do not be one of them.**

Our Approach to Mastering the MCAT
You will need to conquer both the verbal and the science portions of the MCAT to get your best score. But it might surprise you to learn that the Verbal Reasoning and Writing Sample are the most important sub-sections on the test. That is why we dedicate twice as much class time to these sections as does any other national course! We will help you to develop superlative reading and writing skills so you will be ready to write well crafted, concise essay responses. And of course, we will also help you to develop a thorough understanding of the basic science concepts and problem-solving techniques that you will need to ace the MCAT.

Total Preparation: 41 Class Sessions
With 41 class sessions, our MCAT course ensures that you will be prepared and confident by the time you take the test.

The Most Practice Materials
You will receive more than 3,000 pages of practice materials and 1,300 pages of supplemental materials, and all are yours to keep. Rest assured that our material is always fresh. Each year we write a new set of practice passages to reflect the style and content of the most recent tests. You will also take five full-length practice MCATs under actual testing conditions, so you can build your test-taking stamina and get used to the time constraints.

Specialist Instructors
Your course will be led by a team of between two and five instructors—each an expert in his or her specific subjects. Our instructors are carefully screened and undergo a rigorous national training program. In fact, the quality of our instructors is a major reason students recommend our course to their friends.

Get the Score You Want
We guarantee you will be completely satisfied with your MCAT score!* Our students boast an average MCAT score improvement of ten points.**

*If you attend all class sessions, complete all tests and homework, finish the entire course, take the MCAT at the next administration and do not void your test, and you still are not satisfied with your score, we will work with you again at no additional cost for one of the next two MCAT administrations.

**Independently verified by International Communications Research.

800-2Review | www.PrincetonReview.com

ClassSize-8 Classroom Courses for the GRE, LSAT, and GMAT

Small Classes
We know students learn better in smaller classes. With no more than eight students in a Princeton Review class, your instructor knows who you are, and works closely with you to identify your strengths and weaknesses. You will be as prepared as possible. When it comes to your future, you shouldn't be lost in a crowd of students.

Guaranteed Satisfaction
A prep course is a big investment—in terms of both time and money. At The Princeton Review, your investment will pay off. Our LSAT students improve by an average of 7 points, our GRE students improve by an average of 212 points, and our GMAT students boast an average score improvement of 92.5 points—the best score improvement in the industry.* We guarantee that you will be satisfied with your results. If you're not, we'll work with you again for free.**

Expert Instructors
Princeton Review instructors are energetic and smart—they've all scored in the 95th percentile or higher on standardized tests. Our instructors will make your experience engaging and effective.

Free Extra Help
We want you to get your best possible score on the test. If you need extra help on a particular topic, your instructor is happy to meet with you outside of class to make sure you are comfortable with the material—at no extra charge!

Online Lessons, Tests, and Drills
Princeton Review *ClassSize-8* Courses are the only classroom courses that have online lessons designed to support each class session. You can practice concepts you learn in class, spend some extra time on topics that you find challenging, or prepare for an upcoming class. And you'll have access as soon as you enroll, so you can get a head start on your test preparation.

The Most Comprehensive, Up-to-Date Materials
Our research and development team studies the tests year-round to stay on top of trends and to make sure you learn what you need to get your best score.

*Independently verified by International Communications Research (ICR).
**Some restrictions apply.

800-2Review | www.PrincetonReview.com

Online *and* LiveOnline *Courses* for the GRE, LSAT, and GMAT

The Best of Both Worlds

We've combined our high-quality, comprehensive test preparation with a convenient, multimedia format that works around your schedule and your needs.

Online *and* LiveOnline *Courses*

Lively, Engaging Lessons

If you think taking an online course means staring at a screen and struggling to pay attention, think again. Our lessons are engaging and interactive – you'll never just read blocks of text or passively watch video clips. Princeton Review online courses feature animation, audio, interactive lessons, and self-directed navigation.

Customized, Focused Practice

The course software will discover your personal strengths and weaknesses. It will help you to prioritize and focus on the areas that are most important to your success. Of course, you'll have access to dozens of hours' worth of lessons and drills covering all areas of the test, so you can practice as much or as little as you choose.

Help at your Fingertips

Even though you'll be working on your own, you won't be left to fend for yourself. We're ready to help at any time of the day or night: you can chat online with a live Coach, check our Frequently Asked Questions database, or talk to other students in our discussion groups.

LiveOnline *Course*

Extra Features

In addition to self-directed online lessons, practice tests, drills, and more, you'll participate in five live class sessions and three extra help sessions given in real time over the Internet. You'll get the live interaction of a classroom course from the comfort of your own home.

ExpressOnline *Course*

The Best in Quick Prep

If your test is less than a month away, or you just want an introduction to our legendary strategies, this mini-course may be the right choice for you. Our multimedia lessons will walk you through basic test-taking strategies to give you the edge you need on test day.

800-2Review | www.PrincetonReview.com

1-2-1 *Private Tutoring*
The Ultimate in Personalized Attention

If you're too busy for a classroom course, prefer learning at your kitchen table, or simply want your instructor's undivided attention,
1-2-1 Private Tutoring may be for you.

Focused on You
In larger classrooms, there is always one student who monopolizes the instructor's attention. With *1-2-1* Private Tutoring, that student is you. Your instructor will tailor the course to your needs – greater focus on the subjects that cause you trouble, and less focus on the subjects that you're comfortable with. You can get all the instruction you need in less time than you would spend in a class.

Expert Tutors
Our outstanding tutoring staff is comprised of specially selected, rigorously trained instructors who have performed exceptionally in the classroom. They have scored in the top percentiles on standardized tests and received the highest student evaluations.

Schedules to Meet Your Needs
We know you are busy, and preparing for the test is perhaps the last thing you want to do in your "spare" time. The Princeton Review
1-2-1 Private Tutoring Program will work around your schedule.

Additional Online Lessons and Resources
The learning continues outside of your tutoring sessions. Within the Online Student Center*, you will have access to math, verbal, AWA, and general strategy lessons to supplement your private instruction. Best of all, they are accessible to you 24 hours a day,
7 days a week.
*Available for LSAT, GRE, and GMAT

The Princeton Review
Admissions Services

At The Princeton Review, we care about your ability to get accepted to the best school for you. But, we all know getting accepting involves much more than just doing well on standardized tests. That's why, in addition to our test preparation services, we also offer free admissions services to students looking to enter college or graduate school. You can find these services on our website, *www.PrincetonReview.com*, the best online resource for researching, applying to, and learning how to pay for the right school for you.

No matter what type of program you're applying to—undergraduate, graduate, law, business, or medical—**PrincetonReview.com has the free tools, services, and advice you need to navigate the admissions process.** Read on to learn more about the services we offer.

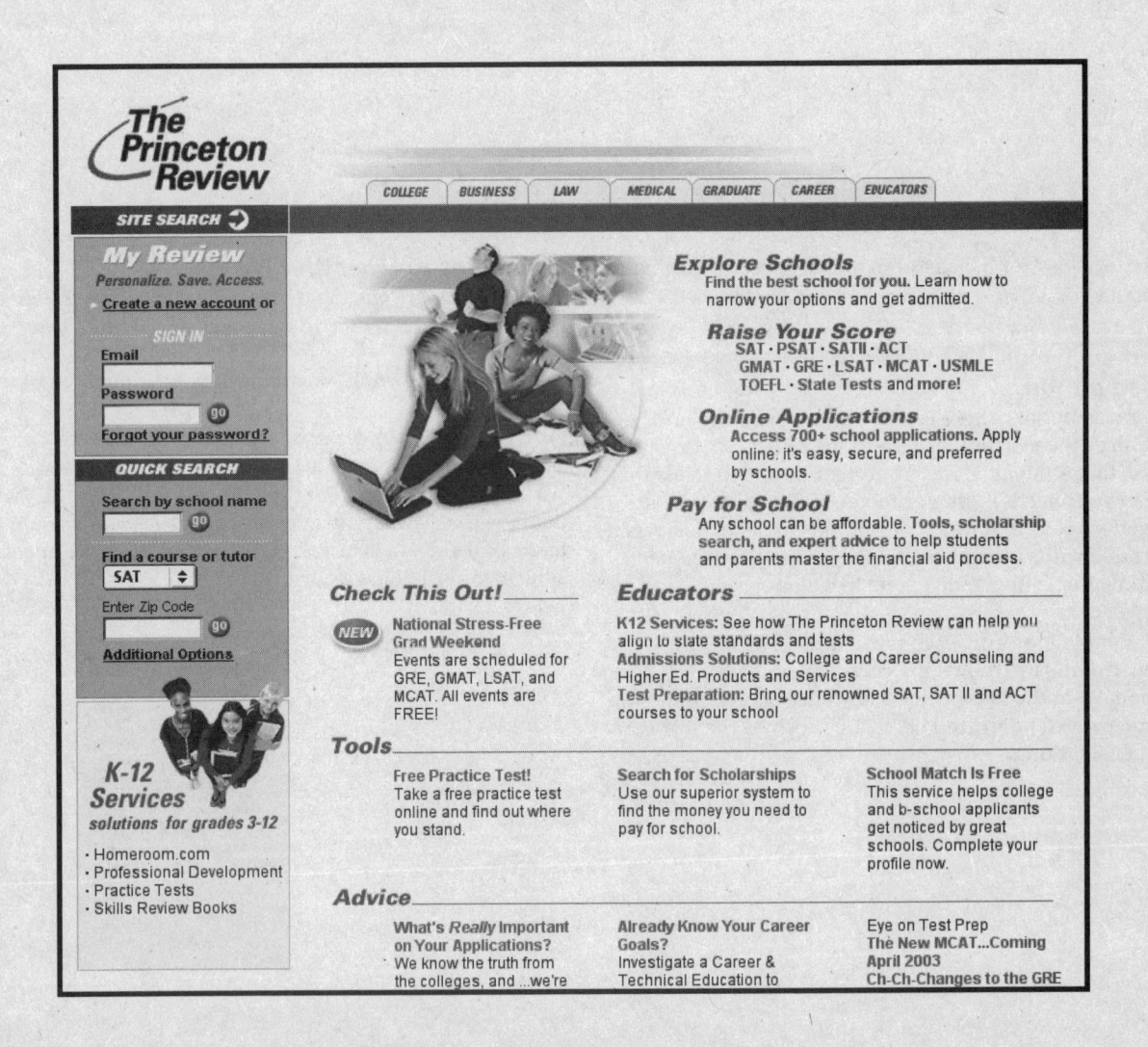

Research Schools
www.PrincetonReview.com/Research

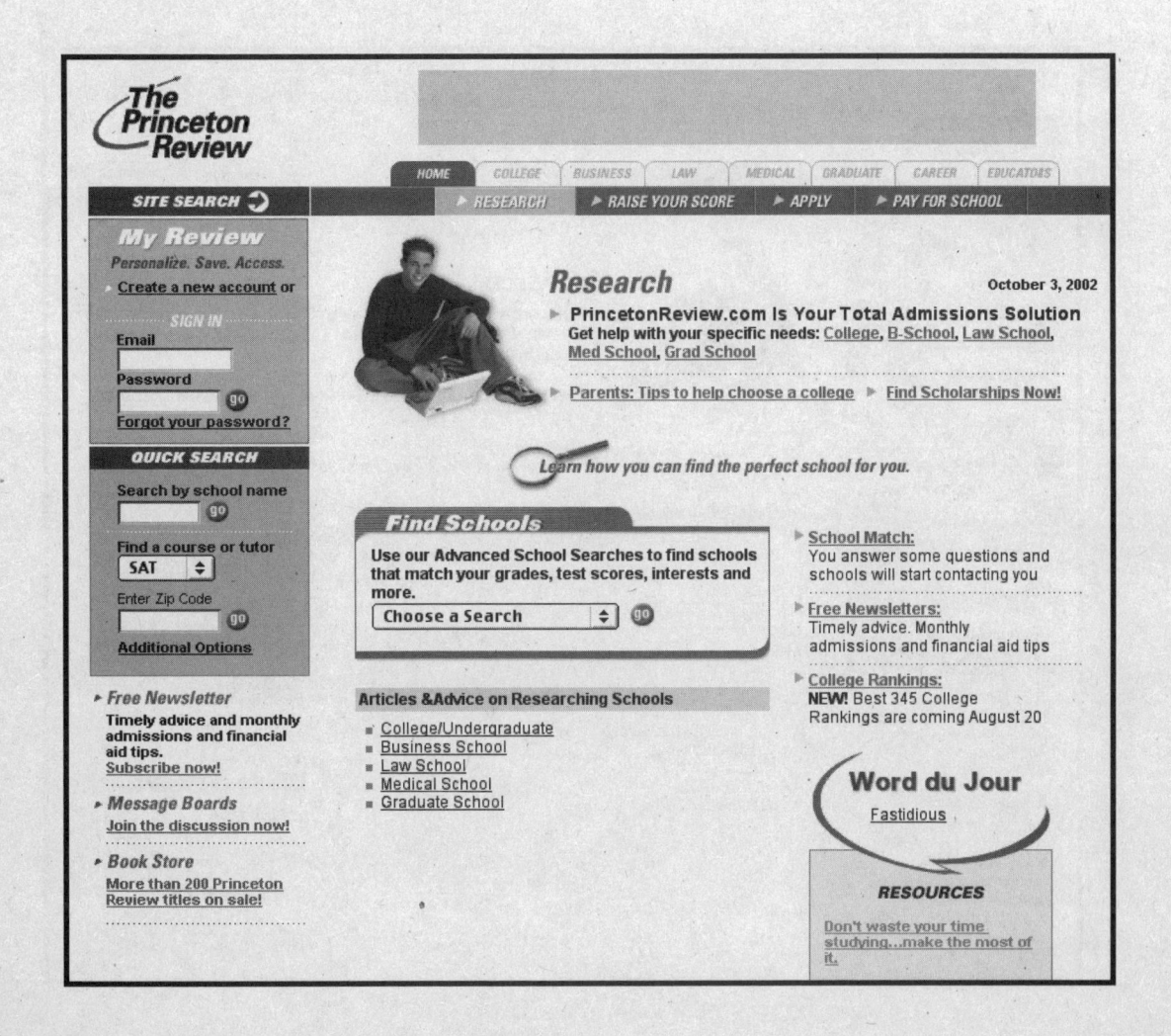

PrincetonReview.com features an interactive tool called **Advanced School Search.** When you use this tool, you enter stats and information about yourself to find a list of schools that fit your needs. From there you can read statistical and editorial information about every accredited business school, law school, medical school, and graduate school.

If you are applying to business school, make sure to use **School Match**. You tell us your scores, interests, and preferences and Princeton Review partner schools will contact you.

No matter what type of school or specialized program you are considering, **PrincetonReview.com has free articles and advice, in addition to our tools, to help you make the right choice.**

Apply to School
www.PrincetonReview.com/Apply

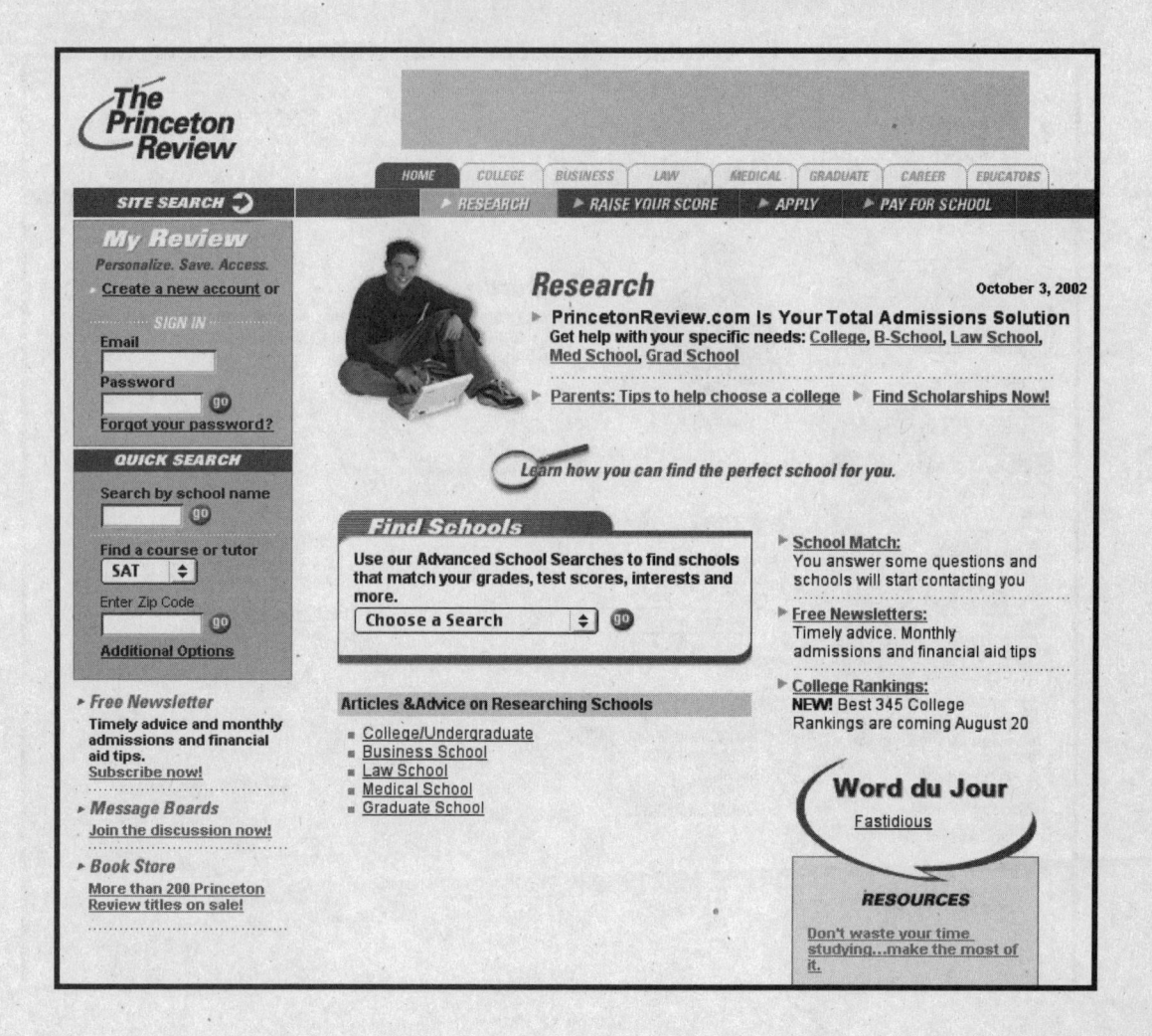

For most students, completing the school application is the most stressful part of the admissions process. PrincetonReview.com's powerful **Online School Application Engine** makes it easy to apply.

Paper applications are mostly a thing of the past. And, our hundreds of partner schools tell us they prefer to receive your applications online.

Using our online application service is simple:

- Enter information once and the common data automatically transfers onto each application.
- Save your applications and access them at any time to edit and perfect.
- Submit electronically or print and mail in.
- Pay your application fee online, using an e-check, or mail the school a check.

Our powerful application engine is built to accommodate all your needs.

Pay for School
www.PrincetonReview.com/Finance

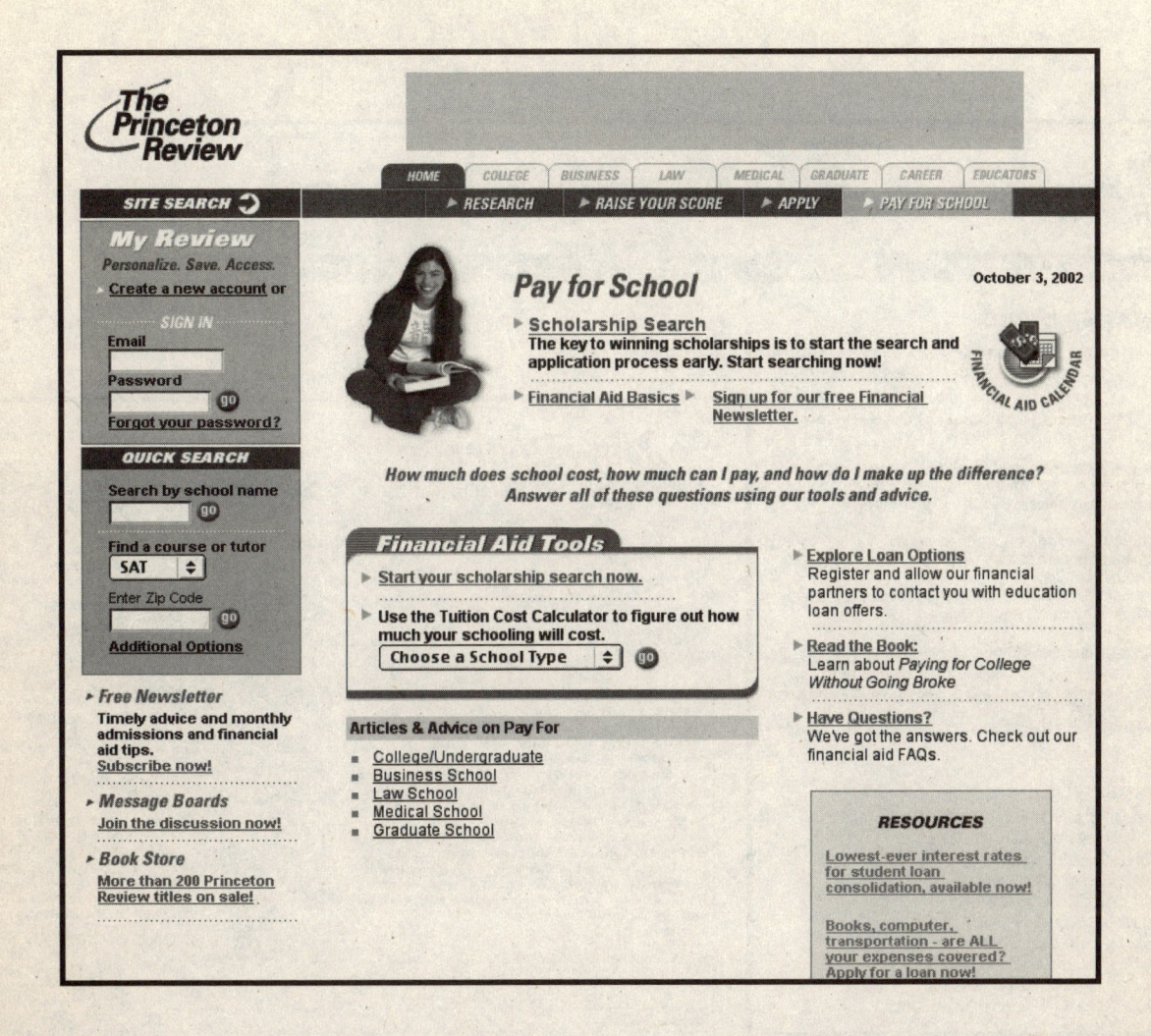

The financial aid process is confusing for everyone. But don't worry. Our free online tools, services, and advice can help you plan for the future and get the money you need to pay for school.

Our **Scholarship Search** engine will help you find free money, although often scholarships alone won't cover the cost of high tuitions. So, we offer other tools and resources to help you navigate the entire process.

Filling out the FAFSA and CSS Profile can be a daunting process, use our **Strategies for both forms** to make sure you answer the questions correctly the first time.

If scholarships and government aid aren't enough to swing the cost of tuition, we'll help you secure student loans. The Princeton Review has partnered with a select group of reputable financial institutions who will help **explore all your loans options**.

If you know how to work the financial aid process, you'll learn you don't have to **eliminate a school based on tuition.**

Be a Part of the PrincetonReview.com Community

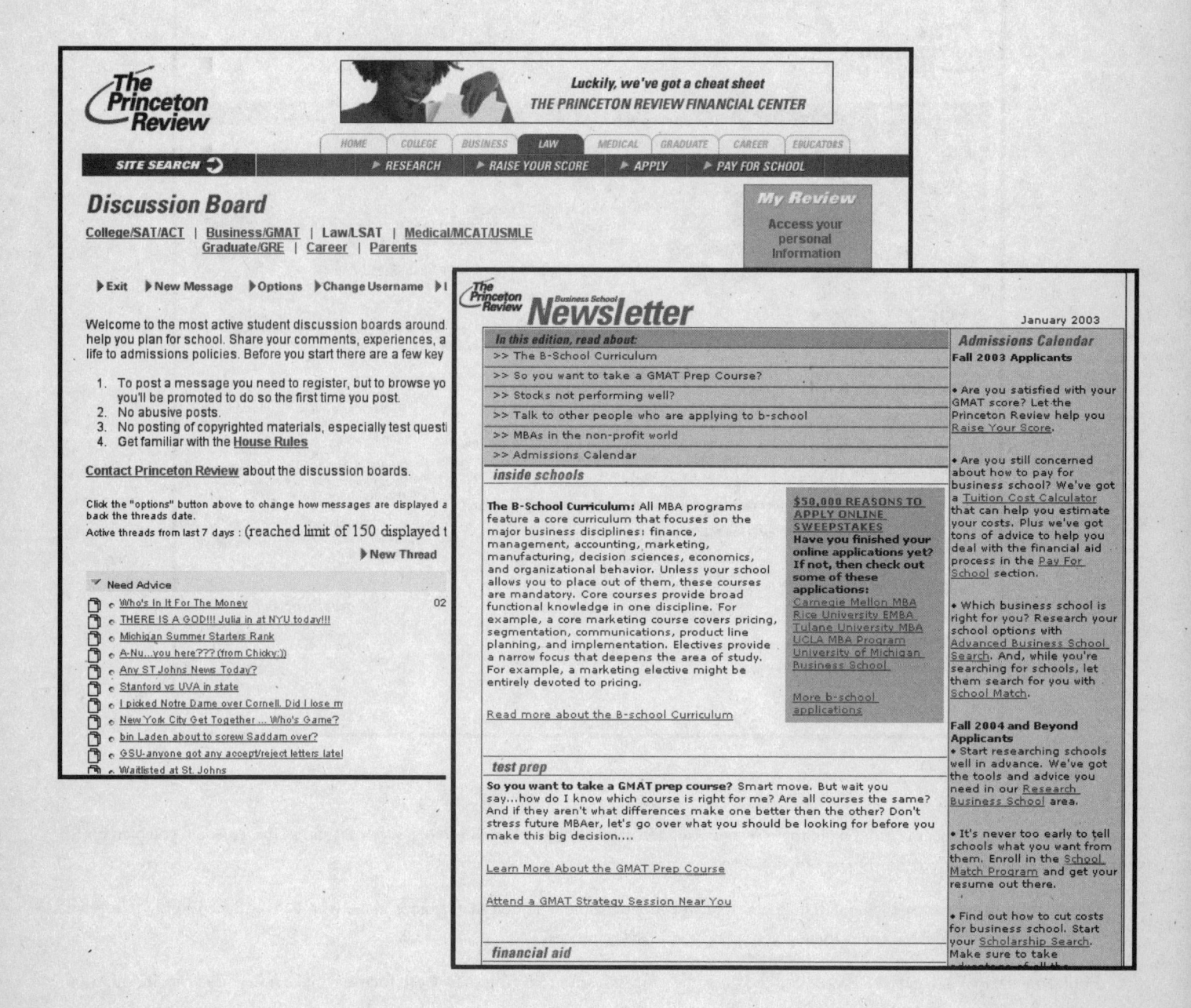

PrincetonReview.com's **Discussion Boards** and **Free Newsletters** are additional services to help you to get information about the admissions process from your peers and from The Princeton Review experts.

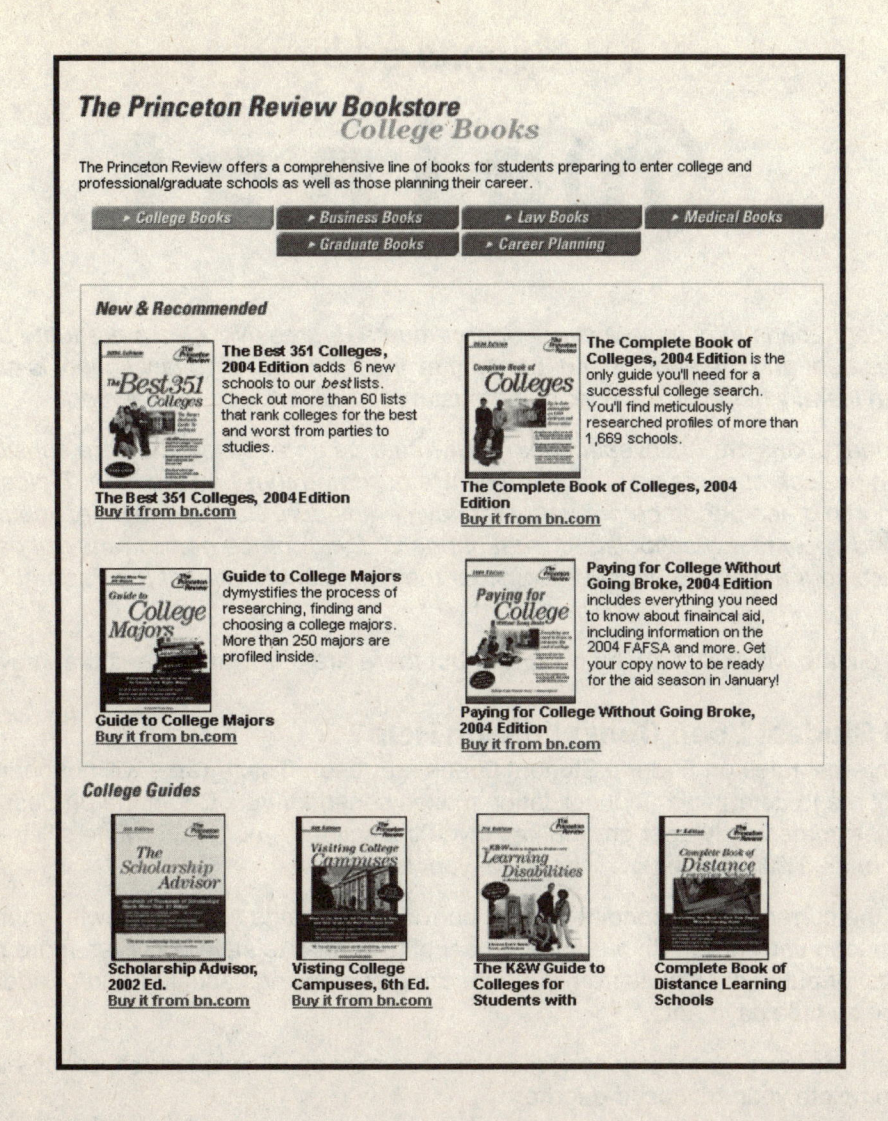

Book Store
www.PrincetonReview.com/college/Bookstore.asp

In addition to this book, we publish hundreds of other titles, including guidebooks that highlight life on campus, student opinion, and all the statistical data that you need to know about any school you are considering. Just a few of the titles that we offer are:

- Complete Book of Business Schools
- Complete Book of Law Schools
- Complete Book of Medical Schools
- The Best 351 Colleges
- The K&W Guide to Colleges for Students with Learning Disabilities or Attention Deficit Disorder
- Guide to College Majors
- Paying for College Without Going Broke

For a complete listing of all of our titles, visit our **online book store**:

www.princetonreview.com/college/bookstore.asp

From Undergraduate to Graduate School—
The Repayment Zone

Sponsored by
nelnet

You used Federal Student Loans to complete your undergraduate degree. Now, as a graduate student, understanding how to manage this debt and the additional debt you may incur by attending law school is crucial to your financial well-being and can literally help you save tens of thousands of dollars upon repayment.

Because Federal Student Loans are an investment in your future as an attorney, they are considered "good debt." However, like any form of debt, at some point in time you are obligated to repay the loan. Typically, Federal Student Loans provide a six-month grace period before your first payment is due. During this time, you may complete graduate entrance exams and apply to law schools. So what happens if your grace period runs out before you know if and where you will complete your advanced degree? Consider the financial benefits of the Federal Consolidation Loan program.

The ideal time to consolidate will likely vary by borrower, but there are a few guidelines that may help you.

How Can Federal Student Loan Consolidation Help?
Each year on July 1, interest rates on Federal Student Loans are reset. These rates will not change again for another 12 months, giving you time to determine if consolidation makes sense for you. Begin the process of researching consolidation companies immediately after graduation. If you consolidate your loans while still in your grace period, you can save an additional .6% in interest over the life of your loan.

While you will give up the current terms, conditions, and borrower programs associated with your loans, remember your new consolidation loan can come with a number of benefits geared to save you even more money, such as interest rate deductions for automatic debits from your checking and savings account and/or additional interest rate reduction for consistent on-time payments.

When you are accepted into law school, your consolidation loan may be eligible for deferment, allowing you to put off repayment until you complete your advanced degree.

No fees are associated with Federal Student Consolidation loans. You may even qualify to consolidate if you're in a period of forbearance, in which you're not making payments because of financial hardship. To determine if you are eligible for consolidation, start by contacting one of your lenders. If all of your loans are with the same lender, you must start there. Otherwise, if your loans were taken directly from the Department of Education, or if you have multiple lenders, you can use any consolidation service. Rates can vary, as can the borrower benefit programs.

Nelnet, the National Education Loan Network, has more than two decades of experience providing education finance solutions to students and their parents. Nelnet's FLEX Consolidation Loan is designed to provide you with a repayment plan and interest rate which could save you as much as 63% on your monthly student loan payments.

Develop a Solid Financial Repayment Plan

Over time, as your career progresses, your salary should follow a steady increase. In theory, the raise in income should allow you to better manage your monthly payments, though your financial obligations will also multiply. You may be buying a home, starting a family, buying a car, setting aside retirement savings, and saving for your kids' education. You will need a clear-cut financial plan that lets you quickly pay down your student loan debt, while still allowing you to meet life's other obligations and personal interests.

First and foremost, consider these lifestyle suggestions:

- Continue to live like a "poor student" for a couple of more years. Keep your pursuit of material things down to a minimum, and focus your finances toward paying down your debt.
- Sharing housing and delaying significant purchases such as a new car can have a big impact on your ability to repay your education loans.
- Plan for significant purchases such as a home. Start putting money in a savings account to make sure you have a minimum down payment when you need it.

Finally, try to live within your means, even when you start to realize the fruits of your education investment.

Lower rates mean big savings

Because Federal Student Loans carry different interest rates, not all consolidation loan rates will be the same. The rate on your loan depends upon when you borrowed the money and how much you borrowed. The combined rate on all your loans is rounded up to the nearest one eighth of one percent, not to exceed 8.25%.

Don't forget the deduction

And there's another benefit for student loan borrowers. In 2003, the IRS will allow up to $2,500 of education loan interest to be deducted from your income tax return, subject to income limits. The income limits before you start to lose the deduction are increased significantly. For singles, the income limits for full deductibility start to phase out when your income hits $50,000 and is phased out completely at $65,000. For married couples filing jointly, the phase out starts at $100,000 and is phased out completely when your income reaches $130,000. We suggest you check with a tax advisor to determine how much interest you can deduct.

Repayment strategies

The maximum repayment term on federal student loans is 10 years. Unfortunately, it is not unusual for students to leave law school several thousands of dollars in debt. If you consider the average student loan borrower is expected to make monthly payments at a rate of 10% of their income, you realize that law students do not fit that average. Paying back five-figure or higher debt in 10 years can be a daunting task. You should make it a goal to repay student loans as soon as possible, so you can start saving and investing for other goals.

With a lower monthly payment, you might want to make additional principal payments and get out from under that loan even faster. There are no prepayment penalties for student loans, but you can only consolidate once unless you go back to school and take out further loans. Taking the time to speak with professional loan advisors like those you'll find at Nelnet, will quickly help you determine if consolidation is the right step for you. Call toll-free at 1.866.485.3366 or visit Nelnet online at *http://www.flexloan.nelnet.net/TPR*. A FLEX Loan Advisor will counsel you on your eligibility and the steps you need to take to consolidate.

Student loans make it possible to invest in your greatest asset, your mind. Taking the time to do some smart financial planning will allow you to capitalize on that investment.

More expert advice from The Princeton Review

Increase your chances of getting into the law school of your choice with The Princeton Review. We can help you get higher test scores, make the most informed choices, and make the most of your experience once you get there. We can also help you make the career move that will let you use your skills and education to their best advantage.

CRACKING THE LSAT
2004 Edition
0-375-76321-X $20.00

CRACKING THE LSAT WITH SAMPLE TESTS ON CD-ROM
2004 Edition
0-375-76326-0 $34.95

COMPLETE BOOK OF LAW SCHOOLS
2004 Edition
0-375-76347-3 $22.00

LAW SCHOOL ESSAYS THAT MADE A DIFFERENCE
0-375-76345-7 $13.95

Available at Bookstores Everywhere.

www.PrincetonReview.com